ANATOMY OF THE
NEW TESTAMENT

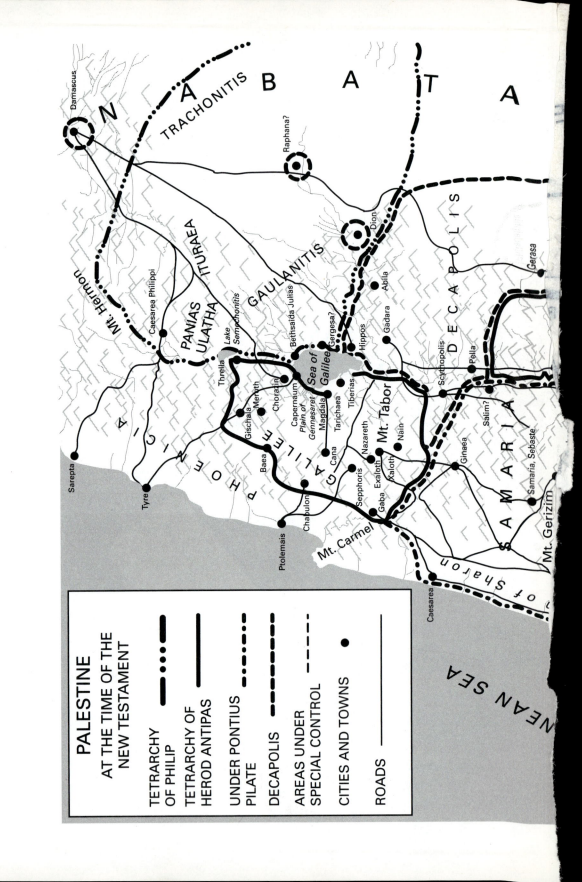

PALESTINE
AT THE TIME OF THE
NEW TESTAMENT

TETRARCHY
OF PHILIP

TETRARCHY OF
HEROD ANTIPAS

UNDER PONTIUS
PILATE

DECAPOLIS

AREAS UNDER
SPECIAL CONTROL

CITIES AND TOWNS

ROADS

N A B A T A

TRACHONITIS

Damascus

Raphana?

Dion

DECAPOLIS

Gerasa

Abila

Caesarea Philippi

Mt. Hermon

PANIAS
ULATHA

ITURAEA

GAULANITIS

Bethsaïda Julias

Gadara

Pella

Lake
Semechonitis

Gergesa?

Hippos

Scythopolis

Thrella

Sea of
Galilee

Choratin

Meroth

Capernaum
Plain of
Gennesaret

Magdala

Tarichaea

Tiberias

Mt. Tabor

Salim?

Gischala

Baea

G A L I L E E

Cana

Nazareth

Nain

Ginaea

Chabulon

Sepphoris

Gaba

Exaloth

Xaloth

Samaria, Sebaste

Mt. Carmel

S A M A R I A

Mt. Gerizim

PHOENICIA

Sarepta

Tyre

Ptolemais

Caesarea

of Sharon

NEAN SEA

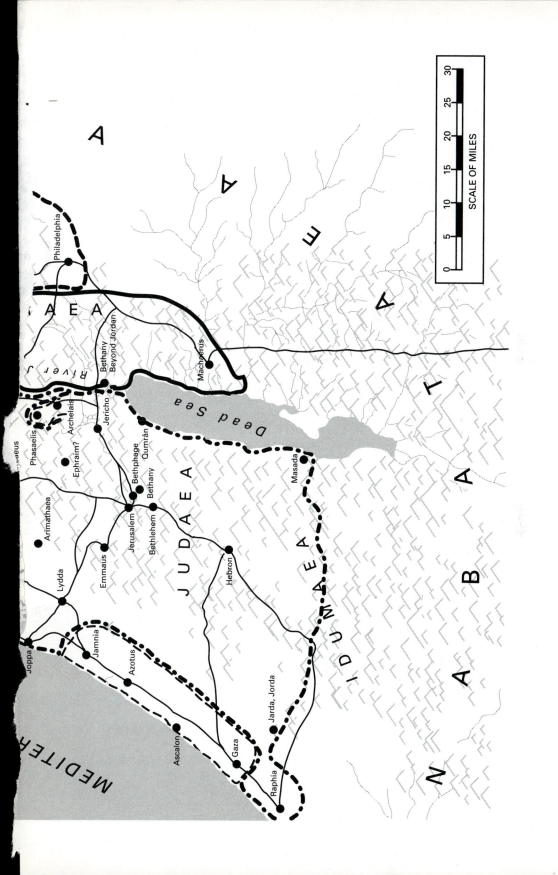

SCALE OF MILES

0 5 10 15 20 25 30

Philadelphia

AEA

Bethany
Beyond Jordan

Machaerus

River J

Dead Sea

Jericho

Archelais

Phasaelis

Ephraim?

Bethphage

Qumrân

Bethany

Arimathaea

Jerusalem

JUDAEA

Masada

Lydda

Emmaus

Bethlehem

Hebron

IDUMAEA

Jamnia

Joppa

Azotus

NABAT

Jarda, Jorda

Ascalon

Gaza

Raphia

MEDITER

ANATOMY OF THE
NEW TESTAMENT

A GUIDE TO ITS STRUCTURE AND MEANING

SIXTH EDITION

ROBERT A. SPIVEY

D. MOODY SMITH

C. CLIFTON BLACK

PEARSON
Prentice
Hall

Upper Saddle River, New Jersey 07458

Library of Congress Cataloging-in-Publication Data

Spivey, Robert A.,
Anatomy of the New Testament / Robert Spivey, Moody Smith, Clifton Black.—6th ed.
   p. cm.
Includes bibliographical references and indexes.
ISBN 0-13-189703-9
1. Bible. N.T.—Introductions.   2. Bible. N.T.—Criticism, interpretation, etc.   I. Smith, D. Moody
(Dwight Moody)   II. Black, C. Clifton (Carl Clifton),   III.   Title.
BS2330.3.S65 2007
225.6'1—dc22   2006016481

Editor-in-Chief: Sarah Touborg
Senior Acquisitions Editor: Mical Moser
Editorial Assistant: Carla Worner
Marketing Director: Brandy Dawson
Asst. Marketing Manager: Andrea Messineo
Marketing Assistant: Bekim Perolli
Senior Managing Editor: Joanne Riker
Production Liaison: Randy Pettit
Manufacturing Buyer: Christina Amato
Cover Design: Jayne Conte

Illustrator (Interior): Preparé Inc.
Director, Image Resource Center: Melinda Reo
Manager, Rights and Permissions: Zina Arabia
Manager: Visual Research: Beth Brenzel
Manager, Cover Visual Research & Permissions:
Karen Sanatar
Composition/Full-Service Project Management:
Caterina Melara, Preparé Inc.
Printer/Binder: R.R. Donnelley & Sons, Inc.
Typeface: 11/13 Garamond

Credits and acknowledgments borrowed from other sources and reproduced, with permission, in this
textbook appear on appropriate page within text (or on pages xxiii–xxiv).

Pearson Education LTD.
Pearson Education Singapore, Pte. Ltd
Pearson Education, Canada, Ltd
Pearson Education–Japan

Pearson Education Australia PTY, Limited
Pearson Education North Asia Ltd
Pearson Educación de Mexico, S.A. de C.V.
Pearson Education Malaysia, Pte. Ltd

10 9 8 7 6 5 4 3 2

ISBN 0-13-189703-9

To
Martha,
Jane,
Harriet

CONTENTS

List of Images, Illustrations, Maps, Charts, Diagrams, and Sidebars

PREFACE

After a decade, we have produced another revised edition of *Anatomy of the New Testament*. For this sixth edition, we welcome the collaboration of C. Clifton Black, Otto A. Piper Professor of Biblical Theology at Princeton Theological Seminary. Black studied *Anatomy* as an undergraduate at Wake Forest University and has adopted it in teaching at the University of Rochester, Southern Methodist University, and Princeton. His present title reflects our continuing commitment to explaining the nature and interests of the New Testament and its individual writings.

Recent cultural and political events have brought to light the broader, public relevance of the task of understanding the New Testament. The culture wars raging in Western societies involve beliefs about what the New Testament affirms or condemns. Yet the New Testament does not speak directly to hot-button issues such as abortion, same-sex marriage, or the Iraq War (2003–). These may be important issues for today, but they were not for the ancient societies and cultures in which the New Testament was produced. The widespread assumption that Jesus or the New Testament's authors would have regarded them as defining issues is misplaced. Beginning with Jesus, the New Testament represents a radical reevaluation, if not rejection, of some moral assumptions and values of that day, even of Judaism, the parent religion. Jesus' early followers were viewed as a destabilizing influence on society. This means that the New Testament interpreter must reckon with historical conditions past and present, as well as with **theological** issues and ethical agendas. Moreover, all reading involves interpretation, whether knowingly or not. We invite the reader to join us in the fruitful, and to us exciting, challenge of interpreting the New Testament. The purpose of *Anatomy of the New Testament* is to foster a sympathetic, but not uncritical, reading of these important ancient writings.

The older, standard questions of "introduction" (authorship, date and place of composition, and so forth) have again been dealt with in summary fashion in notes at the beginnings of chapters or at other appropriate places. If there is agreement on a problem, it is stated. If not, we give our position and reasons for holding it. In any event, such questions are of little concern to readers until they have some knowledge of, and involvement with, the content of the New Testament itself. Thus, the sooner they can get to the text, the better. Readers can return to these questions as they become aware of the relevance of such issues for understanding the text. By then, they will be ready to consult more advanced and detailed works on the subject.

Although the character of *Anatomy* remains the same, significant changes have been introduced in the sixth edition:

- In the Prologue, we pay attention to the question of how our approach is related to the nature, purpose, and reading of the New Testament itself. We invite the reader to join with us in the task of interpretation, or exegesis: "drawing out" the meaning of a text.

- While continuing to emphasize this central task, at a number of points we deal more extensively with historical issues. For example, near the beginning of Chapter 6 ("Jesus the Messiah"), there is a new, highlighted section dealing with what we do not know about Jesus, and why. Popular interest in such questions has been stimulated by films like *The Passion of the Christ* (2004) and such books as Dan Brown's *The Da Vinci Code* (2003), which convey as presumptive fact what is at best exaggeration and at worst baseless fiction. Similarly, in Chapter 5 ("John: The Gospel of Jesus' Glory"), we pay more attention to the historical dimensions of the Fourth Gospel, adding a treatment of its account of Jesus' trial before Pilate. This new section raises questions about the setting and purpose of that Gospel as well as the specific question of who was responsible for the death of Jesus.

- We have revisited and revised every chapter, in some cases (such as Chapter 3, "Matthew: The Gospel of Obedience") adding new material that reflects current trends in contemporary scholarship.

- We have deleted the fifth edition's final, general chapter (on the community of the New Testament) to make room for a full new chapter (9) on 1 Corinthians. This document, more than any other, exhibits the range of problems affecting early Christian churches set in a pagan culture. We continue to deal with such questions in the context of interpreting other New Testament texts, as befits the character and purpose of *Anatomy*.

- The sixth edition's final chapter ends, appropriately, with the Revelation to John, but now includes also 2 Peter and Hebrews. 2 Peter faces questions raised by the fact that Jesus has not returned; Hebrews presents a view of history and **eschatology** quite different from Revelation, yet embodying a similar hope and expectation. Here we address issues such as those raised by the *Left Behind* novels, whose sales are in the millions and which offer a particular construction of Christian hope as though it were the only one.

- A leading question, introducing the discussion of each New Testament passage and intending to provoke the student's thought, has been maintained, although often revised.

- Explanatory boxes or sidebars, dealing with specific questions (such as the Christmas story and what we do and do not know about Jesus), have been introduced into the book's format.

- Key words (like messiah or parable) and technical terms (natural theology, redaction criticism) that appear throughout our discussions have been set in **boldface type** when such terms first appear in a section of a chapter. Definitions for these words may be found in the Glossary at the back of the book.

- New illustrations, photographs, and charts have been added, as aids to better understand the New Testament and the history of its interpretation.

- All bibliographies have been completely revised and brought up to date.

We hope these changes will make this latest edition of *Anatomy of the New Testament* more accessible for its intended reader and enhance its value.

ACKNOWLEDGMENTS

We again wish to acknowledge the source *New Testament Illustrations: The Cambridge Bible Commentary on the New English Bible*, edited by Clifford M. Jones (New York: Cambridge University Press, 1966), for the adaptation of the following figures: "Time Chart of the New Testament," "Diagram of the Synoptic Problem," "Map of Galilee," "Diagram of the Temple," and "Diagram of Jerusalem." Adaptation of the "Diagram of the Formation of the Gospels" is courtesy of *Jesus in the Church's Gospels: Modern Scholarship and the Earliest Sources*, by John Reumann (Philadelphia: Fortress, 1968). Adaptation of the end map of the Mediterranean world is courtesy of *The Good News: The New Testament with over 500 Illustrations and Maps* (New York: American Bible Society, 1953). Adaptation of the end map of Palestine is courtesy of *The Westminster Historical Atlas to the Bible*, edited by George Ernest Wright and Floyd Vivian Filson, revised (copyright, 1945, by the Westminster Press; 1956, by W. L. Jenkins; adapted by permission). Adaptation of the chart displaying repetitive cycles in Revelation is by courtesy of M. Eugene Boring, *Revelation* (Louisville: John Knox, 1999; adapted by permission). Adaptation of the chart, "The Baptism of Jesus," on p. 97 is used by permission of Thomas Nelson, Inc. Several paragraphs from *Interpreting the Gospels for Preaching* by D. Moody Smith (Philadelphia: Fortress, 1980) have been used with the permission of the publisher. Unless otherwise specified, photographs of ancient sites are courtesy of D. Moody Smith and Jane Allen Smith.

For their interest in this book and their encouragement in its revision we are grateful to our editors, Sarah Touborg and Mical Moser, our production editor Caterina Melara, as well as their predecessors: Maggie Barbieri, Ted Bolen, Helen McInnis, Kenneth J. Scott, Charles E. Smith, and John D. Moore. Princeton Theological Seminary graciously granted one of the authors pedagogical relief during those critical months in which the revised manuscript was finalized. Like Sarah Freedman, her predecessor at Duke University Divinity School, Gail Chappell has rendered valuable service at her word processor. At several points C. Kavin Rowe, a graduate assistant at Duke, offered help; at nearly every step along the path of revision, we received inestimable support from David J. Downs, a graduate assistant at Princeton Seminary. In countless ways, Martha Spivey and Jane Smith continue to encourage and support this project, which has now extended across almost four decades. Harriet Black has now joined their selfless ranks. The book's dedication attests our gratitude for their understanding, toleration, and considerable help.

R. A. S.
D. M. S.
C. C. B.
June, 2006

LIST OF ABBREVIATIONS

EH	The *Ecclesiastical History* of Eusebius.
KJV	The King James Version of the Bible.
LXX	The Septuagint (see the Glossary).
NAB	New American Bible
NIB	*The New Interpreter's Bible*, ed. L. E. Keck, 12 volume (Nashville: Abingdon, 1994-2002).
NRSV	The New Revised Standard Version of the Bible.
par., parr.	Parallel or parallels (usually in the Gospels).
REB	Revised English Bible
RSV	The Revised Standard Version of the Bible.
TDNT	*Theological Dictionary of the New Testament*, ed. G. Kittel and G. Friedrich, trans. G. W. Bromiley, 10 volumes (Grand Rapids: Eerdmans, 1964-1976).

TIME–CHART OF THE NEW TESTAMENT*

Significant Pre-New Testament Dates
336–323 B.C. Conquest and Rule of Alexander the Great
167–164 B.C. The Maccabean Revolt
63 B.C. Roman Rule of Palestine Begins

Date	Events	Herods	Governors of Judea	Roman Emperors	New Testament Writings
10 BC	Birth of Jesus (before 4 BC)	Herod the Great 37-4 BC		Augustus (27 BC-AD 14)	
AD		Archelaus (4 BC-AD 6)			
10		Philip the Tetrarch (4 BC-AD 34)	Coponius (6-9) Marcus Ambivius (9-12) Annius Rufus (12-15)		
20	Ministry of John the Baptist	Herod Antipas (4 BC-AD 39)	Valerius Gratus (15-26)	Tiberius (14-37)	
30	Ministry of Jesus Crucifixion of Jesus Paul's Conversion		Pontius Plate (26-36)		
40	Paul's first missionary activity	Herod Agrippa I (37-44)	Marcellus (36-37) Marullus (37-41)	Caligula (37-41)	
50	Council of Jerusalem Paul in Corinth Paul in Ephesus Paul's journey to Jerusalem and arrest		Cuspius Fadus (44-46) Tiberius Alexander (46-48) Cumanus (48-52) Felix (52-58)	Claudius (41-54)	1 & 2 Thessalonians Galatians 1 & 2 Corinthians Romans
60	Paul, prisoner to Rome Paul, prisoner in Rome Paul's martyrdom under Nero		Festus (58-62) Albinus (62-64) Gessius Florus (64-66)	Nero (54-68)	Philippians Philemon
70	Jewish War (66-70) Destruction of the Temple (70) Siege of Masada (72-73)	Herod Agrippa II (53-100)		Galba (68-69) Otho (69) Vitellius (69) Vespasian (69-79)	Mark Colossians Ephesians
80				Titus (79-81)	Hebrews
90	Council of Jamnia Domitian Persecution			Domitian (81-96)	Matthew 1 Peter Luke Acts Gospel of John Letters of John Revelation to John Pastorals
100				Nerva (96) Trajan (98-117)	James Jude 2 Peter

*Chronology is only approximate, especially in regard to dating the books of the New Testament.

Significant Post-New Testament Dates:
Jewish revolt under Bar Kochba (132-135)
Fall of Jerusalem (135)
Pax Romana (27 B.C.-A.D. 180)
Constantine, emperor of Rome (306-337),
  converted and made Christianity the
  official religion of the Roman Empire.

A vellum page of the Gospel of John, from Codex Sinaiticus (fourth century A.D.), now housed at the British Museum. *(Courtesy of The Bridgeman Art Library.)*

THE NATURE OF THE NEW TESTAMENT

The New Testament consists of twenty-seven early Christian writings that with the Old Testament, the Bible of Judaism, constitute the Christian Bible. Although the New Testament is thus comparable to the Old, there are significant differences. The Old Testament is more than three times the length of the New, and the material in it was written over a period of nearly a thousand years. The New Testament was composed in a mere fraction of that time. Most of the Old Testament was written in Hebrew, the language of ancient Israel; the New Testament, in Greek, the language of the ancient Mediterranean world.

THE STRUCTURE AND MEANING OF THE NEW TESTAMENT

Structure

The structure of *Anatomy of the New Testament* reflects the structure of the New Testament itself, but is not identical. **Gospels**, Acts, **Epistles**, and Revelation stand in the same general order as in the New Testament. The structure of the New Testament is keyed to the centrality of Jesus. Thus the Gospels stand first. In Part One, "The Gospels and Jesus," Mark is treated before Matthew, because, for reasons that will become evident, Mark is generally believed to be the earliest of the Gospels. Also in Part One "Jesus the Messiah" is treated last. Obviously, the Gospels are about Jesus, who lived and died before they were written. Yet the character of the Gospels, which are interpretations rather than simply records of Jesus, must first be taken into account.

1

Something similar applies in the case of the Book of Acts and the Epistles, taken up in Part Two, "The Apostles and the Early Church." Jesus is their basis, but the focus is on the life of the **church**, the Christian communities. This is true of the letters ascribed to the **Apostle** Paul, as well as of those ascribed to other apostles (or followers) of Jesus: James, Peter, Jude, and John. It is possible to discern a chronological order among Paul's letters reflected in *Anatomy*'s order, and therefore to observe how Paul's career, thought, and practice developed. The other letters were probably written later than Paul's; thus they are treated after Paul's, as they appear in the New Testament. The Revelation to John, the last book of the Christian Bible, is fittingly positioned. Based on an event and person of the past, the faith of the community that produced the New Testament looks to the future, as does Revelation.

The story of how and why these books were written and at length gathered into the collection we now call the New Testament is a long and complicated one. Each book originated within a particular historical situation. The individual books were preserved, circulated among early Christians, and gradually brought together because most everyday Christians deemed them useful and authoritative in the church. By the beginning of the third century, the four Gospels, Acts, and the letters attributed to Paul were widely regarded as scripture. Probably Paul's letters had also been collected and were being read even earlier (see 2 Pet. 3:15–16; cf. Col. 4:16).

Not until the late fourth century, however, did canonical lists appear containing exactly the twenty-seven books of our New Testament. Christians and churches got along for centuries without the New Testament in exactly the form we have it, and for more than a century without anything approximating our complete collection of Gospels, Acts, Epistles, and Revelation. That they were able to do so testifies to the fact that early Christianity's vitality and strength lay in its enthusiastic faith and community life—two factors much in evidence in the writings of the New Testament themselves.

At first, the early Christians used as their Bible what they later came to regard as the Old Testament: the scriptures of Israel and contemporary Judaism. From the beginning, synagogue and church have appealed to the same scriptures; at times they have heatedly debated their proper interpretation. Christian faith and church life have therefore never been without an authoritative book. The great fourth- and fifth-century **manuscripts** of the New Testament (Sinaiticus, Vaticanus, and Alexandrinus) are complete Bibles, containing the Old and New Testaments. Thus the scriptures of Christianity consist of both testaments. The New Testament is, and always has been, not only incomplete but inconceivable apart from the Old. Even the structure of the New Testament is grounded upon the foundation of the Old Testament.

Meaning

None of the individual writers knew they were writing for a collection of books that would be called the New Testament and compiled centuries later. One speaks of the **canon** of the New Testament and of the New Testament books as canonical. The term "canon" is a Greek word (*kanōn*) meaning "rule" in the sense of norm. The New Testament was formed as a rule of faith and practice for the followers of Jesus. Thus the New Testament as a whole developed along the lines of the major books that became a part of it. For example, the Gospel of Matthew begins with a genealogy, thereby adopting an Old Testament **genre** or form. The biblically knowledgeable reader would understand that Matthew is intended to be scriptural, that is, a normative guide for believers. Similarly, Luke begins with canticles or songs written in a biblical language and cadence. The Acts of the Apostles extends the story of God's dealing with a people beyond the narratives of the Old Testament and the Gospels. Although the New Testament as a whole obviously developed later than its individual writings or books, it stands in continuity with them. Like the major writings that compose it, the New Testament is intended to be normative, that is, canonical. It defines who Jesus **Christ** is and how the believer may follow him. The issues and needs of the church or churches that produced the New Testament over a period of a couple of centuries were not the same as those that led to the writing of the various New Testament books. Between them, however, lies a continuity of purpose and function.

At the same time, neither individual New Testament books nor the New Testament as a whole was ever intended to function as the sole source of authority for Christians or the church. The New Testament itself developed alongside creeds, like the **Apostles' Creed** and the Nicene Creed, which also were authoritative canons or norms, as well as an ordained ministry that watched over the churches' faith and practice. (*Episkopos*, the original Greek term for bishop, literally means "overseer": a supervisor, one who watches over.) In the case of individual New Testament books, their authority functioned together with that of the **apostles** and their successors, as well as the **Spirit**, often called the Holy Spirit. Sometimes, as in 1 John, we see evidence of the meeting or collision of these different sources of authority: for example, right confession and the Spirit in 1 John 4:1–4.

THE TRANSMISSION AND TRANSLATION OF THE NEW TESTAMENT

Transmission

Available technology fundamentally affects people's access to knowledge, what they read and whether they read. There were no printing presses in the West until the middle of the fifteen century. After that, the Bible was the first and foremost book printed and eventually became readily available to the general public. Without printed Bibles, the emphasis of the Protestant Reformation of the sixteenth century on *sola scriptura*, scripture alone, is hardly imaginable. Prior to that time, most people heard scripture in church liturgies rather than reading scripture privately—even if they were able to read.

None of the original copies (*autographa*) of the New Testament books survives. They were written by hand and then copied. Because of the needs of churches, rather than of individual readers, they were copied frequently. Probably books were copied individually at first (e.g., the Gospel of John). Gradually, as the New Testament developed, they were copied and bound together, at first in papyrus, similar to paper, later in codexes that were sewn together like books, ultimately on more permanent vellum (leather). In Christian usage the codex displaced the scroll on which the Jewish scriptures were written. (Thus one speaks of the Jewish **Dead Sea Scrolls**.) Christian use of the codex, instead of scrolls, may have been ahead of its time. In due course, however, codexes replaced scrolls even in general, secular usage.

A codex could accommodate four **Gospels** bound together, in which one could easily refer to a particular Gospel. This practice would have been much more difficult if scrolls were used. It may well be that the use of the codex accelerated the acceptance of a fourfold Gospel canon, which the church has used since the second century.

There are far more copies of the Greek New Testament than of any other writings or documents from antiquity. Over five thousand ancient **manuscripts** of some part of the New Testament are known to exist, together with several thousand copies of ancient translations into such languages as Latin, Coptic, and Syriac. The existence of this wealth of material is reassuring to the modern reader or scholar, but it also presents problems. No two manuscripts are exactly the same: there are many differences in wording, readings, or even content. For example, our most ancient manuscripts of the Gospel of Mark do not contain the so-called longer ending (16:9–20), found in the King James Version and long recognized as a part of the Christian scriptures. Rather, according to these manuscripts, Mark's Gospel ends abruptly with the reported fear of women fleeing from Jesus' empty tomb (16:8). Similarly, John 7:53–8:11, the well-known story of the woman taken in adultery, was not part of the earliest known manuscripts of that Gospel. The question arises: Which ancient authorities are to be followed? To side with the majority seems reasonable, but that solution presents problems: most of the extant manuscripts are relatively late, dependent on the earlier ones, and therefore less reliable. Generally speaking, the most ancient manuscripts are more trustworthy, although this may not always be the case. An early and possibly original reading may be found in later manuscripts.

To assess the relative merits of manuscripts and readings and to decide what stood in the most ancient or original text is the task of textual criticism. Such work is demanding, sometimes tedious, and often uncertain in its results. Nevertheless, the work of textual critics across the past two centuries has produced a text of the Greek New Testament that is certainly much closer to the original than that used by the translators of the famous King James Version, which though published in the early seventeenth century is still widely used, largely because of the grace of its English prose and poetry. Since the invention of the printing press in the fifteenth century, manuscripts are no longer copied, so the creation or reproduction of variant (i.e., differing) readings has ceased. Nevertheless, the task of refining the text goes on, and even in the twentieth century hitherto-unknown manuscripts have been found. That any subsequent manuscript discoveries will produce a radically different New Testament is, however, highly unlikely. Were all the thousands of New Testament manuscripts destroyed, most of the corpus could be reconstructed on the basis of patristic commentaries on its texts, which, again, approximate the New Testament as we now have it. One can be confident that what we read in a responsible modern translation represents substantially what the ancient authors wrote. Yet there remain numerous, significant cases in which the exact wording remains in doubt.

The Most Ancient Manuscripts of the New Testament

The Bodmer papyri (p^{66}, p^{75}), housed in Cologny/Geneva, partially preserve texts of the Gospel of John dating from the beginning of the third century. Rylands papyrus 457 (p^{52}), a fragment of John 18 housed in Manchester (U.K.), dates from the second quarter of the second century. The fragment labeled p^{52} is, to date, the oldest surviving remnant of a New Testament **manuscript**. The most ancient full manuscripts of the New Testament are Codex Vaticanus, now housed in Rome's Vatican Museum, and Codex Sinaiticus, now in the British Museum in London.

Translation

Probably more people have read the New Testament more frequently than any other writing or collection of documents. Among different Christian **churches** or traditions, there are some differences in the definition and contents of the Old Testament. Catholic and Orthodox Bibles contain the so-called **Apocryphal** Books (Sirach, 1 and 2 Maccabees, among others). Since the Reformation Protestants have not recognized these books as canonical; their Old Testament consists only of the books in the Hebrew Bible. Generally speaking, such differences are not widespread with the New Testament, where the same twenty-seven books are read and regarded as authoritative by almost all churches and Christians. Among most of them, the New Testament is read in translation rather than the original Greek. Scholars and serious students read the New Testament in Greek, as do modern Greeks, for whom the **Hellenistic** Greek in which it was composed is still intelligible.

Significantly, this state of affairs is different from the Qur'an within Islam. Many Muslims learn Arabic in order in order to read the Qur'an in its original language, for only that is authoritative. The Christian practice of translating the New Testament assumes that the **revelation** of God resides first of all in the *events* proclaimed rather than in the words used to articulate them. Accordingly, the New Testament has been translated into thousands of languages, beginning in antiquity. Such ancient translations are called versions, the most prominent of which is the Latin. The ancient Latin translation known as the Vulgate was preeminent in the Roman Catholic Church for centuries. Nowadays, however, Roman Catholic scholars and theologians work with the original Greek text, and translations based on the Greek are widely read by members of the Catholic Church.

Of the many English translations, or versions, of the New Testament, the King James, or so-called Authorized, Version (KJV; 1611) still stands as a monument of the English language, despite the fact that its Greek textual basis is now known to be seriously flawed. Without doubt the Revised Standard Version (RSV; 1952), which preserved much of the cadence and style of the King James in modern dress, provided a good compromise between faithfulness to the syntax of the original languages and the modern English idiom. With good reason the RSV has been called the final revision of the King James, though it too has now been revised as the New Revised Standard Version (NRSV; 1989). The NRSV incorporates gender–inclusive language, as well as a number of other changes or improvements. For this reason *Anatomy* now follows the NRSV except where the authors find reason to disagree with its translation. The RSV and NRSV are official translations, authorized by the National Council of the Churches of Christ in the United States of America. In Great Britain there are now comparable, official translations done in the latter half of the twentieth century: the New English Bible (NEB; 1970) and its successor, the Revised English Bible (REB; 1989). Although such translations are not sectarian and are used by Roman Catholics as well as others, they are basically Protestant in origin. A good, modern Catholic translation is the New American Bible (NAB; 1970). There are other reliable translations, though some recent popular paraphrases of the Bible (like *The Living Bible*, 1962) are quite tendentious, theologically or in other ways.

He, She, or It? Gender in Translation

The sixth edition of *Anatomy of the New Testament* is again based on the NRSV, which makes a serious and laudable effort to avoid sexist—androcentric or masculine–oriented—language.

That effort is occasioned by differences between the biblical languages and English. For example, in English the word "man" has traditionally been used to refer both to a male human being and to humanity generally. When the Psalmist asks (8:4 RSV), "What is man that thou art mindful of him, / and the son of man that thou dost care for him?" the NRSV changes this to "What are human beings that you are mindful of them, / mortals that you care for them? " This is done to avoid using the word for a male human being, though "man" also has stood for humanity generally, and thus to avoid presumably sexist language or interpretation. To that end, the NRSV also uses the plural noun "human beings" and substitutes "mortals" for "son of man, " thus departing considerably from the original text.

The original Hebrew of this psalm's verse uses *enosh* and *ben adam*, both terms signifying humanity generally rather than a particular male or female, for which the Hebrew words are *ish, ishah* (man, woman). Similarly, in both places the Greek **Septuagint (LXX)** reads *anthrō pos* ("man" in the sense of human being; cf. "anthropology"). There are also specific Greek words for man and woman (*anēr, gynē*). Ancient societies may have been patriarchal, but their languages reflected the need for a single word to designate a human being or humanity in general, as distinguished from a particular man or woman. Modern English lacks this capability, although German, for example, possesses it (*Mann*, a male; *Mensch*, a human being). The NRSV might have translated Psalm 8:4, "What is a human being that you are mindful of one, / or the offspring of a human being that you care for such a one?" It would thus have been closer to the original, though such a translation obviously borders on the ludicrous.

All translation involves interpretation. There are, however, significant degrees of interpretation and here, as frequently elsewhere, a much higher degree in the NRSV than in the RSV. Communication by spoken (or written) words involves what is heard (or seen), as well as what is intended by the speaker (or writer). The NRSV translators, in order to prevent "What is man . . . ?" from being understood as "What is a male human being?"—or perhaps to avoid any connotation of male dominance—resorted to "What are human beings . . . ?" Yet in avoiding the danger of sexist misreading, a rhetorical price was paid. As social and cultural situations evolve, language will continue to change, as it always has. The rhetorically eloquent "What is man that thou art mindful of him?" may someday make a reentry in subsequent biblical translations.

The task of translation is a demanding one and must continually be redone. Languages grow and change, so that certain words disappear or change their meanings. Thus 1 Corinthians 13 in the KJV the Greek word *agapē* is translated "charity," but in modern versions it is quite properly rendered "love." "Charity" now connotes benevolence or gifts to the poor. Words in one language rarely have exact equivalents in another. For example, the Greek *logos*, translated "**word**" in the prologue of John's Gospel (1:1–18), has a much broader range of meanings in Greek, where under varying circumstances it means "statement," "discourse," "reason," or even "reckoning." Moreover, the punctuation of an English translation—for that matter, of modern Greek editions—has been introduced by modern editors to aid reading. Ancient **manuscripts** had little or no punctuation. Likewise, the chapter-and-verse divisions of the Bible are later, medieval additions. Conventional chapter divisions often accord with sense or narrative divisions remarkably well. Yet the reader and interpreter must remember that they are later impositions upon the text. They may not accord with how the author, or earlier readers, intended or perceived the text to be divided.

READING THE NEW TESTAMENT

A major principle of modern biblical criticism and interpretation is that the Bible should be read like any other book. Of course, different books are appropriately read in different ways, and the Bible itself has been read quite differently by various people or groups. That the Bible should be read like any other book has usually meant that individual biblical books should be read with appreciation for who wrote them, under what circumstances, and for what purpose. Thus the reader must pay attention to the history, character, and literary **genre** of the writing in question.

Still, the overall purpose of the scriptural **canon**, to define Christian life and faith, is very much in accord with that of the New Testament books. Therefore, it is entirely necessary, indeed proper, to read them with a view to understanding their claims about God and God's relationship to individuals, the human race, and the world. This way of reading does not mean that one has to accept the New Testament's claims in order to understand it. Our approach to the New Testament, and that of modern **exegesis** generally, is based on the premise that the reader can understand what the New Testament and its constituent books are about and can appreciate their claims upon human life and allegiances without a prior commitment to belief in them. At the same time, like all culturally important literature—whether Shakespearean drama or the United States Constitution—this scripture rewards a serious and sympathetic reading.

Our situation, however, is quite different from that of antiquity. Although the New Testament was copied frequently, as its thousands of surviving manuscripts attest, these copies were made for churches rather than individuals. Doubtless more Christians heard the New Testament read aloud than read it for themselves. The New Testament itself indicates that these writings were read in church. In 1 Thessalonians (5:27) Paul commands that his letters be read to the congregation. Similarly, in the Letter to the Colossians the readers are told that, when the letter has been read in their congregation, it should be read in the **church** of Laodiceans and that the Laodicean letter should be read in Colossae (4:16). "The public reading of scripture" (1 Tim. 4:13) may imply that some Christian writings were so regarded; in 2 Peter, probably written after **A.D.** 100, Paul's letters are lumped with "other scriptures" (3:16). Even in the **Gospels** there is a word directed to readers (Mark 13:14), probably those who would read the Gospel aloud in church. The author of Revelation expressly states that he expects his book of **prophecy** to be read aloud so that members of the church will hear it (Rev. 1:3). At mid-second century Justin Martyr, who refers to the Gospels as "the memoirs of the apostles," speaks of their being read on Sunday during worship (*Apology* 67, 3)— apparently an established practice that reflects an even more primitive usage. Although private reading of scripture as a devotional act is now common, probably more Christians still hear the New Testament read in church than read it for themselves.

Thus, reading the New Testament intelligently requires an understanding that these books were originally read and heard within Christian churches, as they still are today. Although the New Testament does not have to be read for religious purposes within a religious community, its character demands that it be read with an understanding and appreciation of those purposes and communities.

The task of reading the New Testament is at once simple and complex. It is simple because one can be confident of the New Testament's general purpose, which is not different in principle from that of its individual books. Yet it is complex, because each book's specific situation and purpose are different.

Therefore, in *Anatomy* we encourage a slow and careful reading of the New Testament. In twenty-first century culture, even that may be a lost art requiring discipline to recapture. As one reads, one stops, ponders, and considers different interpretive options. What questions should I put to this text? What questions are inappropriate, thus unfruitful? In the case of a **parable** of Jesus—for example, the Parable of the Good Samaritan (Luke 10:25–37)— one appropriately asks what point is being made or what sort of conduct is encouraged. One need not ask whether that particular Samaritan ever existed. Perhaps he did; perhaps he did not. Either way, his existence is not germane to the parable's purpose.

Meaning is *led out* of a text. There is a Greek word for this, *exēgēsis*. This is the cognate noun for the verb *exēgeomai*, which literally means "lead out," is commonly used to refer to an informed "explanation" or "interpretation." In reading texts and interpreting them, first of all to ourselves, we are engaging in **exegesis**: drawing meaning out of a text. Exegesis is the specific mode of interpretation that deals with written texts.

In discussing specific texts at some length, the authors of *Anatomy* are engaging in exegesis, interpretation appropriate to texts, and inviting the reader to join with us in this task. Limitations of time and space obviously prevent us from dealing with every word of the New Testament. In the case of major New Testament books—the Gospels, Acts, Romans, and 1 Corinthians—a number of typical and representative texts have been chosen, and for every book at least one such text. The overall purpose of *Anatomy of the New Testament* is to assist others in the reading of the New Testament, which merits a sympathetic hearing accompanied by critical awareness.

How to Study the New Testament

The authors of *Anatomy of the New Testament* recommend the following procedure in studying each New Testament book. After familiarizing themselves with important issues concerning the origin of the work in question by reading the background comments in *Anatomy*, readers should then look at the brief outline of the entire biblical document, to gain some prior conception of what it is about. *Then, the New Testament book should be read in its entirety, preferably in one sitting.* Only then is one adequately prepared to dig into the representative texts with which this book mainly deals. In following this procedure, the reader should find the appropriate section of *Anatomy* both a guide and a help in understanding. These **exegetical** sections, which constitute the greater part of the book, will make little sense unless they are read with the New Testament in hand. The questions posed at the head of interpretive sections are intended to provoke thought and to engage the reader with the New Testament's subject matter. Used in this way, students have found *Anatomy* a helpful inducement and guide for studying New Testament. The bibliographies at the end of each chapter, and at the end of the book, offer guidance for continued reflection and study.

This scene from the Arch of Titus in the Roman Forum celebrates Titus's capture of Jerusalem in A.D. 70. The victorious Romans triumphantly bear the sacred objects of the Jerusalem temple, including the menorah, or seven-branched lampstand, symbolizing the presence of God. *(Courtesy of The Art Resource, New York.)*

THE WORLD OF THE NEW TESTAMENT

THE JEWISH WORLD

Jesus was a Jew. So were his first disciples. *Jesus Christ* means Jesus the **Messiah** of Israel, the anointed king of Davidic lineage (cf. 2 Sam. 7:12–15 and Psalm 89:3–4). In fact, the earliest Christians did not think of themselves as members of a new religion separate from Judaism. Yet Jesus and his disciples represented something new within Judaism. This newness consisted not in original or unique ideas but in the aspects of ancient traditions and hopes that were taken up, reinterpreted, and emphasized.

No new movement can be understood, however, apart from its historical antecedents and the factors that helped to produce it. The historical setting of Jesus, early Christianity, and the New Testament was first-century Judaism. A remarkable continuity or similarity exists between the Judaism of today and that of the first century, despite the changes that succeeding centuries have wrought. This continuity is in itself a clue to the character of that ancient faith.

Both Judaism and Christianity are historical religions, and it belongs to the nature of both to emphasize continuity. They share a faith in a God who deals with human beings, individually and collectively, in such a way that God's will can be discerned in history. Crucial to both religions is the idea that God *reveals* or has been *revealed* in history. The holy scriptures of both religions are largely narratives of the past: legends, sagas, and historical accounts. Broadly speaking, they are testimonies to God's historical revelations. The Hebrew Bible (the Christian Old Testament) is a vast collection of legal, cultic, devotional, and narrative material set in a historical framework. It is the literary product of nearly a thousand years of Israel's history. Although the New Testament is much briefer and covers a much shorter period of time, it too tells of people and events in the conviction that God has wrought wondrous deeds in history that are of utmost importance for the future of humanity. Consciously and deliberately the New Testament writers take up the story of the Old Testament and bring it to a culmination. This, of course, is a distinctly Christian, rather than Jewish, culmination.

The limits of the Hebrew Bible had not actually been officially defined in the time of Jesus and earliest Christianity. Yet, according to the New Testament, Jesus himself speaks of "the law and the prophets" (Matt. 5:17) and quotes from the Psalms (Mark 15:34; cf. Psalm 22:1). Thus he seems to have known the threefold division of sacred scripture—**law**, **prophets**, and writings (cf. Luke 24:44)—that is reflected generally in the New Testament. According to tradition, the Hebrew **canon** of the Hebrew Bible was fixed by the **rabbis** at the **Council of Jamnia** in about **A.D.** 90, although in fact the main lines had been established much earlier. Most Protestant churches accept this Hebrew canon. Other, Catholic churches accept as canonical the **apocryphal** or deuterocanonical books contained in the **Septuagint**.

Judaism was a religion of **revelation**, history, and a book. As such, it was a religion steeped in tradition, and this tradition was a means by which Israel identified and understood itself as a distinct and chosen people, the people of the Lord. Moreover, much of the literature of the Old Testament and the **oral** and written **traditions** that developed from it were understood as divine directions intended to regulate Israel's response to the Lord's goodness. The most influential law code the Western world has known, the **Ten Commandments**, begins: "I am the Lord your God, who brought you out of the land of Egypt, out of the house of slavery. You shall have no other gods before me" (Exod. 20:2–3). The statement of what God has done leads to the statement of what the people ought to do in response, forming the basic structure of Old Testament law. A principal activity of many Jewish religious leaders in the time of Jesus was the interpretation and fulfillment of that law.

Revelation and history, tradition and law, although immensely important, were not the whole of Judaism. A part of obedience to the law was the performance of worship worthy of God. The center of this worship in the time of Jesus was the temple in Jerusalem, and the heart of the temple was the **sacrificial** altar, where **priests** offered sacrifice to God. Until its destruction by the Romans in A.D. 70, the temple served as the focal point of Jewish worship. Its importance to the life of first-century Judaism can scarcely be overestimated. Not only was the temple regarded as the center of the universe and the place where the last days were to be consummated; it also served as a means for structuring time, both through the daily sacrifices and the seasonal festivals. Any violation of the temple by the Roman authorities or others was sufficient to cause a major Jewish revolt. Further, the Jewish sect of **Qumran** (see pp. 23–25) originated in part as a reaction to what they considered to be the corruption of temple worship, and Jesus was accused of trying to destroy this sacred institution of Jewish piety (Mark 14:58 par.).

The other major Jewish religious institution was the synagogue. There was but one Jerusalem temple, but there were many synagogues. Even in Palestine, but especially in the **Diaspora**, the synagogue became for most the practical center of Jewish religious life. Although the origin of the synagogue is hidden in obscurity, by the first century it had become a central Jewish institution, a kind of community center for study of the Jewish law, the Torah, and a place for regular weekly worship, including reading and commentary on the **Torah** and prayers for the congregation. Unlike the temple that was presided over by the priests, the synagogue was a lay organization that allowed broader participation, such as Jesus' reading from the Torah in the synagogue (see Luke 4:16) and Paul's extensive use of synagogues in his missionary work (see Acts 18:4).

Excavations at the site of the City of David, south of the Temple Mount. This is the site of King David's capital in the tenth century before the time of Jesus.

Another factor played a large role in first-century Judaism: the land. The small piece of territory at the eastern end of the Mediterranean Sea, which is variously called the Holy Land, Palestine, or Israel, has been the occasion and cause of both hope and frustration for Jews for three thousand years. At least from the days of the Davidic monarchy the land was regarded as God's promise and gift to his people. The promise reached back into the days of the patriarchs Abraham, Isaac, and Jacob, who dwelt in and around the land but did not possess it (cf. Gen. 12:1–3). Yet Israel believed that God had promised the land to her, and in this faith she occupied and defended it. Israel could never rest easy in the land, however, for, subject to frequent threat and attack, she was only secure when the more powerful surrounding nations were momentarily weak or looking in other directions. In the late eighth century B.C. the territories of all the Israelite tribes except Judah were overrun by the Assyrians, and less than a century and a half later the Babylonians invaded Judea, laid siege to Jerusalem, and overthrew it. The Davidic kingship came to an end, and many of the people were deported into Babylonian captivity.

The subsequent history of the land has been a troubled one. In fact, the modern state of Israel represents the first instance of Jewish control of the land since shortly before the time of Jesus, and that control is still contested. Since the Babylonian **exile** the land of Israel has been ruled by other peoples, whether Persians, Romans, or British. The question of the possession and rulership of the land was quite as important in Jesus' day as it is today, for the land was then occupied by the Romans and ruled by puppet-kings and imperial **procurators**. The hope for the restoration of Jewish dominion under Davidic kingship was an important aspect of the background of Jesus' ministry.

A History of Tragedy and Renewal

From the Babylonian conquest of Judea in 587 B.C. to the time of Jesus' death, the Jews in Palestine lived mostly under foreign domination, relieved only by a century or so of relative independence under the **Hasmonean** dynasty just prior to the advent of the Romans in 63 B.C. In the Babylonian conquest many Jews were taken east by their captors to Mesopotamia. Others fled south to Egypt. The so-called **Diaspora**, or dispersion, of the Jews began. From this time onward, Jews in increasing numbers were to be found living outside their Palestinian homeland.

Sources for Reconstructing Jewish History

The concerns of postexilic Israel are reflected in the later Old Testament books and treated directly in Ezra and Nehemiah. The Maccabean period is dealt with in 1 and 2 Maccabees. The *Jewish Antiquities*, a continuous history of the Jews to the Roman War by the first-century Jewish historian Josephus, is doubtless the most valuable single non-Biblical source.

Shortly after the middle of the sixth century B.C. Babylonian overlordship was replaced by a Persian one. Jews were allowed to return to their homeland and to begin the restoration of the Jerusalem temple, which had been destroyed by the Babylonians. Although we have an incomplete picture of Jewish life under Persian rule, conditions were certainly much improved. More than two centuries of Persian domination came to an end late in the fourth century before Jesus, when Alexander of Macedon (northern Greece) and his armies moved east, sweeping everything before them. Alexander overran the Jewish homeland, and over the years he and his successors attempted to introduce Greek culture and customs, as was their practice in all conquered territories. Alexander was as much a missionary of Greek culture as a conquering general. After his death in 323 B.C., his empire broke up as quickly as it had been formed. And although his successors could not preserve political unity, they were able to continue the process of Hellenization, that is, the spreading of Greek culture.

After the division of Alexander's empire by his heirs, the Jews were situated between two rival centers of power—the Seleucids, who controlled Mesopotamia and Syria, and the Ptolemies, who ruled Egypt. The geographical setting of Israel between these two great powers of the Fertile Crescent made struggle over Palestine inevitable. By and large, Jewish Palestine during the third century was controlled by the Ptolemies with a minimum of interference in Jewish internal affairs. After they defeated the Ptolemies in 198 B.C., a similar policy at first characterized the Seleucids' rule. Following a period of changing rulers, however, Antiochus IV (called Epiphanes because he proclaimed himself to be "God manifest") ascended to the Syrian throne in 175 B.C., and the situation changed. Already there were **Hellenizing** Jews in Jerusalem and elsewhere who were all too eager to adopt Greek customs and dress, in part because of the economic and other advantages they thought assimilation would bring (1 Macc. 1:11–15). In due course, however, more pious Jews (*Hasidim*) strongly objected to such accommodation, and the seeds from which conflict would sprout were quickly sown as positions hardened on both sides. Because Antiochus probably saw in such Jewish resistance dangerous opposition to his own rule, he decided to suppress the Jewish religion. Heathen altars were erected in Jewish towns and the Jerusalem temple became the scene of disgraceful conduct and sacrifices (2 Macc. 6:1–6). Resistance was likely to mean death.

In the face of such depredations and threats, Mattathias, the patriarch of the Hasmonean family, rose to the occasion when in 167 B.C., emissaries of Antiochus came to his town of Modein to enforce the command to perform pagan sacrifice (cf. 1 Macc. 2:15–28). Proclaiming that "even if all the nations that live under the rule of the king obey him, and have chosen to do his commandments . . . yet I and my sons and my brothers will continue to live by the covenant of our ancestors," he killed a Jew who had come forward to offer sacrifice, as well as one of the king's officers. Then he and his sons took to the hills in open rebellion. Said Mattathias: "Let everyone who is zealous for the law and supports the covenant come out with me!" (1 Macc. 2:27).

Mattathias died soon thereafter, and his son Judas, called Maccabeus, assumed command of the rebel force. (The family is often called **Maccabean**, after him.) Victorious in combat, in 165 B.C. Judas Maccabeus and his men seized the temple and reclaimed it for Judaism. This victory has ever since been celebrated in the feast of Hanukkah (dedication), even though it was not until 142 B.C. that the last remnants of the Syrian Hellenizers were driven from Jerusalem.

Although the Maccabean or Hasmonean dynasty was generally welcomed as a blessed relief and the fulfillment of long-frustrated expectations, its promise far outstripped its actuality. The propensity of the later Hasmoneans to style themselves as kings and high **priests**, as well as the internecine struggle among them, led to disillusionment. As kings they were not sons of David and as priests they were not descendants of the priestly family of Zadok, and thus they could be viewed as interlopers. When the Romans arrived on the scene about a century after the Maccabean Revolt, their general, Pompey, supported one Hasmonean claimant, Hyrcanus II, against the other, Aristobulus II. Although some supporters of Aristobulus offered fierce resistance, particularly at the temple, the Roman occupation of Palestine and the Holy City would scarcely have been regarded as a disaster by many Jews. For while Roman domination may have been inevitable, the conduct of the later Hasmoneans made it seem initially less distasteful to Jews than it might otherwise have been. The Romans allowed the weak Hasmonean Hyrcanus II to hold the office of high priest and ethnarch. But Palestine was now in fact Roman territory, and the power behind the throne was Antipater of Idumea, a master of political intrigue who had helped engineer the Roman coup in the first place.

These massive walls around the tombs of the patriarchs of Israel (cf. Genesis 23:9) in Hebron, a few miles south of Bethlehem, were originally constructed by Herod the Great (Matthew 2:1–23), who also rebuilt the temple of Jerusalem (John 2:20).

Antipater brought his remarkable career to a culmination by having the Romans declare his son Herod king of the Jews. This Herod ruled effectively, if brutally, from 37 to 4 B.C. and figures prominently in Matthew's story of Jesus' infancy. He is commonly known as Herod the Great, in distinction from the lesser Herods who followed him. During his long and successful rule, Herod accepted the necessity of appealing to Jewish religious sensibilities, at the same time devoting himself to the task of Hellenizing the culture and life of Palestine. He built cities according to the Hellenistic patterns, and he constructed stadiums, gymnasiums, and theaters. In non-Jewish areas (e.g., Sebaste, the ancient Samaria) he built pagan temples. Yet he also rebuilt the Jerusalem temple in a more magnificent style. Despite his efforts, the Jews did not love or trust Herod; nor did he trust them. He executed his Hasmonean wife Mariamne and eventually two of her sons, along with his ambitious and able son Antipater (named for his grandfater), who had married a Hasmonean princess. Obviously Herod feared that the memory of the Hasmoneans would inspire the Jews against him.

After the death of Herod, the kingdom was split into three parts and divided among three surviving sons. Philip became tetrarch of the region northeast of the Sea of Galilee, including Iturea and Trachonitis, and reigned over that largely Gentile area from 4 B.C. until A.D. 34. Herod Antipas became ruler of Galilee and Perea and ruled from 4 B.C. until A.D. 39. Archelaus became ruler of Samaria, Judea, and Idumea, but was deposed after a short reign. Following the deposition of Archelaus in A.D. 6, a Roman **procurator**, or prefect, was installed as ruler of Judea. The procuratorship remained in effect continuously until the brief reign of Agrippa (37–44) and was resumed thereafter. Pontius Pilate (26–36) was the fifth of these procurators, surely one of the worst from the Jewish point of view. He took money from the temple treasury, brought military insignia with the emperor's image into Jerusalem, and ruthlessly destroyed a group of Samaritans who were watching a prophet perform a miracle. It is an understatement to say that he was not overly sensitive to Jewish religious sensibilities.

Yet Roman rule was not unremittingly brutal or oppressive. The procurator of Judea lived not in Jerusalem but on the Mediterranean coast in Caesarea. Although he had final responsibility, much authority was granted to the Sanhedrin, a group of about seventy distinguished Jewish elders—priests, scribes, and laymen. The high priest was the official head of this group and was, as he had been since the Babylonian **exile**, the most important Jewish governmental figure. In the villages, synagogues may have served as law courts, where **scribes** were the authorities for interpreting and applying the **law**, or **Torah**.

Jesus was born during the reign of Herod the Great, lived in Galilee under Herod Antipas, and died in Jerusalem during the procuratorship of Pilate and the high priesthood of Caiaphas. Although Jesus was doubtless influenced by the political conditions of the times, there is little evidence that he made an impact upon them. On the one hand, Jesus and his followers would not have encouraged any who advocated armed resistance against Roman rule. Although Jesus spoke frequently of the **kingdom of God** and aroused hopes that he himself would become king, he evidently did not intend to lead a rebellion (cf. Luke 4:5–8; Matt. 4:7–10; John 6:15; 18:36). For example, he did not explicitly forbid the payment of taxes to Caesar (Mark 12:13–17 parr.; but cf. Luke 23:2). On the other hand, Jesus was executed as a messianic pretender, a claimant to the throne of Israel, and thus a political rebel.

The Zealots

Such resisters have been known as **Zealots**, although recent scholarship demonstrates that a party specifically called "Zealot" does not emerge before **A.D.** 66. It is usually inferred from Josephus that Judas the Galilean founded the sect in A.D. 6. Nevertheless, while isolated Jewish uprisings can be documented, it is unclear that there was any organized party advocating armed revolution during the period with which we are concerned.

Gradually, during the first century, the tension between Roman and Jew heightened. What the Romans regarded as Jewish provocations led to retaliation, which in turn increased the polarization of sentiment. More and more Jews became willing to fight and die, convinced that God would vindicate them in their righteous cause. Jewish Christians, among others, did not share the widespread enthusiasm for war, and when its outbreak seemed imminent those in Jerusalem fled for safety, according to tradition to Pella across the Jordan River. At about this time, James the brother of Jesus was martyred by other Jews (an event recorded by Josephus, *Jewish Antiquities* XX, 200). In A.D. 66, war broke out. Although the Jews fought bravely and enjoyed some initial success, they had little chance against Roman power. In A.D. 70, the Romans took Jerusalem after a long and grueling siege and laid it waste, destroying the temple. A few years later, the last Jewish resistance at the fortress of Masada was overwhelmed. Even then the Jewish will to resist was not broken. Later, word circulated that Emperor Hadrian intended to rebuild Jerusalem as Aelia Capitolina and to erect a temple to Jupiter on the ruins of the Jewish temple. ("Aelius" was Hadrian's middle name, and "Capitoline" recalled Rome's Capitoline Hill, where pagan gods were worshipped.) The Jews then rallied around a leader called Bar Kochba ("Son of the Star"), whom the renowned **Rabbi** Akiba hailed as the **Messiah** of Israel. Once more (A.D. 132–135), the Jews fought fiercely, but after a time were subdued. The Romans went ahead with their building plans and after the new city was complete forbade any Jew to enter it on pain of death. The trend of many centuries reached its logical end. Judaism had become a nation without a homeland over which the Jews themselves ruled.

Because the Jews believed that their land had been given them by the same God who had called them to be his chosen people, those who lived in Palestine chafed under foreign domination. Indeed, the character of Judaism during the time of Jesus and the early **church** was much affected by conditions in the Jewish homeland. Even though Jews generally looked for relief from foreign oppression and the restoration of the Davidic monarchy, many were content to wait upon God for the fulfillment of this hope, some thinking that it was near at hand. Other Jews had already made their peace with Hellenistic culture and Roman rule and probably did not really yearn for their overthrow. To be sure, there were large numbers of Jews living outside Palestine for whom political independence was not a burning issue. Indeed, rebellion in the home-land presented the grim and unwelcome possibility of retaliation against Jews elsewhere.

Moreover, it would be a mistake to view the Judaism of Jesus' time solely in terms of its reaction to an international, and domestic, political situation with unfortunate consequences for Jews. Many Jews continued to be primarily concerned with the right understanding of the law and the proper worship of God. The development of various schools of thought continued under Roman rule, and the Romans were willing to toler-ate this so long as there was not overt dissension or violence. Postexilic developments had already led to the formation of several schools of religious opinion among the Jews, mak-ing for a rather complex situation in the time of Jesus. We must now examine that situa-tion more closely to understand why differing positions and parties existed and how their presence shaped the setting in which Christianity appeared.

A Persistent Obedience

If anything is central to Judaism, it is the **law** (Hebrew *torah*, "law" in the sense of "instruction"). Notwithstanding its human mediation through Moses, the Jew regarded the law as divine **revelation**. "The stability of the World rests on three things, on the Law, on worship, and on deeds of personal kindness" (*Pirke Aboth* 1, 2). Of course, proper wor-ship and the nature of deeds of kindness are defined by the law. Strictly speaking, the law consists of the five books of Moses—the Pentateuch—that stand at the beginning of the Bible. Obedience to the Torah is, and has been, the paramount obligation of the Jew; it is the way to true **righteousness**. Interpretation of the law was historically the province of **priests** and **scribes**. Ezra, the great fifth-century scribe and "scholar of the text of the commandments of the Lord and his statutes for Israel" (Ezra 7:11), was the descendant of an important priestly family (7:1–5). Although most law-observant Jews were members of no sect or special group, the law was so central to Judaism that such groups can be cate-gorized according to their attitude toward it.

The Pharisees

> The Pharisees . . . are considered the most accurate interpreters of the laws, and hold the position of the leading sect. [Josephus, *The Jewish War*, II, 162]

> The scribes and Pharisees sit on Moses' seat; therefore, do whatever they teach you and follow it, but do not do as they do; for they do not practice what they teach. [Matt. 23:2 ff.]

> When Paul noticed that some were Sadducees and others were Pharisees, he called out in the council, "Brothers, I am a Pharisee, a son of Pharisees. I am on trial concerning the hope of the resurrection of the dead." [Acts 23:6]

Probably the single most influential and significant religious group within the Jewish community of New Testament times was the **Pharisees**. The **Gospels** make clear that they were important during the time of Jesus, and they became even more influential after the disastrous climax of the Jewish War (**A.D.** 70). After that war, a **rabbinic** council assembled near the Mediterranean coast at Jamnia. The **Council of Jamnia** became a center for the study and interpretation of the law. Although its influence has sometimes been exaggerated, the council played an important role in the dissemination of the Pharisaic point of view throughout Judaism. The Gospels' portrayal of the Pharisees is doubtless colored by the fact that they usually appear as opponents of Jesus. Yet the representation of them as defenders and interpreters of the law is surely accurate (cf. Mark 2:24; 10:2).

The history of the Pharisees and even the origin of their name is obscure. Very likely they stemmed from the Hasidim, or "pious ones," whose ferocious allegiance to the nation and the law gave impetus to the Maccabean revolt. The word *Pharisee* seems to be derived from a Hebrew verb meaning "to separate." If so, it would appropriately designate the Pharisees as those separated or chosen by God for full obedience to the law. Yet Pharisees did not withdraw from society. Pharisaism was fundamentally a lay movement, and Pharisees emphasized the necessity of obeying the law in all areas or aspects of life. The Pharisees seem to have been the original custodians of the oral law, that is, the law revealed to Moses on Sinai but, unlike the scriptural Torah, not committed to writing. In the Gospels, the Pharisees accuse Jesus of not following the traditions of the elders (Mark 7:5), and Jesus in turn accuses them of preferring such human tradition to the **commandment** of God (7:8,13). Paul, himself a former Pharisee (Phil. 3:5), speaks of how far advanced he had become in the traditions of his forefathers (Gal. 1:14). These traditions of the oral law were eventually committed to writing in the **Mishnah**, though not until more than a century after the period of Christian and New Testament origins. Because they had already begun to understand Judaism primarily as interpretation of and obedience to the law, the Pharisees were well situated to reconstitute and redefine Judaism in the aftermath of the temple's destruction during the Roman War. Although earlier Pharisees may well have shared traditional Jewish hopes for the reestablishment of God's rule over the land of Israel, the Mishnah does not discuss them, but concentrates on specific commands to which obedience is expected.

Two famous and important Pharisaic leaders were Hillel and Shammai, contemporaries and rivals who flourished in the latter part of the first century **B.C.** and the first decade of the following century. Around them gathered rival schools or houses of legal interpretation. Shammai's was known for its stricter, harsher interpretation of the law, whereas the interpretations of the house of Hillel were more liberal. Hillel's school eventually came to dominate. Some of the sayings attributed to Hillel closely parallel sayings ascribed to Jesus. Among these is the negative form of the Golden Rule (cf. Matt. 7:12; Luke 6:31): "What is hateful to yourself do not do to your neighbor. That is the entire Torah. All the rest is commentary. Now go forth and learn" (Babylonian **Talmud**, *Sabbat*

31a). Versions of the Golden Rule are found also in various Jewish and other writings (e.g., the **apocryphal** Tobit 4:15 and Sirach 31:15).

In the New Testament, the Pharisees are frequently spoken of together with the scribes, and the impression is created that they are closely allied if not identical groups. The impression is not false, but the scribes were authoritative custodians and interpreters of the law before the appearance of a distinct group called Pharisees. Moreover, not all Pharisees were scribes. The historic task of the scribes was, however, largely taken up by the Pharisees, whose consuming interest was to interpret and apply the law to every sphere of life. They continued and expanded the traditional interpretations of the law, the fruition of which is to be found in the rabbinic literature, a large body of interpretative material from the earlier centuries of our era dealing with every phase of the law and with almost every aspect of religious and secular life.

The Rabbinic Tradition

The basic document of rabbinic literature, dating from the early third century, is the **Mishnah**. The **Talmud** includes, but is in the main a kind of learned commentary upon, the Mishnah. There are two Talmuds, the Babylonian and the Palestinian. The Palestinian is shorter than the Babylonian and dates from the early fifth century, whereas the latter dates from the late fifth century. In addition, the rabbinic period produced a wealth of **midrash**: biblical interpretation either legal (**halakic**) or illustrative and narrative (**haggadic**) in character.

The Sadducees

> The Sadducees hold that the soul perishes along with the body. They own no observance of any sort apart from the laws. . . . There are but few men to whom this doctrine has been made known, but these are men of the highest standing. [Josephus, *Jewish Antiquities*, XVIII, 16 f.]

> Then the high priest took action; he and all who were with him (that is, the sect of the Sadducees), being filled with jealousy arrested the apostles and put them in the public prison. [Acts 5:17 f.]

A second major group within Judaism, also mentioned in the **Gospels**, is the **Sadducees**. As in the case of the Pharisees, their history and the derivation of their name are not entirely clear. Presumably the name is related to the proper name of Zadok, a high priest appointed by Solomon. Whatever the history of the name and of the group, by New Testament times the Sadducees were the priestly aristocracy. In Acts 5:17, the high priest and the Sadducees are linked, and in 4:1, the priests, the captain of the temple, and the Sadducees appear together. Pharisees and Sadducees were thus religious brotherhoods centering, respectively, upon the authoritative interpretation of the **law** and temple worship. As such, they represented the chief foci of Jewish faith as it existed prior to A.D. 70. Although the temple and its service of worship had declined in practical

Jerusalem looking toward the Western Wall, or Wailing Wall, of the temple area. In the center is the Dome of the Rock, erected in the late seventh century as an Islamic shrine. Probably it stands on the site of the Second Temple of Judaism, which was extensively renovated by Herod the Great during Jesus' lifetime (cf. John 2:20).

importance as the majority of Jews came to live outside the land of Israel, it was nevertheless the symbolic center of Judaism. On the altar, **sacrifices** were offered so that the people might commune with God. **Sins** were dealt with and a right relationship between God and the people restored and maintained. Probably the most graphic example of this priestly function was the yearly ritual of the Day of Atonement, when the high priest alone entered the unapproachable Holy of Holies in the temple and there, as the representative of the people, came into the very presence of the Holy One. On this day, his action signified divine favor in that he entered, met, and was not destroyed by the God of Israel.

As custodians of religious tradition and cultic ceremony the Sadducees were somewhat more conservative than the Pharisees. The priests themselves held office by hereditary right. Moreover, the Sadducees represented established wealth and position. With regard to obedience to the law, they rejected the **oral tradition** and thus the effort of the Pharisees to extend the law's application to every situation in life in a binding way. They accepted only the word of scripture as authoritative. Politically, they were quietists who generally cooperated with the Romans. As members of the establishment it was in their interest to do so. They would have nothing to do with the relatively late doctrine of the **resurrection** of the dead, but rather adhered to the older and more typically biblical (Old Testament) view that death is simply the end of significant conscious life. In this they differed from the Pharisees, as well as from Jesus and the early Christians.

The Essenes

> The Essenes have a reputation for cultivating peculiar sanctity. Of Jewish birth, they show a greater attachment to each other than do the other sects. They shun pleasures as a vice and regard temperance and the control of the passions as a special virtue. [Josephus, *The Jewish War,* II, 119 f.]

In addition to the Pharisees and Sadducees there existed, at the time of Jesus, a group called **Essenes**, whose exact identity and extent are not entirely clear. Two important Jewish writers of the first century, the philosopher Philo and the historian Josephus, speak of them, although they are not mentioned by name in the New Testament. In recent decades, however, our knowledge of Essene or Essene-type groups has been immensely enlarged by the discovery of a monastery and an immense cache of documents at **Qumran**, on the northwest shore of the Dead Sea. Apparently an Essene community existed there at the time of Jesus.

A view of the monastery of Qumran, where the Dead Sea Scrolls were found. *(Courtesy of David Levenson.)*

The Qumran movement, which began sometime during the second or early first century **B.C.**, was characterized by revulsion at the impropriety of the temple worship presided over by an illegitimate high priesthood of **Hasmonean** rather than Zadokite lineage and based upon an erroneous festival calendar. A figure called only the "teacher of righteousness" or the "righteous teacher" was apparently the founder of this group. Unlike the Pharisees and Sadducees, they withdrew from the mainstream of Jewish life, which they regarded as corrupt, and often formed monastic communities. Yet this withdrawal had a positive as well as a negative side. It was a separation not only for the sake of the preservation of holiness but for a positive task and goal. First of all, the members of the community sought to carry out punctiliously the ritual and **ethical** requirements of the law and thus render a more acceptable obedience to God. This obedience was enforced under a strict discipline, and severe punishment was meted out for even minor infractions:

> Whoever has gone naked before his companion, without having been obliged
> to do so, he shall do penance for six months.
> Whoever has spat in an Assembly of the Congregation shall do penance for
> thirty days.
> Whoever has been so poorly dressed that when drawing his hand from beneath
> his garment his nakedness has been seen, he shall do penance for thirty days.
> Whoever has guffawed foolishly shall do penance for thirty days.
> Whoever has drawn out his left hand to gesticulate with it shall do penance
> for ten days. [*Community Rule VIII*, 14-17]

In addition, they looked toward the future vindication of Israel, or at least of their own community as the remnant of the true Israel. This vindication was expected in the form of an **apocalyptic** drama, indeed, a conflict in which the forces of light would overwhelm those of darkness (*War Rule* X–XIX). The victory would never be in doubt, because God was to fight on the side of his elect. Such terms as *light, darkness*, and *elect* highlight the basic character of Qumran thought. Almost everything was seen as a choice between good and evil, with no compromise allowed:

> He has created man to govern the world, and has appointed for him two
> spirits in which to walk until the time of His visitation: the spirits of truth
> and falsehood. Those born of truth spring from a fountain of light, but
> those born of falsehood spring from a source of darkness. All the children of
> righteousness are ruled by the Prince of Light and walk in the ways of light,
> but all the children of falsehood are ruled by the Angel of Darkness and
> walk in the ways of darkness. *[Community Rule* III, 17–21]

This way of perceiving the world, often called *dualism*, was reflected in the group's extremely rigid attitude toward the law, in its implacable hostility toward those regarded as enemies, and in its view of the coming culmination of history. The triumph of the good people over the bad would result in the elimination of evil from the world.

For the purpose of a historical understanding of Jesus, his disciples, and early Christianity, the Qumran documents are quite important. They reveal another Jewish sect of the same period that was engaged in alternately searching the scriptures and the heavens for signs of **God's** approaching **kingdom**. For the Christians, these hopes and expectations found fulfillment, although not in the way anticipated. For the Qumran community and other Essenes there was apparently only disappointment in this world. The monastery was destroyed by the Romans in the war, and the inhabitants hid their sacred scrolls in nearby caves, where they were accidentally discovered nearly two thousand years later.

Because the history of this sect has to be reconstructed on the basis of references and allusions in its own writings and in those of ancient Jewish authors such as Philo and Josephus, its origins and relationships remain somewhat obscure. Recurrently, it is proposed that the **Dead Sea Scrolls** are actually Christian documents and that this and similar facts about them have been intentionally suppressed. Such proposals are baseless. No specifically Christian documents have been found at Qumran, and the writings of the sect do not explicitly mention Jesus or other early Christian figures.

The Qumraners, or Essenes, as they may be called, were not purely passive in their hopes and expectations. Rather, they saw themselves, and particularly their separatist existence in the desert, as the fulfillment of the prophecy of Isaiah 40:3 (cf. *Community Rule*, VIII). They were in the wilderness preparing the way of the Lord. In this respect there is a striking similarity between the Qumran community and the New Testament **church**. In the New Testament, the same Old Testament passage is found on the lips of John the Baptist (John 1:23), who views his task in a similar way. Both the desert community and Jesus and his disciples lived in an atmosphere of apocalyptic or **eschatological** expectation. They looked forward to the coming of God. In fact, there were other similarities between the two groups. Both stood apart from prevailing forms of Jewish piety. Both looked to a central leader or founder, whether Jesus or the unnamed "teacher of righteousness"; in different ways both maintained a distinctive view of the law; both formed a community or sect of believers within Judaism. Of course, the Qumraners withdrew from society generally, while Jesus' disciples and the church did not. Nevertheless, the Qumran discoveries have not only enlarged our view of ancient Judaism, but in several significant ways have brought us closer to the origins of Christianity.

An Abiding Hope

Judaism in New Testament times was characterized not only by a memorable past and earnest efforts to obey the **law** of God in the present but also by its attitude toward the future. The **Qumran** discoveries are important evidence of this hope. As we have already noted, most Jews had definite ideas about the future, which were usually tied to the national destiny.

At one end of the spectrum stood those like the Qumraners, who looked for God's dramatic intervention in history to destroy the wicked and establish forever the righteous Israelites. At the other stood the **Sadducees**, whose position of relative security and comfort in relation to the Roman authorities made them little disposed either to sedition or to an **apocalyptic** outlook. The Sadducees looked for no cataclysmic end of history and no **resurrection** of the dead. In this respect they seem to have been in substantial agreement with the theology of preexilic Israel. From time to time, some, like the **Zealots**, sought to realize their hope for the recovery of national autonomy through armed resistance, perhaps aided by an expected divine intervention. (Such an expectation seems to be reflected in the Qumran community's *War Scroll*.) Apart from such extremes stood the **Pharisees**, who may have hoped for "the redemption of Israel" (Luke 24:21) but who did not expect to initiate it by violent revolution. Although the Pharisees may have abjured the active cooperation with Roman authority in which the Sadducees engaged, they served along with priests and Sadducees on the Sanhedrin, the highest Jewish court of appeal under Roman rule. Moreover, they had a history of political involvement during the **Maccabean** period. According to Josephus (*Jewish War*, II, xvii, 3), Pharisees were prominent among those who attempted to dissuade revolutionaries who were in the process of launching rebellion against Rome. Unlike the **Essenes**, the Pharisees were not monastically inclined.

It is difficult to say with certainty how the Pharisees expected Israel's national destiny to be fulfilled. The **rabbinic** documents, which generally express a Pharisaic point of view, do not look forward to an *imminent* apocalyptic drama whereby God would bring ordinary history to an end and restore the fortunes of Israel. But the rabbinic literature is not necessarily an accurate guide to Pharisaic expectations during the period of Jesus and the writing of the New Testament books. It reflects the attitude of Judaism after the Roman War and the uprising of Bar Kochba, when disappointed Zealot and revolutionary hopes made apocalyptic and **messianic** speculations about such matters unattractive. Yet earlier the Pharisees, like the Essenes, probably cherished such apocalyptic and messianic hopes:

> See, Lord, and raise up for them their king, the son of David, to rule over
> your servant Israel in the time known to you, O God.
> Undergird him with the strength to destroy the unrighteous rulers, to purge
> Jerusalem from Gentiles who trample her to destruction. . . .
> At his warning the nations will flee from his presence; and he will condemn
> sinners by the thoughts of their hearts. [*Psalms of Solomon* 17:23, 24, 27]

In the intertestamental apocalyptic literature, we find the expectation of a decisive culmination of history. The hope was widely shared. This world or this age was to come to a conclusion with the restoration of Israel's fortunes and the resurrection of her righteous dead, marking the inauguration of the messianic age. After a period of several hundred to a thousand years, the general resurrection (that is, of all the dead) would take place as a prelude to the final judgment of God. Then God would usher in the "age to come," the consummation toward which all history was moving. It is too much to speak of a single plan or scheme, but the existence of similar ideas and expectations, if not in systematized form, in the New Testament shows that they were common currency in the Judaism of Jesus' day.

Apocalyptic and similar ideas were not espoused solely out of patriotic interests and hopes. The doctrine of the resurrection of the dead provided a lively individual hope and a means of justifying God's ways. If, as experience dictated, the righteous servants of God's law suffer in this life, they may expect better things when the dead are raised. The doctrine of the resurrection became the hallmark of the Pharisees (cf. Acts 23:6), so that in time a virtual anathema could be pronounced against those who disbelieved it. Belief in the resurrection appears rarely in the Old Testament, notably in Isaiah 26:19 and Daniel 12:2. Thus it is not surprising that the Sadducees did not feel obliged to share it. Nevertheless, the New Testament reports that Jesus (Mark 12:26 f.) as well as Paul (Acts 23:6) believed in the resurrection. In doing so they were following a Pharisaic Jewish tradition.

The whole complex of apocalyptic ideas, including the resurrection of the dead, the dualism of good and evil, the distinction between this age and the age to come, and the destruction of evil and the triumph of good in a cataclysmic **cosmic** upheaval and judgment, cannot be explained fully on the basis of the earlier, Old Testament tradition of Israel, whether historical, **prophetic**, or cultic. The apocalyptic frame of mind has marked affinities with Persian, particularly Zoroastrian, thought. This is especially true of the dualism, cosmic eschatology, and the last judgment. To what extent they may reflect direct borrowing or even more subtle influences is debatable, although such outside influences cannot simply be discounted, especially in view of the exposure of many Jews to foreign influences in the exile and the **Diaspora** after the sixth century B.C. But the oppression and frustration of the Jews in their homeland doubtless provided the necessary seedbed and impetus for such ideas to develop. In due course, this same kind of thinking provided the fertile ground out of which Christianity emerged. For John the Baptist came proclaiming the imminent judgment; Jesus announced the inbreaking of the **kingdom of God** in power; and the early Christians proclaimed that Jesus had risen from the dead and would come again in glory to render judgment (cf. also Daniel 7). Although Jesus surely felt himself to be a son of Abraham, as did the early Christians generally (cf. Gal. 3:29), and consciously stood in the tradition of the law and the prophets, he was the heir of ideas and perspectives that were unknown to the **patriarchs**, Moses, or Amos. Some of these were perhaps "foreign" in the sense of being non-Israelite. Yet the substance and framework of Jesus' message had deep roots in his people's history and faith. Apart from the glory and the agony of that history, Jesus can scarcely be fully understood. In his insistence on obedience to God's will in the present as the key to the future, Jesus exemplifies Israelite faith. Jesus proposed a reinterpretation of both obedience and hope, but in the indissoluble linking of the two he was a true son of Abraham.

Judaism is history, law, tradition, worship, and the land. But perhaps more than anything else, Judaism is and always has been a people of the **covenant**—a people with a unique sense of identity and purpose, a chosen people, with all the distinctiveness as well as the dangers that such a concept implies. Our discussion of Judaism has naturally and perhaps inevitably focused upon the major religious groupings of the first century. But, as we have noted, most Jews were probably members of no definable religious group. To the majority of these people, or at least to the less conscientiously pious among them, the term *people of the land (am ha-aretz)* was applied. They were often looked down upon by those who were more scrupulous observers. Quite possibly Jesus himself was numbered among these humble folk (cf. John 7:15); certainly many of his followers were. In the Gospel of John, they are described as ignorant of the law and accursed (7:49). But although frequently disparaged and even ridiculed, such folk were not necessarily unaware of their heritage and identity. This sense of belonging, together with resistance toward the claims of the religious establishment, is reflected in the attitude of Jesus himself. He was clearly aware of his identity as an Israelite, a Jew, yet he reacted sharply against claims of religious superiority. Like Jesus, the earliest Christians were Jews, and only gradually began to think of themselves in any other way.

Jesus lived and died a Jew. In a real sense his death was the consequence of his unswerving allegiance to the God of Israel at a time when his people lived under foreign, and sometimes oppressive, dominion. His disciples were, of course, Jews, and, as far as we can tell, they continued to regard themselves as such. His own brother James became an important figure in the early church (Acts 15; 21:17-26; Gal. 2) and apparently represented and led that wing of the new community that strongly affirmed its Jewishness. But the early Christian movement spread across the Mediterranean world, making most of its converts among people who never had been, and would not become, Jews. The story of Jesus and of his first followers is, however, inextricably tied, to and rooted in, the Judaism of the land of Israel.

THE GRECO-ROMAN WORLD

Judaism provided the ingredients from which a new faith took shape. The pilgrimage and travail of Israel, its scriptures and its expectations, furnished the essential frame of reference for Jesus and his earliest followers. Yet Christianity soon broke away from Judaism and spread rapidly among **Gentiles** throughout the Mediterranean world. In a sense, it became a universal form of Judaism. But how and why did this happen to the sect of Jesus' followers in particular? The answer to this question remains in part a mystery. Nevertheless, some valid reasons can be discerned by observing the conditions of the world into which Christianity spread.

Language and Culture

Several hundred years before the beginning of the Christian era, in about the third century **B.C.**, the Hebrew scriptures were translated into Greek. This important version is known as the **Septuagint** (abbreviated **LXX**). Most New Testament writers used this translation. According to an ancient legend found in the *Epistle of Aristeas*, the translation was made by seventy-two Jewish elders, working in Egypt for the royal library, because of scholarly appreciation for the importance of the books. In all probability, however, the translation was made on the initiative and for the benefit of the Jews themselves, most of whom could by then read and understand Greek better than their ancestral Hebrew tongue.

Alexander the Great

The Jews had become widely scattered in Egypt and other places as a result of the **Exile**. They spoke Greek largely because of the remarkable influence of one man, Alexander of Macedon. Few individuals have had a greater impact upon the history, culture, and religion of the world than Alexander. Born in 356 B.C., he succeeded to the throne of his father, Philip of Macedon, in 334. Two years later he set out from his home in Macedonia to begin the conquest of the Persian Empire, which for years had menaced and invaded Greece. In eight years, he and his army swept as far south as Egypt and as far east as the Indus River at the westernmost reaches of India, where only logistics and the homesickness of his soldiers halted his advance. Although the Persian Empire and army proved ineffective against the more homogeneous, better disciplined army of Alexander, his military accomplishment cannot be minimized. Courageous, capable of brutality but at times humanely sensitive, he ranks as one of the great military leaders of all time.

Of greater importance than military feats, however, was the cultural revolution that he accomplished. Alexander was not only a soldier but also a man of letters and a student of Aristotle. He intended to establish Greek culture and language in the areas that he conquered, and his success in this respect was remarkable. Alexander's conquests created genuine cultural mixtures throughout the ancient world, with the Hellenic (Greek) element as the common factor everywhere. This achievement was exemplified in the fact that he and his soldiers took women of the East as wives. Following his conquest he seemed content to remain there, and apparently regarded Babylon as his capital. But after a short stay, quite unexpectedly, he died of a fever in 323 B.C. at the age of thirty-three, leaving no legal heir capable of succeeding him. His lieutenants struggled for control of his empire and soon managed to pull it apart. Thus the fruit of his military conquest, although immense, proved ephemeral, for his empire dissolved almost as quickly as it had emerged.

Although Alexander did not succeed in establishing a Macedonian empire that would survive his death, his efforts to spread Greek language and culture and to embed them in the life of the East proved highly successful, especially in the cities. As his heritage

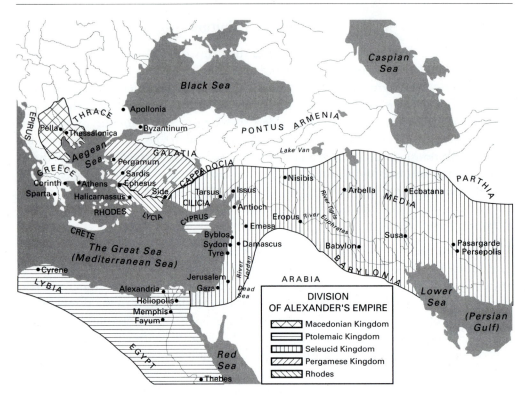

Division of Alexander's Empire.

he left a string of Greek cities across the area of his conquest, outposts of Greek civilization. Probably the largest and most successful of these was the great Egyptian center of
Alexandria, which appropriately bore his name. Here a large colony of Jews settled, and
the first and most important translation of the Hebrew scriptures into Greek was made.
Alexandria is still a great city, the second city of Egypt after Cairo.

Alexander created, for the first time, one far-flung cultural world, and momentarily a political world as well. His conquests made it possible to conceive of humanity as a
unity, and perhaps Alexander himself viewed the world and its people in that way. His
view of himself and his mission can only be inferred from his deeds. He sought out
divine oracles in that connection and gladly received divine honors. Such honors were
reserved only for gods in Greece, but in the East were often accorded to powerful rulers.
It is tempting to see in Alexander one who thought of himself as a **son of God** destined
to unify humanity. Possibly he did, although we cannot safely draw such a conclusion
from the evidence. In any event, Alexander's role as well as his accomplishments sowed
seeds that later made possible the worldwide Christian movement.

The Greek Language

Alexander gave a particular form and character to the world into which Christianity was born. Nothing is more important for history and culture than language, and nothing promotes communication and understanding like a common language. Among other things, Alexander bequeathed to the Mediterranean world a common language, Greek. It was not the Greek of Plato or Sophocles, but another newer and somewhat simpler dialect known as **koine**, or common, Greek. This Greek became the *lingua franca* of the ancient world three hundred years before the time of Christ, much as English is today.

People from widely separated areas, with vastly different backgrounds, could talk to each other in Greek. Perhaps they could not construct complex Greek sentences with perfect syntax and inflection, but they could make themselves understood. Needless to say, this gift of common speech was of considerable importance in encouraging commerce and various sorts of interchange throughout the Alexandrian world. Indeed, in the centers of Greek culture established by Alexander, conscious attempts were made to promote and spread the manners and customs of Hellenic civilization, especially the athletic games. The world that Alexander left was one world in a sense that it had never been before. Previously there had been great overarching empires such as the Assyrian, the Persian, and the Egyptian, and certainly different peoples and cultures had interacted. Yet never before had there been such an attempt to create a common world civilization as Alexander and his successors actually and purposefully brought about. This mixture of Hellenic (Greek) and Oriental elements is called **Hellenistic** civilization.

The importance of this universal Mediterranean civilization for Judaism and its offspring Christianity can scarcely be overestimated. For Judaism it was at once a challenge and a benefit: a challenge in that it threatened just those distinguishing features of life that characterized the Jewish community as such; a benefit in that it made possible greater extension of the scope and influence of Judaism, especially Greek-speaking Judaism. For Christianity it was an immense boon. Without Alexander the rapid spread of Christianity throughout the Greco-Roman world might never have taken place. Certainly the Christian message had a power of its own, and its impact cannot be attributed to favorable cultural factors alone. Nevertheless, it is a striking fact that the spread of Christianity in the first centuries occurred principally in those areas that fell under the sway of Alexander's, or at least of Greek, influence.

The New Testament itself was composed entirely in Hellenistic Greek, although the **Gospels** are in part based on earlier **Aramaic** sources, either written or oral. Except in Palestine and Syria, and perhaps to some extent even there, the preaching of the **gospel** was in Greek. In most places of any importance, Greek was the language that was spoken and understood by both preacher and hearer. Even in Rome, to which Christianity spread at a very early time and which we generally associate with the Latin language,

The Parthenon, certainly the most famous site of Greek antiquity, stands atop the acropolis of the city of Athens. Dating from the fifth century before Christ, it was the temple of Athena. Paul's sermon recorded in Acts 17:22–31 was delivered at the foot of the acropolis and under the shadow of this great building—which he never mentions!

Greek was generally spoken and understood by cultured people. Paul wrote to the Romans in Greek. Not only did Paul and other New Testament writers use the Greek language; they also adopted Greek and Roman modes of persuasive discourse, as described by Aristotle, Cicero, and Quintilian, among others. Much of the New Testament exhorts its audience to perform activities that benefit them: Matthew's Sermon on the Mount (chaps. 5–7) exemplifies such deliberative rhetoric. Jesus' farewell discourse to his disciples (John 14–16) is a good example of epideictic rhetoric, which intends to instill or enhance particular beliefs and values. When Paul invites the Corinthians to judge the character of his ministry among them (2 Cor. 5:11–6:10; 10:1–13:14), he employs judicial rhetoric. All these forms of persuasion rely on careful arrangement of the author's views, crafted in distinctive styles with different kinds of proof. *Logos* refers to deductive or inductive arguments, such as those that open the Letter to the Hebrews (1:1–2:14). *Pathos* attempts to generate emotional responses among a group of listeners: "Now when they heard [his Pentecost sermon] they were cut to the heart and said to Peter and to the other apostles, 'Brothers, what should we do?'" (Acts 2:37 NRSV). Especially in the case of Jesus and the Gospels (e.g., Mark 1:22; 4:41), persuasion relies heavily on the power of the speaker's authoritative character, or *ethos*.

Despite the important role that Greek language and culture played in its spread, it would be incorrect to call Christianity simply a Greek religion. Viewed from the standpoint of its origin and original constituents, it is also Oriental and especially Jewish. It is not, therefore, the purely Greek element, but precisely this combination of Greek and Jewish, West and East, that was characteristic of Christianity in the Hellenistic world.

Life under the Roman Empire

Alexander created a world but did not live to govern it. That task was ultimately performed by Rome. It is true, of course, that the limits of Alexander's conquests and those of the Roman Empire at its height were not the same. Alexander's conquests extended farther to the east, whereas the Roman Empire's orbit stretched far beyond Italy to the north and west. Yet in a sense, the worlds of Alexandrian **Hellenism** and of Rome were one world. Through conquest of Greece and wholesale appropriation of Greek culture in the second century B.C., Rome fell heir to the legacy of Greece just when the empire was emerging as the dominant military force and political power of the Western world. For a half century before **Christ** and nearly half a millennium after, the Roman Empire gave to the Mediterranean world a political unity and stability. That unity, though not unbroken, was as continuous and dependable as any so large and varied a segment of the world has known before or since. The marvel is not that the Roman Empire fell—crumbled is the better word—but that it stood so long. At the time of its greatest extent and vitality—that is, during the New Testament period—the Roman Empire stretched from Syria and Palestine to the British Isles. Of western Europe, only Germany and the Scandinavian countries remained outside the Roman orbit, and only Scandinavia completely outside. The southern- and westernmost parts of Germany came under Roman domination, as did Austria as far north as the Danube.

Roman Peace

The birth and development of Christianity as a world religion came about during the two centuries when Rome was at the zenith of its power (i.e., from 27 B.C., the accession date of Augustus Caesar, to A.D. 180, the year of the death of Marcus Aurelius, the philosopher-emperor). This period, often referred to as the *pax romana* (Roman peace), was a favorable time for the origin of a movement like Christianity. There was enforced peace and internal order. Our present Western systems of law owe more directly to the Romans than to the Hebrews, and the *pax romana* was a time of lawfulness as well as peace. The Romans administered their empire with firmness, occasionally with brutality, but with a certain sensitivity for the varieties of people and customs within their bounds. Local law enforcement and administration were left in the hands of local officials. Where local administration or law enforcement broke down, as in the case of Judea at the time of Jesus, the Romans intervened to make sure that anarchy did not result. Roman officials were not universally good, as we have already noted. Pontius Pilate, for example, left a great deal to be desired. Yet the Romans themselves removed Pilate from power. Although it is true that Jesus died on a Roman cross and that Christians were persecuted by Romans, it is equally true, and probably just as important, that early Christianity benefited considerably from the relatively peaceful and lawful conditions of Roman rule that accompanied its beginnings.

Communication

Early Christianity profited also from the network of roads and sea transportation that the Romans had developed and maintained, largely for military purposes. Again, policing of the roads was left to the various provinces and localities as long as they could do the job, but when and where conditions demanded, the Roman military intervened to keep roads open for travel and free of bandits and other potential harassments. It would certainly be wrong to imagine that travel in ancient times was as easy as it is today. Yet travel between virtually all parts of the empire was possible, and it was easier to go from Jerusalem to Rome in Paul's day than it was to travel from the East Coast to California in this country 150 years ago.

Thus, favorable conditions of language and culture as well as an orderly government and a workable transportation system favored the spread of the Christian gospel in the Greco-Roman world. They help to explain the rapid growth of the church and the ways in which the **gospel** found expression—not the least of which is the New Testament itself, a collection of books written in Greek, and in many cases written from one Christian or group of Christians to or for another. These documents attest not only a lively faith but also a sense of tangible relationship between one Christian **church** and another, which was made possible by the conditions of the time. Moreover, they display a concrete sense of mission to the inhabited world (Greek, *oikoumenē*), a concept not previously unknown but given particular point and form by the vision and work of Alexander the Great and the political reality of the Roman Empire.

Civic Life

Although the classical age of the Greek city-state preceded the time of Alexander and the establishment of his empire, the form of the **Hellenistic** city persisted under Rome and thus into the time of the rise of Christianity and beyond. This urban atmosphere, which featured local political control, temples to the various gods, citizens' assemblies for discussion and debate, the gymnasium for instruction of young men, and stadiums for athletic games, provided the matrix for the rise of the Christian faith. The missionary endeavors of Paul and others within this religious, social, and political synthesis were made possible by common language, political stability, and the accessibility of these cities—some of which had been newly created. At the same time, the spiritual ferment of the times provided an openness to religious messages from a variety of sources, including the early Christians. Consequently, early Christians declared their message in this urban setting, even though the origins of Jesus and the first disciples were much less cosmopolitan.

Domestic Life

Within the Hellenistic city of Roman times the house or household played a central role. It was much larger than the modern nuclear family—perhaps more like the extended family of several generations ago, consisting of more than one or two generations of kinspeople. Moreover, it also included household employees and slaves. The head of the household was of necessity a relatively affluent and influential person. The household provided not only a

The house of a rich person of Pompeii, near modern Naples, and somewhat over a hundred miles south of Rome. The wealthy lived well, much better than the vast majority.

residence but also an important mode of social identity, and even a livelihood for a number of persons who would have otherwise lacked such essentials of everyday life.

The conversion of the head of a household was a major coup for the early Christians. For one thing it would enormously increase the likelihood of conversion of other members of the household. Religion was less a matter of individual, personal choice in the ancient world than it is in contemporary society. Nevertheless, Christianity by its very nature introduced an element of individual decision. One had to confess faith (Rom. 10:10; 1 Cor. 12:3) and be **baptized** (Acts 8:36). Even if one's householder or master were converted, one might remain an unbeliever. This seems to have been the case with Onesimus, whom Paul later converted and sent back a Christian to his master Philemon (Philem. 15–17).

Moreover, the conversion of the head of a household meant that the **church** acquired a place of worship. Paul speaks of several such householders who were hosts to the churches he founded or knew (Rom. 16:3–5, 23). We tend to think of a church primarily as a building. But there were no such buildings available for the earliest Christians. Upon reaching a new city, Paul may have preached initially in synagogues, as Acts portrays him, and perhaps he occasionally even hired a public hall (cf. Acts 19:9); but the principal meeting place of Christian cells or churches was the private home. Thus the householder, who could provide such a place of meeting, was a most important convert for the Christian community.

Religion

According to the Book of Acts, the **Apostle** Paul began his famous speech on the Areopagus by saying, "Athenians, I see how extremely religious you are in every way" (17:22). Indeed, the world of New Testament times was a religious world, and Christianity did not originate in a time of religious decline. Whatever may have been the general state of culture in the first century, religion did not lack vitality and vigorous manifestations. Religions were often integral to ethnic and political identity, and this was true even of Judaism, but not of early Christianity.

A striking characteristic of the religious situation was its variety. This too is represented in Paul's speech, for he mentions the objects of their worship, among which is an altar inscribed to an unknown god, as if the Athenians were taking no chances on omitting, and therefore offending, any deity ("to whom it may concern"). People participated in various rites and ceremonies according to law, taste, or desire. The period was also marked by syncretism: various religious traditions merged together or were interpreted in terms of one another.

Such toleration did not mean that people by and large did not take religion seriously. If anything, just the opposite was the case. Only from the Christian or Jewish point of view would this toleration of, and participation in, a multiplicity of religious cults be taken as idolatry. The exclusivism of Judaism and Christianity was itself regarded as odd and even impious in ancient times, and the refusal of Christians and Jews to worship any god other than their own led their neighbors to brand them as atheists. This persistence in worshiping only one God was perhaps the factor that most clearly distinguished Christians and Jews in the ancient world, and it may have had something to do with the fact that of the religions of that civilization, only Christianity and Judaism survive today. Yet elements of these other religions have survived in Judaism and particularly in Christianity. For example, the date of Jesus' birth is unknown; Christmas is the Christianized version of an ancient Roman rite celebrating the winter solstice and return of the sun. Easter, however, is a distinctly Christian holiday, whose date is determined by the death of Jesus at the Jewish **Passover**.

The specific manifestations of piety in the Greco-Roman world are far too numerous to discuss fully here. Nevertheless, it is important to notice several basic types of religion that were popular and significant. These include the traditional and official religions of the Greco-Roman pantheon (a Greek word meaning a temple dedicated to "all the gods"), the state-inspired worship of the ruler, the more individualistic mystery religions, as well as **Gnosticism**, and **Hellenistic** Judaism. Within and against this background, early Christianity emerged.

Traditional and Official Religion

At the time of Christianity's emergence and the writing of the New Testament books, the traditional religion of the Roman Empire was a complex, somewhat amorphous combination of both Greek and Roman elements. Prior to the Christian era there had been a distinctly Roman religious cult involving especially the gods of the hearth and the family, of which the public religion was an extension and enlargement. This state or city cult was presided over first by the king, and later by a pontifical college made up of several prominent men of the realm. Ancient Greek religion of the pre-Christian period seems to have consisted originally of a variety of local deities, each with a **holy** place. These were later submerged under, or incorporated into, the pantheon of very human gods known to us from Homer, who is the fountainhead of classical mythology. By the beginning of the Christian period an amalgamation of Greek and Roman deities had taken place. It was taken for granted that the Greek and Roman gods were for the most part actually the same gods, even if they had different names, and an equation of the various gods of the Homeric pantheon with Roman gods had been worked out. For example, the three prominent Greek gods, Zeus, Hera, and Athena, were identified, respectively, with the Roman Jupiter, Juno, and Minerva. Moreover, the purely Greek god Apollo was worshiped on the Palatine Hill in Rome.

By the beginning of the Christian era, the traditional piety of Greece and Rome was facing competition from newer religions, especially those of Oriental origin, which were gaining enthusiastic adherents. Moreover, people of some education and intelligence had difficulty taking the **myths** and stories that were told about the gods seriously, at least insofar as they were understood as literal accounts of what actually took place or of the nature of divine reality. Folk of a philosophical bent, especially the Stoics, had been interpreting the myths in an **allegorical** fashion for some time. That is, they took them to be narrative representations of philosophical truths, which really had nothing to do with the stories per se and could stand independently of them. Thus the old gods got a new lease on life. For example, Zeus, the head of the Homeric pantheon, could be identified with "the general law, which is right reason, pervading everything . . . the Supreme Head of the universe" (Zeno, *Fragments,* 162, 152). Stoic monism, according to which God or the *logos* (Greek for *word* or *reason*) pervades the universe much as the soul or animation pervades the body and gives it unity and purpose, was thereby reconciled with a mythology that had quite a different origin and meaning. Especially those stories of the gods consorting and cavorting with one another in ways that sober people came to regard as shameful were allegorized away, making room for the Stoic **ethic**, which centered in willing conformity with that reason or logos that governs the universe and the individual. The Stoics themselves, however, were not coldly rationalistic. Philosophy was for them a vital piety, as it was for many literate Greeks. Although such piety might be grounded in a philosophical pantheism, its expression often took the form of hymns and prayers to a personal God, as can be seen from a portion of Cleanthes' famous *Hymn to Zeus:*

> Thou, O Zeus, art praised above all gods; many are thy names and thine is
>   all power for ever.
> The beginning of the world was from thee; and with law thou rulest over all
>   things.
> Unto thee may all flesh speak; for we are thy offspring.
> Therefore will I raise a hymn unto thee: and will ever sing of thy power.
> The whole order of the heavens obeyeth thy word: as it moveth around the earth:
> With little and great lights mixed together: how great art thou, King above
>   all for ever! [Cleanthes, *Fragment* 537, 1–10]

The ancient Greco-Roman religion survived not merely in Stoic reinterpretation but also in more naive popular worship. As such, it remained the traditional public religion of the Roman Empire, just as its predecessors had been the official cults of old Rome and of the Greek city-states. We find some indication of its survival in the New Testament. According to Acts the people of Lystra, in what is now Asia Minor, hailed Paul and Barnabas as Hermes and Zeus, respectively, upon their performance of a **miracle**. Moreover, a temple of Zeus was located near that city (Acts 14:12 f.). There was in the city of Ephesus a great temple of Artemis (cf. Acts 19:23 ff.), the ruins of which have been unearthed in modern times by **archaeologists**, as have many other temples to the Greco-Roman deities. In addition, the Roman emperor Augustus, who was ruling at the time Jesus was born, made a serious effort to promote the traditional public cult, especially the ancient Roman practices and ceremonies. Upon the death of the high **priest**, he went so far as to assume that office himself, reviving a custom long fallen into disuse, according to which the kingship and high priesthood were united in one man.

There was an increasing tendency to regard the emperor as a divine figure and to place him among the pantheon of gods to whom worship was due. Although Augustus

The ancient tomb of Caesar Augustus, Roman emperor at the time of Jesus' birth, stands beside the (restored) monument to the Roman Peace *(pax romana)*, called the Monument of Peace.

coyly spurned divine honors during his lifetime, they were accorded him upon his death. By the end of the first century, it was no longer a question of ascribing divine honors and worship to deceased emperors. Now such veneration was required for the living emperor as well. Not surprisingly, this led in due course to a confrontation between the young Christian church and Rome, for Rome insisted upon emperor worship as a pledge of allegiance—or devotion—to the emperor and thus to the empire. As Pliny, governor of Bithynia in the early second century, writes to the emperor Trajan, "All who denied that they were or had been Christians I considered should be discharged, because they called upon the gods at my dictation and did reverence, with incense and wine, to your image which I had ordered to be brought forward for this purpose . . . " (Pliny, *Letters* X, 96). It was, in fact, a sort of loyalty oath, one that many Christians could not conscientiously take. When emperor worship is seen against the background of the many gods and many lords of the ancient world (cf. 1 Cor. 8:5), however, and when the benefits accruing to humankind from the emperor's rule are recalled, we can understand why the authorities did not regard divine homage as too much to ask of any subject. Moreover, worship of the supreme ruler was not unknown in earlier times.

Even though Hebrew religious tradition clearly separated the king from the divine, the amalgam of Mediterranean culture and religion included an Egyptian religious tradition in which the Pharaoh appeared as divine and immortal. Indeed, Alexander's unification of the Mediterranean world opened the way to a synthesis in which the king could be titled savior, lord, god. Roman emperors were actually slow to press claims of divinity, until under Domitian (81–96) emperor worship was made a test of loyalty to Rome. Then Christians who understood Jesus as the true bearer of such divine titles began to be persecuted for failure to honor the emperor and the empire. The Romans were perplexed to find peoples who stubbornly refused to participate in emperor worship—the people of Israel who declared their allegiance to the one God of Abraham, Isaac, and Jacob, and the people of the new **covenant** who declared themselves a **messianic** community. Within that context Jews were ordinarily exempted from participation in the emperor cult— but Christians as such were not.

Popular Religion

Although the official religious rites of Greece and Rome were by no means dead at the beginning of the Christian era, they did not represent the principal form of personal piety. Their continued existence, and whatever vitality they had, was probably due largely to the role they played in expressing the political and cultural solidarity of the Roman Empire and the Greco-Roman world. No sustained and systematic attempt was made to establish public religion to the exclusion of private practices and societies, however, and it is in the latter that the burgeoning variety and strength of religion in later antiquity can be most clearly seen.

Mystery Religions   Unfortunately, our knowledge of these practices and societies is quite limited, owing in no small measure to the aura of secrecy that surrounded many of them. This is especially true of the mystery religions, which were gaining in prominence and popularity at the beginning of the Christian era. The vows of secrecy taken by the followers of these religions were meticulously observed. Much of the ancient material on the mysteries comes to us secondhand through Christian and Jewish sources. Consequently, we do not know in detail, or with a high degree of assurance, what they were like.

The most closely guarded secrets of the mystery religions were their rites of initiation, through which the novitiate first received the benefits that the cult deity bestowed. Apparently the candidate somehow reenacted or saw reenacted the cult **myth**: the story about the god or gods on which the cult was based. Through participation in the cult ritual, the candidate received the **salvation** that was the very reason for the cult's being.

Perhaps the best account of the mystery ritual is found in Apuleius, *The Golden Ass* (XI, 22–26), from which the following, deliberately vague description of an Isis initiation is taken:

> Then behold the day approached when as the sacrifice of dedication should be done; and when the sun declined and evening came, there arrived on every coast a great multitude of priests, who according to their ancient order offered me many presents and gifts. Then was all the laity and profane people commanded to depart, and when they had put on my back a new linen robe, the priest took my hand and brought me to the most secret and sacred place of the temple. . . . Thou shalt understand that I approached near unto hell, even to the gates of Proserpine, and after that I was ravished throughout all the elements, I returned to my proper place: about midnight I saw the sun brightly shine, I saw likewise the gods celestial and the gods infernal, before whom I presented myself and worshipped them. Behold now have I told thee, which although thou hast heard, yet it is necessary that thou conceal it; wherefore this only will I tell, which may be declared without offence for the understanding of the profane.

The myth of the cult naturally varied with the different mystery religions. Among others, there were the Eleusinian mysteries of Greece; the cult of Attis and Cybele, originating in Asia Minor; as well as that of Isis and Osiris, which had its origin in Egypt. Most of the cults were based originally upon fertility rites celebrating the return of the growing season. In time, however, the meaning of the cult myth was seen against the background of human life and death, so that through initiation into the mysteries one could assure oneself of a happy destiny beyond death. Scholars once confidently asserted that the common factor in the cult myths was the death and **resurrection** of a deity, in which the initiate participated vicariously through the rites and thus rose from the dead with the god (cf. Rom. 6:1–11). This interpretation has been subject to dispute, but it is probably not completely misleading. Even though early Christian belief in the death and resurrection of Jesus was not based on the cult myths of the mystery religions, it found a kind of parallel there. Thus people could recognize in Christianity, as in the mysteries, an important dimension of personal salvation.

The traditional religions of Greece and Rome, like the religion of Israel, focused primarily upon the ordering of life in this world, and did not promise the adherent a glorious life after death. The mysteries, however, appealed to human hopes and fears in the face of death and offered to those who became initiates the promise of eternal life. Membership in them presumed a belief in their efficacy and required a conscious act of the will, a decision. Thus the mystery religions had a character decidedly different from the traditional official religions and in some respects not unlike Christianity. That is, they were private, they were oriented around hope and assurance for the future, and they were voluntary. To some outsiders, early Christianity may have seemed to be a mystery cult. Unlike Judaism and Christianity, however, the mysteries did not claim the exclusive loyalty of their adherents. A person might worship Zeus and the emperor and at the same time be an initiate of one or more mysteries. In fact, the official religions and the mysteries were complementary; they applied to different spheres of life, the one to public order and morality, the other to the need for emotional satisfaction and the assurance of present and ultimate security of one's personal being and destiny. Thus several Roman emperors, including Augustus, were initiated into the Eleusinian mysteries.

Gnosticism   At some time after the mystery religions moved into center stage, there appeared another important spiritual phenomenon that was in some ways like them. We say "phenomenon," for it is not quite certain that **Gnosticism** should be called a religion. It was found in various places and in various forms. Until fairly recently most of our knowledge of Gnosticism came from Christian writers of the late second, third, and later centuries, all of whom portray Gnosticism as a Christian heresy in which a special knowledge (Greek *gnōsis*—hence the name Gnosticism) is made the key to salvation. Such a description is not entirely inaccurate. The process of salvation in Gnosticism involves, first of all, a knowledge or sense of one's profound alienation from the world. Thus one must find a way out of imprisonment in this world and into the world above. This release can be accomplished only by a special dispensation of knowledge by which the secrets of the way back to one's heavenly home are divulged. In Christian Gnostic systems, Jesus is the heavenly revealer who awakens the adherents from their stupor in this world, reminds them of their heavenly home, reveals the secrets of the way, and also leads them back. The way back was often conceived as a rather long road, a tortuous climb back through the seven or more heavens, in each of which the Gnostics shed another part of the veil of flesh until the divine essence—the very quintessence of their being—arrived safely home.

Gnosticism was once regarded as the acute **Hellenization** of Christianity, a distorted translation of the Christian message into Greek ways of thinking and speaking. Yet recent research and discoveries have shown that Gnosticism is not simply derived from Christianity, and that it owes more to the East, to Syria, Persia, and Babylonia, and perhaps even to Judaism, than to classical Greek culture. In this respect it is not unlike the mystery religions, many of which came from the Orient. The exact nature and origins of Gnosticism are still obscure, however, and remain matters of controversy among historians of religion.

We can, nevertheless, get a fairly clear grasp of the thrust and meaning of Gnosticism. Wherever it appears, in whatever form, it is characterized by an extreme dualism of God and the world. In contrast to the Stoic monism, in which God and the world are essentially related and, indeed, indwell one another, Gnosticism takes God and the world to be separate and incompatible. Far from being the creation of the one God, as in orthodox Jewish and Christian thought, this world is at best an excrescence from the divine world, at worst the creation of an antigod. Its very existence is the antithesis of God's salvation. The mystery religions were primarily motivated by a desire to secure human existence in the face of death. Gnosticism also had this goal in view, but combined with it an abhorrence of evil, which was in general identified with this world and its history.

According to Gnosticism, people live in the world, but at least some of them are not of it. For while human bodies are made of the same substance as the world, there is, or may be, hidden within each one a spark of the divine life. Salvation is then the rescuing of the divine spark from its imprisonment in the material world, and specifically in the flesh. The first and essential step is the recognition that one is not at home in this world, that one's essential being is related to the divine world and can find its way home.

> Therefore if one has knowledge he is from above. If he is called, he hears, he answers, and he turns to him who is calling him, and ascends to him. And he knows in what manner he is called. Having knowledge, he does the will of the one who called him, he wishes to be pleasing to him, he receives rest. Each one's name comes to him. He who is to have knowledge in this manner knows where he comes from and where he is going. He knows as one who having become drunk has turned away from his drunkenness, [and] having returned to himself, has set right what are his own. *[Gospel of Truth 22:3–20]*

There is nothing specifically Christian about this passage, yet early Christianity was deeply engaged with the Gnostic problem throughout the second century, and probably even earlier. In the Gospel of John, Jesus says, "Those who love their life lose it, and those who hate their life in this world will keep it for eternal life" (12:25; cf. Mark 8:35)—certainly a gnosticizing statement about the nature and sphere of salvation. Compared with Jewish hopes of the restoration of Davidic kingship, important aspects of early Christian hope seem closer to Gnosticism. Thus we see traces of the contact and conflict with Gnosticism not only in the Gospel of John but in the Johannine letters, Colossians, and the **Pastoral Epistles**, as well as the extensive anti–Gnostic literature that appears from the time of Justin Martyr in the middle of the second century. A large collection of Gnostic literature going back to the second century (although the actual **manuscripts** are a couple of centuries later) has in this century been uncovered in Nag Hammadi, near the Nile River in southern Egypt. It was obviously used by people who considered themselves Christians. Some of the books, such as the *Gospel of Truth* (quoted above), are apparently Gnostic interpretations of Christianity. Others have little explicit connection with anything we can identify with Christianity, except that they were apparently used by this Gnostic Christian church. *The Gospel of Truth* represents an attractive, if not specifically Christian, piety. It mentions Jesus, and may reflect knowledge of the Gospel of John. In reading it, one can appreciate the attractiveness of such Gnosticism, quite in contrast to the form represented in the accounts of orthodox Christians, who wrote about it in order to refute it. Gnosticism is different from the religion and **theology** of the orthodox church as it developed in the second though the fifth centuries. Evidence of a pre-Christian Gnosticism with a redeemer who descends and ascends (as Jesus does in the Gospel of John) is lacking. Yet the world-denying character of Gnosticism, with the sharp division (or dualism) between God (the divine) above and the world (the carnal or physical) below, certainly existed prior to Jesus and the rise of Christianity, and contributed in diverse ways to the development and theology of that religion.

From Philosophy to Astrology   Among other major religious forces of the first-century Mediterranean world were the philosophical sects, including Pythagoreans, Epicureans, Cynics, and the already mentioned Stoics. The latter two, in addition to advocating reorientation of the moral and spiritual life according to special philosophical–religious tenets, were noted for their itinerant preachers who sought disciples and converts as they traveled from city to city, discussing and debating the nature of the good life. Such teachers, who were quite often accompanied by disciples, sought to convince listeners of the evil of this world and to persuade potential converts of the truth of the contemplative, ascetic life. They shared something of the spirit of **Gnosticism**. These wandering moralists also established a precedent and provided a pattern for early Christian preachers, though the literature of the New Testament attests to the special care with which Christian missionaries sought to distinguish themselves from abuses attributed to such peripatetic philosophers (cf. 1 Thess. 2:9; 1 Cor. 9:4–12; 3 John 6–8). If to some, Christianity seemed to be another mystery religion, to others it may have appeared to be another school of popular philosophy (cf. Acts 17:16–21).

There were, of course, other manifestations of belief and what we might call superstition and magic. These we can only note in passing. Many people in the ancient world were fascinated or oppressed by Fate (Greek, *hē heimarmenē*) or Fortune (Greek, *tychē*). Fortune came to be personalized and venerated as a goddess. The stars were thought to determine the course of people's lives, their fate. As a result, astrology, the "science" dealing with the influence of the stars on life, gained considerable popularity as the key to the secrets of human existence. At the same time, some people relied on magic, invoking on occasion even the names of Yahweh and Jesus. There were also hero cults dedicated to those who had been elevated to the status of gods or demigods. Among these were the healing cult of Asclepius, who claimed many shrines and spas and thousands of devotées who attributed to him **miraculous** cures no less amazing than those attributed to Jesus in the **Gospels**. Although early Christians rejected magic (cf. Acts 8:9–24; 19:19), some educated people dismissed the new faith as exactly that—magic and superstition.

Diaspora Judaism

In the complex religious picture of the Greco-Roman world, Judaism was a significant factor. Most Jews did not live in Palestine, but in other parts of that world. This **Diaspora** or dispersion of Jews to the far corners of the world began as early as 587 **B.C.** with the conquest of Judah and the destruction of Jerusalem by the Babylonians. As conditions within the homeland became more difficult during the later postexilic period and the number of Jews increased, the prospects of living outside Palestine became increasingly attractive.

It is customary and useful to distinguish between the Judaism of the land of Israel and that of the Diaspora. Both shared in most of the basic elements of Judaism mentioned at the beginning of this chapter, yet outside Palestine significant change had taken place, much of which resulted from **Hellenization**. Hellenization, or accommodation to Greek culture, also took place within Palestine. Outside Palestine, however, Judaism of necessity began to take on some of the characteristics of a religion as distinguished from a nation. Nevertheless, the Jewish people succeeded in maintaining their ethnic identity and a certain separateness in their ways and places of living. Yet Jews mingled to some extent with **Gentiles**, were inevitably influenced by them, and vice versa. Adjustments to life in a predominantly Gentile world became necessary.

As we have seen, one of the most important adjustments was in language. Judaism in the Greco-Roman world was largely Greek speaking. The fact that the Hebrew scriptures had been translated into Greek and were read and interpreted in that language doubtless influenced the way in which they were understood. Philo of Alexandria, a contemporary of Jesus and Paul, affords a notable, if perhaps extreme, example of the kinds of changes that could take place. A Jew who never once thought of surrendering that hallmark of Judaism, the **law**, Philo nevertheless interpreted the Hebrew scriptures in terms of Hellenistic philosophy and piety by using the well-established Greek method of **allegorizing**. Thus he could wring meanings from biblical texts of which the original authors would never have dreamed. Hellenistic Judaism had already produced religious books containing some ideas that were more Greek than biblical. For example, one reads in Wisdom of Solomon 3:1–9 of the immortality of the souls of the **righteous** dead, a fundamentally Greek idea. Yet it is set in a biblical context: they are in the hand of God (3:1).

Another adjustment forced on the Jews by the dispersion involved their public worship. Up until the destruction of the temple of Solomon at Jerusalem, the principal form of worship was **sacrificial**, officially performed at the Jerusalem temple, though sometimes actually carried out elsewhere, much to the disgust of some **prophets** and other purists. After the fall of Jerusalem, the destruction of the temple, the deportations, and the flight of refugees, another form of worship began to gain preeminence, that of the synagogue, or individual congregation. Here there was no animal sacrifice, but prayer, scripture reading, and preaching. In New Testament times, synagogues were sprinkled around the Mediterranean world, as well as in Palestine. The Acts of the Apostles portrays Paul, and by implication other Christian missionaries, preaching the **gospel** in the local synagogue whenever he entered a new town.

The synagogues of the dispersion thus provided a ready–made platform for the early Christians, who, without necessarily ceasing to regard themselves as Jews, brought the good news of God's new **salvation** in Jesus the **Messiah** to their fellow Jews and any others who might by chance listen. Inasmuch as new ideas and terms had already crept into the Hellenistic synagogue from the surrounding pagan culture, it need not surprise us to see these also in the New Testament. The New Testament writings, at least in their present form, were addressed to a **church** that had grown up in the midst of the Hellenistic culture of the Roman Empire. The importance of the Greek-speaking Judaism of the dispersion for early Christianity is epitomized in the fact that the New Testament is written in Greek. Moreover, the Old Testament, which is so frequently cited in the New, is usually quoted from the Greek version.

Diaspora Judaism also prepared the way for the universal emphasis and success of the Christian gospel. The Hellenistic synagogue itself did not disdain the missionary enterprise. There is some evidence of a sustained and serious effort to convert Gentiles to Judaism (cf. Matt. 23:15), although Judaism was not focused upon mission and conversion as early Christianity was. And not a few Gentiles were attracted by the antiquity and moral seriousness of the Jewish religion. The technical term for the conversion of Gentiles was *proselytism*, and converts were called *proselytes*. Even where proselytism was not actively pursued, the situation of the Jews in the midst of an alien and potentially hostile culture required that they look outward and have a decent respect for public opinion. One sees such an outward-looking perspective in Philo and perhaps even more noticeably in the great first-century Jewish historian Josephus. His extensive *Jewish Antiquities* is an elaborate exposition and explanation of the entire history and faith of his people for a literate Gentile audience. It is at once our best single historical source for the so-called intertestamental period and a monumental effort to make Jewish history intelligible to the wider world.

First-century Diaspora Judaism was an important movement in and of itself, but it is of extraordinary significance for the Christianity of New Testament times. For the modern student it illuminates the path that Christianity traversed from its beginnings as a sect of Palestinian Judaism to the status of a world religion.

SUGGESTIONS FOR FURTHER READING

Throughout this and subsequent bibliographies, series titles have been omitted to conserve space.

PRIMARY SOURCES

General.   The Old and New Testaments, as well as the Old Testament Apocrypha, are cited usually according to the New Revised Standard Version. Josephus' *Jewish Antiquities* and *Jewish War* are available in original Greek with English translations in the Loeb Classical Library (Cambridge, MA: Harvard University Press), as are the works of Philo, the writings of the Apostolic Fathers, and Eusebius' *Ecclesiastical History*.

The Dead Sea Scrolls.   Two succinct, reliable translations of the Scrolls are recommended: G. Vermes, *The Dead Sea Scrolls in English*, 4th ed. (London: Penguin, 1995); and F. García-Martínez, *The Dead Sea Scrolls Translated: The Qumran Texts in English*, trans. W. G. E. Watson, 2 vols. (Leiden: Brill, 1994–1996). J. H. Charlesworth (ed.), *The Dead Sea Scrolls: Hebrew, Aramaic and Greek Texts with English Translations*. 5 vols. (Tübingen and Louisville: Mohr-Siebeck/Westminster John Knox, 1994–2002), is a comprehensive collection of Qumran materials, with concordances.

Jewish Pseudepigrapha   (see Glossary). J. H. Charlesworth (ed.), *The Old Testament Apocrypha and Pseudepigrapha*, 2 vols. (Garden City, NY: Doubleday, 1983–1985), provides standard translations and commentaries. G. W. E. Nickelsburg and M. E. Stone, *Faith and Piety in Early Judaism: Texts and Documents* (Philadelphia: Fortress, 1983), is a brief selection and discussion of representative intertestamental texts.

Rabbinic sources.   Two English versions are now standard: H. Danby, *The Mishnah* (London: Oxford University Press, 1933), and J. Neusner, *The Mishnah: A New Translation* (New Haven: Yale University Press, 1988). C. G. Montefiore and H. Loew, *A Rabbinic Anthology* (New York: Schocken, 1974), is a helpful introduction and anthology, as is the more recent H. Maccoby, *Early Rabbinic Writings* (Cambridge: Cambridge University Press, 1985).

Greek and Gnostic Writings.   F. C. Grant (ed.), *Hellenistic Religions: The Age of Syncretism* (New York: Bobbs–Merrill, 1955) is still serviceable. For Gnostic sources, consult B. Layton (ed.), *The Gnostic Scriptures: A New Translation with Annotations and Introductions* (Garden City, NY: Doubleday, 1987), and J. M. Robinson (ed.), *The Nag Hammadi Library in English*, 3rd rev. ed. (San Francisco: Harper & Row, 1988).

A superior anthology, now in its fourth revised edition, is C. K. Barrett (ed.), *The New Testament Background: Writings from Ancient Greece and the Roman Empire that Illuminate Christian Origins* (San Francisco: HarperSanFrancisco, 1995).

MODERN STUDIES

Ancient Judaism.   G. F. Moore, *Judaism in the First Centuries of the Christian Era*, 3 vols. (Cambridge, MA: Harvard University Press, 1927–1930), remains worth consulting, as does the updated E. Schürer, *The History of the Jewish People in the Age of Jesus Christ (175 B.C.–A.D. 135)*, rev. and ed. G. Vermes, F. Millar, M. Black, and M. Goodman, 3 vols. (Edinburgh: T. & T. Clark, 1973–1987). More recent, standard treatments include S. Safrai and M.

Stern (eds.), *The Jewish People in the First Century: Historical Geography, Political History, Social, Cultural and Religious Life and Institutions* (Philadelphia: Fortress, 1974–1976), S. J. D. Cohen, *From the Maccabees to the Mishnah* (Philadelphia: Westminster, 1987), E. P. Sanders, *Judaism: Practice and Belief, 63 BCE–66 CE* (Philadelphia: Trinity Press International, 1992), L. L. Grabbe, *Judaic Religion in the Second Temple Period: Belief and Practice from the Exile to Yavneh* (London: Routledge, 2000), and J. C. VanderKam, *An Introduction to Early Judaism* (Grand Rapids: Eerdmans, 2001). Important studies of Jewish eschatology include J. H. Charlesworth (ed.), *The Messiah: Developments in Earliest Christianity and Judaism* (Minneapolis: Fortress, 1992), J. J. Collins, *The Scepter and the Star: The Messiahs of the Dead Sea Scrolls and Other Ancient Literature* (New York: Doubleday, 1995), and J. J. Collins (ed.), *The Encyclopedia of Apocalypticism,* Volume One: *The Origins of Apocalypticism in Judaism and Christianity* (New York: Continuum, 1998). See also G. W. E. Nickelsburg, *Jewish Literature between the Bible and the Mishnah: A Historical and Literary Introduction,* 2nd ed. (Minneapolis: Fortress, 2005), and M. E. Stone (ed.), *Jewish Writings of the Second Temple Period* (Philadelphia: Fortress, 1984).

Hellenistic Judaism.   Among the standard works are V. Tcherikover, *Hellenistic Civilization and the Jews*, trans. S. Applebaum (Philadelphia: Jewish Publication Society, 1959), M. Hengel, *Judaism and Hellenism: Studies in Their Encounter in Palestine during the Hellenistic Period*, trans. J. Bowden, 2 vols. (Philadelphia: Fortress, 1974), E. M. Smallwood, *The Jews under Roman Rule: From Pompey to Diocletian* (Leiden: Brill, 1976), and J. J. Collins, *Between Athens and Jerusalem: Jewish Identity in the Hellenistic Diaspora* (New York: Crossroad, 1983). More recent, important investigations include J. M. G. Barclay, *Jews in the Mediterranean Diaspora: From Alexander to Trajan (323 BCE–117 CE)* (Berkeley: University of California Press, 1996), E. S. Gruen, *Diaspora: Jews amidst Greeks and Romans* (Cambridge, MA: Harvard University Press, 2002), and J. Neusner, *Judaism When Christianity Began: A Survey of Belief and Practice* (Louisville: Westminster John Knox, 2002).

The Greco-Roman World.   A definitive handbook is H. Koester, *Introduction to the New Testament,* Volume One: *History, Culture and Religion of the Hellenistic Age* (Philadelphia: Fortress, 1982); for a concise overview, see C. J. Roetzel, *The World That Shaped the New Testament*, rev. ed. (Louisville: Westminster John Knox, 2002). The broader historical landscape is surveyed by F. E. Peters, *The Harvest of Hellenism: A History of the Near East from Alexander the Great to the Triumph of Christianity* (New York: Simon & Schuster, 1970), F. Millar, *The Roman Near East: 31 B.C.–A.D. 337* (Cambridge, MA: Harvard University Press, 1993), and F. W. Walbank, *The Hellenistic World*, rev. ed. (Cambridge, MA: Harvard University Press, 1993). Traditional and popular religious expressions are considered by W. Burkert, *Greek Religion*, trans. J. Raffan (Cambridge, MA: Harvard University Press, 1985), M. Beard, J. North, and S. Price (eds.), *Religions of Rome*, 2 vols. (Cambridge: Cambridge University Press, 1998), and H.–J. Klauck, *The Religious Context of Early Christianity*, trans. B. McNeil (Minneapolis: Fortress, 2003). A. A. Long, *Hellenistic Philosophy: Stoics, Epicureans, Sceptics*, 2nd ed. (Berkeley and Los Angeles: University of California Press, 1986), is a standard work in its area, as are G. A. Kennedy, *The Art of Rhetoric in the Roman World* (Princeton: Princeton University Press, 1972), and R. S. Kraemer, *Her Share of the Blessings: Women's Religions among Pagans, Jews, and Christians in the Greco-Roman World* (New York: Oxford University Press, 1992). H. Jonas, *The Gnostic Religion*, rev. ed. (Boston: Beacon, 1963), and K. Rudolph, *Gnosis: The Nature and History of Gnosticism*, trans. R. McL. Wilson (San Francisco: Harper & Row, 1983), are important studies. Very useful for general reference is S. Hornblower and A. Spaforth (eds.), *The Oxford Classical Dictionary*, 3rd rev. ed. (Oxford: Oxford University Press, 2003).

PART ONE

THE GOSPELS AND JESUS

Christian faith began with the mission of Jesus of Nazareth, an event that could be understood only in the context of the history of Israel and communicated only by means of the literary and thought patterns of the first-century Mediterranean world. The new religious faith was thus grounded in the story of a particular person, who lived and died in the land of Israel. Yet Jesus was not the founder of the Christian movement in the sense that Martin Luther and John Calvin were the founders of Protestant Christianity or George Washington or Thomas Jefferson were the Founding Fathers of the American Republic. Whether, in any sense, Jesus himself intended to found the Christian **church** is a matter that has been much debated. He did call disciples to follow him. But he would have scarcely intended to found a community separate from Judaism. What is clear is that the Christian faith, shared by the various churches, ancient and modern, but expressed in different forms, would never have emerged without Jesus' ministry, death, and **resurrection**. What Jesus did and taught is important, but also what was done to him. He died at the hands of enemies. That is an indisputable historical fact. He was raised from the dead by God, his Father. That is the prime article of Christian faith, although it is impossible to prove his resurrection was such a fact. The **Apostles' Creed** nevertheless affirms that "The third day he rose from the dead." (Although this creed was not framed by the **apostles**, it represents the apostolic faith that is the basis of historic Christianity.)

In the New Testament and in all four **Gospels**, Jesus is viewed through the dual prism of what his enemies did in order to destroy him and what God did to affirm him and his ministry. The Gospels were written in and for the communities and churches of the ancient Mediterranean world. The New Testament Gospels are all narratives about Jesus, but they do not view Jesus dispassionately. They were written by followers who were passionate in their devotion to Jesus and saw him not so much as a figure of the past, but the Lord of the present. They were intended to bolster the faith and practice of believers and to attract the allegiance of those who might become believers. They were church documents, but not in the somewhat conservative sense one might attach to "church" in the modern world. The earliest church was not a stabilizing factor in ancient societies, but if anything a destabilizing one, as it proclaimed in the name of Jesus, a **crucified** criminal, the in-breaking of God's rule to overthrow the powers that ruled this world.

Perhaps that primal urgency is best expressed in the Gospel of Mark, as Jesus announces: "The time is fulfilled and the **kingdom of God** is at hand; repent and believe the gospel" (1:15 RSV). But other words of Jesus, found only in John's Gospel, state most explicitly his followers' view of him: "I am the way, and the truth, and the life. No one comes to the Father except through me" (14:6).

With this unique perception of Jesus' identity and meaning in view, our study of the New Testament therefore focuses in Part I upon the story of Jesus, first as depicted in the Gospels (Chapters 2, 3, 4, 5) and then as portrayed with the help of historical investigation (Chapter 6). Although the earliest New Testament documents are the letters of Paul, the prior position of the Gospels in the New Testament collection accurately reflects the conviction of the early Christian community that the story of Jesus was the beginning of the faith.

In the Gospel stories matters of life and death, both for individual Christians and for the churches, were filtered through the narration of Jesus' actions and words. From without, the Christians faced problems connected with Jewish leaders in Israel, the Roman government in the empire, and a **Hellenistic** culture that pervaded everyday Mediterranean life. From within, the churches struggled with the relation of the old and the new Israel; the nature of discipleship; the extent of the Christian mission; the place of **miracles**; the nature of power, order, and authority in the community; the relation between faith and ethics; and the delay of the end time. In speaking to these questions, the early Christians acknowledged the authority of Jesus, while at the same time assuming the freedom to retell his story in the light of their changed situations.

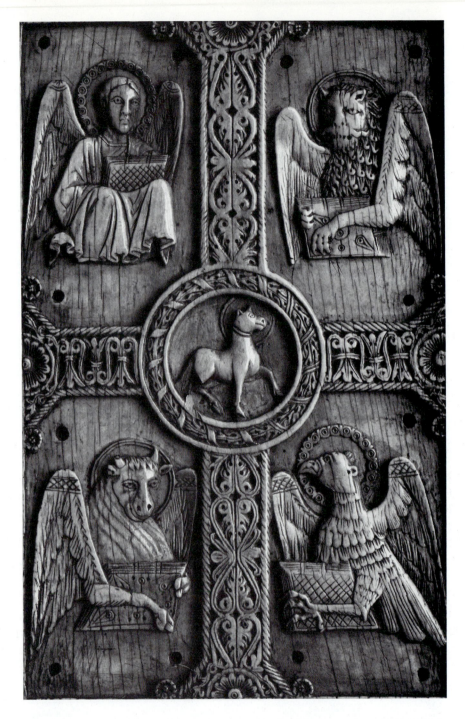

An ivory plaque from a tenth-century German or Northern Italian book cover. *Agnus Dei* (lamb of God), displayed on a cross, between emblems of the four evangelists: Matthew, the man; Mark, the lion; Luke, the ox; and John, the eagle. *(Courtesy of The Metropolitan Museum of Art, Gift of J. Pierpont Morgan, 1917.)*

CHAPTER 2

MARK:
THE GOSPEL
OF SUFFERING

THE GOSPELS, GOSPEL CRITICISM, AND THE ORIGIN OF MARK

The Nature of the Gospels

The New Testament narratives about Jesus are traditionally called **Gospels**. The Greek word for gospel, *euangelion*, means "good news." This word had acquired religious significance in the Roman Empire, chiefly in the cult of the emperor, in which the appearance of the Roman emperor, his accession to the throne, and his decrees were known as "glad tidings" or "gospels." Perhaps the New Testament usage was also derived from the "good news" of freedom from bondage, which Isaiah proclaimed to the people of Israel emerging from the Babylonian **exile** (see Isa. 40:9; 52:7; 61:1). In the New Testament itself, *euangelion* signifies good news of **salvation** through Jesus (see for example, Matt. 11:5; Rom. 1:1; 1 Cor. 15:1; Mark 1:1). Early usage of *euangelion* implied the **oral tradition** of such news (cf. Gal. 1:6–12). Not until years after they were written were New Testament writings called Gospels, but with the appearance of Mark, Matthew, Luke, John, and the **apocryphal** Gospels, the Gospel became a distinctive literary **genre**. The Gospels are not biographies of Jesus in the modern sense, for they lack the typical interest in personal character and in chronological order. Neither are they **myths**, tales of the gods, because Jesus of Nazareth, the central figure of the Gospels, was a historical person. Yet elements of both biography (a story of a particular historical person) and myth (a tale of divine action) are present in the Gospels. Basically the Gospels are religious proclamations based upon historical event.

This is true of the **canonical** (New Testament) Gospels. Whether it was also true of non-canonical Gospels, largely lost or suppressed in antiquity, is not clear. For the most part they have survived only in scattered quotations or fragments. Several so-called Gospels, found in mid-twentieth century at Nag Hammadi in Upper Egypt, have survived in complete, or nearly complete, form. These are not, however, narratives. The *Gospel of Thomas*, probably the best known, is a collection of Jesus' sayings attributed to the Apostle Thomas. Many of these are familiar, because of their similarity to sayings in the Synoptic Gospels. *Thomas* itself may be similar to the hypothetical **Q source** on which Matthew and Luke are thought to have drawn (see below, pp. 131–132).

The *Gospel of Peter*, discovered in the late nineteenth century was a narrative, but only a portion consisting of the trial and death of Jesus survives. Although it has many points of contact with the New Testament Gospels, it is obviously a fictionalized account which lacks their narrative restraint. There are also portions of a hitherto *Unknown Gospel* (referred to as "Egerton Papyrus 2," first published in 1935). Both of these were apparently parts of narrative Gospels. While we do not know that there were no serious rivals to the narrative Gospels of the New Testament, we do not possess them now. Ancient Christian authors mention Gospels of *the Ebionites, Nazaraeans*, and *Hebrews*, but we do not even know for sure whether these are three Gospels or different ways of referring to only one. If there were comparable narratives which presented alternative views of the ministry of Jesus, they do not survive. In the popular media (and in the best-selling novel *The Da Vinci Code*, by Dan Brown) it is frequently suggested that such narrative gospels were suppressed by the growing orthodox church. That they were deliberately suppressed cannot be disproved and is not without some foundation in fact. For example, Bishop Serapion of Rhossus (near Syrian Antioch) is said to have forbidden the use of the *Gospel of Peter* after having read it. Orthodox Christians would have maintained that such Gospels were ruled out because they were fictitious and heretical. From what we know of them, they were fictitious by any reasonable historical standard, and heretical by the rule (**canon** or standard) of orthodoxy.

There was, however, within the first century a serious attempt to conform Gospels to one, synoptic, pattern. Thus we speak of three Gospels, Matthew, Mark, and Luke, as the **Synoptic Gospels**. They literally see the ministry of Jesus together (which is what *synoptic* means in Greek). The odd Gospel out is John, which has important points of contact, or common features, but also differs in significant respects. It is obvious that there is a close relationship involving literary dependency (or use) among the Synoptics. It is not so obvious that John is related to the others in the same way (see "Gospel Criticism: The Relation Among the Synoptics," and chapter 5, esp. pp. 151–154). All tell the story of Jesus, the Synoptics in very similar ways, John quite differently. Matthew and Luke are much longer than Mark, yet they agree with Mark in the general outline of Jesus' ministry. Luke (1:4) says his purpose in writing is "so that you will know the truth of the things about which you have been instructed." In a similar vein, John says he has written "so that you may believe [or come to believe] that Jesus is the Messiah, the Son of God, and that through believing you may have life in his name" (20:31). Both, therefore, claim to be definitive works.

The Gospels are not unprejudiced lives of Jesus. They were written to arouse and confirm loyalty to Jesus, who was no longer physically present among his disciples. Directly or indirectly the Gospels encourage disciples or would-be disciples to follow Jesus by obeying his teaching and embracing his example.

Papias, a bishop of Hieropolis (in present-day Turkey, not far from ancient Ephesus) in the first half of the second century, wrote that he preferred the living, oral tradition to what was written in books (Eusebius *EH*, 111, 39, 3ff). This is a clear indication of what on other grounds seems probable. The words and deeds of Jesus were at first spoken, that is, repeated, before they were written down. Obviously, the Apostle Paul, who lived and worked before the Gospels were written, knew words of Jesus that had been transmitted orally (see 1 Cor. 7:10–12; 9:14; 11:23–26). In another significant statement, Papias wrote, "Mark became Peter's interpreter and wrote accurately all that he remembered, not, indeed, in order, of the things said or done by the Lord" (i.e. Jesus). "Mark" refers to the author of the Second Gospel. Papias goes on to say that Peter used Jesus' sayings as occasion or necessity demanded, thus explaining what was meant by "not . . . in order" (Eusebius, *EH*, 111, 39, 15). Another early Christian writing, the **Didache**, is principally a collection of Jesus' sayings, perhaps from the oral tradition rather than our written Gospels. The Synoptic Gospels are the literary deposit of what had been spoken, taught, and preached.

Eusebius of Caesarea

Eusebius was bishop of Caesarea on the coast of present-day Israel in the early fourth century. His *Ecclesiastical History (EH)* was the first comprehensive history of the church until that time. Eusebius brought the narrative up to his own day. He had no predecessor since the Acts of the Apostles.

Gospel Criticism: The Relations among the Synoptics

Mark is generally thought to be the earliest **Gospel**. This view is based upon a comparison with two other similar Gospels, Matthew and Luke. These are known as the **Synoptic Gospels**. One can evaluate this evidence of their relationships with the help of a *synopsis* of the Gospels, a volume in which the Gospels are arranged in parallel columns for easy comparison. Striking facts emerge from such a study:

1. The order of events in the narratives of Matthew, Mark, and Luke is frequently the same. Where it is not, Matthew and Luke almost never agree with each other against Mark, although each alone may, and frequently does, agree with Mark against the other.

2. A similar observation can be made about the wording of the text in the parallel portions (where all three have basically the same material). Sometimes it is identical in all three, but where it is not, Matthew and Luke only infrequently have the same wording in disagreement with Mark. Yet here the situation is not as clear cut as in the case of order. Occasionally, Matthew and Luke agree against Mark. For example, both Matthew 13:11 and Luke 8:10 have "has been given to know the secrets," instead of "has been given the secret" (Mark 4:10).

3. Sometimes Mark will have a version of a statement or event that is less than flattering to Jesus, and Matthew and Luke will depart from it, usually in different ways. In Mark 5:31, the disciples chide Jesus for asking who touched him in view of the fact that a crowd is surrounding him. In Matthew 9:20–21, the exchange is omitted; in Luke 8:45-46, the disciples' rejoinder to Jesus is softened. Mark 6:5 says that Jesus in his hometown could do no deed of power (miracle), although exceptions are cited. Luke omits this statement completely (cf. 4:24–25), while Matthew softens it from

"could not" to "did not" (13:58). An error is corrected in Mark 1:2 where a quotation of Malachi 3:1 is misidentified as Isaiah. Both Matthew and Luke omit this mistaken identification. One can find other instances in which a questionable statement of Mark seems to have been omitted or altered in Matthew or Luke.

Obviously, Mark often appears to be the middle term between Matthew and Luke. That is, where the latter agree in parallel narratives, they agree also with Mark. Only occasionally do they agree with each other against Mark. Moreover, Mark is much shorter than Matthew or Luke. Although shorter, Mark's individual narratives of the same events are sometimes longer. This is the case with the story of the execution of John the Baptist (Mark 6:17–29), which Mark tells in great detail, while Matthew describes it much more briefly (14:3–12), and Luke only alludes to the imprisonment during which John was executed (3:19–20). It once was thought that the Gospels were written in the order in which they appear in the New Testament, and that Mark had condensed Matthew. But why should Mark expand such an odd episode as the Baptist's death yet condense his narrative as a whole by omitting any description of Jesus' birth or his **resurrection** appearances, and by radically reducing the presentation of Jesus' teaching? Given the existence of either Matthew or Luke, why would Mark have proceeded as he did in composing his Gospel? It has been suggested that Mark conflated (combined) them only where they agreed. Yet Matthew and Luke often agree in the teachings of Jesus they present, and Mark does not follow them. They are largely lacking in Mark. There is no Sermon on the Mount (Matthew) or the Plain (Luke) in Mark.

Although the content of this teaching and related material in Matthew and Luke is quite often similar, the arrangement is different. The different use and arrangement of this material in Matthew and Luke would seem to indicate that neither used the other as a source. For example, their versions of the Lord's Prayer are unaccountably different (Matt. 6:7–13; Luke 11:1–4). Luke's Sermon on the Plain (Luke 6:17–49) is similar to Matthew's Sermon on the Mount (chapters 5–7), though much shorter. Yet most of the content of Matthew's Sermon is found elsewhere in Luke, if not in the Sermon on the Plain.

If neither Matthew nor Luke has used the other, they must have drawn upon a common source other than Mark. This source no longer exists independently, and is usually called **Q** (German *Quelle,* meaning "source"). The twentieth-century discovery of the *Gospel of Thomas* among the Nag Hammadi **Gnostic** documents has provided a parallel to the hypothetical Q, for Thomas is a collection of Jesus' sayings without narrative framework. In addition to Mark and Q, both Matthew and Luke had access to special traditions either oral or written: these materials, distinctive to each, are sometimes referred to as M and L. This most widely accepted solution of the **synoptic problem** is called the two-document (Mark and Q) or four-document (Mark, Q, M, and L) hypothesis.

This is the simplest and most probable solution of the synoptic problem, but it is not universally accepted. A number of scholars, for example, think that Matthew and Luke used an earlier and somewhat different version of Mark. (This would account for their agreements in wording against Mark.) Some find Q an unnecessary hypothesis, and believe Matthew used Mark, and then Luke wrote, knowing both Mark and Matthew. It is rarely proposed that Luke preceded Matthew, although at some points (e.g. the Lord's Prayer) Luke's version seems to be the earlier and less developed.

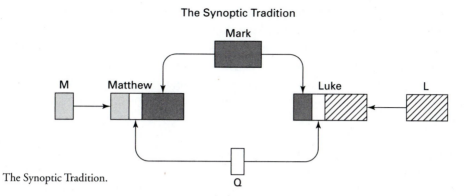

The Synoptic Tradition.

All these positions assume some significant literary relationship. Oral transmission is insufficient to account for the similarities in the order of episodes, as well as the verbatim (word-for-word) agreements among the Synoptic Gospels. This is not nearly so clear when the Gospel of John is brought into the picture, for the differences between it and the Synoptics are much greater and more difficult to account for.

Unless the stories of and about Jesus are fabrications—and that is extremely unlikely—the period between Jesus and the writing of the Gospels was bridged by oral transmission of stories and sayings about Jesus. These fall into discrete patterns or forms: **miracle** stories, pronouncement stories (a narrative setting culminating in a saying of Jesus, as for example in Mark 2:15–17 or 12:13–17), or **parables** of various types and lengths. Similar forms appear repeatedly, doubtless a product of oral transmission. The Synoptic Gospels have been created by the stringing together—better, the arrangement—of these units of formerly **oral tradition**. The study of this process, with a view to discovering the form and formation of these units is known as *form criticism* (based on the German *Formgeschichte*, "form–history"). While there doubtless was a relation between form and function, the form is easier to determine than the function. Nevertheless, one can assume that these sayings and episodes had a real function in the preaching and teaching of the early churches.

Increasingly, attention has also been paid to the way the individual units of tradition have been assembled into the present Gospels. Originally, this was conceived of as editing, hence the term *redaction criticism*. (*Redaktion* means "editing" in German; *Redaktionsgeschichte*, the "history of editing.") It has been suggested, however, the *composition* would be a better term, because it would better do justice to the formative role each evangelist played in composing his Gospel. The Synoptic Gospels do not differ randomly, but reflect the different purposes of their authors, who in large measure were using the same material or traditions.

Mark places a great emphasis on Jesus' movement toward his death (8:27–10:51), and he sometimes groups similar narratives or materials together (if they did not come to him already assembled). For example, chapters 2 and 12 of Mark consist of controversy stories; Jesus debates his opponents. Mark 4 consists of parables; Mark 5 of miracles stories; Mark 13 of (**apocalyptic**) sayings about the future. Mark 14–15 is the **Passion** Narrative, the story of Jesus' arrest, trial, and death. Matthew and Luke follow Mark generally, but do not regard

Mark's narrative as set in stone. Matthew interjects five discourses or sermons of Jesus, beginning with the Sermon on the Mount (chapters 5–7: cf. 10:1–42; 13:1–52; 18:1–35; 24:3–25:46). Luke, like Matthew, has a sermon of Jesus (6:17–49) toward the beginning of his narrative, although it is not Jesus' first public act, as in Matthew. Instead of presenting Jesus teaching in five sermons or discourses, Luke spreads it through a long narrative of Jesus' journey to Jerusalem (9:51–19:27), and includes a number of parables, the most famous of which, the Good Samaritan (10:25–37) and the Prodigal Son (15:11–32), are found nowhere else.

Attention to the Gospels as a whole, how the evangelists have arranged and edited their materials, has proven quite profitable in understanding and interpreting them. The Gospel writers had real people and concrete communities, churches, in view as they wrote. Whether one or all of them wrote for specific communities (churches) or for a much wider readership is debated. Nevertheless, they clearly wrote for practical, religious, as well as **theological**, reasons. Who is Jesus? What does it mean to follow Jesus, believing that he is the **Messiah** or **Son of God**? In the conflicted religious and cultural settings of the ancient world these were pressing, practical questions.

Ancient readers would have recognized the Gospels as "lives" (Greek *bios*; pl. *bioi*). And they were, but they were also quite distinctive. One cannot find exact parallels to the Gospels in antiquity, and this fact is a consequence of the distinctive claims they make for Jesus and their concentration on his role and destiny. He was crucified, as certain a historical fact as we can know. He was raised from the dead, a fundamental article of faith for those who believed in him. We are told nothing of Jesus' appearance, background, personal development, or education, all staples of ancient, as well as modern, biography. Could Jesus read? We may think so (cf. Luke 4:16–20), but most ancient Mediterranean peasants could not. Maybe Jesus, even as a child, was exceptional (cf. Luke 2:41–52). The Gospels whet modern readers' appetites, but do little more.

One may compare other ancient literature that is in some ways similar. The narrative about King David in 1 and 2 Samuel is perhaps the earliest specimen of biographical, historical, prose. In it we learn much more about David—his loves, his hates, his physical character, not to mention his sinning—than we do about Jesus in the Gospels, which give us nothing to satisfy our natural curiosity. Speculation about Jesus' intimate relation to Mary Magdalene is just that: speculation. There is no basis for it in the Gospels. The dialogues of Plato differ from the David narrative in that they present Socrates as a nearly ideal figure. Like the Jesus of the gospels, his dedication to truth and his sense of calling leads to his own death, which he accepts. Also, there is room to debate how much goes back to the historical Socrates and how much is Plato's development, as is the case with Jesus and the evangelists. Nevertheless, one gets in Plato's dialogues, as well as the David narratives, a fuller portrayal of a real human being than one finds in the Gospels. In analyzing and interpreting the Gospels one must constantly be aware of their character and purpose.

Gospel criticism takes it as fundamental that the Gospels are based upon, or arise out of, three settings in life. First, there is the setting of Jesus' actual historical ministry. This setting was real, and its importance is not to be dismissed. In the case of most sto-

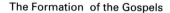

The Formation of the Gospels

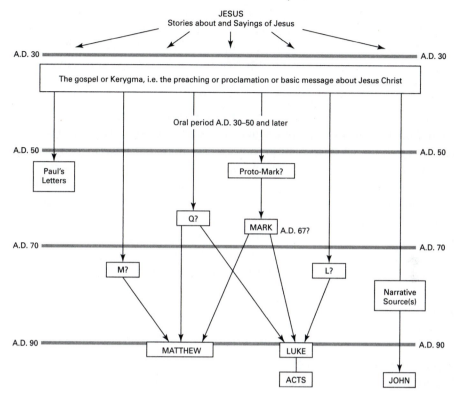

The formation of the Gospels, according to the most widely accepted theory of synoptic relationships.

ries and sayings of Jesus, however, that setting is impossible to reconstruct except in a general way. Second, there is the setting in the life of the early church (**Sitz im Leben**) that preserved the Gospel tradition. Without doubt, tradition was preserved and transmitted because it performed a valued function in the religious community. This is the insight of form criticism, which deals with this period of oral, or informal, transmission. Third, there is the situation of the evangelists themselves. These situations gave rise to the Gospels. The Gospels are not to be viewed as the products of these settings pure and simple; they are more than the last stage in the development of the tradition of Jesus in the church. The evangelists sought to speak with relevance and power to their own situations, while being faithful to Jesus. Less than the other Gospels, particularly Luke (1:1–4) and John (17:20; 20:29; 21:24–25), Mark indicates little explicit awareness of its readers (but see 13:14). Yet all of chapter 13 seems to carry an urgent message to its readers, as well as Jesus' contemporaries.

Utilizing the insights of modern criticism, our method for determining the message of each Gospel consists of four steps. (1) *Outlining the structure*: By determining the anatomy or basic outline (its beginning, climax, and end), we can begin to discern the intention and meaning of the Gospel. A detailed outline, not always possible, would involve ordering the separate sayings or episodes, known as **pericopes**, into the overall structure. (2) *Identifying emphases*: Some emphases are obvious because of their frequency throughout each Gospel; other emphases become evident in examining the Gospel's order and structure. Identifying such emphases is not only informed by the structure; it also serves to test any theory of the structure. Any overall interpretation of a writing must take into account dominant emphases. (3) *Distinguishing tradition from redaction*: By discerning which earlier material is selected and how it has been shaped, we can arrive at probable conclusions about the author's intention. This technique of criticism is more difficult to employ in the case of the Gospel of Mark, because we do not have the sources of tradition that Mark used. Yet by isolating traditional forms, form criticism helps in discerning that Gospel's traditional basis. (4) *Imagining the historical context*: Some historical situation or combination of situations provided the impetus for the writing of each Gospel. On the basis of our knowledge of early Christian history and the culture in which Christians lived, we imagine an occasion that most likely fits the origin of the Gospel in question. Such historical judgments must correspond to the life of the ancient rather than the contemporary church.

All four of these methodological steps mutually inform and correct each other. No neat, simple procedure removes the necessity for common sense and historical imagination as primary ingredients for understanding the Gospels.

Background of the Gospel of Mark

Mark, then, is the earliest Gospel, or at least the earliest to have survived. Moreover, it is not ascribed to an **apostle**, but to a Mark, who may have been a companion of the apostles, particularly Peter. The letter of 1 Peter mentions "my son Mark" (5:13), without identifying him further. In his church history, Eusebius of Caesarea gives two significant quotations about Mark from earlier Christian writers. Papias had written that Mark was Peter's interpreter (*EH*, III, 39, 15; see earlier, p. 55). Later, Clement of Alexandria stated that Mark at the urging of others in Rome (presumably Christians), wrote down what Peter had preached and distributed the Gospel to those who had asked him (*EH*, VI, 14, 6–7). The association of Mark the evangelist with Rome thus goes back to the first half of the second century (Papias). That this Mark is the same as the John Mark mentioned in Acts 12:25 and 15:37-39 or the Mark mentioned in Col. 4:10; 2 Tim. 4:11; and Phlm. 24; as well as 1 Peter 5:13, is possible, but not certain.

In all probability, the author's name was Mark (a common Roman name). If a pseudonym (false name) had been given to the author of this Gospel, a name of one of the apostles would likely have been chosen. Exactly who this Mark was remains undecided.

External (to the Gospel itself) evidence points strongly to Rome as Mark's place of origin. If one looks within the Gospel, there is no explicit evidence. But events in Rome during the mid-sixties admirably fit Mark's emphasis upon persecution. The suffering of Jesus (8:31; 9:31; 10:33 ff.), the centrality of the cross (chaps. 14 and 15), and the necessity for a suffering and serving discipleship (8:34–38; 9:33–50; 10:38–45; 13:9–13) seem to reflect an urgent message to a persecuted community. Tacitus, the first-century Roman historian, describes persecution of Roman Christians in the mid-sixties by the emperor Nero, who evidently, in order to enlarge his palace complex, started a great fire that burned much of Rome:

> Therefore, to scotch the rumour, Nero substituted as culprits, and punished with the utmost exquisite cruelty, a class loathed for their abominations, whom the crowd styled Christians. Accordingly, arrest was first made of those who confessed [to being Christians]; next, on their disclosures, vast numbers were convicted, not so much on the count of arson as for hatred of the human race. Every sort of derision was added to their deaths: they were wrapped in wild beasts' skins and dismembered by dogs; or they were fastened on crosses, and, when daylight failed were burned to serve as lamps by night. [*Annals,* XV, 44]

Mark's Gospel fits such a situation of persecution in Rome. Quite possibly it was written there shortly before the destruction of Jerusalem by Titus in A.D. 70.

On the other hand, Jesus addresses his disciples and warns them about difficulties and dangers lying immediately ahead in Mark 13. Here, Judea and the readers are mentioned explicitly (13:14), and the setting of the war between Jews and Romans in Palestine (66–70) fits this description of oncoming events rather well. Moreover, Galilee has a special importance, not only as the place of Jesus' ministry, but into the future (e.g. 14:27–28; 16:7). Obviously, Mark's roots are in the land of Israel, where Jesus lived and worked. At the same time Mark's Gospel seems to have been published and read in Rome at an early date. If it had become recognized as the Gospel of the Roman church, with the prestige and authority of Peter, its use independently by Matthew and Luke becomes understandable. The names of two otherwise unknown figures, Alexander and Rufus, the sons of Simon of Cyrene who carried Jesus' cross (15:21), also may link Mark to Rome. Paul in Romans 16:13 sends greetings to a Rufus who is evidently a prominent member of that church. In its present textual form, Mark seems to presuppose a **Gentile**, rather than Jewish Christian audience: women could initiate divorce (Mark 10:12); Jewish practices require explanation (5:41: 7:3–4, 11). It is perhaps noteworthy that traditions linking the Gospel of Mark to Rome describe it as the preaching of Peter. This seems to correspond to its actual character. The evidence of chapter 13, which has some bearing either upon the Gospel's, or its tradition's, place of origin, also has implication for the time of its composition. Is it just before the outbreak of hostilities in the Roman War, or perhaps even while they were taking place? A date in the late sixties (66–70) again becomes quite plausible. Such a date would also fit a Roman origin.

On similar grounds it is likely that the other Synoptic Gospels are later, for they contain more explicit references to the destruction of Jerusalem in the year 70. Matthew 22:7 speaks of destroying "those murderers" and burning "their city," presumably references to the Jewish authorities who put Jesus to death and the subsequent destruction of Jerusalem. Luke 21:20-24 describes quite explicitly the siege and sack of Jerusalem. Such allusions or references are missing in Mark, which probably dates from a very few years before or possibly during that traumatic event.

PROLOGUE: THE SPIRIT AND JESUS IN THE WORLD (1:1–15)

Why does Mark's Gospel begin with Jesus' baptism by John?

Mark's opening hardly sounds like an objective biography of Jesus of Nazareth. Neither an apology (as in Luke 1:1–4) nor a genealogy of Jesus (as in Matt. 1:1–17), the opening of Mark could scarcely attain a higher note of faith. Jesus Christ is named as though Christ were his last name. His name, however, was Jesus, and **Christ** is a bestowed title of honor, meaning "anointed one" or "**Messiah**." Any lingering expectation of a neutral history is dispelled by the final title, "**Son of God**," which appears in many though not all ancient manuscripts. The significance of this designation for Mark becomes clearer at the climactic point of the opening story when Jesus is told by a voice from heaven that he is "my Son, the Beloved" (vs. 11). The key introductory phrase of the opening verse, however, is probably "the beginning of the good news." By the prologue's end (vs. 14) this phrase has become "proclaiming the good news of God." Something has enabled "the beginning of the good news" to become "proclaiming the good news." (NRSV properly uses "good news" to translate *euangelion*, "**gospel**.")

Mark starts, strangely, not at the beginning but in the middle of things. Mark begins with Jesus' **baptism** when he was already an adult, instead of with Jesus' birth or childhood. Mark did know something about Jesus' earlier life, for later we are informed about Jesus' occupation and family (Mark 6:3). In Mark's view the baptism of Jesus is the crucial initiatory event for Jesus.

The Old Testament **prophecy** (1:2–3) points forward toward some kind of fulfillment. (Although Mark declares that the prophet Isaiah spoke these words, they are actually a combination of Malachi 3:1, Exodus 23:20, and Isaiah 40:3.) Something will happen. In fact, by the end of the prologue, the verb tense has shifted to the Greek perfect, "The time is *fulfilled*, and the **kingdom of God** "*has come near*" (1:15). Again, we apparently have an indication of the crucial importance of Jesus' baptism by John.

John the baptizer stands at the center of the next section (1:2–8). John is a wild man. He is in the wilderness, preaching judgment and repentance. He wears clothes of the wilderness, camel's hair and a leather girdle (cf. the description of Elijah in 2 Kings 1:8); he eats food of the wilderness, locusts and wild honey. As John speaks of the one who comes after him (vs. 7), he clearly stands at the beginning of the Gospel (cf. Acts 1:22; 10:37), as different as he may be from Jesus.

A striking feature of this section is its remarkable emphasis upon repentance for all the people of Judea and Jerusalem, as if a full-scale national repentance were taking place. Mark probably views this repentance as an anticipation of the coming Messiah. John's decisive act is to baptize the people in the river Jordan. Through this rite of baptism, a cleansing or preparation takes place. Moreover, John declares that this baptism with water would be completed later by one who would baptize with the **Spirit**. Earlier we read a prophecy about John the baptizer (vss. 2, 3); now John himself prophesies (vss. 7, 8). Just this fact of his prophesying indicates that the Spirit is appearing. In first-century Judaism the Spirit, often the enabler of biblical prophecy (cf. Isa. 61:1–2; Ezek. 2:2; 11:5; Hos. 9:7), was thought by many to have departed Israel with the last prophets (Haggai, Zechariah, and Malachi) and was expected only in the last days (cf. Acts 2:17-22 and its use of Joel 2:28-32). As John clearly points to the approach of another, Jesus, he also foreshadows an irruption of the end time, the time of the active Spirit.

A different mood pervades the next section (vss. 9–13). Previously we had John the Baptizer, the crowds, and baptism in the river; now Jesus alone appears. The heavens open, the Spirit descends, and a voice from heaven speaks; Mark has shifted to "cosmic language." At his baptism, the Spirit descends upon Jesus and a voice says, "You are my Son, the Beloved; with you I am well pleased." This utterance combines portions of Psalm 2:7 and Isaiah 42:1. Thus Mark proclaims the occurrence of a cosmic event in which the Son of God is designated. Does this mean that Jesus did not become Son of God until his baptism? Mark offers no opinion; the text asserts simply that at this baptism God's Spirit rested upon Jesus, declared as Son of God.

The title *Son* was used commonly as a designation for Israel in the Hebrew Scriptures (Exod. 4:22; cf. Jer. 31:9 and Hos. 11:1) and for those who especially represented the people of Israel, such as the king or high **priest**. Typically, sonship did not mean biological descent from God but signified special selection by God for a task. The appropriate response of sonship, therefore, is obedience to the task. This Hebraic understanding of sonship suggests that the voice from heaven revealed to Jesus that God had chosen him for a task. In fact, the unexpected climax of Mark's introduction occurs when the Spirit drives Jesus into the wilderness where he is tempted by Satan (vs. 12). The Spirit did not offer Jesus triumph and resolution; instead the Spirit brought conflict with the power of evil, with Satan.

The importance of the Spirit's expelling Jesus into the wilderness is underscored by the fact that Jesus was already in the wilderness at his baptism. Why then does Mark emphasize the wilderness motif? Both Moses (Exod. 34:28) and Elijah (1 Kings 19:8) spent forty days on Mount Sinai; moreover, the people of Israel wandered forty years in the wilderness before they could enter the Promised Land. Jesus' sojourn in the wilderness may then anticipate the founding of a new Israel, a new religious community.

The most striking feature of the Markan temptation story, especially in comparison with the temptation stories in Matthew (4:1–11) and Luke (4:1–13), is its lack of narrative detail. In this Markan episode, Jesus' activity is overshadowed by the supernatural conflict between the Spirit and Satan. The outcome of this conflict, however, has already been anticipated in Jesus' baptism. By Jesus' act of submission to John's baptism the Spirit has come and with this coming, Satan already is being defeated (see 3:23–29; cf. 10:38).

In these successive sections of Mark's introduction, the Spirit is the decisive factor. The Spirit is promised by John the Baptist and is already emerging in his prophecy (1:2–8). During Jesus' baptism (1:9–11) the Spirit descends upon him. In the temptation (1:12–13) the Spirit drives Jesus into conflict and victory over Satan. A likely clue to the meaning of Mark's introduction appears in the answer Jesus later gives to the accusation that he is in league with Satan: "But no one can enter a strong man's house and plunder his property without first tying up the strong man; then indeed the house can be plundered" (Mark 3:27). Jesus' baptism and temptation manifest an initial conquest of Satan by the Spirit. Therefore, the way is cleared for Jesus' later conflicts with the demons, his religious opponents, and even his disciples. After Jesus' obedient submission to baptism, the Spirit drives him into a conflict that eventually will result in final victory.

The note of future victory resounds in the conclusion of Mark's introduction (vss. 14–15), where instead of "the beginning of the good news" we now hear of "preaching the good news of God." (For Mark's other uses of *euangelion*, "good news" or "gospel," see 1:1, 15; 8:35; 10:29; 13:10; 14:9.) After Jesus' baptism and temptation, the preaching of the good news of God can take place, because the Spirit has become active in Jesus' obedience. The crucial phrase, "the kingdom of God has come near" (vs. 15), means neither that victory has fully arrived nor that triumph remains entirely future; Mark proclaims that God's ruling presence is now nearer than it was before. This message, this gospel, rather than Jesus himself, is the object of belief (vs. 15). Therefore, Mark concludes his introduction with Jesus' preaching the good news of God that demands repentance and belief. The introduction has suggested to the reader that the gospel concerns a victory (the Spirit over Satan) to be won only through conflict (the wilderness) and obedience (the baptism of Jesus). The rest of Mark's Gospel narrates Jesus' present triumph in conflict through his exorcisms, debates, and suffering, in order to effect the future triumph of the disciples, if they will repent and believe.

Faith and Believing in Mark

There is a significant difference between New Testament Greek and the English language. Greek has one basic stem that connotes both the English noun "faith" (*pistis*) and the verb "to believe" (*pisteuein*). In English, however, there is no verb "to faith"; we must use "believe." In English the noun "belief" also means "things believed." Jesus calls people to believe that the good news is a fact, that it is real. Yet more than that: he also means for them to *trust* in that reality. The English word "trust" is both a noun and a verb: one has trust, and one trusts. Thus, where one sees "believe" in English versions of the New Testament, that translation usually connotes trust as well. It means believing something is true and also trusting in that fact. Thus, when Jesus calls for people to repent and believe in the good news (Mark 1:15), that gospel is to be believed and also trusted.

THE GOSPEL OF POWER: JESUS OPPOSES HIS ENEMIES (1:16–8:21)

Now that the **Spirit** has met Satan in the temptation of Jesus, the public action of Jesus can begin. Jesus came preaching that the **kingdom of God** is drawing near, and this kingdom proclamation by its very nature aroused opposition. Forces are at work against the emergence of the kingdom, for the old order does not easily yield. So Jesus calls and commissions disciples to be with him and to share his work (1:16–20; 3:13–19).

In the first half of the Gospel of Mark (1:16–8:21), opposition to Jesus comes in the main from two camps—the demons and the **Pharisees**. Jesus opposes the demons with exorcism and the Pharisees with debate. Consequently, the first half of Mark centers upon Jesus' **miracles** and teachings. Indeed, as we shall see, miracles and teachings are mingled within individual units of tradition because both are means for opposing his enemies. The two opposing forces differ in that the demons recognize Jesus and do battle against him, whereas the Pharisees, though also antagonistic to Jesus, do not recognize his true identity.

In the second half of Mark (8:22–15:47), the major opposition to Jesus is not that of enemies but rather of friends, his disciples. To be sure, the disciples did not put Jesus to death; the chief **priests**, elders, and **scribes**, along with the Roman authorities, were responsible for his **crucifixion**. Still, the disciples did oppose Jesus because they failed to understand why he had to suffer and die. Unless we keep in mind the disciples' misunderstanding opposition, the full meaning of Jesus' actions and teachings against the demons and the Pharisees will be missed. Mark's Gospel depicts an opposition of enemies met by direct action through exorcisms and debates. The opposition of friends is met by indirect persuasion, even apparent defeat in death.

This preference for persuading rather than compelling the disciples relates to a major problem in the first half of Mark. After several disclosures of divine healing power, Jesus curiously commands keeping these miracles secret (1:43 f.; 3:12; 5:43). This is an aspect of what is called the messianic secret in Mark (see "The Messianic Secret," p. 76). In effect, the Jesus of Mark avoids the making of disciples by powerful deeds. After demons had been exorcised and opponents silenced in debate, the task of making true disciples still remained.

In this first half of Mark, miracles dominate. There are nature miracles, such as stilling the storm (4:35–41; 6:45–52) and feeding the multitudes (6:30–44; 8:1–10); there are healing miracles, such as the healing of the leper (1:40–45) and the raising of the dead girl (5:35–43); and there are miracles of exorcism, the driving out of demons (1:21–28; 5:1–13; see also 1:34; 3:22). The exorcisms likely provide the key to understanding the miracles in this Gospel. Mark summarizes the activity of Jesus in Galilee as that of preaching and casting out demons (1:39), and Jesus appoints the Twelve to the same tasks (3:14, 15; 6:13). Evidently, for Mark, miracles are essentially the same as exorcisms and thus do not constitute a separate class of acts or events. All Jesus' actions represent his overcoming the power of evil.

A crucial question related to these mighty acts is whether Jesus performs such acts with the power of Satan or of God (3:20–30). For Mark, Jesus performs exorcisms with the help of God; anyone who denies this source of Jesus' power (cf. 3:30) must be on the side of Satan. Now that the strong man, Satan, has been bound by the Spirit, Jesus is to plunder the house, to rid the world of demons (3:27). In demon exorcism we are to recognize a transcendent battle taking place in the life of Jesus and his contemporaries. Demons inhabit human beings; they are part of human history. Yet their power comes from beyond, from Satan. Similarly, Jesus exorcises demons, but he claims a power from beyond; for in Mark he is the **Son of God**, the one upon whom the Spirit descended in his **baptism**.

Encounter with Demons and Sickness (1:21–45)

Are Jesus' miracles in Mark signs of his compassion—or something more?

The first exorcism in Mark (1:21–28) follows the calling of disciples and is set within the context of Jesus' teaching in the synagogue on the Sabbath. Opposition between the teaching of the **scribes** and the authority of Jesus characterizes this scene. At first no one truly recognizes Jesus except the demon, who cries out, "I know who you are, the Holy One of God" (1:24; cf. 3:11; 5:7). Perhaps the demon used this exalted title of Jesus to gain power over him. In the ancient world, knowledge and use of the name gave the speaker magic power. Two memorable scriptural attempts to gain control through knowledge of the name are Jacob's wrestling with the angel (Gen. 32:29) and Moses at the burning bush (Exod. 3:13). More obviously, the demon's recognition of Jesus involves immediate opposition: an enemy has appeared ("Have you come to destroy us?"). The result of Jesus' appearance is heightened activity by the demon, resulting in the man's convulsing and crying out. Jesus and the demon have absolutely nothing in common, only antagonism.

This exorcism implies a "before and after" motif, which occurs explicitly in other Markan accounts of Jesus' **miracles** (see 6:45–52). Before the exorcism there is opposition, violence, crying out; afterward there is silence, victory, and the spread of Jesus' fame. Yet this particular exorcism does not end with a neat resolution of all difficulties. We are perplexed because the bystanders label the exorcism "a new teaching," instead of "a mighty deed." This response makes the encounter something more than exorcism of an unclean spirit, for the question of Jesus' authority is thus brought to the fore (see 1:22, 27). Clearly for Mark, Jesus' action and teaching are not finally separable. Moreover, the inconclusive result ("... and they kept on asking one another") suggests that the exorcism had produced no final resolution. Jesus still had to debate with the **Pharisees**. This episode ends, perhaps ironically, on the note of the spread of Jesus' fame, a fame that will lead not to apparent success but to death.

A brief healing episode (1:29–31) and two summary sections (1:32–34; 1:35–39) separate Jesus' first exorcism from the next major healing event (1:40–45). The healing of the disciple Simon's mother–in–law focuses attention upon the disciples who cannot

The larger covered ruin in the excavated town of Capernaum is known as Simon Peter's house (cf. Mark 1:29–31). Since this photograph was taken, a modern church has been built, suspended over the house.

heal. At this point, the disciples are impotent, even though the ill woman is one of their relatives. Jesus' healing enables her to serve. As we learn later, the disciples also have to become servants, though in a different way (see 9:35; 10:35–45; 12:1–11). Therefore, even this brief episode may point beyond itself to the necessity for service by the disciples, something that becomes possible only after they allow themselves to be served by Jesus' death (10:45). A summary section of healing and exorcism follows (1:32–34). The people flock to a healer, the healings take place publicly; curiously, Jesus "would not permit the demons to speak, because they knew him."

In the following section (1:35–39) Jesus retires to a lonely place to pray. In response to the disciples' demands, Jesus acknowledges only that he will go to preach in the next towns. The narrative also mentions that he continued "casting out demons" (vs. 39). Evidently Jesus' primary mission is preaching (1:14) and even the casting out of demons is secondary to it. This section (beginning with 1:21) concludes a connected series of episodes taking us through a day to the evening (1:32–34) and the following morning (1:35–39). Perhaps Mark places this series here because it presents typical acts of Jesus.

A key action of Jesus throughout the Gospel is praying. On three other occasions in Mark, Jesus prays. Each time, the motif of faithful discipleship is the common thread of the diverse incidents. After the feeding of the five thousand, Jesus prays (6:46); the immediate consequence is his calming appearance to the disciples terrified by the storm. At the healing of the epileptic boy, Jesus tells the disciples that they are unable to heal because they have not prayed (9:29). Jesus mandates prayer, particularly prayers of forgiveness in an era when (for Mark) the temple is defunct (11:22-26; 11:15–17; cf. 13:1–2). In Gethsemane, Jesus also prays for strength to accept his impending death, while the disciples sleep (14:32–42). To become disciples, they will have to "keep awake and pray"

(14:38). For Mark, Jesus' primary mission is neither healing nor exorcising demons; Jesus brings near the **kingdom of God** to effect *discipleship*.

The subsequent episode tells of Jesus' healing of a leper (1:40–45). No demon appears in this healing miracle; the conversation takes place between Jesus and a man. Here for the first time Jesus is moved with pity, and when the man speaks to Jesus, there seems to be something like the element of faith: "If you choose, you can make me clean." In distinction from the exorcism, this healing shows Jesus in touch with the person to be healed, moving more closely within the human realm and eliciting the response of faith. As in the case of the exorcism, the meeting with Jesus produces results; the victim is made well of leprosy and made fit for communion with others. Once again Jesus enjoins silence (cf. vs. 34), but this time he is not obeyed. Although this scene depicts Jesus as acting out of compassion and the man's incipient faith, somehow things are still not right. Because the healed man goes "to spread the **word**," Jesus can no longer move about openly. Instead of righting everything, the healing seems to deter Jesus from his mission—that of preaching the good news of God and making true disciples—that is, believers in the good news (1:15).

To summarize: the Markan exorcisms and healings depict one phase of a struggle that erupts with Jesus' mission. The purely transcendent struggle between the **Spirit** and Satan, foreshadowed in the temptation (1:12–13), now occurs at the transcendent–historical level of the "Holy One of God" versus the demons (1:24). As we shall see, that conflict moves farther within history in the opposition between Jesus and the **Pharisees** and eventually between the suffering **Son of Man** and his disciples. While **miracles**, Jesus' most public deeds, inspire an impressive reception (1:28), they also produce inconclusive results, especially among the disciples.

In these passages, Jesus' demand for silence about his miracles is critical for understanding how Mark used the stories of Jesus' miracles. We have in Mark an apparent contradiction: the healing tradition does not convey the crucial aspect of Jesus' ministry, yet much of Mark's Gospel, especially the first half, consists of miracle stories. Why then does Mark combine this miracle tradition with injunctions to be silent about the miracles (the so-called messianic secret)? For Mark the heart and center of Jesus' ministry is his suffering and death on the cross. Moreover, the winning of true disciples can take place only through the suffering death of Jesus. Belief in Jesus' power to effect miraculous healings was a given in Mark's **church**. Mark neither doubts nor disdains the miracle tradition of Jesus; however, he locates that tradition within the special perspective of Jesus' death (see 9:9). Therefore, according to Mark, Jesus does not want people to extoll his miraculous deeds; instead, he characteristically enjoins silence about them.

Mark's Christian contemporaries knew of divinely empowered miracle workers; moreover, **apocryphal** stories of Jesus also emphasized his magical powers. In the *Infancy Gospel of Thomas* the child Jesus is pictured as a stupendous miracle worker: He makes sparrows of clay; he kills a lad who disturbs a pool he made; he destroys a child who strikes his arm; he stretches a short beam into a longer one to aid Joseph, his carpenter–father.

Such a popular, one-sided emphasis on Jesus as a divine miracle worker is rejected in the Gospel of Mark, not by ignoring that role but by setting it within the context of Jesus' **passion**. Thus Mark suggests that the fundamental miracle of discipleship, that is, of believing, comes not through Jesus' miraculous powers but rather through his death.

Miraculous signs, though not denied, are insufficient to turn followers of Jesus into genuine disciples. Later in Mark, Jesus replies to the Pharisees who come seeking a sign from heaven, "Why does this generation ask for a sign? Truly, I tell you, no sign will be given to this generation" (8:12). According to Mark, public signs of power are not the basis of faith.

Debate with the Pharisees (2:1–3:6)

How are the debates in Mark like the miracles?

Communication takes place in many ways. Debate persuades by allowing the listener to hear both sides. Debate, therefore, communicates in conflict, and the Gospel of Mark is an example of such communication by conflict. In Mark, Jesus' teaching takes place primarily in debate, with the Pharisees (his enemies) or with the disciples (his friends). The debates with the Pharisees and the **scribes** have parallels with debates in the writings of the **rabbis**; however, the key for understanding the Markan debates is the exorcisms. Earlier we were puzzled by the people's astonishment at Jesus' *teaching* (1:22) when the story related the driving out of an unclean spirit. Mark seems deliberately to commingle healing action and teaching authority so that Jesus' conflicts (with demons, Pharisees, and disciples) are all of a piece. The healing of the paralytic (2:1–12) demonstrates that healing action ("Stand up and take your mat and walk") and authoritative teaching ("Your sins are forgiven") are inextricably interwoven, suggesting that Jesus has to wrestle with the stubbornness of the Pharisees as well as crippling disease. Indeed, the community of Markan Christianity, as represented in the disciples, is both to perform works of power (6:13) and to practice forgiveness (11:25).

The prelude for this section is once again the calling of disciples, in this case a tax collector named Levi (2:13 f.; cf. 1:16–20). (Levi does not appear in the later Markan list of the twelve disciples [3:16–19]; in Matthew 9:9, however, the Levi of Mark's story has become Matthew, who is named as one of the Twelve.) The closely related, subsequent episode shows Jesus eating at table with sinners and tax collectors (2:15–17). Sinners presumably had in some flagrant way broken the Mosaic **law** (cf. Luke 7:36–50). Tax collectors were hired by those agents who purchased the right to collect taxes for the Roman government and in turn were allowed to extract heavy taxes from the Jewish people. Evidently the two groups were social outcasts, yet Jesus and his disciples ate at table with them. The scribes and the Pharisees object to the disciples about Jesus' conduct, though not to Jesus himself. (Perhaps the involvement of the disciples at this point indicates that the issue was still a live one in the early church.) Even though not addressed directly, Jesus replies with an answer that silences everyone. He comes to the sick; that is the physician's duty (2:17). Jesus' opponents fail to grasp that a new society of disciples, those who follow Jesus, is being formed. The ancient rigid distinctions of clean and unclean (see Leviticus 11:1-15:33), especially the procedure for forgiveness (see vs. 7), are being swept away in the new community that Jesus inaugurates.

The following section (2:18–22), concerning fasting, probes this new society further. This time Mark distinguishes not only between Jesus and the Pharisees but also between Jesus' disciples and those of John the Baptist. Both the Pharisees and the disciples of John fast. As the bringer of good news, Jesus asserts that the time for fasting is now past, for his disciples now experience a new reality ("the bridegroom"). The statement (vs. 20) implying that they will fast after Jesus' death may in the Markan context refer to the suffering and persecution that the disciples will have to endure. In the second half of Mark, Jesus speaks unequivocally about the necessity of suffering. Indeed, Jesus' words (especially vs. 20) do not allow the reader to forget the impending death. The final words of the episode (2:21 f.) mark an end to the debate and an answer to the conflict over fasting. Everything stresses newness—the bridegroom is present, new cloth and new wine are available; fresh skins are needed, for the old cannot determine the new. The old order must make way for the new; real disciples know and act upon this "newness."

The first two episodes of this section stressed the breaking forth of a new society in connection with Jesus; the following two episodes focus on unorthodox Sabbath activity. Even though it is the disciples who have violated the Sabbath (2:23–28), the Pharisees now debate directly with Jesus. Jesus answers their charge by quoting scripture, citing the example of David and his men eating the holy bread. (Mark seems to have erred in that Ahimelech, not Abiathar, was high **priest** at the time of this incident: thus, 1 Sam. 21:1–6). The criterion, suggested by the David episode, is that need takes precedence over flat adherence to the law. Moreover, the first half of Jesus' final word ("The sabbath was made for humankind, not humankind for the sabbath"—vs. 27) also bears out this view, which in isolation sounds quite modern—that is, human considerations take precedence over legalistic ritual. Yet the final clause ("so the Son of Man is lord even of the sabbath") indicates that we have in Jesus' saying something more than a general humanitarian principle. The appearance of the **Son of Man** signifies the beginning of the end time, the irruption of a new age (cf. Dan. 7:13 and Mark 13:26). Jesus' disciples can now violate the Sabbath, because they are beginning to live out of the new time being ushered in with Jesus: the time for joy (vs. 19), the time for wine (vs. 22), and the time for forgiveness of sinners (vs. 17; cf. vs. 10).

The next episode places the debate with the Pharisees in the context of healing (3:1–6). In the synagogue, the stronghold of the Pharisees, Jesus is being watched—the Pharisees are not at first named. The atmosphere is that of a test of Jesus (cf. also 8:11; 10:2; 12:13, 15), similar to his time of testing in the wilderness. A comparison of this episode with the previous exorcism of the unclean spirit (1:21–28) illuminates how debate-conflict is both similar to and yet also different from demon-conflict. Jesus commanded the demon to be silent (1:25). Now, before the healing is performed, his opponents are silent before his question, "Is it lawful to do good or to do harm on the sabbath, to save life or to kill?" (3:4). After the exorcism, even though there was questioning of his authority, Jesus' fame spread (1:27 f.). Now, after Jesus' Sabbath healing, his enemies plot to destroy him (3:6).

The remainder of the first half of Mark may be characterized as a development of what is already implied in the opening scenes of the Gospel. The old order's resistance to Jesus' message and action frees the good news to appeal to new multitudes, even those from Tyre and Sidon lying beyond Palestine (3:7–12). When rejected by the established religious authorities, Jesus forms the new Israel, founded upon the twelve disciples (**3:13–19a**). Whoever doubts the authenticity of this new community fails to see the clear manifestations of God's work through Jesus' casting out demons (3:28–30). Moreover, no one can rely upon a guaranteed privilege that reckoned physical descent as assurance of God's favor (3:31–35).

Nothing avails to eliminate the opposition to Jesus by the Jewish leaders. His **parables** about the breaking in of God's word are closed ciphers to all except the joyful few who really hear Jesus' word about a new society (4:1–20, esp. vss. 8 f. and vs. 20).

Even those who hear must receive further private instruction (see 4:33 f.), because Mark has in view the necessity for perseverance to the end (cf. 13:9–13). The hope for such endurance rests in the amazing power that accompanies Jesus ("Who then is this, that even wind and sea obey him?": 4:41). This power protects the disciples from the violent sea (4:35–41) and casts the fearsome unclean spirit Legion into the sea (5:1–13). Oddly, the people beg Jesus to leave their neighborhood because of his demon exorcism (vs. 7). Moreover, instead of the usual command to silence, Jesus urges the restored demoniac to tell his friends about the mercy God has shown (5:19–20).

This injunction to *speak* about God's action contrasts all the more with the ending of the next episode (5:21–43), which explicitly enjoins *silence*. The episode of the demon Legion (5:1–20) emphasizes, however, the destruction of the old and the people's fearful response to that loss. In the double episode of the raising of Jairus' daughter and the healing of the woman, we find the typically Markan technique of intercalation, inserting one story or comment into another, presumably in order to interpret the one by the other (see also 2:1–12 and 14:53–72). Thereby two central themes of Mark's second half, the necessity for faith (vs. 34) and the **resurrection** from the dead (vs. 41), are highlighted and connected. The command to silence is appropriate to these themes. Although the people still figure in this narrative as they did in the exorcism, the center of attention is beginning to shift more clearly to the response of disciples (see vss. 31, 37, 40). The disciples' importance becomes more evident in the following stories: Jesus is rejected by his own people (6:1–6); he appoints the Twelve for a mission of healing and exorcism (6:7–13); John the Baptizer is beheaded by Herod and his body is given to his disciples (6:14–29), perhaps in anticipation of the role for which Jesus is beginning to prepare his disciples. The disciples' return from their mission and the miraculous feeding of the multitudes (6:30–44) may be viewed as a foreshadowing of the **Lord's Supper** and Jesus' death and resurrection.

Conflict with the religious leaders becomes most acute in the following chapter, where the Markan Jesus abolishes the crucial distinctions of purity embedded in Judaism's cultic law (see 7:11–23). Moreover, the extension of Jesus' powers in exorcising the demon from the daughter of the (**Gentile**) Syrophoenician woman (7:24–30) foreshadows an extension of the new religious community beyond Israel's borders.

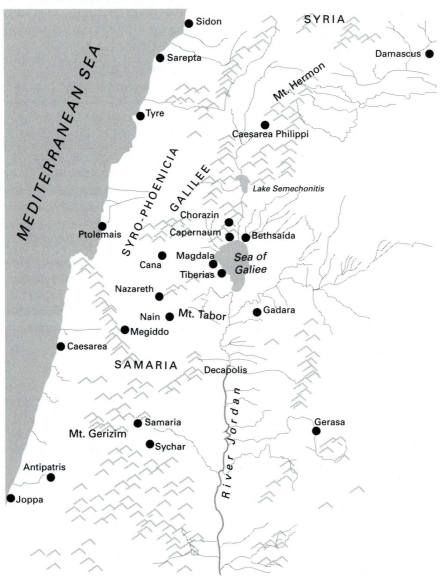

Galilee, Samaria, Syro-Phoenicia, and Syria.

Summing up: this brief journey through some of the remaining portions of Mark's first half (up to 8:21) suggests that the debates with the Pharisees are matters of life and death (2:15–3:6). For Mark the new reality, especially the new society that will emerge in Jesus' disciples, represents a freedom toward the law that defenders of the old reality could not tolerate. Consequently, the religious leaders resist; they plan Jesus' death. Jesus opposed the demons more successfully and more easily than he did the Pharisees. Ironically, the reaction of the Pharisees and other authorities to Jesus, their rejection and the plotting of his death, becomes the means for the accomplishment of Jesus' victory in making disciples (8:31; cf. 8:34). For even though the disciples remain close to Jesus throughout the first half of Mark, they have yet to learn the secret of Jesus' power. That realization came only with Jesus' death and resurrection.

THE POWER OF SUFFERING: JESUS AND HIS DISCIPLES (8:22–15:47)

The second half of Mark's Gospel centers upon the **passion** of Jesus. The passion story includes Jesus' decision to go to Jerusalem (10:32–34), the events of the last days in Jerusalem (11:1–14:72), and finally his death on the cross (15:1–47). Jesus' predictions of the passion begin in Chapter 8. When we observe that the passion of Jesus thus embraces almost one-half of the Gospel, the characterization of Mark as "a passion story with an extended introduction" seems particularly apt. In the first half of Mark, Jesus has dealt with his opponents, the demons and the **Pharisees**. In the second half, the human opponents will deal with Jesus. They put him to death by the Roman form of capital punishment—**crucifixion**. Yet these last chapters do not dwell on the opponents of Jesus. Instead, the disciples and their understanding of Jesus become central.

At three crucial moments Jesus predicts the sufferings he must undergo: "Then he began to teach them that the Son of Man must undergo great suffering, and be rejected by the elders, the chief priests, and the scribes, and be killed, and after three days rise again" (8:31; cf. 9:31; 10:33 f.). The disciples' continued misunderstanding of or inability to accept this prediction becomes clear in Gethsemane just before the arrest, trial, and crucifixion. They could not watch and pray while Jesus was grappling with temptation (14:38–41). The terse, seemingly final, verdict on the disciples is pronounced immediately after Jesus' arrest, "All of them deserted him and fled" (14:50). Indeed, Peter, the closest disciple, denied Jesus not once but three times (14:66–72).

The disciples' denial and flight occur because of their inability or unwillingness to acknowledge that their own discipleship must share the same quality as Jesus' suffering. Mark's Gospel speaks not only about the nature of Jesus' messiahship but also about the nature of discipleship; Mark's second half implies that there is no victory apart from suffering and conflict.

Structural considerations show that Mark 8:22–10:52 is the central, pivotal part of this Gospel, introducing its second half. This long section begins with the story of the blind man who at first sees men like trees walking. It ends with the gift of sight to blind

Bartimaeus, who then chooses to follow Jesus. Before this point in the Gospel is reached, Jesus' **miracles** are recounted in much detail. His teaching is frequently mentioned but not extensively described, except in scenes of controversy such as Mark 7:1–23, when Jesus denounces the Pharisees and the tradition of the elders. Mark contains a number of controversy scenes and stories. We have noted how these are related to the exorcisms, which are characterized by struggle between the demons and Jesus. With the initial story of Jesus' bestowing sight (8:22–26), decisive new factors enter the picture. First, in response to Jesus' question, Peter confesses Jesus as **Messiah** (8:27–30). Then Jesus repeatedly predicts his approaching suffering and death as the **Son of Man**. Jesus appears transfigured before his disciples (9:2–8), a foretaste of his **resurrection**, but they are far from understanding the meaning of this and other things that are transpiring.

Indeed, Mark's second half mirrors and emphasizes the disciples' lack of understanding, both of Jesus and of themselves. This is nowhere more evident than when Jesus instructs them in the meaning of discipleship (8:31–38; 9:33–37; 10:35–45). Whenever the Twelve, notably James and John, seek preferment, Jesus admonishes them by his own example: "Whoever wishes to be great among you must be your servant, and whoever wishes to be first among you must be slave of all. For the Son of man came not to be served but to serve, and to give his life a ransom for many" (10:43–45).

Immediately afterward, Jesus enters Jerusalem (11:1–11). The passion week is beginning. Mark's central section (8:22–10:52) clearly introduces a new phase of the Gospel. The structure, the arrangement of the material, and the emphases that emerge in the narrative show that a distinctive teaching about messiahship and discipleship is being set forth and emphasized. The theme of the true character of Jesus' messiahship leads to the reiterated and heavily emphasized teaching about discipleship. This section is a fitting introduction to the second half of the Gospel, which presents Jesus' death. The reader is learning what that death implies for Jesus' messiahship and for true discipleship.

Two Stages of Discipleship (8:22–9:9)

Why does Jesus respond as he does to Peter's confession?

The point of transition from the first portion of Mark to the second can be located in the episode at Caesarea Philippi, where Peter confesses Jesus as the **Christ** (the **Messiah**) and Jesus answers by declaring that his mission is one of divinely ordained suffering and vindication (8:27–33). The preceding episode, the healing of the blind man at Bethsaida (8:22–26), dramatically symbolizes what follows. This story stands out as the only two-stage healing in the Gospels. When Jesus first heals, the man sees only dimly and men look like trees walking; then Jesus applies a second touch and the blind man sees everything clearly. The unique manner of this healing seems to prefigure the "seeing" of the disciple Peter in the next episode. Peter sees that Jesus is the Christ; however, he does not yet understand the suffering nature of Jesus' messiahship (vs. 32). Peter, like the other disciples, must go through a second stage of "healing" before he can become a true disciple (cf. 8:34 ff.).

Peter's confession occurs on the way to the villages of Caesarea Philippi, located at the far northern end of Palestine where **Hellenistic** influence was prevalent. The location suggests that underneath Jesus' query about his identity may lie the question of whether his ministry should extend beyond the borders of Israel. After his death it will (13:10). At any rate, the answers of others (John the Baptist, Elijah, a prophet) are inadequate (cf. 6:14 f.). When Jesus turns the question to the disciples, Peter, speaking for them, answers, "You are the Messiah." Jesus then charges them not to tell anyone who he is (8:30). Previous commands of silence concerned his exorcisms and healings; now Jesus commands silence about his identity.

Within the Gospel itself the messianic secret focuses the reader's attention on the question of the nature of Jesus' messiahship and consequently upon the nature of Christian discipleship. The disciples, including Peter, misunderstood the role of Jesus as the

Caesarea Philippi (above) is the site of Peter's confession of Jesus as the Christ (Mark 8:27–30). It lay some 25 miles north of the Sea of Galilee, at the origin of the Jordan River (foreground).

Christ. As the **Son of Man** (the **apocalyptic**, heavenly figure; cf. Daniel 7:13–14) Jesus must suffer many things and be killed, and after three days rise (8:31). Peter's rebuke of Jesus leads to Jesus' rebuke of Peter (vss. 32 f.). The disciples' expectation of a miracle-working Messiah who delivers his followers from all unpleasantness into great reward (cf. 10:32–45) is rejected. The messianic secret restrains and tones down the **miracle**-tradition of Jesus precisely because the reader is being forced to acknowledge and accept Jesus' suffering. In fact, the community of Christians, followers of Jesus, is for Mark not possible until after Jesus' **crucifixion** and **resurrection**.

The Messianic Secret

Mark 8:29-30 serves as the focal point for what has become known in New Testament research as the problem of the "messianic secret." This broad term, first popularized by William Wrede (1901), comprises Jesus' commands to keep silent about his **miracles** (1:34, 44; 3:12; 5:43; 7:36) and his identity (8:27–30; 9:9), his private instruction to the disciples (7:17 f.; 9:39 f.; 10:10), and his private interpretation of **parables** (4:10 ff., 33 f.). The two most frequent proposals for understanding the messianic secret are (1) that Jesus commanded silence to keep the uninstructed multitudes from learning about his nonpolitical messiahship and perverting it into a political one, or (2) that Jesus did not in fact understand himself to be the **Messiah**; the secrecy motif is an attempt to explain, from the standpoint of the early church's faith, that Jesus was the Messiah, why Jesus was not publicly recognized as such, and why the Jesus tradition was relatively devoid of messianic claims. The first explanation depends entirely on the argument from silence, for there is nothing about such a motivation in the text. In the second case, there is, of course, a tension between Jesus' relative silence about his own role and the evangelists' (and **church's**) faith in him as the **Christ**. But both these solutions betray a modern preoccupation with the question of whether, or in what sense, Jesus thought that he was the Messiah. Moreover, they fail to take account of the several types of material grouped under the "messianic secret" motif. In Mark, the question is not *whether* Jesus was Messiah, but *why* he was the kind of Messiah he was.

The subsequent section on discipleship (8:34–9:1), spoken not only to the disciples but also to the multitudes, characterizes following Jesus as fellowship in service and suffering. Thus the character of Jesus' messiahship determines what discipleship must be. In becoming followers of Jesus, the disciples have taken the first step; however, they have not yet realized the full implications of discipleship. Victory can be realized only in conflict. Just as the **Spirit** fought Satan, and just as Jesus opposed demons and **Pharisees**, so too the disciples must continue to struggle until the end. That, according to Mark, cannot be far off: "There are some standing here who will not taste death until they see that the **kingdom of God** has come with power" (9:1; cf. Mark 13:24–37). Nowhere, however, does Jesus himself connect the coming kingdom with his title, Christ. In Mark at least, Jesus is not to be understood primarily as the political messiah, the expected restorer of Israel (see 8:29; 13:21 f.; 14:61; 15:32). The most frequent Markan designation for Jesus is the Son of Man. As Son of Man he exercises freedom over the law (2:10, 28), goes to his suffering and death (8:31 and passim), and will come again as **eschatological** judge (8:38; 13:26; 14:62). Thus the community Mark envisions is one that awaits the end time.

Jesus' teaching after Peter's confession (8:34–9:1) focuses upon the nature of discipleship rather than on the identity of the one whom the disciples follow. Not until the following episode, the transfiguration scene (9:2–9), does Mark return to the question of Jesus' identity. There Jesus, with three disciples, climbs a high mountain where he is transfigured. His clothes become glistening white, like those of the angels; moreover, even Moses and Elijah appear to speak with him. According to Israel's tradition, Moses gave the law from a mountain (Exod. 19:16 ff.) and Elijah prophesied from a mountain (1 Kings 19:9 ff). Thus Jesus converses with the two men representing Israel's heritage of the **law** and the **prophets**. Again the disciples misunderstand (vs. 6), not realizing that the coming of Jesus in some way fulfills the law and the prophets, for Jesus alone remains (vs. 8).

The climactic statement of the transfiguration scene, by the voice from the cloud ("This is my Son, the Beloved; listen to him!" [vs. 7]), alludes to the kingly tradition of Israel (cf. Psalm 2:7). If any other Old Testament figure was worthy of this distinguished company on the mountain, it would be David, the king of ancient Israel (cf. 2:25; 10:47 f.; 12:35 ff.). Possibly his exclusion prevents any political misunderstanding about the role of Jesus. At any rate, the voice announces to the disciples that Jesus is the eschatological king of Israel, the true final king. Jesus is **Son of God** with kingly power. At another crucial revelation of Jesus' identity in Mark, similar words have been spoken (1:11). Indeed, Mark's opening, "The beginning of the good news of Jesus Christ, the *Son of God*" (1:1), has already coupled this designation with Jesus. Such kingly power has to be viewed, however, in the context of the injunction "Listen to him" (vs. 7). In the following teaching (9:9–13), Jesus not only charges the disciples to be silent but explicitly links his power with both John's suffering ("Elijah has come" [vs. 13]) and his own (vs. 12). The final Markan designation of Jesus as Son of God occurs at the cross (15:39). Jesus' kingly power fulfills the law and the prophets by enduring suffering (see 14:21, 27).

A definite scheme thus appears: At the **baptism**, Jesus is declared Son of God by a voice from heaven. At the transfiguration, Jesus is announced as Son of God by a voice from the cloud to three major disciples. At the cross, Jesus is ironically proclaimed Son of God by a **Gentile** centurion. By implication, the kingdom comes with power (9:1) when the Son of God's suffering is accomplished and is both affirmed and imitated by the inclusive community that exists after Jesus' death and resurrection.

Faith to Produce Healing (9:14–32)

Why is the father's attitude superior to that of the disciples?

From this point to the end of the Gospel, the disciples are often in the foreground (see esp. 9:33–41; 10:23–31; 13:1 ff.) and always in the background. In 9:14–32, the healing of an epileptic boy, Mark combines two stories. The one shows how a father's faith enables his son to be healed; the other draws a contrast between the master's ability and the disciples' inability to heal, in order to present an example of genuine faith for the disciples. They are unable to heal because they do not yet understand the nature of true faith (cf. 9:32).

The argumentative disciples form a contrast with the beseeching father. He cries out, "I believe; help my unbelief!" (vs. 24), thereby demonstrating that all things are possible to the believer (vs. 23). Of course, this prayer for healing originates from the crisis of the father's desperate need. The disciples cannot heal because they do not pray (vs. 29). Prayer is characteristic of Jesus (1:35; 6:46). Later the ability to pray seems almost equivalent to the act of faith: "So I tell you whatever you ask for in prayer, believe that you have received it, and it will be yours" (11:24; cf. 11:22–26). The necessity for prayer becomes evident in the major Markan prayer episode, Jesus in Gethsemane (14:32–42). The disciples are to wait while Jesus prays (vs. 32), but they are also warned to pray (vs. 38). Jesus asks that suffering (the cup; cf. 10:38-39) might pass from him; however, he prays that God's will, not his own, be done. The disciples cannot heal, because they neither pray nor believe; they do not experience the suffering of Jesus. The necessity for such suffering is made explicit at the close of this healing episode (9:30–32). Again, Jesus predicts further conflict, but the disciples "did not understand what he was saying, and were afraid to ask him" (vs. 32).

In fact, fear dominates the disciples (cf. 4:40; 5:15; 9:6, 32; 10:32; 16:8). Probably such fear underscores the condition of the community to which the Gospel is addressed. Mark's Gospel was likely written to a **church** undergoing persecution (see above, pp. 60–61). According to Mark, this fear can be overcome by faith (vs. 23). The worst the disciples had to fear from persecution was death. In the healing of the epileptic boy, however, even the verdict, "He is dead" (vs. 26), proves false, because of the father's faith. Moreover, although Jesus, as the **Son of Man**, will be killed, after three days "he will rise" (vs. 31). If the disciples truly follow Jesus, then they too will go through persecution into victory. Indeed, the end time will be one of vindication (see 13:20 f.) if they continue and endure.

For the time being, however, the disciples are afraid. Out of their fear and lack of faith they dispute about greatness (9:34), are not open to lowly children (10:13), and deter nondisciples from casting out demons (9:38). They have yet to understand that Jesus' messiahship demands discipleship of service (vs. 41) to one another (vs. 50).

Jesus Approaches His Death (10:1–14:72)

What theological belief holds the themes of this narrative together?

As Jesus goes into Judea (10:1) and enters Jerusalem (11:1), he moves inevitably toward his suffering and death. Mark's narrative of the events leading up to and including Jesus' **crucifixion** is dominated by four separate but interrelated themes: fulfillment of the old, desertion by the disciples, victory through failure, and the necessity of Jesus' death. While characteristic of Mark, each is also traditional in the sense that it was shared by other Christians. This section of the Gospel sums up the Markan themes we have seen from the beginning.

Fulfillment of the Old

The **Pharisees** try to trap Jesus by raising the question of divorce (10:2–12), but Jesus declares that the will of God is communicated through the scripture rather than being identical with the scripture. (Jesus is not a literalist; some aspects of scripture are more important than others.) A man who obeys the **law** goes away sorrowful because his allegiance is finally to himself rather than to God (10:17–22). Jesus triumphantly enters Jerusalem, Israel's **holy** city, but only to disrupt the holy temple (11:15–19), even as he curses a fruitless fig tree (11:1–14; cf. Hosea 9:10, 16–17)—another Markan intercalation. Indeed, Jesus cannot accept the crowd's accolades ("Blessed is the coming kingdom of our ancestor David!" [11:9]) because Christ is not the Son of David (12:35–37) in a political sense. The kingdom that Jesus announces brings the end of history (chap. 13) rather than the restoration of Israel's kingdom. Israel's religious leaders reject this leader and the new society created by him (12:1–12); they quibble about taxes (12:13–17) and **resurrection** (12:18–27), and ignore God's coming near. In the narration of the **passion** itself, there are many allusions to the Old Testament. Scripture is fulfilled, but in ways that could hardly have been anticipated.

Desertion by the Disciples

The disciples continue to follow Jesus; however, they question his "hard" sayings (10:23–31) and follow only in fear (10:32). Just before Jesus' trial they all flee (14:50). Mark underscores that fact with the elliptical tale of the young follower of Jesus who flees away naked (14:51–52). The most crushing rejection of Jesus occurs in Peter's denial (14:53–72), especially tragic when viewed against Jesus' prediction and Peter's protest (14:26–31). While Jesus is put on trial before the council, Peter is tried and found wanting.

Victory Through Failure

The disciples are, however, the closest followers of Jesus. In spite of their desertion, Jesus will still come to them in Galilee after his death. In fact, the Last Supper anticipates such a reunion (14:12–28). The disciples may confidently look forward to it. Their confidence has several grounds: Jesus shows mercy, even to little children (10:13–16); the God who can do all things is at work (10:23–31); the only requirements are a recognition of need (10:46–52; cf. 9:23), the practice of forgiveness (11:25), and a letting go of self (12:41–44)—that is, a response of faith (11:20–26). Indeed, the transfiguration scene (9:2–13) probably represents a proleptic glory that both Jesus and the true disciples will share.

Necessity of Jesus' Death

The disciples' paralyzing fear in the face of persecution (see 13:9, 19) cannot be taken as final, for Jesus' death by crucifixion is the way in which God's victory will be achieved for them (10:32–45). This death is not only predicted by Jesus but is also prepared for by the anointing with costly ointment (14:1–9) and celebrated in the Last Supper (14:12–25). It occurs at the instigation of one of the disciples (14:10 f.). Although Jesus himself prays that his death may be avoided, he accepts the cross as God's will (14:32–42). In the scenes immediately before and during the crucifixion, Jesus' innocence is apparent (14:53–65; 15:1–15) and his behavior is exemplary (15:16–32). Thereby Mark shows the injustice of the human agents in Jesus' death and the perfect submission of Jesus to a death that ultimately triumphs through God's will.

Judas's Betrayal of Jesus

Judas lives in infamy as the betrayer of Jesus. According to Mark 14:11 the betrayal was for money. Matthew 26:15 specifies thirty pieces of silver. John adds that Judas was the keeper of the common purse, the treasurer of Jesus' group (12:6; cf. 13:29). The later **Gospels** tell more about Judas and portray Jesus as fingering him specifically as the betrayer, which does not yet happen in Mark. By contrast, in John (13:27) Jesus virtually commands him to get on with the deed. Continuing this trend of embellishing the portrait of Judas, the newly discovered *Gospel of Judas* (second-century) has Jesus commend him above the other disciples. Until the *Gospel of Judas*, that disciple is increasingly vilified, though in Matthew (27:3-10) Judas repents of his deed, returns the money, and hangs himself. Similarly, according to Acts (1:15-20), Judas committed suicide, if not by hanging. Is it possible that Judas's motivation was not greed and his intention was not Jesus' execution? Various motivations have been suggested, but we lack the necessary evidence to corroborate any of them. That Jesus and Judas plotted together, as the *Gospel of Judas* has it, is unlikely, since the rest of that **Gnostic** Gospel contains so much that is historically improbable. In the *Gospel of Judas*, Jesus' death apparently allows him to put off his body and assume a purely spiritual state—a typically Gnostic goal that has little basis in earliest Christianity or its ancient Jewish matrix.

Significantly, the context in which Mark's reader views Jesus' suffering in his trial and death (chaps. 14–15) is the prediction of the suffering and future triumph of the **church** of Jesus (chap. 13). This address by Jesus, known as the "little **apocalypse**," maintains a tension between the imminence of the end (vss. 14, 26, 29, 30, 35) and the recognition that the time of its coming is unknown. Not even Jesus knows exactly when it will come (vss. 7, 21, 32). Mark's apocalyptic look into the future is an explicit warning to the church against understanding Christian existence as present power, even in miraculous acts (see vss. 6–8, 21–27). The present consists of self-sacrificial suffering that, because it is acknowledged, accepted, and not avoided, will eventually lead to triumph. The Markan community that faces persecution is bolstered by its belief in the imminent end of history and the final triumph with Jesus in the fulfilled **kingdom of God**.

The Cross of Jesus (15:33–47)

What is the meaning of Jesus' last words?

The Markan account of the **crucifixion** seemingly depicts an action accomplished by Jesus' opponents. Jesus remains passive. Pilate's question as to whether he is the king of the Jews is answered enigmatically (15:1–5). Jesus makes no plea for his life before the crowd when Barabbas is released (15:6–15). He does not protest the scourging (15:16–20). Someone else, another Simon, carries his cross (15:21). Furthermore, he does not even acknowledge those who mock his helplessness on the cross (15:29–32). The one action of Jesus upon which Mark centers is his loud cry from the cross: "My God, my God, why have you forsaken me?" (15:34; cf. Psalm 22:1). Mark underscores the cry's importance by first giving it in Jesus' native **Aramaic** and then translating it into Greek. The meaning of this cry can only be understood from the context. The setting for Jesus' death is somber. At noon darkness comes over the whole land for three hours before he dies (vs. 33; cf. Amos 8:9). Although it generally took twelve or more hours for someone to die by crucifixion, Jesus died after only six (Mark 15:25, 33,34–37). At the critical moment, Jesus shouts this cry of apparent despair. Someone rushes to give him vinegar while others mockingly ask whether Elijah will come to help. Then he "gave a loud cry and breathed his last" (vs. 37). In reading the text, we observe that Jesus gave two loud cries just before his death. Possibly "My God, why have you forsaken me?" was a later addition spelling out what the "loud cry" was. If so, then Mark, or the tradition lying behind Mark, added these words for a specific reason. Whatever the answer to the question of the cry's origin, clearly this shout is the Markan key to Jesus' death.

Traditionally these words (vs. 34) have been considered the "cry of dereliction," the cry of despair at abandonment by God. Yet these words may be a cry of victory, for they are the opening words of Psalm 22, which begins in despair but ends on a note of triumph: "All the ends of the earth shall remember and turn to the Lord; and all the families of the nations shall worship before him. For dominion belongs to the Lord, and he rules over the nations" (Psalm 22:27f.). Perhaps so, but the **theological** truth of such reasoning should not remove the element of despair and real suffering. Clearly the Psalmist suffers, and Jesus suffers; Mark intends for the reader to perceive Jesus' sense of despair, even to the point of apparently being abandoned by God. Thus Jesus' last fearful word in Mark maintains tension to the very end. No premature miracle rescues Jesus from this final struggle with God himself (cf. 14:36).

The preceding scene at the cross (15:29–32) stresses the Markan perception of the necessity for suffering. Here Jesus is mocked because he cannot save himself, although he has claimed to save others. The mockers ironically make Mark's point. Suffering cannot be avoided for Jesus, the disciples, and Mark's persecuted church, because thereby others can be saved (see 8:35).

Yet Mark claims, for Jesus and the **church**, victory in suffering. The mockery over his boast of destroying and rebuilding the temple in three days (15:29 f.) is answered by

The Church of the Holy Sepulchre, which in its present form dates from the eleventh century, stands within the walls of present-day Jerusalem, but outside the city walls of Jesus' day, (cf. John 19:20; Hebrews 13:12), as excavations have shown. It is the traditional site of Jesus' crucifixion (Golgotha) and tomb.

the tearing apart of the temple curtain at Jesus' death (vs. 38), for that death extends God's **revelation** and relation with Israel to all people. Fittingly, the **Gentile** centurion confesses Jesus as "**Son of God**" (vs. 39). The extension of God's **salvation** to all answers the mocking of those waiting for Elijah to take Jesus down. God has come down to open the temple. The principal actor in the passion is neither Jesus nor the people and officials, but God. In Jesus' suffering, God is acting to effect triumph. We might have anticipated this conclusion. Even when Jesus cried out in despair (vs. 34), his cry was addressed to God; he was praying. In Mark, prayer or faith makes all things possible, even victory in the face of apparent defeat (cf. 14:34 f.; 9:29; 11:24).

Mark effectively depicts four responses to Jesus' death: those of God (vs. 38), the centurion (vs. 39), the women (vss. 40 f.), and Joseph of Arimathea (vss. 42–47). The most explicit of these is that of the centurion. Unlike the disciples, who were earlier afraid (4:40; 6:50; 10:32), the centurion boldly acclaims Jesus as the Son of God. This affirmation occurs directly after Jesus' death. Possibly the centurion was impressed with the manner in which Jesus died, but the Markan text mentions no such impression. Conceivably the centurion spoke in derision or contempt. We cannot know. What we do know, however, is that "Son of God" is a key Markan designation of Jesus (1:1). At the **baptism**, such sonship meant obedience to God (1:11); at the transfiguration such sonship announced the kingly power of Jesus (9:7); and now at the crucifixion the centurion proclaims Jesus as God's Son precisely at his death (cf. also 3:11; 5:7). Thereby Mark manifests Jesus' suffering messiahship as the key to discipleship.

The women confirm that Jesus is dead, for the Twelve have all fled and they are the only ones left. Moreover, the Galilean women make peculiarly good and apt Markan witnesses of Jesus' death. We are told that they "used to follow him and provided for him" (vs. 41; cf. 1:31). Of course, "following" is another way of expressing discipleship (cf. esp. 1:17), and their "providing" picks up Jesus' emphasis upon "service" (the same Greek word, *diakonein* or *diakonia,* is used for both): "For the Son of man also came not to be *served* but to *serve,* and to give his life as a ransom for many" (10:45). Furthermore, Jesus charged his disciples, "Whoever wants to be first must be last of all and *servant* of all" (9:35). These women are the first followers of Jesus to see his death, witness his burial, and hear the **resurrection** report. They were apparently also the first followers to accept Jesus' way of service. Possibly women played a prominent role in the Markan church. The way of discipleship receives further explication in the action of Joseph of Arimathea, a respected member of the Jewish council (vs. 43). In contrast to the chosen disciples, he has courage (cf. 14:50). Furthermore, he seeks the **kingdom of God**, whereas the disciples appear to be seeking their own welfare (cf. 10:35–45).

The **passion** narrative ends with conclusive evidence of the death of Jesus. Pilate learns from the centurion that Jesus has died quickly (15:44). The body is laid and sealed in the tomb, with women as witnesses (vs. 47). Yet already in the centurion, the women, and Joseph of Arimathea, something new is being born.

EPILOGUE: THE FUTURE VICTORY (16:1–8)

Why do the women respond in fear?

After Jesus' death the Christian reader expects a happy ending: resurrection and glorious triumph. The note of victory is in fact present in Mark's epilogue, but it is restrained. Among the Gospels, only Mark fails to record an appearance of Jesus to the women or disciples. Our interpretation omits Mark 16:9–20, because this passage is doubtless a later addition to the text. The Gospel abruptly ends with verse 8. The only evidence contradicting the natural assumption that the death is final is the empty-tomb story, which in itself is ambiguous. The absence of Jesus' body does not necessarily prove his resurrection (cf. Matt. 28:13–15).

The opening verses (1–4) create the atmosphere for the incident. The women are going to perform a pious deed, to anoint the body of Jesus. Evidently burial was hasty, and they could not anoint the body on the **holy** Sabbath. At the first opportunity ("very early"), they go to the tomb. They have come to honor the dead Jesus, but their plans are upset. Mark portrays a young man sitting in the open tomb, who, from his apparel, must be an angel, a messenger from God. Naturally the women are quite amazed, but the messenger chides them for their perplexity (vs. 6a). Earlier encounters with Jesus evoked similar awe and amazement from the crowds (1:27; 9:15), the **Pharisees** (12:17), and the disciples (10:24). This response, however, falls short of the required act of faith. Amazement and awe at Jesus' numinous quality are not enough. Neither is the reaction of fear (16:8) an adequate response to Jesus, whether on the part of Jesus' opponents (11:18) or his disciples (4:40; 9:6, 32). Amazement and fear are already linked at the first explicit reference to Jesus' unalterable movement toward Jerusalem (10:32). True discipleship consists of more than awe at the numinous or fear at the realities of human finitude. Something more, a response of faith, a victory through suffering, is required according to Mark (cf. 4:40; 10:52; 11:22).

The women, disciples, and Peter are promised that something more will occur. Jesus will go before them into Galilee (16:7). Of course, they have no guarantee other than the messenger's word (cf. 14:28) that he will appear in Galilee. The precise reason for the choice of Galilee is not certain. Perhaps the disciples are to meet Jesus in Galilee, rather than Jerusalem, to gather forces for the **Gentile** mission. The precise meaning of the promise that they will see Jesus is also unclear. Perhaps the disciples are to await the second coming of Christ, the **parousia**, when **God's kingdom** will fully come (cf. chap. 13). More likely, they will await a resurrection appearance of Jesus ("there you will see him"; cf. 14:28). Indeed, the first resurrection appearances to the disciples were likely in Galilee (Matt. 28:16; cf. John 21:1). Whatever the exact meaning, the promise stresses the future. Everything has not yet happened; a future victory awaits. The Markan story of Jesus does not promise to deliver the **church** from persecution, even though in Jesus' life and death a first victory has been won. Satan was bound, demons were exorcised, opponents were defeated in debate, disciples were gathered. Moreover, the future promises a second, complete victory. But the future can still only be assured through faith. In the present the church faces strife and persecution (see 13:19).

Mark's concluding words ("for they were afraid") corroborate this interpretation. Even though manuscript evidence decisively supports it, some scholars challenge this ending because it sounds like a half-sentence. In addition, the end of a manuscript, especially a papyrus scroll, could easily be lost. Although inferior manuscripts provide what was deemed a more satisfying ending to Mark (cf. 16:9–20), Matthew and Luke appear to know only the version ending at 16:8. Their respective resurrection appearance stories do not parallel Mark's longer ending (16:9–20). Most important, the ending of Mark at verse 8 fits this Gospel. The women are left with fear, the normal and ever-present fear of a church undergoing persecution in the mid-to-late-sixties, perhaps at Rome. Of course, Mark wishes to encourage endurance, faith, and prayer in spite of fear, but the Gospel does not command faith only at its end. Instead, Mark's whole Gospel implies the need for faith in a final victory, because an initial triumph through suffering has occurred in Jesus. Mark is realistic enough to acknowledge fear and hopeful enough to proclaim the breaking of fear's power through faith in that future final victory promised by the suffering and resurrected Jesus.

CONCLUSION

A summary of our interpretation of the Gospel of Mark can best be made by reviewing the results of our four-step methodology.

In *structure* this Gospel presents a series of conflicts between Jesus, allied with God's **Spirit** (1:1–15), and opponents at various levels: Satan, demons, **Pharisees**, and finally disciples. The major Markan watershed is Peter's confession at Caesarea Philippi (8:22 ff.); from this point attention shifts to Jesus' relationship with his disciples. The first half of Mark shows Jesus' movement toward apparent success both in **miracle** and debate, whereas in the second half, he moves toward apparent failure in death, as the disciples persist in misunderstanding.

We have found at least five themes or *emphases* in Mark: (1) the miracles of Jesus; (2) his **passion**; (3) the messianic secret; (4) the call to a discipleship of suffering and service; and (5) the confession of Jesus as **Son of God**. Our interpretation reconciles the apparent contradiction of the first two emphases (the "strong Jesus" of miracles versus the "weak Jesus" of death) through the third emphasis, the secrecy motif, which suggests Jesus' use of persuasion rather than dramatic demonstration in making true disciples (the fourth emphasis). Mark took over the miracle tradition of Jesus but set it within the perspective of Jesus' passion, thus implying that the creation of the disciples' faith could occur only if Jesus abandoned miracles and accepted suffering as God's will. The fifth emphasis, Jesus as Son of God, gathers up all the others, and they in turn define Jesus' sonship.

The messianic-secret motif occurs precisely at those points where the tradition was most susceptible to presenting Jesus as a divine man with power to overcome any difficulty. In effect, Mark opposed such an attitude about Jesus and the life of discipleship. God's declaration of Jesus' sonship at the **baptism** and at the transfiguration is affirmed by a human only at Jesus' death. (Note how the occurrences of "Son of God" confirm the Markan structure: 1:1, 11; 9:7; and 15:39.) *Jesus is Son of God in suffering and death.* Consequently, for Mark the nature of discipleship and of the Christian community is marked by faith that believes in spite of unbelief (9:24; cf. 5:34–36; 11:23 f.) and by a faithful remnant who suffer in the watchful, prayerful expectation of the final coming of the **kingdom of God** (13:33 ff.; 14:38).

Although we do not have the Markan sources of tradition from which to study his *redaction* of that material, we can see that such motifs as the messianic secret and the predictions of Jesus' suffering, death, and resurrection either occur in Mark's transitional sections or otherwise give evidence of the evangelist's hand. Moreover, we may safely assume that Mark selected and arranged the tradition in order to accomplish his purposes. Thus there is the dominance of the miracle tradition in the first half of Mark's Gospel and of the passion story in the second.

Whether or not the Gospel was written at Rome, Mark reflects the *historical setting* of a **church** undergoing persecution. This crisis and time of **apocalyptic** expectation required a steadfast community of faithful and watchful disciples. Jesus **Christ**, the Son of God, had himself gone through persecution and no escape had been offered him. Jesus triumphed through his suffering, and the same victory is promised to the faithful disciple: "For whoever would save his life will lose it; and whoever loses his life for my sake and the gospel's will save it" (8:35).

SUGGESTIONS FOR FURTHER READING

THE SYNOPTIC GOSPELS

A basic tool for study of the Synoptics is B. H. Throckmorton, Jr., *Gospel Parallels: A Comparison of the Synoptic Gospels*, 5th ed. (Nashville: Thomas Nelson, 1992). Also very useful is K. Aland, *Synopsis of the Four Gospels: English Edition* (New York: United Bible Societies, 1982), which includes the Gospel of John. A classic analysis of Synoptic sources and interrelations is B. H. Streeter, *The Four Gospels: A Study of Origins*, rev. ed. (London: Macmillan, 1930). E. P. Sanders and M. Davies, *Studying the Synoptic Gospels* (Philadelphia: Trinity Press International, 1989), offers an up–to–date, cautious, inductive approach to the Synoptic problem, as well as modern approaches to Gospel interpretation. J. M. Robinson, P. Hoffmann, and J. S. Kloppenborg (eds.), *The Critical Edition of Q* (Minneapolis: Fortress, 2000), is the most ambitious reconstruction and analysis of that hypothetical Gospel source. The standard, critical collection of apocryphal Gospels, as well as apocryphal acts and apocalypses, is W. Schneemelcher (ed.), *The New Testament Apocrypha*, trans. R. McL. Wilson (Louisville: Westminster/John Knox, 1991–1992). H. Koester, *Ancient Christian Gospels: Their History and Development* (Philadelphia: Trinity Press International, 1990), treats canonical and apocryphal Gospels on the same level. An important inquiry into the genre of the Gospels is R. A. Burridge, *What Are the Gospels? A Comparison with Graeco–Roman Biography* (Grand Rapids and Dearborn, MI: Eerdmans/Dove, 2004). G. N. Stanton, *Jesus and the Gospel* (Cambridge: Cambridge University Press, 2004), considers the transition from earliest proclamations to four Gospels. A revisionist assessment of the Gospels' circulation among early Christian communities is presented in R. Bauckham (ed.), *The Gospel for All Christians: Rethinking the Gospel Audiences* (Grand Rapids: Eerdmans, 1998).

THE GOSPEL ACCORDING TO MARK

Note: Commentary series identified in the General Bibliography are not mentioned at the ends of chapters. In general, commentaries on the Greek text are not listed.

Among the many superb **commentaries** on Mark, especially recommended are E. Schweizer, *The Good News According to Mark*, trans. D. H. Madvig (Richmond: John Knox, 1970), R. A. Guelich, *Mark 1–8:26*, and C. A. Evans, *Mark 8:27–16:20* (Dallas and Nashville: Word/Thomas Nelson, 1989–2001), M. D. Hooker, *The Gospel According to Saint Mark* (London: A & C Black, 1991), J. Marcus, *Mark 1–8: A New Translation with Introduction and Commentary* (New York: Doubleday, 2000), J. R. Edwards, *The Gospel According to Mark* (Grand Rapids: Eerdmans, 2002), and F. J. Moloney, *The Gospel of Mark: A Commentary* (Peabody, MA: Hendrickson, 2002).

Overviews of disputed questions in Markan interpretation are offered by D. H. Juel, *The Gospel of Mark* (Nashville: Abingdon, 1999), D. J. Harrington, *What Are They Saying About Mark?* (New York: Paulist, 2004), and F. J. Moloney, *Mark: Storyteller, Interpreter, Evangelist* (Peabody, MA: Hendrickson, 2004). W. R. Telford (ed.), *The Interpretation of Mark*, 2nd ed. (Edinburgh: T & T Clark, 1995), assembles important essays on the Gospel. M. Hengel, *Studies in the Gospel of Mark* (Philadelphia: Fortress, 1985), A. Y. Collins, *The Beginning of the Gospel: Probings of Mark in Context* (Minneapolis: Fortress, 1992), and C. C. Black, *Mark: Images of an Apostolic Interpreter* (Minneapolis: Fortress, 2001) explore aspects of Mark's **history and tradition**. Still important for studying Mark's appropriation of traditional motifs are W. Wrede, *The Messianic Secret,* trans. by J. C. G. Greig (Cambridge: Clark, 1971), J. M. Robinson, *The Problem of History in Mark* (Philadelphia: Fortress, 1982; originally published in 1957), and U. W. Mauser, *Christ in the Wilderness* (Naperville, IL: Allenson, 1963). H. C. Kee, *Community of the New Age: Studies in Mark's Gospel* (Philadelphia: Westminster, 1977), is a pioneering treatment of the Gospel's **social setting**; more recent, differently framed inquiries include C. Myers, *Binding the Strong Man: A Political Reading of Mark's Story of Jesus* (Maryknoll, NY: Orbis, 1988), and J. K. Riches, *Conflicting Mythologies: Identity Formation in the Gospels of Mark and Matthew* (Edinburgh: T & T Clark, 2000). Important **literary approaches** include M. A. Tolbert, *Sowing the Gospel: Mark's World in Literary–Historical Perspective* (Minneapolis: Fortress, 1989), R. M. Fowler, *Let the Reader Understand: Reader–Response Criticism and the Gospel of Mark* (Minneapolis: Fortress, 1991), and E. S. Malbon, *In the Company of Jesus: Characters in Mark's Gospel* (Louisville: Westminster John Knox, 2000).

W. Marxsen, *Mark the Evangelist: Studies on the Redaction History of the Gospel*, trans. R. A. Harrsiville, et al. (Nashville: Abingdon, 1969), is fundamental for its **redaction-critical** approach; C. C. Black, *The Disciples According to Mark: Markan Redaction in Current Debate* (Sheffield: Sheffield Academic Press, 1989), has challenged many assumptions of Marxsen and his successors. On Markan **theology** generally, the syntheses by D. H. Juel, *A Master of Surprise: Mark Interpreted* (Minneapolis: Fortress, 1994), and W. R. Telford, *The Theology of the Gospel of Mark* (Cambridge: Cambridge University Press, 1999), are commendable. On the still controversial question of Mark's **use of Scripture**, compare the different analyses of J. Marcus, *The Way of the Lord: Christological Exegesis of the Old Testament in the Gospel of Mark* (Louisville: Westminster/John Knox, 1992), and R. E. Watts, *Isaiah's New Exodus in Mark* (Grand Rapids: Baker, 2000).

Master of the Life of Saint John the Baptist (1320/1330), by Rimini. The National Gallery of Art, Washington. *(Courtesy of © 2006 Board of Trustees, National Gallery of Art, Washington, Samuel H. Kress Collection, 1939.)*

CHAPTER 3

MATTHEW: THE GOSPEL OF OBEDIENCE

Background of the Gospel of Matthew

Like the Gospel of Mark, Matthew contains no direct reference to its author and place of origin. The earliest apparent reference to Matthew's Gospel is a report from Papias (ca. **A.D.** 130):

> Matthew collected the oracles in the Hebrew language, and each one interpreted them as best he could (Eusebius, *EH*, III, 39, 16). . . . Matthew, had first preached to Hebrews, and when he was on the point of going to others, he transmitted in writing in his native language the Gospel according to himself (*EH*, III, 24, 6).

This information is, however, unclear and of uncertain value. In fact, it does not seem to be a reference to our Matthew, which was written in Greek. Because our Gospel is based upon the Greek text of Mark and the **Q** sayings **source**, it is unlikely that it was written by Matthew, an **Aramaic**-speaking disciple and eyewitness (cf. Mark 3:18 par.). Possibly Papias means that Matthew collected Jesus' sayings, which is what the Greek word (*logia*), translated "oracles," means.

The Gospel was probably at first anonymous, inasmuch as the present titles were added only as the Gospels were incorporated into a fourfold canon. Authorship may have been attributed to Matthew, one of the twelve disciples, because only this Gospel distinguishes Matthew as a tax collector (10:3; cf. Mark 3:18), making the incident of the calling of a tax collector (who is Levi in Mark 2:14) a story about Matthew (Matt. 9:9). We do not know the reason for this change other than to give some prominence to Matthew.

The author was familiar with Jewish Christianity and wrote for a Greek-speaking audience. Possibly he was a Christian **scribe**, similar to the Jewish scribes of the **law** (see 13:52). He took over and expanded the Markan framework by adding two types of material: sayings common also to Luke (Q source) and his own special Matthean tradition, which came from **oral tradition** or from a written source or sources. As a result, the prominence of Matthew's narrative portion is equaled, if not exceeded, by its sayings material. The Jesus of Matthew is at least as much a teacher as an actor. Our five-part outline of Matthew (excluding the Introduction, 1:1–2:23, and Conclusion, 26:2–28:20) apparently reflects the evangelist's own design. The end of each major discourse section is clearly marked by an editorial conclusion (see 7:28 ff.; 11:1; 13:53; 19:1 ff.; 26:1 ff.) Although much of the material found in the five discourse sections is paralleled in Luke, the organization into discrete discourses belongs to Matthew alone. For example, although Luke contains most of the sayings of Jesus found in Matthew's Sermon on the Mount (chaps. 5–7), only a part of them appears in Luke's shorter Sermon on the Plain. The Sermon on the Mount as such is known only from Matthew.

Like Luke, Matthew begins his narrative with an account of Jesus' birth, but the nativity stories of the two Gospels are quite different. Only Matthew informs us of Joseph's embarrassment at the prospect of the birth of Jesus before his marriage with Mary is consummated (1:18–25), the visit of the wise men (Magi) from the East (2:1–12), or the departure of the Holy Family to Egypt (2:13–15). Such famous sayings as Jesus' pronouncement of comfort to the weary and heavy-laden are found only in Matthew (11:28–30), together with a number of **parables** (13:24–30, 36–43, 44, 45–46, 47–50, 51–52; 18:23–35; 20:1–16; also 25:31–46, if it is to be considered a parable). Among the Gospels only Matthew relates, in connection with Jesus' death, the fate of Judas (27:3–10, cf. Acts 1:18–20), Pilate's washing his hands of Jesus' blood (27:24), the placing of guards at Jesus' tomb (27:62–66), and the subsequent bribing of them (28:11–15). Finally, the charge of the risen Jesus to his disciples from a Galilean mountain is found in Matthew alone (28:16–20). There are other distinctively Matthean materials, but these are typical.

The provenance of Matthew's Gospel is generally thought to be Syria, probably the city of Antioch. The oldest witness to the use of this Gospel may be Ignatius, bishop of Antioch. Although he does not cite it by name, his letters (A.D. 110–115) contain bits of distinctively Matthean material. In all probability, Matthew was written after A.D. 70, for its addition to the parable of the marriage feast ("The king was angry, and he sent his troops and destroyed those murderers and burned their city"–22:7; cf. Luke 14:21) apparently refers to the destruction of Jerusalem in that year. Because Mark was probably composed shortly before Jerusalem's fall, some time would likely have elapsed before Mark's authority became sufficient for the anonymous author of Matthew to use it as a primary source. Consequently, a date of about A.D. 80–90 seems likely. Indeed, the obvious tension between the Christianity of Matthew and the Judaism of the **Pharisees** (cf. Matt. 23) also suggests a date after the Roman destruction of the temple in A.D. 70.

At this time Judaism retrenched in the face of the threat of possible extinction and began to develop toward a **rabbinic**, Pharisaic uniformity. Sectarian movements within Judaism, such as Jewish Christianity, became suspect and eventually may have been read out of the developing normative Judaism.

Clearly this Gospel is more systematically and intricately organized than Mark. Matthew emphasizes fulfillment of **prophecy**, Jesus as teacher, and the place of the law and final judgment within the Christian congregation. These broad interests suggest a churchly Gospel, written to guide the community in a time of transition as it faced problems pertaining to organization, separation from Judaism, and disappointed **eschatological** hopes. Matthew serves the **church**; probably for that reason the church placed it first in the New Testament **canon**. Because it is written to offer the church direction, Matthew may be compared with a roughly contemporary document, the *Community Rule* of the **Qumran** community. Matthew's method of Old Testament interpretation also resembles that found at Qumran, particularly in the *Habakkuk Commentary*.

OUTLINE OF MATTHEW

Introduction: The New Obedience (1:1–2:23)

The Higher Righteousness (3:1–7:29)
Fulfilling Righteousness (3:13–17)
Teaching Righteousness (5:17–20)

True Discipleship (8:1–11:1)

The Kingdom of Heaven (11:2–13:52)

The Forgiving Church (13:53–19:2)
Peter as the Rock (16:13–23)
Discipline in Community (18:15–22)

Judgment: Doing God's Will (19:3–26:1)
Condemnation of Hypocrisy (23:1–39)
Doing Mercy without Calculation (25:31–46)

Conclusion: Obedience and Resurrection (26:2–28:20)
The Great Commission (28:16–20)

INTRODUCTION: THE NEW OBEDIENCE (1:1–2:23)

Matthew's Gospel begins with his special tradition, which appears to be largely legendary: a genealogical list of Jesus' ancestors; a story of Jesus' birth; exotic wise men from the East, their encounter with Herod and worship of the baby Jesus; the flight to Egypt; the slaying of the innocent children; and the return to Nazareth. These matters may seem preliminary to the real work of Jesus, which for Mark began at Jesus' **baptism** and ended at the **crucifixion**. But these "Christmas stories" bear the heart of Matthew's message, his good news.

The genealogy (1:1 ff.) helps in understanding the birth story (1:18–25). At first glance, this list of Jesus' ancestors looks rather unpromising for determining Matthew's intent and purpose. We notice that the genealogy is divided into three sets of generations of fourteen each: from Abraham to David, from David to the Babylonian deportation, and from Babylon to the Christ (vs. 17; unaccountably, the last set contains only thirteen generations). Abraham is the father of the Jewish people, for Israel's God is the God of

Abraham, Isaac, and Jacob (see Gen. 12:1–3; cf. Matt. 3:9; 22:32). The **Christ** who climaxes this genealogy fulfills the hope of Israel; therefore, the age of fulfillment is dawning with the birth of the expected **Messiah**. This Christ is also descended from David, the great king in Israel's history. Indeed, the Lord promised through the prophet Nathan that David's offspring would be established in a kingdom forever (2 Sam. 7:12–17). Thus Jesus Christ will fulfill Israel's hopes, prefigured in Abraham and David (see 1:1). Yet the Babylonian **exile**, the next major division in the genealogy, meant disaster for Israel's hope of establishing a political kingdom in which God's rule would triumph. Perhaps for Matthew, the deportation raises the question of whether fulfillment of Israel's hopes will take a form other than that of a Davidic political kingdom.

What's behind Matthew's Genealogy?

Genealogy is a biblical **genre** (cf. 1 Chron. 1-9, the longest Old Testament genealogy, as well as Gen. 5:1-32; 10:1-11:32, among others). That Matthew provides such a genealogy says something about how he regards his book. It may well be intended as biblical, that is, authoritative, for Christians in Matthew's own day and even beyond. One might suppose that Matthew's Gospel aims to prove that Jesus was the Messiah because he was descended from Abraham and especially David. Yet, according to the following verses, Joseph does not father Jesus, even though the genealogy would have to be traced through him to function as proof of Davidic lineage. Originally this tradition, separated from 1:18–25, might have proved the Davidic descent of Jesus and therefore his messiahship. In the Matthean context, however, biological descent from David through Joseph cannot be maintained. (Cf. Luke 3:23, which betokens awareness of the problem of descent through Joseph.) Joseph's legal status as the father of Jesus is probably what counts for Matthew.

The inclusion of women in the genealogy suggests a possibility of the unexpected; the Christ who comes may not correspond to the image of the Messiah for whom Israel was waiting. In the ancient world, descent was traced through the male; yet aside from Mary (vs. 16), four women appear in the genealogy: Tamar (vs. 3), Rahab and Ruth (vs. 5), and the wife of Uriah (vs. 6). Moreover, these are quite unusual women. Tamar disguised herself as a harlot to seduce her father-in-law Judah so that she could bear children, Perez and Zerah (Gen. 38). Rahab, the prostitute of Jericho, saved Joshua's two spies and consequently preserved her own life when the walls of Jericho fell (Josh. 2, 6). Ruth, the Moabite woman who was loyal to her Hebrew mother-in-law, gained her future husband Boaz one night during the grain festival (Ruth 3). And "the wife of Uriah" is none other than Bathsheba, who bathed in the right place during "the spring of the year" and thus became David's wife (2 Sam. 11–12). Possibly each of these women, at least Rahab and Ruth, would be perceived as foreigners. In spite of their origins and questionable moral actions, God acted through each.

Within this setting, Matthew's story of Jesus' birth takes place. The genealogy indicates that Jesus' significant ancestry includes not only the men, especially Abraham and David, but also the women: Tamar, Rahab, Ruth, Bathsheba, and finally Mary. Moreover, there are Jews *and* **Gentiles** in this lineage.

The birth story itself (vss. 18–25) centers on Joseph's response to the pregnancy of his betrothed Mary. Although Matthew explicitly talks about a virginal conception (vss. 18, 20, 23, 25), the story focuses not upon wonder at the virgin Mary but, rather, on how Joseph will react to the dilemma posed by the question of whether she is pregnant from unfaithfulness or the power of God. That question is posed not only within the birth story itself but also by the preceding section. Inclusion of the women in Matthew's genealogy raises the question of how God works to achieve his purposes, and at the culmination of the birth story Joseph must decide whether Mary's pregnancy is by God's action.

Joseph at first thinks that he has been wronged by Mary. "Being a righteous man," he decides to divorce her quietly (vs. 19). According to Jewish **law**, engagement, like marriage, could be severed only by divorce (Deut. 24:1–4). A man could do one of two things: he could bring his betrothed to public trial, where conviction of infidelity might carry the penalty of death by stoning, or he could divorce his betrothed privately. Joseph generously opts for the latter course. At this moment, however, the angel intrudes, and through a dream Joseph learns about a higher **righteousness** (see also 3:15; 5:20; 5:33). He hears that this conception is from the **Holy Spirit**, the agent of God's activity on earth. Furthermore, this son of Mary is to be named Jesus, whose name implies one who will "save his people from their sins" (vs. 21).

The Name "Jesus"

The name "Jesus" is a transliteration of *lēsous*. This, in turn, transliterates *Yeshua* or *yehoshua*, which comes into English as Joshua, the protégé of Moses who led the Israelites into the land of Canaan. The Old Testament book of that name recounts his deeds. The name is similar in Hebrew to the term for **salvation** or deliverance (*yeshuah*). Thus, Matthew 1:21 is a play on Jesus' name that requires knowledge of Hebrew to be fully understood and appreciated.

Matthew then continues with a reference to the fulfillment of Hebrew prophecy (vss. 22–23). These opening two chapters, which narrate Jesus' birth, are characterized by Matthew's use of a formula for Old Testament scripture citation (see also 2:6, 15, 18, 23; in addition, 4:15–16; 8:17; 12:18–21; 13:35; 21:5; 26:56; 27:9–10). Matthew applies these formula or fulfillment quotations to the story of Jesus in order to link his mission and message with the story of Israel. Thus the theme of Jesus as the savior of his people is developed in the quotation from Isaiah 7:14 (vss. 22 ff.). The birth of Jesus fulfills the Old Testament and signifies Emmanuel ("God is with us"). This linkage of Jesus as savior from **sins** and Jesus as a sign of God's presence also occurs near the opening of the Matthean **miracle** section (8:1 ff.). There, another quotation from the prophet Isaiah ("He took our infirmities and bore our diseases": 53:4; Matt. 8:17) affirms that Jesus is the bringer of God's forgiveness (cf. Matt. 9:1–7). Still another, subsequent statement by Jesus sounds like a promise of Emmanuel: "For where two or three are gathered in my name, I am there among them" (18:20). This, too, is immediately followed by Jesus' declaration of the necessity for limitless forgiveness (18:21 ff.).

This good news of forgiveness does not imply, however, that Matthew understands the Christian **gospel** to be devoid of human responsibility, for the heart of this story is

Joseph's response. Joseph responds to God's presence as experienced in a dream. Matthew states simply that when he "awoke from sleep, he did as the angel of the Lord commanded him; he took her as his wife" (vs. 24). Joseph obeyed; he practiced a higher righteousness. Throughout Matthew, beginning in this opening scene and ending with the last words of Jesus to the disciples (28:20), the themes of obedience and righteousness recur (see 5:17–20; 7:15–27; 21:28–32; 28:20).

The first half of chapter 2 (vss. 1–18) is dominated by the "wise men from the East," and the entire chapter is organized around a series of geographical places: the East, Jerusalem, Bethlehem, Egypt, and finally Nazareth. The wise men come to pay homage to the newly born king of the Jews. Perhaps they are Zoroastrian priests or Babylonian astrologers; without doubt they are Gentiles. Whereas Joseph demonstrated the reaction of a loyal, just Jew to the birth of Jesus, now we see the response of wise Gentiles (see 28:19). They have come to worship him as they would a king or a god (2:2, 8, 11; cf. 14:33; 28:17). Their reaction to Jesus' birth contrasts with that of Herod, the political king, who can think of Jesus only as a threat to his rule. And with good reason, for the unusual star's appearance serves as a sign of a crucial event (cf. Numbers 24:17): the old age, typified by Herod's kingdom, yields to the new, manifested in the birth of Jesus. The midpoint of this chapter, a turning point of the narrative (vss. 13–15), discloses Matthew's intent. After the wise men have left, an angel of the Lord again appears to Joseph. This time Joseph is told to flee to Egypt, and again he obeys (vs. 14). By his response to the revelatory dreams, the story moves forward in fulfillment of the scripture (vs. 15).

The sixth-century Church of the Nativity in Bethlehem marks the traditional site of Jesus' birth. It was originally built in the fourth century by the Emperor Constantine and rebuilt by the Emperor Justinian in the sixth.

All this occurred in order "to fulfill what had been spoken by the Lord through the prophet, "'Out of Egypt I have called my son'" (vs. 15: cf. Hos. 11:1). Originally this verse recalled Israel's being brought out of Egypt. Now "my son" refers, not to Israel, but to Jesus. Moreover, chapter 2 suggests that Jesus is to be understood as a new Moses. Moses lived in Egypt before leading the people to the promised land; Jesus also fled to Egypt before coming to Nazareth. The Hebrew male children were killed at the birth of Moses; Bethlehem's male children were killed at the birth of Jesus (2:16–19; cf. Exod. 1:15–2:10). Yet the text seems to imply something more than a Moses–Jesus typology. Jesus is not a new Moses, but a new Israel. The Old Testament equated **God's Son** with the people, not Moses (Exod. 4:22). Whereas in Judaism Moses was honored and respected, in the new community Jesus is worshiped (2:11; 28:17).

Jesus and Moses

Matthew suggests various parallels between Jesus' work and that of Moses. The "forty days and nights" of fasting in the wilderness temptation (4:2) picks up the "forty days and nights" Moses also fasted when he wrote the commandments from God (Exod. 34:28). In the **antitheses** (5:21–48) Jesus elaborates commandments of Moses; indeed, the entire Sermon is from the Mount (cf. Exod. 19:2 ff.). Finally, the five-part structure of Matthew (see the outline, above) parallels the Pentateuch, the five books of Moses. On the other hand, it should be noted that in Matthew's first two chapters the Exodus texts dealing with the birth and childhood of Moses are not cited. On balance, the Moses analogy is present within Matthew; nevertheless, this Gospel primarily proclaims the formation of a new Israel.

In his own demonic way Herod recognizes the new era's breaking in. He tries without success to kill the new Davidic king (vss. 16 ff.). Fittingly, the chapter ends with Jesus in Nazareth (vs. 23). From this point, the focus of the narrative narrows, and a particular history replaces the **prophetic**, **eschatological** overview of the Gospel's introduction. Whether the first two Matthean chapters contain history in the sense of observed and reported events is debatable. In any case, the narrative does proclaim Matthew's understanding of the new Christian way. This way of radical obedience becomes possible with the appearance of Jesus, who both is and brings into existence the new Israel.

THE HIGHER RIGHTEOUSNESS (3:1–7:29)

Like the four other major Matthean sections, this one consists of both narrative and discourse. The narrative includes the baptism, temptation, preaching, and calling of disciples by Jesus (3:1–4:25). The discourse is the Sermon on the Mount (5:1–7:29). By this arrangement, Matthew uses Jesus' discourse to interpret the narrative, which he has basically taken over from Mark. Our interpretation of this overall section, as a depiction of higher **righteousness**, is borne out by a comparison of Matthew's treatment of John the Baptist with Luke's.

Both Matthew and Luke report John the Baptist's reaction to some who come out to be baptized by him (3:7–10; cf. Luke 3:7–9, from the **Q source**). According to Luke, John's scathing attack is directed against the multitudes because they are not bearing fruit that befits repentance. Characteristically, Matthew has John the Baptist assault the **Pharisees** and **Sadducees**, who in the time of Jesus were distinct and important groups. Through his presentation of the incident, Matthew stresses that even Israel's leaders are not bearing good fruit. Therefore, they are liable to condemnation, and their claim to descent from Abraham will be of no avail against final judgment (vss. 9 ff.). A higher righteousness is demanded.

This discussion of the necessity of bearing fruit receives further elaboration in the discourse of the Sermon on the Mount: "Every good tree bears good fruit, but the bad tree bears bad fruit" (7:17; cf. 7:18–20). Matthew prefaces this statement with an attack upon false **prophets** who appear in sheep's clothing, pretending to be righteous (7:15 ff.). These false prophets rely upon their record of prophesying and casting out demons in the face of God's judgment (7:21–23). But their activity is of no avail unless they produce fruits—that is, deeds of righteousness, such as loving the enemy (5:44), not being angry with one's brother (5:22), praying without hypocrisy (6:5), not judging (7:1), and so on. Although the Matthean words of Jesus clearly define the higher righteousness (5:20) that Jesus demands, hearing is not enough; doing is indispensable (7:24). Therefore, Matthew moves from an emphasis on redefining righteousness to the necessity of practicing it. Higher righteousness is more than knowledge; it consists also of doing.

Fulfilling Righteousness (3:13–17)

Why does Jesus seek baptism by John the Baptist?

Jesus' first act in the Gospel of Matthew occurs in connection with his **baptism**. In comparing Matthew's baptism story (3:13–17) with that of Mark (1:9–11), we note four distinct Matthean characteristics: (1) the preaching of John the Baptist and Jesus are identical; (2) Jesus explicitly decides to be baptized; (3) his baptism fulfills all righteousness; and (4) the voice from heaven apparently speaks, not to Jesus, but to John the Baptist.

According to Matthew, both John the Baptist and Jesus proclaim, "Repent, for the kingdom of heaven has come near" (3:2; 4:17). (Matthew's preference for "kingdom of heaven" rather than "**kingdom of God**" reflects his characteristically Jewish reserve about using the name of God.) Such identical messages show clearly that Matthew presumes a close relationship between John and Jesus. Yet Matthew also makes clear that John the Baptist's message is **prophecy**, "Prepare the way of the Lord, make his paths straight" (3:3; Isa. 40:3), whereas Jesus' coming is fulfillment, "The people who sat in darkness have seen a great light, and for those who sat in the region and shadow of death light has dawned" (4:16; Isa. 9:1 ff.). Nevertheless, John the Baptist's injunction to bear good fruit (3:10) is supported and elaborated by Jesus at the close of the Sermon on the Mount (7:16). Moreover, Matthew's Jesus, unlike Mark's, decides to leave Galilee to be baptized by John (vs. 13). What happened without explanation in Mark (1:9) occurs in Matthew because of Jesus' deliberate decision and action (cf. vs. 14).

The Baptism of Jesus

Matt. 3.13-17	Mark 1.9-11	Luke 3.21-22	John 1.29-34
[13]The Jesus came from Galilee to the Jordan to John, to be baptized by him. [14]John would have prevented him, saying "I need to be baptized by you, and do you come to me?" [15]But Jesus answered him, "Let it be so now; for thus it is fitting for us to fulfil all right-eousness." Then he consented. [16]And when Jesus was bap-tized, he went up immediately from the water, and behold, the heavens were opened and he saw the Spirit of God descending like a dove and alighting on him; [17]and lo, a voice from heaven, saying.	[9]In those days Jesus came from Nazareth of Galilee	[27]Now when all the people were baptized,	[29]The next day he saw Jesus coming toward him, and said, "Behold, the Lamb of God, who takes away the sin of the world! [30]This is he of whom I said, 'After me comes a man who ranks before me, for he was before me,' [31]I myself did not know him; but for this I came baptizing with water, that he might be revealed to Israel."
	and was baptized by John in the Jordan. 10 And when he came up out of the water, immediately he saw the heavens opened and the Spirit descended upon him like a dove;	and when Jesus also had been baptized and was praying, the heaven was opened, [22]and the Holy Spirit descended upon him in bodily form, as a dove,	[32]And John bore witness, "I saw the Spirit descend as a dove from heaven, and it remained on him. [33]I myself did not know him; but he who sent me to baptize with water said to me, 'He on whom you see the Spirit descend and remain, this is he who baptizes with the Holy Spirit.'
	[17]and a voice came from heaven,	and a voice came from heaven,	[34]And I have seen and have borne witness that this is the Son of God."
"This is my beloved Son, with whom I am well pleased."	"Thou art my beloved Son; with thee I am well pleased."	"Thou art my beloved Son; with thee I am well pleased."	

The story of the Baptism of Jesus nicely illustrates the similarities and differences among the Gospels, as well as Matthew's distinctive material and emphasis (3:14-15). The Johannine account actually contains material found in the broader Synoptic setting and is not as distinctive as at first may appear (*Adapted from B. H. Throckmorton, Jr. [ed.], Gospel Parallels, 4th ed. [Nashville: Thomas Nelson, 1979].*)

In Matthew, John's protest about the inappropriateness of his baptizing Jesus is answered by the first words of Jesus, "Let it be so now; for it is proper for us in this way to fulfill all righteousness" (vs. 15). This answer, appearing only in Matthew, explains why the presumably sinless Jesus needed a baptism for repentance (cf. 2 Cor. 5:21; Heb. 4:15).

Grappling with the Messiah's Baptism

The apologetic motif we find in Matthew 3:14-15 also occurs in accounts of Jesus' baptism in noncanonical Gospels. In the **apocryphal** *Gospel of the Ebionites*, John asks Jesus to baptize him *after* the voice speaks from heaven. *The Gospel According to the Nazaraeans* reports the following exchange: "Behold, the mother of the Lord and his brethren said to him: 'John the Baptist baptizes unto the remission of sins, let us go and be baptized by him.' But he [Jesus] said to them: 'Wherein have I sinned that I should go and be baptized by him? Unless what I have said is [a sin of] ignorance.'" In the canonical Gospel of John, Jesus' baptism is not mentioned.

Jesus' reply in Matthew may also be understood as his acceptance of a requirement for the whole nation, to establish an identity between himself and his people. In any case, Jesus' baptism in Matthew is no routine of going through the motions. Jesus himself initiates the action and says that this baptism is "to fulfill all righteousness" (cf. 5:17), a central Matthean theme. Therefore, we need to look more carefully into Jesus' reply.

In Matthew "**righteousness**" refers to that conduct which is in agreement with God's will and well pleasing to him. It is rightness of life before God. Matthew does not speak about righteousness merely as a preliminary step toward the **kingdom** of heaven, but rather as the very substance of this kingdom (see 5:6, 10, 20; 6:33). The fulfilling of all righteousness should be understood in the context of the preceding verses (3:11ff.), where John declared that he himself only baptized with water for repentance, but that after him would come one who would baptize with "the Holy Spirit and fire." The **Holy Spirit**, of course, signifies God's presence (see 1:18), and fire depicts judgment, as the context implies ("unquenchable fire"). The coming of Jesus, then, is the sign of both God's presence (cf. 1:23) and his judgment. The relationship between the two was already anticipated in John the Baptist's previous speech (3:7–10). Judgment comes to whoever does not bear fruit. But, as this passage makes clear (3:13–17), God's presence now makes it possible to bear fruit, because the Holy Spirit has come with Jesus. Jesus willingly undergoes baptism, for because of the Spirit's presence he can now be obedient (bear fruit) and fulfill all righteousness, being well pleasing to God (vs. 17).

The unexpected plural in Jesus' answer to John, "it is proper for *us* in this way to fulfill all righteousness," refers both to Jesus and John the Baptist. John the Baptist is obedient ("he consented"—vs. 15). Jesus obeyed in his decision to come from Galilee to be baptized, and John the Baptist complied with complete Jesus' obedience. With their fulfillment of all righteousness, the Spirit of God appears visually to Jesus and aurally to John the Baptist (in Mark 1:11 the voice spoke to Jesus).

This interpretation of the story of Jesus' baptism is supported by the following temptation story (4:1–11). The beloved **Son of God**, announced in the baptism, now acts as the Son in response to each temptation. "If you are the Son of God" (vss. 3, 6) does not really imply that Jesus might not be the Son of God. The baptism (3:17) left no doubt that Jesus was. The only doubt concerns the *nature* of that sonship: whether Jesus will act in obedience to God or on his own authority. Just as obedience characterized his baptism, so the temptations show the Son of God acting in accordance with the will of God (vss. 4, 7, 10).

After the temptation, Jesus first goes to territory close to the **Gentiles** (4:12–16). There he begins to preach (vs. 17) and calls disciples (vss. 18–22), who respond by following him (vss. 20, 22). A brief summary section of healings (vss. 23–25; cf. Mark 1:21–3:11) shows how he attracts crowds from everywhere and leads into the first discourse, the Sermon on the Mount.

Teaching Righteousness (5:17–20)

How does the righteousness proclaimed by Jesus exceed that of the scribes and Pharisees?

The Sermon on the Mount (Matt. 5–7) has been acclaimed as the heart of Christian faith. This section contains the first and most important discourse of Matthew. In all probability, the Sermon was not spoken by Jesus on one occasion, for much of the same material is scattered throughout the Gospel of Luke (see, for example, the Sermon on the Plain, Luke 6:17–49, but also 12:22–34). Hence the arrangement of the tradition probably reflects Matthean interests and concerns.

The significance of the Sermon on the Mount for Matthew is illustrated by the fact that Matthew's **passion** story picks up motifs already prepared for in the Sermon. For example, in Gethsemane Jesus prays word-for-word the third petition of the Lord's Prayer: "Your will be done" (26:42; cf. 6:10). Jesus also advocates peace in the confrontation at his arrest (26:52; cf. 5:39). Moreover, Jesus never relaxes the commandments; he is innocent and righteous (27:4, 19, 24; cf. 5:19). Further, Jesus refuses to reply to the high priest's request for an oath (26:63; cf. 5:34). All these instances are Matthean additions not found in the Markan text.

Two aspects of staging characterize this discourse. First, Jesus appears as a **rabbi**, a teacher (5:2). This initial depiction of Jesus contrasts with that of Mark, where Jesus initially appeared as a **miracle** worker and healer (Mark 1:21 ff.). Second, the Sermon is delivered from the Mount. Two other crucial events, the transfiguration scene (17:1 ff.; similarly, Mark 9:2 ff.) and the final word to the disciples (28:16 ff.; only in Matthew), occur on a mountain in Matthew's Gospel. The Sermon's delivery from the mountain is reminiscent of Moses' receiving the **law** on a mountain in the wilderness (Exod. 19). According to Matthew, a new teaching comes from the mountain—a **righteousness** higher than that delivered by Moses.

In addition, two observations about the Sermon's content show its character and meaning. First, it begins with a series of nine **beatitudes**, or blessings (5:3–12). Of these, the first three describe the condition of those for whom Jesus' message is good news: "the poor in spirit," "those who mourn," and "the meek" (5:3–5). These conditions should not be understood as requirements for blessing. Rather, Matthew declares God's unmerited grace or blessing, and future participation in the kingdom of heaven is promised simply to those who have need. Even the last six *beatitudes* (5:6–12), which might be taken as **ethical** requirements, are still within the setting of unconditional blessing. All merit is ascribed to God's astonishing generosity. Thus the opening of the Sermon on the Mount stresses God's favor rather than his demand. Second, the Sermon on the Mount ends with a clear call to obedience (7:15–29): "You will know them by their fruits" (7:16). Entrance into the kingdom of heaven will reward whoever "does the will of my Father in heaven" (7:21); the wise man hears Jesus' words and does them (7:24). Hence the grace of God does not make obedience unnecessary.

We now turn to the word of Jesus about the **law** and **prophets** (5:17–20), which appears only in Matthew. In the first three verses Jesus declares his complete acceptance of the law and the prophets. Nothing will pass away from the law until all is accomplished. No one may relax one of these commandments or teach anyone else to do so. This complete acceptance of the law is difficult to understand in view of later criticism of the law. The final verse demanding a "higher righteousness" (vs. 20) already hints at criticism, but other passages are more explicit. John the Baptist is identified with the law and the prophets; yet he who is least in the kingdom of heaven is greater than he (11:11–15). Matthew follows Mark in Jesus' criticism of the law's distinction between clean and unclean: "Listen and understand: it is not what goes into the mouth that defiles a person, but it is what comes out of the mouth that defiles" (15:10; cf. Mark 7:14 ff.; though Matthew omits Mark's comment [7:19] that Jesus declared all foods clean). Nevertheless, Jesus' words (vss. 17–19) make clear that he expects nothing less than fulfillment of the law.

In another passage, (22:34–40; cf. Mark 12:28–34), Jesus discusses the nature of the law and the prophets and says that the first and great commandment is love of God, and the second love of neighbor. *All* the law and the prophets depend on these commandments (vs. 40). This conclusion, which appears only in Matthew, suggests that the "higher righteousness" that Jesus teaches consists of a primary relation with God and a secondary relation with other people. This view of higher righteousness helps to explain Jesus' later castigation of the **scribes** and **Pharisees** (chap. 23). By any "normal" measure, the scribes and Pharisees made up the most observant group within Israel, during both the time of Jesus and that of Matthew. Only by the extraordinary norm of the love of God and the love of neighbor, which nevertheless is derived from the law and the prophets, could they be denounced. Of course, in Jesus' call for a higher righteousness this high standard is set for his own disciples.

At the **baptism**, Jesus and John the Baptist fulfilled all righteousness (3:15) by their respective acts of obedience. Here in the Sermon, "whoever does them and teaches them will be called great in the kingdom of heaven" (vs. 19b). Matthew understands the congregation of Christ's followers as founded not only upon Jesus' action but also upon his teaching. Jesus' closing words in the Gospel reiterate this theme: "Go therefore and make disciples of all nations . . . teaching them to obey everything that I have commanded you" (28:19 ff.).

The key to Jesus' teaching about fulfillment of the law and the prophets lies, of course, in the enigmatic last verse of this passage (5:20), where Jesus calls for righteousness higher than that of the scribes and Pharisees. The rest of the Sermon elaborates this higher righteousness, which becomes explicit in six **antitheses** (5:21–48; only in Matthew), so designated because of the antithetical form in which they are cast: "You have heard that it was said . . . ; But I say to you. . . ." These antitheses indicate that Jesus pays attention to a person's intention as well as to the actual deed. His words therefore advise the hearer to root out evil thoughts so that evil actions will not follow. Such good advice seems easier to give than to heed. It is sometimes difficult to refrain from killing, committing adultery, and hating one's neighbor; it is almost impossible to refrain from anger, lust, and hate of one's enemy. These words are not, however, a counsel of despair, for the extremely radical nature of their demand elicits from the hearer the recognition that these are more than human commands. In a sense, the antitheses set forth both the will and the presence of God. The commandments are transparent, such that God shines through them. Indeed the Sermon's opening beatitudes already indicated the present blessings of God. Moreover, Jesus' subsequent teaching emphasizes the availability of God in prayer (6:5–15) and everyday life (6:25–34). Therefore, the final, seemingly impossible requirement, "Be perfect, therefore, as your heavenly Father is perfect" (5:48), is Jesus' call to align oneself with the perfection or righteousness of God, which God not only requires but also manifests. With the demand for the higher righteousness comes the gift of God's presence. In Matthew, Jesus does not introduce a new teaching so much as draw out the radical implications of the old.

Matthew develops the entire Sermon under the implied rubrics of love of God and love of neighbor as fulfillment of the law and the prophets (cf. 7:11 ff.). The antitheses call for an unlimited concern for the neighbor (vss. 21–48; see also 7:1–5), whereas the remaining sections of the Sermon point to the one gracious source of life. What is impossible apart from God becomes a fulfillable promise in his presence (6:33). The Sermon on the Mount begins with the promise of blessings (5:1–12) and ends with the demand for obedience (7:24–27). This tension characterizes the Jewish Christianity of Matthew and is actually typical of the New Testament as a whole. God's grace does not nullify human responsibility; it enables people to obey. Jesus does not set aside the commandments of God; he points the way to their fulfillment.

TRUE DISCIPLESHIP (8:1–11:1)

In Matthew's first major section, Jesus appeared as Messiah of the word (chaps. 3–7); in the second he appears as Messiah of the deed. Matthew has brought together ten **miracle** narratives (chaps. 8–9), accounts of Jesus' actions that lead naturally into the missionary discourse (chap. 10) describing the deeds required in discipleship (10:42).

This movement from Jesus' miracles to the disciples' working is reflected in Matthew's threefold division of the miracle section. The first part (8:2–17) portrays Jesus as bearing the infirmities and diseases of all people—the leper, the centurion's servant, the disciple's mother-in-law. By his healings Jesus fulfills the prophet Isaiah's word, "He took our infirmities and bore our diseases" (8:17; cf. Isa. 53:4). The middle and dominant division (8:18–9:17) places the disciples at the center of action. The initial episode (8:18–22) concerns "following," that is, discipleship. Next Jesus responds to the plight of the perishing and faithless disciples (8:23–27). Then his power is manifest in the exorcism of the two demoniacs (8:28–34) and the healing and forgiveness of the paralytic (9:1–8). After these miracles Jesus immediately calls the disciple Matthew, who as a tax collector is socially unacceptable; indeed, Jesus has come not to call the righteous, but sinners (9:9–13). Therefore, Jesus' disciples rejoice rather than fast as John's disciples do (9:14–17). In distinction from the previous division's emphasis on the disciples, the third and final part of the miracle section (9:18–23; cf. Mark 5:21–43) concerns faith. Indeed, Matthew has stripped down the narration about the raising of the daughter and the

A view of the ruins of the town of Capernaum, a major site of Jesus' ministry, which was excavated by archaeologists of the Franciscan order in the twentieth century.

healing of the woman with the hemorrhage (9:18–26) to a bare minimum, thus emphasizing the essential point of the father's faith. The same is true of Matthew's treatment of the healing of the two blind men (9:27–31; cf. Mark 10:46–52). Moreover, faith is implicitly the subject of the final healing of the mute demoniac (9:32–34). Without faith there is no miracle.

Matthew's miracle stories portray a compassionate healer, drawing out disciples who believe in working with God rather than the prince of demons (9:34). Thus Jesus calls out faithful disciples who will continue his own work. In other words, he calls for faithful disciples to join him in the labor of alleviating the suffering of people. The view that Matthew seeks to define discipleship within this section (chaps. 8–10) is confirmed by the opening, transitional verse: "When Jesus had come down from the mountain, great crowds *followed* him" (8:1; cf. Mark 1:39 ff.). "Following"—discipleship—then becomes the theme of the succeeding Matthean miracle section (chaps. 8 and 9).

The missionary discourse (chap. 10), which immediately follows the miracles, links the twelve *disciples* directly with the acts that Jesus has just performed: "Then Jesus summoned his twelve disciples and gave them authority over unclean spirits, to cast them out, and to cure every disease and every sickness" (10:1; 8:16–17). Finally, the closing transitional sentence of this section reads, "Now when Jesus had finished instructing his *twelve disciples*, he went on from there to teach and proclaim his message in their cities" (11:1; only in Matthew). The Twelve are to carry on the ministry of Jesus.

The composition and character of Matthew's missionary discourse (chap. 10) suggest that this tradition does more than simply report Jesus' instructions to his twelve disciples. This discourse concerning the nature of true discipleship is intended also for the disciples in the **church** of Matthew's time. This is evident in the changes Matthew has made in the Markan tradition (cf. Mark 6:7–13). First, Matthew has no report of the disciples' actually carrying out the mission that he gave them. Although his Markan source contained the statement that "they went out and proclaimed that all should repent . . . ," Matthew lacks even that (Mark 6:12 ff.; cf. Matt. 10:14 ff.). For Matthew, this missionary task was delivered to the community that came into existence with the death and **resurrection** of Jesus (28:19 ff.). Second, Matthew inserts a passage from Jesus' **apocalyptic** discourse concerning the future end of the world (Mark 13:9–13) into the missionary discourse (Matt. 10:17–25) as instruction for the congregation in its present situation. In Matthew, these words are spoken by Jesus to the church for application to the time between Jesus' resurrection and his **parousia**; thus Matthew changes an apocalyptic warning into churchly instructions.

Perhaps the most puzzling of Jesus' sayings within this discourse is the injunction to the disciples, "Go nowhere among the **Gentiles**, and enter no town of the Samaritans, but go rather to the lost sheep of the house of Israel" (10:5–6, only in Matthew; see also 15:24). This imperative contrasts sharply with the risen Jesus' concluding words at the close of Matthew, "Go therefore and make disciples of all nations. . ." (28:19). Although restriction of Jesus' mission, and that of the disciples, to the confines of Israel may simply reflect an earlier stage of the tradition that Matthew retains without agreement, another suggestion for Matthew's intent seems more plausible. Within the discourse itself Jesus also predicts that the disciples "will be dragged before governors and kings because of me, as a testimony to them *and the Gentiles*" (10:18; cf. Mark 13:9 ff.). This narrative, in the future tense, makes sense if Matthew conceives of Jesus' ministry as basically directed toward the people of Israel, but the ministry of the disciples and the early church as directed to both the people of Israel and the Gentiles. (See 1:1–25 with its emphasis on the heritage of Israel, the descent from Abraham, and 2:1–23 with its emphasis on the extension to Gentiles, the worship of the wise men.) This interpretation also helps account for the omission by Matthew of Mark's report of the disciples' actually going on the missionary journey. For Matthew that mission, in its full significance, occurs only after Jesus' death and resurrection.

In this treatment of discipleship, Matthew has shown Jesus as the Messiah in deed, whose miracles alleviate the suffering of humanity (8:16 ff.). In turn, the disciples are to respond with obedient deeds. They realize true discipleship insofar as they acknowledge Jesus' lordship and follow him, performing acts of mercy toward others (10:42; cf. Mark 9:41).

THE KINGDOM OF HEAVEN (11:2–13:52)

Were Matthew presenting a historical narrative in the usual sense, we might next expect information about what happened to the disciples after they responded to Jesus' missionary imperative (chap. 10). Instead, we read of Jesus' further activity and the reactions, both positive and negative, that he elicits: first, the relationship of John the Baptist and Jesus (11:2–19); next, chastisement of the cities that rejected Jesus (11:20–24); then, pronouncements of blessing upon those who accept the yoke of Jesus (11:25–30); next, controversy with the **Pharisees** involving a series of **miracles** (chap. 12); and, finally, a series of **parables** initially addressed to the crowds, but adapted by Matthew for the disciples (chap. 13).

The key to this section lies not so much in the order of events as in the way in which Matthew has brought his own special interests to them. Four emphases stand out.

1. The section is devoted overall to the character of the **kingdom** of heaven. The opening incident raises the **Christological** question, "Are you the one who is to come, or are we to wait for another?" (11:3). However, Jesus' answer and the ensuing discussion transform that question into one about the nature of the kingdom. Although John the Baptist is greater than anyone else born of woman, "yet the least in the kingdom of heaven is greater than he" (11:11). Moreover, in a later debate with the Pharisees about whether Jesus casts out demons by God or Beelzebub, the climactic answer again focuses on the kingdom: "But if it is by the Spirit of God that I cast out demons, then the kingdom of God has come upon you" (12:28). Finally, the discourse of this section unveils the "secrets of the kingdom of heaven" (13:11). The seven kingdom parables, with which this section ends, show that, for

Matthew, understanding of Jesus as the **Christ** comes through understanding Jesus' proclamation about the kingdom of heaven.

2. This kingdom of heaven is a kingdom of mercy. Jesus answers John the Baptist's disciples by enumerating his merciful deeds (11:5; cf. Luke 7:22). Furthermore, Jesus' demand for discipleship is a yoke that is gentle and restful, because Jesus himself is gentle and lowly in heart (11:28–30; only in Matthew). Sabbath observance is understood within the context of mercy (12:7 ff.; cf. 9:13 and Hos. 6:6). Indeed, Jesus' parable of the sower proclaims God's abundant mercy: the sower generously sows seed everywhere without distinction, and the seed on good soil bears grain prodigiously (13:3–8).

3. The kingdom of heaven is, however, not mercy only; judgment also occurs. Chorazin, Bethsaida, and Capernaum will be brought down on the day of judgment because they rejected the words of mercy (11:20–24). Jesus' opponents, especially the Pharisees, will be brought to account on the day of judgment because they have not borne the good fruit—that is, acts of mercy (12:33–37). Indeed, this present generation is an evil one (12:45; only in Matthew). Finally, at the close of the age "all causes of sin and all evildoers" will be gathered out of the kingdom and thrown "into the furnace of fire, where there will be weeping and gnashing of teeth" (13:41-42; only in Matthew; cf. 8:12; 13:50; 22:13).

4. Jesus' disciples are the ones who will realize the true nature of the kingdom of heaven. Those who have been gathered to Jesus learn that the kingdom offers both mercy and judgment. They are the infants who learn that this yoke is easy (11:28–30; only in Matthew). They are the true family of Jesus. Matthew alone records Jesus' saying that the *disciples* are his mother and brothers (12:49; cf. Mark 3:34). Matthew also directs the final six kingdom parables to the disciples, for they are the ones who know the kingdom's secrets (13:10–17). Indeed, Matthew omits Mark's castigation of the disciples, "Do you not understand this parable? Then how will you understand all the parables?" (Mark 4:13). In Matthew, the opposite point is true—the disciples *do* understand; therefore, when Jesus asks them, "Have you understood all this?" the only possible answer is "Yes" (13:51). Matthew then concludes, "Therefore every scribe who has been trained for the kingdom of heaven is like the master of a household who brings out of his treasure what is new and what is old" (vs. 52; only in Matthew). The new refers to the kingdom of mercy, new in comparison with Pharisaic insistence on strict Sabbath observance (cf. 12:12b). The old refers to the kingdom of judgment, the old expectation of judgment under the criterion of obedience to the will of God (cf. 12:50). Therefore, the **scribe** trains for the kingdom by accepting the new mercy and by carrying out the old obedience. Matthew speaks to the church in the time between **resurrection** and the **parousia**, a time of mercy and judgment. The disciples have no security other than the gracious presence of Christ (cf. 10:40; 28:20). They are to work between the times so that at the future judgment they will be found merciful. Matthew thus prepares for the subject matter of his next section, the **church**.

THE FORGIVING CHURCH (13:53–19:2)

The **kingdom** of heaven has been characterized as an **eschatological** reality, already present in mercy and expected in judgment (11:2–13:52). Now, stress falls upon the **church**, the community of disciples living between the **resurrection** and the **parousia**, those who are closely identified with the the kingdom of heaven's mercy.

Here, as in every other section of Matthew, narrative is informed by discourse. What Jesus teaches controls his own actions and those of his opponents and disciples. The concluding discourse (17:22–19:1) centers upon the nature and authority of the church. Fittingly, then, the the narrative's climactic action (13:53–17:21) is Jesus' establishment of Peter as the rock upon which the church is built (16:17–19). We receive clues as to the nature of this section simply by observing the heightened role of Peter. For example, Matthew takes over Mark's story of Jesus' walking on the water (14:22–33; Mark 6:45–52) and, instead of using it as an occasion to illustrate the disciples' misunderstanding (Mark 6:51 ff.), shows Peter's amazing, albeit faltering, courage in trying to walk on water. When he sinks from fear, Peter cries out with a **Christological** confession, "Lord, save me" (14:30). Partly because of Peter's action, at the story's end the other disciples worship Jesus and confess, "Truly, you are the Son of God" (14:33). Matthew's stress on the Christological foundation of the church is evident in the exalted titles for Jesus in this part of the Gospel: "Lord" (15:22; 16:22; 17:4, 15), "**Son of God**" (14:33; 16:16), "**Son of Man**" (16:13, 27 ff.), and "Son of David" (15:22). All are Matthew's distinctive additions to his inherited tradition.

The increased emphasis on Peter is matched by a more prominent role for the disciples throughout this section. Perhaps the clearest evidence is Matthew's treatment of the two feedings of the multitudes. In the feeding of the five thousand (14:13–21; cf. Mark 6:30–44), Matthew omits the question in which the disciples misunderstand Jesus (Mark 6:37). In Matthew, the disciples immediately understand, but they doubt their ability to supply bread for the multitudes: "We have nothing here but five loaves and two fish" (14:17). Moreover, in Matthew the disciples actually fetch the food (14:18). Finally, only Matthew depicts the disciples' duplication of Jesus' action in distributing the loaves to the crowds (vs. 19b; cf. Mark 6:41). Similarly, in the feeding of the four thousand (15:32–39; cf. Mark 8:1–10), again the disciples immediately understand their task; they are concerned only about their ability to accomplish it (vs. 33; cf. Mark 8:4). Once more the disciples actually give the bread to the people in imitation of Jesus (vs. 36; cf. Mark 8:6). Matthew also omits distribution of the fish to the crowds (Mark 8:7), thereby bringing his account closer to the actual celebration of the **Lord's Supper** in the church's life. By implication, the disciples are ministers of the church. Through Matthew's use of the tradition, these events in the life of Jesus are in the process of becoming events in the life of the church. By using the framework of Mark (Mark 6:14–9:32), by abbreviating and adding other material, especially that not found in other Gospels, Matthew has turned this section into a discussion about the church.

Peter as the Rock (16:13–23)

How and why does Matthew's account of Peter's confession differ from Mark's?

Only in Matthew does Jesus explicitly accept Peter's confession at Caesarea Philippi (cf. Mark 8:27–33). Indeed, the source of Peter's insight is said by Jesus to be none other than "my Father in heaven" (16:17). Furthermore, Peter has the keys to the **kingdom**: whatever he binds and looses—that is, his solemn decisions in matters of discipline—will be upheld on the judgment day (vs. 19; cf. 18:18). Without going into the much-debated question of the authenticity of 16:17–19, we contend that Matthew speaks here not so much of Petrine primacy, and the founding of the episcopacy (order of bishops) through Peter, as of the primacy of the church (cf. esp. 18:17–18). Peter represents the disciples, and the disciples in turn represent the **church**.

In spite of this praise of Peter for his recognition of the **Messiah**, after Jesus' announcement that he must suffer (vs. 21), the two engage in controversy (vss. 22 ff.). Although Matthew may seem to be simply following Mark, so that Peter's difficulty with Jesus should be overlooked, this explanation is not sustained by scrutiny of the text. Matthew could have omitted the rebuke by Peter and the retort of Jesus, as did Luke (9:18–22). Moreover, Matthew not only includes the rebuke by Peter but also increases Peter's opposition to Jesus' suffering by adding Peter's words, "God forbid it, Lord! This must never happen to you" (vs. 22). At one moment in Matthew, Peter is literally praised to the heavens; at the next, he is thrust into the company of Satan (vs. 23).

Matthew's tension between praise and blame for Peter is deliberate. Although the church has accepted Jesus as the Lord and the **Son of** the living **God** and has thus been granted authority to bind and loose on earth, individual Christians, like the disciple Peter, have to accept Jesus' suffering. Even Peter is not spared suffering. Christians must imitate Christ. Even though the church has authority to bind and to loose (cf. John 20:23), disciples cannot avoid Christ's way. Thus Matthew's earlier identification of Christ with the role of the suffering servant (12:18–21) takes on new meaning, for the disciples must also become suffering servants (cf. 5:10–12).

The inescapability of suffering as a disciple is depicted in Jesus' definition of discipleship as taking up one's cross and following him (16:24–28). To his Markan source (cf. Mark 8:34–9:1) Matthew adds that, when the **Son of Man** comes in glory, "he will repay everyone for what has been done" (vs. 27). Matthew's emphasis on obedience implies that although the church exists between the **resurrection** and the second coming, with great power to bind and to loose, every disciple is still accountable to the Judge for what he has done. Peter is pronounced blessed, but his blessedness, along with that of all disciples, will have to endure and be judged.

To sum up this episode, confession of Christ leads to the founding of a church whose authority is binding. The disciples, however, must be neither complacent nor self-righteous. They must do the will of God to prepare for the future judgment. The nature of the church that has been so founded becomes transparent in the following discourse.

Discipline in Community (18:15–22)

How does discipline make community life possible?

Just as Peter's confession of the **Christ** was not simply an occasion for praise and rejoicing, so too Matthew's depiction of the disciples' liberation from the **Pharisaic** interpretation of the **law** (15:1–20) does not mean the creation of a community without discipline. Matthew's concluding discourse for the **church** (17:22–19:2) asserts that the Christian disciple comes under discipline of the churchly community. The incident of the temple tax (17:24–27), which serves as a transition to the discourse, illustrates the point. In this distinctively Matthean scene that follows a prediction of suffering (17:22), Jesus and Simon Peter discuss whether the temple tax should be paid. Although "the children are free" (17:26), Jesus orders the paying of the tax in order not to give offense (17:24–27). The members of the church possess freedom, yet freedom is restricted by the necessities of a community (cf. 1 Cor. 10:23 ff.).

In agreement with the preceding, our present passage (18:15–22) indicates that it may be necessary for the church to exclude people in exercising its authority to bind on earth (18:18). This power of excommunication does not exist for the purpose of condemning people, for the church acts under rules (vss. 15 ff.) and always in forgiveness (vss. 21 ff.). This concern for the individual Christian is indicated by the talk about "children" (18:3) and "little ones" (18:5, 10, 14). These "little ones" are to be received, not because they are actual children, but rather because they are the disciples, the members of the congregation, who journey from the privilege of forgiveness (18:10–14) to deeds of obedience (18:5–9). Indeed, these same little ones are blessed in the **beatitudes**. They are poor in spirit; they are mourning and meek (5:3–5); they yearn after **righteousness**, mercy, purity in heart, and peace, knowing that they are blessed (5:6–12). Matthew sets the discipline of the church in the context of God's grace. Even the community that exercises discipline consists of "little ones" who are in constant need of mercy (18:14).

Therefore, the passage containing the most rigorous word of discipline in Matthew—"Let such a one be to you as a Gentile and a tax collector" (vs. 17b)—closes with the most definite promise of Christ's presence: "For where two or three are gathered in my name, I am there among them" (vs. 20). The church exists, then, not only with authority to bind and to loose, but also in the authority of Christ's gracious presence. Consequently the church's most characteristic activity is that of worship (2:2, 8, 11; 8:2; 9:18; 14:33; 20:20; 28:9, 17). Such worship, adoration of the Lord, allows the church to bind or loose by offering forgiveness on the authority of Jesus. Therefore, Matthew concludes his exhortation for discipline in the church community with a word of Jesus about the radical necessity to forgive (18:21 ff.) and with a long parable (only in Matthew) about the punishment of the wicked servant who does not forgive (18:23–35).

The church is founded upon the confession of Jesus as the Christ. In its exercise of authority for judgment and discipline, the constant limiting factor is Jesus' demand for forgiveness (cf. 6:14 ff.). Matthew's congregation of believers is the forgiving church.

JUDGMENT: DOING GOD'S WILL (19:3–26:1)

Matthew's discussion of the **church** as the forgiving community leads into a final major section: the church facing the last judgment. The judgment theme is found in Jesus' **apocalyptic** pronouncement (chap. 24), especially in the command of watchfulness for the coming end (24:36–51), and in the parables of the wise and foolish bridesmaids (or virgins), the talents, and the great judgment (chap. 25). The church, which exists in the blessedness of forgiveness, also lives under the threat of judgment. In that light, the disciples are called to do God's will.

Although again Matthew is dependent upon Mark's framework (Mark 10–13), his use of **Q** and his special M tradition and his shaping of all the material have made this section a manual on how the church meets judgment by doing the will of God. For example, the opening unit of tradition, the debate with the **Pharisees** about divorce (19:3–12; cf. Mark 10:1–12), places a discussion about doing God's will in the proper Jewish–Christian context of the **law**. Several other episodes also concern interpretation of the law: the rich young man (19:16–30), paying taxes to Caesar (22:15–22), the **resurrection** question (22:23–33), the great commandment question (22:34–40), and the "woes" against the **scribes** and Pharisees (chap. 23, esp. 23:23 ff.).

To do the will of God, one must properly understand the nature of the law. Matthew is concerned about discerning the will of God in the law and, most important, obeying it. In discussion with the Pharisees, Matthew has apparently softened Jesus' radical prohibition against divorce (cf. Mark 10:10–12) by allowing it on the grounds of unchastity (19:9; cf. 5:32). Yet in the very next episode Matthew shows a demand for obedience to the law more stringent than that of his Markan source, for the young man must be perfect (19:21; cf. Mark 10:21). The will of God cannot be equated with either a stricter or more lenient interpretation of the Jewish law. The one thing necessary for the doing of God's will is God's presence and empowerment: "For mortals it is impossible, but *for God* all things are possible" (19:26).

For Matthew, the disciples' reward for doing God's will is different from any idea of reward as so much accumulated merit. Instead, Matthew proclaims that there are no degrees of reward; the only and final reward (25:41-46) is eternal life in God's presence, which disciples already anticipate by doing God's will. These claims are graphically dramatized by the **parable** of the laborers in the vineyard (20:1-16; found only in Matthew), in which all the workers receive a full day's wage, irrespective of how many hours they worked. That scandalous outcome illustrates the last of the Sermon on the Mount's **antitheses**: disciples should conduct themselves with that complete integrity by which God acts in impartially bestowing his blessings (5:43-48). None of the laborers in this parable earn what they deserve; all receive in equal measure a righteous God's incomprehensibly generous gifts. One may depend on God's faithfulness, but one cannot circumscribe God's goodness.

To a degree greater even than one of his sources, Mark (11:1–12:44), Matthew emphasizes Jesus' entry and early teaching in Jerusalem with severe criticism of those,

The Damascus Gate of Jerusalem, located on the north side of the old city. The walls are medieval, not ancient.

notably the Pharisees, who reject Jesus' authority, do not bear fruit (21:19), or, if they do, keep it for themselves (21:33-44). Thus even pious Jews cannot escape judgment. That warning is repeatedly emphasized in Matthew's Gospel, deftly woven together from his several sources: Mark (Jesus' entry into Jerusalem, followed by his condemnation of the temple, 21:1-13; teaching on faith, 21:18-22; the parable of the wicked tenants, 21:33-46; debates with religious authorities, 21:23-27; 22:15-45), as well as Q (the parable of the king's marriage banquet, 22:1-10), and Matthew's special tradition (the children's acclamation of Jesus as Son of David, 21:14-17; the parable of the two sons, 21:28-32; the parable of the wedding garment, 22:11-14).

A final indication of Matthew's preoccupation with judgment in this portion of his Gospel is its narrative setting in the territory of Judea and the city of Jerusalem (see 19:1; 21:1, 10; 24:1). At Jerusalem the condemnation of Jesus takes place, but that judgment ultimately turns against Jesus' enemies and in favor of his disciples—if they continue to do God's will (cf. 20:20 ff.; 24:1 ff.). Jesus' return as the **Son of Man** will determine whether disciples are sheep or goats, accepted or rejected (25:31 ff.). The test for discipleship is the same one Jesus had to pass: the doing of God's will, not one's own (26:39). Further examination of 23:1-36 and 25:31-46 confirm this understanding of Matthew's view of judgment.

Condemnation of Hypocrisy (23:1-39)

Why does Jesus assail his pious contemporaries so harshly?

The climax of this entire section of Matthew (19:3–23:39) is Jesus' chastisement of the **scribes** and **Pharisees** in Chapter 23. Here Jesus' critique of the religious establishment of his day reaches its apex in this Gospel. Matthew 23:1-39 falls into three sections. The first is an indictment of Israel's leaders (vss. 1-12) for the very failings against which Matthew has repeatedly inveighed: a disjunction between exhortation and practice (vs. 3b; cf. 2:8; 7:4; 12:34 ff.; 21:28 ff.), laying burdens upon others, while doing nothing to relieve them (vs. 4; cf. 11:28-30; 18:10 ff.), an ostentatious piety and prideful arrogance (vss. 5-7.; cf. 3:9; 6:2, 5, 7, 16, 19; 8:11 ff.). The second part of Jesus' speech scolds Israel's scribes and Pharisees as hypocrites in matters of **righteousness** (vss. 13-15, 23-36), blind guides (vss. 16, 17, 19, 24, 26), whitewashed tombs (vs. 27), and—recalling John the Baptist's denunciation—"snakes, brood of vipers" (vs. 33; cf. 3:7; 12:34). The final segment of this diatribe is a lament pronounced over Jerusalem (cf. 2:5; 21:10) and its forsaken, desolate house (i.e., the temple; 21:12-17; cf. Isa. 51:17; Jer. 4:14; 13:27; 15:5). As in the parables recounted in 22:40-43 and 22:7, Matthew associates the holy city's destruction with its rejection of its own **Messiah**.

Alongside 27:25, in which the Jewish multitudes cry that Jesus' blood be on them and their children, Matthew 23 raises for modern readers the specter of anti-Semitism. Possibly such passages have been pressed, far beyond Matthew's comprehension and intention, to serve anti-Jewish sentiments. Some modern interpreters regard Matthew's fiery rhetoric at these points so far beyond the pale as to be irredeemable. Rather than pretend that such portions of Matthew do not exist, we must understand them on their own terms. First, Jesus' invective against his adversaries likely has some basis in historical fact. In any case, it is in line with Old Testament prophets' denunciation of Israel's leaders in their own day (see Isa. 5:1-30; 10:1-3; 30:1-15; Amos 5:18-20; 6:1-7). Jesus, a Jew, renders a scathing critique against fellow Jews. Second, the controversy between Jesus and his adversaries in Matthew 23 is colored by the Matthean **church**'s debate with the Pharisaism of its own day. Because it reflects heated controversy between competing synagogues (cf. 10:17; 12:9; 13:54; 23:34) or perhaps between rival factions within a single synagogue, Matthew's Gospel cannot be branded as "anti-Jewish" in any meaningful sense. Again, this reflects a controversy *within* ancient Judaism. Third, while offensive to many modern readers, sweeping condemnation and caricature of whole groups was par for the course among competing religious parties in antiquity (as may be seen in the writings of such Jews as Philo, Josephus, and the **Qumran** sect). Finally, it is important to recognize that in Chapter 23, Jesus—the Matthean community's sole authoritative teacher (vs. 8)—addresses his comments first and foremost "to the crowds and to his disciples" (vs. 1). Woes pronounced upon Jewish leaders of Jesus (and Matthew's) day do not condemn all Jews for all times and in all places. Indeed, in Matthew's Gospel they serve as warnings to *Jewish Christian* leaders, lest *they* succumb to such hypocrisy and corruption (Matt 23:37-39; cf. 5–7; 18; 24–25).

Like the wicked tenants in Matthew 21:33-44, the scribes and Pharisees in Matthew 23 do not honor Jesus as the vineyard-owner's Son (21:38-39); they try to justify themselves by their obedience rather than by acknowledging the gracious God. Matthew underscores the necessity for obedience, but additionally asserts the need for belief in the giver of all obedience—God through **Christ** (cf. 21:42). Only thereby will the community of Jesus' disciples, be delivered from self-righteous, possessive, and corrupted obedience (see 18:1-35).

Doing Mercy without Calculation (25:31–46)

Why are both the sheep and goats surprised?

Matthew's understanding of judgment and the end time is contained in the final discourse (chap. 25), which comments upon the preceding **apocalyptic** discourses (chap. 24; cf. Mark 13). The **parable** of the ten bridesmaids (25:1–13; only in Matthew) and the parable of the talents (25:14–30; cf. Luke 19:12–27) provide a framework for viewing judgment. The prospect of judgment may be wrongly met in one of two ways—either in relaxed carelessness about the future, as seen in the five foolish virgins, or in paralysis caused by anxiety over the severity of the judge, as seen in the wicked and slothful servant.

The judgment itself is depicted in the final parable (25:31–46; only in Matthew), which tells about the shepherd who will separate the sheep from the goats. The standard of separation is simply whether the one judged has performed acts of mercy for a fellow human being (25:35 ff.). The element of surprise in this parable is that neither the righteous nor the unrighteous realized that their deeds of mercy were acts performed (or not performed) for the Lord (vss. 37 ff.). The climactic word of Jesus, "Truly, I tell you, just as you did it to one of the least of these who are members of my family, you did it to me" (vs. 40), alludes to the fact that mercy for the neighbor, and service to others, is service to Christ (cf. 7:21–23). Therefore, the true disciple shows mercy to others without calculation, without thinking such deeds will somehow cause God's judgment to be more favorable. Such noncalculation grows out of a relation with **Christ** in which anxiety is diminished and the disciple responds to whatever human need is at hand, especially to the neighbor (10:40–42).

Those who show mercy act without calculation, without thought that thereby they will ensure their future blessedness (cf. Matthew 7:21-22). They are merciful because they have been shown mercy; moreover, their deeds for the neighbor are deeds for Christ, who is present in the least of the brethren. Thus Matthew pictures the church in the time between the first and second comings. The church's role of obedience in that time has been most clearly anticipated in the death and **resurrection** of Jesus, Lord of the congregation, who serves as the paradigm for the Christian life. In a real sense Matthew 20:1-16 and 25:31-46 express the outer limits of New Testament **soteriology**, disallowing **righteousness** through **works** on the one hand and righteousness through dogmatic confession on the other.

CONCLUSION:
OBEDIENCE AND RESURRECTION (26:2–28:20)

At the outset of this conclusion, Matthew gives clear indication that Jesus' **passion** occurs at the bidding of God. The passive voice ("will be handed over to be crucified," 26:2; see also 26:18) suggests divine causation. The action of both Jesus and the other characters is guided by a power not their own. For example, the woman who anoints Jesus' head with the expensive ointment (26:6–13) prepares his body for burial even though her action might ordinarily be understood as an expression of mere sentiment or as an anointing of kingship (see 27:11, 29, 37, 42). Ironically, however, her anointing for death is also an anointing of the congregation's future Lord. Further, Matthew hints at the victory of the **resurrection** by reminding the reader that Jesus is the **Son of God** (27:40, 43; only in Matthew). The power of resurrection over death is also evident in the supernatural events surrounding Jesus' death: the earth shook, rocks were split, saints were raised from the dead and appeared to many in the holy city (27:51–54; cf. Mark 15:38 ff.).

Matthew subtly transforms the Markan passion story so that the element of Jesus' suffering, impossible to eradicate, is modified by Jesus' obedience, which in turn becomes a paradigm for disciples. Insofar as Jesus acts or speaks in the passion, he voluntarily accepts his death; he obeys God's will. He could have called legions of angels, but "how then would the scriptures be fulfilled?" (26:54, 56; cf. Mark 14:48–50). Matthew adds to Mark's account of Jesus' accepting the cross ("yet not what I want but what you want"—26:39; cf. Mark 14:36) a reinforcing word of obedience, "My Father, if this cannot pass unless I drink it, your will be done" (26:42). Thus Matthew shows that in his passion Jesus fulfills the "higher **righteousness**" he set forth in the Sermon on the Mount (6:20; cf. 7:24); Jesus acts as the one who fulfills "all righteousness" (3:15). Matthew's Jesus not only demands obedience; he also enacts obedience. His resurrection and establishment as Lord of the congregation are based upon faithful obedience to God.

The Great Commission (28:16–20)

How do Jesus' final words convey the message of the Gospel of Matthew?

In the final words of Matthew (28:16–20) the resurrected Jesus charges the disciples—that is, the Christian congregation—with the task of teaching all nations to observe what he has commanded (28:20). Such observance is now possible because Jesus has fully obeyed. At death the bruised reed did not break; he brought judgment to victory (12:20; only in Matthew).

Matthew follows Mark in depicting the burial of Jesus and the subsequent discovery of the empty tomb by the women. To this he adds the appearance of Jesus to the women (28:9 ff.) and an account of the efforts of the Jewish leaders to make it appear that the body was stolen (28:11–15; cf. 27:62–66). The second and final appearance of the risen Jesus is obviously of greatest importance for Matthew. It occurs in Galilee

(26:32; 28:7) at a mountain (5:1; 15:29; 17:1). The disciples' reaction to this climactic moment is described briefly: "They worshiped him" (see 2:2; 18:26; 28:9) "but some doubted" (vs. 17). The report of doubt strikes the reader as inappropriate, since the disciples have just worshiped Jesus. In other resurrection appearances doubt also occurs, but in those instances some further action of Jesus overcomes the doubt (Luke 24:41; Mark 16:14; John 20:25). Here the expression of doubt is simply followed by the word of Jesus.

Before exhorting the disciples to action, the risen Jesus declares, "All authority in heaven and on earth has been given to me" (vs. 18). Jesus' authoritative announcement has an implicit reference to the **cosmic** enthronement of the **apocalyptic Son of Man** depicted in Daniel: "And to him was given dominion and glory and kingship, that all peoples, nations and languages should serve him; his dominion is an everlasting dominion that shall not pass away, and his kingship is one that shall not be destroyed" (7:14). The combination of authority, dominion, and extension to all nations makes this passage relevant to Jesus' word. Jesus' authority in heaven and on earth exists until "the end of the age," that is, while the **church** exists. Previously, Matthew dealt with the subject of authority as an aspect of Jesus' earthly activity: he taught with authority (7:28 ff.), he healed with authority (8:9), he forgave with authority (9:6, 8). Now the authority of the resurrected Jesus is expressed precisely through the disciples' earthly task of making obedient disciples. The new thing about this authority is that with Jesus' resurrection it is extended to include all the nations.

The resurrected Jesus' word to the disciples—"teaching them to obey everything that I *have commanded you*" (vs. 20a; cf. 24:34 ff.)—refers them to his previous teaching. The risen Lord's words are rooted not in heavenly visions but in words already spoken by the earthly Jesus. Yet Matthew does not allow the authority of the resurrected Jesus to rest simply with his activity on earth. Accordingly, the disciples, in the presence of the Resurrected One, will extend his authority to all nations. The church's mission extends beyond those who claim election simply because of membership in the chosen people Israel (3:9; 21:33–43; cf. 2 Cor. 11:15–29).

Matthew's distillation of the resurrected Jesus' authority to the simple command to make disciples, **baptize**, and teach obedience (28:19, 20a) may contain another subtle warning. In the spurious ending of Mark's resurrection account (16:9–20), Jesus gives a commission to his disciples that includes preaching, baptizing, and performing charismatic acts of healing, exorcism, and speaking in tongues. On the surface, these phenomena seem much more impressive as evidence for the authority of Jesus and his disciples than Matthew's simple obedience. However, Matthew has already prepared the reader for this more austere concept of authority, for he has denied that marvelous manifestations were proof of faith and obedience (7:21–23). True discipleship will be demonstrated, not in ecstatic activity, but rather in obedience. More than ever the disciples themselves are called to obey the words Jesus commanded. What at first appears simply as a call to missionary endeavor on closer inspection turns out to be a call for discipleship that embraces obedience.

Looking now more directly at the imperative from the risen Jesus (vss. 19, 20a), we find that the task is divided into three stages: making disciples, baptizing them, and teaching them to observe all that Jesus has commanded. Matthew definitely emphasizes the first and the third stages, for he sees the church as the community of discipleship (13:52; 16:13–20; 27:57), which consists of lowliness, readiness for suffering, and above all obedience (10:40–42; 16:24–27; 18:1–6; 22:11–14). The esteem in which Matthew holds discipleship is illustrated by the fact that he recognizes only one level of church membership. In first-century Judaism the ambitious disciple hoped one day to become the teacher or **rabbi**. But in Matthew, Jesus says to his disciples, "But you are not to be called rabbi, for you have one teacher, and you are all students" (23:8; only in Matthew). Doubtless Matthew understood Jesus' warning to apply also to matters of rank and office in the church. Although Matthew never has the disciples address Jesus with the title teacher or rabbi (instead their more customary form of address is "Lord"), there can be little doubt that the final words to the disciples establish once and for all that the Lord of the congregation is, in the last analysis, the only Rabbi or Teacher.

The Gospel According to Matthew has thus come full circle. The initial emphasis on Joseph's radical obedience (1:24) has been expanded through the body of the Gospel to spell out the way of **righteousness** (3:15; 5:6, 20; 6:33) that is fulfilled in obedience (7:21; 21:28–32; 25:31–46). The disciples are to observe all that Jesus has commanded. Yet this radical demand becomes possible because in Jesus, his mission and message, God has come near (1:23; 18:20). Above all, the way of righteousness was fulfilled by the action of Jesus, particularly his obedient submission to death (20:26–28). Therefore, the final word of the resurrected Jesus assures the disciples that the Lord of the congregation both is and will be with them until the close of the age. The continuing presence of Jesus with the congregation means that these final words are not a farewell from Jesus. As long as the church continues, the risen Jesus lives and abides in his disciples' obedience to his teaching.

CONCLUSION

In summary, our investigations demonstrate that Matthew's **Gospel** is an interpretation of the tradition of Jesus based upon Mark, the **Q** collection of sayings, and other traditions. Matthew's interpretive procedure does not mean, however, that he did not stand in the service of the Jesus tradition that he received. Matthew clearly intends to remain faithful to it. Both Matthew and Luke combine the predominantly narrative Gospel of Mark with the predominantly discourse collection of Jesus' sayings known as Q. Thereby these Gospels serve as a check against any inclination within the early Christian community toward making Christianity into a kind of mystery religion dominated by the pattern of a dying and rising god. In effect, Matthew and Luke are saying that Christian faith involves a particular teaching.

Matthew's stress on the words that Jesus spoke binds the Christian **revelation** to the historical Jesus, one whose past words and actions demand and promise obedience. The Christian congregation, therefore, knows its unity and origin in the historical Jesus. Even though Matthew may contain words of Jesus that were never spoken by him during his ministry, in binding the narrative and discourse traditions, it limits in principle the revelation of Christian faith to Jesus of Nazareth. Matthew and the other **canonical** Gospels thereby preserve the distinctive character of Christian faith, the so-called scandal of particularity: a particular person at a particular time and place is claimed as the relevation of the creating and judging God of the universe.

We can now review our use of four approaches in understanding Matthew's Gospel.

The *structure* of Matthew is clear-cut. The Introduction (1:1–2:23) sets the tone for the rest of the Gospel. The coming of Jesus establishes a new and more radical obedience, first exemplified by Joseph; moreover, this obedience takes place within a new Israel, where Jew and **Gentile** (wise men) worship together. Matthew then sets forth the Gospel in five major sections, each consisting of narrative discourse and reminiscent of the five authoritative books of Moses. Book 1 (3:1–7:29) depicts the "higher **righteousness**" that Jesus both effects (the **baptism**) and demands (Sermon on the Mount). Book 2 (8:1–11:1) previews the life of discipleship by showing that the **miracles** of Jesus call for deeds of love and service in the disciples' mission. Book 3 (11:2–13:52) puts earthly activity into the perspective of the **kingdom** of heaven. Present mercy stands within the context of future judgment; the followers of Jesus are to train for this future event. Book 4 (13:53–19:2) locates this present mercy in the context of the forgiving **church**, where the basis for discipline and exclusion becomes the unwillingness to practice forgiveness. Book 5 (19:3–26:1) appropriately concludes with the expectation of future judgment on the basis of deeds, not beliefs. Furthermore, the doers of mercy are those who live in faith without thought of reward. The Conclusion (26:2–28:20) reports Jesus' obedient submission to death and God's response—the **resurrection**. Finally, the risen Jesus commissions the disciples to obey and to teach obedience, with the knowledge that he abides with them until the age's end.

Matthew's carefully worked out structure displays this Gospel's *major emphases*. We may now bring them together under three headings: the new obedience, its source, and its community. Matthew advocates a higher righteousness, which is a new obedience. The higher righteousness enables and requires radical obedience, and the spelling out of this obedience becomes clearer in Matthew's treatment of the **law**. Nowhere does he claim that the law has been abolished; on the contrary, the law is affirmed. Without deeds, professions of loyalty to Jesus are empty (7:21). Yet Matthew emphasizes the love of God and the love of all peoples, which must not be neglected through preoccupation with carrying out legal details. Thereby Matthew seeks to make the will of God present and alive.

The second major emphasis is upon the source of higher righteousness, the Lord Jesus. In one sense, the Jesus of Matthew is a more majestic figure than is the Jesus of Mark. Matthew tends to abbreviate Mark's miracle stories; consequently, he make them even more inexplicable as human events. Yet this abbreviation is a primary means for emphasizing the importance of Jesus' teaching. Even in the miraculous acts, Jesus is a teacher, an extraordinary first-century **rabbi**. This teaching makes Jesus an authoritative, majestic figure. Matthew's Jesus, however, is also lowly and obedient. He fulfills scripture by becoming the suffering servant who not only teaches obedience to disciples but actually performs it. The mighty Lord goes to his death in obedient lowliness, thereby fulfilling the way of higher righteousness.

The third and final emphasis follows from the preceding: the higher righteousness fulfilled in Jesus Christ requires realization in the congregation. This community of Jesus' followers learns that the present is determined by the mercy of God's presence, even for the sinner. The **beatitudes** proclaim God's love for the poor in spirit, the meek. The church knows itself as the "little ones," who obediently await the final judgment in the presence of Jesus.

Our comprehensive interpretation has depended upon observation of Matthew's *redaction* of the tradition. Among other things, **redaction criticism** shows that Matthew's treatment of the disciples is significantly less harsh than that of his predecessor Mark. Yet our study suggests that Matthew has a more realistic view of the disciples' actual behavior than has Mark. Matthew recognizes that the disciples do "understand" Jesus; after all, they followed him. Nevertheless, they were still of "little faith" (see 8:23–27; 14:31; 16:8; 17:20) because they had not yet acted in obedience. According to Matthew, they could not obey until Jesus completed his own obedience through death and resurrection.

The general *situation* that produced the Gospel of Matthew is implicit in the document itself. Matthew's Gospel arises out of Judaism; yet Matthew insists that Jesus' message differs from the Judaism of the **Pharisees**. This insight explains the tension between the Gospel's emphasis on the law and the role of Israel on the one hand (e.g., 5:18 ff.; 10:6), and its espousal of a higher righteousness and universal mission on the other (5:20; 28:16 ff.). Matthew calls for a higher level of obedience to the law than that required by those noted for their observance, that is, the Pharisees. Only against a Jewish background can the origin of Matthew's position be understood.

Although Jewish, the **eschatology** of Matthew cannot be classified as **apocalyptic** in the usual sense. Matthew's church did not cherish the belief that the end of the world was just around the corner and that people should gird themselves by extreme piety and **ethical** effort for an imminent encounter with God. True, Matthew emphasizes the coming of the final day (chap. 24; cf. also 4:17; 26:28), yet he also speaks about a time of waiting for the church. For Matthew the church's era is truly significant (see 24:6, 36 ff., 42 ff.). Indeed, the close of Matthew (28:16–20) would make no sense if the evangelist expected the end immediately.

Matthew strikes out in more than one direction. On the one hand, he attacks Pharisaic Judaism's interpretation of the law. On the other, Matthew would have rejected a Christianity developing without regard for its roots in Israel and the Old Testament into an unrestrained and undisciplined spiritualism. Such a Christianity developed later, and Matthew may have already sensed its danger. At any rate, Matthew understood Christian faith to be firmly rooted in the historical Jesus. While rejecting Pharisaism, he used the teaching of Jesus to oppose any lack of moral responsibility. Matthew called his congregation to the obedience that Jesus had both commanded in his teaching and embodied in his **passion**.

It is evident from Matthew that his church is a community with Jewish roots. Standing within this community, Matthew maintains the Jewish themes of righteousness and obedience to the law; but he sets them within the context of faith in Jesus Christ, in whom they are fulfilled. Because of God's action through Christ and his continuing presence with the congregation, the end of Christian faith is not at all unlike the way. Thus, the **kingdom** of heaven is both present and future. Matthew's Gospel mirrors not only the life of Christ but also Matthew's view of the life of the Christian community.

SUGGESTIONS FOR FURTHER READING

High quality **commentaries** on Matthew are abundant. For the student who can use Greek, W. D. Davies and D. C. Allison, *A Critical and Exegetical Commentary on the Gospel According to Saint Matthew*, 3 vols. (Edinburgh: T&T Clark, 1988–1997), is a rich mine of exegetical information and insight. The first two of U. Luz's three volumes on Matthew are available in English: *Matthew 1–7: A Commentary*, trans. W. C. Linns (Minneapolis: Augsburg, 1989), and *Matthew 8–20: A Commentary*, trans. J. E. Crouch (Minneapolis: Fortress, 2001). Another technical commentary, somewhat more conservative in tenor, is D. A. Hagner, *Matthew*, 2 vols. (Dallas: Word Books, 1993, 1995). Also valuable is H. D. Betz, *The Sermon on the Mount: A Commentary on the Sermon on the Mount, Including the Sermon on the Plain (Matthew 5:3–7:27 and Luke 6:20-49)* (Minneapolis: Fortress, 1995). Rich in theological exposition are E. Schweizer, *The Good News According to Matthew*, trans. D. E. Green (Richmond, VA: John Knox, 1975), D. R. A. Hare, *Matthew* (Louisville: John Knox, 1993), M. E. Boring, "Matthew: Introduction, Commentary, and Reflections," *The New Interpreter's Bible*, volume 8 (Nashville: Abingdon, 1995), pp. 87–505, D. Senior, *Matthew* (Nashville: Abingdon, 1998); C. S. Keener, *A Commentary on the Gospel of Matthew* (Grand Rapids: Eerdmans, 1999), and F. D. Brunner, *Matthew: A Commentary*, Volume One: *The Christbook, Matthew 1–12*, Volume Two: *The Churchbook, Matthew 13–28*, rev. and expanded (Grand Rapids: Eerdmans, 2004).

Other Studies. A pioneering exercise in **redaction criticism**, G. Bornkamm, G. Barth, and H.–J. Held, *Tradition and Interpretation in Matthew*, trans P. Scott (Philadelphia: Westminster, 1965), is still worth reading. The classic studies by W. D. Davies, *The Setting of the Sermon on the Mount* (New York: Cambridge University Press, 1964), and K. Stendahl, *The School of St. Matthew and Its Use of the Old Testament* (Philadelphia: Fortress, 1968) remain significant, particularly for their insight into Matthew's **Jewish milieu.** The latter subject has seen important contributions, with divergent outcomes: J. A. Overman, *Matthew's Gospel and Formative Judaism: The Social World of the Matthean Community* (Minneapolis: Fortress, 1990), and G. N. Stanton, *A Gospel for a New People: Studies in Matthew* (Edinburgh: T&T Clark, 1992), argue that the Evangelist's community is caught in religious and ethnic transition. A. J. Saldarini, *Matthew's Christian–Jewish Community* (Chicago and London: University of Chicago Press, 1994), understands the Gospel as an essentially Jewish product; D. C. Sim, *The Gospel of Matthew and Christian Judaism: The History and Social Setting of the Matthean Community* (Edinburgh: T&T Clark, 1998), as essentially Gentile. D. Senior offers judicious **appraisals** of that and other disputed topics in *What Are They Saying about Matthew?* rev. ed. (New York: Paulist, 1996), and *The Gospel of Matthew* (Nashville: Abingdon, 1997).

Ulrich Luz surveys *The Theology of the Gospel of Matthew*, trans. J. B. Robinson (Cambridge: Cambridge University Press, 1995), as well as *Matthew in History: Interpretation, Influence, and Effects* (Minneapolis: Fortress, 1994). **Theological insights** are gleaned by J. P. Meier, *The Vision of Matthew: Christ, Church, and Morality in the First Gospel* (New York: Paulist, 1979), B. Przybylski, *Righteousness in Matthew and His World of Thought* (Cambridge: Cambridge University Press, 1980), J. D. Kingsbury, *Matthew: Structure, Theology, and Kingdom* (Minneapolis: Fortress, 1989), D. C. Allison, *The New Moses: A Matthean Typology* (Minneapolis: Fortress, 1993), J. H. Neyrey, *Honor and Shame in the Gospel of Matthew* (Louisville: Westminster John Knox, 1998), and B. Byrne, *Lifting the Burden: Reading Matthew's Gospel in the Church Today* (Collegeville, MN: Liturgical, 2004).

The Supper at Emmaus (1606), by Michelangelo Merisi (Caravaggio; 1573–1610). *(Courtesy of Brera Gallery.)*

CHAPTER 4

LUKE:
THE GOSPEL
OF WITNESSING

Background of the Gospel of Luke

An early tradition about Luke's **Gospel**, from the Muratorian Canon (a catalogue of New Testament writings originating in Rome about **A.D.** 200) states that both the Gospel According to Luke and the Acts of the Apostles were written by the same author. This view is supported by the opening verses of each book, which in both cases contain dedications to a certain Theophilus, and by Acts' reference to a "first book" (1:1). The two books definitely display a kinship in style and emphasis. Yet neither Luke nor Acts specifies the author's identity. Luke–Acts is an anonymous two-volume work. Presumably these books were composed to be read together, although in the **canonical** arrangement their original close connection is interrupted by the Fourth Gospel. Together Luke–Acts comprises approximately one-fourth of the New Testament.

To be accepted by the church at the end of the second century, a Gospel needed a claim to **apostolic** authority. According to tradition, Mark rests upon the authority of one great apostle, Peter;. Similarly, Luke rests on the authority of another, Paul. In the letters ascribed to him, Paul mentions as a companion "Luke, the beloved physician" (Col. 4:14; Philemon. 24; 2 Tim. 4:11). This Luke may have accompanied Paul on some of his missionary journeys. The occasional use of "we" in Acts (e.g., 16:10 ff.) suggests the author is a participant in the events, although this is not certain.

If some doubt attaches to the relationship with Paul, a few things may be said with certainty about the author of the Gospel according to Luke. He was more self-consciously an author than were the writers of either Mark or Matthew. The preface (1:1–4) makes explicit the literary aim of the Gospel: it is dedicated to Theophilus and speaks knowingly of previous works on the same subject. Probably the author of Luke was a **Gentile** Christian. He spoke Greek as his native tongue and knew something of **Hellenistic** literary convention. On the other hand, Luke seems to know little about Palestinian geography. In 17:11 he apparently conceives of Samaria as lying north of Galilee or, alternatively, of the two provinces as lying side by side on an east–west axis with a corridor between them. Sometimes Luke has Jesus preaching in Judea (4:44) or attracting hearers from there (5:17; 6:17), as though Judea were nearby.

Although Luke used the Gospel of Mark, as did Matthew, he used this source more critically. Whereas Matthew took over practically all of Mark, Luke used only about half. Like Matthew, Luke used the sayings source **Q**. In addition, there is a considerable body of tradition found only in Luke.

The material found only in Luke (usually designated L; see pp. 56–57), beginning with the preface (1:1–4), is typical of that Gospel. A birth narrative, parallel with Matthew's but significantly different, follows (1:5–2:40; see "The Christmas Story," p. 127). Only Luke gives us a story from Jesus' childhood, as he describes the boy Jesus in the temple (2:41–52). Several of the best-known **parables** of Jesus are found only in Luke: the good Samaritan (10:29–37); the prodigal son (15:11–32); the rich man and Lazarus (16:19–31); and the **Pharisee** and the publican (18:9–14), among others. Only Luke mentions Zacchaeus, short of stature and sinfully rich, who climbed a tree to catch sight of Jesus (19:1-10). Several of these parables and stories emphasize God's love and the importance of repentance. In the **passion** and **resurrection** narratives, only Luke mentions Jesus' going before Herod (Antipas) in Jerusalem (23:6–12), as well as the dramatic resurrection appearance to two disciples on the Emmaus road (24:13–35).

A number of Lukan stories have affinities with John's Gospel. The parable of Lazarus recalls Jesus' raising Lazarus from the dead (John 11:1–44). Only Luke and John mention the sisters Mary and Martha (Luke 10:38–42; John 11:1–44). Luke's story of the miraculous catch of fish (5:1–11) is echoed in John's account of the risen Jesus appearing to disciples beside the sea (21:1–14). Only Luke (24:36–49) and John (20:19–29) recount appearances of Jesus to the Twelve in Jerusalem; only they deal with Jesus' ascension (Luke 24:50-51; Acts 1:1-11; John 20:17, cf. vs. 27). Finally, these evangelists in particular emphasize that women were among Jesus' earliest followers (Luke 8:1–3; John 19:25–27; 20:11–18; cf. 4:7–42). Oddly, John reflects knowledge of much of the narrative and historical data otherwise distinctive of Luke, but little if any of its considerable teaching material, found only in the Third Gospel.

As in the case of the other **Synoptic** Gospels, the exact dating of Luke is difficult. Like Matthew, Luke seems to know about the actual destruction of Jerusalem (cf. Luke 21:20 and 19:43 f.). The earliest date for Luke would therefore be sometime after the city's fall in A.D. 70. Because the introduction of Acts alludes to the Gospel (1:1), Luke was presumably written before the final version of Acts. The letters of Paul were written in the middle of the first century but were not assembled before the end of the century. It is unlikely that the author of Luke–Acts knew the Pauline **epistles**. At least he does not mention them. Nor does what he writes indicate knowledge of events of the second century. Therefore, a date sometime before the end of the first century is probable. According to the preface (1:1–4), Luke apparently belongs to the third stage of the Christian tradition: he speaks of eyewitnesses, collectors ("ministers of the word"), and his own composition. If so, then a date only shortly before the turn of the century would be appropriate. Luke–Acts was likely written sometime between A.D. 80 and 100. Little can be said about the geographical origin of Luke other than that it probably did not originate in Palestine. Although the occasion of Luke's writing is unknown, the evangelist's general purpose may be inferred from the fact that this is the only Gospel with a sequel, an Acts of the Apostles. The rest of this chapter and Chapter 7 examine this purpose more closely. We may, however, anticipate our study by suggesting that Luke presents a view of the history of **salvation** extending from the time of Israel through the life of Jesus and continuing in the history of the **church**. The good news for Israel is extended through Jesus and the apostles to all people.

The outline or structure of the two-volume work Luke–Acts depicts this history of salvation in an explicit manner, for the Gospel can be characterized as a movement from Galilee to Jerusalem:

Introduction:	Birth of John and Jesus in Jerusalem	1:1–2:52
Part One:	Gathering Witnesses in Galilee	3:1–9:50
Part Two:	Journey to Jerusalem	9:51–19:27
Part Three:	Jesus' Triumph in Jerusalem	19:28–24:53

The Acts of the Apostles as a movement from Jerusalem to Rome (see p. 243):

Introduction:	Birth of Church in Jerusalem	1:1–2:47
Part One:	Witnesses within Israel	3:1–12:25
Part Two:	Journey to the Gentiles	13:1–21:14
Part Three:	Paul's Triumph in Rome	21:15–28:31

Obviously, the author of Luke–Acts uses geography as a key for communicating the story of the triumphal march of the new religious movement, from the obscurity of Galilee through the capital city of ancient Israel to the very center of the Roman Empire. Indeed, the journey theme, occurring as it does in the middle sections of both Luke and Acts, reflects the evangelist's intention of writing a narrative to depict the sweep of God's victorious action, primarily through Jesus and Paul. Luke has expanded the Markan story of Jesus' journey to Jerusalem (Mark 8:27–10:52) into a dominating motif and metaphor for Jesus and the early church (Luke 9:51–19:27).

PREFACE:
A TIME FOR TRUE REMEMBERING (1:1–4)

In what sense did Luke intend to write history or biography?

With a preface of a sort not found in the other Gospels, yet common in the writings of antiquity, Luke makes the reader conscious of his predecessors and purpose (1:1–4). That the preface was a literary convention can be seen from a comparison of the opening sentences of Luke and Acts with prefaces of the first-century Jewish historian Josephus. His *Against Apion*, Book I, opens with the following statement:

> In my history of our Antiquities, most excellent Epaphroditus, I have, I think, made sufficiently clear to any who may peruse that work the extreme antiquity of our Jewish race, the purity of the original stock and the manner in which it established itself in the country which we occupy today. . . . Since, however, I observe that a considerable number of persons . . . discredit the statements in my history concerning our antiquity, . . . I consider it my duty to devote a brief treatise to all these points, in order at once to convict our detractors of malignity and deliberate falsehood, to correct the ignorance of others, and to instruct all who desire to know the truth concerning the antiquity of our race.

Book II begins:

> In the first volume of this work, my most esteemed Epaphroditus, I demonstrated the antiquity of our race, corroborating my statements by the writings of the Phoenicians, Chaldeans, and Egyptians. . . . I also challenged the statements of Manetho, Chaeremon, and some others. I shall now proceed to refute the rest of the authors who have attacked us.

Not only Luke's Gospel but also the Acts of the Apostles begins with such a preface. Thus the parallel with Josephus is even more impressive. The very fact that

Luke followed the prevailing literary fashion of his day indicates part of his purpose: to make his Gospel acceptable to the literate individual. Still, the preface has a more definite purpose.

With the statement that many others have undertaken to compile a narrative about the things that he will relate, Luke forgoes any claim to originality. Indeed, originality is not the point. Nor does he claim a divine **revelation** superseding all other previous accounts. Yet the opening verses give the unmistakable impression that he means to write a Gospel superior to its predecessors. Although there have been other compilers, as well as eyewitnesses and ministers of the word, Luke purposes to write an account more adequate than anything yet presented. Among Luke's many sources were most likely Mark, the **Q source**, and special Lukan tradition.

Luke's historical situation can be inferred from the statement concerning his predecessors (vs. 2). In all, there are three stages of the **gospel** tradition. The first stage of eyewitnesses consists of those who have been with Jesus most intimately, for example, the twelve **apostles** (6:12 f.; cf. Mark 3:13 f.). Later we learn that apostles are those eyewitnesses who were with Jesus from the baptism to the **ascension** (cf. Acts 1:21–26). The second group, ministers or servants of the word, pass on the eyewitness tradition by preaching. Although in Acts, ministers of the word are first of all the apostles themselves, there are other ministers, such as Stephen and Philip, who preach the word. The final stage, in which Luke himself stands, is that of compilers of the tradition. With the advantage of hindsight the compiler is able to see what is most important and worthy of being preserved. Although Luke stands within that third phase, he intends to surpass all the rest. By "following all things closely" (vs. 3), he expects to give both an orderly and truthful account of the life, death, and **resurrection** of Jesus (vs. 4). Not only does Luke consider this compilation of the tradition more adequate than that of its predecessors; he also considers this third stage the most advantageous perspective. In some ways it offers a more comprehensive and truer perspective than that even of eyewitnesses, although the latter are certainly indispensable.

Luke stresses that he is going to write an "orderly account" (vs. 3). This cannot mean that he is going to arrange his account differently, for Luke generally follows Mark's order. Probably Luke refers to his general scheme for placing Jesus within history, so that Jesus fulfills the story of Israel and initiates the story of the **church**. Perhaps the "Theophilus" to whom he addresses this work (vs. 3) is an actual person: an esteemed or eminent citizen, perhaps Luke's patron. Alternatively, the name "friend of God" (which is what *Theophilus* means) stands for the religious reader who as a **God–fearer** is interested in Christianity (see Acts 10:2, where Cornelius, the first named **Gentile** convert, is said to "fear God"). Whoever Theophilus may have been, he was certainly someone who had a preliminary knowledge of the Christian faith and was willing to read both the story of Jesus and that of the early church. He represents all who wished to know the truth about these things (literally, "words" [vs. 4]). The implied reader is an interested inquirer, if not a new convert.

Luke's preface suggests his purpose. He seeks to write a Gospel of Jesus that will serve as the foundation for belief. Luke understands himself as living at a time in which true remembering needs to take place; he wishes to recover and reformulate roots so that the certainty and continuity of Christian faith from the beginning up to the present can be established: from Israel through Jesus to the church. The reader must hear the full Christian story.

INTRODUCTION: A UNIVERSAL STORY (1:5–2:52)

The first two chapters of Luke are concerned primarily with the birth stories of John the Baptist and Jesus of Nazareth. This tradition is not contained in the other **Synoptic** Gospels, even though another infancy narrative is, of course, found in Matthew. The persons and incidents in these chapters for the most part disappear in the rest of the Gospel. Nevertheless, these opening episodes set the tone for what follows and suggest who Jesus really is.

This Gospel opens with a **priest** named Zechariah, who will be father of the Baptist, in the temple at Jerusalem (1:5 ff.), a city of crucial importance to Luke. Like none of the other Gospels, Luke begins in Jerusalem. In the central journey section, Jerusalem is the destination (9:51). There in his last days Jesus takes over the temple (19:47; 21:37 f.; 24:53; only in Luke). Jesus' **resurrection** appearances occur in Jerusalem and its vicinity rather than in Galilee, as Matthew states (24:6; cf. 24:13, 18, 33) and Mark clearly implies (14:28; 16:7; cf. John 21:1). Finally, the disciples wait in Jerusalem until the **Holy Spirit** manifests itself so that they may witness to the rest of the world (see Acts 1:4, 8).

A prominent characteristic of Luke's opening chapter is the twofold nature of figures and events. The birth of Jesus is coupled with the birth of John. A **revelation** occurs to Mary, the mother of Jesus; a revelation is also given to Zechariah, husband of Elizabeth, mother of John the Baptist. John is the forerunner, Jesus is the fulfillment (1:45). The babe in Elizabeth's womb leaps at the meeting with Mary, mother of Jesus (1:39–45). Elizabeth calls Mary "the mother of my Lord" (Greek *kyrios*), indicating far-reaching knowledge of who Jesus is, and will be. John is the "prophet of the Most High" (1:76); Jesus is the "Son of the Most High" (1:32). The two are not, however, set against one another but are in continuity. John the Baptist serves as a **witness** and a **prophet** to Jesus (cf. 1:80 with 2:40, 52; also see 3:4 ff.). In addition, both Simeon (2:22 ff.) and the prophetess Anna (2:36 ff.) testify to Jesus.

Luke also sets the story within the context of world history: "In the days of Herod" (1:5), "In the sixth month" (1:26), "In those days a decree went out from Caesar Augustus" (2:1; cf. 3:1). At the same time Luke emphasizes the role of women and the humble: Elizabeth and Mary are in the foreground; the shepherds come and worship Jesus (1:53; 2:8 ff.; cf. 6:20; 7:22). A romantic, idyllic quality pervades this section where salvation emerges among humble folk, women exult in childbirth, and shepherds come to worship a baby in a manger, or feeding trough.

The Christmas Story

Luke's story of Jesus' nativity is distinctive in its emphases, but it is usually regarded in relation to the somewhat similar nativity story in the first two chapters of Matthew's **Gospel** (see "Background of the Gospel of Luke," pp. 121–123). Taken together, this forms the Christmas Story with which most people today are familiar. Because the particulars of the two stories in Matthew and in Luke differ widely, each narrative should be taken on its own terms. Yet both share common features, which explains why the stories are often merged in pageants, liturgy, and Christian consciousness generally.

In both Gospels, the angel of the Lord (called Gabriel in Luke) announces the forthcoming conception and birth of Jesus, saying that the child will be conceived by the **Holy Spirit**, that is, by God's action rather than that of a human father (Matt. 1:18-24; Luke 1:26-35), even though Mary is engaged to Joseph. (Strictly speaking, both Evangelists are more interested in Jesus' virginal *conception*, not his virginal *birth*.) In Matthew, the recipient of the angelic announcement is Joseph; in Luke, Mary. These differences reflect the fact that, in Matthew, the principal human figure in the narrative is Joseph, while in Luke it is Mary. In both accounts, Jesus is born in Bethlehem (Matt. 2:1; Luke 2:4-5), the Judean city of King David. In Matthew that seems to be the parents' home; in Luke, however, they must travel there from their home in Nazareth of Galilee. (Probably in this respect Luke is more accurate historically: throughout the Gospels, Jesus is known as "Jesus of Nazareth.") In both, although in quite distinct ways, Jesus is presented as the fulfillment of Israelite hope and **prophecy**. After his birth, the baby Jesus is worshipped or adored, in Matthew by wise men from the East who visit him in a house (Matt. 2:1-12), in Luke by lowly shepherds (Luke 2:8-20) who find him in a stable's manger. In both accounts Jesus is designated as the future ruler or **Christ** (Matt. 1:21-23; Luke 1:31-33), the one anointed as Israel's king.

While Jesus' birth is mentioned elsewhere in the New Testament (e.g., Gal. 4:4; John 18:37), no allusion is made to these infancy stories, not even elsewhere in Matthew and Luke. In the Gospel of John, which emphasizes Jesus' sonship, Jesus is nevertheless called the son of Joseph (1:45) as well as the **Son of God**. Joseph is mentioned in Matthew, Luke, and John, although not in Mark, which, like John, has no infancy narrative. Paul and Mark at least know Jesus was of the line of David (Rom. 1:3; Mark 10:47–48; cf. Matt. 1:29; Luke 1:27); John may also be aware of this feature (7:42).

The next earliest reference to Jesus' **Virgin Birth** lies outside the New Testament: in letters to other churches by Bishop Ignatius of Antioch (ca.115-120), written while being transported as a prisoner to Rome, presumably to be martyred (*Ephesians* 7.2; 19.1; *Smyrnaeans* 1.1). Probably Ignatius' belief was grounded in the Gospel of Matthew, which he seems to have known (cf. Ignatius's *To the Ephesians* 19.1-3 with Matt. 2:2, 7).

The familiar **Apostles' Creed** speaks of Jesus' having been "conceived of the Holy Spirit [and] born of the Virgin Mary." Although in its present form this creed does not go back to the apostles, its roots lie in the middle of the second century. The fourth-century Nicene Creed, perhaps the most widely used creed in Christendom, combines John's language about incarnation and divine sonship (John 1:14, 18) with the virginal conception of Jesus: ". . . incarnate of the Holy Spirit and the Virgin Mary." So the Christian doctrine of the **Incarnation**—Jesus as God in the flesh—was eventually anchored in the doctrine of the Virgin Birth, some time after the New Testament books were written, even though the New Testament itself does not express that linkage. The **theological**, properly **Christological**, affirmation that Jesus is the Son of God did not begin with the birth stories in Matthew and in Luke, but after Jesus' death and the belief in his **resurrection** (see Rom. 1:4).

Twofold Witness to Jesus (2:22–40)

What do Simeon and Anna, who receive Jesus in the temple, represent or embody?

The Simeon episode (2:22–35) shows that Jesus' parents were **law**-abiding adherents of the Jewish faith (cf. 2:39). After Jesus' circumcision on the eighth day (2:21), attention turns to the purification of the mother of a son, which according to Jewish law took place on the thirty-third day after circumcision or the fortieth day after birth (Lev. 12:2–8). Although purification actually is for the mother, not the child, this story depicts the parents as bringing the child Jesus "to do for him according to the custom of the law" (vs. 27). Perhaps Luke is unfamiliar with Jewish practices, or perhaps this manner of narration enables Luke to keep Jesus the center of attention even when the mother's purification would be taking place.

As the scene begins, it presents a contrast between the old man Simeon, who has been patiently waiting for the consolation of Israel, and the child Jesus. Upon seeing Jesus, he exclaims, "Lord, now lettest thou thy servant depart in peace" (2:29–32 RSV). The astonishment of Jesus' father and mother at Simeon's words (2:33) is itself surprising, for they already knew that Jesus was to be a **messianic** figure (1:32 ff.; 2:13 ff.). Further, Simeon's speech contains a new item, for Jesus' coming is "a light for revelation to the **Gentiles**" (vs. 32). Jewish parents would understandably be surprised, especially since the news comes from a devout fellow Israelite (vss. 34 f.). Even this point is not entirely novel, however, for Simeon's speech goes back to Isaiah, who made similar prophecies (52:10; 42:6; 49:6). The principal point of this episode, and of the entire introduction, is that Jesus will bring **salvation** for all people, even Gentiles. He is meant for old and young, for women like Mary and Elizabeth, and for priests and shepherds.

In this episode's final part, the old prophetess Anna appears (2:36–38). She is exemplary for her chaste widowhood as well as for her great piety. Again we have Luke's twofold witness: An old man and an old woman praise Jesus. Her actions are similar to those of the early Christians who also went to the temple in order to worship and pray (cf. Acts 2:46–3:1). Furthermore, what she anticipates—"the redemption of Jerusalem" (vs. 38)—is effected in the early **church** by the life of Jesus (cf. 19:28–24:53, esp. 24:21). Antiquity, represented by the old woman and the old man, foresees the new salvation and calls attention to that redemption's ancient roots in Israel. It is noteworthy that Luke chooses a woman, as well as a man, to **prophesy** redemption, for he has already emphasized the role of women throughout the infancy narrative.

Initial Victory in the Temple (2:41–52)

What impression is conveyed by Jesus' first action in Luke?

The one boyhood story of Jesus contained in any of the **canonical** Gospels places Jesus in the temple. (The **apocryphal** Gospels contain numerous stories of Jesus' infancy, sometimes grotesque and occasionally distasteful.) This Lukan emphasis upon the temple was already apparent in the initial scene with Zechariah and the preceding encounters with

The modern Church of the Annunciation of the City of Nazareth (above) stands above the site of excavations of the village of Jesus' day, which is mentioned in no ancient source earlier than the Gospels (cf. John 1:46).

Simeon and Anna. After Jesus' first action, a triumphant demonstration before **rabbis** in the temple, his parents question him because his unexplained absence has caused them great anxiety. He replies, "Did you not know that I must be in my Father's house?" (2:49). The temple is Jesus' inheritance because he fulfills the hope of Israel.

Strikingly, the question is posed by Jesus' mother (2:48) rather than his father. Throughout the introduction, Mary rather than Joseph takes the lead. In the purification episode, Simeon speaks to Mary (2:34). In fact, Mary is mentioned twelve times in the opening two chapters. And, finally, "his mother kept all these things in her heart" (2:51). Yet in the rest of the Gospel she is not particularly important and is even rebuked (8:19 ff.). The fact that her womb bore Jesus and that her breasts were sucked by him is declared insignificant in comparison with those "who hear the word of God and keep it" (11:27 f.; only in Luke). Luke's emphasis upon Mary does not stress the virginal conception; the narrative concentrates on a series of wonders rather than one particular miracle.

The consistent flow of marvels underlines the fact that "with God, nothing will be impossible" (1:37).

The essential point of the birth stories, around which Luke's introduction is built, is the overwhelming power of God. Luke uses the **miraculous** birth of Jesus (Luke 1–2) to introduce Jesus' life in the same way as he uses the miraculous birth of the **church** (Acts 1–2) to introduce the church's mission. The outpouring of the **Spirit** upon various people at Jesus' birth is matched in Acts by the Spirit's descending upon **apostles** and disciples. The close of the introduction anticipates further developments (2:52). This verse echoes an earlier one (2:40). Further manifestations of God through the Spirit are thereby foreshadowed, for what was begun by the Spirit (cf. 1:15, 35, 41, 67; 2:25, 26) is now to be accomplished in the ministry of Jesus. The characters passively receive the Spirit; God's power acts in Jesus' birth. Only with the final episode, Jesus in the temple, does someone act with authority. And Jesus' action paves the way for Luke's first major section, in which Jesus gathers witnesses in Galilee for the journey to Jerusalem and the temple.

The Geography and Theology of Jerusalem

Jerusalem has a central role in the New Testament and in the Old. The site was already inhabited in 3000 B.C., and David seized it from the Jebusites and made it his capital about a millennium before the time of Jesus. Down to the present day Jerusalem remains important for Jews, Muslims, and Christians—and thus all too frequently a focal point of conflict.

Jerusalem sits astride a mountain range, about 2,500 feet above sea level. Although during the Israeli presence trees have been cultivated and the city looks green, this has not always been the case. Photographs taken in the middle to latter part of the nineteenth century show much less vegetation and betray the relatively arid climate. Jerusalem gets about half as much rain as a typical city on the east coast of the United States. It is situated in rough terrain at an altitude higher than any American city except Denver. Unlike other major ancient Mediterranean cites such as Rome, Athens, Alexandria, and Ephesus, it was not on, or easily accessible to, the coast. It was not an important trade, business, or commercial center. The importance of Jerusalem hinged on its religious and, therefore, political role, in ancient times as today.

From the days of King Solomon until its destruction by Roman armies in the year A.D. 70, a period of roughly a thousand years, its religious importance hinged on the temple. Destroyed by the Babylonians in the early sixth century, the temple was rebuilt about a half-century later, and then enormously enlarged by Herod the Great during a long period extending into the time of Jesus' ministry (John 2:20). **Sacrifices** were offered there daily by **priests**, but, perhaps just as important, the temple was the site of the gathering of Jews at the three great pilgrim feasts: **Passover** and Unleavened Bread, **Pentecost** (Weeks), and Tabernacles (Booths).

The earliest Christians gathered in Jerusalem after Jesus' death and **resurrection** (Acts 1-5: Gal. 1:18–2:10). Until its destruction in the Roman war, Jerusalem was the site of the central church of Christianity, as Paul, who was **apostle** to the **Gentiles** and not to the Jews, acknowledges (Rom. 15:14-33). The seer of Revelation looks forward to a New Jerusalem, which comes down from God out of heaven (21:2) and in which there is no temple; for its temple is the Lord God Almighty and the Lamb, that is Christ (21:22). In

Luke–Acts, Jerusalem is the center, to which Jesus moves throughout his ministry, and from which the **gospel** spreads after his death and resurrection. In John, Jesus himself displaces the temple as the locus of God's **revelation** (John 1:14: "the Word became flesh and tented [or tabernacled] among us"; cf. 2:19-22), and in John's narrative Jesus is more frequently seen in Jerusalem and the temple (7:14; 10:23).

Thus Jerusalem remains a **holy** place for Christianity, as well as for Judaism and also Islam. In Islamic tradition, the temple mount, the Dome of the Rock, is believed to be the place from which Muhammad once ascended into heaven. In fact, both the Dome of the Rock and the al–Aqsa mosque are ancient Islamic shrines.

GATHERING WITNESSES IN GALILEE (3:1–9:50)

Thus far any source behind Luke's narrative has been his special tradition. At this point (3:1) the major source becomes Mark's Gospel. In addition, we continue to assume that the special Lukan material (L) reveals something of this Gospel's purpose. The portion of Luke 3:1–9:50 (especially 6:17–7:35) that is found also in Matthew but not in Mark is probably derived from the **Q source**. We would be on fairly uncertain ground in trying to deduce Luke's aims and purposes from his use of this source, simply because we do not possess Q. Thus, we shall largely confine our distinguishing of tradition from redaction to Luke's use of the Markan source.

What May Q Have Included?

To this point we have referred to the **Q-source** hypothesis without presenting the close parallels between Luke and Matthew that are not attested in Mark. The following chart graphically displays those parallels. Luke is given first, because in order and form it often seems to represent an earlier or less developed version. In places where both Luke and Matthew use Mark, Luke also follows its order more closely than does Matthew.

John Preaches Repentance	Luke 3:7–9, 11 // Matt. 3:7–10
John Announces the Messiah	Luke 3:16–17 // Matt. 3:11–12
Satan Tempts Jesus	Luke 4:2–12 // Matt. 4:2–11
Jesus Blesses Poor, Hungry, Persecuted	Luke 6:20–23 // Matt. 5:3, 4, 6, 11, 12
Discipleship Is Love for Enemies	Luke 6:27–36 // Matt. 5:39–42, 44–48
The Pitfalls of Judging	Luke 6:37–42 // Matt. 7:1–5
A Tree Is Known by Its Fruit	Luke 6:43–46 // Matt. 7:16–21; 12:33–35
Hearers and Doers of the Word	Luke 6:47–49 // Matt. 7:24–27
Jesus Heals a Centurion's Servant	Luke 7:1–10 // Matt. 8:5–13
John Questions Jesus	Luke 7:18–23 // Matt. 11:2–6
John, the Preparer for Jesus	Luke 7:24–35 // Matt. 11:7–19
Discipleship Is Leaving Everything	Luke 9:57–60 // Matt. 8:19–22
Discipleship Is Extending Jesus' Work	Luke 10:2–12 // Matt. 9:37–38; 10:7–16

Jesus Pronounces Doom on Unrepentant Cities	Luke 10:13–15 // Matt. 11:21–23
Discipleship Is Sharing Jesus' Rejection	Luke 10:16 // Matt. 10:40
Jesus Thanks the Father for the Gift of Wisdom	Luke 10:21–22 // Matt. 11:25–27
Discipleship Is Sharing in the Gift of Wisdom	Luke 10:23–24 // Matt. 13:16–17
Jesus Teaches How to Pray	Luke 11:2–4 // Matt. 6:9–13
The Father Will Answer His Children's Prayer	Luke 11:9–13 // Matt. 7:7–11
Jesus' Exorcisms Show God's Kingdom Is Present	Luke 11:14–23 // Matt. 12:22–30
The Danger of the Return of the Unclean Spirit	Luke 11:24–26 // Matt. 12:43–45
The Sign of Jonah and the Wisdom of Solomon	Luke 11:29–32 // Matt. 12:38–42
Sayings about Light and Darkness	Luke 11:33–36 // Matt. 5:15; 6:22–23
Jesus Pronounces Doom on the Pharisees	Luke 11:39–44 // Matt. 23:25–26, 23, 6–7, 27
Jesus Pronounces Doom on the Lawyers	Luke 11:46–52 // Matt. 23:4, 29–31, 34–36, 13
Discipleship Is Fearless Confession of Jesus	Luke 12:2–12 // Matt. 10:26–33; 12:32; 10:19–20
Discipleship Is Trusting God, Not Possessions	Luke 12:22–34 // Matt. 6:25–33, 19–21
The Unexpected Return of a Householder	Luke 12:39–46 // Matt. 24:43–51
Jesus Brings Division, Not Peace	Luke 12:51–53 // Matt. 10:34–36
Signs of the Times	Luke 12:54–56 // Matt. 16:2–3
The Kingdom of God Is Like Leaven in Bread	Luke 13:20–21 // Matt. 13:33
Entry into the Kingdom of God Is Difficult	Luke 13:25–29 // Matt. 7:13–14; 25:10–12; 7:22–23; 8:11
Jesus Laments over Jerusalem	Luke 13:34–35 // Matt. 23:37–39
The Banquet in the Kingdom of God	Luke 14:16–23 // Matt. 22:2–10
Discipleship Is Hating Family, Bearing a Cross	Luke 14:26–27 // Matt. 10:37–38
The Joyful Shepherd	Luke 15:4–7 // Matt. 18:12–14
God or Mammon?	Luke 16:3 // Matt. 6:24
The Violence of the Kingdom of God	Luke 16:16 // Matt. 11:12–13
The Permanence of the Law	Luke 16:17 // Matt. 5:18
Discipleship Means Unlimited Forgiving	Luke 17:3–4 // Matt. 18:15, 21–22
The Power of Even a Little Faith	Luke 17:5–6 // Matt. 17:20
The Surprise of the Day of the Son of Man	Luke 17:23–37 // Matt. 24:26–27, 37–41; 10:39; 24:40, 28
The Fate of a Nobleman's Servants	Luke 19:12–26 // Matt. 25:14–29
Jesus' Followers Will Share His Kingdom	Luke 22:28–30 // Matt. 19:28

Luke locates the beginning of Jesus' ministry in two spheres, that of world history (3:1; cf. 2:1) and that of God's **word**. That word is first preached by John, the son of Zechariah (Luke 3:2 ff.). Luke's account of the Baptist's activity is similar to Matthew's, but with some remarkable differences. For example, whereas Matthew carefully showed that Jesus was baptized by John to fulfill **righteousness** (Matt. 3:13 ff.), Luke minimizes the fact that Jesus was baptized by John (cf. Luke 3:20 f.). At the same time, John the Baptist preaches exactly the same message of repentance and forgiveness (3:3), which becomes the heart of Jesus' own proclamation (chap. 15; 24:47). As the opening birth stories already indicate, this Gospel shows a high regard for John (cf. 7:28). Yet the Baptist still belongs to the old Israel (16:16), for he is the one who points ahead to the new time of Jesus (3:16).

Characteristic Lukan emphases abound in this section. Jesus is a universal savior: the genealogy goes from Jesus back to Adam, the first man (3:38), not to Abraham (Matt. 1:1 f.). Jesus is an example of piety: whenever a crisis arises, he is at prayer (5:16; 6:12; 9:18, 28 f.). Moreover, the **Spirit** descends upon Jesus while he is praying almost as if the Spirit were summoned by prayer rather than by the **baptism** (3:21; cf. Mark 1:9 f.). Luke apparently seeks to establish the practice of prayer as a basis for the **church**'s continuing life (see Acts 1:14; 2:42). Emphasis upon the church's contemporary situation may be reflected in Luke's omission of Mark's summary of Jesus' preaching, "The time is fulfilled, and the **kingdom of God** has come near; repent, and believe in the good news" (Mark 1:15). Although Luke also mentions the kingdom in this section, in Luke Jesus rarely preaches about the kingdom as if it were imminent (see 4:43 and 8:1; cf. 9:27). This loss of a sense for the kingdom's imminent coming is related to Luke's greater emphasis on the church, and on God's saving activity through history.

Jesus' gathering of disciples in Galilee is a focal point of this section of the narrative. Many people flock to him (4:15, 42; 5:1, 15); some are in opposition (5:30; 6:2) and remain only in the crowd (6:17; 7:11), but he gathers the disciples (5:1–11). Indeed, from those disciples he calls together the Twelve, whom he "named **apostles**" (6:13; cf. Mark 3:14). Here in his own territory Jesus gathers those who will be **witnesses** to carry on his work after his death. (At Jesus' **ascension**, two men in white robes address the disciples as "men of Galilee": Acts 1:11.) The continuing importance of women is shown by their inclusion alongside the Twelve as part of Jesus' retinue (8:1-3). Later they too, along with the Twelve, will be witnesses: "The women who had come with him *from Galilee* followed, and saw the tomb, and how his body was laid; then they returned, and prepared spices and ointments" (23:55 f.; see 23:49). Luke seeks to establish certainty of witness (cf. 1:4): there are people who had accompanied Jesus all the time, from his baptism until the day when he was taken up (see Acts 1:21 f.).

The Offense of Jesus' Preaching (4:16–30)

Why do the people of Nazareth try to kill Jesus?

In Mark, Jesus' first public act is to exorcise a demon (1:21–28); in Matthew, it is to deliver the Sermon on the Mount (chaps. 5–7); in Luke, it is to preach in his home synagogue at Nazareth. This episode's special importance is indicated by its position at the beginning of Jesus' public ministry. Moreover, Luke uncharacteristically departs from the Markan order by moving forward and expanding Mark's simpler narrative (cf. Mark 6:1–6).

Jesus appears as a pious Jew: "He went to the synagogue, as his custom was, on the sabbath day" (vs. 16). He there reads from the **prophet** Isaiah, whose message from the

Old Testament (61:1–2; 58:6) proclaims the end time; the **Spirit** acts, good news is preached to the poor, and a new age has dawned. After finishing, Jesus says, "Today, this scripture has been fulfilled in your hearing" (4:21; only in Luke). In other words, **salvation** has appeared with Jesus, who comes to preach good news to the poor, release the captive, and proclaim the arrival of deliverance. The **kingdom** is not merely imminent; it has, in some sense, already arrived. That the kingdom is good news for the poor, for the depressed and deprived, is an emphasis that recurs elsewhere in the Gospel (e.g., 1:52–55; 6:20–21, 24–25; 14:13, 21). It is characteristic of Luke's Jesus.

The reception accorded Jesus by the people of Nazareth is indeed startling. They at first accept him as the one who brings salvation (vs. 22). In Luke's source (Mark 6:1–6), the people immediately took offense at Jesus' claim to authority. In Luke, "Is not this Joseph's son?" (vs. 22), seems at first to proceed rather from surprise than anger (cf. Mark 6:3). Nevertheless, in Luke, too, Jesus is eventually rejected, not because he claims authority but because he extends salvation to the wrong people, to outsiders.

Clearly, Jesus thinks he will be expected to perform **miracles** as he has in Capernaum (vs. 23; although Luke has not yet reported any of Jesus' miracles). Jesus rejects any such request, declares that a prophet is not acceptable in his own country, and then speaks of the miracles in the Old Testament that the prophets Elijah and Elisha performed—not for the people of Israel, but for foreigners. Immediately, the audience's anger is aroused. Jesus' proclamation extends deliverance beyond Israel to the **Gentiles**. They drive him out of the city and intend to kill him, but he escapes (vss. 29 f.). We might now expect Jesus to leave Palestine to preach to Gentiles, but Luke, like the other canonical Gospels, reports no major mission outside Israel. For Luke the matter is resolved: Jesus' saying finds fulfillment in the **church**'s mission; Acts makes clear that the Gentiles hear the word (Acts 11:18; 13:46; 22:21; 28:28).

The incidents that follow this opening scene further reveal Luke's program. What Jesus has done in Nazareth, he now proceeds to do in Capernaum (4:31 ff.). He refused to perform a miracle at Nazareth, but in this synagogue and on this Sabbath, he heals. Jesus heals now because he is on his way toward his goal. When the people try to hold him, he says, "I must preach the good news of the kingdom of God to the other cities also; for I was sent for this purpose" (4:43). Precisely because this preaching to other cities cannot be done by Jesus alone, the necessary conclusion of the opening Nazareth scene is the calling of disciples. When Jesus' ministry has concluded, these disciples will be the instruments for spreading the message beyond Israel to the cities of the Gentiles.

A comparison between the calling of disciples in Luke (5:1–11) and in Mark (1:16–20) shows that the stories are quite different. Luke alone includes a miracle, that of the great catch of fish. Stress is laid, however, upon the consequence of the miracle, Simon Peter's confession of **sin**: "Depart from me, for I am a sinful man, O Lord" (vs. 8). After this repentance, Simon Peter and those with him become fishers of men or true disciples. But the **Pharisees** and their **scribes** upbraid them for eating with "tax collectors and sinners" (5:30). Jesus defends his disciples' conduct, however: "I have not come

The ruin of the synagogue of Capernaum, probably built in the fourth century, stands on the same site as the one visited by Jesus according to the Gospels (cf. Luke 4:31-37).

to call the righteous, but sinners to repentance" (5:32). The opposition to Jesus and his purpose is here graphically portrayed.

Another example of Luke's repentance motif is the story of the woman "who was a sinner" (7:36–50). Although this story has some affinities with Mark (14:3–9; cf. John 12:1–8), its present form has a distinctly Lukan cast. In Luke, the sinful woman who shows great love to Jesus serves as the occasion for a **parable** of Jesus that stresses that someone who has been forgiven more then loves more (7:41-43). Yet the actual incident first mentions the woman's love, then Jesus' forgiveness (cf. 7:47 f.). That her love is an expression of repentance is clear from the story: she is a sinner, she weeps, she kisses the feet of Jesus. Her repentance and love and Jesus' forgiveness contrast with the moralism of Simon the Pharisee, their perplexed host.

Jesus' presence elicits two kinds of response, either rejection by those who cling to a narrow view of **righteousness** or repentance by those who accept his promise of **salvation**. Those who repent become witnessing disciples to the forgiveness that Jesus brings.

Sure Witness to the Word (8:1–21)

In what sense is the parable of the sower really about the work of the church?

In the introduction of this passage, a number of witnesses are gathered around Jesus: the Twelve and the women who not only follow Jesus but also support him from their own financial resources (8:1–3). At its close, the mother and brothers of Jesus who come to see him are told, "My mother and my brothers are those who hear the word of God and do it" (8:21). This sequence is designed by Luke to demonstrate that true disciples not only hear Jesus' word but also go out to become preachers of this **word** (8:15; cf. 1:2; Acts 6:1–7).

In comparing this section with its parallels in Mark (4:1–34; 3:31–35), a major difference becomes evident: Luke shifts the position of the discussion about the true mother and brothers of Jesus hearing God's word (8:19–21) so that it now follows, rather than precedes, the parable of the sower. The change reflects Luke's concentration upon the theme of the word of God. For example, in Luke's interpretation of the parable of the sower, Jesus says more directly than in Mark, "Now the parable is this: The seed is the word of God" (8:11; cf. Mark 4:13 f.). Mark says only that the sower sows the word.

Luke's version of the sower parable (8:4–8) unfolds much as in Mark (4:1–9) except that Mark emphasizes response to Jesus' teaching in parables, whereas Luke stresses response to Jesus' message of the word of God. By a series of slight changes Luke transforms the passage into an exhortation for careful and sure **witness** to the word of the **gospel**. Such clauses as "the seed is the word of God" (8:11; cf. Mark 4:13), "then the devil comes and takes away the word from their hearts that they may not believe and be saved" (8:12b; cf. Mark 4:15), and "they are those who, hearing the word, hold it fast in an honest and good heart, and bring forth fruit with patience" (8:15; cf. Mark 4:20) show Luke's intention to emphasize the importance of hearing and holding to the word of God. By slight alterations Luke makes his point. By the same token, the saying about not hiding the lamp (8:16) refers in Luke to those who hear the word and patiently bring forth fruitful witness (8:15; cf. Mark 4:20). Gathering sure disciples in Galilee assures the faithful continuation of the word of God in the witness of the church.

The next episodes in Luke, basically following the order of Mark, are a series of miracles: the miracle of calming the waves (8:22–25), the driving out of the demons at Gerasa (8:26–39), the healing of the woman with the flow of blood (8:43–48), and the raising of the dead daughter (8:40–42, 49–56). This series culminates when Jesus "called the twelve together and gave them power and authority over all demons and to cure diseases, and he sent them out to proclaim the kingdom of God and to heal" (9:1–2). The witnesses are gathered and convinced; even Herod begins to wonder (9:7–9). The crowds are filled, for after the feeding of the five thousand "twelve baskets of broken pieces" are left over (9:10–17). Only then are the disciples asked to affirm that Jesus is the **Christ** of God (9:18–20).

The conclusion of the first part of Luke, "the gathering of witnesses in Galilee," begins a discussion of Jesus' identity, especially the necessity of his suffering (9:21–27, 43b–45). At the close of this first major section, instead of Mark's "whoever is not against *us* is for *us*" (Mark 9:40), Luke's Jesus says, "whoever is not against *you* is for *you*" (9:50). These are clearly instructions for the early church. Luke anticipates the separation of Jesus from his disciples in the post-**resurrection** period after Jesus has **ascended** into heaven (cf. Acts 1:9–11).

WITNESS TO THE WORD ON THE JOURNEY TO JERUSALEM (9:51–19:27)

The Galilean witnesses gathered by Jesus must journey with him to Jerusalem. Luke's second major section, which narrates that journey, seems much longer than the short distance (about sixty miles) and the brief time (about three days) that it would take to travel by foot from Galilee to Jerusalem. Although Jesus is on the way to Jerusalem all this time, he seems to make little physical progress (9:51; 10:1, 38; 13:22, 33; 17:11; 19:11).

Luke's reason for such an extensive account of the journey is not simply an interest in geographical matters, for it is difficult to answer questions about Jesus' itinerary from Galilee to Jerusalem on the basis of information in the text. For instance, despite Luke's interest in Samaritans (10:29–37), we are left uncertain how Jesus went through Samaria, which lies on the most direct route from Galilee to Jerusalem (cf. 9:52–53; 17:11). As the journey progresses Luke does make clear, however, that certain people are present with Jesus throughout the trip. Continuity in **witness** to the work and **word** of Jesus is thereby assured (cf. 23:49).

The opening verse is a key to this section: "When the days drew near for him to be taken up, he set his face to go to Jerusalem" (9:51; only in Luke). Jesus goes to Jerusalem because "today, tomorrow, and the next day I must be on my way; because it is impossible for a prophet to be killed outside of Jerusalem" (13:33; only in Luke). As **prophet** to Israel, Jesus goes to die at Jerusalem, the capital of Israel. The journey turns out to consist largely of instruction in the purpose and meaning of Jesus' mission and death.

A comparison of the structure of Luke's **Gospel** with that of the Acts of the Apostles reveals a striking similarity that helps to illuminate the reason for the journey. In Acts:

- First, the **Spirit**'s appearance and the gathering of witnesses in Jerusalem
- Second, journeys of missionaries, especially Paul
- Third, Paul's arrest and trial ending in Rome

In Luke the order is similar:

- First, gathering of witnesses in Galilee
- Second, the journey to Jerusalem accompanied by preaching the word
- Third, Jesus' arrest, trial, **crucifixion**, and **resurrection** in Jerusalem

Luke–Acts shows a continuity of witness stretching from Galilee to Rome. Luke's journey motif emphasizes an orderly, gradual spread of the new faith.

Throughout this section Luke stresses the theme of witness, in two senses: (1) a witness *observes* something; (2) a witness *testifies* to something. These senses correspond to his distinction between "eyewitnesses and ministers of the word" (1:2). The first two episodes (9:51–56 and 9:57–62; mainly special Lukan material) indicate the necessity of following Jesus closely—that is, of *observing*. The mission of the seventy (10:1–17) implies that the Twelve remained with Jesus even during the sending out of the seventy (10:1; note "others"); moreover, the disciples are singled out: "Then turning to the disciples Jesus said privately, 'Blessed are the eyes that see what you see!'" (10:23; cf. Matt. 13:16). Other passages point out that disciples are always with Jesus so that his journey has been faithfully observed (11:1; 12:1, 22, 41; 16:1; 17:1, 5, 22; 19:28–40). By and large, these passages belong to the editorial work of Luke. By the end of this section the emphasis includes not only faithful observation but also faithful testifying to what has been observed (19:11–27).

This entire section (9:51–19:27) is a depiction of Jesus' telling the disciples about the word of God. They learn that women matter (10:38–42). Luke's interest in women's relationships with Jesus doubtless reflects Jesus' own practice, as well as that of the earliest **church**. Prayer is also a vital part of Jesus' life and that of those with him (11:1 ff.). The **kingdom of God** becomes present whenever Jesus casts out demons (11:20). Physical closeness to Jesus guarantees nothing by itself; the blessed are "those who hear the word of God and obey it" (11:27 f.). True disciples cannot be satisfied with the old rules of piety (11:37–12:3). Riches are clearly a barrier to hearing the word that Jesus proclaims (12:13–34; cf. 14:33; 16:11, 14, 19–31; 18:22–30; 19:1–10). Watchfulness and faithfulness are demanded over a long period of time (12:41–49), though repentance is necessary now (13:1–9). Jesus' ministry must continue for a considerable time (13:10–35); furthermore, the world's end is not in sight (17:20 ff.). The **messianic** banquet with Jesus will include great multitudes, the unexpected (14:13), the **Gentiles** (14:23; cf. 17:18 and 10:33); but not all will enter (14:25–35). The dynamic of *repentance* and *forgiveness* is elaborated in sayings found only in Luke: Jesus' word from the cross (23:34, omitted in some ancient **manuscripts** though nevertheless true to the Lukan spirit), his promise to the criminal on the cross (23:39–43), and his charge to **resurrection** witnesses (24:47). The following, special Lukan material from the journey gives the heart of Jesus' instructions, especially concerning repentance and forgiveness.

Jesus' Word about the Present (15:1–32)

What is the common theme of these three parables?

After Jesus says "Let anyone with ears to hear listen!" (14:35), we learn that "all the tax collectors and sinners were coming near to listen to him" (15:1). Into the heart of the journey section, Luke inserts three parables, of which only the parable of the lost sheep is found in any other Gospel (Matt. 18:12–14). These parables clarify and extend Jesus' **word**, which the disciples are to transmit to others. The **Pharisees** and the **scribes** have been irritated by Jesus' association with **sinners** (vs. 2). In contrast, the parables emphasize joy and openness to all (cf. 15:7, 10, 32), a prominent motif within Luke (cf. 1:14, 44; 2:10; 6:23).

The first two parables pose an interesting problem of interpretation, for the general conclusion of each speaks of a sinner's repenting (15:7, 10), yet such repentance is hardly exemplified in the parables themselves. A lost sheep or a lost coin does not repent. The usual explanation is that the general conclusions anticipate and more properly belong to the third parable, that of the prodigal son. Moreover, this last parable contains the key passage concerning repentance, for the prodigal son repented: "when he came to himself" (15:17).

An opposite conclusion could, however, be drawn: Luke's very purpose in using the two introductory parables was to *prevent* an incorrect reading of the parable of the prodigal son in terms that make repentance primary. The first two parables unmistakably emphasize the initiative of the one who seeks out the lost. Whether this is Jesus or God is not crucial—probably both are intended—for the decisive announcement is that **salvation** is present (see 4:21; 10:9, 11; 11:20; 17:20; 18:30; 19:9; 23:43). Luke is addressing the charge made against Jesus that he eats with sinners (vs. 2). Jesus claims that it is precisely the avowed sinner who recognizes what is happening and, unlike the Pharisees and scribes, receives God's forgiveness.

A more appropriate title for the familiar parable of the prodigal son might be the parable of the prodigal *father*. The parable runs smoothly and understandably through the son's realization that he would be better off as one of his father's hired servants (vss. 17 f.), at which point he returns home, confessing himself a sinner. The story's surprise lies in the way the father receives him. Instead of greeting him self-righteously ("I told you so") with a demand that he demonstrate his repentance, the father runs out—scandalously, for an oriental **patriarch**—to embrace him, giving orders to bring the best robe, the ring, shoes, and the fatted calf. He will have a feast for his son. There is joy and merriment for one who was lost and is now found (vs. 24).

To prevent our missing the point, the elder son is then introduced (vs. 25). He is angry: he cannot understand his father's joyful reception, much as the Pharisees and scribes cannot understand Jesus' association with sinners. But the father exclaims, "Son, you are always with me, and all that is mine is yours. It was fitting to make merry and be glad, for this your brother was dead, and is alive; he was lost, and is found" (vs. 32). The elder brother fails to recognize the joy and salvation that is already present. Thus *he* now needs to repent and accept the good news of God's forgiveness (15:7, 10, 25–32). Only then is God's word truly heard.

These same themes of forgiveness and repentance recur in the remaining portions of Jesus' journey. The rich man tries too late to repent (16:19 ff.), and the once poor Lazarus cannot help him. Unexpectedly, some do repent because the **kingdom** is in their midst (17:11–21). The one who hears Jesus' word keeps knocking at the door (18:1 ff.), admitting that he is a sinner in need of God's mercy (18:9 ff.). Things turn out unhappily for those who are self-satisfied (18:18–23), yet whoever calls on the mercy of Jesus will receive sight (18:35-43). Even a rich chief tax collector will be saved if he sees himself as a sinner (19:1-10). The word Jesus proclaims during this journey effects salvation. Those who are close to him will testify to what they have heard and seen: "Today salvation has come to this house, because he too is a son of Abraham" (19:9).

At times, Luke seems to be saying that already salvation has fully arrived. But he knows there is more to come; the history of the church will be unfolded by those acting under God's **Spirit**. Although Jesus' final days in Jerusalem are coming, Luke does not think that nothing else remains to be done. Hence he closes this journey section with the parable of the pounds.

Jesus' Word about the Future (19:11–27)

In what sense does the nobleman of this parable represent Jesus?

In Jesus, salvation is present (10:18; 11:20; 17:20). But how does the presence of salvation in him relate to the coming **kingdom of God**? The opening of the parable of the pounds does not suggest the expectation of an imminent kingdom (19:11; cf. 21:8; Acts 1:6 ff.). Seemingly, present salvation and future kingdom are distinguished in the thought of Luke: the kingdom is still coming, but at an undisclosed time in the future.

In this parable the nobleman goes into a *far country* to receive kingly power, a hint that in Luke's eschatology the king will return again only after a long journey. Before leaving, he gives ten pounds to ten slaves, one pound each, with explicit instructions to trade with the money. (The pound was a fairly large sum, about three-months' wages for a day laborer.) The citizens of his country do not want him to be their king; they resist by sending an embassy after him, to oppose him. The parable is relatively complex (cf. the much simpler parallel in Matt. 25:14–30), for the unhappy citizens appear only at the beginning and the end of the parable and the relation between citizens and slaves is unclear. The parable's point at first seems to be that, when he returns, the king condemns the slave who in fear of him as a severe judge, had simply stowed the gift away. But concentration upon the future severity misses the point. Although the king does deal severely with this slave and with his enemies at the end (vs. 27), the one who waits and makes use of the gift of salvation—that is, who continues his **witness** to a forgiving God—over a long period of time need not fear.

Throughout this section Jesus' word brings forgiveness for whoever will receive it: sinners, those in the highways and hedges, a prodigal son, or foreigners. But if they do not see and testify to this **word**, judgment will surely come. A joyful present and a threatening future have been proclaimed as they journeyed to Jerusalem. Now Luke brings Jesus into the city where he must die and be **resurrected**.

THE TRUE ISRAEL THROUGH THE PASSION AND RESURRECTION (19:28–24:53)

In Luke's third and final section, two distinctive motifs emerge: first, Jesus' triumph in the temple; second, Jesus' innocence. The temple motif is not new in Luke (see the introductory section, esp. 2:41-52). Now, however, he reiterates his emphasis more insistently. Jesus is teaching daily in the temple (19:47; 20:1; 21:37 ff.; 22:53); even after his **resurrection** the disciples return to the temple to bless God continually (24:53). Moreover, the **apocalyptic** discourse takes place in the temple rather than on the Mount of Olives, as in Mark and Matthew (21:5–28; cf. Mark 13:1 ff. and Matt. 24:1 ff.). In Luke, Jesus does not budge from the temple. Why does Luke so emphasize Jesus' frequenting the temple?

In the Acts of the Apostles, the earliest **church** is also centered in the temple (Acts 2:46; 3:1 ff.; 5:20). Apparently, Jesus establishes himself in the temple in order that the early church may also operate from this base. Luke thereby also shows that the new faith

The Golden Gate of the Jerusalem temple, here seen from Garden of Gethsemane, is, according to Christian tradition, the site of Jesus' entry into Jerusalem, recorded in all the Gospels (cf. Luke 19:28-40).

in Jesus represents the true Israel and is the authentic extension and continuation of Israel's dominant religious institution. (The temple had probably been laid waste at least a decade before Luke wrote.) The evangelist thus assures both Jewish and **Gentile** believers of the antiquity and continuity of the new faith. The disciples, who return to the temple immediately after the resurrection appearances to bless God and to await the power of the **Spirit** (24:53), are neither fanatics expecting the end of the world nor political revolutionaries against the Roman Empire. This latter emphasis becomes more explicit in Acts, but is present already in the Gospel.

The second major motif of this **passion** and resurrection section, the trial and death of the *innocent* Jesus, fits this view. Special Lukan details illustrate his emphasis on Jesus' innocence. Only in Luke does Herod Antipas interrogate Jesus and find no substance to the charges against him (23:6-16). At Jesus' trial before Pilate, the elders of the people accuse Jesus of having forbidden the giving of tribute to Caesar (23:1–5; cf. Mark 15:1–5), but an earlier debate established the falsity of this charge (20:20–26). In Mark, Pilate, the Roman **procurator**, finds Jesus not guilty on one occasion (15:14); in Luke this verdict of innocence occurs three times (cf. 23:4, 14–16, 22). Furthermore, in Luke the centurion at the cross says, "Certainly, this man was innocent" (23:47), whereas in Mark he says, "Truly this man was the **Son of God**" (15:39; cf. Matt. 27:54). The subtle way in which Luke opposes Jesus to Barabbas suggests that Jesus was not an insurrectionist like Barabbas (cf. Luke 23:19, 25 with Mark 15:7). Jesus' climactic word from the cross establishes his innocence: "Father, forgive them; for they do not know what they are doing" (23:34; in many, though not all **manuscripts** of Luke). Luke further underlines Jesus' innocence as one of the thieves from the cross says, "We are getting what we deserve for our deeds, but this man has done nothing wrong" (23:41; only in Luke). This major theme receives further, unqualified substantiation in Acts: "This man . . . you crucified and killed by the hands of those outside the law" (Acts 2:23; cf. 8:32 ff. and 17:30).

The innocent Jesus is falsely accused, tried, and executed. Instead of concentrating upon the guilt of those responsible for this miscarriage of justice, Luke focuses upon Jesus' triumph even under adversity. At the cross, Jesus' general word of forgiveness (23:34) and his forgiveness of the repentant thief (23:39–43) show that guilt need not be overwhelming. Moreover, this Lukan passion story is the working out of God's plan for the true Israel. ("This Jesus, delivered up according to the definite plan and foreknowledge of God": Acts 2:23; cf. 3:18; Luke 22:22.) Jesus dies a martyr's death, prefiguring the martyrdom of others in the early church, especially Stephen and James (cf. Acts 7:54–8:3; 9:1; 12:1 ff.). But through all these events God's word of "repentance and forgiveness of sins" is being preached to all nations (24:47). God's plan is thus fulfilled.

The True Inheritors (20:9–19)

Who are the inheritors to whom the vineyard will be given?

In focusing intently upon the passion events up to and including Jesus' death and **resurrection**, Luke is obviously in company with the other Synoptic Gospels. In the **parable** of the wicked tenants, Luke shows his understanding of the reason for Jesus' death and resurrection.

In the preceding passage (19:47–20:8), the chief **priests** and the **scribes** have challenged Jesus' authority for teaching daily in the temple. Comparing the parable's opening with its Markan source (Luke 20:9; cf. Mark 12:1; Matt. 21:33), we are struck by Luke's distinction between the people *to* whom this parable is spoken and the chief priests and the scribes *against* whom it is spoken (cf. 20:19). In Mark's version (12:1–12), the parable is clearly a polemic against the chief priests, scribes, and elders, because they have rejected God's servants, the **prophets** and even the "beloved son" (Mark 12:6). The identity of the Markan "others" who will receive the vineyard is indefinite, though the reader may surmise that they are the **Gentiles** (Mark 13:10; cf. Matt. 21:43).

In Luke, however, this parable is addressed not to Jesus' opponents but to the people (vs. 9), "spellbound by what they heard" (19:48). Moreover, the people strongly protest the destruction of the former tenants and the giving of the vineyard to others: "When they heard this, they said, 'Heaven forbid!'" (20:16b; only in Luke). This protest serves, however, to allow Jesus to restate his conclusion (vss. 17 f.) and to imply that the people finally accept Jesus' word, for the leaders acknowledge that the people are on Jesus' side (vs. 19) while they themselves are not.

Throughout this section Luke consistently portrays the people as being sympathetic to Jesus. They are the ones who praise God (18:43); they listen in the temple (19:48; 21:38); they observe Jesus' defeat of the authorities (20:26). They stand by watching at the **crucifixion**; it is the rulers who scoff (23:35). Within biblical and Jewish tradition, reference to "the people" carries with it the connotation of God's chosen people, the peo-

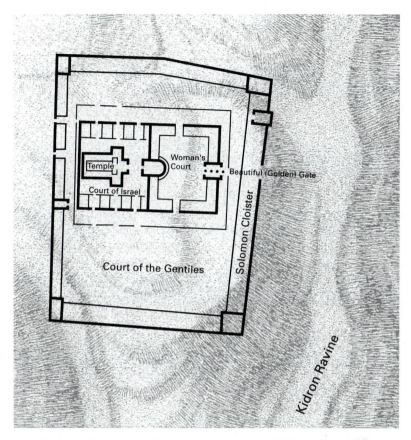

The Temple and Its Precincts. The Garden of Gethsemane lies across the Kidron Valley, at the foot of the Mount of Olives.

ple of Israel (cf. Luke 1:68; 2:32). Consequently, the alignment of the people with Jesus implies that Jesus' word is finally accepted by Israel.

In the Book of Acts, Luke clarifies the identity of the "others" (Luke 20:16). They are the true inheritors, for they are the "Israelites" and the Gentiles who hear the preaching (Acts 2:22; 3:12; 13:16, 46–48). The last speech of Paul, at the conclusion of Acts, implies that the Gentiles have become the true people of God, because the old Israel has rejected the preaching (28:26–28). Yet Luke clearly shows by this parable that the people are on Jesus' side, so that "others," the inheritors, include both Jews and Gentiles. In Luke, a parable concerning the rejection of Jesus becomes also a parable stressing the true inheritors—those who *hear*.

Luke nonetheless emphasizes rejection in this parable, and in his own special way. Omitting the last lines of Mark's quotation (12:10; cf. Psalm 118:22) and adding an allusion to Isaiah (8:14–15), Luke underscores the judgment that occurs for those who do not truly understand or interpret the scripture. They cannot tell the true Israel from the false. This necessity for rightly interpreting the scripture is the subject of our final Lukan passage.

Fulfilling the Scripture (24:13–35)

Why is the risen Jesus not recognized immediately?

Before turning to the climactic "Emmaus-road" story, we need to observe the way in which Luke prepares for this scene. Throughout the passion, especially after the parable of the wicked tenants, two themes mutually reinforce each other: (1) these events necessarily happened; (2) they were closely and surely **witnessed**.

Definite things must happen before the end can come (Luke 21:12) to fulfill scripture (21:22; 22:37; 24:25–27, 32). These things are done at the bidding of God, who alone is in command of the situation (21:18, a Lukan addition picking up 12:7). God's direction of events is implicitly claimed by the assurance that these things happen to fulfill scripture: "Was it not necessary that the **Messiah** should suffer these things and then enter into his glory?" (24:26; cf. 22:15 f.).

Not only must these things happen, but they also have to be observed by the disciples, that is, the **apostles**. For after Jesus is gone, they will have opportunity to bear testimony (21:13; 24:48; cf. Mark 13:10). To ensure this witness, the apostles and women of Galilee are Jesus' constant companions. For Luke it is especially important for the apostles to be with Jesus (22:14; cf. Mark 14:17). We learn in Acts that an apostle is one who "beginning from the baptism of John until the day when he was taken up from us" was constantly with Jesus (Acts 1:21–26). The apostles continue with Jesus in his trials (22:28); they follow Jesus to the Mount of Olives (22:39; cf. Mark 14:26), and even when they fall asleep it is "for sorrow" (22:45; cf. Mark 14:37). Luke omits Mark's statement, "And they all forsook him and fled" (14:50). At the **crucifixion**, "all his acquaintances and the women who had followed him from Galilee stood at a distance and saw these things" (23:49; cf. Mark 15:40 f.). Luke insists that ministers of the **word** based their testimony on eyewitness reports. They observed in order that the truth about these things might be known (see Luke 1:1–4).

Witness and Eyewitness

Along with the **Gospel** and **Epistles** of John, Luke emphasizes the importance of **witness** or testimony to Jesus that is based on eyewitnesses and eyewitness accounts. Luke (1:2) traces the testimony of his own Gospel back to those who were eyewitnesses (*autoptai*), a term that appears nowhere else in the New Testament. For Luke, eyewitnesses were qualified to be **apostles**, those having accompanied Jesus during his ministry (Acts 1:21-25).

John's programmatic statement that the **word** became flesh is followed by a claim to have seen his glory (1:14). Whether this is tantamount to an eyewitness claim has been debated, but it is apparently interpreted as such in 1 John 1:1, with reference not only to seeing but also to hearing and even touching. At the end of the Gospel, the truth of the Beloved Disciple's testimony is attested (21:24); earlier this same figure's witness is based on what he saw (19:35). While Luke traces his own testimony back to an earlier eyewitness, such a witness seems to be a more direct source of the Gospel of John.

The story of the empty tomb, which precedes the story of the Emmaus road, bears out these preliminary observations (24:1–12; cf. Mark 16:1–8). Two men greet the women instead of a single young man (cf. Mark 16:5). This twofold witness guarantees authenticity (see p. 128). Subtly, Luke also modifies what had been a prediction of Jesus' future appearances in Galilee into a statement about what Jesus said while he was in Galilee (24:6; cf. Mark 16:7). This change brings his text into harmony with the evangelist's view that the **resurrection** appearances took place in Jerusalem (cf. Matt. 28:16). Luke's Gospel shows a clear, straightforward development: beginning in Galilee, extending to Jerusalem, and from there to the rest of the world (24:47). Moreover, Luke's story of the empty tomb points ahead to Jesus' confirmatory appearances to the disciples, for when the apostles first hear the report from the women, "these words seemed to them an idle tale, and they did not believe them" (24:11). Luke's stress upon both continuity and certainty required more than an account by fearful women. (Luke 24:12, if authentic, and 24 report a visit to the tomb by apostles that nevertheless proves inconclusive, as does the visit reported in John 20:2-10.) Full recognition of the resurrected Jesus occurs only when his followers meet him on the road to Emmaus (24:13 ff.). That this meeting takes place "on the road" is in keeping with Luke's journey motif. Furthermore, we hear twice in this episode about "the things that have happened" (24:14, 18); indeed, testing them, Jesus asks, "What things?" (24:19). These lines recall the Gospel's introduction, for this was to be a narrative about "the things which have been accomplished among us" (1:1; cf. 1:4).

The puzzle of this story is the men's initial nonrecognition of Jesus. Perhaps they were kept from recognizing him because God willed it thus (vs. 16). Yet why should God want to keep them from recognizing Jesus? Probably they failed to recognize him because of their preoccupation with the tragic events of preceding days (vss. 19–21). Jesus proceeds to interpret the scriptures to show that the **Christ** indeed had to suffer to enter into his glory (vss. 26 f.). Jesus' role in God's plan was that of a suffering servant (see 22:37; Isa. 53:12). Even this disclosure, however, does not enable them to recognize Jesus—though later they recall, "Were not our hearts burning within us while he was talking to us on the road, while he was opening the scriptures to us?" (vs. 32).

The crucial moment of recognition comes only during the meal: "Their eyes were opened, and they recognized him; and he vanished from their sight" (vs. 31). Later their report confirms that the decisive act was "the breaking of the bread" (vs. 35). There are at least two immediate possibilities for understanding the significance of the "breaking of the bread." (1) Jesus performed a familiar act that they had often observed; therefore, they recognized him. (2) The "breaking of the bread" was a **sacramental** communal act of worship in the early **church** (Acts 2:42, 46), and Luke thereby implies that the believer knows the resurrected Jesus primarily in the **Lord's Supper**. Neither view is wholly satisfying, for neither is explicit in the text.

A different interpretation takes its cue from the act of *eating*. In the following story (24:36–43), even though Jesus appears directly to the disciples and tells them to look at his hands and feet, they still "disbelieved for joy" (vs. 41). Only after he has eaten does he pronounce his farewell address (vss. 44–49). Again, eating seems to be crucial for full recognition. During the Last Supper with the apostles (22:14–19), Jesus said, "I have earnestly desired to eat this **Passover** with you before I suffer; for I tell you I shall not eat it until it is fulfilled in the kingdom of God" (vss. 15 f.; only in Luke). Evidently, Jesus would not eat until suffering was accomplished. That he now eats with the disciples implies that his suffering has been completed and he is now raised to glory. Therefore, in Luke, scripture's interpretation emphasizes the necessity for suffering (24:26 f.), and Jesus' eating with his disciples (24:30, 35, 42 f.) emphasizes that the suffering is accomplished, the glory of Jesus begun. Now they can recognize him. With that sure foundation, the church can now receive its charge from the risen Christ.

Jesus' final words to the disciples suggest the plausibility of this interpretation (24:44–49). Israel's redemption is effected by Jesus' suffering, which fulfills scripture (vss. 45 f.). Repentance and forgiveness of **sins** are to be preached, beginning from Jerusalem and extending to all the world (vs. 47). The **witnesses** who have observed and who will now testify await only the coming of the **Spirit** (vss. 48 f.; Acts 1:8). Because Jesus' word and deed are now accomplished and because his followers can perpetuate the witness, the new Israel returns to the temple with joy and with Jesus' blessing (24:50–53).

CONCLUSION

Of all the **Gospel** writers, Luke is the most interested in preserving the truth about the life of Jesus. But for him, as for most historians in the first century, truth is not simply equated with historical data. The purpose of Luke's Gospel, like that of Mark and Matthew, is religious proclamation and reflection, not simply historical reporting. Luke wrote so that careful observation and a comprehensive and true outlook would be available to the **church** of his day.

Luke's *structure* is distinctive. Only Luke follows his Gospel about Jesus with a second volume on the early church. In itself this structure indicates Luke's interest not only in Jesus but also in the church he originated. A long-range perspective on the life of Jesus is also suggested by the preface, where Luke writes of three stages of the tradition: eyewitnesses, ministers of the word, and the writing of the Gospel.

In Luke's introduction Simeon, an Israelite who has long awaited **salvation**, is finally rewarded by Jesus' appearance to him in the temple. Toward the close of Luke's story, Jesus frequents the temple and, in effect, triumphs in Israel's central religious institution. After Jesus' death and **resurrection** the disciples return to the temple to wait for the **Spirit's** coming, which will empower their preaching of repentance and forgiveness to all people. Their testimony to Jesus' message is certain, because they have observed its beginning and end, from Galilee to Jerusalem.

This overall view of Luke is confirmed by the threefold division of the Gospel itself: gathering **witnesses** in Galilee (3:1–9:50), witness to the **word** on the journey to

Jerusalem (9:51–19:27), and the establishment of the true and renewed Israel through Jesus' **passion** and resurrection (19:28–24:53). These main divisions show how the old is incorporated into the new. Israel is on a journey through the Old Testament, culminating in the life of Jesus and moving into the early church.

Luke's repeated *emphases* support our proposed structure for the Gospel. These include (1) the new faith as the true Israel, (2) the history of salvation's expansion to include world history, and (3) the necessity for accurate, ongoing witness.

1. Luke affirms that the new religion is the true Israel. What happened to Jesus occurred according to God's word, known through scripture. Thus Jesus' first public act was to preach fulfillment of the **prophet** Isaiah in the synagogue at Nazareth (4:16 ff.). Moreover, in the resurrection appearances Jesus interpreted his suffering as a fulfillment of scripture (24:27, 44). These things are presented as sure because all were predicted and foretold. The witness of Jesus began and ended with correct interpretation of the scripture. A further emphasis supporting the theme of the true Israel is the centrality accorded the temple and Jerusalem. The Gospel opens with Zechariah in the Jerusalem temple; at the introduction's close, Jesus is also in Jerusalem and in the temple (2:41–52). The journey section of the Gospel presses toward Jerusalem: "he set his face to go to Jerusalem" (9:51; cf. 13:33). The passion narrative centers on Jesus' teaching in the temple (19:47 f.). In addition, the Gospel concludes with the disciples' return to the temple in Jerusalem (24:52 f.). This elaborate picture of Jesus in the temple and in Jerusalem implies that Jesus embodies the true Israel and that his followers are the authentic people of God.

The character of this New Israel as the nonsubversive, legitimate extension of the old receives confirmation in the elaborate detail showing Jesus' innocence of any wrongdoing. Jesus did not forbid the paying of tribute to Rome (20:19–26). Indeed, in the persons of both Pilate and the centurion, Rome proclaimed Jesus' innocence (23:4, 14 ff., 22, 47). And the repentant thief declared Jesus innocent of any wrongdoing (23:41). This theme of innocence is extended and enlarged in Acts, particularly in Luke's portrayal of Rome's favorable disposition to the new religious movement. Paul is declared thoroughly and completely innocent (Acts 25:25; 26:31 f.), even as Jesus was (Luke 23:47). Certainly any educated Roman reader would conclude that Christianity and Rome were not at cross-purposes.

2. Luke's second major emphasis is that the true Israel aims to embrace the whole world. For Luke, the world outside Israel is not an adversary, but a mission field: Luke–Acts progresses from Galilee to Jerusalem and on to Rome. Furthermore, Luke records traces of world history (2:1; 3:1; Acts 24:27) to keep this final goal in view. Involvement with the world occurs by God's acting in the Spirit through the person of Jesus (Luke) and through eyewitnesses and ministers of the word (Acts) to bring the **gospel** to all people (Luke 24:47 and Acts 2:38 f.). Luke's Christianity is universalistic: Simeon speaks about salvation "to the **Gentiles**" (2:32); Jesus' genealogy goes back to Adam (3:38); and in his opening sermon Jesus speaks favorably of Gentiles (4:24–29). Of course, the second volume shows the new religion's extension beyond the confines of Israel to the known world (Acts 10:1–11:18).

3. The final major Lukan emphasis is witness (1:2), consisting of accurate observation (eyewitnesses) and truthful testimony (ministers of the word). **Apostles**, disciples, and women accompanied Jesus throughout his ministry; they in turn became or were followed by preachers who declared Jesus' own themes of repentance and forgiveness (Luke 15; 24:47; Acts 2:38). Forgiveness begins with God's initiative, irrespective of human action; Jesus' actions embody this forgiveness in the present (7:48). Yet forgiveness elicits a human response of repentance. Whoever receives Gord's merciful forgiveness acts without anxiety for God's coming judgment (19:1–10). In Jesus salvation becomes available (4:21; cf. 23:43); therefore, the ministers and preachers of the early church testify to what God has done and continues to do in Jesus. As witnesses they preach good news (2:10; 3:18; 4:18; 7:22; 16:16) of forgiveness and repentance.

Luke's *redaction* of the tradition has been used as a key in the establishment of Luke's emphases. Luke's shaping of Mark—for example, in the parables of the sower (8:4–21) and the wicked tenants (20:9–18)—discloses his emphasis on the word of God (8:11) and the true Israel (20:9). Especially noteworthy are the special Lukan additions, already noted, which serve to emphasize Jesus' innocence and his proclivity to forgiveness.

There have been many attempts to identify precisely Luke's *historical situation*, none of which is conclusive. Our interpretation, instead of precisely locating the historical situation in which the Gospel was written, views it in the context of early Christianity generally. It was not designed primarily to convert the unbeliever but speaks principally to Christians and "almost" Christians, showing the continuity and certainty of the Christian faith. For Luke, the journey of Christian faith is made in joy and victory. The life and work of the church of Luke's time is authentic, in accordance with the scriptures, because the true Israel is emerging as the world is slowly and surely responding to the good news. The forgiving Jesus is presented as both fulfillment of the old and originator of the new. His witnesses have not been arbitrarily chosen. They were prepared for their task, and their present successes show the sweep and power of the new way.

Luke's Gospel has something of the romance about it. There are women as well as men, some of questionable repute; there are journeys and quests; there are successful adventures. At the Gospel's end the disciples are in the temple blessing God and waiting for the Spirit's coming with power for the mission. At the end of Acts of the Apostles, Paul is preaching in Rome and things will turn out well. Luke idealizes the story, no doubt, but he thereby testifies to the faith and history of Jesus and the early church. What was founded by Jesus, observed by the apostles, and proclaimed by them will continue without faltering until all have come into the **kingdom of God** and the fellowship of the Lord Jesus Christ "quite openly and unhindered" (Acts 28:31).

SUGGESTIONS FOR FURTHER READING

LUKE–ACTS AS A TWO-VOLUME WORK

M. P. Bonz, *The Past as Legacy: Luke–Acts and Ancient Epic* (Minneapolis: Fortress, 2000), considers classical antecedents of Lukan literature. A different approach, adopting modern strategies of reading, is R. C. Tannehill, *The Narrative Unity of Luke–Acts*, Volume One: *The Gospel According to Luke* (Philadelphia: Fortress, 1986), and Volume Two: *The Acts of the Apostles* (Minneapolis: Fortress, 1990). See also W. S. Kurz, *Reading Luke–Acts: Dynamics of Biblical Narrative* (Louisville: Westminster John Knox, 1993). Recent scholarship has revisited **Luke's portrayal of Israel**: thus, J. T. Squires, *The Plan of God in Luke–Acts* (Cambridge University Press, 1993), D. Ravens, *Luke and the Restoration of Israel* (Sheffield, England: Sheffield Academic Press, 1995), D. P. Moessner (ed.), *Luke and the Heritage of Israel: Luke's Narrative Claim upon Israel's Legacy* (Harrisburg, PA: Trinity Press International, 1999), and J. B. Tyson, *Luke, Judaism, and the Scholars: Critical Approaches to Luke–Acts* (Columbia: University of South Carolina Press, 1999). On **Luke's depiction of women**, see T. K. Seim, *The Double Message: Patterns of Gender in Luke–Acts* (Edinburgh: T & T Clark, 1994), I. R. Reiner, *Women in the Acts of the Apostles: A Feminist Liberation Perspective*, trans. L. M. Maloney (Minneapolis: Fortress, 1995), B. E. Reid, *Choosing the Better Part? Women in the Gospel of Luke* (Collegeville, MN: Liturgical, 1996), A.-J. Levine and M. Blickenstaff (eds.), *A Feminist Companion to Luke* (Sheffield: Sheffield Academic Press, 2002), and *idem*, *A Feminist Companion to the Acts of the Apostles* (London: T & T Clark, 2004). For investigation of **various theological issues**, L. E. Keck and J. L. Martyn, *Studies in Luke–Acts*, rev. ed. (Philadelphia: Fortress, 1980), and R. Maddox, *The Purpose of Luke–Acts* (Edinburgh: T & T Clark, 1982), remain important.

THE GOSPEL OF LUKE

Commentaries.   E. Schweizer, *The Good News According to Luke*, trans, D. E. Green (Atlanta: John Knox, 1984) is a very useful commentary, as are L. T. Johnson, *The Gospel of Luke* (Collegeville, MN: Liturgical, 1991), R. C. Tannehilll, *Luke* (Nashville: Abingdon, 1996), J. B. Green, *The Gospel of Luke* (Grand Rapids: Eerdmans, 1997), and C. H. Talbert, *Reading Luke: A Literary and Theological Commentary on the Third Gospel* (Macon, GA: Smyth & Helwys, 2002). The standard technical commentaries are J. A. Fitzmyer, *The Gospel According to Luke*, 2 vols. (Garden City, NY: Doubleday, 1981, 1985), and F. Bovon, *Luke 1: A Commentary on the Gospel of Luke* 1:1–9:50, trans. C. M. Thomas (Minneapolis: Fortress, 2002).

Other Studies.   The pioneering study of Lukan theology is H. Conzelmann, *The Theology of St. Luke*, trans. G. Buswell (London: Faber & Faber, 1960), whose verdict that Luke divides history into three periods, centered on Jesus, has been challenged and refined. A balanced assessment of Lukan belief is found in J. B. Green, *The Theology of the Gospel of Luke* (Cambridge: Cambridge University Press, 1995). P. F. Esler, *Community and Gospel in Luke–Acts: The Social and Political Motivations of Lucan Theology* (Cambridge: Cambridge University Press, 1987), inquires into the specific Christian community for which Luke–Acts was written. K. E. Bailey, *Poet & Peasant and Through Peasant Eyes: A Literary–Cultural Approach to the Parables in Luke*, combined edition (Grand Rapids: Eerdmans, 2000), attempts to recapture the Middle Eastern culture in which Luke's parables would have resonated.

See also Suggestions for Further Reading at the end of Chapter 7.

Christ in Glory, a tapestry adorning the apse of the Coventry Cathedral, England, designed by Graham Sutherland. It is 78 feet long, 38 feet wide, and weighs nearly a ton. *(Courtesy of Getty Images Inc.—Hutton Archive Photos.)*

CHAPTER 5

JOHN: THE GOSPEL OF JESUS' GLORY

Background of the Gospel of John

Like Luke (1:1–4), John contains a statement about its author (21:24). He is the disciple whom Jesus loved, who reclined at the Last Supper on Jesus' breast (21:20; cf. 12:23). He is described as a true witness: obviously an eyewitness of the events leading up to and including Jesus' death (19:25–27). This stands in contrast with Luke, who makes clear he was not one of the eyewitnesses, but was dependent on them.

Within a century of the Gospel's composition (ca. **A.D.** 175), ancient Christian authorities began to identify the author as John the disciple of the Lord, and presumably a son of Zebedee (cf. Mark 1:16–20). Yet this beloved disciple is never named in the Gospel itself, nor do the Sons of Zebedee appear until the concluding scene (21:2). According to later Christian writers, this John lived in the city of Ephesus until a ripe old age and there composed this Gospel. The Revelation to John, unlike the Gospel, identifies its author as John of Patmos (1:1, 9), but not as an **apostle** with such a close relationship to Jesus. Yet Patmos is off the coast of present-day Turkey, not far from where ancient Ephesus lay. The three letters of John are similar to the Gospel (but not to Revelation) in language, style, and theology (see pp. 411–415), but the author's name is never called. They presume a lively interchange among churches, but none is specifically named. Revelation, on the other hand, names seven cities in which there are churches (1:11), including Ephesus. One can well imagine that the Fourth Gospel was written in Ephesus. Yet the earliest letter to the church at Ephesus (by Ignatius of Antioch in the early second century) makes much of the Apostle Paul's importance, but does not mention John at all. The bottom line: much is said about the authorship of John in antiquity, but nothing is certain. By the end of the second century, however, it was widely agreed that the Gospel was written by the Apostle John, in Ephesus, toward the end of the first century. It was also thought to be the latest of the Gospels, intentionally written with the others in view.

This ancient view works well at the macro-level. John makes explicit what is implicit in the **Synoptics**, especially in the portrayal of Jesus, particularly his teaching. All the evangelists believed that Jesus was the **Christ**, the **Son of God** (Mark 1:1), but in John, Jesus teaches about himself and his role. He teaches **Christology**. This stands in some contrast with the others, especially Mark, where Jesus seems unwilling to talk about himself at all, but maintains the Messianic Secret.

At the micro-level this ancient view does not work nearly as well. Aspects of John's narrative simply contradict the Synoptics. In the latter, Jesus' ministry seems to last no more than one year. He goes up to Jerusalem at the only **Passover** mentioned in those Gospels, and there he dies. Otherwise, he is never in Jerusalem. In John, on the other hand, at least three annual Passovers occur (2:13; 6:4; 11:55); in each case Jesus goes up to Jerusalem, where he spends a great deal of time. There is another major difference in the chronology or calendar: in the Synoptic Gospels the Last Supper is the Passover meal (Mark 14:12–17 parr.). In John, however, Jesus dies before the Passover meal is eaten (18:28; 19:14). In either case John could be correct. In all the Gospels, Jesus' ministry begins with his encounter with John the Baptist. (In all the Gospels except John it is explicitly said that John **baptized** Jesus.) In John's Gospel, however, Jesus' superiority over John is emphasized even more than in the others (1:15, 30; 1:20–28; 3:28–30). Yet only in John is Jesus himself said to have baptized (3:22, 26; 4:1). Does the Fourth Gospel emphasize Jesus' superiority all the more because it was known in some circles that Jesus himself had baptized—that at one time he was a disciple and follower of the Baptist?

If John the evangelist knew the other Gospels, he evidently chose to go his own way, independently of them. If he knew Mark or the others, he knew them as Gospels on the same level as his own, not as **holy** scripture. John obviously did not use Mark in the way Matthew or Luke did, appropriating large parts of it.

If not Mark or the Synoptics, what sources did John use? There is, of course, the eye-witness claim (21:24; cf. 19:35), which, though it cannot be taken at face value, should not be dismissed outright. At the same time, the state of the present, **canonical** text seems to reflect a process of literary growth. Chapter 21 is obviously a later addition, one that speaks to issues raised by the basic Gospel (chaps. 1-20), which were apparently discussed by the community of Jesus' followers who produced it (cf. 21:23–24). If chapters 15-17 were simply missing, the connection between the apparent ending of the conversation in 14:31 and the exit of Jesus and his disciples in 18:1 would be entirely smooth. As things now stand, it is not; chapters 15–17 intervene. Chapter 6 finds Jesus in Galilee, whereas just before he has been in Jerusalem. Did John's Gospel grow in stages? Was there ever an earlier version? One can see the Synoptic Gospels grow from Mark to Matthew, or to Luke. Is such growth hidden within John? This is a widely held and plausible point of view. The Fourth Gospel reflects the existence of a circle of Christians—that is, **churches**—in which the story of Jesus had evidently been known and cherished. This is true of the Letters of John, and perhaps also of Revelation, which, although distinctive and different, has points of contact with the other Johannine literature. Yet a consensus on the existence of such an earlier version of the Gospel and process of its development is much broader than any agreement on its exact character and extent.

The characterization of the opponents of Jesus as "the Pharisees" or simply "the Jews" is unique to this Gospel. **Pharisees** appear in the other Gospels, but along with **Sadducees**, **scribes**, Herodians, and others. In particular, the impression that "the Jews" are singled out as opponents of Jesus has had dire implications for Jewish–Christian relations through the centuries. Yet the Gospel shows an awareness that Jesus was a Jew (4:9), as were his disciples and John the Bapist, who came baptizing in order that Jesus be revealed to Israel (1:31). If "the Jews" is often a negative term, "Israel" is always used positively. Such language and division reflects a time after Jesus himself, who shows no awareness of the division between himself and his followers and "the Jews" as opponents. Does John represents a breakaway Jewish sect? If so, it would be similar to the **Essenes** who produced the **Dead Sea Scrolls**. In fact, the **theological** vocabulary of **Qumran**, as found in their *Community Rule* (cols. 3 and 4) is quite similar to John's: world, spirit, truth and falsehood, light and darkness.

Jesus' potential followers hesitate to commit themselves to him for fear they will be expelled from synagogues (9:22; 12:42; cf. 16:2). Such a threatening situation did not exist during Jesus' lifetime. More likely it existed during the period after the disastrous Jewish–Roman war (A.D. 66-70). At that time Jerusalem and the temple were sacked and burned, and all vestiges of self-government suppressed. In the period immediately following, in which Judaism retrenched and reformed, the Pharisees and their allies became the dominant party. Perhaps followers of Jesus, who did not share their fellows' dedication to the **law**, and who now also included **Gentiles**, would have become suspect.

The Gospel of John has left many tracks and traces of its origin, as many or more than any other Gospel. Yet the trail fades as we draw near to the Gospel itself. It was apparently well known to the author of the Johannine **Epistles**, who echoes its language but nevertheless does not quote it directly or exactly. Probably the Elder (so idenitified in 2 and 3 John) wrote only a few years after the Gospel began to circulate. In the period A.D. 115–120 Ignatius, Antioch's bishop, wrote letters to seven prominent churches while making his way as a prisoner to Rome, where he expected martyrdom. He too reflects the language of John's Gospel, though less frequently. At mid–second century Justin Martyr only rarely echoes the language of John, although he seems to know the other Gospels well, referring to them as apostolic memoirs. The paucity of references to John is striking.

Yet John's Gospel was known and read in the middle of the second century by heretics such as **Montanists** and **Gnostics**. The Montanists believed in the immediate arrival of the **Spirit**, or **Paraclete** (Advocate or Counselor), promised by Jesus in John as a specific event in the readers' own time. The **Gnostics** denied the creation of this world, believed by them to be irredemably evil, by a good God; some attempted to use an interpretation of John to defend their position. In his commentary on John, Origen, the early third-century theologian of Alexandria, attacked the Gnostic Heracleon, who had also written a commentary on John. Perhaps because of John's use by heretics, Gaius, a late second-century Roman churchman, rejected John; another Christian writer, Hippolytus, soon wrote a defense of the Gospel and Apocalypse (or **Revelation**) of John.

John's early use is also attested by the discovery of **manuscript** fragments. The oldest fragment of the New Testament is a small piece of John 18 dating from ca. A.D. 125–50 (designated p^{52}). There are nearly complete manuscripts of John (ca. 200) as old and as long as those of any part of the New Testament. Around A.D. 170, Tatian, a Christian scholar, composed a harmony (combination) of all four Gospels, using Jesus' three-year ministry in John as the framework. It was called the *Diatessaron*, which literally means "through four." A few years later Bishop Irenaeus of Lyons wrote a denunciation of heresy (*Against Heresies*) in which he defended John as worthy to stand with the other three Gospels (in what would soon be called the New Testament). By the time we cross the threshold into the third century, most churches have accepted John along with the three Synoptics.

OUTLINE OF JOHN

Introduction (1:1–51)
The Prologue: Jesus Christ as the Word (1:1–18)
The Appearance of John the Baptist (1:19–51)

The Revelation of Jesus' Glory before the World (2:1–12:50)

Nicodemus (3:1–21)   The Healing of the Man Born Blind (9:1–41)
The Response to Jesus' Signs Turns
Hostile (5:1–47)

The Revelation of Jesus' Glory before the Community (13:1–17:26)

The Last Supper (13:1–38)   Jesus' Last Will: The Prayer of
The Promise of the Paraclete (14:15–17, 26;   Consecration (17:1–26)
and 16:12–14)

Jesus' Last Appearance before the World: His Hidden Glorification (18:1–19:42)
The Trial before Pilate (18:28-19:16)
The Execution of Jesus by Crucifixion (19:17-42)

Jesus' Return to His Disciples (20:1–31)

Appendix: The Gospel Continues (21:1-25)

INTRODUCTION (1:1–51)

The Gospel of John falls into several rather well-defined parts. The first chapter stands apart from the body of the Gospel as a kind of introduction. It in turn falls into two major parts: the prologue and the witness of the Baptist to Jesus. Jesus receives his first disciples from John, who directs them to him, telling them that Jesus is the lamb of God who takes away the **sin** of the world (1:29; cf. vs. 34). The chapter ends on a note of expectation: the **revelation** of God will take place in Jesus' ministry (1:51). The prologue sets the stage for it.

The Prologue: Jesus Christ as the Word (1:1–18)

Why is Jesus called "the Word"?

The prologue has a rhythmic, almost poetic character. Moreover, there is a peculiar chainlike progression in the repetition of key words in verses 1–5 and 9–12. The translation of the prologue in Raymond Brown's commentary (see below, p. 184) admirably preserves both the strophic form and this chainlike sequence (vss. 1–5):

> In the beginning was the *Word*;
> the *Word* was in God's presence, and the *Word* was *God*.
> He was present with *God* in the beginning.
> Through him all things *came into being*,
> and apart from him not a thing *came to be*.
> That which had *come to be* in him was *life*,
> and this *life* was the *light* of men.
> The *light* shines on in the *darkness*,
> for the *darkness* did not overcome it.

The prologue's poetic mood is broken, however, by 1:6–8 and 15 (set off in NRSV by a separate paragraph in the one case and by parentheses in the other), which refer not to the **Word**, the subject of the rest of the prologue, but to John the Baptist. Quite possibly we are dealing here with an early Christian hymn that the evangelist has annotated with references to the Baptist and incorporated into the Gospel. (Other such hymns appear in Phil. 2:6–11; Col. 1:15–20; and 1 Tim. 3:16.) Its language, style, and theology are "Johannine"; that is, the basic hymn and the Gospel appear to share a common perspective and vocabulary. The prologue falls into distinct sections that correspond roughly to its thematic divisions. In verses 1–5, the theme is God, creation, and the Word; in verses 6–8, John the Baptist; in verses 9–13, the Word in the world; and in verses 14–18, the community's confession of the Word.

Given this structure, the meaning of the prologue hinges on an understanding of its key term *Word* (Greek, *logos*) and its relation to the rest of the Gospel. Who or what is the Word? In the first place, the Word is Jesus **Christ**. That said, several related questions are cast into sharp relief. In verses 1–5 does the author intend to speak of the man Jesus of Nazareth? He can hardly mean that Jesus of Nazareth was with God before all creation and was the mediator of all creation. Where, moreover, does this concept of the Word originate? It may be understood against the background of Greek philosophy, in which the term and concept of *logos* were important. Or it might be seen against the backdrop of the Old Testament and Jewish concept of the word of the Lord. It is clear that the Word *denotes* Jesus Christ; what more remains to be determined.

The Greek philosophical meaning of *logos* is not related directly to John's use of the term. Nevertheless, the fact that *logos* comprehends such varied meanings as explanation, argument, principle, thought or reason, language, speech, and divine utterance is relevant. So is the use of the term in late Jewish and other religious texts to designate God's agent in creation and world government. Moreover, in the **Hellenistic**–Jewish Wisdom of Solomon (9:1–2) *word (logos)* as God's agent in creation is identified with *wisdom (sophia)*. It is clear enough that the *logos* of John is God's speech, his self-disclosure to the world and, as the text makes plain, the means through which God creates. This range of meaning is the background of the evangelist's usage.

The most obvious and immediate reference point for the concept of God's Word is the creation story of Genesis 1, which also opens with the phrase "in the beginning." Like Genesis, John speaks of the creation. Although Genesis does not say that God created all things by the Word, it does portray each stage of creation as resulting from God's speaking. "Then God said, 'Let there be light'; and there was light" (Gen. 1:3). The fact that in Genesis God first creates *light* is paralleled by John's emphasis on light throughout the prologue. Moreover, the motifs of darkness and light appear together in both places. In Genesis, God speaks and there is light where darkness had theretofore prevailed: God

The mosaic above the lintel of a door in the monastery of St. John on the Island of Patmos shows John, who is described there as "apostle" and "theologian," with the beginning of the Gospel of John in Greek.

separates the light from the darkness (1:3–5). This leads to an account of the beginning of night and day. In John's prologue, however, the opposition between light and darkness develops into a sharply defined dualism, which is characteristic of the Gospel as a whole: distinctions are drawn between the forces of light and darkness, truth and falsehood, God and Satan, and so on. Such dualism was common not only to Zoroastrianism, **Gnosticism**, and late Platonism, but also to certain forms of Judaism. That a similar, dualistic worldview could arise even within first-century Palestinian Judaism has been shown by the discovery of the **Qumran** scrolls, in which a view of the world, human beings, and events very similar to that of John's Gospel is presented. The affinity between John and Genesis reveals the common ground on which they stand. But the striking dualism of John is equally significant, for it shows that John belongs in a first-century religious world.

Nevertheless, it would be wrong to leave the impression that understanding the prologue first requires understanding the Greek use of *logos*, the Old Testament creation story, or first-century sectarian Judaism. All these are informative, but John speaks clearly and directly apart from them. John has always been a popular Gospel for Christians, most of whom have not had the faintest conception of its cultural background. (The prologue is a traditional Christian lectionary reading for Christmas Day.) The text as it stands is richly suggestive and evocative. Any Christian reader would know that the Word was Jesus Christ before reading further in the Gospel, even though Jesus is not named until the prologue has moved from the **cosmic** or the metaphysical plane to the historical (vs. 17).

The movement from the rather abstract, if dramatic and impressive, talk about the *logos* to the level of historical events takes place by stages. Verses 1 and 2 deal with the relation of the Word to God, which is defined in the closest possible terms without John's quite saying that *logos* and God are simply equivalents. The statement, "the Word was God," is immediately qualified by "He was in the beginning with God." The Word participates in God without exhausting God's being. (Different versions render the key phrase variously: "the Word was God" [KJV, RSV, NRSV]; "what God was, the Word was" [NEB].) In verses 3 and 4 the most exalted status and functions are attributed to the Word, God's agent in creation, yet at the end of the Gospel Jesus is worshiped as Lord and God (20:28). Through the Word, the God who creates will now save the world from its evil and folly.

John's affirmation that the light shines in darkness (vs. 5) is the first hint of the advent of Jesus into the world. The ensuing description of the mission of John the Baptist (vss. 6–8), who heralded his coming, confirms this. It is followed by a more explicit reference to Jesus' appearance (vs. 9): "The true . . . light was coming into the world." The following paragraph (vss. 10–13) succinctly summarizes the world's and his own people's rejection of Jesus. Yet there are some who believe (vss. 12–13), whose happy destiny is to become children of God.

Why Does John the Baptist Interrupt John's Hymn to Christ?

John the Baptist is important both positively and negatively. Positively, John is the primary witness to Jesus, "a man sent from God." Moreover, "everything that John said about this man was true" (10:41). John's place as the forerunner of Jesus was established in the **Synoptic** tradition. The Fourth Gospel goes beyond the Synoptics to see in John the **witness** of Israel's true tradition and heritage to Jesus. Still, there is also a negative aspect of this Gospel's portrayal of John. The evangelist goes out of his way to make sure the reader understands that John was not the light (vs. 8), and John himself will deny that he is the Christ (vs. 20). Such demurrals are found only in the Gospel of John (cf. 1:19-34; 3:25-30). Quite possibly the evangelist, or the Johannine community, confronted other Jews who believed that the Baptist was the **Messiah**, or Elijah, or the **prophet** (vs. 21). Some such group is in fact mentioned in the Book of Acts (18:25; 19:3-5)—in Ephesus of all places, the traditional site of the Fourth Gospel's composition.

The brief description of the Word's mission in the world (vss. 9–13) takes on a richness of color and specificity in light of the Gospel's narration of Jesus' ministry, conflicts, and death and **resurrection**. Apart from that narrative these few lines remain bland or opaque. Read with that story in view, they are poignant and touching. Particularly moving is the simple assertion: "He came unto his own, and his own received him not" (vs. 11 KJV). Jesus' public ministry, as well as his **passion**, is the evangelist's spelling out of his tragic destiny. The dualism of the Gospel, its sharp distinction between light and darkness, truth and falsehood, is epitomized in the distance between the people who rejected him (vss. 10–11) and those who received him (vss. 12–13).

The prologue's final paragraph (vss. 14–18) is introduced by the most important **theological** statement of the Gospel, and one of the New Testament's crucial affirmations: "And the Word became flesh and lived among us" (vs. 14). John still does not mention Jesus by name, although the knowledgeable reader will know to whom this refers. Modern interpreters have debated whether John intends emphasis to fall upon the **Incarnation**, the Word's becoming human flesh, or upon the manifestation of divine glory, which occupies the latter part of the verse. Actually, John is ambiguous at this point, although 1 John makes clear that the real humanity of Jesus, his fleshliness, is of crucial importance (1:1–3; 4:1–3). In affirming that Jesus is full of grace and truth, John combines a typical Pauline term (*grace*; Greek, *charis*) with his own favorite designation of Jesus, *truth* (cf. 14:6).

At this point a **Christological** motif that will recur in the Gospel makes its first appearance. Neither "lived among us" (NRSV) nor "dwelt among us" (RSV, KJV) quite catches what is implied by John's language. He uses a verb (*skēnoun*) that could well be translated "tented" or "tabernacled" among us, evoking the whole tradition of the tabernacle or tent and later the temple in which the glory of Israel's God was believed to dwell (Exod. 40:35; Num. 14:10; 1 Kgs 8:11; cf. Isa. 6:1–3; Ezek. 1–3, esp. 1:28; 2:12; 3:23). John repeatedly suggests that, as the glory of God once tabernacled in a tent or building, it now dwells in Jesus. He reveals that Jesus himself spoke of the temple of his body

(2:21), when his hearers naturally thought he was speaking of the Jerusalem temple. When the Samaritan woman asks Jesus where one ought to worship, whether on "this mountain" (Gerizim, the site of the Samaritan temple) or in Jerusalem, Jesus answers, in effect, neither (4:20–23). True worshipers will worship in **spirit** and truth, says Jesus, subtly pointing ahead to the time when his followers will pray in his name (14:13–14).

In the prologue's concluding lines, the Baptist reiterates his witness (vs. 15), and John testifies about the grace received from Jesus (vs. 16; cf. vs. 12–13). Then Jesus is compared and contrasted with Moses (vs. 17), the new with the old. The reader is left to puzzle about the status of the **law** given through Moses. On the one hand, it seems to pale before the grace and truth embodied in Jesus Christ (vs. 17; cf. vs. 14), now mentioned by name for the first time. Jesus will speak of "your law" (8:17; i.e., the law of the Jews). Yet John continues to assume its validity (7:19–24; 10:34–36), at least for Jews. John's fundamental belief, however, is that the law or scripture, when rightly read, points ahead to Jesus (5:39, 45–47). The final statement expresses John's distinctive theological point: Jesus, the only Son, and he alone, has seen and revealed God (vs. 18). Uncertainty as to whether John wrote "only [begotten] Son" or "only [begotten] God" does not obscure this point. Text-critical criteria actually favor the latter reading. **Manuscript** attestation for it is strong, and to call Jesus *theos* (God) completes the circle begun in verse 1, where the *logos* (Word) is called God. Moreover, at the end of the scenes in which the risen Jesus appears to the disciples as a group, Thomas, who has at first doubted, confesses Jesus as "my Lord and my God!" (20:28). Even though there is an epilogue to the Gospel (chap. 21), that verse, with verses 30-31, looks very much like its original conclusion.

After reading the prologue one is prepared to encounter the distinctive figure of Jesus in John's Gospel. He incarnates, "makes flesh," the Word that was with God and is God (vs. 14). The prologue is a theological confession of who Jesus is. Yet it is also a narrative, perhaps a narrative overture in which the story of the Word foreshadows the story of Jesus' ministry. If that story is already known, the reader can instantly see Jesus behind the text (e.g., in vv. 5, 6-8, 9, 10, 11, as well as v. 14). John's language is mysterious to the outsider but takes on additional meaning once one knows the key, who is Jesus. One must know who Jesus really was and is.

The Appearance of John the Baptist (1:19–51)

How and why is the Fourth Gospel's portrayal of John the Baptist different?

Immediately after the prologue, John's narrative properly begins. There are points of positive contact with the **Synoptic Gospels**, along with striking differences. In every Gospel, Jesus' ministry begins with his encounter with John the Baptist (cf. also Acts 10:37; 13:24). In all probability Jesus' meeting with John was important for Jesus historically and the starting point of his public activity.

Still, John significantly diverges from the Synoptic accounts. In the Fourth Gospel, John is called simply that; he is never given the title "Baptist" (or "Baptizer"). Indeed, in this Gospel Jesus is never said to be baptized by John, although that may be assumed (1:31). Also, John is not described as an **apocalyptic** preacher and ascetic, announcing God's judgment, as he is in the other Gospels (Mark 1:2-8; Matt 3:1-12; Luke 3:2-17). Instead, John bears **witness**: first against himself (1:19-28), in the face of questioning about his identity and role by **priests** and Levites sent by the Jews (1:19, 24). The latter will appear repeatedly; sometimes they seeem identical with those called **Pharisees**. (In vs. 24 the Pharisees are said to have sent these emissaries.) To them John denies that he himself is the **Christ**, or Elijah, or the **prophet** (vss. 20-21). He is not himself an important figure in the drama of **salvation**. Instead, John's function is to bear witness, to point to the one who is important: Jesus.

Accordingly, he directs his own disciples to Jesus (1:29-34). John may actually have done this. At least, it is possible that at some point disciples of John went over to Jesus. Now John himself takes up the narration, describing a scene quite similar to the Synoptic accounts of Jesus' meeting with John. This episode with John is much longer in the Fourth Gospel than in the Synoptics (see Mark 1:16-20 parr). Perhaps an interchange between Jesus' disciples and those of John lies in the background, and the evangelist wants to portray John as instrumental in Jesus' calling of his disciples. Although highly stylized, John's account is in an important respect more plausible historically: in the Synoptic version, no reason is given for why the disciples should have left their work and followed Jesus.

In the Fourth Gospel they are sent by John. Then there is a process in which disciples recruit other disciples, and they come to discover more fully who Jesus is (1:35-51). John has already told them that Jesus is the Lamb of God, who takes away the **sin** of the world (1:29, 36). But this is an enigmatic statement. Is the Lamb the **Passover** lamb or some other, **sacrificial** lamb? Apparently, the reader is expected to understand, or perhaps to puzzle over it. Andrew leads his brother Peter to Jesus, whom he already designates as the **Messiah** or **Christ** (v. 41). In the Synoptics Jesus is not revealed as the Christ until Peter's confession, halfway through the Gospels' narrative (Mark 8:27-30 parr). He is then called the one spoken of in the law and the prophets, "Jesus son of Joseph from Nazareth" (1:45). In response, Nathanael indicates that Nazareth was a humble village (1:46): "Can anything good come out of Nazareth?" When Jesus reveals to Nathanael his uncanny knowledge of him (vv. 47-48), Nathanael responds by addressing him as "**Rabbi**," the **Son of God** and the King of Israel (v. 49). Jesus' mysterious response points to a future **revelation** of God in him (vv. 50-51).

In the introduction, the prologue first introduces Jesus in a **cosmic** dimension (1:1-18). Then he is presented as the fulfillment of Israel's hopes and expectations (1:19-51). Obviously, the prologue is addressed to the reader. But now not only the reader, but the actors in the drama, the disciples, become aware of the historic, biblical role that Jesus will play. They learn this much sooner than in the narratives of the other Gospels. Yet even though they know, they do not, until the end, really understand (cf. 14:5, 8; 16:29-33).

THE REVELATION OF JESUS' GLORY BEFORE THE WORLD (2:1–12:50)

Jesus' public ministry in John is characterized by **miracles** and controversy, both of which are found in the other Gospels. But in contrast to the **Synoptics**, where Jesus takes a dim view of the desire for signs, in John, the miracles are just such revelatory signs. **Parables** and other forms of public teaching, familiar from the Synoptics, are notable by their absence from John. Jesus does not teach a hostile world, but confronts it with his astonishing deeds and lofty claims. Thus heated controversy arises over who Jesus is, and such controversy is distinctive of John.

Before the controversy begins, however, there are two quite different, but related, episodes that open Jesus' public ministry. In one, Jesus seemingly saves a host embarrassment by changing water into wine (2:1–11). In the other, he drives vendors and money-changers out of the Jerusalem temple (2:13–22). The former has no parallel outside the Fourth Gospel; the latter is found also in the Synoptics, though not until the end of Jesus' ministry. Indeed, this difference may have something to do with the fact that, while John has Jesus go to Jerusalem for the annual **Passover** or Feast of Unleavened Bread three times, the Synoptics depict the ministry in a year or less—Jesus goes up to Jerusalem for Passover only once, at the end. (The tradition that Jesus' ministry lasted three years is solely a product of the Gospel of John.)

The very different stories have in common one major motif: Jesus' confrontation and transformation of Judaism's institutions. The water he transforms into wine was kept in "six stone water jars for the Jewish rites of purification" (2:6). The wine produced is obviously the best of all; contrary to common practice, the best is kept until last (vs. 10). Probably the incident symbolizes the salvation or life that Jesus brings (cf. 15:1–11, where Jesus is portrayed as the vine). The temple that will be destroyed and raised up in three days is actually the temple of Jesus' risen body, although not even the disciples will understand until after his **resurrection** (vss. 19–22). These stories are epiphany stories: episodes in which Jesus manifests himself before his people, in the one case at a celebration of one of the most important events of human life, in the other at Judaism's center, the headquarters of those called "the Jews" who will oppose Jesus and his claims. At this point in the narrative, however, there is little of the heated controversy and hostility on both sides that will appear later.

Nicodemus (3:1–21)

Why does Jesus seem rude to Nicodemus?

Jesus' encounter with his own people, culture, and religious tradition is most graphically represented in the story of his conversation with Nicodemus, who is described as a **Pharisee** and a leader (or ruler) of the Jews (3:1).

The most striking aspect of this episode's beginning is that Nicodemus' apparent openness or friendliness to Jesus (vs. 2) is met by Jesus' abrupt retorts. Far from responding in a polite way, Jesus rejects Nicodemus' kind approach (vs. 3) and seemingly refuses to answer his questions in terms Nicodemus can comprehend (vss. 4–8). Nicodemus' puzzled question, "How can these things be?" (vs. 9), is really not hard to understand. Furthermore, Jesus' subsequent rejoinder (vs. 10) is either incredulous or sarcastic, or both. From that point on, Jesus goes into a kind of monologue (vss. 11–21), and, in fact, it is difficult to discern where Jesus stops talking and the evangelist begins. With the veiled prediction of his **ascension** (vss. 13–14), Jesus speaks of himself in the third person. It is as if the evangelist were describing Jesus' life-giving work from a later perspective. Indeed, Jesus had already switched from the singular "I" to the plural "we" (vs. 11), as if he were speaking with, or on behalf of, the community of his followers.

The Nicodemus episode is typical of a literary technique that appears frequently in the Fourth Gospel and characterizes its understanding of **revelation**. Nicodemus *misunderstands* Jesus. Already the steward did not know the origin of the good wine (2:9). Nor did the Jews understand Jesus' word about the destruction of the temple (2:20). Apparently, neither did the disciples understand until after Jesus was raised from the dead (vs. 22). Now, the impressively credentialed Nicodemus is equally in the dark (cf. 3:1: "He came to Jesus by night.") Later on, the woman of Samaria will think that Jesus is offering her a new water-delivery system rather than supernatural, life-giving water (4:15).

This technique of misunderstanding says something important about revelation in the Fourth Gospel. Old assumptions, standards, or traditions cannot comprehend Jesus, or the revelation of God in Jesus, even when applied in a positive way. Therefore, although Nicodemus is prepared to credit Jesus as a teacher sent from God on the basis of his signs (vs. 3), Jesus rejects this kind of acceptance. No one can see the **kingdom of God** unless he is born from above. In John, Jesus uses an ambiguous Greek word (*anōthen*) that can mean either "again" (or "anew," RSV) or "from above" (NRSV). Obviously birth from above is a new birth, but the point is its source or origin. Nicodemus misunderstands Jesus, and takes the point to be mere repetition (vs. 4). He misunderstands the heavenly, because he interprets it solely in terms of the very earthly reality of physical birth. This exemplifies another characteristic feature of John: Jesus' interlocutors misunderstand him because they try to interpret the new in terms of the old, and the otherworldly in this-worldly terms. But Jesus can be understood only on his own terms. He is self-authenticating. One believes his claims or one does not. Jesus fulfills ancient expectations, but at the same time transcends them. Thus he speaks of the necessity of being born of water and the **Spirit**, probably meaning the water of **baptism** as well as the accompanying gift of the **Holy Spirit**. By mentioning the Spirit, Jesus invokes divine causality. Coming to believe in Jesus, conversion, is finally the work of the Spirit, that is, of God.

As Nicodemus vanishes from the scene, the evangelist speaks directly about the revelatory event of God's sending his Son in order that those who believe may have eternal life (3:16). After this thematic statement, which encapsulates John's **theology** or **soteriology** (doctrine of **salvation**), the evangelist reflects upon the meaning of the sending of the Son, God's purpose in sending him and its actual results (vss. 17–21). Doubtless the author now interprets the effect of Jesus' appearance against the background of his own knowledge and experience of who has accepted him and who has not. John here insists that the purpose of God's sending Jesus was salvation, not condemnation or judgment. Yet some people reject the light (vs. 19; cf. 1:5, 9) and incur judgment for themselves. In doing that, or by accepting the light, people reveal who they really are (vss. 19–21).

John's statements can be oversimplified and taken to mean that people who were already good accepted Jesus, and people who were bad rejected him. Were that the case, however, Jesus' coming would have changed nothing. Doubtless the meaning is that a person's true character—being in the light or being in darkness—is revealed only in how one responds when the light—Jesus—comes. Otherwise, who or what that person is cannot be known. Thus Jesus not only reveals himself and reveals God; he also reveals the true character of every person he encounters (cf. 4:16–19, 29). His coming brings life, salvation, or judgment. Jesus' (first) coming is already the **eschatological**, or final, event in every person's history.

We now seem to know the meaning of Jesus' coming into the world, as expressed in his encounter with Nicodemus. Nicodemus did not understand, and presumably perished. Yet later this same Nicodemus returns to defend Jesus' right to a fair hearing (7:50–52) and finally—in John only—helps bury him (19:39–40). The coming of the Light and **Word** into the world is misunderstood and creates division. It seems a simple, black-or-white affair. Yet John understands that with people things are not always so straightforward, at least not immediately so. Thomas, one of the twelve disciples, will have great difficulty understanding and believing Jesus, but will ultimately trust him (20:28). People may initially believe, but time and further events must unfold before they come to adequate faith. John has now given the reader a basis for understanding the issues involved and appreciating the complex unfolding of controversy and conflict that will surround Jesus' public ministry and lead eventually to his death.

The Response to Jesus' Signs Turns Hostile (5:1–47)

Is opposition to Jesus understandable? On what basis?

Jesus has performed signs that perplex, but do not yet enrage, the Jews who witness them (cf. 2:23-25). He then engages in conversation with a woman of Samaria (4:1-42). This act astounds his disciples—not so much that he talks with a Samaritan, but with a woman (4:27). While in Cana of Galilee, Jesus heals an official's son in Capermaum, and his entire household comes to faith (4:46-54). In the story of the healing of the ill man at the pool by the Sheep Gate and its aftermath (5:1-47), however, an aura of sharp hostility arises.

Because of Jesus' having performed a healing on the Sabbath, he is "persecuted" by "the Jews" (5:16). When Jesus likens his own working to the Father's (God's) working (v. 17), he is accused of making himself equal to God (v. 18). Jesus' statement in itself does not necessarily imply such a claim, but instead of renouncing it Jesus wholeheartedly embraces it (5:19-24), saying that he is only doing the will of the one (God) who sent him. As the Father raises the dead and gives life, so does the Son (v. 21). The theme then shifts to that of testimony or **witness** (v. 31); Jesus claims the testimony of God the Father (v. 37), whose **word** is to be found in the scriptures that Moses wrote (5:39, 45-47). The Jews could scarcely be more amazed—and understandably angered. While none of the episodes narrated in John 2–4 has evoked great hostility against Jesus, the healing of the invalid at the pool (5:1-18) and its ensuing dispute (5:19-47) sets the tone for the remainder of the Gospel. Now the tension between Jesus and "the Jews" will be unremitting, and this has to do with the claims Jesus makes for himself, which are the claims the Johannine community makes for him.

According to John 5, Jesus claims the status of God's final and definitive **revelation**. It is Jesus who makes God finally and fully known to human beings under the conditions and limitations of human life and death. Jesus is not to be judged by previous revelations, even those to Israel recorded in scripture and hallowed by sacred tradition. Rather, they are to be judged by him. Therefore, Jesus' claim to reveal God cannot in principle be validated by appeal to other authorities. Later (10:30) Jesus will say that he and God the Father are one. In the claims he now makes he is already suggesting that. In 10:33 his opponents seek to stone him to death for blasphemy, as also here (5:18) they seek to kill him.

In chapter 9, we see an outstanding example of how Jesus' works are not so much a proof as a watershed. Everything depends on whether one acknowledges them to be real and valid. The final test of Jesus' work for the man born blind is that now he sees (9:25). One who sees cannot deny sight any more than he can deny his previous blindness.

The Healing of the Man Born Blind (9:1–41)

How do these miracle stories present the message of the Fourth Gospel?

Between the healing of the invalid at the pool (chap. 5) and the present episode, the hostility against Jesus (5:18) has continued to mount. During the bread discourse, Jesus' conversation partners seem more perplexed than hostile, but by the end even some of his disciples are turning away from him (6:66). At the subsequent Festival of Booths (chap. 7) the authorities make an attempt to arrest Jesus, who is aware that his life is in danger (7:19), but are unsuccessful. Chapter 7 is a tightly woven story about Jesus in the Jerusalem temple: it is tied in with what preceded (7:1), has a clear narrative framework, and a conclusion that relates to what has occurred earlier in the account (7:45; cf. vs. 32). Chapter 8 is a more loosely connected series of arguments and counterarguments between Jesus and the Jews, or the Jews who had believed in him (vs. 31). Its continuity derives largely from the bitterness of the exchanges and the fact that Jesus is still in the temple. There is no explicit connection between this chapter and the previous one, and no new incident or episode begins the discussion. The break and the need for some fresh opening narrative are so obvious that some ancient scribe inserted at the beginning the now famous story of the woman taken in adultery (7:53–8:11), which is missing in the oldest and most reliable **manuscripts**. Similarly, the chapter ends abruptly with "the Jews" unsuccessfully attempting to stone Jesus (8:59), who hides and leaves the temple. There is then no explicit connection with what follows; thus the story of the healing of the blind man (chap. 9) begins with Jesus simply walking along. We can later infer the locus of the narrative from the fact that Jesus tells the man to wash in the pool of Siloam, in Jerusalem and south of the temple mount (9:7, 11). These locations are still known.

The healing itself (9:1–7) is in many respects similar to the **Synoptic miracle** stories. The story is introduced with only the vaguest connection with the preceding scene. Such a brief introduction is common in the Synoptics. The idea that sickness or deformity is punishment for **sin** (vss. 2 f.; cf. vs. 34) is an ancient one, and dies hard (cf. Luke 13:1–5; Exod. 20:5). Although Jesus rejects this belief (vs. 3), his own interpretation of the man's blindness is scarcely more acceptable to modern sensibilities. Here we have one of two remarkable parallels to the Lazarus story (see chap. 11), where the sickness of Lazarus is said to be for the glory of God and of the Son (11:4). The point, however, is not that God deforms people to show his own power, but that in and through such misfortune the power of God manifests itself (cf. Gen. 50:20). The second parallel (9:4 f. corresponding to 11:9 f.) consists of a subtle allusion to Jesus' coming death. Already its inevitability has been indicated by the evangelist's passing references (2:22; 7:39) and by the Jews' attitude in controversy with Jesus (5:18; 8:37, 40, 59). As his public ministry draws toward its close, Jesus' last acts of healing are cast under the shadow of the cross.

Jesus' affirmation, "I am the light of the world" (vs. 5, cf. 1:5, 9; 8:12), shows the close connection between the prologue and the Gospel proper. This statement belongs to a group of "I am" sayings that are distinctive of the Fourth Gospel (e.g., 6:35; 10:11; 11:25; 14:6; 15:1) and reflect the Johannine view that Jesus proclaims himself and his dignity. By contrast, in the Synoptics Jesus proclaims not himself but the **kingdom of God**, and such "I am" statements are not found. Obviously, the theme of light is closely related to Jesus' gift of sight.

The miracle itself is described briefly and with restraint (vss. 6 f.). In Mark also, Jesus is said to heal with spittle (8:23); once in Luke (17:12–15) the healing likewise takes place after Jesus has sent the persons involved away. For the evangelist the significance of the pool of Siloam lies not in its proximity but in the Hebrew meaning of its name, "Sent." In John, Jesus is frequently described as the one sent by God (e.g., 3:17). The man's obedience to Jesus and the results are described as succinctly as possible. In fact, the basic miracle story is much less elaborate and detailed than are many similar stories in the Synoptic tradition. This brevity may indicate that John possessed a primitive miracle story in simple form.

After the brief account of the miracle, there follows an extended dialogue concerned with questions fundamental to Johannine **theology**. The Synoptic miracle stories concisely report the reaction to Jesus' miracles. By contrast, John develops the theological issues that arise as a consequence of the miracle. This emphasis is reflected in the literary form: a traditional story forms the basis of, and affords the springboard for, a developed dialogue. That dialogue, unlike anything in the Synoptics, is quite typical of John. Much the same pattern of events plus interpretation is observable in chapter 5. Indeed, it is characteristic of this Gospel's style.

There are several interrogations of the blind man (9:8–12, 13–17, 18–23, 24–34). First the man's neighbors question him (vss. 8 ff.), then the **Pharisees** (vss. 13–17). Then the man's parents are questioned by the Jews (vss. 18–23). Finally, the Jews return to question the man himself a second time (vss. 24–34). Probably no distinction is to be drawn between Pharisees and Jews in this instance. John's characteristic designation of those who oppose Jesus and his work is simply "the Jews." When he does mention a particular sect of Judaism, it is the Pharisees. John tends to equate Jews and Pharisees, though the reason for this is not obvious.

If, however, John was written after the Roman war (**A.D.** 70), the main Jewish opponents of Christianity would have been Pharisees. The other principal sects—**Sadducees**, **Zealots**, and **Essenes**—were either dissolved or sharply reduced in size and influence as a result of that conflict. Thus John's reference to the Pharisees probably indicates that they were the group most actively competing with or opposing Christianity at the end of the first century. We shall see some indication of that before the end of this chapter. By contrast, the Synoptic material still views Jesus' ministry from the standpoint of Palestinian Judaism before the temple's destruction, although the evangelists themselves do reflect a later time and distinctively Christian interests.

A brief narrative (vss. 8–12) reports more of the healed man's background and conveys the astonishment, even disbelief, of his neighbors (vss. 8 f.). The man calmly and certainly identifies himself as the blind beggar whom they have known, and describes how and by whom he has been healed. When brought before the Pharisees (vss. 13–17), his assurance and simplicity are impressive (vs. 15). For the first time we learn that the healing had been performed on the Sabbath (vs. 14), a common feature of the Synoptic tradition, where Jesus is more than once accused of illegally performing healings—and therefore working—on the Sabbath (cf. also John 5). The division among the Pharisees (vs. 16) is typical of the division that Jesus causes. Some reject him out of hand, because he violates their preconceptions of what a **holy** or **righteous** man must be: "He does not observe the sabbath." Others are at least open to the testimony of his works, to see them as "signs" signifying who Jesus is. The question is then put to the blind man (vs. 17): "What do you say about him? It was your eyes he opened." Earlier the man has simply spoken of "the man called Jesus." Now he says that Jesus is a **prophet**. That term serves to indicate that Jesus is not a sinner, as his detractors contend, but a man sent from God.

The mounting opposition to Jesus next takes the form of the Jews' refusal to believe that the man had actually been born blind (vs. 18). So his parents are called to testify (vss. 18–23). They are obviously not anxious to involve themselves, but they do give a minimally truthful testimony. The man who claims to have been healed by Jesus the prophet is, in fact, their son who was born blind (vs. 20). For all questions about how or by whom he was healed, however, the parents refer the questioners back to their son (vs. 21).

The evangelist now interjects an explanation of the parents' reticence (vss. 22 f.) that does not really fit the time of Jesus, but rather the end of the first Christian century. Only after the destruction of Jerusalem and the formation of the rabbinic **Council of Jamnia** might people have actually been forced to leave the synagogue for professing Jesus to be the **Messiah** or **Christ**. The theme of being cast out of the synagogue occurs more than once in John (12:42; 16:2; cf. Luke 6:22) and is probably a reflection of that situation. Despite the parents' timidity, the attempt to discredit the man's claims, and indirectly to discredit Jesus, comes to grief on the hard fact that a change has occurred in him. He was born blind, but is so no longer.

The same hearing continues and the man is called a second time (vss. 24 ff.). The serenity of the man healed contrasts with the obviously hostile jury. He simply recites what he knows on the basis of what he has experienced. He was blind, but now he sees (vs. 25). This most effective and infuriating response drives the questioners now to take a new tack (vs. 26): "What did he do to you?" Perhaps they suspect that Jesus has used spittle in the act of healing and is therefore guilty of adopting the tricks of an illegal sorcerer. The man's reply is intentionally cutting (vs. 27) and draws a trenchant retort (vss. 28 f.). Actually, the Jews' claim to be the true disciples of Moses would not have been accepted by the evangelist (cf. 5:45–47). That the man is Jesus' disciple has not heretofore been suggested. Nevertheless, it will turn out to be true.

The opponents' rejection of Jesus (vs. 29) is based upon a religious certainty that harks back to an earlier **revelation** that is viewed as unchanging. But Jesus cannot be judged by earlier revelation and tradition. That Jesus' opponents do not know the origin of Jesus is altogether typical of John's thought. To know Jesus' true origin is to know that he is sent by God. The Jews ironically do not know the truth of their observation that they are ignorant of Jesus' origin (cf. 3:31 ff.; 6:42; 7:27, 41 f., 52; 8:23, 57 f.). The man's sardonic response to the statement of the Jews, who view themselves as heirs of established authority (Moses), appeals only to his own experience (vs. 30). His further clarification (vss. 31–33) strikes home, because it is based on presuppositions that the questioners-turned-accusers also share. The response of the man healed is so telling that the Jews lash out in anger, venting their rage upon him. They cast him out—possibly out of the hearing room, but more probably out of the synagogue or the Jewish community (cf. vss. 22 f.). The latter interpretation fits with what follows (vss. 35 ff.). After the man healed has been ejected for refusing to repudiate Jesus, Jesus himself returns to him.

At this point the man still has no special theological knowledge about Jesus. In Jesus' question (vs. 35) we find one of the fairly numerous instances of the term **Son of Man** in John's Gospel. As in the Synoptics it appears on the lips of Jesus himself, presumably as a self–designation. The man's answer to Jesus' question is typically guileless (vs. 36). Only now does Jesus reveal his full and true identity (vs. 37). The man's response (vs. 38) indicates that he understands Son of Man to be a **messianic** title. "Lord, I believe" is a **Christological** confession, as is made plain by the statement that at this point the man worshiped Jesus. Jesus' final words (vss. 39–41), now addressed not so much to the man as to the total situation, are a commentary on his whole mission.

Do You See?

What are we to make of Jesus' strange statement that he has come in order that those who do not see may see and in order that those who do see may become blind (vs. 39)? This chapter's traces of Jewish–Christian polemic in the latter part of the first century lead us to the conclusion that the same situation is in view here. Those who do not see are not the physically blind, for in that case the import of Jesus' statement would be the absurd notion that as he goes about giving sight to the blind, so he also puts out the eyes of those who see. Obviously the blindness and sight referred to here are of a different order. At the beginning of this story (vs. 5) Jesus declared that he is the light of the world. He gives sight to those in darkness, but those who try to walk by their own light are blinded. To receive sight, to see the true light, one must recognize one's condition of blindness. Those who insist upon their prior revelatory knowledge ("we see") and their right to judge Jesus become blind because of this pretension. Their rejection of Jesus proves their blindness, whereas their insistence that they see confirms their guilt (9:41). From here it is only a step—perhaps the evangelist has already taken that step, but at least he lays the basis for it—to the application of this principle to humankind at large. The pretension that one already sees prevents the self-knowledge and recognition of one's true condition that is the first step to genuine sight. So the effect of Jesus' appearance is to blind such people (vs. 39), at least until they are ready to recognize their actual state.

John's **theological** perspective helps us to understand Jesus' apparently anomalous assertion in 9:41. Elsewhere it is explicitly said that he does not come in order to judge (see 3:17 f., where the word *condemn* translates the same word, Greek *krinein*, "to judge"; also 12:47). From 5:22 onward, however, it is clear that the Son *does* judge. The difficulty is resolved if we recognize that the ultimate purpose of Jesus' coming is not judgment but salvation (3:16 ff.). Yet from this, judgment inevitably results—because some reject the **salvation** that is offered and persist in evil (3:19 ff.). This negative statement of Jesus' purpose is doubtless influenced by the context, as it follows a narrative in which hostility toward Jesus and his work has been vigorously expressed.

John 9 is a paradigm of Jesus' public ministry, portraying in dramatic form the prologue's statement (1:5) that the light shines in darkness and the darkness has not overcome or comprehended it. Moreover, verses 9–13 of the prologue take on concreteness in the light of this story. At the same time we see a movement or progression in Jesus' ministry. The hostility that has already become evident (cf. chaps. 5 and 8) could not be made plainer than it is here. Also, John's portrayal of Jesus as the giver of sight and, by implication, of light, prepares the way for the final manifestation of Jesus as the giver of life (chap. 11). The principal point of John 9 does not lie in its contribution to historical knowledge of Jesus' ministry. The questions addressed arise not from Jesus' own time but out of encounters between Jews who were followers of Jesus and the majority who were not. This point is clear from Jesus' concluding word (9:39–41): he succinctly characterizes his whole mission as one of judgment.

In the background of 9:1-41 stands John's distinctive view of Jesus as the light and life of the world. The miracle itself is indispensable: it manifests the fact that Jesus really changes people. The healed man's stubborn insistence upon the fact of his healing bears eloquent testimony to this conviction. He grounds his relation to Jesus on what has actually happened to him, even though he cannot give this experience adequate expression until Jesus reveals himself to him; only then does he acknowledge and worship the Christ whose reality and activity on his behalf he has already confessed. As Jesus here manifests himself as the light of the world by giving sight to the blind, so later (chap. 11) he appears as the **resurrection** and the life by raising the dead. Interestingly, in chapter 9, Jesus himself remains in the background. The story's real hero is the nameless man who is healed. This is true of this particular miracle story as of no other in John. Neither the restored man of chapter 5 nor even Lazarus in chapter 11 emerges as a hero.

John's Characterizations

While no other Johannine **miracle** story offers an exact parallel to the healed man's heroism (chap. 9), this account does bring to light an important Johannine characteristic—namely, the author's interest in the various types of people who confront Jesus. Clearly many of the characters who encounter Jesus are typical and perhaps symbolic. There is Nathanael, the true Israelite in whom there is no guile (1:47 ff.). There is Nicodemus, the teacher of Israel, who at first cannot comprehend Jesus and yet later defends him and finally returns to help bury him (3:1 ff.; 7:50; 19:39). In contrast to Nicodemus stands the nameless Samaritan woman, the representative of a heterodox Judaism (4:7 ff.), whose dim perception of Jesus is nevertheless superior to that of Nicodemus. Still, if the characters are symbolic, they are also lifelike.

Yet the Jesus of John lacks the humanity of the other characters. This is all the more surprising in view of the intensely human—if authoritative—Jesus who emerges at many points from the **Synoptic** account. The Johannine Jesus behaves strangely by human standards (see 2:4; 7:2–10; 11:6). John's portrayal of Jesus is not designed to represent his humanity for the benefit of the readers' curiosity or to make him personally more familiar. John does not deny that Jesus was really human. He has a mother and father (1:45; 6:42). Yet John's primary interest and emphasis are focused by his conviction that through Jesus God is speaking to the world. The single-mindedness of this **theological** concept is etched sharply against the background of John's perceptive presentation of humanity in all its color and concreteness. At this he is a master, and that is nowhere more apparent than in the story of the man blind from birth.

THE REVELATION OF JESUS' GLORY BEFORE THE COMMUNITY (13:1–17:26)

Jesus' glory is revealed throughout his public ministry, but the world cannot perceive this glory for what it is. The disciples see and believe, but their understanding before Jesus' death and resurrection is necessarily limited. During the final period of his ministry Jesus reveals himself directly and explicitly to his disciples. Even then their perception is still limited, but ultimately they **witness** the risen Jesus and come to more adequate faith.

A view of Jerusalem from the ridge of the Mount of Olives, as Jesus would have approached the city from Bethany.

After bestowing sight upon the blind man, Jesus describes himself as the gate and shepherd of his sheep (his followers). Consequently he again falls into furious debate with the Jews, after which he withdraws across the Jordan to escape their wrath (10:40–42). When, however, he learns of the mortal illness of his friend Lazarus, he returns to the Jerusalem area, to Bethany, where his friend lives. Meanwhile, Lazarus has died, as Jesus knew he must (11:11–15).

The raising of Lazarus from the dead (11:1–44) leads directly to the authorities' plotting Jesus' death (11:45–53). No longer does he move freely in Judea, but now retreats to a town called Ephraim (11:54) near the wilderness. As **Passover** draws near (12:1) Jesus returns to Bethany, where he is entertained in the home of Lazarus by Lazarus' sisters Martha and Mary. Mary anoints the feet of Jesus, over Judas's protest (12:1–8). Subsequently Jesus enters Jerusalem in a procession, recounted also in the **Synoptic Gospels** (12:12–19).

At this point, an interlude: Jesus appears among the festival crowd, making mysterious pronouncements about his coming death that are scarcely understood by the onlookers (12:20–36a). Then the evangelist declares Jesus' public ministry to be at an end.

Despite all the signs he did, the result is unbelief (12:37), as the **prophet** Isaiah had predicted (12:38–40). Jesus cries aloud, effectively summarizing his ministry or God's saving purpose in that ministry (12:44–50). He again announces that he has come as a light into the world (vs. 46), not to judge or condemn it, but to save it. His mission, he reiterates, has been to deliver the message God has given him. From now on Jesus is with his disciples only, except for the inevitable confrontation with the Jewish religious authorities and with Pontius Pilate, the Roman governor.

The Last Supper (13:1–38)

What is the relationship between the foot washing and the Lord's Supper?

Jesus withdraws with his disciples to the Last Supper, even as he does in the **Synoptics**. John indicates the imminence of the end (13:1). Judas is now primed to betray Jesus (vs. 2), and Jesus himself is confident in the full knowledge of his divine commission and destiny. The Johannine account of the Supper is parallel to the Synoptic, but with some significant differences. In fact, as the events of Jesus' ministry close in upon his imminent death, John and the Synoptics move closer together in their narratives. Yet in the Synoptic Gospels, the Last Supper is a Passover meal, introduced by a brief narrative about its preparation (Mark 14:12–25 parr.). In John, the meal occurs on the evening before the Passover was to be eaten (13:1–29; 19:31).

The most astonishing difference in the Johannine account, however, appears at the outset. Instead of instituting the **Lord's Supper** with words familiar from the Synoptics (Mark 14:22–25 parr.) and Paul (1 Cor. 11:23–26), Jesus washes his disciples' feet (13:4–11). Only in John does Jesus perform this act (but cf. Luke 12:37). John's reasons for seemingly substituting the foot washing for the institution of the Lord's Supper are not clear; still, the meaning of the act itself is plain enough.

As Jesus comes to Simon Peter (vs. 6), that disciple protests having his feet washed by his master, or lord. When Jesus tells Peter that he does not understand now but will later, this remark is apparently a veiled reference to Jesus' **crucifixion** and **resurrection**, after which the disciples will indeed understand (cf. 2:22). Yet Peter is still in the dark and continues to protest that Jesus will not wash his feet (vs. 8), at which point Jesus makes clear to him that the act he intends to perform is necessary if they are to have a continuing relationship. Even in yielding to Jesus (vs. 9), Simon reveals that his understanding is scarcely better than that of Nicodemus or the woman of Samaria. Jesus does reassure him (vs. 10), but this reassurance likely falls on deaf ears, at least for the moment, as Simon Peter cannot yet understand the depths of what Jesus is saying. At least he does not demonstrate understanding of the hidden meaning of Jesus' deed. The washing of the disciples' feet—the humble, slave's service that Jesus performs upon his disciples—symbolizes the service he performs in his death. Only after he has done it, however, will the disciples understand its meaning (vs. 7). The noting of the exception to Jesus' dictum that all the disciples are clean (vss. 10–11) is typical of the Fourth Gospel, where Jesus is betrayed by Judas, but only with Jesus' prior knowledge and at his behest.

After first presenting the foot washing as a preenactment of his own suffering service for the disciples, Jesus then interprets his deed from yet another angle of vision (vss. 12–17). As Teacher and Lord he declares that the foot washing is for the disciples an example of how they should serve one another (vs. 15). In other words, there is first a **theological** (or **soteriological**) interpretation and then an **ethical** one; the two are very closely entwined. As Jesus has served the disciples, they must serve one another. This principle is reiterated time and again in John (13:34; 15:12–14) as well as in 1 John (3:16). Whether Jesus instituted a rite of foot washing is debatable, but the broader, theological and ethical implications of his act are clear enough.

Then comes the prediction of Jesus' betrayal by Judas (13:18–20), followed immediately by Jesus' identification of Judas as the betrayer (vs. 21–30). The parallel accounts in the Synoptics (Mark 14:18–19 parr.) differ in detail but are recognizably similar. If anything, the Johannine version of the episode is more elaborate. Jesus puts the finger on Judas specifically, which is not at all the case in Mark. Further, Jesus reveals the betrayer's identity only to the Beloved Disciple ("the one whom Jesus loved"—vs. 23), as it becomes evident that the other disciples present do not share this information (vs. 28–29).

Who Is the Beloved Disciple?

Found only in the Fourth Gospel, the Beloved Disciple repeatedly reappears in the narrative from this point on: perhaps at the door of the high **priest**'s house (18:15–16); at the foot of the cross (19:25–27); at the empty tomb (20:2–10); at the appearance of the risen Christ by the sea (21:7); and finally with Peter and the risen Jesus at the very end of the Gospel (21:20–24). It is as if everywhere Peter goes, the Beloved Disciple goes; moreover, everything Peter can do, the Beloved Disciple can do better. Even though the Beloved Disciple constantly outdoes Peter, Peter is not denigrated or played down. It is just that the Beloved Disciple has a special place. Tradition has identified him with John the son of Zebedee, but that identification is never explicitly made in the Gospel itself. Perhaps the Beloved Disciple is an ideal or symbolic figure. Certainly he is that: he is the ideal disciple. Yet he seems also to be the special link between the Johannine Christian community and Jesus (cf. 19:35). The fact that it was rumored that he would not die, yet apparently had died (21:21–22), speaks on the side of his having been a historical figure. The Johannine community would not have invented someone whose death then had to be explained.

After the identification of the betrayer to the Beloved Disciple—and to the reader—Jesus announces his glorification (13:31–33). His glory is revealed only in his death and resurrection; that is, these events are the **revelation** of Jesus' glory. In fact, Jesus is here announcing his impending death. To the outsider such talk is enigmatic. The informed (i.e., believing) reader, however, knows its meaning. Just at this point Jesus issues the new commandment to his disciples, which echoes the command to love elsewhere in the

New Testament, also outside the Johannine literature (John 15:12; cf. Gal. 5:14; Rom. 13:9; Mark 12:33 parr.; Matt. 5:44). In John, however, the command is directed particularly to the circle of Jesus' own disciples. Their love for one another is a **witness** to the world of who, and whose, they are (13:35). Only in the Gospel of John does Jesus issue the love commandment at this point in the narrative. Jesus has manifested his own self-giving love, symbolized in the foot washing, and now he commands his disciples to show that same love to each other (vs. 34). The Johannine version of the Lord's Supper begins and ends on the theme of love. Indeed, only in the Fourth Gospel is the narrative of the Last Supper framed by the theme of love in such an explicit way. Almost as an afterthought Jesus predicts Peter's denial (13:36–38), as he does in all the Gospels.

John's emphasis on Jesus' love for the disciples and the importance of their love for one another dominates his account of the Last Supper. That may explain why the traditional narrative of the institution of the Lord's Supper is omitted, seemingly in favor of the foot washing. In the words of institution Jesus indicates that he gives his body and blood for his followers (cf. Mark 14:22, 24; 1 Cor. 11:24–25). In the foot washing, Jesus' self-giving service, motivated by his love for his disciples (13:1), is made even more explicit. Obviously John knows the tradition of the **Eucharist**; otherwise, the words in which Jesus' disciples are commanded to eat his flesh and drink his blood (6:52–58) are incomprehensible. In the narrative of the Last Supper, however, John calls attention to the meaning of the Eucharist precisely by omitting it, offering instead a story that dramatizes both Jesus' **saving** work and the obligation of mutual love that Jesus places upon his followers.

The Promise of the Paraclete (14:15–17, 26 and 16:12–14)

How can the Paraclete be identical with Jesus?

The farewell discourses (14:1–16:33) speak to the disciples' basic problem: How they can maintain their union with Jesus in light of the loss of his physical presence and their continued existence in a hostile world? At the start, Jesus assures them that ultimately they shall be with him (14:1–4); at the end, he tells them that he has overcome the world (16:33). Afterward, his prayer concludes with the petition that his followers may be with him in his **eschatological** glory (17:25). In the meantime, however, the disciples are not bereft of his presence. Jesus will send the **Paraclete**, the **Spirit** of truth (14:16 f.) or **Holy Spirit** (14:26), to be with them.

"Paraclete" transliterates the Greek term found in the gospel: *paraklētos*, which literally means "one called to the side of." English versions render the word "Comforter" (KJV), "Counselor" (RSV), or "Advocate" (NRSV). In terms of ancient usage "advocate," which stands closest to the literal meaning of the word, seems most appropriate. In 1 John 2:1, Jesus is called our "advocate with the Father," and in that context this translation seems exactly right. When the Paraclete is first mentioned in the Gospel, he is called "another Paraclete" (14:16), as if, indeed, Jesus were the first. Thus the NRSV translates "another Advocate."

According to Jesus the function of the Paraclete is not so much to plead a case before God as to remind, to teach, to comfort, or to counsel the disciples. (Thus the KJV and the RSV translators reasonably opted for the English term "comforter" or "counselor.") The Paraclete performs those functions because he, in effect, continues the ministry and **revelation** of Jesus himself. "I will not leave you orphaned," says Jesus, "I am coming to you" (14:18; cf. 14:16). In the farewell discourses Jesus speaks repeatedly of his own departure and coming again to the disciples (14:2–4, 18; 16:7, 16). This reminds one of the tradition of Jesus' exaltation and future return known to us from the New Testament's **apocalyptic** texts (e.g., Mark 13:26–27; 1 Thess. 4:13–18; Rev. 22:20). Such hopes were maintained also in the Johannine community, even apart from the Book of Revelation (John 21:22–23; 1 John 2:28; 3:2). John reinterprets those hopes. The coming of Jesus is essentially a spiritual coming, his reappearance as the Paraclete or the Holy Spirit.

When Jesus says that the Paraclete will teach the disciples everything and remind them of what he has said (14:26) or that the Paraclete will guide them into such truth as they cannot yet bear (or understand, 16:12), in effect he makes the Paraclete the continuation or extension of his own revelation and presence. Jesus' continuing ministry through the Spirit or Paraclete is absolutely essential to the Johannine **church**: it maintains union with Jesus (17:20–23, cf. 10:16).

The Spirit's coming is contingent on Jesus' physical departure in death (16:7). Only after his death will the disciples, or the church, be so empowered and truly understand what has taken place in his ministry. All along, the evangelist has informed the reader that the disciples would only later understand what was happening, in retrospect (2:17–22; 12:16; 13:7; cf. 14:29), after the Spirit's coming (7:39). John takes cognizance of what was surely the fact that Jesus' ministry, in its full **theological** significance and meaning, could not be comprehended at the time by eyewitnesses or even his disciples. The same notion is expressed in Mark's idea of the messianic secret: Jesus' true identity as **Messiah** is not known until Peter's confession (8:27–30)—but even after it is known, it is not understood. In John, Jesus' messianic role is announced and apparently understood by the disciples, who believe in him (2:11) yet remain strangely uncomprehending, even throughout the farewell discourses. At their conclusion, Jesus responds to the disciples' affirmation of him by predicting their desertion (16:32), while suggesting that they will ultimately represent him in the world (vs. 33).

The farewell discourses and subsequent prayer of Jesus are extremely important for understanding the Fourth Gospel. In a sense, they displace the apocalyptic discourse of the **Synoptic Gospels** (Mark 13 parr.) and offer a rather different outlook on the future. The community of Jesus' followers is to look not to the imminent future for God's apocalyptically conceived interventions in history; rather, it is to look immediately inward to the present manifestation of the Father and the Son in the church through the Spirit (cf. 14:22–23). What is revealed through the Paraclete is Jesus' further relevance, what Jesus continues to say to the church. John's Gospel itself may be viewed as a part of this ongoing revelation. While remembering the earthly Jesus of Nazareth (20:31; cf. 1 John 1:1–3; 4:1–3), John presents not so much the historical Jesus as the risen and exalted Jesus as he continues to commune and communicate with his disciples.

Jesus' Last Will: The Prayer of Consecration (17:1–26)

Why is Jesus' final utterance cast in the form of a prayer?

Jesus' last prayer in John is a carefully wrought exposition of his legacy to his disciples. His own death is mentioned in its peculiarly Johannine significance as the glorification and consecration of the **Son of God**. In the Synoptic Gospels Jesus prays in Gethsemane, "Abba, Father, for you all things are possible; remove this cup from me; yet not what I want, but what you want" (Mark 14:36; cf. John 12:27 f.). Although the Synoptics better reflect the actual, human historical situation of Jesus, the Johannine prayer vividly illumines the message of the Fourth Gospel.

With the announcement that the hour has come (17:1; cf. 12:23; 13:31–32), Jesus signals, in a typically Johannine way, the imminence of the **crucifixion** as also the hour of his glorification. The glorifying of the Son is now to take place in his death and exaltation to heaven. In John, crucifixion, **resurrection**, and exaltation are entwined as the moment of **revelation**. God glorifies Jesus by turning his death into victory; the glory that Jesus thereby shares is nothing less than God's imposing power as he makes it known to all people. Already the **Word**'s becoming flesh and dwelling among humankind has been subtly compared with God's glory dwelling in the temple (1:14; cf. 2:19 ff. and 4:20 ff.). Now the close connection between the Father and the Son allows the evangelist to assert that Jesus shares in God's eternal glory (cf. esp. vs. 5).

The definition of *eternal life* (vs. 3) shows the distance between John and any **apocalyptic** worldview. Eternal life is an **eschatological** concept; in chapter 3 it appears in conjunction with the term **kingdom of God**, so familiar from the Synoptics. The phrase "eternal life" also occurs in the Synoptics (cf. Mark 10:17), where it refers to the life of the age to come (Mark 10:30). Although in John eternal life is not robbed of its future dimension (14:1–7; 17:24), the evangelist emphasizes its present reality as knowledge of the only true God and Jesus Christ (vs. 3).

The Son glorifies the Father—that is, renders the praise and service due him—by obediently doing his work (vs. 4). Now he prays, "Father, glorify me" (vs. 5; cf. vs. 1). The new element in this petition is the reference to Christ's **preexistence**, his being with the Father before creation. There is thus a close connection between chapter 17 and John's prologue (1:1). The meaning of Jesus' glorification is that God fully accepts and affirms Jesus' work.

Throughout the farewell discourses, the disciples remain full of misunderstandings and uncertainties. Jesus' own piercing retort (16:31 f.) reveals the inadequacy of their final solemn affirmation (16:29 f.). The evangelist knows well that the disciples will desert Jesus and that they cannot fully understand the things he tells them until he has departed from them (16:7–15; 16:31 f.). In the prayer, on the other hand, Jesus views his disciples as if they had already moved into this deeper understanding. The post-resurrection **church** comes into view: Jesus' statements to his disciples are now made on the basis, not of their conduct during his earthly ministry, but of their post-resurrection faith, which is about to become a reality. Jesus prays for his disciples and also for those who will believe their preaching (17:20).

As Jesus looks toward future believers (vss. 20–23), he reiterates the need for unity, what will subsequently be called the unity of the church. Precisely this unity is for the sake of the world's believing (vs. 21) and knowing (vs. 23) the truth in which Jesus and the disciples have been unified. The Johannine church looks inward in love and faith to assure itself of its basis and ground, but then looks outward to the world, as Jesus himself was sent into the world.

JESUS' LAST APPEARANCE BEFORE THE WORLD: HIS HIDDEN GLORIFICATION (18:1–19:42)

The death of Jesus must now take place. It is Jesus' glorification (12:16, 23; 17:1), his being lifted up (3:14; 8:28; 12:32-34). The language is mysterious to the outsider, but the Johannine believer will understand. It alludes both to Jesus' **crucifixion** and **resurrection**. He is lifted up upon the cross and raised from the dead. His disciples will know this, but the world does not.

Jesus goes out across the Kidron valley to a garden (18:1), unnamed here but in other Gospels (Mark 14:32 parr.) called Gethsemane, which lies opposite the temple mount. There he is arrested (18:2-11), taken first to Annas, a former high **priest** (18:12-23), then to Caiaphas the current high priest (vv. 24, 28). The hearing before Annas is inconclusive; we learn nothing of what went on before Caiaphas. By contrast, Mark 14:53-65 and Matthew 22:57-67 presents a full-scale trial of Jesus before the Sanhedrin, the Jerusalem "supreme court," presided over by the high priest. In John, however, the principal trial is before Pilate (18:28-19:16; cf. Mark 15:1-15 parr). Here the question of Jesus' alleged crime and suitable punishment is brought out and discussed, with input from Pilate, the chief priests, and Jesus himself.

What are the causes of Jesus' death? Who is responsible? In John's Gospel, both the chief priests and Pilate have roles to play. Yet Jesus' destiny is finally in God's hands (19:11). The **Son of Man** must be lifted up (3:14), for it was God who gave his only Son (3:16). The reader has known this conclusion early on, for throughout the narrative there are hints (3:22; 7:39; 12:16; 32-33).

The Trial before Pilate (18:28–19:16)

How does Pilate typify the world's opposition to Jesus?

Elements of the Markan narrative appear in John's longer account. As in the **Synoptics**, Pilate asks Jesus, "Are you the King of the Jews?" (18:33; Mark 15:2 parr). On the other hand, in the Fourth Gospel Jesus' account of his kingdom is wholly distinctive (John 18:36), and Jesus defines his mission as testifying to the truth (v. 39). Pilate appears perplexed and perhaps also cynical, as he responds (v. 38), "What is truth?" Either way, Pilate is utterly ignorant of the fact that Jesus himself is the truth (14:6; cf. 8:31-32). This recalls the Johannine motif of misunderstanding: Jesus talks in plain speech, which, however, is unintelligible to outsiders, people like Pilate who are without a clue as to who he really is (see 3:1-10; cf. pp. 161–163).

Excavations near the Citadel of Jerusalem on the western wall of the city. This is close to the likely location of the trial of Jesus, probably in Herod's palace.

Only in John is the venue of this event Pilate's headquarters (the *praetorium*)— probably the Herodian palace on the city's western side, although this is uncertain. Jesus' (Jewish) accusers, the chief **priests** (19:6), refuse to enter the palace lest they be defiled and unable to eat the **Passover** (18:28). The date according to the Jewish Calendar is thus identified. This represents a sharp difference from the other Gospels, where the **Lord's Supper** is the Passover meal (Mark 14:12). In John that meal is still anticipated (cf. 13:1). John might have changed the date so that Jesus would die with the Passover lambs (cf. 1:29, 35). Historically speaking, however, this whole series of events would more likely have taken place before the festival began rather than during it. (Mark 14:2 indicates that Jesus' enemies sought to get him out of the way before it began.) In any event, John seems quite insistent on this chronology (19:14, 31).

Pilate's initial question is to "the Jews" who have brought Jesus before him (18:29-31). Their response (v. 30) assumes that Jesus is guilty unless proven innocent; and the latter, they are confident, will not happen. When Pilate wants to throw the whole process back to Jesus' Jewish opponents (vs. 31), they admit their reason for bringing Jesus to him is that they themselves do not have the power to put anyone to death. Only Luke (23:2) has the Jewish authorities explicitly state the charges against Jesus, including claiming that he himself is **Christ**, a king; Pilate then seizes upon this issue. Matthew, Mark, and John leave the reader to infer the charges.

Historical facts are again mixed with Johannine interpretation. Jesus had Jewish opponents, as all the Gospels attest, but the Roman authorities could not have cared less about such controversies so long as they did not disturb the peace. Yet Jesus was crucified ("under Pontius Pilate" says the **Apostles' Creed**), and John's reference to "the kind of death" he was to die (vs. 32) alludes to **crucifixion**. Jesus is to be lifted up from the earth, that is, crucified (12:32-3). Moreover, crucifixion was a typically Roman, not Jewish, form of execution, usually reserved for political rebels. Nevertheless, John portrays the Jewish authorities as assuming culpability for his death, as they try to convince Pilate of its necessity (19:6-16; cf. Matt. 27:25). Thus John stereotypes both Pilate and the Jews. Still, Pilate ultimately decided there was reason enough to have Jesus crucified—though John depicts him as succumbing to pressure applied by the chief priests, alternately called "the Jews."

Their reasons for wanting Jesus executed (19:7) seem of no interest to Pilate, who three times declares Jesus innocent (18:38; 19:4, 6). They know, however, that Pilate cannot ignore the charge that as a kingly pretender Jesus represents a challenge to Roman power (i.e., the emperor or Caesar; 19:12; cf. Luke 23:2). Pilate seems scarcely willing to take seriously the charge that Jesus is a real threat. When they persist, Pilate incredulously asks whether they want him to crucify their own king (v. 15). They reply that they have no king but Caesar. John portrays the chief priests as choosing Rome over Israel, thus abdicating their own responsibility. Pilate yields and hands Jesus over for crucifixion, apparently to the Jews (v. 16). Nevertheless, John describes the execution as carried out by Roman soldiers (19:18, 23-24), which it doubtless was. The trial concludes with the controversy between Pilate and the chief priests, with Jesus himself making a definitive statement about the source of all power (vs. 11).

This entire episode is similar to that in the Synoptics, with elements that are distinctly Johannine. The latter predominate in John 19:6-16. The Synoptic-like elements seem to provide the historical basis, and the distinctly Johannine parts appear as theological interpretations that tend to assign responsibility and blame for Jesus' death to the Jews. Yet, as we have observed, the death of Jesus is finally viewed as a necessity, ordained by God. Moreover, although the conversations between the chief priests and Pilate are hardly stenographic records, John may disclose some of the historical dynamics of the situation. Here "the Jews" refers primarily to the chief priests (19:6-7, 14-15). In all likelihood, the chief priests, not the Jewish people as a whole, actually did play an active role in having Jesus condemned (cf. 11:45-53). In the early scenes of the Acts of the Apostles, the chief priests, described as **Sadducees** (Acts 4:1-7), take the lead in opposing followers of the crucified Jesus who have remained in Jerusalem (cf. 5:17-18).

The Execution of Jesus by Crucifixion (19:17–42)

How and why is John's account of Jesus' death distinctive?

John's narrative of these events closely parallels the other Gospels (Mark 15:21-41 parr.), with typical differences. In all four Gospels Jesus is crucified at the Place of the Skull, in Hebrew (or **Aramaic**) *Golgotha*. He is crucified with two other condemned criminals; a sign is placed on the cross that identifies him as King of the Jews. The soldiers gamble for

A modern scene along the Via Dolorosa in Jerusalem, the traditional path of Jesus from his trial by Pilate to the crucifixion at Golgotha. Whether the various stations of the cross are accurate is open to historical investigation and admits of no general answer.

his clothes. The male disciples have fled. The only witnesses to these horrific events are the women who had followed Jesus. Mary Magdalene is mentioned in Matthew, Mark, and John; Mary the mother of Jesus, in John only (19:25-27). Only in John, Jesus delivers his mother into the Beloved Disciple's care. Thus, only in John is Jesus' mother portrayed as appearing at the beginning and end of his ministry (cf. 2:1-11).

There are other typically Johannine touches. Jesus carries his own cross, needing no help from Simon of Cyrene (Mark 15:20 parr). Golgotha is said to be near but not inside the city (19:20; cf. Heb. 13:12). The chief **priests** try to get Pilate to change the inscription on the cross, but he refuses (vs. 21-22). The casting of lots for Jesus' seamless tunic is narrated in detail (vv. 23-25a). One of the soldiers pierces Jesus' side (19:31-37). Only in John is Joseph of Arimathea, who buries Jesus' body in all four Gospels, joined by Nicodemus—a character unique to John (cf. 3:1-10; 7:50-52).

Similarly, there are surprising, if sometimes typically Johannine, omissions. Jesus is not mocked while hanging on the cross (Mark 15:27-32a parr). He does not cry out to God (Mark 15:34 par), nor does he utter a loud cry at his death (Mark 15:37 parr). There is no darkness at noon (Mark 15:33 parr); no rending of the temple veil (Mark 15:38 parr); no confession of the centurion (Mark 15:39 parr). Moreover, in John, Jesus appears in control until the end (19:30), as he has been all along. One gets no sense of Jesus' suffering on the cross.

JESUS' RETURN TO HIS DISCIPLES (20:1–31)

Is Jesus' resurrection expected?

Every Gospel recounts the discovery of the empty tomb by women; in John it is Mary Magdalene only, though she is mentioned in every Gospel account (cf. Mark 16:1-8 parr). Only John describes male disciples visiting the already discovered empty tomb (John 20:2-9; but cf. Luke 24:12, which is textually doubtful, and 24:24). Yet only John presents Mary Magdalene alone as the first witness of the risen Jesus (20:14-18; cf. Matt. 28:9-10). John's dramatic scene implies a special relationship between Jesus and Mary.

Jesus addresses Mary by name (cf. 10:3), and Mary responds, "Teacher," or "my Teacher." Apparently she reaches out to Jesus, who tells her not to hold on to him, because he has not yet **ascended** to the Father, but to go and make the announcement "to my brothers" (vss. 16-17). Mary then does so, telling Jesus' disciples (i.e., his brothers). Later Jesus will invite his disciple Thomas to touch him (20:27), implying that his ascent has been accomplished. We are not told whether Thomas actually touched Jesus.

John then recounts two successive Sunday meetings with the disciples, at the first of which (20:19-23) Thomas was not present. Thomas then demands tangible proof that what his colleagues have seen is actually the risen Jesus himself (vv. 24-25). A week later, again on the first day of the week, they gather once again, with Thomas in attendance (vv. 26-29). When Jesus challenges Thomas to receive tactile proof (v. 27), he utters the highest confession found in the Gospel, or for that matter in the rest of the New Testament: "My Lord and my God!" (v. 28). Jesus' response, however, is not to congratulate Thomas, but to point ahead to those who have not seen, but will come to believe (v. 29).

The Gospel apparently ends with a statement about its character and purpose (20:30-31). Clearly this is a formal conclusion, after which the ancient (or modern) reader would expect nothing more.

APPENDIX: THE GOSPEL CONTINUES (21:1–25)

What does the Appendix accomplish in concluding the Gospel?

This final section contains two distinct elements: a **resurrection** appearance of Jesus by the Sea of Tiberias (i.e., Galilee; 21:1–14) and a conversation between Jesus and Simon Peter in which Jesus reveals to Simon his own fate and the role of the disciple Jesus loved (21:15–25).

This chapter's narrative is continuous, but its connection with what precedes is difficult to understand, even if the conclusion of 20:30-31 is omitted. Abruptly one finds Peter returning to his work of fishing and the other disciples going with him (21:3). They are in Galilee by the Sea. Just previously, however, they have twice seen the risen Jesus in Jerusalem, and been sent out by him, even as the Father sent Jesus (20:21). (Incidentally, John has heretofore said nothing about the disciples having been Galilean fishermen. This account seems to reflect knowledge of the disciples in the **Synoptic Gospels**: Mark 1:16–20 parr). Also, only here are the Zebedee brothers mentioned (21:2); they too seem to be imports from the Synoptics. This entire scene also answers the expectation of Mark 16:7 (cf. Mark 14:28) that the risen Jesus would appear to his disciples in Galilee, their home country. Was this scene originally an *initial* resurrection appearance, as apparently in the *Gospel of Peter,* not the third in John's series (vs. 14)?

In the subsequent conversation, Peter is required to confess his love for Jesus three times (vv. 15–19), corresponding perhaps to his three denials of Jesus (cf. 18:17, 25, 27). After Peter has been informed of the manner of his own death (21:18–19), he turns and sees the Beloved Disciple: "Lord, what about him?" (v. 21). This is a natural question, bespeaking nevertheless some rivalry between the two, doubtless because of their leadership roles after Jesus' death. What Jesus says to Peter about this disciple (v. 22), and the following comment (v. 23), imply that this disciple lived a long time, probably beyond Peter, but then died without Jesus' having returned. This disciple's death likely caused consternation in the Johannine **church**. Perhaps it played a part in the revision of end time, **eschatological** expectation we now find in John.

The Gospel then concludes with a ringing affirmation of this disciple whom Jesus loved as a true **witness**, whose followers can vouch for him (v. 24). He also is designated as the author, although the statement could mean "caused these things to be written." Either way, this disciple is said to be responsible for the existence of this Gospel. Yet it remains the case that he is neither here nor elsewhere identified with John. The Fourth Gospel's attribution to "John" does not occur until the last quarter of the second century (ca. A.D. 175). The concluding rumination about the number of books that could be written (vs. 25) seems to presuppose the existence of other Gospels known to this author, perhaps one or more of the Synoptics.

CONCLUSION

John's *structure* is quite simple (see p. 154). Commentators can scarcely agree on details, but its basic twofold division is obvious. Jesus reveals his glory to the world and gathers his disciples, who follow him without fully understanding him (chaps 2–12). Then he retreats with his disciples to reveal himself more fully to them (chaps. 13–21). The **passion** narrative (chaps. 18–19) only seems to break this pattern. Jesus' **crucifixion** is a public event, but there is no **revelation** to the world. Yet Jesus' being lifted up on the cross (12:32–33; cf. 3:14) is necessary for his disciples or anyone to understand (8:28). The Johannine pattern of Public Ministry followed by the Passion Narrative is found in all four Gospels, but in John that distinction and demarcation is sharpest.

John's *emphases* appear in the episodes discussed above. First, Jesus' appearance is the revelation of God's glory, superior to anything that has preceded or will follow (1:1–18). It is the expression of God's love and the gift of life (3:16; 5:21), while at the same time bringing judgment (3:17 ff.). It is the fulfillment of Israel's hope (1:19 ff.), although Jesus' Jewish disciples cannot yet comprehend this (1:50 f.). If they can hardly understand, it is scarcely surprising that the learned **Pharisee** Nicodemus cannot, well-disposed though he may be (3:1–10). He wants to fit Jesus into his previously established religious pattern. He is a teacher of Israel (3:10) and should understand, but what is required is a transvaluation of values, a reversal of assumptions previously held. The Bible (Old Testament) and Jewish tradition do not make the revelation in Jesus understandable. Rather, Jesus makes them understandable. Ordinary expectations are thrown into reverse.

Jesus brings healing (9:1–41). In fact, Jesus appeared as a *thaumaturge*, a doer of mighty deeds or miracles. As such, he is the giver of life. But his acts are not really comprehended. As in the Nicodemus episode, they do not lead to belief in Jesus. Instead they provoke rejection and hostility, except on the part of his disciples. That Jesus actually does such deeds is questioned (9:18). The parents of the man born blind testify, truthfully but circumspectly. Finally, they put the ball back into their son's court (9:23). They fear that association with Jesus will result in expulsion from Judaism, represented by the synagogue. This *historical situation* bespeaks a time later than Jesus' own day, when **Christ**-confessors and Christ-deniers—both still Jews— were in conflict. Even after Jesus' departure in death, Christians still belonged to synagogues. In the Epistle of James (2:2), "assembly" translates the Greek word for "synagogue" (*synagogē*). The **Apostle** Paul speaks of being lashed by Jews, apparently punishment administered to him as a Jew (2 Cor. 11:14; cf. Deut 25:3), probably in a synagogue. Nevertheless, in John "the Jews" generally are the enemies of Jesus. They reject his claims. John reflects a parting of the paths, in which two religions with common roots went their separate and often hostile ways.

This rejection is finally incomprehensible, and John often uses the language of election or predestination to explain it (cf. Rom. 8:28–30): "You did not choose me, but I chose you," says Jesus (John 15:16). At the same time, he has just made obedience to his own commandments the test of the disciples' seriousness and, in effect, their election (15:9–10).

Any attempt to separate *redaction* from *tradition* in the Fourth Gospel becomes problematic, because we do not possess John's sources. This holds true even if John knew the **Synoptic Gospels**, because he so often does not appropriate them but moves off in other directions. Thus John is rightly called a maverick Gospel, unaccountably different from the others.

Nevertheless, a distinction between tradition and redaction is useful. There is evidence that John has grown by stages. To some extent we can discern a process of development. Also, some parts of the narrative seem more basic, and thus traditional. For instance, in the trial before Pilate the latter's question, "Are you the King of the Jews?" (19:33) is basic, pivotal, and found in all four Gospels. John's distinctive material (19:34–38a) presupposes, and is an elaboration of, the issues raised by that question. Throughout the passion narrative John runs fairly close to Mark or the Synoptics. When John departs, he is sometimes supplying his distinctive embellishment or interpretation. At other points, however, John may deliberately follow a different tradition. Thus John omits Mark's long account of Jesus' Jewish trial before the Sanhedrin and high **priest**, a narrative that would have served his purposes well. It has Jesus condemned for blasphemy by the highest Jewish authorities, as he is elsewhere in John (Mark 14:53–65; esp. v. 63; cf. John 10:33).

Earlier in John, the stories of Jesus' **miracles** (signs), not unlike those in the Synoptics, are followed by extensive discourses or debates, quite unlike anything found there (see 5:1–9, followed by 5:10–47, esp. vss. 17–30; also 9:1–7, followed by 9:8–41, esp. vss. 13–34). In such cases, it is a reasonable judgment that the miracle stories themselves are taken from preexisting tradition, while the subsequent discussion is added later and reflects the evangelist's setting.

The separation of tradition and redaction is no more difficult than in the case of Mark, whose sources we do not possess, but more difficult than with Matthew or Luke, whose sources we either possess (Mark) or can infer from **Q**. All along, as Johannine texts have been examined in this chapter, the **redaction-critical** method has actually been followed where possible.

Returning to the *historical setting* (or *settings*) of John, it may have shifted during the Gospel's composition, if that process was spread over a period of years. There seems to have been a time when the setting was a conflict within Judaism about whether Jesus was the expected **messiah** (3:1–21; 9:1–41), with sharp divisions emerging. Other parts of the Gospel reflect primarily inner-Christian concerns and issues (chaps. 13–17). In the passion narrative (chaps. 18–19), historical tradition is more predominant than elsewhere in the Gospel, and the hostility of Roman, as well as Jewish, authority is evident. By then, perhaps, Johannine Christianity was breaking into a larger world. In the last chapter (John 21), inner Christian tensions come to light. (Such tensions apparently grew in the period of the Epistles of John.) The prologue takes the longest view of all, perhaps reflecting a later time in the history of composition, as does chapter 21. Yet the issues in the prologue are different, **cosmic** rather than church-political. The opposition of Jesus' own people is noted (1:11), but the **gospel**, and this Gospel, have now passed to a broader stage (1:12–13). The **theological** implications of Jesus' appearance in history are now emphasized (1:14, 16–18). Although the reference to Moses and the **law** (vs. 17) can be taken negatively, this is not the only or necessary interpretation. Moses' ministry can be, and in the history of interpretation has been, understood as preparation for the gospel (cf. Gal. 3:23–29). John's ambiguity is typical of this Gospel.

In later decades, John's Gospel, which may have begun within sectarian boundaries in a seedbed of controversy, became the hallmark of Christian orthodoxy ("right teaching") as the theme of the **Incarnation** (as in 1:14) became the subject of the great Christian creeds of the fourth and fifth centuries, particularly the so-called Nicene Creed. This Creed dealt with the relationship of Jesus the incarnate **Word** to God, and declared him to be only (*monogenēs*), or only begotten, Son. The same term is used in John 1:18. The key term of the Creed, *homoousios* (the same being) is not found in John, but it is a proper understanding of the statement that the Word was God (*theos*) in John 1:1 (cf. 20:28). The Nicene Creed has become the classic statement of orthodox Christian faith, still recited at Mass or Holy Communion by millions of Christians today.

SUGGESTIONS FOR FURTHER READING

Commentaries on John are quite numerous. The work of R. E. Brown, *The Gospel According to John*, 2 vols. (Garden City, NY: Doubleday, 1966, 1970), remains the standard commentary for the student who does not use Greek. (Inability to read Greek will inhibit the use of Rudolf Bultmann's important commentary, as well as those of C. K. Barrett and Rudolf Schnackenburg.) See also Brown's revised introduction, *An Introduction to the Gospel of John*, ed. F. J. Moloney (New York: Doubleday, 2002), as well as Moloney's own commentary, *The Gospel of John* (Collegeville, MN: Liturgical Press, 1998). D. M. Smith's *John* (Nashville: Abingdon, 1999), a briefer commentary, will also prove useful. The most recent technical commentary is C. S. Keener, *The Gospel of John: A Commentary*, 2 vols. (Peabody, MA: Hendrickson, 2003), which is exhaustive in its command of secondary as well as primary sources.

Other Studies.   C. H. Dodd, *Historical Tradition in the Fourth Gospel* (New York: Cambridge University Press, 1963), is still the fundamental work in that area. J. L. Martyn, *History and Theology in the Fourth Gospel*, 3rd rev. ed. (Louisville: Westminster John Knox, 2003), is extremely important for the **historical setting and purpose** of the Gospel, as is R. E. Brown, *The Community of the Beloved Disciple* (New York: Paulist, 1979). Applying **newer literary criticism** to the Fourth Gospel, R. A. Culpepper, *Anatomy of the Fourth Gospel: A Study in Literary Design* (Philadelphia: Fortress, 1983), breaks fresh ground. J. Ashton, *Understanding the*

Fourth Gospel (Oxford: Clarendon, 1991), utilizes the insights of Martyn and others in offering a **comprehensive interpretation** of the Gospel, as does J. Painter, *The Quest of the Messiah: The History, Literature, and Theology of the Johannine Community*, 2nd ed. (Nashville: Abingdon, 1993). M. M. Thompson, *The God of the Gospel of John* (Grand Rapids, MI: Eerdmans, 2001) raises a centrally important **theological** issue. For a concise, more general statement, see D. M. Smith, *The Theology of the Gospel of John* (Cambridge: Cambridge University Press, 1995).

D. M. Smith, *John among the Gospels*, 2nd rev. ed. (Columbia, SC: University of South Carolina Press, 2001), charts the course of the discussion of this modern yet very ancient problem. G. S. Sloyan, *What Are They Saying About John?* (New York: Paulist, 1991), admirably reports on the most **important recent research** on the Fourth Gospel. For an excellent collection of essays on various aspects and issues, see *Exploring the Gospel of John*, ed. R. A. Culpepper and C. C. Black (Louisville: Westminster John Knox, 1996). See the ends of Chapters 12 and 13 for bibliography on the Epistles of John and Revelation.

Jesus of the People. © Copyright 1999 by Janet McKenzie. *(Reproduced by kind permission of the artist.)*

CHAPTER 6

JESUS
THE MESSIAH

INTRODUCTION: THE TRADITION ABOUT JESUS

To write a life of Jesus is impossible, for we cannot reconstruct the course of Jesus' ministry in any detail or understand his psychological development. The nature of the **Gospel** sources does not permit this kind of historical endeavor. Moreover, sources for the historical Jesus outside the Gospels, both **canonical** and extracanonical, are meager.

What Do We Know about Jesus from Sources Outside the New Testament?

We learn little about him from contemporary secular and Jewish sources. Perhaps the most important attestation of Christianity, and therefore of Jesus, in Roman historical writings is found in the *Annals* of Tacitus (early second century), who refers to his execution. The first-century Jewish historian Josephus recounted Jewish history during the period of Jesus' life; although he described the **Essenes** and John the Baptist in some detail, he barely mentioned Jesus. Josephus certainly refers to "James, the brother of Jesus who was called the **Christ**" (*Jewish Antiquities*, XX, 200). In that work (XVIII, 63–64) there is a fuller reference to Jesus that is at least in part the product of Christian embellishment, for it has Josephus affirm that Jesus was the Christ and that he rose from the dead. Polemical references in the Jewish **Talmud** contain little independent tradition about Jesus. Samuel Sandmel trenchantly summed up the situation: "Accordingly, though Jesus was a Jew, there are no Jewish sources of any value about him" (*Judaism and Christian Beginnings* [1978]). More accurately, they add nothing to our knowledge of Jesus beyond confirmation that he existed, was a Jew, and was executed. Although no early non-Christian source questions Jesus' historical existence, at the same time the literature takes little notice of him.

At first glance the **apocryphal** Gospels appear to provide extensive sources for the historical Jesus. These Gospels, which did not become part of the Christian **canon**, can be divided into three basic types: (1) later, popular Gospels, like the *Infancy Gospel of Thomas*, which contain imaginative stories about Jesus (including his hidden childhood) that served to satisfy pious curiosity and to entertain the faithful; (2) **Gnostic** Gospels, like the *Gospel of Philip*, the *Gospel of Judas*, and the Nag Hammadi *Gospel of Thomas*, which present a secret teaching of Jesus that elaborates a way of **salvation** higher than that given in the common Gospel tradition; (3) a few Gospels, such as the *Gospel of the Hebrews* and the *Gospel of Peter*, which are possibly early or embody early traditions but are known only through surviving fragments (*Peter*) or brief quotations in other sources (*Hebrews*). The *Gospel of Thomas* does contain a number of sayings of Jesus that are probably authentic, but many are found also in the canonical Gospels in somewhat different form. Although the apocryphal Gospels seem to offer much additional teaching and narrative material, with the possible exception of the *Gospel of Thomas*, they are of little help in reconstructing the historical Jesus.

In fact, apart from the canonical Gospels, we find little tradition about Jesus within the New Testament. Some **agrapha**—sayings attributed to him and preserved outside the Gospels—may be authentic: for example, "It is more blessed to give than to receive" (Acts 20:35). Still, these are relatively few and do not greatly affect understanding of him. On several occasions Paul refers to the tradition of the Lord that he had received (1 Cor. 11:23–26; 15:3 f.; cf. 7:10, 12, 25). Probably Paul knew more Jesus tradition than at first appears. Nevertheless, the rarity of Paul's citation of Jesus' words or deeds proves the rule: little tradition of Jesus can be identified with certainty in the latter half of the New Testament.

Thus the principal sources for knowing the historical Jesus are the canonical Gospels, but they do not include the information necessary for what we think of as a biography. In previous chapters, we have learned that the Gospels are dominated by their religious and **theological** perspectives; they serve chronological, psychological, or purely factual interests in limited ways, if at all. With the exception of the infancy narratives in Matthew and Luke, which differ widely, they tell us nothing of Jesus' life before the beginning of his brief ministry. These Gospels proclaim the good news in the form of the story of Jesus.

Among the canonical Gospels, John stands out as obviously different. Not only does it recount a two- or three-year ministry—as against only a year or less in the **Synoptics**—but, as we have seen, its portrayal of Jesus is unique. Whether addressing disciples or others, the Johannine Jesus speaks mostly of himself. His themes are **Christological**; that is, John's Jesus elaborates his dignity and role as **Messiah** and **Son of God**. This portrayal of Jesus is surely more the product of early Christian faith and reflection than of history or historical tradition. With the exception of the **passion** narrative, most of John's content is without parallel in the other Gospels, and vice versa.

Still, we have also observed that the Fourth Gospel may provide us with some data that are historically correct, even where it contradicts the Synoptics. For example, Jesus probably visited Jerusalem more than once in his career. Among the Synoptics, Matthew and Luke appear to rely upon Mark for the framework, outline, or order of Jesus' ministry. Where they depart from Mark in this respect, they also differ from each other. Matthew and Luke are not, therefore, independent sources for the course of Jesus' ministry. It is a measure of John's independence of the others that its framework differs widely from that of Mark.

In this chapter, we attempt to reconstruct a single portrait of Jesus of Nazareth that emerges out of the Gospel portraits. Our justification for this procedure lies not only in contemporary historical interest in Jesus but also in the fact that the four Gospel portraits stand at the beginning of the New Testament. In ancient Gospel **manuscripts** there is one general heading, "The Gospel," followed by "According to Matthew," and so forth. Although their portraits are obviously different, the Gospels invite an encounter once again with the same Jesus of Nazareth, a real and distinct historical figure. Although there are four Gospels, the New Testament suggests that there is but one **gospel** message and one Jesus.

Kerygma, Gospels, and Jesus of Nazareth

New Testament Christianity was founded upon belief in the **resurrection** of the **crucified** Jesus; his apparently ignominious death was regarded as the decisive act of God for the **salvation** of humankind (1 Cor. 15:3). This faith was at first held in anticipation of his imminent return in glory to judge and to rule. From the beginning Christians felt impelled to announce to others the good news (**gospel**) of what God had done in Jesus. This proclamation or ***kērygma*** was based on what God had done through Jesus rather than on what Jesus himself had done. Its power did not rest in new knowledge or wisdom but rather in an event—Jesus' death and resurrection.

That event is the seed from which the **Gospels** ultimately grew. They presuppose, and to a remarkable extent are based upon, early Christian faith and preaching. The words with which the Fourth Gospel closes are equally applicable to the others: "These [things] are written so that you may come to believe that Jesus is the **Messiah**, the **Son of God**, and that through believing you may have life in his name" (John 20:31). This too was the purpose of the proclamation of the gospel generally. Even the traditions of Jesus that came to the Gospel writers from **oral tradition** and written sources were already, down to individual units, shaped by the interests of the church. (This insight is the lasting contribution of **form criticism**; see Chapter 2, pp. 57–60.) In fact, early Christians remembered the tradition of Jesus only because they were convinced that God had acted for them in this man, especially in his death and resurrection.

In studying the Gospels, it is important to keep in mind the history of Christian faith and experience they presuppose. In earlier generations, Christian readers have more or less shared this faith and have read the Gospels with that proper major premise in view. Yet pre-conceptions and prejudices have often distorted such reading. Whether or not modern readers share the faith of those early Christians, they can understand what it was and how it influenced the telling of the story. One must bear in mind also that the Gospels in their present form are not, for the most part, the product of the earliest witnesses but appeared only as, or after, those witnesses passed from the scene (Luke 1:2; John 21:20–24). The Gospels are the legacy of those primal witnesses as it was bequeathed to the **church**.

The Basic Tradition of Jesus

Unless one is determined to regard everything in the Gospels as historical—and that can be accomplished only by dogmatic desire, not by critical judgment—some means for identifying the materials that stem from Jesus himself must be established. Several criteria of **authenticity** have proved useful.

1. The oldest material will usually be found in the *cores* of stories, **parables**, or sayings proper, as distinguished from introductions, endings, and transitions, which are often the work of later editors or authors. (This criterion proves more useful in the **Synoptics** than in John, where narrative and discourse are often more smoothly woven together.) For instance, in Mark 4 the introduction (vss. 1–2) is likely editorial. The general statement about parables (vss. 10–12) together with the interpretation (vss. 13–20) is probably a later development of the tradition. The former explains the mystery of unbelief; the latter interprets the parable so that it explains the success or failure of the **church**'s later preaching of the gospel. The parable itself (vss. 3–9), how-ever, is in all probability the kernel that originates from Jesus. (This parable, lacking introduction or subsequent interpretation, is found in the *Gospel of Thomas*, 9.)

2. An important criterion is *cultural, religious, and linguistic appropriateness* or *intelligibility*. Is what is attributed to Jesus intelligible in a first-century Palestinian Jewish environment, in which **Aramaic** was the commonly spoken language? In general, Jesus' debates about the meaning of the **law** are intelligible in that context. Also the term **Son of Man**, evidently Jesus' favorite self-designation, is a known idiom in Aramaic and Hebrew but not in Greek. Likewise, **kingdom of God**, an important theme of Jesus' preaching, is a biblical concept. On the other hand, the saying of Jesus in the *Gospel of Thomas* (37) encouraging nudity can scarcely be ascribed to the historical Jesus, for it flies in the face of Jewish custom and does not cohere with his other teaching (see criterion 5, below). Moreover, a quotation of scripture that too closely follows the **Septuagint** (a Greek translation) becomes at least suspect (cf. Matt. 13:14–15), since Jesus would more likely have cited the **targums** (in Aramaic translation), if not the original Hebrew.

3. The criterion of *dissimilarity* accords a high probability of authenticity to sayings of Jesus or similar materials that are unlikely to have been derived from contemporary Judaism and that are not easily ascribed to the early church—although something unheard of or unthinkable in a Jewish milieu would hardly be authentic. Thus, the terms *kingdom of God* and *Son of Man* are easily ascribed to the historical Jesus as authentic. Although both can be found in first-century Judaism or earlier, neither occupies as important a place as it does in the teachings of Jesus. At the same time, neither term has anything like the importance in the teaching of the early church, as attested in New Testament writings outside the Gospels, that it has in the Gospels and especially in the sayings of Jesus. This criterion is helpful if used with care and discrimination. Obviously, since Jesus himself was Jewish, sayings based on Jewish premises are not for that reason to be eliminated.

4. The criterion of *multiple attestation* means the occurrence of sayings, concepts, narratives, or other materials in more than one stream of tradition (as distinguished from where Matthew or Luke is simply following Mark). Again, *Son of Man* and *kingdom of God* appear not only in all the Gospels but also in their underlying sources: that is, in Mark (used by Matthew and Luke), **Q** (used by Matthew and Luke), M (distinctively Matthean material), L (distinctively Lukan material), as well as the relatively independent Gospel of John and even the *Gospel of Thomas* (86). Something similar could be said of Jesus' **miracles**, his teaching about obedience to God, and his **crucifixion**: all these also appear in different streams of tradition. Even though the specific healing miracles of John are found in none of the other Gospels, they too strongly attest the fact that Jesus was known as a healer.

5. Any reconstruction of Jesus' career or of his teaching must finally take account of the principle of *coherence*. It is important that any given saying or fact about Jesus should cohere with an emerging picture of him. For example, the portrayal of Jesus as one accused of breaking the Sabbath coheres with those instances in which on other grounds he clashes with the authority of **scribes**, tradition, or even scripture. Thus, we seek to portray with greater detail the one coherent, historical figure who stimulated the tradition in all its variety.

The Jordan River as it flows south
out of the Sea of Galilee.

We possess in considerable quantity traditional materials, basic to the Synoptic
Gospels and found also in John, that pertain to Jesus' *miracles*, his *teaching*, and his
death. The existence of these three separate strands of the fundamental tradition raises
the question of their interrelationship. A coherent picture of Jesus must somehow show
how these three major, traditional areas unite in one historical figure. How, for example,
does the powerful Jesus who performs miracles relate to the Jesus who is powerless to
prevent his own death? This particular problem is already recognized and dealt with, theologically, by the Gospels' authors.

The basic tradition of Jesus includes not only facts but meaning. The early Christians did not feel free to read any meaning into Jesus. They saw his deeds, words, and
death in the light of their commonly held conviction that he was the **Messiah**. Therefore, in our presentation we speak of the healing Messiah, the teaching Messiah, and the
suffering Messiah. All the Gospels unanimously and unequivocally see all three main

aspects of Jesus' mission and message as messianic, and our reconstruction takes this viewpoint into account. The reconstruction of such a portrait does not, however, prove that Jesus claimed to be the Messiah, much less that Jesus *was* the Messiah; it only makes this messianic claim comprehensible.

In an important sense this claim that Jesus is the Messiah represents the conviction that he is the *Christian* Messiah. That is, Jesus himself—his fate, and belief in and about him—colored decisively the conception of messiahship that Christians held and attributed to Jesus. At the same time early Christians never ceased believing that he was also the Messiah of Jewish and biblical expectation, and in this conviction they constantly appealed to scripture to prove their point.

In this chapter, we must depend on the portraits of Jesus that appear in the Gospels. In the belief of the church that produced the New Testament, they complement rather than contradict one another: each evangelist looked at the same Jesus from a different perspective. They were concerned less about exactness in detail than about being true to their basic conceptions of Jesus. It is not inappropriate for the same freedom and loyalty to attend our study of the tradition of Jesus.

THE HEALING MESSIAH

The reader of the Gospels quickly learns that Jesus was a **miracle** worker. This impression is particularly strong in Mark, where miracle working seems to be his chief activity prior to the final week in Jerusalem, and in John, where the astounding character of the miracles and their faith- (or opposition-) evoking quality are obvious. Yet when one reads some of the **apocryphal** Gospels, like the *Gospel of Peter* or the *Infancy Gospel of Thomas*, one is struck by the **canonical** narratives' relative restraint. Whatever one thinks of the possibility of miracles in the modern world, the tradition of Jesus as miracle worker is probably rooted in his own activity (see Acts 2:22; 10:38).

In all likelihood individual miracle stories of the Gospels, most of which are self-contained **pericopae**, were grouped together before their incorporation into our canonical Gospels. By this means Jesus could have been presented as a man endowed by God with special powers, a type familiar to the **Hellenistic** world and not unprecedented in Judaism. This presentation of Jesus implies not only an interest in miracles but a correspondence between his activity and that of his followers. That is, there were miracle working and miracle workers in the **church** (e.g., Acts 3:1–16; 1 Cor. 12:9-10, 28; 2 Cor. 12:12). Although it had some popular acceptance, such a presentation of Jesus could not and did not survive in independent form, for it lacked any distinctively Christian element and substituted wonder for faith. Moreover, taken alone it did not deal with the central scandal of Jesus' life, the fact of his **crucifixion**, which was well known among **Gentiles** and Jews who had heard of him. Nevertheless, the presentation of Jesus as miracle worker had some factual basis and did attest to the Christian conviction that God was at work in him. Although understanding the relation of Jesus to early Christianity remains the central problem of Christian origins, the reality of that relation is hardly a matter of doubt. Early Christianity stemmed from Jesus. Its literature reflects a constant harking back to him as the basis of its faith. The preservation of so many miracle stories testifies to this fact. At the same time Christianity quickly became a religion *about* Jesus rather than a movement of which Jesus was personally the leader and founder. Christians preached the gospel of Jesus to Jews and then Gentiles with a view to gaining their allegiance to Jesus or, more properly, eliciting their faith in Jesus as Lord, **Christ**, or **Son of God**. Probably the miracle stories were preserved in such numbers because they called attention to Jesus' extraordinary nature and could be used to commend him as a person of divine origin and mission.

The most characteristic miracles in the **Synoptics** are Jesus' healings, especially the exorcism of demons, which Mark emphasizes and are noticeable for their absence in John. Miracle stories comprise a large part of each of the Gospels. Nearly one-third of Mark's Gospel is devoted to them. Matthew and Luke report practically all the Markan miracles and add several more; the Gospel of John contains yet other miracles, there called *signs*. In Peter's first speech to the **Gentiles**, no mention is made of Jesus' teaching, but the good news does include "how God anointed Jesus of Nazareth with the **Holy Spirit** and with power; how he went about doing good and healing all that were oppressed by the devil" (Acts 10:38). Even the **Talmud** acknowledges that Jesus healed, but dismisses his work as that of a sorcerer: in the most famous talmudic statement about Jesus (Babylonian Talmud, *Sanhedrin* 43a), he is said to have been hanged for sorcery and leading Israel astray. Demon exorcism and healing were manifestly among Jesus' principal activities.

Yet there has always been a certain ambiguity about miracles. When after many healings the crowds gathered around Jesus, his family "went out to restrain him, for people were saying, 'He has gone out of his mind.' And the **scribes** who came down from Jerusalem said, 'He has Beelzebub, and by the ruler of the demons he casts out demons'" (Mark 3:21 f.). Thus healing miracles could be considered the work of God or of the devil; they do not prove **messiahship**. Indeed, according to one major New Testament emphasis, Jesus' power is not in mighty works, but in his **crucifixion** and death. Christ crucified is "to those who are called, both Jews and Greeks . . . the *power* of God and the wisdom of God" (1 Cor. 1:24). Moreover, to desire miracles as proof of Jesus' messiahship is to seek after signs (cf. 1 Cor. 1:22). Thus, when the **Pharisees** come to Jesus demanding a sign, he replies, "An evil and adulterous generation asks for a sign; but no sign will be given to it except the sign of the **prophet** Jonah" (Matt. 12:39; cf. Mark 8:12). Despite such reservations about signs in the Synoptics and Paul, miracles function positively as signs of who Jesus is in John's Gospel. This is only one of the many differences between the Fourth Gospel and the others. In all likelihood the Synoptics are closer to Jesus' own view, whereas in John later controversy about Jesus' identity has led to the use of the miracle tradition in a different way.

Before looking more closely at miracles in the Gospels, we need to understand the first century's view of miracles so that the miracle tradition is set within its environment. This, in turn, will set the stage for our final section when we look at miracles from a modern perspective.

Miracles in the First Century

In the first century, indeed in the New Testament itself, Jesus is not the only miracle worker. For example, in the Acts of the Apostles, Luke says that Simon the Magician did great wonders and amazed people by his magic. Moreover, he tried to buy the **Spirit** from the **apostles** and was refused, because according to Peter the gift of God could not be obtained with money (Acts 8:9–24). Simon desired the Spirit because the disciples performed signs and great miracles (Acts 5:12). The Apostle Paul and others performed wonders (2 Cor. 12:12). Even some **rabbis**, who were known primarily as teachers, performed miracles. Onias the Circlemaker, a rabbi in the first century B.C., is reported to have made it rain for Israel neither too fiercely nor too gently, but in moderation. A famous miracle worker in **Hellenistic** literature was Apollonius of Tyana, a Pythagorean philosopher who lived during the first Christian century. He is reported to have miraculously exorcised a demon from a young man who later became a philosopher and a miracle worker himself. Of course, the Old Testament reports healings and other miracles: especially significant are those of Elijah (e.g., 1 Kings 17:17–24) and Elisha (2 Kings 4:18–37), which are not unlike those of Jesus.

Jesus as Miracle Worker in Apocryphal Gospels

Within an ancient context, Jesus' miracles are not quite so unusual. In fact, some early Christians felt constrained to enlarge the miracle activity of Jesus beyond what is reported in the **canonical Gospels**. Consequently, some **apocryphal** Gospels attribute to Jesus bigger and more fantastic miracles. In the *Infancy Gospel of Thomas*, Jesus fetches water for his mother with a garment instead of a pitcher. When the carpenter Joseph discovers that one of the boards for a bed is too short, his son Jesus corrects the situation by stretching the board to the proper length. In the same Gospel, Jesus makes twelve clay birds that become real birds after he claps his hands. When a young boy disturbs a pool of water in which Jesus is playing, Jesus withers him as if he were a tree. Under the influence of popular piety Jesus became a real magician. Probably miracle stories served both to entertain the pious and to support their belief that Jesus was the **Christ**, the **Son of God.**

It is understandable, therefore, that the Gospels portrayed Jesus as a miracle worker, especially given the fact he had been known as a healer during his lifetime. Very likely his healings and exorcisms first attracted attention to him. The tendency to enlarge upon the miracles of Jesus, observable in the apocryphal Gospels, may already have been at work in the earliest tradition. Whether the Gospels have furthered or checked this tendency is a good question. Obviously, John highlights Jesus' miracle-working power. Matthew, on the other hand, reduces the dimensions of the miraculous by abbreviating many of Mark's miracle stories.

Miracles in the Synoptic Gospels

In modern usage, a miracle is an occurrence contrary to known scientific laws. Because the evangelists wrote at a time in which there was no commonly accepted concept of "known scientific laws," they understood miracles as deeds of power, wonders, mighty works, and signs. These strange, remarkable happenings caused people to be amazed and terrified, and to wonder whether these occurrences were manifestations of God's power (the good) or that of Satan (the evil). For convenience's sake, we may nevertheless speak about miracles in the Gospels, for the term's modern use roughly corresponds to the reported events.

To understand miracles in Jesus' ministry, we must first take account of the view of the world and history in which they are set, then attempt to classify the miracles according to type, and finally explore the relation of miracles to faith. We deal primarily with the **Synoptics** rather than with John, because in their estimate of miracles they are probably closer to Jesus' own position.

The Eschatological Context

The proclamation of the **kingdom of God** was central to Jesus' preaching and teaching (Mark 1:14). Jesus himself appears to have linked his mighty works to the appearance of the kingdom: "But if it is by the finger of God that I cast out the demons, then the kingdom of God has come to you" (Luke 11:20; cf. Matt. 12:28). At the same time his work is a manifestation of his having overcome the powers of Satan, or evil: "When a strong man, fully armed, guards his castle, his property is safe. But when one stronger than he attacks him and overpowers him, he takes away his armor in which he trusted, and divides his plunder" (Luke 11:21–22; cf. Mark 3:27). When asked on John the Baptist's behalf whether he is the coming one—that is, the **Messiah** or charismatic leader who would inaugurate God's rule—Jesus replies: "Go and tell John what you have seen and heard: the blind receive their sight, the lame walk, lepers are cleansed, the deaf hear, the dead are raised, the poor have good news brought to them" (Luke 7:22; cf. Matt 11:4–5). He instructs his disciples that in healing the sick they should say to them, "The kingdom of God has come near to you" (Luke 10:9). In Jesus' own view, then, his miracles are signs of the breaking in of the **eschatological** kingdom.

The breaking in of God's kingdom in Jesus' miracle activity is not, however, the kingdom's final realization. The miracles signify an inaugurated kingdom, not a completed one. This setting of Jesus' miracles within the context of such an "inaugurated eschatology" means that the miracles point to the working of God rather than to the status of Jesus. God's kingdom, not the rule of Jesus, is inaugurated. Moreover, from the standpoint of Jesus' opponents, these miracles or wonders are ambiguous and could be viewed as the work of Satan as well as of God. Jesus refuses to use the miracles as signs to validate himself (Mark 8:11 f.; Matt. 12:39). Similarly, the temptation stories show Jesus declining to elicit support by the performance of miracles or spectacular feats (Matt. 4:1–11; Luke 4:1–13). The healings bear witness to the kingdom's appearance; God's extraordinary presence is consistently and continually proclaimed in Jesus' message.

Types of Miracles

Having discerned the framework of the **kerygma** of the kingdom in which the **miracles** occur, we turn for a closer look at the actual miracle stories themselves. The Synoptic Gospels contain basically four types: exorcisms, healings, resuscitations, and nature miracles. All except exorcism are found also in John. The first three have to do with human subjects; the fourth involves inanimate matter. Generally speaking, the exorcisms pertain to what we would call mental disorders; the healings refer to physical diseases. For our purposes they both can be treated under one heading—healings.

In Mark's Gospel *exorcisms* (1:21–28; cf. 32–34) and *healings* (1:29–31, 40–45; cf. 32–34) are narrated in rapid succession; these acts are closely related, and both belong to the essence of Jesus' **saving**, or healing, work. In the exorcism of the demon at Capernaum's synagogue and the cleansing of the leper, similar elements characterize each narrative. There is a forceful approach to Jesus (vss. 23–24; cf. vs. 40); Jesus responds vigorously or compassionately (vs. 25; cf. vss. 41, 43); the evil spirit or force departs (vs. 26; cf. vs. 42). In the one case there is an immediate crowd reaction (vs. 27); in the other none is reported. Yet in both stories Jesus' fame is said to spread throughout the area (vss. 28, 45). In both, Mark portrays Jesus as responding immediately to a dire situation or need, albeit one that presumably has existed for some time prior to the encounter with him. In both, Jesus acts and speaks decisively to overcome the evil spirit or disease.

Even though in both stories Jesus acts as an authoritative, **charismatic** figure, in neither case does the question of his **messiahship** arise. Whether the command to silence (vs. 44; cf. vss. 25, 34) originates with Mark or Jesus himself, its effect is to subordinate the role of Jesus' healing to his primary proclamation of the nearness of God's kingdom. As best we can tell, this order of priorities goes back to Jesus himself.

The question of whether the miracle described in Mark 1:40–45 actually happened should be considered in light of the fact that the "leprosy" spoken of need not have been the incurable Hansen's disease called leprosy. Moreover, in antiquity similar miracles were attributed to others. Nevertheless, such considerations are not decisive in determining what may have occurred. There is an overall impression of authenticity, stemming from the fact that the miracle is narrated with restraint and without calling attention to itself. It is pointless to offer scientific or psychological explanations of what happened; although these cannot be ruled out in principle, they are pure speculation in the face of the text's silence about most matters of detail.

The Gospels report three *resuscitations*: the raising of the widow of Nain's son (Luke 7:11–17), of Lazarus (John 11:1–44), and of Jairus' daughter (Mark 5:21–43 and parr.). The latter story is interrupted by an account of the healing of a woman with a hemorrhage (Mark 5:25–34 parr.). Yet this break is not accidental, for the interlude illustrates the power of believing (cf. 5:36). The woman, who is ritually unclean (Lev. 15:25), approaches Jesus from behind. Strikingly, the healing of the woman with the hemorrhage occurs without Jesus' being aware of her presence. Consequently, Jesus did not intend the miracle (5:28–30). If the miracle happens without Jesus' intent, then in a sense the miracle happened to Jesus as well as to the woman. This healing of the woman makes the implicit point that belief in Jesus is actually faith in the power that works through Jesus rather than in Jesus himself (5:30, 34).

The role of belief or faith is then taken up in the raising of Jairus' daughter (5:36). Jesus' raising of the seemingly dead girl may rest upon an actual incident in which he aroused a girl who was in a coma (cf. vss. 35 f., 39), although it is now impossible to be certain. As it stands, however, it raises the question of whether belief in God goes so far as to affirm Jesus' victory over death. Thus the story of Jesus' raising of Jairus' daughter may have used an actual occurrence of healing to affirm a central matter of faith: God's power to raise the dead. Such faith becomes the center of attention in the Fourth Gospel. There Jesus claims the God-given power to raise the dead (5:25–29), and then most dramatically exercises that power as he restores Lazarus to life, calling him forth from the grave (11:43). Even in the Synoptics Jesus speaks of the dead being raised, among other deeds of power (Matt. 11:5; Luke 7:22).

Resuscitation or Resurrection?

Like the Bible generally (cf. Isa. 26:19; Dan. 12:2), the New Testament distinguishes between resuscitations and **resurrection** from the dead. The former results in the restoration to human life of those who will eventually die. The latter refers to an irreducibly **eschatological** event: God's giving to the dead a new and different kind of life that can never again be terminated by death (cf. Matt. 28:20; Acts 1:9-11; 1 Cor. 15:20 ff.).

Two examples of *nature miracles* are the feeding of the five thousand (Mark 6:30–44; cf. Matt. 14:13–21; Luke 9:10–17; John 6:1–14) and the stilling of the storm (Mark 4:35–41 parr.). In the Gospels' accounts of the feeding of the multitudes, the evangelists have exercised freedom in detail regarding the miracle's occasion. They agree, however, that Jesus is surrounded by hungry throngs at a place where food is not accessible. We cannot isolate an earlier, nonmiraculous version of the story; the central point is that of a miraculous feeding, possibly with **eucharistic** overtones. It is beside the point to explain this story as some kind of picnic in which Jesus and his disciples encouraged the people to generosity. Jesus may have taken part in such meals with the disciples and a large multitude. Still, the question of whether such an incredible miracle took place remains unanswered. The form of this story clearly reflects the early **church**'s eucharistic practice (see Mark 6:41). Therefore, the miracle may be a post-**resurrection** story, based upon Christians' experience in the **Lord's Supper** that the living Christ feeds hungry multitudes (cf. Luke 24:28–35; John 21:9–14). Such conjecture is supported by the fact that this nature miracle concentrates more upon Jesus' person and action than do most other miracle stories. This kind of emphasis on Jesus, characteristic of the Fourth Gospel (6:15 ff.), may reflect a concern of the early church more than the attitude of the historical Jesus. Again, however, compassion toward the multitudes is what we would expect of

Jesus of Nazareth. The essence of the story accords with our evolving picture of the historical Jesus. The form, however, reflects interests of the early church. In this case, as in others, one can well imagine that an actual event has been elaborated in a miraculous mode, though we cannot move beyond conjecture. It is also worth noting that a similar amazing feeding was attributed to the prophet Elisha (2 Kings 4:42–44). Conceivably, the biblical story has been transferred to Jesus, with different details. More likely, the Elisha account has influenced the telling of the Jesus story (cf. the barley loaves in 2 Kings 4:42 and John 6:9).

The stilling of the storm on the Sea of Galilee also belongs in the category of nature miracles (Mark 4:35–41 parr.). Its present form may obscure an earlier story about the exorcism of a storm–demon. Jesus silences the storm as he silenced the demon (4:39; cf. 1:25). As it now reads, however, it demonstrates Jesus' authority over nature and challenges the disciples' lack of faith (4:40 f.). Moreover, Jesus' action seems to embody that **salvation** the Old Testament ascribes to God: "You silence the roaring of the seas, the roaring of their waves, the tumult of the peoples" (Psalm 65:7; cf. 89:9). The entire miracle story makes Jesus the object of religious awe. Probably we have here a **Christological** confession, occasioned not so much by a single incident out of Jesus' life as by the total impact of Jesus, particularly his death and resurrection. Again this conclusion does not mean that no actual historical event lies at this story's root. Doubtless Jesus was frequently in a boat on the Sea of Galilee with his disciples. Yet any specific event that may have formed this story's basis is no longer accessible to us.

Miracles and Faith

All three types of **miracle** story—healings, resuscitations, and nature miracles—convey a consistent theme: the response of faith. But what is the relation between faith and miracles? In many cases faith seems to be the triggering mechanism that produces miracles. God is always ready to perform miracles; consequently, if a person has faith, miracles occur. One can find support from the Gospels for this understanding: "And [Jesus] could do no deed of power there, except that he laid his hands on a few sick people and cured them. And he was amazed at their unbelief" (Mark 6:5 f.). Jesus replies to the woman healed of her hemorrhage, "Daughter, your faith has made you well; go in peace and be healed of your disease" (Mark 5:34 parr.). The disciples' astonishment at the withered fig tree prompts Jesus to say, "Have faith in God. Truly I tell you, if you say to this mountain, 'Be taken up and thrown into the sea,' and if you do not doubt in your heart, but believe that what you say will come to pass, it will be done for you" (Mark 11:22 f.; cf. 1 Cor. 13:2). In John, of course, it is the other way around. Miracles as signs stimulate faith, although they sometimes evoke resistance (John 9; cf. 2:23–25). But traces of the other view of the relation of miracles and faith appear even in John (4:48 ff.; 5:6; cf. 14:13 f.).

Yet before we conclude that according to Jesus faith produces miracles or whatever else the believer wishes, we should remember that in the Gospels even Jesus did not have his own way. The temptation stories set the tempo for Jesus' entire life in that he refuses to assert his own power. Moreover, in Gethsemane Jesus prays, "**Abba**, Father, for you all things are possible; remove this cup from me; yet not what I want, but what you want" (Mark 14:36 parr.). Because the cup was not removed, we can only conclude that faith is not presented as an automatic device for accomplishing the will of Jesus or of the believer. Faith's ultimate object is God and his will. In the Gospels, faith means that one trusts, accepts, and responds affirmatively to God's coming. If in some instances faith appears as the condition for a miracle, or vice versa, the reader ought not to conclude that this represents the fundamental understanding of faith in the Gospels or in the ministry of Jesus. The faith that Jesus demands is belief in the good news of his announcement of the coming of God and the **kingdom**. Everything else depends on such faith (Mark 1:15; 8:34–38; Matt. 12:28). After his departure from them, the believers' faith was directed to Jesus himself, or to what God was accomplishing through him.

Undoubtedly Jesus did perform miracles or deeds of power: demons were cast out, the sick healed. People were amazed at his actions (Mark 1:27; 2:12; 9:15). Yet these extraordinary acts were ambiguous and did not prove that Jesus was the **Messiah**. Some people saw them as the devil's work; others saw and did not believe (Mark 3:22). These events, like many at that time and many since, aroused temporary wonder, amazement, and faith. In themselves, however, the miracles did not produce the faith that changed **sinners** into persons who obeyed and trusted God instead of themselves, forgave their enemies, and lived out of the assurance of God's favor.

Miracles in a Modern Perspective

Most people regard a **miracle** as a breach of scientific, natural law. Taken literally, however, such language can be misleading, because scientific laws are statements about cause and effect based on empirical observation. Out of observation and experiment a law is formed. With more testing it is found inadequate, so the law is reformulated; again it is found inadequate, reformulated again, and so forth. We need to keep in mind that scientists themselves realize that the models or laws that the scientific process constructs are only aids toward understanding reality. These laws are impersonal oversimplifications, pragmatically useful but not determinative of reality. To mistake natural laws for reality itself pushes the observer into a flat scientific—actually, unscientific—view of the world in which all complexity and mystery are abolished for the sake of clarity and certainty.

Miracle stories convey mystery. They speak about extraordinary events, situations in which things are more than they seem. Miracle stories claim that a power is at work which is personal concern—understood in the New Testament as the will of God. The point of miracle stories is not scientific explanation; their point is beyond all such explanation. Thus we do the miracle stories no service if we "explain" them historically in order to remove their mysterious character.

According to the Gospels, Jesus' miracles were real, specific, and discernible events. Yet they occurred in an atmosphere of **eschatological** expectation and faith. When wrenched from that context, they look like the works of a magician or a sorcerer. In his own time and for the earliest **church**, the question of miracle could not be separated from faith in Jesus' preaching and power, both of which had to do with the dawning of God's kingdom. Faith could not—and cannot—prove the miracles happened. Faith in God's rule provides the context in which their meaning can be discussed. Apart from this eschatological context, Jesus' miracles, if they are not rejected outright, must be viewed as occult phenomena with rough parallels in ancient and modern times. If, however, one believes that the new age really was dawning in Jesus, a basis is provided for understanding the miracles. Early Christians believed this was happening. In their time and subsequently, such faith has lent reality and meaning to accounts of the miraculous.

THE TEACHING MESSIAH

The earliest extant documents of Christianity, Paul's letters, contain surprisingly little teaching that Paul attributes to Jesus himself. Though Paul could have worked at a time or in places where no extensive tradition or body of Jesus' sayings was known or used, occasionally he does cite a word of Jesus (1 Cor. 7:10; 9:14; 11:23–26). Thus the practice of preserving and referring to Jesus' own words cannot have been unknown to him (cf. Rom. 12:14–21; 13:8–10). He may have known more of the Jesus tradition than he reveals. Still, the focus of Paul's preaching and teaching is elsewhere, preeminently upon the meaning of the **crucifixion** and **resurrection**.

Aside from Paul's own example, there are stronger indications that Jesus' sayings were preserved and transmitted among his followers. All the Gospels, including John, portray Jesus as a teacher and contain evidence of the existence of the teaching material in earlier, pre-Gospel forms. The Gospel of Matthew's famous Sermon on the Mount (chaps. 5–7) is paralleled in Luke by a Sermon on the Plain (6:20–49), which, although much shorter, is obviously an alternative, probably earlier, recension of much of the same material. Therefore, the Sermon on the Mount seems to be neither a single utterance of Jesus nor a composition of Matthew. Rather, it is based upon a traditional collection of Jesus' sayings, which Matthew has doubtless augmented. Traces of similar sayings of Jesus may be found, for example, in the Epistle of James. But the most impressive evidence for collections of Jesus' sayings is the parallel materials of Matthew and Luke, of which the Sermon on the Mount (or Plain) is only a part. This parallel material was scarcely copied from one Gospel by the author of the other, but was drawn by both from the same or a similar source. This was probably a collection of Jesus' sayings that lacked narrative structure or framework, called by scholars the **Q source** (see Chapter 2, pp. 56–57). As we have noted, a similar collection of Jesus' sayings, the **apocryphal** *Gospel of Thomas*, was found among the Coptic **Gnostic** manuscripts uncovered at Nag Hammadi in upper Egypt.

The shape of some narratives in the Gospels suggests that they functioned primarily to preserve a saying of Jesus. Smaller complexes or groups of sayings in the Gospels may once have circulated as separate units before having been incorporated into a Gospel. Probably some ancient and genuine materials found their way into Gospels, such as the *Gospel of the Hebrews* or the *Gospel of the Egyptians*, which are known to us from early Christian writers but that are otherwise lost. Someday, perhaps, copies of these long-lost Gospels may become known.

The collection, preservation, and transmission of Jesus' sayings, whether in oral or written form, demonstrate that some early Christians regarded Jesus as a **rabbi**, a teacher (cf. John 1:38), whatever else he may have been. For some, Jesus has always been the supreme teacher. Thus before the Gospels were even written there were collections of Jesus' sayings, his teachings.

Was Jesus an Apocalyptic Prophet?

Our portrait of the healing **Messiah** has suggested the urgency with which Jesus preached and taught, as he proclaimed the nearness of the **kingdom of God**. Recent research, centered in the North American Jesus Seminar, has disputed an equation of God's kingdom with the end of history. Whether **apocalyptic eschatology** should be translated into modern idiom as the end of history is a valid question. Nevertheless, any attempt to understand Jesus' teaching that does not take account of the kingdom's centrality, as well as the air of expectation it engendered, is fundamentally flawed. Certainly in the **Synoptic Gospels** Jesus' proclamation is set in the context of apocalyptic eschatology: the view that God will soon intervene in human affairs in some decisive way, to change their course and character, and to establish his rule.

The Proclamation of the Kingdom of God

In the **Synoptics** Jesus' message centers on the **kingdom of God**. "Now after John was arrested, Jesus came into Galilee, proclaiming the good news of God, and saying, 'The time is fulfilled, and the kingdom of God has drawn near; repent, and believe in the good news'" (Mark 1:14 f.). That formulation may be Mark's, but it accurately summarizes Jesus' message. After the **scribe** applauds Jesus' summary of the **law** in the twin commandments to love God and neighbor, Jesus replies, "You are not far from the kingdom of God" (Mark 12:34). In the **Beatitudes** Jesus proclaims, "Blessed are you who are poor, for yours is the kingdom of God" (Luke 6:20; Matt. 5:3). Concerning John the Baptist, Jesus says, "Truly, I tell you, among those born of women no one has risen greater than John the Baptist; yet the least in the kingdom of heaven is greater than he" (Matt. 11:11; Luke 7:28). In one petition of the Lord's Prayer Jesus prays, "Your kingdom come. Your will be done, on earth as it is in heaven" (Matt. 6:10; cf. Luke 11:2). Jesus' exorcisms suggest the kingdom's coming: "But if it is by the finger of God that I cast out demons, then the kingdom of God has come to you" (Luke 11:20; Matt. 12:28). Obviously, Jesus' proclamation is pregnant with the kingdom of God. We should keep in mind that *kingdom* (Greek *basileia*) also means kingship, rule, or reign. The emphasis is on God's ruling rather than on a territory or people ruled. Still, the meaning of Jesus' kingdom proclamation is debatable.

We must deal head-on with two major questions concerning Jesus' concept of the kingdom. First, did he announce the kingdom as present or future, or some combination of the two? Second, was the kingdom primarily an ethical goal, to be attained by human decision and effort, or an **apocalyptic** event to be brought about on God's initiative only?

Both questions were put forward most cogently and relentlessly by Albert Schweitzer (1875–1965), the great biblical scholar and humanitarian. Schweitzer persuasively argued that nineteenth-century historians and theologians had interpreted the Gospels in accord with their own prejudices, which were read into the text and had produced a Jesus who was the projection of modern **ethical** ideals. Moreover, Schweitzer insisted that Jesus' own view of the kingdom of God was of a future, cataclysmic, apocalyptic event, which God himself would inaugurate to bring to an end all worldly history and conditions. Interpreting the Gospel accounts from the standpoint of their many apocalyptic passages (e.g., Mark 13; 8:38), which he read in the light of ancient Jewish apocalyptic texts, Schweitzer sharply rejected the notion that God's kingdom was either a fully present reality or an ethical goal. For Schweitzer, Jesus' ethic applied only to the brief interim before the kingdom's advent. Only under such emergency conditions could one think of turning the other cheek or giving up one's coat and cloak (Matt. 5:39 f.).

While the questions of the time and manner of the kingdom's coming and its ethical implications are closely related, we shall reserve the latter for treatment under Jesus' radical demand. In considering the former question, we shall group the varied sayings according to their present or future orientation to reach tentative conclusions about Jesus' temporal emphasis. As a check on our findings, we briefly investigate seven kingdom **parables** (Matt. 13). We shall then be able to say more precisely how Jesus' kingdom proclamation is oriented to the present and future.

The Kingdom As Present and Future

Altogether the three Synoptic Gospels contain well over a hundred references to the kingdom of God. This contrasts with fewer than forty references in the rest of the New Testament, including the Fourth Gospel, where the kingdom is not a prominent element of Jesus' teaching. As we would expect, Matthew and Luke, which embody the bulk of Jesus' teachings, contain more references than does Mark (54 in Matthew, 41 in Luke, 19 in Mark).

Despite numerous sayings about its future coming, the kingdom of God is occasionally said to be somehow present in Jesus' mission and message. Several passages refer to Jesus' activity as indicative of the kingdom's presence. Thus Jesus says that his exorcisms by the finger or **Spirit** of God show that "the kingdom of God has come upon you" (Luke 11:20; Matt. 12:28). As we can be reasonably certain that Jesus did perform exorcisms, it is probable that he himself was responsible for relating them to the kingdom's presence. On another occasion, when Jesus was asked by **Pharisees** when the kingdom was coming, he is said to have replied, "The kingdom of God is not coming with things that can be observed; nor will they say, 'Look, here it is!' or 'There it is!' for in fact, the kingdom of God is among you" (Luke 17:20 f.; cf. *Gospel of Thomas* 3 and 22). The final phrase ("among you") may be translated "within you," but such a translation does not fit the rest of Jesus' kingdom teaching. Evidently the present already contains what the Pharisees seek in the future. After the seventy go out upon their mission and find that they too can conquer demons, Jesus says to them, "I watched Satan fall from heaven like a flash of lightning from heaven" (Luke 10:18). Satan's defeat marks the beginning of the end time (cf. Mark 3:27; Rev. 20:1–3). In some sense the kingdom is present. This point is confirmed by Jesus' parables, as we shall see.

Nevertheless, in Jesus' message the kingdom of God has also a future dimension, and the evidence for this futuristic emphasis is quite clear. In addition to the passages cited above, after the confession of Peter at Caesarea Philippi Jesus instructs the disciples, "Truly, I tell you, there are some standing here who will not taste death until they see that the kingdom of God has come with power" (Mark 9:1 parr.). At the Last Supper, Jesus says to the disciples, "Truly, I say to you, I shall not drink again of the fruit of the vine until that day when I drink it new in the kingdom of God" (Mark 14:25 parr.). Jesus speaks frequently about entering and receiving the kingdom of God. Such sayings also fit the concept of a future or coming kingdom (Matt. 5:20; 7:21; 18:3; 19:23; 25:34; Mark 9:47; 10:15; 15:43; Luke 9:62; 12:32; 18:17).

If we can associate with the kingdom other references to the coming of the end time—such as the coming of the **Son of Man**, the tribulations of the last day, the coming of the judgment—then we have an abundance of indirect evidence that Jesus understood the kingdom as future. The **apocalyptic** discourse (Mark 13 parr.) speaks repeatedly of the impending future tribulation that ushers in God's rule. Although it contains much material that did not originate with Jesus, it would scarcely have obtained its present form had he not proclaimed the future, coming kingdom of God. One surprising thing about the apocalyptic discourse, however, is the near absence of the term *kingdom* itself (though cf. Luke 21:31).

On the basis of individual sayings and related apocalyptic references in Jesus' teaching, we can only conclude that he himself proclaimed the kingdom as coming. But this conclusion must be coupled with Jesus' message of the kingdom as also present. There is a tension between present and future in the Gospels that apparently goes back to Jesus himself. There are intimations of the kingdom in the present, but its power will be manifest to all only in the future.

Jesus and Apocalypticism

In the Synoptic tradition Jesus proclaims the **kingdom** as both present and future. If understood against the background of Jewish apocalyptic thought, Jesus was no ordinary apocalyptic thinker.

Ancient Jewish Apocalypticism

Two traits characterize apocalyptic teaching—*but Jesus fully shares only the first of them.* First, apocalypticism looks toward a future consummation of history that God will command. Second, this event is typically set in a dualistic framework and occurs as the final climax of an overall "plan" for history. Jewish apocalyptic literature, which developed during the period between the **Maccabean** uprising and the final destruction of Jerusalem after the Bar Kochba rebellion (167 **B.C.–A.D.** 135), embodied the fundamental hope that God would overthrow all wordly kingdoms and rule directly over humankind. Thus history as we know it would end. The early stages of such apocalyptic thought can be seen in the Book of Daniel (chaps. 7–12); its further development is evidenced in the **apocryphal** *4 Ezra* and the *War Scroll* of the **Qumran** community, as well as the Book of Revelation. This view reflects pessimism about any possibility of humans' extricating themselves from the present evil age. The powers of Satan, represented by foreign powers dominating the Jewish people, had won the upper hand. The only hope was the advent of God's new age, in which the old powers would be annihilated and God's reign established. This worldview deals in dualistic contrasts: good and bad, new and old, God and Satan. In its perspective on history and God's plan, it presumes that the world has become progressively more evil, descending from an initial paradise to the present hell on earth. This evil, instigated by humankind and God's adversary Satan, is especially rampant against God's elect in the last days. But God's plan, visible only to the discerning elect, calls for a final intervention in which everything will be reversed, so that the oppressed will triumph and their oppressors will be destroyed. Therefore, apocalypticism calls for repentance in the face of the terrible judgment of the imminent end.

Jesus' expectation is related to ancient Jewish apocalypticism, but apart from the apocalyptic discourse (Mark 13 parr.) he does not lay out a scenario. John the Baptist, the angry preacher of judgment (see Matt. 3:1–12), deserves the title of apocalyptist more than Jesus. Yet the fact that he was baptized by John suggests that Jesus had been convinced by the Baptist's preaching of a coming judgment. With its graphic and detailed description of the end time, the Book of Revelation is quite appropriately called the Apocalypse (see Rev. 21:1–8). Jesus is an **eschatological** teacher who proclaims the imminent kingdom (Mark 1:15 par.; Matt. 8:11 f. par.). Yet Jesus proclaims neither knowledge of God's plan nor a pessimistic, dualistic rejection of this world. (Schweitzer attributed to Jesus such a dualistic worldview but in so doing ignored much of his teaching, some of which fits and some does not.) Jesus rejects the apocalyptic penchant for looking for signs and speculating about the exact time for the end (Mark 8:12; cf. Matt. 16:1; Luke 11:29; 17:20 f.). Even in the so-called apocalyptic discourse, which is largely the product of a later time, Jesus refuses to speculate (Mark 13:32). When **Pharisees** ask Jesus about the time of the kingdom's coming, Jesus replies that the kingdom is not coming "with things that can be observed," for it is already in their midst (Luke 17:20 f.). John the Baptist's disciples inquire whether Jesus himself is the sign that the apocalyptic end time has arrived (Matt. 11:2–6; Luke 7:18–23). Jesus' only answer is to describe what he is doing. Because his acts of preaching and healing are good news, they are hardly the dreadful, cataclysmic signs of the world's end.

Jesus strongly implies that the kingdom is inaugurated in his ministry. It is in the process of being realized, but it has not yet fully come, for its completion is still future. Such was the secret of Jesus' message about the kingdom. His parables bear out this viewpoint.

The Kingdom and the Parables

In our discussion of Jesus' proclamation of the kingdom, we have thus far deliberately ignored the numerous kingdom **parables**. It is not too much to say that if Jesus taught anything, he proclaimed the **kingdom of God** and that if he taught in any specific form, he spoke in parables.

Before examining a representative group of kingdom parables in Matthew 13, we need to understand something of the nature of a parable. Jesus spoke parables to drive home points by way of analogies drawn from the everyday world. The parables are not stories told to illustrate general truths; they are sharp words with implied directives for concrete situations. Our use of religious language to interpret the parables must not lose sight of the fact that parables seldom mention God or use religious language. In the parables Jesus talks about **eschatology** in everyday language, implying that we meet the unexpected—God—within this world.

The parables of Jesus accumulated redactional additions during the course of their oral and written transmission. This material was added to make them meaningful to later situations. One way in which the early **church** made Jesus' parables applicable was by **allegorizing** them, giving them new meaning by making each point of the parable refer to some Christian truth. In Matthew the interpretations of the parables of the sower (13:18–23) and of the weeds in the field (13:36–43) are examples of such allegorization. This sort of interpretation, however, may not be true to the parables' original intent.

Jesus' parables focus one's attention not on the particulars but on the story's total impact. By contrast, allegory allows the particulars to dominate by referring each element to some previously known framework of meaning. If, however, the many elements of the parable are viewed as a whole, it is impossible to translate the parable into other terms; any generalization about a parable is always secondary. Consequently in our interpretation of certain parables, we need to keep in mind that genuine understanding occurs simply in reading and hearing the parables. The directive, the stimulus to action or to repentance, that they imply is clear enough in most parables. We need here to ask only about the view of the kingdom that they imply or assume.

Chapter 13 of Matthew serves our purpose well, for the evangelist has gathered there a collection of Jesus' kingdom parables. Although Matthew uses Mark as his source, he includes material not found in Mark. The kingdom parables (as distinguished from their interpretation) probably originated with Jesus. Interestingly, Matthew's redaction of Mark 4:10–12, by making the parables a means of clarifying Jesus' message rather than obscuring it (Matt. 13:13; cf. vss. 34–35), doubtless comes closer to Jesus' actual purpose than does Mark. Mark is preoccupied with the motif of secrecy in Jesus' mission and message.

The *parable of the sower* (Matt. 13:3–8; cf. Mark 4:3–8; Luke 8:5–8; *Gospel of Thomas* 9) requires some knowledge of Jesus' time and place to be understood. First, the harvest image was already connected with the eschatological notion of world history's culmination, for the end time was viewed as the harvest time (cf. Isa. 9:1–7; Psalm 126). Second, the yield of grain (13:8) was excessively large: a tenfold yield would have been a good harvest; a yield of seven and a half, an average one.

Assuming that this parable was spoken by Jesus, we may dispense with the interpretation (13:18–23), for it is quite difficult to imagine that this allegory conveys what the parable meant to its first hearers. For example, the identification of the birds with "the evil one" is artificial and would have been unlikely to occur to Jesus' listeners. The parable points more simply to activity taking place in the present: seed being sown, but much seed being lost. Jesus speaks this parable about the sower not to encourage endurance from people already committed to him (cf. vs. 21) but to declare what is happening in their midst. The parable's unexpected element is the size of the harvest (vs. 8). Since a good yield would be tenfold, these results are incredible. Even now the sowing is taking place; moreover, the future harvest will be beyond imagination. Evidently the parable's movement portrays in everyday, yet unexpected, language Jesus' proclamation of the kingdom. The present is for Jesus the time of the kingdom's hidden coming; the future will witness an unbelievable consummation of that kingdom. Deliverance lies not only in the future but already is present in a hidden way.

The *parable of the weeds in the field* (Matt. 13:24–30; cf. *Thomas* 57) also has an allegorical interpretation that is clearly secondary—it is actually separated from the parable itself—and does not belong to Jesus' message (13:36–43). According to the interpretation, Jesus warns against false security by vividly depicting the punishment and reward of the last judgment. But this interpretation obscures the story's surprising point. Again we have a parable of the harvest. This time, instead of announcing a magnificent future yield and thereby claiming hidden significance for the present sowing, the parable depicts the future as a time of judgment, a process of separation (vs. 30). But the present is a time when judgment cannot be exercised (vs. 29). Actually the weight of the parable falls on the latter point. Final judgment belongs to God, not to human beings (cf. Matt. 7:1; Luke 15). Any attempt to bring judgment into the present misses the point of Jesus' proclaiming the kingdom as inaugurated (cf. Matt. 13:44 ff.; Mark 2:18 ff.), even though not realized.

The following twin parables, the *parable of the mustard seed* (Matt. 13:31 f.; cf. Mark 4:30–32; Luke 13:18 f.; *Thomas* 20) and *the parable of the leaven* (Matt. 13:33; cf. Luke 13:20 f.; *Thomas* 96), also speak about present and future. Exaggeration has occurred in the Matthean and Lukan accounts, for in fact the mustard seed becomes a large shrub only about nine feet in height, rather than a tree. Moreover, the specified measure of meal is a huge quantity of flour, approximately fifty pounds (cf. Gen. 18:6). Many modern interpreters have viewed these parables as depicting the growth of the kingdom of God, which starts small but over the course of years grows through human effort until it encompasses the whole world. But such an interpretation misses both the eschatological urgency of Jesus' message and the thrust of the images themselves. Jesus uses the tiny and insignificant mustard seed and leaven to surprise the hearer with the astounding results: a tree that shelters the birds and enough dough to feed a host of people. These are parables not of growth but of contrast. Jesus contrasts the small, present beginning with the great result to come. The process of growth is nowhere mentioned, so that the "how" of this great result remains a mystery.

The twin *parables of the treasure* (Matt. 13:44; cf. *Thomas* 109) and *the pearl* (Matt. 13:45 f.; cf. *Thomas* 76) elaborate the theme of present response to the kingdom. No calculation is involved. The finder of the treasure and the finder of the pearl have in common the knowledge that their find overshadows all else. The finders understand themselves not as surrendering everything but as gaining the one essential thing: the treasure or the pearl. In one case, the laborer accidentally finds the treasure in the field; in the other, the merchant finds the pearl after a great search. But in both cases, all is forgotten in the joy of finding the treasure and the pearl.

These two parables, dealing with present response to the kingdom, are followed by the *parable of the net and the fish*, which relates to the future (Matt. 13:47–50; cf. *Thomas* 8). Jesus' original parable probably consisted simply of the image of throwing the net, then gathering and sorting the good and bad fish (vss. 47–48). Matthew's redactional addition (vss. 49–50; cf. Matt. 8:12; 13:42; 22:13) correctly interprets this parable in the light of final judgment. The future orientation becomes evident when this parable is seen alongside the *parable of the weeds and the wheat* (13:24–30), for the latter's secondary point is that judgment can and will take place in the future.

To summarize: Jesus' parables, like his kingdom message, stress the present as well as the future. A small beginning now will be fully consummated in the future. This present beginning is a time for great joy. Whoever seeks to control the future by immediate judgment loses the future reward. Whoever discerns the present activity of God will be astonished at the final results.

We may now draw some conclusions about the kingdom of God in the proclamation of Jesus. First, God's rule, not human effort, was foremost in his conception of the coming kingdom. Jesus never viewed the kingdom of God as a movement slowly evolving within history, which could be brought about by human adherence to moral principles. When in John's Gospel Jesus says that his kingdom is not of this world (18:36), the **Synoptic** teaching is transposed to a Johannine key but is not falsified. For Jesus the kingdom was both present and future, yet its future nature was not described in **apocalyptic** imagery, any more than its presence was conceived as a purely inner or spiritual reality. The kingdom involved both God's action and human response. The kingdom's present, hidden reality challenged disciples to accept it now, and thus enabled them joyfully to anticipate the future. God was the primary actor; somehow in the words and deeds of Jesus God was at work to effect a magnificent, future consummation. Jesus' eschatological message proclaimed an "already" and a "not yet." Already in Jesus' activity the kingdom is inaugurated, but it has not yet fully come.

The Expectation of Jesus' Return

Both Paul (e.g., 1 Cor. 15) and the **Synoptic Gospels** (e.g., Mark 13), as well as the Book of Revelation, reveal the early Christians' expectation that the risen Jesus would soon return in glory to reveal his true identity, hold judgment, and inaugurate the **kingdom of God**. This return is often spoken of as the **parousia** (Greek for "appearance"). Understandably, therefore, many Christians regarded the present as only an interim, a time of waiting or preparation for the consummation. This expectation is expressed in the phrase, apparently common in early Christian worship, "Our Lord, come!" (1 Cor. 16:22; cf. Rev. 22:20).

Although this **apocalyptic** expectation was clearly important to many, if not most, of the first generation of Christians, remarkably it did not become a part of the earliest Christian confessions, as far as can be judged from the New Testament. Still, apocalyptic traditions began to grow, perhaps as soon as it was apparent that the end was delayed in coming, and perhaps in part to explain the delay. Embryonic forms of such traditions are found in 1 Thessalonians 4:15–18, 1 Corinthians 15:23 ff., and 2 Thessalonians 2:3–12. A more developed example is Mark 13 and the parallel material in Matthew and Luke, called the Little Apocalypse because of its similarity to the Apocalypse of John (Revelation).

Early Christian Prophecy

As we have seen, Jesus himself spoke of impending **eschatological** events, particularly the kingdom's coming, but the growth of apocalyptic tradition in early Christianity was largely the work of Christian **prophets** or seers. Paul speaks of prophets and ranks them second only to **apostles** (1 Cor. 12:28). The best-known Christian prophet is John of Patmos, the author of the Book of Revelation. It is noteworthy that John sometimes speaks in the name of Jesus himself (esp. chaps. 1–3). Probably prophets regularly spoke in Jesus' name, *ex ore Christi* ("out of the mouth of Christ"). Although based on some genuine words of Jesus, the Synoptic apocalypses are largely the work of such prophets; the warnings against false prophets in these discourses (Mark 13:22; Matt. 24:11) attest their origin among "true" prophets. The necessity for criteria to test early Christian prophets is recognized in 1 John 4:1–3, as well as in the writings of the **Apostolic Fathers** (see *Didache* xi, 7–xiii, 7). The work of Christian prophets was not limited to apocalyptic utterances, but they originated and thrived in the atmosphere of eager expectancy that pervaded early Christianity.

That Paul also expected history's consummation in the near future cannot be doubted in view of his apocalyptic statements and the way he takes up such traditions. Moreover, scattered throughout the Gospels are sayings of Jesus that anticipate the end, including a distinct group in which he speaks of the coming of the **Son of Man** (e.g., Mark 8:38), by which Christians have assumed he meant his own return. To what extent the latter sayings express Jesus' own viewpoint is debatable. It is clear, however, that they would never have been preserved, or formulated, by Christians had not they themselves lived in a state of eschatological expectation. Most likely, this expectancy was rooted in Jesus' own anticipation of God's coming rule.

The antiquity of this apocalyptic, eschatological material is confirmed by the fact that it is to a considerable extent preserved in the Gospels: documents for which the expectation of Jesus' imminent return had already become a problem. Luke thinks of Jesus' ministry as the center of time and presents his own era as the period of the **church**'s life and mission, analogous to that of Israel. Obviously, in Acts, Luke has expanded the short interval before the Lord's anticipated return in view of the continuation of history's normal course. The Fourth Gospel shows that the whole eschatological question was being reconsidered in some Christian circles (see John 11:23–26; 14:22–24). Perhaps the death of the aged Beloved Disciple (21:20–23) provided the catalyst for this process. That there was a problem, or perplexity, among many Christians because Jesus had not returned is evident from the explanation given in 2 Peter (3:4–9). Mark, the earliest Gospel, clearly manifests a lively hope and expectation (1:15; 8:38–9:1), although there are already signs of an awareness of some delay (13:32, 37).

The Radical Demand of the Kingdom

As we have seen, the heart of Jesus' message was proclamation of a kingdom *both* present *and* future. It included God's action and the necessity for human response. Yet how does the good news of the inauguration of God's **kingdom** relate to the **ethical** demand of Jesus? Is the urgency of the demand undercut by the proclamation of God's presence?

The Sermon on the Mount

The most concentrated expression of Jesus' radical statement of God's will occurs in the Sermon on the Mount (Matt. 5–7). The "higher **righteousness**" (5:20) is defined by prohibitions against anger (5:22), the lustful look (5:28), divorce (5:32), and oaths (5:34). Jesus also commands nonresistance to evil (5:39) and love for one's enemies (5:44). All this reaches a stunning climax: "You, therefore, must be perfect, as your heavenly Father is perfect" (5:48).

Such words of Jesus (5:21–48), called the **antitheses** because they are set over against the **law** of Moses or its common interpretation, are so radical that they would hardly have originated in the early **church**. Further words, such as the prohibitions against anxiety (6:35), the command not to judge (7:1), and the injunction to do the Father's will (7:21), strike the reader as extraordinarily demanding. Basically, they must be from Jesus, despite the fact that they appear only in Matthew. Their radical character can hardly be ascribed to Matthew or to the transmission of his tradition, because this Gospel and its tradition show a more conservative treatment of the matter: Jesus fulfills the law and the **prophets** (5:17).

Is Jesus' radical demand a call for righteousness *for* the kingdom or *of* the kingdom? Does this call for obedience to God's will lay down conditions *for entrance into* the kingdom, or does it show those deeds that signify *the presence of* the kingdom? If the former, then the kingdom truly is future. If the latter, then the kingdom may be both present and future.

We have already presented our basic understanding of the Sermon in the treatment of Matthew (see Chapter 3, pp. 99–101). Although some material in Matthew 5–7 may come from the evangelist or his tradition, rather than from Jesus, the Sermon taken as a whole does not misrepresent Jesus. Two conclusions are unavoidable. On the one hand, no hint whatsoever is given in the Sermon that anything less than obedience to the demands of Jesus is required. On the other hand, we do not read that this obedience is to take place through the unaided effort of the hearer of Jesus' words. The validity of these observations may be elaborated from several perspectives. First, the opening **Beatitudes** proclaim that God loves those who eagerly receive what is graciously occurring in the present. God's blessing, as present action, operates to effect higher righteousness, greater obedience. Second, although this new reality means a deeper regard for the life of one person with another (Matt. 5:21–48), still this new life, according to Jesus, is built on the relationship that the Father has already established with his people (5:48). Third, barriers to the relationship with God—hypocrisy, ostentatious prayer, anxiety about one's own destiny—must be eradicated (Matt. 6). Seeking first the kingdom and the Father's righteousness enables one to find freedom and enjoyment in the present. Fourth, the future belongs to God (7:1; cf. 7:7). God's grace accompanies Jesus' command; yet whoever encounters the grace of God must still bear good fruit (7:19) and face God in the future judgment (7:24–27).

Reward is not just some future prize for good deeds done in the present; reward already belongs in right relationship with God. Present blessings and obedience simply become expanded and enlarged in the future. Jesus' proclamation of the kingdom seeks to elicit a response from his hearers, a response defined as doing the will of God. Thus the righteousness that Jesus demands is not righteousness *for* the kingdom, not even the proper attitude with which to unlock the kingdom. Instead, Jesus demands righteousness *of* the kingdom. This kingdom is only partially present, inaugurated, but the kingdom's power is already at work. The Sermon reveals that Jesus speaks as one convinced that the kingdom is breaking into the present and will be consummated in the future both as the act of God and the response of obedient people.

Jesus and the Law

Indirect support for the unity of Jesus' **kingdom** preaching and **ethical** teaching may be seen in the fact that Jesus' words, especially in the Sermon on the Mount, express an attitude toward the law only possible for one convinced that the **eschatological** time was beginning. In the **antitheses** Jesus opposes his understanding of the law to that of Moses, even though no ordinary **rabbi** would dare assume that kind of authority. Jesus' "but *I* say to you" implies that for him the present is a time for the law's radical reinterpretation. Characterized by the command to love one's enemies and by prohibitions against lust, anger, and oaths, this reinterpretation is rooted in the dawning of God's kingdom. Nowhere does Jesus' daring become more evident than in his apparent abolition of the law's crucial distinction between clean and unclean: "Listen to me, all of you, and understand: there is nothing outside a person that by going in can defile, but the things that come out are what defile" (Mark 7:14f. par.). With God's coming near, distinctions of the sacred and the profane, the clean and the unclean, are no longer valid. Jesus' message urges his hearers to seek and to do God's will in the law, in view of the coming kingdom.

Rejection of the distinction between clean and unclean represents the most extreme position taken by Jesus over against the law. Such a rejection did not immediately take hold throughout the early church. The **Apostle** Paul apparently embraced it (cf. Gal. 2:10–14) but does not cite Jesus' word in support of his position. On the other hand, Paul's quotation of Jesus is the exception rather than the rule. Moreover, this sweeping overhaul in understanding the law agrees in tenor not only with the antitheses of the Sermon on the Mount but also with such radical injunctions as the command to let the dead bury their dead (Luke 9:59–60; cf. Matt. 8:21–22). This last exhortation is a sharp departure from ancient Jewish custom and piety.

The solution, therefore, to the problem of eschatology and ethics in Jesus' message entails a recognition that the kingdom is both present and future. The kingdom is present in blessing; therefore, no one can afford to spend time in calculating the end of time. God is present; therefore, people have to respond, to hear, and to obey today. Yet the kingdom is also future. Final judgment can be exercised by no one other than God. The urgency of Jesus' demand derives not primarily from the ancient law—although the law is not rejected in principle—but from the onset of the kingdom or rule of God, a prospect that dominates the future.

The Relationship of Jesus to His Message

To repeat: the heart of Jesus' message is the proclamation of God's inaugurated **kingdom**. The person of Jesus does not stand at the center of his message. Jesus points to God, not to himself, for he speaks not about his own person but about God's rule. The **Synoptic Gospels** show little interest in Jesus' personality or self-consciousness, for they are concerned with his mission and message. Yet it would be a mistake to infer that the question of Jesus' identity is of little or no importance. The relationship of Jesus to his proclamation of the kingdom is an important question raised by the tradition itself. The authors of the Gospels have an answer to that question: Jesus was the **Messiah** or **Christ**.

The New Testament unequivocally maintains that Jesus' identity is related to his work. In other words, the question "Who was he?" cannot be separated from the question "What did he do?" At least in the Synoptics, **eschatology** and **ethics**, rather than **Christology** as such, constitute the center of Jesus' proclamation. In his message, Jesus proclaims God's kingdom and calls people to obey God; in his deeds he manifests the kingdom's power. Thus Jesus presents himself as the crucial figure in the history of God's dealing with Israel and with humanity.

The Question of Jesus' Messianic Consciousness

A logical starting point for understanding Jesus' view of himself lies in various **Christological** titles used either by Jesus or by his contemporaries. The major titles are **Son of God**, Savior, Lord, **Messiah** or **Christ**, **Son of Man**, and **prophet**. Of these, the first three appear only rarely if at all in the Synoptics. *Son*, in the sense of Son of God, is common in John's Gospel although Savior and Lord are not. Of course, the Johannine Jesus proclaims himself, his messianic dignity and sonship, whereas in the other Gospels he does not. But John's presentation can no longer be taken at its face value as historical. Had Jesus actually spoken in the terms he employs in John, it is impossible to understand why the other Gospels and traditions should so little reflect that fact, inasmuch as the faith they too affirm is enunciated by the Johannine Jesus. Therefore, our inquiry into Jesus' self-consciousness must begin with the Synoptics, and the last three titles—Messiah or Christ, Son of Man, and prophet—are most important for this investigation.

Messiah (Christ). As we saw in Chapter 1, not all hopes for Israel's restoration were tied to the figure of a national Messiah. Nevertheless, the basic messianic hope of first-century Israel was the hope for such a figure, usually thought to be an heir of King David and perhaps Son of God (see Psalm 2:7). Messiah simply means "anointed" in Hebrew, as Christ (*christos*) does in Greek. While others in Israel were anointed, in this case the term refers particularly to the anointing of the Davidic king. He was expected to overthrow Israel's political enemies, establish the chosen people in a new and perfect reign of David, and inaugurate the **kingdom of God**. Of Jesus' actions the entry into Jerusalem (Mark 11:1–10 parr.) and the subsequent overthrow of the moneychangers in the temple (Mark 11:11–19 parr.) are most susceptible to such political interpretation. The most significant evidence for the political character of Jesus' messiahship, however, is the fact that he was executed as a messianic pretender, a political threat to the Roman government and the status quo (John 11:47–50). At the trial Pilate asks him, "Are you the King of the Jews?" (Mark 15:2), and the inscription over the cross describing the charge against him read "King of the Jews" (Mark 15:26; cf. 15:18, 32). Nevertheless, the total impression of the tradition works against viewing Jesus as a messianic political figure. At the temptation, the devil is rebuked when he offers Jesus political power (Matt. 4:8–10 par.). Moreover, Jesus denies that he is seeking to establish an earthly kingdom (Mark 10:42–44; cf. John 18:36). Despite the one blow struck in his defense, Jesus himself offers no resistance at his arrest, trial, and death (Mark 14:47–49; cf. Matt. 26:52). If Jesus was arrested and executed as a politically subversive messianic pretender, this fact only shows how thoroughly his opponents misunderstood or misused him.

From New Testament times onward Christians and others have assumed that Jesus claimed to be the Messiah of Jewish expectation. But this assumption is questionable on two grounds. First, Jewish future expectations, and specifically messianic expectations, were likely much more complex than the New Testament testimony would lead us to believe. To what expectation, if any, did the career and claim of Jesus correspond? The probable answer is that early Christians rewrote the messianic script in the light of Jesus' actual career. Second, the New Testament evidence that Jesus claimed messiahship is not as overwhelming as one might suppose.

Although at least three incidents recounted in the Synoptics apparently indicate that Jesus espoused a messianic claim—the confession of Peter at Caesarea Philippi, John the Baptist's question to Jesus, and Jesus' answer to the high **priest** at the trial—close examination in each case shows that matters are not as simple as they may at first appear. In Mark's account of the confession at Caesarea Philippi (8:27–33), Peter says that Jesus is the Messiah; Jesus does not, however, accept the title without qualification. When John the Baptist sends emissaries to Jesus to determine whether he is the one to come—the Messiah—Jesus does not give a direct answer. Although Jesus' response is usually taken as affirmative, he points only to his activity and does not claim or accept any title (Luke 7:18–23; Matt. 11:2–6). In the trial scene Jesus answers the high priest's question about messiahship positively (Mark 14:62), but the historicity of this exchange is at least dubious. Moreover, the Matthean and Lukan versions of the incident do not contain this clear, affirmative answer (Matt. 26:64 and Luke 22:67), and it is possible that their text of Mark did not. In view of the unanimous testimony of the New Testament writers that Jesus was the Christ, it is quite striking that the Synoptic writers so seldom portray him as making or even accepting messianic claims. That is true even of the Fourth Gospel. Whether Jesus thought of himself in explicitly messianic terms, or when he began to think in such terms, is a question difficult to decide. It is clear enough, however, that he did not measure the response to his message and action by the titles that hearers and observers might confer upon him.

Son of Man. At first the situation seems quite different with the title **Son of Man**, which appears frequently in Jesus' speech as a self-designation. As a rule, no one else used this title as a designation for Jesus. In fact, it is rarely used by anyone else in the entire New Testament. Consequently, "Son of Man" appears to be the title by which Jesus designated and understood himself. Yet this seemingly obvious conclusion requires further scrutiny in the light of the term's background and its varied uses in the Synoptic tradition.

The term *Son of Man* (**Aramaic** *bar nasha*) was apparently not uncommon in the Aramaic speech of Jesus' time, although it is an oddity in Greek. It seems to have served as an indefinite pronoun meaning "anyone" or "a man." Perhaps it could also stand as the personal pronoun "I," although this is still disputed among experts in the Aramaic language. In any event, this term clearly could have been used by Aramaic-speaking contemporaries of Jesus, and thus by Jesus himself. Because the term is so frequently used of Jesus in the Gospels and only rarely by anyone other than himself, the assumptions (a) that it was used by Jesus and (b) that it appears in the Gospels because Jesus used it seem valid. Beyond that, it is impossible to say anything with certainty, for there is no consensus about the matter in modern Gospel and Jesus research. Interestingly enough, aside from the use of the term in Daniel 7:13 (cited in Mark 14:62 parr.), in the Book of Ezekiel God frequently addresses the prophet as "Son of Man." (Unfortunately, in both

Daniel and Ezekiel the NRSV obscures the potentially important **christological** reference by translating the term "mortal" or "human being.")

In order to grasp the varied functions of this title, it is useful to classify Son of Man sayings in the Gospels according to three basic types, even though these do not quite comprehend all the various usages: (1) sayings that speak of a future, glorious Son of Man; (2) those that speak of the present, suffering Son of Man; and (3) those that speak of an authoritative earthly Son of Man. By and large, the usages do not overlap; that is, they occur in separate sayings or traditions.

1. According to Mark, after Peter's confession at Caesarea Philippi Jesus says, "Those who are ashamed of me and of my words in this adulterous and sinful generation, of them the Son of Man will also be ashamed, when he comes in the glory of his Father with the holy angels" (8:38; cf. Luke 9:26 and Matt. 16:27). Here is the *future, glorious Son of Man.* The **apocalyptic** discourse of Mark 13 (parr. in Matt. and Luke) brings out details of the Son of Man's coming: how he will "send out the angels, and gather his elect from the four winds, from the ends of the earth to the ends of heaven" (Mark 13:26 parr.). Other apocalyptic Son of Man sayings are found in Luke 12:40; 17:22–30; 18:8; 21:36; Matthew 13:41–43; 19:28; 24:29–44; 25:31 ff. The nature of the relationship between Jesus and this Son of Man remains unclear, although the fact of a relationship is clearly asserted: "And I tell you, every one who acknowledges me before others, the Son of Man also will acknowledge before the angels of God" (Luke 12:8 f; cf. Matt. 10:32 f.). In the apocalyptic Son of Man sayings Jesus never explicitly says that *he* is the Son of Man, nor is that a necessary inference, although most readers, as well as the evangelists, assume that identification. In fact, Jesus seems to speak of the Son of Man as someone other than himself.

2. The sayings about the *present, suffering Son of Man* are more stereotyped and less varied than are those in the first category. They teach "that the Son of Man must undergo great suffering, and be rejected by the elders, the chief priests, and the scribes, and be killed, and after three days rise again" (Mark 8:31 parr.; 9:31 parr.; 10:33–34 parr.; see also Mark 9:9 par.; 14:21 par.; 14:41; Matt. 17:22 f. and Luke 9:44; Matt. 26:45 and Luke 22:48). After the final saying of this type Jesus speaks explicitly of his redemptive mission, "For the Son of Man came not to be served but to serve, and to give his life a ransom for many" (Mark 10:45 par.; cf. Luke 22:27). Here the Son of Man is clearly Jesus.

3. A less clearly defined type deals with the *earthly activity of Jesus as Son of Man,* apart from his suffering (see Luke 11:20 f. and Matt. 12:40; Matt. 13:36 ff.; Luke 19:10.). In this role Jesus has authority to forgive sins (Mark 2:10 parr.) and is lord of the Sabbath (Mark 2:27 f. parr.). Also, the earthly Son of Man is accused of being a glutton, a drunkard, a friend of tax collectors and sinners (Matt. 11:18 f.; Luke 7:33 f.). In addition, as Son of Man, Jesus has nowhere to lay his head (Matt. 8:20; Luke 9:58).

How are we to understand the Son of Man sayings and the relationship among the three types? Are they all authentic words of Jesus? Did one group of sayings or the other originate in the early **church**? How is it possible to relate the suffering Son of Man and the future glorious Son of Man, especially when Jesus speaks of the latter as if he were someone other than himself?

Because references to the *apocalyptic Son of Man* appear in all strata of the Synoptic tradition (Mark, **Q**, and the material distinctive to Matthew and Luke) as well as in John (5:27), the case for the authenticity of these sayings appears to be strong. Yet this conclusion has been seriously challenged on the basis of the fact that *Son of Man* does not appear in the tradition alongside, or in association with, sayings about the **kingdom of God**. This must be regarded as a striking and potentially significant fact.

Moreover, the once generally held view that there existed a pre-Christian Son of Man, Messiah, or messianic expectation, in the Old Testament or ancient Judaism has been increasingly questioned. Daniel's figure of the Son of Man (7:13–14), a heavenly apparition, is in that book explicitly identified with "the holy ones of the Most High" (7:18), the righteous remnant of Israel. In certain Jewish apocalypses such as *1 Enoch* (48:2 ff.) and *4 Ezra* (chap. 13), a messianic figure is called "Son of Man," or simply "Man" (*4 Ezra*), but the question is whether the use of the phrase indicates the existence of an established messianic category. Even when viewed over against the numerous references to the coming, or apocalyptic, Son of Man in the Gospels, the relatively few instances of the term in earlier or contemporary Jewish sources do not constitute a strong case for it as a Jewish messianic category. Thus it is not clear from Jewish sources that "Son of Man" was already a title for the Messiah before Jesus.

If one assumes that this coming Son of Man is simply Jesus, who will return after his death, it is not necessary to think that the title represents a Jewish apocalyptic, messianic idea. One might infer that, in those instances where he speaks of a coming Son of Man, Jesus was simply referring to himself. And thus Jesus anticipated and foresaw not only his earthly fate but also his future **resurrection** and ultimate **parousia**. That is the traditional Christian view.

If, however, one questions whether Jesus would have foreseen so explicitly his own fate after death and doubts the authenticity of many of the other Son of Man sayings, especially those predicting his suffering—as modern criticism has—then the traditional view presents problems. Under those circumstances it is no longer clear that in the apocalyptic Son of Man sayings Jesus referred to himself. Indeed, when viewed alone, those sayings do not obviously designate Jesus. But if he did not refer to himself, it is necessary to suppose that there was a category of expectation—the heavenly, coming Son of Man—which Jesus assumed that his readers would know and understand. As we have just observed, the evidence for such a category in Judaism outside the New Testament is not altogether clear. Alternatively, it has been suggested that Jesus never used the title or term for himself at all; rather, it came into being as a Christological title in a branch of the early church and was placed upon his lips. Yet if that were the case, it is strange that

"Son of Man" now appears as a title *only* in the Gospels, nowhere else in the New Testament, and only on Jesus' lips. One would think that it should have survived elsewhere.

Most modern critical scholars agree that the *suffering Son of Man sayings* in their present form are stereotypical; they clearly project Jesus' fate as the Gospels recount it and as faith believed in it, and are likely the product of the later, post-resurrection church, if not of Mark himself (upon whom Matthew and Luke rely). This does not necessarily mean that Jesus took no thought of the future, or specifically of the prospect of his own fate. In a number of Synoptic passages set before and during the **passion** week, Jesus seems to contemplate or anticipate his death (e.g., Mark 14:22–25, 36; Luke 13:31–35). In such **pericopae**, moreover, Jesus does not characteristically refer to himself as the Son of Man. In fact, in one such case he evidently calls himself a prophet and links himself with the prophets of old (Luke 13:33–34).

Not surprisingly, the Son of Man sayings that represent Jesus as acting with *authority,* and some of those in which he refers to himself as Son of Man in an almost offhand way (e.g., Matt. 8:20; Luke 9:58), are once again moving into the center of attention. It may be that such sayings as Mark 2:10 and 2:27–28 agree with the later church's understanding of Jesus' authority, as many modern interpreters have thought. But they may also reflect Jesus' own speech, or at least his authoritative self-understanding. Because there are real difficulties in accepting the suffering Son of Man sayings as authentic, and because it is difficult to suppose that Jesus either spoke of his own return from heaven (the traditional view) or that he used "Son of Man" to refer to a mythical, apocalyptic figure other than himself, the origin of these Son of Man categories in Jesus' own speech becomes doubtful. Yet it is difficult to conceive how this language could have arisen in the early church apart from Jesus, especially when in the Gospel narratives only Jesus uses the term. Consequently, these less easily categorized sayings may well hold the key to Jesus' view of himself as an authoritative messenger of God's kingdom. Just as Jesus spoke of the kingdom of God as something his hearers would know about, without defining it, so he may have spoken of himself as Son of Man, allowing his followers to discern in his word and works the designation's true significance. Thus the title itself does not evoke messianic traditions that would detract from, or misinterpret, his kingdom proclamation. Understandably, early Christians would have subsequently used the term in sayings about Jesus' death and second coming.

Prophet. There remains the possibility that Jesus thought of himself also as a **prophet**. As we have noted, God addresses Ezekiel as "Son of Man" precisely in his prophetic role (Ezek. 2:1; 3:4, 17). *Prophet* is not usually taken to be a messianic title but, rather, a role or function. One thinks first of all of Israel's prophets, whose words and deeds are recorded in the Old Testament. They pronounced warnings and judgments against injustice and inequity, and foretold God's intervention in human affairs for weal or woe. Certainly Jesus' conduct closely paralleled that of Old Testament prophets in certain respects, as some of his contemporaries recognized (Mark 6:15 parr.). Furthermore, Jesus almost certainly referred to himself as a prophet (Mark 6:4 parr.; cf. Luke 13:33), and one of his disciples is portrayed as describing him as "a prophet mighty in deed and word before God and all the people" (Luke 24:19).

In important respects Jesus is aptly characterized as a prophet, particularly a prophet of the kingdom of God. In the view of some modern scholars, he was an apocalyptic prophet, although we have noticed that "apocalyptic" can be applied to Jesus only with significant qualifications. The prophetic role also coincides with an ancient expectation of the appearance of a prophet like Moses (Deut. 18:15–22). Such a prophet came to be associated with Jewish **eschatological** hopes for God's intervention in history, and that expectation was taken up by early Christians (cf. Acts 3:22).

Some Christians, and others, have gladly recognized Jesus as a prophet, if not *the* prophet of Deuteronomy. But in Peter's confession (cf. Mark 8:27–30) the prophetic title (vs. 28; cf. 6:15) seems to be rejected in favor of designating Jesus as **Christ** (**Messiah**). Thus, most Christians have regarded as inadequate the view that Jesus was a prophet. In doing so, however, they tend to attach to his messianic dignity associations that derive more from Christian confession and worship than from the concept's historic, Jewish background. In any event, whatever else Jesus may have been, his career recalls the role of the prophet in the great Israelite tradition.

Jesus emphasized obedience to God and his rule, and did not expound upon his own titles or dignity. Yet he must have reflected upon his own role in the mission on which he embarked. The crucial aspect of Jesus' self-concept becomes clear in his reply to the inquiry of John the Baptist's disciples, "And blessed is anyone who takes no offense at me" (Matt. 11:6; Luke 7:23). In context, Jesus says that he asks nothing more than acknowledgment of the **miracles** that are occurring and the good news being proclaimed. In other words, the center of Jesus' message is the eschatological **salvation** offered to the hearer. Although Jesus did not announce himself or proclaim his own messianic dignity, his message and actions were based upon convictions about his unique mission and calling. Thus, to question Jesus' so-called messianic self-consciousness is not necessarily to take the position that his identity, role, and importance in the history of God's dealing with his people were matters unimportant to him. If anything, the fact that Jesus called disciples speaks to the character and strength of Jesus' purpose and self-consciousness.

Jesus' Call To Discipleship

Jesus' authoritative self-consciousness is implicit in his call to discipleship. Jesus gathered disciples (Mark 1:16–20), crying out, "Follow *me* and *I* will make you fish for people" (Mark 1:17; Matt. 4:19; cf. Luke 5:10). He summoned Levi the tax collector with a curt "Follow me" (Mark 2:14; Luke 5:27 f.; cf. Matt. 9:9). Jesus speaks; people drop what they are doing and follow then or not at all (cf. Luke 9:59–62). The Gospels report that the **Pharisees** had disciples (Matt. 22:16), as did the later **rabbis** and John the Baptist (cf. Mark 2:18 parr. and John 1:35). Yet despite certain analogies with other leaders and teachers, Jesus stands out as one who called disciples with an unprecedented authority.

Jesus called disciples to a close, personal relationship with himself (Mark 1:17; 2:14). The source of that authoritative action lay in his proclamation of the dawning of the **kingdom** (Mark 1:15), for this sense of God's immediate presence gave impetus to the call. Henceforth, the disciples had a new allegiance: the old had to be left behind, whether careeer, possessions (Mark 10:17–31 parr.), or sacred obligations (Matt. 8:22 par.). Discipleship promised no easy way. The disciples were called to proclaim the kingdom and to heal the sick (Mark 6:7–13; cf. Matt. 10:1–11:1; Luke 9:1–6; 10:1–12), following Jesus in service and suffering (Mark 10:32–45 parr.). Nevertheless, the relation to Jesus promised a blessed future for whoever, without shame, remained close to him (Mark 8:38; cf. Matt. 16:27 and Luke 9:26).

The Authority of Jesus: A Summary

1. It is clear that Jesus *acted* with authority in the exorcisms and healings as well as in calling his disciples. Most important, these acts were all the more authoritative by virtue of their position in the context of Jesus' proclamation about the dawning of God's kingdom.

2. Jesus indirectly *claimed* an unprecedented, immediate relationship with God. An indication of this close relationship was Jesus' use of **abba**—the child's intimate, everyday word for father—to address God. A second indication of such an intimate relationship was Jesus' remarkable use of **amen** to introduce a pronouncement (see for example Matt. 5:18, 26). Ordinarily, *amen*—"so be it"—was a liturgical response. In Jesus' usage, however, it is a solemn assurance, like the swearing of an oath. Thus even Jesus' style of teaching claimed an unprecedented authority.

Abba

This way of speaking to God was unusual, and the **Synoptics** record only one instance of it: in Gethsemane, where Jesus prayed, "*Abba*, Father, for you all things are possible; remove this cup from me; yet not what I want, but what you want" (Mark 14:36). Yet Paul used the **Aramaic** *abba* (Rom 8:15; Gal 4:6), probably because it occurred in the ancient Jesus tradition that he knew. Moreover, since Jesus refers to God as Father rather frequently, it is probable that he often used this intimate form of address in prayer, including the Lord's Prayer (Luke 11:2). Ultimately, Christian **trinitarian** language about God (Father, Son, and **Holy Spirit**) is rooted in this relationship and mode of speech. To be sure, Christian trinitarian doctrine developed over several centuries after the **Gospels** were written.

---

3. Jesus authoritatively grants *forgiveness* to all sorts of people. The forgiveness of God was, of course, nothing new to Judaism, but Jesus proclaimed a more radical forgiveness. Without hesitation he admitted sinners into his fellowship (Mark 2:13–15; Luke 15:2). For him all people were basically in need of forgiveness because no one could merit God's favor (Mark 2:17; Luke 18:9–14). Beyond this, the Gospels present Jesus himself as speaking a word of forgiveness over sinners, even the unrepentant (Mark 2:5; Luke 23:34). In so doing, he assumed a unique position of authority (Mark 2:7). While proclaiming God's kingdom both as judgment and forgiveness, Jesus spoke primarily in the latter terms: "I have come to call not the righteous but sinners" (Mark 2:17 parr.; cf. Luke 7:36–50).

4. The final evidence for Jesus' assumption of authority is his *radical interpretation of the law*. Jesus was and remained a Jew in his obedience to the law, as the Gospel tradition attests. Yet Jesus radically interpreted the law in at least three particular respects. First, he denied that impurity could invade an individual from external sources (Mark 7:1–23 par.). Such an extreme qualification of the ancient world's distinction between clean and unclean constituted an attack upon the law's cultic dimension, whether or not Jesus acknowledged it. Second, Jesus set his own authority over that of Moses, especially in the **antitheses** of the Sermon on the Mount (Matt. 5:21–48; cf. Mark 10:2–9). Jesus, however, does not contradict Moses so much as he goes beyond him in the radical nature of his demand. Third, Jesus set scripture against scripture and by so doing assumed authority over its written word (Mark 10:2–12; cf. Matt. 19:3–12). Nevertheless, Jesus' authoritative actions and attributes should be viewed within the context of ancient Judaism. The impression that he stood outside Judaism is a reasonable inference from the Gospel of John, but not from the **Synoptic** tradition.

How could Jesus assume such authority? The probable explanation is rooted in and proceeds from the central proclamation of Jesus concerning the irruption of God's kingdom. This emergent rule of God rendered all other authority provisional and transitory. The preaching of the inaugurated kingdom gave to Jesus' message a fresh, revolutionary quality that inevitably offended those who respected traditional authority.

Healings were occurring; disciples were being called; forgiveness was being offered; a new community of "forgiven sinners" was being formed; the law was being radically reinterpreted. Something new was appearing in many forms. Jesus' treatment of the law typified his opposition to the status quo, which was the primary source of opposition to him. Jesus touched a nerve in first-century Judaism. Eventually the separation of his followers ("Christians") from the old religious community resulted. Understandably, certain Jewish leaders rejected Jesus and his authority; opposition led ultimately to his being handed over to be **crucified** by the Roman government as a politically dangerous revolutionary. To this last, dramatic chapter of Jesus' ministry we now turn.

THE SUFFERING MESSIAH

Our efforts to reconstruct the historical Jesus have been guided by the principle of coherence. According to tradition, Jesus of Nazareth was a man who healed, taught, and suffered a criminal's death. Our portrait of him must include these three elements in a coherent, understandable way, if **historical criticism** is to make sense of the tradition. The necessity for coherence becomes a problem when we turn to the final element in that tradition, the death of Jesus. Why was Jesus **crucified**? Was his death simply the tragic end of a man who had gone about doing good, both in deed and word? How was it possible that one who had performed **miracles** could die in such weakness? How could one who evidently attracted crowds of followers have been completely deserted in the last days? Such questions were potentially embarrassing. Yet rather than conceal Jesus' death, the early Christians proclaimed it.

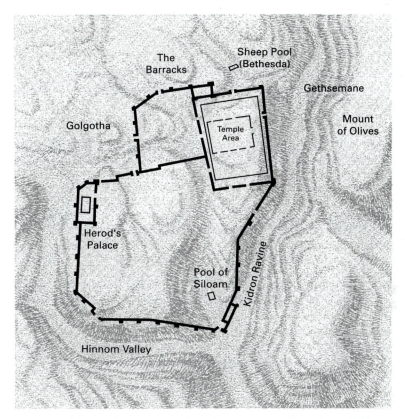

Jerusalem in the Time of Jesus. The exact location of the city walls is, however, a matter of some uncertainty, although it is generally agreed that Golgotha, the site of Jesus' execution (as commemorated by the Church of the Holy Sepulchre), was outside them, as this map shows.

Some indications of answers to these questions have already become apparent. The teaching **Messiah** turned out to be something more than an instructor in good works, piety, and universal kindness. At the center of Jesus' teaching was the kingdom proclamation. As that kingdom's herald, Jesus claimed an authority that astounded some and threatened others. The challenge of Jesus' authoritative message and activity met resistance that finally culminated in his death.

Already we have observed that the healing Messiah possessed authority. But without faith in the power of God's rule, healing did not take place. Jesus' healings were an expression of the power of that inbreaking **kingdom of God**. Still, the healings that Jesus effected demonstrated not only his sovereignty but his service to God and others. The Gospel of Matthew aptly and succinctly characterizes the miraculous healing power of Jesus with the passage from Isaiah (53:4): "He took our infirmities and bore our diseases" (Matt. 8:17). Surprisingly, that same passage could be applied to the death of Jesus (Matt. 26:28; cf. Rom. 5:8; John 3:16). The miracle-working Jesus and the crucified Jesus complement, rather than contradict, each other.

We have come to recognize Jesus' limited use of power by the way in which the miracle tradition is treated in both Mark and Matthew. The heightened miracle tradition in the first half of Mark did not succeed in producing true discipleship. Jesus' disciples became truly faithful only after his death and **resurrection**. Matthew condenses the Markan miracle tradition to focus attention on Jesus' word rather than on his miraculous power. Each **Gospel** affirms that Jesus worked miracles, yet each sets the miraculous within the framework of a ministry that concludes with Jesus' **crucifixion**. Jesus' power did not deliver him from that apparently ignominious end. Jesus' words and works led unerringly to his death.

Jesus was executed by the Romans during or just before the annual Jewish **Passover** feast. The exact date is uncertain, although it was probably A.D. 30, give or take a year or two. Jewish authorities played a role in Jesus' arrest and trial, as the Gospels allege, although Christian sources show a tendency—which must be viewed critically—to shift responsibility from the Romans to the Jews. Even though the Gospels state that Jesus had foreknowledge of his impending death, and Christian belief takes it for granted that he willingly consented to die, the execution of their leader obviously took his disciples by surprise and left them in disarray (Mark 14:27). The inscription on the cross ("The King of the Jews": Mark 15:26) indicates that Jesus was condemned and died as a messianic pretender. Yet his fate contrasted sharply to normal expectations about a king (1 Cor. 1:23). Other messianic pretenders met similar fates (Acts 5:35–39; cf. 21:38) without gaining the recognition to which they aspired. Why should Jesus differ from them? Why should his followers continue—or begin—to insist that he was the Messiah or **Christ**? The most obvious answer is that they believed him to have been raised by God from the dead and set at God's own right hand (Acts 2:24 ff.; 1 Cor. 15:4). Grant that, however, and further problems arise. Why should belief in a resurrection mean that the resurrected one was the Messiah? The bestowal of that title would follow only if the claim had previously been made, or at least entertained by the disciples. Moreover, even a report of his resurrection, which certainly was not universally believed (cf. Matt. 28:11 ff.), did not fully explain the tragic fate of Jesus as the Messiah, the one destined to rule over an earthly kingdom of Israel.

Dating Jesus

The actual dates of Jesus' life do not precisely correspond to the **B.C.–A.D.** or B.C.E.–C.E. ([Before] Common Era) scheme of dating that we commonly use. This scheme, according to which our era begins with the year of Jesus' birth, was introduced in the sixth century. Unfortunately, the date of Jesus' birth was incorrectly calculated, if, as both Matthew (2:1) and Luke (1:5) indicate, Jesus was born before Herod's death (4 B.C.). The exact date of Jesus' birth, as well as his **crucifixion**, is unknown.

For those followers who believed in Jesus' resurrection, the tragic implications of the crucifixion were overcome. But there remained the task of convincing others that his ignominious death did not contradict the traditions and expectations of Israel's Messiah. To accomplish this task, believers in Jesus turned to the scriptures. Thus the earliest references to Jesus' death were often accompanied not only by the proclamation of his resurrection but also by the assertion (1 Cor. 15:3) or a demonstration (Luke 24:25–27; Acts 2:24 ff.) that he had died "in accordance with the scriptures." That is, Jesus' death was in accord with God's will as revealed in the Bible. Doubtless the earliest Christians had to explain Jesus' crucifixion because it was a problem: a "stumbling block," as Paul says, to other Jews (1 Cor. 1:23). Even the proclamation of Jesus' resurrection could not be made credible until the stigma of the cross was removed or explained (Gal. 3:13; 2 Cor. 5:21). It is surely significant that the Gospels' **passion** narratives are studded with Old Testament quotations and allusions. Their fundamental purpose was to expound, to whatever audience, the importance and necessity of Jesus' death as the accomplishment of God's will. Probably such references were found already in the preaching, teaching, and controversies of the primitive **church**.

For the earliest believers, however, the cross was not just a liability to be explained. It was regarded as the focal point of **salvation**, the event and means of God's **redemption**. This understanding of the cross as a redemptive event was a part of the confessional tradition Paul had received ("He died for our sins in accordance with the scriptures"; 1 Cor. 15:3; cf. Rom. 4:25 and Heb. 13:20). It also lies at the heart of the ancient words of institution of the **Lord's Supper** (1 Cor. 11:23 ff. ; cf. Mark 14:22 ff.). From the beginning, or very near it, Jesus' death on the cross has been an important element of Christian preaching and liturgy, as Paul's views on **baptism** (Rom. 6:3–11) and the Lord's Supper (1 Cor. 11:17–34) attest. Jesus' crucifixion is, therefore, a recurring motif throughout the New Testament: particularly in Paul's letters but also in the Gospels, where the relative length of their narration of Jesus' final week in Jerusalem indicates its importance. Many New Testament scholars have long regarded it probable that the Gospels' passion narratives were based upon earlier narrative traditions or sources. The prominence of Jesus' death in early Christian preaching and liturgy, apparent from other sources, suggests that some recitation of the narrative of Jesus' death became fixed in **oral tradition** long before the evangelists wrote. If so, this would explain the existence of two parallel narratives of the passion in Mark and John, which often differ unaccountably, as well as other independent passion traditions found in Matthew and especially Luke, both of whom based their accounts on Mark.

The Passion and Death of Jesus

Although the Fourth Gospel records (perhaps correctly) several trips to Jerusalem, the **Synoptic Gospels** give the impression that Jesus journeyed from Galilee to Jerusalem only at the close of his ministry. This journey occupies a central place in these Gospels.

As we discovered, Luke made that journey the crucial middle section of his Gospel (Luke 9:51–19:29). Mark's tradition describes the journey to Jerusalem as a decisive and awesome step: "They were on the road, going up to Jerusalem, and Jesus was walking ahead of them; and they were amazed, and those who followed were afraid" (Mark 10:32; cf. Matt. 20:17; Luke 18:31).

Why did Jesus make this final visit to Jerusalem? Some New Testament interpreters take at face value the Markan view that Jesus went to Jerusalem to die. Some, like Albert Schweitzer, suggest that the conviction dawned upon Jesus before Caesarea Philippi that he must go to Jerusalem and die in order to bring in the **kingdom of God**. Although the thesis is intriguing, it has no explicit basis in the Gospels. It is a deduction from Jesus' prediction in Mark (8:31), taken at face value; but so far as we can tell from the Synoptics themselves, Jesus did not act in Jerusalem as if he were carrying out a preconceived plan to die. The hypothesis rests in part upon the view that Jesus took upon himself the role of the suffering servant of Isaiah 53: "For the Son of Man came not to be served but to serve, and to give his life a ransom for many" (Mark 10:45). It is quite possible, however, that this saying reflects the faith of the early church rather than Jesus' self-consciousness. In that case, it is a confessional statement, in retrospect, of what Jesus accomplished.

As an alternative hypothesis we suggest that Jesus went to Jerusalem to preach the coming kingdom of God, for no person with a message for Israel would fail to take it to the capital city. Whether or not Jesus believed he was the **Messiah**, he clearly understood himself as the kingdom's herald. His proclamation of the coming of God's rule was, in effect, a radical questioning of the prevailing religious, social, and political order. It was a challenge to the temple and its authorities, as well as to conventional interpretation of the **law**. In carrying out this mission, Jesus could hardly have been blind to the possibility that his own death might result (cf. Luke 13:33). But Jesus' kingdom proclamation does not center on his own role, and the traditions of the kingdom say nothing explicitly about his intention to die. The view that Jesus sought to bring in the kingdom through his suffering lacks support in the Gospels themselves.

The Events of Jesus' Passion and Death

Unlike other traditions in the Gospels, the **passion** narrative, beginning with Jesus' entry into Jerusalem (Mark 11:1; Matt. 21:1; Luke 19:28; John 12:12-19), constitutes a full, detailed narrative covering a period of days. The narrative seems true to life. Jesus' opponents have the upper hand, and Jesus dies. The impression of accuracy is heightened by the Gospels' remarkable concurrence in sequence of events and in details, an agreement much more precise than in earlier portions. This becomes even more pronounced with Jesus' arrest, trial, and **crucifixion**. Moreover, John's Gospel (esp. chaps. 18–19) agrees much more closely with the Synoptics here than at any other point.

Overlooking Gethsemane from the Mount of Olives. The Garden of Gethsemane is the place where Jesus was arrested according to the Gospel accounts (Mark 14:32–50; cf. John 18:1).

In their general order the major episodes of the Synoptic passion story are as follows:

- The triumphal entry into Jerusalem (Mark 11:1–10)
- The cleansing of the temple (Mark 11:15–19)
- The controversies about authority (Mark 11:27–33; 12:1–12, 13–17, 18–27, 28–34)
- The apocalyptic discourse (Mark 13)
- The anointing of Jesus (Mark 14:3–9)
- The Last Supper (Mark 14:12–25)
- Jesus in Gethsemane (Mark 14:32–42)
- Jesus' arrest and trial (Mark 14:43–65)
- The release of Barabbas (Mark 15:6–15)
- Jesus' crucifixion and burial (Mark 15:16–47)

The narrative follows a sequence that must be broadly historical: the crucial events must have occurred in the order in which they are presented—entry into Jerusalem, temple cleansing, the subsequent question about authority, the Last Supper, Gethsemane, Jesus' arrest, his crucifixion, and then the burial. With some confidence, therefore, we may proceed to the following reconstruction of Jesus' activity and reception in Jerusalem.

Jesus' entry into Jerusalem was open to dangerous misinterpretation. The crowds' acclamation, "Blessed is the coming kingdom of our ancestor David!" (Mark 11:10; cf. Matt. 21:9; Luke 19:38), suggests that Jesus was a political king who would restore Israel's fortunes by leading a revolution to overthrow Roman domination. With respect to these hopes, Jesus' first action after entering Jerusalem was ambiguous: he went into the temple and drove out the traders and moneychangers (Mark 11:15 ff.). This event must have taken place in the Court of the **Gentiles**, which ordinarily was well policed with a Roman garrison stationed nearby. How Jesus was able to get away with such a thing—in effect, an attack on the temple—is a major, unresolved historical question. The question is particularly difficult if Jesus' act is viewed as an armed assault; that, however, is improbable. Aside from the fact that the whole Jesus tradition scarcely supports this interpretation, it is by no means clear what Jesus would have hoped to gain for an armed revolt by expelling moneychangers and vendors from the temple precincts. If, however, the central focus of Jesus' mission and message was proclamation and inauguration of the **kingdom of God**, it is reasonable to suppose that he would have gone to the Holy City, and to the holiest place in the city, to announce that kingdom's coming (cf. Mal. 3:1: "See, I am sending my messenger to prepare the way before me, and the Lord whom you seek will suddenly come to his temple.").

It is usually assumed that the temple's corruption provoked his hostility against its custodians. But the selling of animals for **sacrifice** and the currency exchange were a necessity for continued cultic worship. Indeed, it was a convenience for the many pilgrims at the feast. Further, it is often assumed that vendors and moneychangers were overcharging or cheating the people, even though this is nowhere explicitly stated in the Gospels. The more likely implication of Jesus' act is that, for whatever reason, he was attacking the whole temple cult and sacrificial system. Such an attack should be understood, not as Jesus' advocacy of a higher form of religion, but rather as manifestating his belief that, in view of the advent of God's kingly rule, present modes of worship and obedience were called into question. Radical opposition to the temple would then be a logical extension of Jesus' rejection of cultic, particularly purity, **laws**.

Nor would such opposition have been unprecedented in Israel's history. In Jeremiah 7 the **prophet** lashes out at those who seek false security in the temple. In the Synoptic version of the temple incident, Jesus quotes Jeremiah's words (Jer. 7:11). Jesus' acute consciousness of God as king defined his ministry and linked him to the prophetic tradition. For good reason people took him to be a prophet (Mark 6:15; 8:28; cf. Matt. 21:11; Luke 24:19), and he identified himself with that role (Mark 6:4 parr.; Luke 13:33–34). Understandably, the religious leaders reacted with hostility to his action (Mark 11:18); at the trial they accused him of having come to destroy the temple (Mark 14:57 f.; cf. 13:2). Perhaps the charge was accurate (cf. Acts 6:14; John 2:19).

The events leading to Jesus' death center more on the question of what authority Jesus possessed than on the specifically messianic question (Mark 11:28). Jesus' opponents tried to fit him into the category of a political revolutionary (Mark 12:13–17) and to engage him in theological disputes (Mark 12:18-27, 28–34). But Jesus continued to threaten their security by proclaiming the immediacy of God's rule (Mark 12:17, 27, 34), which demanded the response of the whole person (cf. the poor widow in Mark 12:41 ff.). Jesus preached the dawning of God's kingdom rather than a political, spiritual, or moral ideology. That emphasis becomes most evident in the passion story's **apocalyptic** discourse, in which the final days herald the triumphant coming of God's rule and the world's judgment (see esp. Mark 13:24–26, 32 f.). This discourse's position in the passion story authentically elaborates the **eschatological** aspect of Jesus' last message.

It is uncertain whether the Last Supper Jesus shared with his disciples was a **Passover** meal. It is presented as such in the Synoptics but not in John, where it takes place the evening *before* Passover (John 13:1; 19:31; cf. Mark 14:2). In any event, the setting makes clear that the meal was eschatological: "Truly, I tell you, I will never again drink of the fruit of the vine until that day when I drink it new in the kingdom of God" (Mark 14:25). This word of Jesus indicates that by this time he knew his death was imminent. His overwhelming conviction about the immediacy of God's reign attracted followers but also aroused adversaries who now sought his death. The proleptic anointing of Jesus' body for burial (Mark 14:3 ff.) and his betrayal by Judas (Mark 14:10 ff.) point to his impending fate. Not only had ordinary piety been offended; Jesus' kingdom proclamation made him vulnerable to misunderstanding or misrepresentation as a political revolutionary. It has sometimes been suggested that Judas' betrayal resulted from his disappointed realization that Jesus was not going to lead an armed revolt against Rome. But about Judas' motivation one can only speculate: the texts are silent except to imply he did it out of greed (esp. Matt. 26:14–16; see also "Judas's Betrayal of Jesus," Chapter Two, p. 80).

A scene within the Garden of Gethsemane. Some of the olive trees (Gethsemane means "oil press") in that garden are now hundreds of years old.

In Gethsemane Jesus prayed that he might escape death if he would not thereby betray God's rule and will (Mark 14:36; cf. 8:35). Soon thereafter Jesus was alone, deserted even by his closest disciples (Mark 14:37, 30; esp. 14:66–72). The Gethsemane story may not be the report of an eyewitness—who was present to witness Jesus' prayer?—yet it makes sense of Jesus' last hours. In substance if not in detail, it must have a historical basis. It is hard to imagine that the intensely human portrayal of Jesus' feelings was simply invented: the church's **Christology** was moving in another direction.

The dramatic episode of Jesus' arrest is told simply and starkly by Mark (14:43 ff.), followed closely by Matthew, who adds a memorable word of Jesus addressed to the would-be defender who has just cut off the ear of the high **priest**'s slave: "Put your sword back into its place: for all who take the sword will perish by the sword" (Matt. 26:52). Luke's version seems to have Jesus stop Judas before he can kiss him (Luke 22:47–48); John has no betrayer's kiss at all. Yet in John (18:1 ff.), as in the other Gospels, Judas takes the lead in Jesus' arrest. Not surprisingly, the Gethsemane scene, interrupted by the arresting party in the Synoptics, is missing from John, where Jesus is in total control of events. At this point the remaining disciples desert Jesus (Mark 14:50, presumably Peter, James, and John: cf. vs. 33), although Peter follows the arresting party to the place where the council has gathered (14:53–54), only to deny him (14:66–72). Like the Gethsemane scene, Jesus' betrayal by one of his disciples and his denial by another would scarcely have been invented by the early church.

The Jewish trial scene (Mark 14:55 ff.) raises difficult historical questions; our subsequent conclusions must remain conjectural. Although the authorities, including the high priest, condemned Jesus because he claimed to be the **Messiah**, no other record exists of any Jewish court ever condemning anyone as a messianic pretender. The claim itself was not a crime against Judaism, even if events proved it erroneous. Jesus was executed not by the Jewish form of capital punishment, stoning (cf. Acts 5:26; 7:58; John 10:31), but rather by Roman **crucifixion**. Probably Jesus was only arraigned before Jewish authorities and then delivered to the Romans, who executed him as a messianic pretender ("King of the Jews"). The narrative of the evening Sanhedrin trial in which Jesus was condemned to death (Mark 14:58 ff.) is full of irregularities that were illegal by later Jewish (**Mishnaic**) standards. Luke and John do not report it. Although Jesus' radical view of obedience and his seeming disregard for tradition doubtless aroused opposition among **Pharisees**, as the Gospels report, Mark's account of Jesus trial and death—indeed, of the passion week—indicates little or no opposition on their part. It is now the chief priests who lead the opposition against Jesus.

The trial before Pilate (Mark 15:1 ff. parr.) is marked by Jesus' seeming unwillingness to speak, the mortal hostility of the chief priests, **scribes**, and elders, and Pilate's ineffectual effort to give Jesus a fair hearing. The crowd is manipulated by the chief priests, who are the villains in the account, to ask for the rebel Barabbas' release and Jesus' crucifixion.

In Matthew, Pilate protests his own innocence, and the people shout (27:25): "His blood be on us and on our children," a statement sometimes construed as Jewish

The Jaffa Gate is adjacent to the Citadel of Jerusalem, the likely location of Jesus' trial before Pilate.

assumption of guilt for the death of Jesus. Actually, it is part of a trend in Matthew, and in the Gospels generally, to shift blame for Jesus' death from Roman to Jewish authorities. In Matthew "the people" are presumably the people of Jerusalem only; the reference to Jesus' blood on their heads is probably an allusion to Jerusalem's coming destruction by the Romans (A.D. 70), in which thousands of Jerusalemites died. This is another indication that Matthew wrote after that event (cf. 22:7).

Crucifixion in Context

Crucifixion was the ultimate, utterly horrible form of capital punishment in antiquity. Herodotus attributed its practice to the Persians (I, 128; III, 125), though there is plenty of evidence attesting its use throughout the ancient world. The Roman Empire adopted the practice without inventing it. Although occasional reference is made to its practice among Jewish executioners (e.g., Alexander Jannaeus), it appears to have been rare, perhaps even suspended during the reign of Herod the Great (of whom the Jewish historian Josephus reports no crucifixions). Jewish reluctance to crucify its criminals was probably influenced by Deuteronomy 21:23, which interprets "hanging from a tree" as tantamount to separation from the people Israel, and the perception that such brutal execution was at home among **Gentile** barbarians.

Crucifixion was primarily a military and political punishment. Generally, the Romans used it in executing rebels and other seditionists against the empire, dangerous criminals, as well as among slaves and others in lower classes. Except in cases of most heinous transgression, Roman law forbade its use on Roman citizens. For them, alternative executions were prescribed, like burning or beheading.

Even among those who acknowledged its extreme cruelty (Cicero, *Against Verres* V, 64), crucifixion was tolerated for its grisly effectiveness as a deterrent. To that end, it was carried out publicly, on an elevation or another prominent place, with maximum sadism. Often after having been flogged or otherwise abused, the victim was stripped naked, and then lashed or nailed at the hands and feet (or wrists and ankles) to a gibbet. There he could hang for days, slowing dying of trauma or exposure to the elements. If, after time, the agonizing victim still had not died, a *coup de grace* was administered: the breaking of the victim's legs (see John 19:31 ff.). This allowed the body to slump downward without resistance, making it impossible for the victim to raise his chest cavity and breathe. Typically, the corpse was allowed to serve as food for beasts or birds of prey, without burial. Such dishonor of a victim's body was the ultimate disgrace an ancient could imagine.

Crucifixion by order of the Rome's Judean **procurator** (A.D. 26–36) Pontius Pilate is one of the bedrock historical data in the life of Jesus. The most likely motivation for Pilate's decision to dispose of Jesus in this manner would have been suspicion of political insurrection, to which a blind eye could not be turned. Within this context, nonbelievers could only have regarded Christian claims that Jesus was—and by his **resurrection** remained—"the crucified **Messiah**" as the height of oxymoron. Paul acknowledges this in 1 Corinthians (1:18-31). Rather than apologizing for their leader's most ignominious death, Christians rather quickly interpreted Jesus' crucifixion as the ultimate expression of God's willingness to engage humanity in its utter degradation (Phil 2:5-11) and, by doing so, to bequeath freedom to all of God's children (Rom 8:32).

After the summary trial, Jesus is routinely beaten (Mark 15:15), mocked by Roman soldiers (15:16–20), and led out to Golgotha (**Aramaic**, "the skull") where he is crucified (vss. 21–32) and again mocked, this time by passersby (vs. 29). According to the Markan account Jesus died rather quickly (15:44) and with a loud cry (15:37). After his death Joseph of Arimathea, whom Mark identifies as a member of the Sanhedrin (15:43), requested Jesus' body. Pilate granted this request, and Jesus' body was taken down on the evening of the crucifixion. Joseph then buried Jesus, according to Matthew (27:60) in Joseph's own new tomb.

In all likelihood the story of the burial is based upon a kernel of historical fact. It is simple, brief, and direct. The principal character, Joseph of Arimathea, is mentioned in all the Gospel accounts, including John, where Nicodemus joins him in burying Jesus (19:39). He appears only here and is unknown from other sources. Just that fact leads us to trust the reports; otherwise, it is difficult to account for the introduction of this figure to perform the important task of burial.

The series of connected incidents in the passion tradition makes narrative and even historical sense, and the events absorb our interest purely as story. Yet the passion narrative should not be read as a neutral, detached account of Jesus' last days in Jerusalem. The **church**'s faith interprets the meaning of Jesus' passion and death. The conviction that somehow God is at work in the very death of Jesus governs the telling of the story.

The reader does not look away from the episodes to grasp this dimension and understand their meaning. Rather, the events contain their own meaning, their own depth dimension, conveyed by the story but not identical with it. Jesus really died, and his death clarified for his disciples who he was. Probably Jesus did not enter Jerusalem with the express intention of dying but, rather, to proclaim the coming **kingdom of God**. But if Jesus' death were not understandable as the outcome of his life, then there would be no reason why the Christian faith should be tied to this historical person's death. Why not *anyone's* death? Indeed, why any death at all?

In ascribing to Jesus predictions of his suffering and death (Mark 8:31; 9:31; 10:33), his followers maintained, in effect, that he willed his own death by his life. That is, Jesus' death climaxed and actualized his proclamation of the irruption of God's kingdom. Jesus' radical sense of God's nearness, his consequent break with traditional standards of **righteousness**, his association with sinners, and his assault upon the temple aroused a reaction that eventuated in his death. To be sure, Jesus did not go about his mission in Jerusalem blindly. He knew that his message and action had set in motion forces that might cause his death, even if he did not seek it.

So far we have concentrated on Jesus' death. Yet his full identity was seen only in the light of his **resurrection**. Our reading of the Gospels confirms that the resurrection cannot be separated from the death. For early Christian faith the passion and resurrection were one story. Whether the early Christians were right, whether the story was true, remains, irreducibly, a matter of faith. That Jesus died on a cross is virtually indisputable. Yet whether that cross was really God's act for human salvation depends on whether the resurrection report is believed. Without the cross, the resurrection is meaningless. Without the resurrection, the cross remains only a tragedy.

The Resurrection of Jesus of Nazareth

According to the New Testament, the **resurrection** is central for faith: "If Christ has not been raised, then our proclamation has been in vain and your faith has been in vain" (1 Cor. 15:14; cf. 15:17). Without the resurrection there would have been no **Gospels**, no history of the **apostles**, no letters, no vision of the future, and no **church**. The origin of New Testament faith is the victory over death realized in Jesus of Nazareth.

Resurrection in Context

The **eschatological** expectation of a resurrection from the dead, in some cases only of the righteous dead, is basically biblical and Jewish in origin (Isa 26:19; Dan 12:1-3). In such literature resurrection is presented as a hope rather than as an accomplished fact. For his disciples, Jesus' resurrection was a fulfillment of that hope.

Resurrection from the dead—God's giving of a new kind of life to that which had truly died—differs from the immortality of the soul, the notion that the human soul is impervious to death. The latter belief was widespread in antiquity and also found its way into Jewish thought and literature (cf. Wis. 3:1-4). The triumph of life over death was a central theme of ancient mystery religions (see Chapter 1, pp. 40–41). None of them, however, depicted the restoration to life of a known historical personage, but only a figure of the primeval past.

To date, no Jewish writings, beyond those later classified as Christian, have been discovered that intrinsically link messiahship with resurrection. One could, and some Jews did, hope for the one without inferring the other. Jesus' anointing as God's **Messiah**, or **Christ**, based on his resurrection from death and subsequent **ascension**, appears to have been a distinctively Christian conclusion (see Acts 2:32-36; Rom 1:3-4).

Although the modern mind might find congenial the view that the resurrection stories are simply interpretations of Jesus' true identity as the one sent by God and have nothing to do with an actual event, the nature of the resurrection tradition resists such a conclusion. This tradition does not read like a **myth**. Its realistic quality invites, even demands, historical investigation. To maintain that the event of Jesus' resurrection is removed from **historical criticism** denies the factual claim of early Christian faith. On the other hand, to maintain that historical investigation can *decide* about the resurrection denies the event's uniqueness and mystery. Whether Jesus' resurrection occurred is, as I. T. Ramsey observed, a question "for the answering of which evidence is relevant, but the evidence might all be believed without the question itself being answered in the affirmative" (*Religious Language* [New York: Macmillan, 1957], 149). Bearing in mind the important—but not decisive—role of historical criticism in investigating the resurrection, we turn to the nature of that tradition and to the problem of the nature of the resurrection itself.

The Resurrection Tradition

The major New Testament sources of the resurrection tradition are 1 Corinthians 15:3–8, Mark 16:1–8, Matthew 28:1–20, Luke 24:1–53, and John 20:1–21:25. These sources present a bewildering array of material. The variety of the resurrection tradition itself poses a problem. Our first task is to understand the discrepancies and similarities within the resurrection tradition, then to look at the two major types of resurrection tradition: the empty tomb reports and the accounts of resurrection appearances. Only then can we classify the traditions with respect to their various emphases and attempt a preliminary understanding of the nature of the resurrection.

Discrepancies within the New Testament's resurrection traditions are obvious. According to Paul's tradition (1 Cor. 15:3 ff.) Jesus appeared first to Peter, then to the Twelve, and so on. In the **Synoptic Gospels** no appearance to Peter alone is narrated (but cf. Luke 24:34 and John 21). In Mark and Matthew, only the women visit the tomb of Jesus. Luke adds that Peter followed alone (24:12; cf. 24:24). In John, Mary visits the tomb; and then Peter and the Beloved Disciple follow. In Mark and Matthew, Jesus appears (in Mark he will appear) to the disciples in Galilee; in Luke 24 and John 20 he appears in Jerusalem. Paul's tradition reports resurrection appearances to the five hundred and to James; the Gospels make no mention of such events. Both Matthew and John report a first resurrection appearance to women outside the tomb. Mark and Matthew do not report Jesus' eating with his disciples; Luke and John do. According to

Luke, Jesus vanishes from the sight of two disciples on the road to Emmaus. Both Luke and John hand on the tradition that Jesus passed through closed doors. Such obvious discrepancies raise questions about the nature of the resurrection tradition. Does a substantial historical core exist, or do these reports represent only the early Christians' imagination?

Paul's tradition of a number of eyewitnesses to appearances of the risen Christ does not claim that the witnesses saw the resurrection itself—Jesus' vivification or his emergence from the tomb—but rather that they saw the resurrected Christ. (By contrast, the **apocyphal** *Gospel of Peter* 10:38-42 offers an obviously fantastic account of his emergence from the tomb.) Paul admits, however, that he was untimely born (1 Cor. 15:8): his own witness of the risen Jesus was unusually late. Paul's tradition places the initiative for the appearances not with those to whom the risen Christ appeared but with the Resurrected One himself. Moreover, the resurrection is said to have taken place "on the third day" (vs. 4). Although this time reference was probably not meant to be exact, it stresses that the resurrection occurred shortly after Jesus died. The phrase "in accordance with the scriptures" (vs. 3) declares that what happened in Jesus was not the death and resurrection of just any man but of one who fulfilled God's promise to Israel. The tradition also makes quite explicit that he who was raised and appeared to his followers and Paul is the same Jesus who really died and was buried. The Christ of faith is linked by this resurrection tradition to the historical Jesus. Remarkably, Paul does not mention the empty tomb.

In Mark (16:1–8) no resurrection appearance is reported. Instead there is only the story of the empty tomb, in which the young man announces that Jesus has risen and will appear to the disciples in Galilee. Again, the initiative is with Jesus. This tradition is characterized by the women's frightened awe at finding the tomb empty (vss. 5, 6, 8). They came piously to pay homage to the dead body, but the crucified Jesus had departed ahead of them.

Enlarging upon Mark, Matthew's story of the empty tomb (28:1–8) includes a resurrection appearance to the women (vss. 9–10; cf. John 20:14–18), which is followed by an appearance to the disciples in Galilee (28:16–20). Here the dominant mood is one of joy and worship. In contrast, we read that the chief **priests** and elders have made elaborate precautions to prevent the theft of Jesus' body (27:62–66; 28:11–15). The resurrected Jesus speaks to his disciples about their future tasks and affirms his identity with the historical Jesus (". . . teaching them to obey everything that I have commanded you," vs. 20).

Luke (24:1–53) contains the most elaborate tradition of the resurrection in the Synoptics. The empty tomb is subordinated to the resurrection appearances, for, as Luke puts it, "these words seemed to them an idle tale, and they did not believe them" (vs. 11). In the Emmaus road story (vss. 13–35), two disciples do not recognize Jesus by his physical appearance. They only know him when, taking the initiative, he explains the scriptural basis for his death and resurrection and performs the familiar act of blessing, breaking, and giving the bread (vss. 30–31, 35). Jesus then eats with his disciples to demonstrate he is not a disembodied spirit (vss. 36–43), even though he has just been reported to have vanished and appeared again in the same context (cf. vss. 31, 36). Like Matthew, Luke includes Jesus' final instruction to his disciples, which expresses Luke's own understanding of the gospel message: "Repentance and forgiveness of **sins** is to be proclaimed in his name to all nations, beginning from Jerusalem" (vs. 47). Luke's account ends with Jesus' departure (vss. 50–53; cf. Acts 1:9–11). As in the other accounts, in Luke, something happens because of the resurrected Jesus' initiative. Furthermore, it is again made clear that the risen Jesus could not be known apart from his historical life and death. More elaborately than in Matthew, in Luke the **church**'s task is explained and handed over to the disciples.

In John's account (20:1–21:25) Mary Magdalene comes alone to the tomb; Peter and the Beloved Disciple follow later (20:1–10). Then Mary receives an appearance of the risen Christ, whom she recognizes only after he speaks her name (vss. 11–18). Curiously, she is told not to hold him (vs. 17), for he has still to **ascend** to the Father. Before departing to the Father, Jesus gives the disciples the **Holy Spirit** (20:22), after having demonstrated that he is the same Jesus who has been crucified. This point is underscored in the appearance to Thomas (20:26-29). The first Johannine resurrection appearances, like those in Luke, take place in or near Jerusalem. The appendix to John, however, contains an appearance in Galilee (chap. 21; cf. Mark 14:28; 16:7) in which Jesus directs his disciples to make a catch of fish on the lake (21:1–14; cf. Luke 5:1–11). This Galilean appearance seems to be the initial one, despite the statement of John 21:14. The disappointed disciples have returned to work (21:3; cf. *Gospel of Peter* 14:58-60). After the catch Jesus eats with them in a scene that is faintly **eucharistic**. Finally, there follows an encounter in which the risen Jesus questions Peter three times about his love for him (21:15–23). The effect is to restore the fallen Peter, who had denied Jesus (18:17, 25-27).

The basic elements of the **Gospel** tradition are the empty tomb narratives and the appearance stories. The empty tomb story appears in all four Gospels, even though Paul does not mention it in the earliest report of the resurrection appearances. Quite possibly that story circulated later than the reports of appearances. This conclusion rests partly on evidence within the resurrection stories themselves that the tradition of the empty tomb was not initially known to the disciples (e.g., Luke 24:34; cf. John 21:3). Its inclusion in the Synoptics can be attributed to their dependence on Mark; its appearance in John may be due to a separate tradition. Moreover, we should keep in mind that the empty tomb was at most an ambiguous witness to the resurrection. It attests only the absence of the body, not the reality or presence of the risen Jesus. Matthew elaborates a defense against the rumor that the disciples stole Jesus' body (28:11–15). Perhaps such a rumor circulated quite early as a response to Christian claims. Interestingly, it takes for granted that a tomb had been found empty. According to the best New Testament evidence, however, the early disciples were convinced of Jesus' resurrection, not by the empty tomb, but by the appearances. These appearances of the risen Christ attest most accurately the nature of the resurrection tradition. In effect, the disciples exclaimed, "He appeared to me!" Their faith had been crushed by Jesus' death, and they had fled. Yet something had happened at the resurrection, and their faith was restored as belief that God had raised Jesus from the dead.

The appearance traditions present a varied picture with respect to the mode of Jesus' resurrection. Jesus ate with the disciples; they could see and touch the marks of the nails. Yet he could pass through closed doors and vanish from their sight. It is a misnomer

The Maccabean steps lead from the Temple Mount down to the Kidron Valley (cf. John 18:1). It is possible that Jesus descended these steps on his way to the Garden of Gethsemane on the night of his arrest.

to speak of the "physical" resurrection. Paul claimed that the appearance to him was of the same nature as the appearances to Peter, the Twelve, and so on (see Acts 9:1–9; 22:4–11; 26:9–18)—but how could that be a physical appearance? Indeed, 1 Corinthians 15 describes the resurrected body as a spiritual, not a physical, body, explaining that flesh and blood—the physical body—cannot inherit God's **kingdom** (vs. 50; cf. vss. 35–58). The decisive emphasis in all accounts is that the one who appeared was the same Jesus who had also died and been buried. Faith believed that the risen Jesus was no figment of his followers' imagination; *Jesus* had been raised from the dead. Therefore, the disciples knew that death had been conquered. Exactly *how* remained a mystery, but *that* it was conquered Paul was as certain as the evangelists: "But thanks be to God, who gives us the victory through our Lord Jesus Christ" (1 Cor. 15:57).

To sum up: the varied resurrection traditions point to some basic facts about the resurrection. The death of Jesus had left the disciples in confusion (Luke 24:4) or fear for their lives (Mark 14:50). At Jesus' death, he was completely alone, forsaken by all of them (cf. John 16:32). After his resurrection, however, the disciples were changed and made new. This transformation is implicit in the various traditions. It was not their own doing. They attributed it to the risen Jesus who had appeared to them: the same Jesus they had known in his life and death.

CONCLUSION

This chapter's fundamental working assumptions have been two. (1) Although the **Gospels** are religious, **kerygmatic** documents, they have not deliberately perverted or falsified the object of their attention, Jesus of Nazareth. (2) By working with three major areas of the tradition of Jesus—his healing, teaching, and suffering—it is possible to understand the nature of each and their unity in the one historical figure Jesus. Thus the criterion of coherence is crucial for our portrait of Jesus. We have sought to represent the mystery of Jesus of Nazareth, a unique historical person. In the consequent portrait, we have consistently attempted to understand the connection between the mission and message of Jesus and the **church**'s message about him.

Jesus performed **miracles** of healing, out of compassion rather than for power, but they were expressions of God's power and rule. Jesus proclaimed the irrupting **kingdom of God**, without claiming to know the future or making humankind's response insignificant. Jesus demanded forgiveness of enemies, fellowship with sinners, radical obedience to the heart of the **law**, while announcing God's blessing to the poor, the repentant, the believing, and the merciful. Jesus called disciples and followers without promise of immediate reward, but with a command to service. Jesus went to Jerusalem to proclaim the kingdom, neither seeking nor rejecting the death that came. According to the faith of the first and subsequent generations of Christians, God raised Jesus from the dead.

SUGGESTIONS FOR FURTHER READING

Most popular books about Jesus, especially lives of Jesus, are in fact historical novels that rely upon the more or less disciplined imaginations of their authors. Certainly the **principal sources** of reliable information about Jesus are the canonical Gospels. Extant apocryphal Gospels, not found in the New Testament, are assembled in E. Hennecke, *New Testament Apocrypha*, I, ed. W. Schneemelcher and trans. R. McL. Wilson, rev. ed. (Philadelphia: Westminster/John Knox, 1991). J. M. Robinson (ed.), *The Nag Hammadi Library in English,* 3rd rev. ed. (San Francisco: Harper & Row, 1988), offers a complete translation of the Nag Hammadi corpus, including Gnostic Gospels and many other writings. A definitive collection of texts and translations is available in W. D. Stroker, *Extra-Canonical Sayings of Jesus* (Atlanta: Scholars Press, 1989). H. Koester, *Ancient Christian Gospels: Their History and Development* (Philadelphia: Trinity Press International, 1990), offers an appreciative treatment of the apocryphal Gospels.

J. P. Meier, *A Marginal Jew: Rethinking the Historical Jesus*, Vol. 1: *The Roots of the Problem and the Person* (New York: Doubleday, 1991), lays an excellent foundation for approaching the question of the historically reconstructed Jesus. G. Theissen and A. Merz, *The Historical Jesus: A Comprehensive Guide*, trans. J. Bowden (Minneapolis: Fortress, 1998), is a compendious handbook for all the issues raised in this chapter.

A monument of New Testament scholarship, A. Schweitzer, *The Quest of the Historical Jesus*, ed. J. Bowden, trans. W. Montgomery, et al. (Minneapolis: Fortress, 2000; German original, 1913), remains the most devastating critique of its predecessors and the most vigorous exponent of **the eschatological character of Jesus' teaching**. Important contributions in that vein are M. Hengel, *The Charismatic Leader and His Followers*, trans. J. Greig (New York: Crossroad, 1980), and the collection of essays in B. Chilton (ed.), *The Kingdom of God in the Teaching of Jesus* (Philadelphia: Fortress, 1984). C. Allen, *The Human Christ: The Search for the Historical Jesus* (New York: Free Press, 1998), is a lively, accessible portrayal of the evolution of the figure of Jesus in the church, the academy, and popular culture.

Many of the **classic reconstructions of Jesus** of the eighteenth through twentieth centuries are now hard to find. Three of the most important—all, originally volumes in a Lives of Jesus Series edited by L. E. Keck—have been restored to print by Sigler Press (Mifflintown, PA): F. Schleiermacher, *The Life of Jesus*, trans. S. MacL. Gilmour (1997), D. F. Strauss, *The Life of Jesus Critically Examined*, trans. G. Eliot (1994), and J. Weiss, *Jesus' Proclamation of the Kingdom of God*, trans. R. H. Hiers and D. L. Holland (1999). Weiss's eschatological interpretation anticipated Schweitzer's. Also of historical importance are R. Bultmann, *Jesus and the Word*, trans. L. P. Smith and E. H. Lantero (New York: Scribner's, 1934), and G. Bornkamm, *Jesus of Nazareth*, trans. I. and F. McLuskey with J. M. Robinson (Minneapolis: Fortress, 1995).

Six **recent studies of Jesus** typify the diversity of current research. E. P. Sanders, *Jesus and Judaism* (Philadelphia: Fortress, 1985), sets Jesus firmly in the context of first-century Judaism and its apocalyptic eschatology. M. J. Borg, *Jesus: A New Vision* (San Francisco, Harper, 1987), portrays Jesus as a specific religious type, a holy man, and denies that he expected the kingdom's imminent advent as the end of history. J. D. Crossan, *The Historical Jesus: The Life of a Mediterranean Jewish Peasant* (San Francisco: Harper, 1991), highly values some of the apocryphal Gospels, particularly the *Gospel of Thomas*; by contrast, G. Stanton, *The Gospels and Jesus*, 2nd ed. (Oxford: Oxford University Press, 2002), approaches Jesus through the canonical Gospels' portrayal of him. While L. T. Johnson, *The Real Jesus: The Misguided Quest for the Historical Jesus and the Truth of the Traditional Gospels* (New York: HarperCollins, 1997), finds little of positive value in the historically reconstructed Jesus, L. E. Keck, *Who Is Jesus? History in Perfect Tense* (Columbia: University of South Carolina Press, 2000), expands on such reconstruction to reclaim a Jesus with contemporary theological and moral significance. Most similar to Sanders's approach is J. P. Meier's magisterial *A Marginal Jew: Rethinking the Historical Jesus*, 3 vols. (New York: Doubleday, 1991–2001), which awaits the publication of its fourth and fifth volumes.

For decades the work of G. Vermes has viewed Jesus afresh against his **Jewish background**; most recently, see *Jesus in His Jewish Context* (Minneapolis: Fortress, 2003). Most contemporary scholarship on Jesus deals seriously with the content and meaning of his **teaching**, as well as his understanding of his own role. The twentieth-century classic, J. Jeremias, *The Parables of Jesus*, trans. S. H. Hooke, rev. ed. (New York: Scribner's, 1966), remains worth consulting; a more recent treatment is A. J. Hultgren, *The Parables of Jesus: A Commentary* (Grand Rapids: Eerdmans, 2000). On **Jesus' self-presentation**, see especially D. R. A. Hare, *The Son of Man Tradition* (Minneapolis: Fortress, 1989), and M. de Jonge, *God's Final Envoy: Early Christology and Jesus' Own View of His Mission* (Grand Rapids: Eerdmans,

1998). On Jesus' **mighty works** in their social context, consult H. C. Kee, *Miracle in the Early Christian World: A Study in Socio-Historical Method* (New Haven: Yale University Press, 1983), and G. Theissen, *The Miracle Stories of the Early Christian Tradition*, trans. F. McDonagh (Philadelphia: Fortress, 1983). Theissen's *The Gospel in Context: Social and Political History in the Synoptic Tradition*, trans. L. M. Mahoney (Minneapolis: Fortress, 1991), updates Bultmann's techniques, tracing the Gospel tradition into Jewish Palestine and toward the historical Jesus. E. Bammel and C. F. D. Moule (eds.), *Jesus and the Politics of His Day* (Cambridge: Cambridge University Press, 1984), is a rich mine of information on specific problems attached to events recounted in **the Gospels' passion narratives**. Bammel has edited another valuable collection of essays, *The Trial of Jesus: Cambridge Studies in Honour of C. F. D. Moule* (London: SCM, 1970), which affirms the Gospels' basic historical reliability. M. Hengel, *Crucifixion: In the Ancient World and the Folly of the Message of the Cross* (Philadelphia: Fortress, 1977), provides commentary on a wealth of ancient sources; G. S. Sloyan, *The Crucifixion of Jesus: History, Myth, and Faith* (Minneapolis: Fortress, 1995), stresses the admixture of history and theology. R. H. Fuller, *The Formation of the Resurrection Narratives*, 2nd ed. (New York: Macmillan, 1980), explores the development of early traditions. R. N. Longenecker (ed.), *Life in the Face of Death: The Resurrection Message of the New Testament* (Grand Rapids: Eerdmans, 1998), is a survey of the New Testament's various interpretations of Easter. R. E. Brown, *The Birth of the Messiah*, rev. ed. (New York: Doubleday, 1993), and *The Death of the Messiah: From Gethsemane to the Grave: A Commentary on the Passion Narrative in the Four Gospels*, 2 vols. (New York: Doubleday, 1994) are basic works.

PART TWO

THE APOSTLES
AND THE EARLY CHURCH

The critical question for the origin of Christian faith is "How did the proclaimer become the proclaimed?" How did Jesus, who proclaimed the irrupting **kingdom of God**, become himself the subject of proclamation in the **apostles'** preaching? Of course, Jesus' death and belief in his **resurrection** were critical factors. In studying the Acts of the Apostles and the Pauline letters, we have an opportunity to reflect about both the Christian **church**'s historical development and the theological grounding upon Jesus who was proclaimed as **Christ**.

In one sense, the writing of Acts and its subsequent acceptance into the Christian **canon** represent a decisive step in the formation of the early church. Acts provides a continuing stress on history, as does the Gospel of Luke, and a new emphasis on the importance of the church alongside Jesus Christ. New Testament faith has both personal and corporate dimensions; it is concerned not only with the individual but also with the Christian community. We shall see how Acts wrestles with such questions as the scope of the Christian mission, the relation of the church to Judaism, the Christians' attitude toward the Roman Empire, and the connection between the power of the **Spirit** and the church's apostolic authority (Chapter 7). Then we shall observe how Paul, the first great Christian theologian, develops such related questions as the human condition and the nature of **sin**, the work of Christ in bringing God and humanity together, the marks of Christian community, and the tension between present life in Christ and the future end of history (Chapters 8–10).

In studying the post-Pauline writings (Chapters 11–13), it becomes evident that the movement from the apostles to the later church is characterized by a concern for giving the community institutional form as Christians prepare themselves for a long period of existence in the world. In these writings we see a tightening of discipline and doctrine, the development of orthodoxy over against heresy. The affirmation of the goodness of creation, the demand for action as well as belief, insistence upon the indispensability of the scriptures of Israel, the subordination of extreme religious behavior for the common good, the distinction between clergy and laity, the right ordering of family relations, Christians' respect for and fear of the state, the inspiring figure of Jesus as suffering servant and as the one victoriously seated in the heavens, the call for brotherly love, and the dramatic call for faith in God's final victory—all these reflect the range and depth of the coming of age of the church under the leadership of the apostles and their successors.

239

"The Apostles St. Peter and St. Paul," by El Greco (Domenico Theotocopoli, 1541–1614), Hermitage, St. Petersburg, Russia. *(Courtesy of Art Resource, N.Y.)*

CHAPTER 7

ACTS: MISSION AND WITNESS

Background of the Acts of the Apostles

Acts was written by Luke, the author of the **Gospel**, probably within the last two decades of the first century. Acts ends with Paul's debating and preaching while under arrest in Rome. We are not told about his ultimate fate, but there are strong hints (cf. Acts 20:22-25, 38) that Luke knew of Paul's death, even though he did not report it. Paul arrived in Rome about A.D. 59 and, according to the last statement of Acts (28:30 f.), remained there two years. Presumably, he died in the early sixties during the reign of the Emperor Nero nearly a decade before the quelling of the Jewish rebellion against Rome. Luke wrote his Gospel after that rebellion, and the Book of Acts was composed subsequently (Acts 1:1). Luke used Mark as a source for his own Gospel, and Mark itself was not composed until about A.D. 65 or later (see Chapter 2, pp. 54–57).

By his own account (1:1–3) Luke used sources in composing his narrative of Jesus' ministry. Luke may also have had sources for Acts. The detailed account of Paul's journeys in chapters 13–28 is probably based on some record of Paul's travels. The several passages in which the narrator speaks of "we" (16:10–17; 20:5–15; 21:1-18; 27:1–28:16) imply, if they do not prove, that he was at those points Paul's companion. In addition, Luke knew traditional stories from the church's earliest days (e.g., 3:1–10; 5:1–11). Whether he had any traditions of the speeches he records is another question, to be considered as we examine some of them. Following the practice of ancient historians, Luke likely composed these speeches with considerable freedom, impressing them with his own literary style and thought. He has skillfully tied the narrative together with summary statements (e.g., 2:43–47), speaking in general terms of the early church's activities.

Like the Gospels, Acts is a narrative, a story, and it may profitably be read as such. Yet Acts is more than just a story, even as the Gospels are. In and through that story, the author's understanding of the meaning and truth of the subject matter can be perceived. Within a schematic presentation Luke gives us a great deal of information about the early church. A comparison with Paul reveals that, although Acts may contain some inaccuracies, it is in touch with actual historical events. Still, Luke apparently did not know a great many things about the origin of Christianity that we may infer from other documents, and he seems to have deliberately omitted some things that did not accord with his understanding of the essence of apostolic Christianity.

For example, Luke does not explain how Christianity reached Rome, although Christians are already there when Paul arrives (Acts 28:14 ff.). Paul's letter to the Romans also makes it clear that Christians were there before him. Presumably, Christianity also reached Egypt at a rather early date, but we learn nothing about this development from Acts. Nor do we learn anything about any expansion of Christianity to the East. In fact, we are told nothing very specific about the founding of the church in Antioch (11:9), probably the first important early Christian center outside Jerusalem. After chapter 12, all activity is centered around Paul and those associated with him, for Luke uses Paul to personify the entire **Gentile** mission.

The prominence given Paul should be seen against the fact that Acts relates little about the activities of the Twelve **Apostles**. Except for Peter they are all shadowy figures. True, John accompanies Peter in the early chapters, but he is at best a silent partner. The report about James in chapter 12 includes neither the reasons for his martyrdom nor the conditions under which it took place. There is, of course, a list of the eleven apostles (Acts 1:13), but little is said about what happened to the group individually or as a whole. Probably Luke concentrates on Paul at least partly because he has information about him and lacks reports about the Twelve. In some cases, however, other factors may have been at work in the selection of material.

Paul's letters indicate that there was considerable disagreement and even hostility toward his Gentile mission on the part of some of the more conservative members of the Jerusalem community, who believed that adherence to Judaism was the prerequisite for Christian observance. Luke does not avoid reporting this dispute. As we have noticed, the question of the gospel's proclamation to Gentiles is raised throughout the Book of Acts, although the sharp edge of that controversy is consistently dulled. In every instance (cf. chaps. 11, 15, 21) the problem is amicably settled without harsh words or bitterness. Yet it keeps recurring. How much Luke knew of the extent of these controversies is hard to say. Surely he should have known a great deal had he been Paul's companion. In any case, he portrayed the life of the early church and the development of the Christian mission as more harmonious and free of disagreement and friction than they actually were. Doubtless for the sake of the gospel as he understood it, Luke exercised some selectivity in reporting events in the early church.

OUTLINE OF ACTS

Introduction: A New Beginning (1:1–2:47)

Jesus' Departure (1:1–11)   Spirit, Gospel, and Church (2:1–47)
The Apostolic Witness (1:12–26)

The Growth of the Church and Its Witness (3:1–12:25)

Stephen's Martyrdom (6:1–7:60)   Mission to the Gentiles (10:1–11:18)

Christianity's Triumphal March (13:1–21:14)

Paul's Speech at Pisidian Antioch (13:17–41)   Paul's Speech in Athens (17:16–34)

Jerusalem to Rome (21:15–28:31)

INTRODUCTION: A NEW BEGINNING (1:1–2:47)

The first two chapters of Acts lay out and define the themes and principal concerns that are fundamental to the rest of the book. For this reason they merit careful examination. Numerous issues may be raised as one studies these chapters, but our basic question concerns what Luke emphasizes and underscores in his narrative.

Jesus' Departure (1:1–11)

Why is the return of Jesus delayed?

The beginning of the Acts of the Apostles (1:1–2) harks back to Luke's earlier work, the Gospel, which is also addressed to Theophilus. The brief description, "all that Jesus did and taught, from the beginning until the day when he was taken up to heaven," corresponds to the content of the Gospel. The "many proofs" of the **resurrected** Christ (vs. 3) are found in the final chapter of Luke (24:36 ff.; perhaps in 24:44 ff.). Even without such clear indications, however, there would be strong reasons for supposing that the two books are by the same author, for they are written in the same style and from the same general point of view. The story that began with Jesus will now be continued; the Gospel seems to anticipate and presuppose a continuation of the story. The reader will now be told what form that continuation took.

Despite obvious points of contact, there are apparent discrepancies and inconsistencies between the resurrection accounts of Luke 24 and the narrative of Acts 1. Nothing is said about forty days of resurrection appearances in the Gospel; nor is there any mention of the **kingdom of God** in all of Luke 24 (cf. Acts 1:3). The command to stay in Jerusalem (vs. 4) appears also in Luke 24:49, but the word of Jesus about the **baptism** of John and baptism by the **Holy Spirit** (vss. 4 ff.) is not found in Luke 24 (but cf. Luke 3:16). Is Luke simply careless? Probably the explanation lies rather in a difference of emphasis and purpose.

Luke's interests come to light in Acts 1:6-11. The hope that the two disciples on the road to Emmaus had already voiced (Luke 24:21) is now put in the form of a question: "Lord, is this the time when you will restore the kingdom to Israel?" The disciples seem to be asking whether Jesus as **Messiah** will now fulfill the traditional hopes of the Jewish nation with the inauguration of the kingdom of God on earth. Jesus does not answer directly. Instead he replies that it is not for them to know the times and seasons that the Father has fixed by his own authority (cf. Mark 13:32). In other words, these matters must not be their primary concern. Such hopes as they have will be fulfilled in God's own way, at the time of his choosing. Thus the disciples' expectations are effectively put off.

The reason for this delay is then given (vs. 8): "But you will receive power when the Holy Spirit has come upon you; and you will be my **witnesses** in Jerusalem, in all Judea and Samaria, and to the ends of the earth." The time of the kingdom is not yet, because the **gospel** must first be preached throughout the world. The witnesses to Jesus have a mission to perform. The coming of the Spirit has already been mentioned (vs. 5); now its specifically missionary function is spelled out. The Spirit empowers the disciples for their mission, which is described in stages: Jerusalem, Judea, Samaria, and the ends of the earth (vs. 8). These stages correspond to the plan of the Book of Acts, in which the mission of the church unfolds by degrees: first in Jerusalem and its environs, then Samaria, then Syria, Asia Minor, Greece, and finally Rome. With Paul's preaching of the gospel in Rome the Book of Acts comes to an end. This commissioning of the disciples for a worldwide mission is in close agreement with Luke 24:47, where the risen Jesus tells them that repentance and forgiveness are to be preached in his name to all nations, beginning from Jerusalem.

Luke's description of the **ascension** of Jesus (vss. 9–11) has become the model for its conception and artistic representation in the church. But the ascension is portrayed in this way only in Acts. Even in the Gospel of Luke it is described much more enigmatically (24:51). Here Luke carefully reconstructs the scene to drive home a point. The ascension is now viewed not from the standpoint of Jesus but of the waiting disciples. Jesus indeed ascends to heaven and will return in like manner. The disciples ("men of Galilee"), however, are not to stand looking up into heaven in expectation of him, for they have already been given a task. They can perform it with the assurance that their ultimate hopes and expectations will not be disappointed, for Jesus will return in God's good time. Yet the interval gains importance as the period of the church and its mission. To that work the disciples' and the reader's attention is directed.

From the Temple Mount looking south over Hakeldama, the Field of Blood, which is the traditional site of the death of Judas (cf. Matt. 27:8; Acts 1:19).

The Apostolic Witness (1:12–26)

What is the significance of the selection of a twelfth apostle to replace Judas?

The disciples returned from the Mount of Olives, where the **ascension** apparently took place (though cf. Luke 24:50 ff., which locates it differently, at nearby Bethany). They gathered in an upper room in Jerusalem (vss. 12–14). The list of disciples present agrees with that found in Luke 6:14–16 with one obvious exception—Judas Iscariot, Jesus' betrayer (cf. vss. 16–22; contrast Matt. 27:3-10). It is a bit strange that Peter describes in such detail the fate of Judas to his fellow disciples. Presumably most of them were in as good a position as he to know what had occurred; moreover, they would surely have known who Judas was—so why was it necessary for Peter to identify him so thoroughly? Peter's apparent aside (vss. 18 and 19) underscores the difficulty, for here Peter seems to translate the **Aramaic** word *Hakeldama*, "Field of Blood," which would certainly not have been necessary for his Aramaic-speaking hearers, and refers to "their language," as if his hearers spoke a language different from that of Jerusalem's inhabitants. This cannot have been the case. The whole aside has to be understood as a notation addressed to the reader, and for this reason verses 18 and 19 appear in parentheses and outside the quotation marks in the NRSV. In the Greek text, however, the words were not set apart; the author evidently felt no obligation to distinguish clearly between Peter's words to his hearers and his own message for his readers. Probably he would not have considered such a distinction nearly so important as we would. Thus, as we read Luke's account, we may well ask to whom the speeches of the chief characters are directed and to what extent they are means by which Luke sets before the *reader* the meaning of the events that are unfolding. To understand the speeches we must always ask what role they play in the unfolding of the Book of Acts.

The Old Testament quotations (vs. 20; cf. Psalms 69:25 and 109:8) form not only the culmination of the first half of Peter's speech but also the transition to its second part (vss. 21–22), in which he sets forth a course of action. A replacement for the disqualified and defunct Judas must be chosen: "Let another take his position of overseer." Furthermore, the replacement must have a specific qualification: he must have accompanied Jesus and his disciples during his ministry up to the time of his ascension. He may then become a **witness**, with the **apostles**, to the **resurrection**. In the selection of the new apostle (vss. 23–26), two candidates are put forward by the group, but the final choice is left for God (or Jesus, depending on who is here meant by "Lord"). The replacement will be no less an apostolic figure than the eleven original disciples.

Luke is careful to show that the number of the original twelve apostles was again filled out before the beginning of the **church**'s missionary activity. (The word *apostle* comes from the Greek *apostolos*, cognate to the verb *apostellein*, "to send out": the apostles are literally "those sent out.") The concept of *twelve* apostles probably originates with the *twelve* tribes of Israel (cf. Luke 22:30 and Matt. 19:28). Perhaps Luke was aware of this connection with the Old Testament and the Israelite nation, because for him the church, led by the apostles, was the new Israel. Yet Luke, like Paul, seems more interested in the close relation between apostleship and the resurrection of Jesus (Acts 1:22; cf. 1 Cor. 9:1; 15:8). Unlike Luke, however, Paul did not believe that having been a disciple of Jesus was an indispensable qualification of an apostle. Paul himself had not been, and he distinguishes between the Twelve and the apostles in 1 Corinthians 15:5, 7. Although Paul evidently regarded the Twelve as apostles, he did not limit apostleship to them. Nevertheless, precisely this identification of apostles with the twelve disciples of Jesus has informed the Christian understanding of "apostle" and "apostleship" down through the centuries. The church has come to share Luke's view that there existed a complete and fully qualified group of twelve apostles identical with the inner circle of Jesus' disciples.

After Matthias is selected he plays no role in the story—nor do many of the Twelve. In fact, the Twelve were not the only early proclaimers of the gospel of Jesus Christ. Not even in Acts do they play the predominant role in preaching; only Peter appears as a real, flesh-and-blood figure. Luke, who has written to Theophilus in the first place so that he may know the truth of the things of which he has been informed (Luke 1:4), uses the concept of the Twelve to assure the reader of the legitimacy, historical accuracy, and therefore the truth of the Christian message.

In chapter 1 Luke has done two principal things. First, he has explained the meaning of Jesus' departure and of the indefinite period before his return. Second, through his treatment of the reconstitution of the twelve apostles, he has shown that there is continuity between Jesus and his disciples on earth. The apostles guarantee this tradition, for they have firm connections with Jesus of Nazareth, of whose resurrection and life they are witnesses. Luke can now turn his attention to the description and exposition of the earliest missionary preaching of the Christian church. The messenger (Jesus) has become the message.

Spirit, Gospel, and Church (2:1–47)

How does the coming of the Spirit relate to Peter's proclamation?

Chapter 2 falls into two main parts: verses 1–13, a depiction of the descent of the **Holy Spirit** upon the disciples and the reaction of the bystanders; and verses 14–42, an account of the earliest missionary preaching by Peter. The remainder of the chapter (vss. 43–47) gives a brief general description of the life of the Jerusalem church. It is one of the author's typical summary reports.

The day of **Pentecost**, coming on the fiftieth day after the Sabbath of the **Passover** (according to the Jewish calendar), would be the forty-ninth day after the **resurrection** and, according to the Lukan chronology, a little over a week after the **ascension** of Jesus. (According to Acts 1:3 Jesus' resurrection appearances continued over a period of forty days.) In the Gospel of John, however, the Holy Spirit comes, not at Pentecost and after the ascension of Jesus, but directly from the risen Jesus himself on the Sunday following his **crucifixion** (John 20:19–23). Indeed, the ascension as such is not described in John (cf. 20:17). Luke evidently separates into chronological sequence events or experiences— the resurrection of Jesus, the ascension, and the bestowal of the Holy Spirit—that were not so divided in the memories of other early Christians.

Luke regarded the coming of the Holy Spirit (cf. vss. 1–4) as a **miracle**. Yet we should not assume that he attached primary importance to such signs as the wind and fire. For him the most marvelous thing was the inspiration of the apostles and their speaking in tongues. Only highly unusual accompanying circumstances could do justice to this remarkable event. The rushing of the wind and the tongues "as of fire" are subordinate to the main miracle of inspired speech.

In all probability Luke is describing a genuine experience of early Christianity. We learn also from Paul that the gift of the Spirit was associated with speaking in tongues (1 Cor. 14). Paul assumes that without interpretation, **glossolalia** is unintelligible to the hearer, as indeed it generally is when practiced by pentecostal Christians today. In Luke's view, however, a miracle of translation has also occurred. Although no explicit connection is made, from ancient times commentators have seen in the miracle of understanding at Pentecost the resolution of the confusion of tongues at the Tower of Babel (Gen. 11:1–9).

The description of the circumstances under which the multitude came together and the course of events as a whole reveal Luke's own perspectives and interests. When the disciples are gathered in one place, the Spirit descends and they immediately begin pro-claiming "God's deeds of power" (vs. 11) in all the languages of those Jews who have come from far and wide to dwell in Jerusalem, presumably for the feast of Pentecost. These people hear the commotion and come together. Some inquire sincerely as to what all this means (vs. 12). Others understandably attribute the uproar to new wine (vs. 13). Luke thus provides as auspicious an occasion and hearing as possible for Peter's sermon or speech. Although Jewish, the audience is thoroughly cosmopolitan and representative of the eastern half of the Mediterranean world, the mission field of early Christianity (vss. 8–11). To this great congregation Peter addresses himself, standing with the Eleven (vs. 14) to emphasize the authoritative character of his speech. The speech is not only Spirit-inspired but also **apostolic**. Indeed, this speech of Peter (2:14–42) is the disciples' first missionary sermon.

After Peter first explains that the Christians are not drunk (vss. 14–16), he declares that their speaking fulfills what was spoken by the Old Testament **prophet** Joel. There then follows a long quotation from the Book of Joel (2:28–32), a description and pre-diction of what will happen in the days when God restores the fortunes of Judah and Jerusalem (Joel 3:1). Not only will there be the standard **apocalyptic** signs (vss. 19–20) but also the pouring out of God's Spirit (vss. 17–18), which results in visions, dreams, and especially prophecy. Apparently Luke understands the speaking in tongues of the apostles and their companions as the prophecy of which Joel spoke.

This first **gospel** preaching begins with an appeal to the Old Testament. This is typical of the New Testament as a whole, for the gospel is understood as the fulfillment of an ancient promise. Jesus **Christ** is the culmination of what God has been doing from creation on in the history of Israel. So even the gift of the Spirit and the speaking in tongues are set forth as fulfillment of Old Testament prophecy. As this text states, Jesus' earliest followers believed themselves to be possessed of prophetic power and authority. Thus they were able to perceive and declare the fulfillment of the words that the prophets and writers of the Old Testament cast out ahead of them, so to speak. These early preachers implicitly claimed a better understanding of Old Testament texts than their human authors could have had.

The prophetic word (vss. 17–21) was doubtless understood to concern both the present manifestation of the Spirit and the forthcoming signs of the end, as well as the appeal of preaching for conversion in the light of these startling occurrences (vs. 21). Before this appeal could be made, however, its specific basis had to be set forth, for Peter has so far said only that the time for fulfillment of the Old Testament prophecies and of God's promises to his people has come. The distinctively evangelical element appears in verses 22–24. Most surprising is the brevity of the reference to Jesus' ministry (vs. 22). Jesus himself is not presented as the acting subject. Rather he is the means or agent through whom God acts, even in his **miracles**. The divine purpose at work in the crucifixion is made quite clear (vs. 23), and the same purpose is also discerned in the resurrection (vs. 24) as the Old Testament proof from prophecy (vss. 25–28) demon-strates. The author recognizes that the words of the Psalm (16:8–11) were generally believed to have been spoken by David about himself, but he maintains (vss. 29–31) that they were actually meant to apply to Jesus.

Only after the presentation of Old Testament proof is the disciples' witness to the resurrection mentioned (vs. 32). Even then it is passed over briefly. Emphasis falls, rather, upon the ascension of Christ to heaven (vs. 33), again confirmed by the Old Testament (vss. 34 ff.; from Psalm 110:1), and upon the gift of the Spirit. Apparently, Peter does not draw a sharp distinction between the raising of Jesus from the dead and his ascension, or exaltation, to heaven. In Luke's own mind, however, the distinction is very clear. Jesus is first raised from the dead; then, after forty days, he ascends into heaven. Luke's view probably represents a later development in relation to what is attributed to Peter.

The speech reaches its pinnacle and conclusion in verse 36. Once again God is the subject who acts upon Jesus. Jesus becomes, or at least is recognized as, "Lord and **Messiah**" only with the resurrection and exaltation. This point of view is rather uncommon in the New Testament, for Jesus is usually regarded as having been the Messiah during his earthly ministry. Yet just because this verse does not conform to that common conception, and because it would scarcely have been set forth at a time when that conception was widespread, it may well present a primitive point of view. Certainly the crucifixion and resurrection were pivotal points in primitive Christian experience and faith.

Peter's appeal for conversion and repentance follows naturally (vss. 37–42). As he has already indicated ("the entire house of Israel," vs. 36) and as the situation demands, that appeal is still addressed to Jews. Yet there is already a hint that it will not be limited to them (see vs. 39). The hearers are called upon to repent and to be **baptized**, and the gift of the Spirit is promised. No explanation is given as to why believers had to be baptized. By every indication, baptism was practiced from the very beginning, yet we do not know precisely why or how it became the ritual of initiation into the **church**.

Baptism: The Mysterious Origin of an Initiatory Rite

Paul, whose letters are the earliest New Testament writings, mentions **baptism** as a matter of course, as if it were a long-accepted practice. In Matthew 28:19, Jesus commands it. But Paul did not know Matthew, and that command very likely reflects early Christian practice. At best there is no explanation of why baptism should be commanded. Acts mentions some disciples, presumably Christians, who knew only the baptism of John the Baptist and had not received the **Holy Spirit** (19:1–7). In the **Gospels** and the missionary speeches of Acts, John's baptism marks the beginning of Jesus' own ministry, and John's baptism in water is contrasted with Christ's baptism in the Holy Spirit. All this suggests that Christian baptism is somehow rooted in the baptism of John. Yet Christians may have practiced baptism quite apart from John's influence: the Jewish community of that era may have baptized new converts, as well as circumcising males. The **Qumran** community also practiced baptism or lustrations (washings), but their rite was repeatable, whereas early Christian baptism—or at least the form with which we are familiar—was a once-for-all ceremony.

Whereas the practice of baptism was universal, the call to repentance has a particularly Lukan ring. Of course, Luke was not the first to set forth a relation between baptism and repentance or to describe conversion in terms of repentance. The understanding of repentance as the essential element of Christian conversion is, however, quite characteristic of Luke. Although repentance and forgiveness were already possible for the Jew (cf. Psalm 51), Luke believed that God's forgiveness and the possibility of repentance were made known in an unprecedented, universal way in the coming of Jesus. Baptism "in the name of Jesus Christ" (2:38) was the symbolic expression of repentance and the acceptance of God's forgiveness. The act itself implies a washing away of **sin**.

Peter's Pentecost sermon is the first of a number of speeches in the Book of Acts. Ancient historians sometimes used a speech by a leading figure as a literary device to convey something to their readers that they thought was important for an understanding of persons or situations (see above on 1:16–20). Such a procedure was understood by the reader and not considered dishonest or fraudulent. Luke's composition and use of speeches conform with this ancient practice, although he may have drawn upon earlier sources to varying degrees.

At the end of Peter's speech and the account of the conversions, Luke presents a glimpse of the life of the early Jerusalem church. Such general summaries were probably composed by Luke. They recur frequently in Acts and usually reflect such knowledge of the early church as could be gathered by the author from the traditional stories that he narrates. For instance, the reference to common ownership (vss. 44 ff.) is probably a generalization based upon the stories of Barnabas and Ananias and Sapphira (4:36 ff.; 5:1–6). The signs and wonders, as well as their attendant "awe" (vs. 43), are exemplified in such miracle stories as 3:1–10, 9:32–35, and 9:36–43. The general favor that Jesus' followers found among the people (2:47) is also mentioned in 4:21 and 5:33–39. Such matters as the great number of converts, the breaking of bread, and attendance in the temple are included in the summary without the direct support of traditional stories. This is not to say that Luke simply manufactured them; he may have believed he had a right to describe these activities and attribute them to the early church on the basis of what he knew of Jesus and the disciples, and of what he knew of the church of his own day. Of course, Luke may have possessed more detailed information from earlier days that came to him in the form of traditional narratives. In that case, his editorial summaries might contain historically valuable material. Yet we have already noted that Luke did not hesitate to set forth the ascension in distinct and different ways, in the Gospel and Acts, apparently supplying details as needed.

The immediate success of the witness to Jesus at the very heart of Judaism, the constant presence of his followers around the temple, and the table fellowship and piety of Christians all represent typical Lukan motifs. Especially significant is the emphasis on the new faith's acceptance and prominence in Judaism's Holy City, for in Luke's view the church is the new and true Israel. Luke's conception of the piety and life of the early church appears in 2:42–47.

In the opening chapters of Acts, Luke accounts for the departure of the risen Jesus from his disciples, the reason that he has not yet returned, the existence and mission of the church, and the foundation of that church upon the apostolic witness. He then proceeds to report the bestowal of the Spirit upon the disciples and to give an extended example of the preaching of the apostolic church, followed by a brief characterization of its life. This preaching—Peter's speech—contains elements that became characteristic of Christian preaching in subsequent ages: the announcement and demonstration of scripture's fulfillment, the centrality of the crucifixion and resurrection, a characterization of the historic ministry of Jesus, the announcement of the Spirit's coming, and an appeal for repentance and conversion, which includes the offer of forgiveness.

Ruins of the wall of the Jerusalem temple, viewed from the southeast.

THE GROWTH OF THE CHURCH AND ITS WITNESS (3:1–12:25)

Our initial insights into the way Luke works, as well as his interests and goals, may be tested for their adequacy in illuminating the rest of Acts. The first major section (chaps. 3–12) depicts the gradual extension of the church beyond the confines of Judaism and Palestine.

Stephen's Martyrdom (6:1–7:60)

What is the importance of Stephen and the Hellenists for the development of the narrative?

The power manifest in the preaching and healing activities of the **apostles** in Jerusalem is portrayed in chapters 3–5. The stories found there are not told simply for their own sake; they show important aspects of the church's life and mission that Luke wants his readers to know. They depict the apostles' preaching and healing in Jerusalem, especially in the vicinity of the temple, the center of the Jewish religion. The location is significant, for Luke wants his reader to understand that Christianity emerged out of the very heart of Israel and that it is the true expression of the ancient faith. The refusal of the apostles to be silent, even when officials warned or punished them (4:19 and 5:29), shows how strong was the sense of mission in the very earliest congregation. Yet in chapters 3–5, that mission is confined to Judaism, indeed to the city of Jerusalem.

In chapters 6–7, however, the basis is laid for the extension of that witness. Chapter 6 describes the "complaint" of Hellenists against Hebrews: their widows had been overlooked in the daily distribution, which must have been the church's way of caring for its poor and disadvantaged (6:1). Who are these Hellenists and Hebrews? It is clear that both are Christians. Beyond that, complete certainty is not possible. Probably "Hebrews" refers to **Aramaic**-speaking disciples. If so, then "Hellenists" likely means Greek-speaking believers (note the Greek names, vs. 5), although, as soon becomes apparent, these groups are distinguished by factors other than language. The seven Hellenists appointed to serve tables and to see that their widows were not slighted did not stick strictly to their jobs, as Luke's narrative makes clear.

Stephen first appears not as a waiter, or even an administrator, but as a wonder worker and especially a debater, incurring the hostility of the Jews (6:8–15). (Traditionally, the seven have been considered the first *deacons*, a group in the early church [Phil. 1:1; Rom. 16:1], for the same Greek word, *diakonos*, means "waiter" or "deacon.") The charges made against him (vss. 11, 13 ff.) indicate a sharp break on the part of some Christians with Jewish institutions. The accusation about destroying the temple (vs. 14) has a familiar ring, for according to Mark 14:58 it was first leveled at Jesus himself (cf. Mark 13:2; 15:29; John 2:19). Insofar as Stephen is accused of questioning the validity of the **law** (6:13), he stands with the Apostle Paul and later **Hellenistic** Christianity against Jewish or Judaizing Christians. Whatever Stephen's views, he held them with great tenacity. If anyone had hoped that Stephen's appearance before the council, the Jewish Sanhedrin, would exonerate him of the charges against him, those hopes would have been cruelly dashed by Stephen's speech.

That speech (7:1–53) is in its present form the composition of Luke himself. It does not directly answer the high priest's question (7:1), and the council probably would not have endured such a long, and from their point of view, largely superfluous and defamatory, speech in response to so simple a question. The speech contains an extensive statement of Stephen's **theological** position, which is by implication that of the Hellenists, and perhaps also of Luke. Although it does not deal with the charges leveled against him, it sheds some light on how such charges may have arisen, for Stephen denounces the past disobedience of the Israelite people, questions the necessity of the temple (vss. 47 ff.), and concludes with a strong denunciation of Jesus' betrayal and murder. The final reference to the law (vs. 53) is almost an afterthought.

The reaction of Stephen's hearers to such a speech was predictable. The account of his subsequent death, traditionally the first Christian martyrdom, includes a bit of information about a young man named Saul, who held the coats of those who were stoning Stephen (vss. 58 ff.). This Saul, under his Roman name Paul, became the great Christian apostle to the **Gentiles**. Around him the second half of Acts revolves. We know from Paul's own letters (esp. Gal. 1:11–24) that he was a persecutor of the **church** before he himself became a Christian, and it is not impossible that he was in Jerusalem and present on this occasion. If so, history has seldom witnessed stranger ironies. Stephen, the first Christian critic of Judaism, is martyred in the presence of the one who was to become the decisive figure in Christianity's separation from Judaism.

The bulk of chapter 8 describes the missionary harvest reaped as a result of the persecution that broke out after Stephen's martyrdom. Philip makes converts in Samaria (cf. Acts 1:8), and on the road south from Jerusalem to Gaza he converts an Ethiopian eunuch to Christianity and baptizes him on the spot. Others also went out from Jerusalem preaching the word, but Luke tells us only of the instances involving Philip. His statement (8:4; cf. 11:19–21) very likely conveys exactly what happened in this first demonstration of the maxim that the blood of the martyrs is the seed of the church.

According to Luke's account, the **gospel** has now spread outside Jerusalem into the territories of ancient Israel (Judea, Samaria, and Galilee). Thus we are prepared for the next step, the evangelization of the Gentiles. Now the Apostle to the Gentiles must appear at center stage. So we are next told of Paul's conversion (chap. 9). Aside from Jesus' **crucifixion**, this is the best-attested event in the entire New Testament. There are no fewer than three accounts in the Book of Acts (cf. also chaps. 22 and 26). In addition, there is the account from Paul's own hand in Galatians (1:11–17), as well as other allusions to the event in his letters (e.g., 1 Cor. 9:1; 15:8).

With Paul's appearance, we reach a point in the narrative at which it is possible to check the accuracy of the Acts account and also to learn something more about the methods and intentions of Luke as an author. The comparison of Acts with the evidence of

Paul's letters is a complex and difficult task, and one that we shall not undertake in detail. Nevertheless, the consensus of scholarship allows us to adopt the general principle that, where Acts contradicts or cannot be made to fit what Paul says, the critical reader must prefer Paul. He provides firsthand information, whereas the Book of Acts is secondary.

Luke's primary purpose in writing was not that of a contemporary historian or journalist. He was not much interested in the complexity of events and phenomena that constituted early Christianity. Reporting accurately everything that happened would not have accomplished his purpose. He wished to tell the story of how Christianity spread in a way that would not only inform the reader but also edify the church and bring it to a better understanding of the ways in which God had accomplished his purpose in its history. Hence, in describing Christianity's expansion, Luke concentrates on Paul, the imposing missionary figure of the previous generation about whom he has some information and of whom he can presuppose familiarity on the part the Christian reader. Luke knows, however, that Paul did not inaugurate the Gentile mission.

The Apostle Peter

All the **Gospels** agree that Peter was among the first disciples called by Jesus, that he confessed Jesus to be the **Christ** (or, as John puts it, "the Holy One of God"), but that he also betrayed Jesus and fled. Only John (chap. 21) tells of his restoration, but already Mark (16:7) hints at it. It is clear enough that Peter was the leader among the disciples of Jesus. This leadership continued after Jesus' death, despite Peter's denial of Jesus and cowardly flight at his arrest.

According to Paul's description (Gal. 1:18–2:10), Peter, or Cephas (**Aramaic**), was a leader of the Jerusalem **church**. This agrees with Luke's description in Acts (e.g., 2:14-42). Yet it is also clear that the leadership of this church soon passed to James, the brother of Jesus. According to tradition, Peter was martyred in Rome, of which he was, according to tradition, the first bishop. (The bones of an elderly man, claimed by the Roman Church to be Peter's, are interred beneath the altar of St. Peter's Cathedral in the Vatican.) Peter's coming martyrdom is hinted at in John 21:18-19 and 2 Peter 1:13-15.

Vignettes of Peter are found in the **Synoptics**, John, Paul's letters, and Acts. Although they differ widely, a coherent picture of Peter the man emerges from them. Two New Testament **epistles**, 1 and 2 Peter, are ascribed to him. Of these, 2 Peter is almost certainly a later writing in his name. A stronger case can be made that 1 Peter is genuine, if the work of an amanuensis or secretary.

Mission to the Gentiles (10:1–11:18)

Why is Cornelius's conversion described at such length and with much repetition?

Luke portrays Peter as the founder of the **Gentile** mission and the representative of the "liberal" position that the **gospel** can be preached to those outside the bounds of organized Judaism, presumably without their first becoming members of the Jewish congregation. Thus, Peter's position is close to that of Paul, who struggled so valiantly for the principle that Peter seems to have established with relative ease. If Peter actually secured so large a victory at the outset, however, we might wonder why Paul had so much difficulty. In fact, Paul himself had less than unstinting admiration for Peter, whose tolerant conduct among Gentiles was at first what we would expect on the basis of this Acts narrative but who later seems to have reversed his field (cf. Gal. 2:11 ff.). In the light of Paul's struggle and his description of Peter's conduct in Galatians (see Chapter 8, pp. 286–289), we might ask whether Peter actually won a victory as a result of this incident, or whether he himself was as fully committed to the Gentile mission as Luke would lead us to believe. Nevertheless, Acts indicates that the question about the status and obligations of Gentile converts did not die easily. It is the chief subject matter of chapter 15, and in chapter 21 Paul is arrested in Jerusalem for the last time in an incident growing out of this controversy.

Acts narrates a lengthy account of the conversion of Cornelius and the subsequent discussion of its meaning. The complexity of the narrative stems in some measure from Luke's editorial work, which may weave together older, traditional material. The long account can, of course, simply be read as an interesting story. One need not ask what purpose it serves at this point in the narrative. But such an approach would ignore the most important question. Furthermore, one should ask why so much of the story, especially the reports of visions, is repetitious.

The vision of Cornelius at Caesarea instructs him to summon Peter from Joppa (10:1–8). Even while his emissaries are on the way, Peter in turn has a vision (10:9–16). Cornelius' men then explain to Peter the purpose of their mission and bring him with them to Caesarea (10:17–19). After Cornelius has explained the details of his own vision (10:30–33), Peter delivers what amounts to a missionary sermon. The **Holy Spirit** descends upon those standing about, and Peter commands that they be **baptized**. Upon returning to Jerusalem, Peter is criticized by the circumcision party for going to uncircumcised men and eating with them. So, to justify his actions, Peter recounts the entire course of events (11:1–18). On hearing this, his critics have no further argument. Indeed, they glorify God and fall into line with the position Peter has espoused.

Although Cornelius's vision (10:1–8) does not require explanation, it is worth observing that he was a Roman officer and thus a representative of the power and prestige of the empire. He is also described as "a devout man who feared God" (vs. 2), which may mean that he was a Gentile associate of a Jewish synagogue who had not formally become a Jew. That he remained a Gentile is clear from the subsequent narrative and discussion of his conversion to Christianity.

Cornelius's overture to Peter is made at the direction of an angel, who comes at midafternoon (vs. 3) while Cornelius is at prayer. Cornelius sees him clearly. There can be no mistaking the divine origin of the instruction to be delivered. Of the character or appearance of the angel we are told nothing; Luke is interested only in the message's origin and authority, which the angel symbolizes. In Acts several such messages are delivered in visions, also an indication of divine authorization. Thus, in the narrative's next stage Peter sees another vision while standing on the housetop at midday, as Cornelius's emissaries approach the city of Joppa.

The meaning of Peter's vision (10:9–16) is not so obvious as that of Cornelius. In fact, Peter is said to be puzzled about it (vs. 17). In itself the vision seems to indicate that all animals may be eaten without regard for Jewish custom and **law**. There is little reason for Peter to be perplexed about this, except in view of the approaching mission from Cornelius, about which, as yet, he knows nothing. Luke and the reader know about it, however. Therefore, the perplexity at this point is really more appropriate to the reader than to Peter, a sure sign that Luke has his reader in mind. Peter's perplexity disappears by the time he reaches Cornelius at Caesarea (vss. 28 ff.). In the meantime the **Spirit** has instructed him to go with the three men who have come from Cornelius, for the Spirit has sent them. Peter accompanies them to the house of Cornelius, who has already gathered his close friends and family for what he obviously expects will be an important occasion. This is underscored by the way in which he greets Peter (vs. 25). Peter's response is like that of Paul and Barnabas in a similar situation (14:15). Only at this point do we discover that Peter has now understood the meaning of this vision on the rooftop at Joppa: "God has shown me that I should not call anyone profane or unclean" (vs. 28). The vision evidently had primarily to do with the status of human beings rather than of animals. This interpretation of the vision becomes possible only in the light of subsequent events. A new meaning is given to the vision, different from the one that had seemed obvious, but which had left Peter "puzzled" (vs. 17). God shows no partiality. Yet the specific point about dietary laws may also be relevant, for the barrier to table fellowship between Jew and Gentile has been breached (cf. 15:23–29).

This point is not, however, immediately developed. Instead, we hear Cornelius describe his vision to Peter (10:30–33). So Peter first tells Cornelius his vision, or its meaning (vs. 28); and then Cornelius tells Peter his. (Compare a similarly repetitious recounting of dreams in Genesis 40 and 41.) Luke would not have recounted all this had it not served his purpose; even if his report were strictly historical, there must have been some reason for him to give such an overly complete account. He could have simply reported that Cornelius recounted to Peter his vision and all that had happened in connection with it. The probable clue to Luke's procedure is found in verse 33: "So now all of us are here in the presence of God, to listen to *all that the Lord has commanded you to say.*" Luke is concerned to show that the initiator of all these events is God. No one acts until moved to do so by the divine initiative, and Cornelius anticipates nothing else from Peter but what he has been commanded of God. The abundance of visions and reports of visions emphasizes that what is taking place is something other than the working out of a human scheme to evangelize the Gentiles. Thus the break with the past in offering the gospel to the Gentiles comes about by the will and action of God, who gives explicit guidance and direction to this drama's major protagonists.

Now that all has been properly prepared, Peter delivers his sermon (10:34–43), which has much in common with the other missionary speeches of Acts. The initial statement, however, applies specifically to the present, unprecedented situation (vss. 34 ff.), making clear that God is favorably disposed toward what is about to happen. In addition, the tenor of the speech sets it somewhat apart from similar pronouncements. After his opening remark Peter introduces the main body of his speech, the Christian message, with the phrase "you know" (vs. 36), thus making his presentation of the gospel a kind of review of matters with which his audience is already familiar. Apparently the Gentiles have not been converted up to this point because the time has not been right. In the latter part of the speech (vss. 39 ff.), emphasis falls on the **crucifixion** and **resurrection** of Jesus and on the authority of the **witnesses** and their obligation to proclaim the gospel of forgiveness of sins in Jesus' name to all (vs. 42). This statement implies that Peter's own proclamation to these Gentiles is fully justified.

Before Peter can make the characteristic appeal for repentance and conversion (cf. 2:37–42), the Holy Spirit descends upon his hearers (vs. 44), who promptly begin speaking in tongues (vs. 46). All this is witnessed by Jewish Christians (vs. 45), who are amazed that God should give the Spirit even to Gentiles. That these people, Gentile though they be, should be baptized is now a foregone conclusion (vss. 47 ff.). Jewish Christians are in no position to object, inasmuch as they themselves have observed the manifestation of the Spirit. That the Spirit should be given before baptism could only be taken as an unmistakable sign of God's will in the matter.

Peter returns to Jerusalem, where he encounters the criticism of the circumcision party (11:1 ff.), those who assumed that all Christian believers should be circumcised and otherwise qualify as Jews. In response to them he explains fully what happened. Again Luke is not content simply to say that Peter gave an explanation, but gives a full account of it. We now get the *second* rendition of Peter's vision (vss. 4–10) and the *third* of Cornelius's (vss. 13–15). Thus Luke drives home the significance of the events he is recounting. In fact, the whole point of Luke's narrative really comes to focus in Peter's somewhat repetitious response to his critics. Only here does the sense of the preceding narrative finally become entirely clear: God wills the conversion of worthy Gentiles to Christianity. Although it is not obvious from the question (vs. 3) that this is what the Jewish Christians are challenging, their final concession (vs. 18) indicates that for Luke precisely this question is settled by the conversion of Cornelius.

A closer examination of some details confirms this observation. In 11:14 Cornelius's account of his vision is expanded to include as its central point the expectation that Peter will preach the gospel to him and his household. This expectation was not expressed in the earlier accounts (cf. 10:33 and 10:3–6). In Peter's report of his own sermon (11:15), the Holy Spirit no longer falls upon the Gentiles toward the conclusion of his speech (cf. 10:49), but at the beginning—a further indication of the divine initiative. The Spirit's descent is then likened to **Pentecost** (chap. 2). This is a new dispensation of the Spirit of God, in fulfillment of Jesus' own promise (11:16; cf. 1:5). Peter draws its full implications for the church's missionary practice: "If then God gave them the same gift that he gave us when we believed in the Lord Jesus Christ, who was I that I could hinder God?" (vs. 17). Peter had no idea of preaching to Gentiles. Rather, the Gentile mission originated in an epoch-making **revelation** by God of his purposes for the church and the gospel. Moreover, the vision follows the conversion of Paul (9:1–31, esp. vs. 15), the **Apostle** to the Gentiles. This interpretation of the meaning and significance of Cornelius's conversion and its aftermath is borne out in Luke's report of the Jerusalem Council, where Peter defends the Gentile mission on the basis of the Cornelius episode (see Acts 15:7–9).

CHRISTIANITY'S TRIUMPHAL MARCH (13:1–21:14)

Luke now narrates the movement of Christianity from the East to the West, from Antioch in Syria to Greece, making the transition from Jerusalem to the West seem natural and normal. He skillfully dovetails these two major parts of his account so that the coming mission to the Gentiles is prefigured by the conversions of Cornelius and Paul and by the speech of Stephen. Already the **Pentecost** scene, with the descent of the **Spirit** and the preaching of Peter before the representatives of many lands, points ahead to the wider missionary effort. After the center of action shifts away from Jerusalem, we are kept aware of the authority and vitality of the Jerusalem **church** and of the contact between it and the Gentile mission (15:1–35). The church's work and geographical distribution become diverse, but its origin, loyalty, mission, and purpose are one. Luke shares this conviction with other New Testament writers but expresses it in a unique way.

This portion of the Gentile mission falls into several sections, defined by Paul's various activities:

1. First missionary journey: Cyprus and Asia Minor (13:1–14:28)
2. Jerusalem Council (15:1–35)
3. Second missionary journey: entry into Greece (15:36–18:22)
4. Third missionary journey: Ephesus and Greece (18:23–21:14)

Note how this part of Acts shows the progress of **gospel witness** across the world. The concentration on Paul's missionary journeys in Acts typifies Luke's perspective. The gospel is on the move.

Paul's Speech at Pisidian Antioch (13:17–41)

How is Paul's turning to the Gentiles typical of the Book of Acts?

In chapters 13 and 14, we find the first description of missionary activity beyond Palestine and Syria. Paul and Barnabas are commissioned, not by the Jerusalem church, but by the church at Antioch (13:1–3), and sent off under its auspices. This church had already been founded by those fleeing Jerusalem during the persecution of the Hellenists (cf. 11:19–20). It is perhaps understandable that the Jerusalem church had some reservations about the activities of the Antioch church and that Antiochene Christians harbored some resentment toward the mother church. After all, Jewish Christians had been able to remain in Jerusalem after the founders of the Antioch church had been driven out, presumably because of their radical views about their ancestral traditions (see Acts 7).

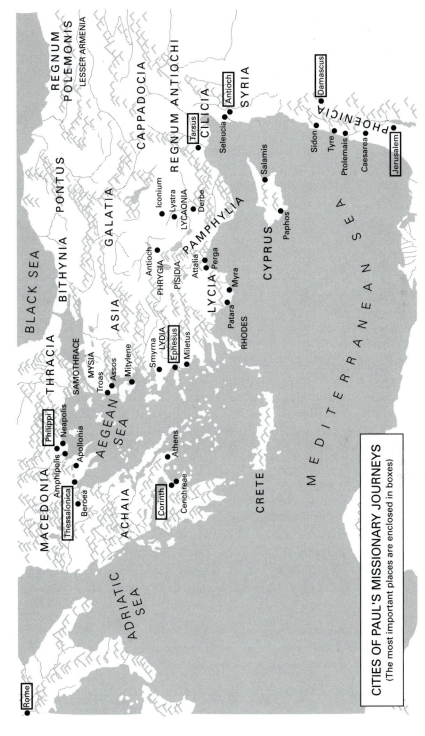

CITIES OF PAUL'S MISSIONARY JOURNEYS
(The most important places are enclosed in boxes)

Cities of Paul's Missionary Journeys. (The most important places are enclosed in boxes.)

The most important incident of chapter 13 is the sermon of Paul (13:17–41) in the synagogue at Pisidian Antioch in Asia Minor (present-day Turkey). Throughout Acts and until the end of his missionary labors in Rome, Paul is portrayed as appealing first to the Jews in every city he visits. Although such a procedure fits almost too well with Luke's conviction about the relation of Christianity to Israel, the **Hellenistic** Jewish synagogue doubtless provided an almost indispensable foothold for the earliest Christian preaching. In keeping with the setting, Paul's sermon is an address by an Israelite to Israelites, although some **God-fearers** are also present (vs. 16). It is designed to portray Jesus, the son of David, as the culmination of their history of **salvation**, the one promised by God. In proof of this, Paul calls upon the Old Testament to show how the ancient prophecies are now fulfilled in him, especially in his **resurrection**. Many of the Jews believe (vs. 43) but some do not, and, characteristically, the nonbelievers work systematically to undermine him (vs. 45). This resistance moves Paul and Barnabas to condemn these recalcitrant Jews and to turn forthwith to the Gentiles, still quoting the Old Testament (Isa. 49:6) to justify their action (13:44–47).

In 14:15–18 Paul and Barnabas are at Lystra, making their first address to a purely pagan audience. This speech has less in common with the sermon of chapter 13 and the earlier missionary speeches than with Paul's address to the Athenians (see pp. 261–266). At the end of chapter 14, Paul and Barnabas return to Antioch. The question of whether non-Jewish converts to Christianity had to be circumcised in accordance with Jewish law was not raised in the Cornelius affair (10:1–11:18), although we were left with the impression that they were not. Now at the beginning of chapter 15 a group of Christians from Judea who insist upon circumcision arrives in Antioch. Their appearance provides the occasion for the resolution of this and related questions in favor of Paul and Barnabas at the Jerusalem Council. Circumcision is not required. Yet a related question is again raised against Paul in chapter 21.

At the end of the Jerusalem Council (chap. 15) and after a sharp dispute over John Mark, Paul and Barnabas separate. Paul returns to the scene of their earlier missionary activity, taking Silas with him (15:36–41). Thence he heads west and, reaching Troas, sees the vision of the man from Macedonia (16:9) that leads him to extend his missionary effort to Europe. Macedonia and Greece henceforth become, with Ephesus, the main focus of Paul's missionary activity until his imprisonment and subsequent journey to Rome. His chief missionary accomplishments are in the Greek cities of Philippi (chap. 16), Thessalonica (17:1–9) and Corinth (chap. 18), and in the Asian city of Ephesus (chap. 19). Luke, however, gives an extended account of the relatively brief visit of Paul to Athens.

Paul's Speech in Athens (17:16–34)

How and why does Paul's preaching in Athens differ from other missionary sermons in Acts?

Obviously, Luke regards Paul's stay in Athens as an important event. As a mission field, Athens is certainly not typical, for Paul's efforts there seem to have borne little fruit.

Nevertheless, Luke's account of his visit occupies a prominent place and includes the longest rendition in Acts of a sermon before an entirely **Gentile** audience.

Although Athens in the first century was not large even by ancient standards—its total number of citizens may not have been more than five thousand—Luke's brief description of the character of the city shows some awareness of the nature as well as of the city's historical importance. Still, he reports that Paul was not at all impressed by Athens and was shocked by the profusion of idols he found there (vs. 16). His displeasure led him to engage in debate, not only in the synagogue, as had previously been his custom, but even in the public marketplace (vs. 17). Although Luke does not say so explicitly, this area is presumably the same marketplace where centuries before Socrates engaged his fellow Athenians in discussions. Perhaps Luke is aware of a certain parallel here, even though he does not mention Socrates' name, for we read that Paul is accused of being a preacher of "foreign divinities" (vs. 18). The Greek could as well be translated "strange demons" and thus corresponds closely to that *daimōn* (in this case, "good spirit") which led Socrates to raise those simple, pointed, and troublesome questions that at length roused the ire of his fellow Athenians and led to his execution as an atheist.

Paul's lack of appreciation of Athenian culture is no greater than the Athenians' misunderstanding of him, as his encounter with the Stoic and Epicurean philosophers shows (vs. 18). The epithet that some of them apply to him, "babbler," literally means "cock-sparrow." It was a term of derision for a person who, without real understanding, picks up ideas from here and there, as the sparrow picks up seed, and then passes them off as his own. That this estimate of Paul is an offhand judgment based on no genuine understanding of him may be inferred from the fact that the philosophers seem to take Jesus and the **resurrection** to be two gods. (This is not quite as absurd as it may seem: the Greek word *anastasis*, resurrection, is feminine in gender, and pagan gods frequently had goddesses as consorts.) In the light of this beginning, the Athenians' desire to hear Paul's teaching in greater detail is difficult to understand. Luke suggests that it only stems from their insatiable curiosity about anything novel (vss. 20 ff.).

The Athenians take Paul to the Areopagus (vs. 19), where he makes his speech. At the time of Paul a court was held on the Areopagus ("hill of Ares," the Greek god of war and equivalent to the Romans' Mars), a small promontory west of the more famous Acropolis. Although it has been suggested that Paul was himself taken there to be tried, this is nowhere explicitly stated (although the verb *took hold of* in verse 19 could imply arrest). The whole affair does not read like a legal proceeding. Rather, Paul is put on display, almost as if he were some kind of freak, by a crowd of intellectual dilettantes.

Paul's initial remark (vs. 22) should probably not be taken in a negative or sarcastic sense. Rather, as the following verses show, it is the point of contact with the pagan audience that Paul hopes to follow up and develop in his delivery of the Christian message. This becomes clear when Paul concedes that the "unknown god" is worshiped in a valid, if inadequate, way by the Athenians (vs. 23). The time has now come, however, for the

In the center of the picture, taken from the acropolis of Athens, is the Areopagus (Hill of Ares, or Mars Hill), according to Acts 17:22 the site of Paul's address to the Athenians.

unknown God to be revealed in the Christian preaching. A right understanding of this God will mean the recognition of the erroneous character of the pagan worship that has heretofore been offered (vss. 24 ff.). This point of view is not, of course, unique to Christianity. It is also Jewish, and this part of Paul's speech may owe something to earlier Jewish missionary propaganda. Furthermore, although the idolatry and polytheism described here may have been practiced and taken seriously by many people in the ancient world, the cultured Greek would have also shared something of Paul's attitude. In fact, verses 24 ff. may owe as much to Stoic philosophy as to Judaism and the Old Testament.

The concepts (esp. in vss. 26–29) actually fit better into the Stoic view of the cosmos (world) than into the biblical–Jewish conception of the history of **salvation**. Verse 26 pertains to characteristic Stoic ideas of God's providence, verses 27 and 28 to God's **immanence** or presence in the world. Moreover, just at the point at which we might have expected a quotation from the Old Testament, Paul quotes the Greek poet Aratus (vs. 28; cf. *Phaenomena*, 5; Cleanthes, *Hymn to Zeus*, 4). Thus does Paul accommodate his message to what is familiar and acceptable to his Greek hearers. At the same time, he drives home the argument against idolatry (vs. 29). Although verses 26–28 are now frequently cited as biblical proof of the unity of all peoples under God, in this context they are probably not intended primarily to set forth that idea. Rather, they are an argument from the evidence of the existence of God in human beings in creation to a conclusion concerning the nature of God and the proper knowledge and worship of the Creator. God orders the world and humanity (vs. 26) in such a way that they should be disposed to seek him (vs. 27), and so indwells the creation that this seeking is by no means futile (vss. 27 ff.). Indeed, as the quotation from Aratus shows, the idea of divine immanence is understood to imply that humankind already has a close relationship to God: "For we too are his offspring." Probably Luke takes this to mean that man is God's **creature, in** line with the Old Testament and Hebraic point of view and not in the sense of **kinship** that the poet originally intended. Nevertheless, creaturehood here already implies the possibility of knowing and having access to God.

Only in verses 30 and 31 does Paul turn from these arguments about **natural theology**, which many Hellenistic Jews or even pagans might have found perfectly congenial, to the distinctly Christian message. The whole history of paganism down to the moment in which Paul speaks is described simply as "times of human ignorance" that God has overlooked (vs. 30). The pagan world will presumably incur no guilt as a result, provided that it now repents. No mention at all is made of the ministry and **crucifixion** of Jesus in this preaching of repentance; only the coming judgment is invoked, and only in connection with that is Jesus mentioned. Even then Paul alludes to him only as the man whom God has appointed to judge the world, giving assurance of this "to all by raising him from the dead." At the mention of the resurrection of the dead, Paul is interrupted; some hearers become contemptuous (the Jewish and Christian notion of resurrection is foreign or distasteful to them), but others remain curious (vs. 32). Paul departs (vs. 33), and although we have the impression that his preaching to the Athenians was something less than a success, he does make a few converts (vs. 34).

This speech is notable on several counts. First, it differs from the missionary speeches of chapters 1–13 in its total lack of reference to the Old Testament and the history of Israel. Second, in important respects it is remarkably dissimilar to the thought of the genuine letters of Paul. Third, it has certain affinities with the speech ascribed to Paul and Barnabas in 14:15–18. In fact, this is one of the rare places in the New Testament where a positive though highly qualified estimate of pagan piety and culture is expressed or implied and a natural theology is set forth. Each of these points deserves further comment.

We have already noticed that at just the point we would have expected Paul to refer to the Hebrew scriptures, he quotes a pagan poet. The Old Testament would have been of little use in confirming the truth of the Christian message before a non-Jewish audience who did not accept its authority in the first place. The appeal to this purely Gentile audience had to be made on the basis of arguments from **Hellenistic** natural theology and Greek literature. This shift does not mean that the use of scripture in Christian preaching was regarded either by Paul or Luke as a purely apologetic device. There is ample reason to suppose that both regarded it as **revelation** in and of itself. Yet the non-Jewish hearer could only be brought to assent on other grounds. Similarly, in the brief missionary sermon of Paul and Barnabas before a non-Jewish audience at Lystra (14:15–18), there is no reference or allusion to scripture or the narrative of salvation history. In recounting the speeches to Gentile audiences in this way, Luke may be following a common procedure or could be influenced by a common practice of the Hellenistic Christian mission in his own day. Yet, if his letters are any indication, Paul did not limit his use of the scriptures to situations in which he was addressing Christians of Jewish background only.

This observation leads directly to our second point. The first three chapters of the Epistle to the Romans suggest that Paul's attitude toward the pagan world was not that portrayed in the Areopagus speech. Whereas in this speech, pagan piety and the possibility of a natural theology are the point of contact and, in fact, the basis of his preaching, in Romans practically the reverse is true (see Chapter 10, pp. 349–354). In Romans, the knowledge of God is in principle possible because of creation and the natural order, but the possibility of such knowledge is not the basis of Christian preaching. Rather it is grounds for condemnation, because, although present, it does not lead to a proper acknowledgment of God (1:18–23). The difference is stark: in Acts, the hearers are credited with worshiping God without knowing him, while in Romans, the human race is charged with knowing God but not worshiping him. Whereas in Acts 17:30, the past prior to the gospel's proclamation is simply a period of ignorance for which no blame is assigned, in Romans, human history is the history of **sin**. Further, when the salvation event is announced in Acts 17:31, Paul speaks primarily of the coming judgment, with a backward look at the resurrection. In Romans 3:21 ff., the salvation event is described in terms of the cross.

Admittedly, in Acts, Paul's speech is interrupted, but we have the impression that with the mention of the resurrection and judgment he has said all he meant to say. Thus in many important respects Paul's Areopagus speech seems the antithesis of Paul's theology in Romans. This observation naturally leads to the question of whether this speech is Paul's or whether Luke has put into Paul's mouth what he considers to be an appropriate and typical missionary sermon to Gentiles. In order to ascribe the speech to Paul, one may surmise that after this occasion Paul gave up this apologetic approach. Yet there is little indication in all the genuine Pauline letters that the **Apostle** himself ever espoused such a theological position as we find in the Acts speech. It is much easier historically to understand the Areopagus speech as the composition of Luke. This, of course, does not mean that Paul did not visit Athens and preach there (cf. 1 Thess. 3:1).

Accordingly, Luke seems to present what he considers a typical missionary sermon to Gentiles. This conclusion is supported by our third point: namely, that the Areopagus speech has its closest affinities with the speech of Paul and Barnabas to a pagan audience at Lystra (14:15–18). The Lystra speech manifests certain specific points of agreement

This photograph was taken from the top of the theater of Ephesus, looking down over the stage. A hostile crowd is said to have dragged companions of the Apostle Paul here; a crowd gathered, and a riot was barely avoided (Acts 19:28–41).

with the Areopagus address. Especially striking are the concept of divine creation (vs. 15), the notion that God has tolerated the idolatry of the Gentiles in times past (vss. 15 ff.), and the belief that the beneficent natural processes attest a divine author (vs. 17). Except for the lack of direct reference to **Christ**, the Lystra speech is quite similar to the one at Athens. And like the latter, it is dissimilar to the speeches of chapters 1–13 and unlike the theology of the Pauline epistles.

Both the Athens speech and the Lystra speech are most unlike Pauline theology and the rest of the New Testament in their ascription of a positive and significant role to a natural knowledge of God, an intuition both possible and extant apart from the Jewish and Christian traditions. They are also unique in regarding the history of humanity prior to the coming of Christ and the preaching of the **gospel** as one of ignorance rather than sin. The revelation in Christ is not the revelation of God's wrath (cf. Rom. 1:18) and of human sinfulness, but of a coming judgment and the necessity of repentance (Acts 17:30 ff.) and forgiveness. Thus, for Luke the human predicament is not quite so desperate as for Paul, and pagan culture and piety are allowed to play a positive, preparatory role for the gospel's presentation.

The idea of a valid general revelation apart from Israel and the Old Testament, although rare in the New Testament, was taken up and developed by Christian apologists and theologians of the second and third centuries. It has persisted among Christians down to the present. For Luke, the entire world and its history provide the scope for the Christian mission and message. Its roots are to be found not only in the history of Israel but also in general human history and culture. Luke's Gospel traces the genealogy of Christ back to Adam. In Acts, the necessary presuppositions of Christian preaching are found in a popular philosophic view of God and the world, as well as in the Old Testament.

JERUSALEM TO ROME (21:15–28:31)

What is the outcome of Paul's arrest and trials?

This final major section of Acts is devoted entirely to the fortunes of Paul from his last visit to Jerusalem until his arrival as a prisoner in Rome. According to Luke, Paul was taken into custody by the Romans to rescue him from an angry Jerusalem mob. Certain Jews accused him of "teaching everyone everywhere against our people, our law, and this place," as well as defiling the temple by bringing Greeks into it (21:28). From the point at which Paul is arrested near the temple in Jerusalem (21:33) to the end of the book, he is a Roman prisoner. (Probably he, like Jesus, died at the hands of the Romans, although Luke does not tell us.) At first Paul is held for a couple of days in Jerusalem. Then he is transferred to Caesarea, the site of the Roman governor's headquarters (chaps. 24–26); finally, on the basis of his own appeal as a Roman citizen to trial by Caesar, he is sent to Rome (chaps. 27–28). At each stage Paul's innocence is affirmed (23:29; 25:25; 26:31 ff.). There the story simply ends, with Paul a prisoner in Rome, albeit with certain freedoms and privileges. As we take leave of him he is still "proclaiming the kingdom of God and teaching about the Lord Jesus Christ with all boldness and without hindrance" (28:31).

With the exception of the sea voyage to Rome (chap. 27), the larger portion of chapters 22–28 is devoted to extensive descriptions of Paul's defense of himself before representatives of Judaism and Rome. It is as if the prophecy of 9:15 were being literally fulfilled: "He is an instrument whom I have chosen to bring my name before Gentiles and kings and before the people of Israel." Luke describes Paul's hearings and speeches in considerable detail. Paul's conversion, reported in full in chapter 9, is repeated with some variations in chapters 22 and 26. In the course of many scenes and speeches, several themes are often reiterated. First, Paul has not betrayed Judaism; rather, he understands his whole mission to pertain directly to the fulfillment of Israel's hope. Second, Paul's mission to the **Gentiles** is not simply his own idea but the direct result of divine causation and directive. Thus Paul's conversion is always closely linked to his commission to preach to the Gentiles—as it is by Paul himself (Gal. 1:15 ff.). Third, Paul's innocence of any crime is established with certainty. The various hints and assertions tending to exonerate Paul are well summarized in the conversation between Agrippa and Festus (26:32), where Agrippa says that Paul could have been released had he not appealed to Caesar. Finally, although it has tragic overtones (e.g., 20:22–25, 38), the fact that Paul must stand before the emperor (27:24) is not finally a tragedy but, rather, the culmination of Christianity's triumphant spread across the known world, which constitutes the high point of Acts. Though some might regard Paul's imprisonment and journey to Rome as the result of the work of evil men or the quirk of a cruel fate, for Luke they are the fulfillment of God's will.

The Roman forum. In antiquity the forum was a center of civic life and government. According to tradition, Paul was held in the Mamertine prison, which is at the opposite end of the forum from the Arch of Titus (see p. 10).

CONCLUSION

The *structure* of the Acts of the Apostles must be considered in conjunction with Luke's Gospel. At the same time, the division between the Gospel and Acts is more than a convenient literary device. It marks a major division in Luke's **theology** and perception of history. Luke envisages a drama of three distinct phases: the period of Israel and her **prophetic** message; the fulfillment of this prophecy in the earthly mission of Jesus; and the mission of the **church**, likewise a fulfillment of ancient prophecy. Luke's threefold division of the history of **salvation** can be discerned from the shape and structure of his writing. Scripture, the Old Testament (cf. Luke 1:5–2:51 esp.), constitutes the first part of a story of salvation that finds its culmination in the coming of Jesus as the **Christ** (the Gospel). But this fulfillment was not limited to the historic appearance of Jesus of Nazareth; it embraced also the existence and mission of his church (Acts).

The basic structure of Acts itself is quite simple. After Jesus' **ascension**, Matthias's election, and the **gospel**'s inaugural preaching by Peter, all of which take place in or around Jerusalem, there are three principal divisions. The first deals with the establishment and growth of the church within Palestine (chaps. 3–12), the second with the church's expansion to the **Gentile** world (13:1–21:14), and the third with Paul's victory against opposition (21:15–28:31). Even as the journey of Jesus to Jerusalem forms the central part of the Gospel, so also the missionary journeys of Paul make up the central portion of Acts. Just as the last part of the Gospel deals with the arrest, trial, and death of an innocent Jesus, so too the last seven chapters of Acts narrate the arrest of an innocent Paul, his trials, and the eventual journey to Rome. The motifs of journeying and **witnessing** thus predominate in Acts as also in Luke's Gospel.

The *emphases* of Acts are intricately bound to its structure and are intimately related to those of the Gospel. Indeed, the same emphases—Christianity as the new Israel, worldwide expansion, and the importance of witnessing—are developed somewhat further in Acts. In the Gospel, Luke is tied to the tradition of Jesus, which he cannot radically change. In Acts, however, he can with a relatively free hand tell the story of the church's advance so as to bring out its meaning and truth.

Luke was deeply convinced that Judaism should have become Christianity, and, as it had not, that the promises to Israel were being fulfilled through **Christ** in the church. Thus the new faith is the proper and genuine continuation and fulfillment of the old. The many quotations from, and allusions and references to, the Old Testament clearly convey this emphasis. In fact, the culmination of Paul's ministry in Rome, recounted in chap. 28, is his application of the famous Isaiah 6:9–10 passage to those Jews who had not believed his preaching (vss. 25–28). The majority of Israel has forfeited its inheritance to the Gentiles by rejecting the gospel, and the young Christian church has now become the true Israel. This conviction is mirrored in Luke's Gospel, in which Jesus begins his ministry with a clear indication that he is to be rejected by the Jews and accepted by

Gentiles (4:16-30). Yet this negative view is tempered all along in Luke and Acts by the common people's reception of Jesus and the **apostles**.

Acts is often called "the first church history," and in a sense it is. Yet it is history of a very special kind. It is written from a definite theological perspective with certain purposes in view. When all allowances are made for Luke's motivations and interests, however, it is apparent that a major part of Luke's purpose in Acts is to tell an interesting and for the most part happy story. He describes the establishment of Christianity and its progress across the Greco-Roman world during the apostolic age. The scope of the gospel is universal, and it will not be denied. Although we hear of persecutions and martyrdoms in the course of this story, the storyteller's attitude remains confident and optimistic throughout, and the narrative ends on a positive note (28:30 ff.). The gospel knows no obstacle too great and no enemy too powerful to impede its successful march from Jerusalem to Rome. The universal emphasis, which is subtly conveyed in Luke's Gospel (cf. Luke 3:38; 4:24–30), becomes the principal subject matter of Acts.

Luke's central emphasis upon the gospel's universality implies an emphasis on witnessing. Again, what is handled somewhat indirectly in the Gospel becomes a major theme of Acts. In Acts 1, Luke's primary concern is to show that in the apostolic group, the Twelve, a firm basis for the witness to Jesus had been established. Matthias, selected by God to replace Judas, is qualified for his role by virtue of intimate, long-time knowledge of Jesus. To assure the gospel's universal scope, the apostles and others bear witness that evokes persecution, as the Gospel has already led to expect. Indeed, the witness (Greek, *martys*, genitive *martyros*) may even become a martyr, as in the case of Stephen, not to mention Peter, Paul, and others who are arrested and otherwise harassed. Although Luke takes full account of such dangers, he does not dwell upon them, for he is fully convinced that such opposition fails utterly to impede the gospel's spread and the church's growth. If anything, resistance expedites that spread and growth.

How Did Peter and Paul Die?

The tradition of Paul's martyrdom is found only in extracanonical documents: *1 Clement* 5.7; *Acts of Paul* 10; Eusebius, *EH*, ii, 22. The ancient Roman church St. Paul Outside the Walls (see p. 372) commemorates the supposed site of Paul's burial. The present structure was rebuilt in modern times after fire destroyed the fourth-century building. That Peter should suffer martyrdom is suggested, though not reported, in the New Testament (John 21:18–19). According to tradition his remains lie under the altar of St. Peter's basilica in the Vatican.

The method of **redaction criticism**, which can be so profitably applied to Luke's Gospel, yields less fruit in Acts. Although we can identify the Gospel's major sources (Mark and **Q**) with some certainty, it is quite difficult to separate tradition from redaction in Acts. Nevertheless, the assumption that sources and traditions of some sort lie behind Acts is probably warranted, and evidence of the author's editing can surely be found in the summary reports, transitions, and especially in the overall structure. It is also likely that the speeches in their present form are largely Luke's composition. The material of Acts is permeated with Luke's own point of view, which can usually be identified with reasonable confidence.

What of the *historical occasion* or *situation* of Acts? While the author probably writes for the general reader, the needs and purposes of the church are nevertheless in the forefront. No doubt he expected the work to be useful to the church for apologetic or missionary purposes. As an apologist, Luke wants to show that Christianity is not a subversive movement. In the Gospel he goes out of his way to prove that Jesus was innocent of any crime (Luke 23:47). A similar motif appears in Agrippa's statement about Paul to Festus, the Roman procurator: "This man could have been set free if he had not appealed to Caesar" (26:32). Christians are arrested not because the authorities have seen them commit a crime but because of their involvement in some public incident, and often because of the accusations or actions of others, whether Jews or Gentiles. That Luke should have had some interest in showing Christians innocent of any crimes against the state is thoroughly understandable. After all, Jesus had been crucified by the Roman authorities, whatever role the Jewish leaders may have played, and this fact was widely known. From the outset Christianity stood under the suspicion of being a subversive movement, and this suspicion could only have been heightened by Christians' refusal to participate in worship of the Roman emperor. Luke intends to show that the charge of political subversion is groundless.

Luke's literary aspirations, reflected in his books' formal prefaces and in their style and tone, make it very hard to pin his work down to a definite time and place of origin within early Christianity. Because of his apologetic concern to show Jesus and the church politically innocent in relation to the Empire, a Roman origin has sometimes been suggested. This suggestion is plausible and possible, though not compelling. But the same widely shared literary style and historical interests that make Acts difficult to locate specifically within the first century contribute to our understanding of its general setting. The character and quality of this book suggest a Christianity well on its way to becoming an established world religion. Indeed, subsequent history confirmed the worldwide vision of Luke–Acts, for within less than three centuries that new faith would become the official religion of the Roman Empire.

SUGGESTIONS FOR FURTHER READING

Commentaries.   E. Haenchen, *The Acts of the Apostles: A Commentary*, trans. H. Anderson, R. McL. Wilson et al. (Philadelphia: Westminster, 1971) remains the best commentary on Acts as a theological work. By comparison, I. H. Marshall, *The Acts of the Apostles: An Introduction and Commentary* (Grand Rapids: Eerdmans, 1980), takes a more positive view of its historical value. The finest technical commentary is C. K. Barrett, *A Critical and Exegetical Commentary on the Acts of the Apostles*, 2 vols. (Edinburgh: T & T Clark, 1994 and 1998), compressed by its author into *The Acts of the Apostles: A Shorter Commentary* (Edinburgh: T & T Clark, 2002). See also J. A. Fitzmyer, *The Acts of the Apostles: A New Translation with Introduction and Commentary* (New York: Doubleday, 1998). Excellent, less technical studies are L. T. Johnson, *The Acts of the Apostles* (Collegeville, MN: Liturgical, 1992), F. S. Spencer, *Acts* (Sheffield, England: Sheffield Academic Press, 1997), and B. R. Gaventa, *Acts* (Nashville: Abingdon, 2003).

Other Studies.   Predictably, Acts has prompted extensive research into **the milieu of early Christianity**. F. J. Foakes–Jackson and K. Lake (eds.), *The Beginnings of Christianity*, 5 vols. (London: Macmillan, 1920–1933), is a scholarly landmark. Many of its concerns are revisited in B. W. Winter (ed.), *The Book of Acts in Its First Century Setting*, 5 vols. (Grand Rapids: Eerdmans, 1993–1995), with volumes devoted to literary character (B. W. Winter and A. D. Clarke), Greco–Romanism (D. W. J. Gill and C. Gempf), Roman jurisprudence (B. Rapske), Palestine (R. Bauckham), and the Diaspora (I. Levinskaya). Scholarly consensus on **Acts' historical reliability** remains elusive. H. J. Cadbury, *The Book of Acts in History* (New York: Harper & Row, 1955), set the terms for much subsequent debate. M. Hengel, *Acts and the Earliest History of Christianity*, trans. J. Bowden (Philadelphia: Fortress, 1979), and C. J. Hemer, *The Book of Acts in the Setting of Hellenistic History* (Tübingen: Mohr–Siebeck, 1989), stress the value of Acts for reconstructing early Christian history. Less sanguine about that prospect are R. I. Pervo, *Profit with Delight: The Literary Genre of the Acts of the Apostles* (Philadelphia: Fortress, 1987), and G. Lüdemann, *Early Christianity According to the Traditions in Acts: A Commentary*, trans. J. Bowden (Minneapolis: Fortress, 1989). The state of the question is assessed in D. Marguerat, *The First Christian Historian: Writing the 'Acts of the Apostles,'* trans. K.McKinney, G. J. Laughery, and R. Bauckham (Cambridge: Cambridge University Press, 2002).

M. Dibelius, *The Book of Acts: Form, Style, and Theology*, ed. K. Hanson, trans. M. Ling (Minneapolis: Fortress, 2004), is a collection of pioneering essays in the **literary and theological interpretation** of Acts. Another important contribution in that vein is C. H. Talbert, *Literary Patterns, Theological Themes, and the Genre of Luke–Acts* (Missoula, MT: Scholars, 1974). See also J. Jervell, *The Theology of the Acts of the Apostles* (Cambridge: Cambridge University Press, 1996).

See also the "Suggestions for Further Reading" at the end of Chapter 4.

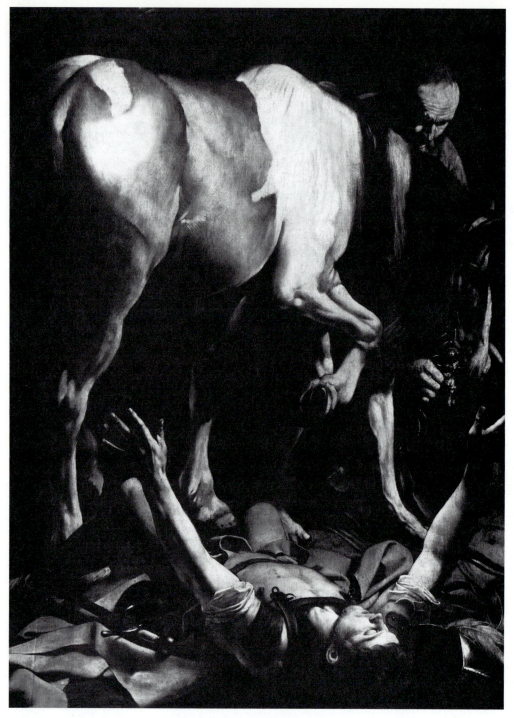

"The Conversion of St. Paul," by Michelangelo Merisi da Caravaggio, 1571–1610, Santa Maria del Popolo, Rome, Italy. *(Courtesy of The Art Resource, New York.)*

CHAPTER 8

PAUL: APOSTLE TO THE GENTILES

An Apostle's Life: Notes on Paul's Career

In studying Acts, we have already been studying Paul. The Acts of the Apostles presents Paul as the **Apostle** to the **Gentiles**, a role he ascribed to himself or was granted to him by the Jerusalem apostles (Gal. 1:15–16; 2:7–9). Doubtless there were other important missionary preachers—among them, Barnabas, Apollos, Prisca (Priscilla), and Aquila—all of whom are mentioned by Paul and in Acts. Nevertheless, Paul stands out in Acts and in the New Testament generally as the leading figure in Christianity's earliest expansion into the Greco-Roman world. While Paul's own understanding of himself and his mission may at some points differ from what is found in Acts, the Paul of his letters and the Paul of Acts are recognizably the same figure.

His importance was not lessened, but perhaps enhanced, by the fact that he was a center of controversy, as quickly becomes apparent from the reading of his letters, especially Galatians and 2 Corinthians. To some extent Paul's controversial character is subdued in Acts, but Luke nevertheless narrates an initial controversy that arose because of the preaching of the **gospel** to Gentiles (Acts 15) and later Paul's arrest because of disturbances attending his final visit to Jerusalem (Acts 21).

To understand the importance of Paul's work, we need to think our way back to the very beginning of Christianity, when there was no consciousness of its being a new religion distinct from Judaism. Like Jesus and his Galilean disciples, Paul was a Jew; moreover, he was a **Pharisee** (Phil. 3:5). Like Jesus, he did not set out to found or spread a new religion, but to announce what God was doing within the framework of the old. Thus neither Jesus nor Paul uses the terms *Christianity* or *Christian*. Paul only rarely speaks of Judaism (Gal. 1:13) because he assumes it as his religious background. Both Jesus and Paul presuppose Israel and the history and tradition known from scripture as the basis or matrix of God's new **revelation**.

To be a Jew, or an Israelite, meant to be born one, although then as now people converted to Judaism. Male circumcision had become the chief physical mark of being Jewish long before the time of Jesus and the origin of Christianity, although it had also been practiced by other ancient Near Eastern people. Establishing his **covenant** with Abraham, God specifies: "Every male among you shall be circumcised" (Gen. 17:10). In the biblical narrative, circumcision precedes by centuries God's giving of the **law** (Exod. 20:1-21). In Galatians, Paul puts the giving of the law four hundred thirty years after the covenant with Abraham. But as circumcision was the physical mark of being Jewish, obedience to the law was Israel's affirmation of having been chosen by God as a special people. Ironically, it was Paul, who, although acutely conscious of being Jewish, saw in **God's** sending of Jesus as his **Son** (Gal. 4:4) a radical challenge to the role of circumcision and the law. Paul ultimately played a leading role in preaching Jesus to Gentiles without requiring them to be circumcised, raising crucial questions about the continuing status of the biblical law.

Whether Jesus anticipated the spreading of God's word to the Gentiles before the appearance of the **kingdom** in power is a debated question. Quite likely he did not (Mark 9:1; Matt. 10:23). By contrast, Paul was himself converted in Damascus, Syria, outside the Holy Land, and learned to be a Christian from people who were neither Jesus' disciples nor closely associated with them. (The version of the gospel that Paul first heard is summarized by him in 1 Cor. 15:3–7.) Paul's initial, positive experience with Christianity seems to have taken place in the company of people who already represented the Gentile, or **Hellenistic**, missionary thrust of Christianity (cf. Acts 11:19–20). Paul quite naturally became involved in this missionary enterprise (Acts 11:21–26), for he himself was not a native of Palestine but of Tarsus, near the Mediterranean coast in present-day Turkey. His native language was Greek, in which all his letters are written and in which he was able to express himself fluently and in quite precise terms. Whether a significant part of his education took place in Jerusalem, as Luke suggests in Acts (22:3), is debatable, but by Paul's own testimony he was a serious student of Jewish traditions and law (Gal. 1:14; 2 Cor. 11:22; Phil. 3:4–6).

Precisely because of this dedication to his ancestral faith, Paul was at first a vehement, vigorous opponent of Jesus' followers. In his own letters, as well as in Acts, Paul's role as persecutor of the early church is made unmistakably clear (Gal. 1:13; 1 Cor. 15:9; Acts 9:1–2; cf. 7:58; 8:1). Doubtless Paul saw the new religious movement as a renegade Jewish sect, a dire threat to Judaism's integrity. The reasons for his view are not entirely clear. Acts does not tell us why precisely, and neither does the Apostle. Christians tend to assume that allegiance to the **crucified** Jesus as **Messiah** would have been grounds for Paul to persecute Christians, as such allegiance would entail a defection from Judaism in order to embrace Christianity. But such an assumption, though reasonable from a later perspective, does not fit the situation of the first generation of **Christ**-confessors, who did not believe that by embracing Jesus they ceased to be Jews. Possibly some Jews would have believed Jesus' crucifixion rendered him accursed, hence unfit to be Messiah (cf. Paul's quotation of Deut. 21:23 in Gal. 3:13). However, simply the belief that a certain person was the Messiah would not disqualify one as a Jew, even if that belief turned out to be false.

Perhaps Paul persecuted believers in Damascus because he opposed their illegitimate manner of opening doors to Gentiles. If such believers, open to fellowship with Gentiles on the latter's terms, were converting Gentiles without requiring them to become Jews, it was no wonder that they caused offense within the Jewish community and to Paul the Jew. But Paul's view of Jesus and his followers before his conversion remains largely hidden from us. In his letters Paul does not speak directly of the motivations that led him to persecute the **church**. We may only make inferences from his postconversion statements and from Acts.

The watershed of Paul's life was, of course, this conversion, which changed him from persecutor of Jesus' followers to one of them. Although we must guard against viewing this event as a conversion *from* Judaism *to* Christianity, the controversy that marked Paul's career and that dogged him to the end of his days centered precisely on the question of the relation and implications of Jesus and the claims made for him to traditional Jewish thought and practice. Paul would later say that Christ was the end of the law (Rom. 10:4). What exactly he meant has been debated ever since, and is not entirely clear from his own writings. Nevertheless, it is beyond doubt that, at some point after his conversion, Paul began preaching a version of the gospel to Gentiles that did not require them to become Jewish. That is, his converts did not have to accept circumcision and the ritual provisions of the law. Thus Paul became the founder of predominantly Gentile churches. At the same time he desired to maintain communion with Jews, particularly Jewish Christians in the church. It was this loyalty to both commitments, to a Gentile mission and church and to historic Israel, that kept Paul at the center of controversy. We see that controversy reflected dimly in Acts, very much in the foreground of Galatians, 2 Corinthians, and Philippians, and rather more in the background of Romans and 1 Corinthians.

When we turn from the **Gospels** and Acts to Paul, we move into a different literary world, from narratives that deal with historical events to letters that were communications from Paul to churches he had founded or in which he had strong interest. The analogy of modern letters is helpful as a beginning point in understanding Paul's, although there are differences of form and purpose. We should remember that Paul's letters are more than personal, occasional writings. They are means by which he intended to extend and exercise apostolic care and authority over the churches. Doubtless Paul expected each to be read before the entire church in solemn assembly (1 Thess. 5:27; cf. Col. 4:16).

The difference between Paul's letters and the Gospels are not, however, merely literary. Although Paul speaks frequently of Jesus, Jesus Christ, or our Lord Jesus Christ, surprisingly he tells us little if anything about Jesus that we do not know from the Gospels. Indeed, there are only occasional allusions to sayings or incidents that we know from the Gospels (e.g., 1 Cor. 7:10–11; 11:23–25; Gal. 4:4). If we were dependent on Paul for our knowledge of Jesus, the pickings would be rather slim. This fact is all the more startling because Paul is our earliest witness to Jesus and the early Christian movement. His letters were written only a couple of decades after Jesus' death and a decade or two before the earliest Gospel, Mark. Doubtless Paul knew more about Jesus than he conveys in his letters, but how much more is a matter of uncertainty and debate. When he refers to his own missionary preaching, he underscores the centrality and importance of Jesus' death (1 Cor. 1:17–18; 2:1–2). Moreover, his account of the gospel tradition that he received and passed on reflects the centrality of Jesus' **passion** (1 Cor. 15:3–7). This focus mirrors Paul's **theological** interests as expressed in 1 Corinthians (see Chapter 9) and especially in Romans (see Chapter 10), where he expounds his views most fully. There Paul concentrates his attention on what God has done in Jesus, particularly by his death and **resurrection**.

Upon reflection, the disproportionate attention given Jesus' death in the Gospels, particularly in Mark and John, corresponds to Paul's emphasis. What is lacking in Paul's letters is equivalent attention to Jesus' life, teaching, and deeds. Remarkably, although Paul clearly knows of Jesus' teaching, he never mentions the **miracles** or mighty works of Jesus that loom so large in the Gospel narratives. In this respect Paul seems unique, but in all probability his intense concentration upon Jesus' death and resurrection as God's deed reflects the principal emphasis of the faith and preaching of many first-generation Christians. (This emphasis in turn accounts for the large role of the passion narratives in the Gospels.) In the narratives of the earliest missionary preaching in the Book of Acts, Peter and Paul are portrayed as concentrating mainly on Jesus' death and resurrection, although his mighty deeds, but not his teaching, are mentioned in passing (see Acts 2:22–36; but cf. 13:17–40, where Paul does *not* mention Jesus' deeds).

Acts gives us a clear picture of Paul and of the course of his missionary career. It is possible to make an approximate correlation of Luke's account of Paul's career with Paul's own letters, to bring his life and work into relation with the main events of the epoch in which he lived, and thus to gain a general conception of Pauline chronology. On the basis of an ancient inscription found at Delphi in Greece, Gallio's proconsulship in Corinth can be dated about A.D. 51–52. According to the Acts report, while Paul was in Corinth for eighteen months on his second missionary journey (15:36–18:21) he was arrested and brought before this same Gallio (18:12 ff.). Thus we can arrive at an approximate date for Paul's first visit to Corinth, the surest fixed point of Pauline chronology. We may confidently place Paul's career in the middle third of the first century. Probably he was converted in the early thirties and died in the early sixties. Within this period there is less certainty about the exact dating of events. While it is possible to construct Paul's itinerary by combining data from his letters and Acts—and we have made an attempt to do this (see p. xxv)—the data do not fit together perfectly, and the results remain subject to doubt.

More of the New Testament has been ascribed to Paul than to any other author. The Pauline authorship of Hebrews, which does not actually claim to be from Paul, is universally rejected among critical scholars, however, and that of the Pastorals (1 and 2 Timothy and Titus) generally so, with 2 Thessalonians, Colossians, and Ephesians considered doubtful. Therefore, Luke would seem to have been the most prolific New Testament author. Yet slightly more than one-half of Luke's total work is about Jesus and therefore embodies much pre-Lukan tradition. Of the rest, more than one-half is about Paul. That so much later literature was ascribed to Paul and that his chief rival for literary productivity devoted so great a portion of his second work to a description of Paul's career are accurate indications of his significance. Paul was not only the most important missionary of the first Christian generation; he was also its most productive literary figure. Moreover, he was a notable organizer, man of affairs, and thinker. We would know a good deal about him if we had only the Book of Acts. Fortunately, we also have at least some of his letters, which reflect not only his activities and thought but also his own personality.

In this chapter, Paul's letters to churches he founded provide the basis for consideration of important aspects of his career, thought, and work. We focus on portions of letters that display Paul's understanding of his own mission and its results. But they also reflect how Paul was received and assessed in the churches that he founded, and by his colleagues in mission, some of whom approved his work while others did not.

- The Thessalonian letters reveal a Paul not yet at the center of controversy. 1 Thessalonians shows how Paul viewed the conversion of the Thessalonians and how he valued and nurtured their new life as a community of believers.
- Galatians reflects a Paul plunged into the heat of controversy. Revealing his life and soul as testimony to the truth of the gospel as he understands it. Here we learn a great deal about Paul's personal history, self-understanding, and relation to the Jerusalem church. Also from Galatians emerges the clearest picture of the nature of the opposition Paul faced from the Jerusalem, or conservative, wing of the church. There were many who assumed that believing in Jesus meant remaining or becoming Jewish, although Paul did not agree.
- 2 Corinthians also reflects Paul's controversy with opponents and at the same time provides unparalleled insights into the self-consciousness of Paul as an apostle. We shall devote an entire chapter to 1 Corinthians. While it reveals a great deal about Paul, his sense of mission and responsibilities to his churches, it also mirrors the practical issues raised by Paul's gospel message. Paul could speak of the rule of God (Rom. 14:17), as Jesus did. But some of his hearers may have thought that the kingdom had already arrived. Paul did not. Moreover, he viewed the issues of life, against the background of his Jewish upbringing, as moral issues. While he no longer believed a human being could be reckoned **righteous** before God by obedience to the biblical **law**, he never ceased regarding the law as the path of moral rectitude. Corinth presented a real challenge to Paul, and in this sense it was typical of many Gentile churches. How were faith in the gospel and obedience to God to be lived out as one faced practical questions in life within the new Christian communities, as they encountered the challenges of the world outside?
- Philippians is not a controversy letter. Paul is on good terms with the church at Philippi, as with that at Thessalonica, but—as chapter 3 makes clear—Paul's opponents still loom in the background, casting a pall over an otherwise friendly letter. Although it is difficult to arrange Paul's letters in chronological—and relative—order, the sequence of treatment here roughly follows that in which they were written. Romans (Chapter 10) almost certainly followed all these letters, except Philippians.

THESSALONIANS: FAITH AND THE FUTURE

Background of the Thessalonian Letters

The Thessalonian letters are the earliest of Paul's extant letters and probably the earliest New Testament books. Certainly 1 Thessalonians is authentic; questions about whether Paul wrote 2 Thessaloinians will be noted below, although we shall interpret it as if he did.

Thessalonica was an important, thriving seaport city and the capital of the Roman province of Macedonia. It was, moreover, a business and trade center on the Egnatian Way that connected Rome with the East. Paul had founded a church there, as his letters make clear.

According to Acts (17:1), Paul and his companions arrived in Thessalonica after they had preached and been arrested in Philippi (16:12–40). Paul's preaching in the synagogue of Thessalonica is said to have been persuasive to some, but sharp opposition arose that resulted in his expulsion from the city, apparently after a period of less than a month (17:1–10, esp. vs. 2). Paul then set out for Athens in the province of Achaia to the south and, after a brief stay there (17:16–34), arrived in nearby Corinth (18:1), where he was joined by Silas (Silvanus) and Timothy (18:5). Some such travels are noted also in 1 Thessalonians (2:2; 3:1, 6), although the itineraries of Paul and his companions suggested there do not entirely agree with Acts. Nevertheless, we are probably reading about the same events in the two sources, and Acts helps fix the place of origin of the Thessalonian letters, namely at Corinth (18:5). In writing both letters Paul is joined by Silvanus and Timothy (1 Thess. 2:2; 2 Thess. 1:1), the companions named in Acts. Paul's stay in Corinth can be dated in A.D. 50 or 51, for it coincided with the proconsulship of Gallio (Acts 18:12).

The letters, especially 1 Thessalonians, suggest that Paul worked among his Thessalonian converts much longer than the few weeks mentioned in Acts (cf. 1 Thess. 1:5–6; 2:1–12). Otherwise, it is difficult to see how he came to know them so well. As in other cases where Paul and Acts stand in some tension, Paul's own account is to be preferred as the earlier and more direct testimony.

There are, however, reasons for doubting the authenticity of 2 Thessalonians. Its relationship to 1 Thessalonians is unclear and the **apocalyptic** mythology of 2:1–12 is unlike anything else we find in Paul. The emphasis upon the letter's *genuineness* and authority (cf. 2:1; 3:14 f., 17) suggests that the author protests too much, thus arousing suspicion. Yet the supposition of *pseudonymity* (i.e., that another person wrote under Paul's name) does not immediately or altogether clarify the letter's situation and interpretation. It may be that 2 Thessalonians was written shortly after 1 Thessalonians and that it addressed a similar situation and problem. But 2 Thessalonians (2:1-12) also faces the challenge of those who believe that the day of the Lord has already come.

OUTLINE OF 1 THESSALONIANS

Salutation (1:1)
Personal and Related Matters (1:2–3:13)

Thanksgiving (1:2–10)
Paul's Missionary Work (2:1–16)
Timothy's Mission (2:17–3:10)
Prayer (3:11–13)

Exhortation and Encouragement (4:1–5:27)

> *General Instructions (4:11–12)*
> *The Return of Jesus (4:13–5:11)*
> *Final Instructions and Prayers (5:12–27)*

Concluding Benedictions (5:28)

The Return of Jesus (1 Thess. 4:13–5:11)

How is Paul's apocalyptic scenario relevant to the Thessalonians' situation?

As Paul's earliest letter, 1 Thessalonians offers valuable clues about the character of his missionary preaching and how conversion and belonging to the new community of Christians were understood. At the outset Paul speaks of how his converts turned from idols "to serve a living and true God" (1:9). This description obviously fits **Gentile** rather than Jewish converts. Despite the impression left by Acts, where Paul preaches in the synagogue in Thessalonica (Acts 17:1–3), we can only conclude that the Thessalonian church was made up mainly, if not exclusively, of Gentiles. Paul describes them as waiting for Jesus' return from heaven (1:10), thus suggesting concerns dealt with toward the end of the letter.

The still graceful ruins of the temple of the Greek god Apollo at Delphi in the mountainous territory north and west of Athens and south of Thessalonica. Delphi was the home of the famous Delphic oracle, whose origin antedates Christianity by centuries. When Paul speaks of the Thessalonians' "turning from idols" (1 Thess. 1:8) he probably had such sources of revelation in mind.

The Thessalonian Christians have become imitators of Paul, of his companions, and of the Lord, meaning Jesus (1:6), as well as of persecuted Christian churches of Judea (2:14). Thus there is solidarity among Christians, and this point is driven home by Paul's expressions of personal affection and concern for his converts (2:17–20). The Thessalonians themselves have proved their own affection and love (1:3; 4:9–12). The imitation of Paul (1:6) has as its end the perfecting and **holiness** of the Thessalonians—that is, their complete dedication to God. Paul reminds them that they learned from him and his companions how they ought to live and please God (4:1). The instructions he has given them are simple and unexceptional (4:2–8) and might have been approved by some morally serious Gentiles as well as by Jews.

Amidst a lengthy exhortation, consisting of rather brief general admonitions and reminders only loosely tied together, we find a sustained discussion of the return of Jesus (4:13–5:11). The purpose of the discussion is similarly hortatory. That is, Paul intends to bolster and encourage the Thessalonians (5:11) by reminding them of a central aspect of his teaching, namely, hope.

There is not only discouragement but anxiety over Christians who have already died. Apparently in the earliest days of the new faith many thought that believers would not die until the Lord returned. As time passed, more and more Christians died, and their deaths could not be attributed to a fall from faith (cf. 1 Cor. 11:30). Paul reassures his readers that those members of the community who have died in faith are not lost (esp. 4:13–18). When the Lord (i.e., Jesus) returns, the "dead in Christ" (4:16) will rise and together with those who are left alive will ascend to meet the descending Lord in the air (4:17). Thus the dead in Christ, believers who have died, suffer no disadvantage. With these words the readers may comfort one another (4:18).

If Paul is not quoting directly from Jesus himself (vs. 15: "by the word of the Lord"), he nevertheless intends to convey the substance of what Jesus had said. The early Christians believed that Jesus had spoken of his return in glory and preserved sayings that expressed this intention (e.g., Mark 8:38; cf. Matt. 10:33; Luke 12:9). Moreover, collections of such sayings, attributed to Jesus, grew up among Christians (Mark 13 parr.). In these discourses Jesus described in detail his coming, or **parousia**, and the events leading up to it. Probably the brief word of the Lord to which Paul refers is an early form of this **apocalyptic** tradition, which, although it flowered quickly and luxuriantly, had roots in the authentic sayings of Jesus. In 1 Corinthians 15:20–28 and 2 Thessalonians 2:1–11 we find other descriptions of the end time. Although neither of these is traced back to Jesus, in each case Paul seems to be drawing on common Christian beliefs and perhaps traditions about the events leading up to the end.

The present passage is intended as a source of encouragement for the Thessalonians. For unbelievers the day of the Lord may be wrath (1:10; 5:2 f.), but for those in Christ it is joy and vindication. In the second part of this rather long discussion of the parousia (5:1–11), Paul describes the way in which Jesus' imminent coming should affect not the dead but the Thessalonians who are alive. The day of the Lord (cf. Amos 5:18–20) will come suddenly, as a thief in the night (5:2; cf. Matt. 24:43; Luke 12:39; Rev. 3:3; 16:15; 2 Pet. 3:10); its coming will be a cause of dismay for those who have not believed or are not prepared (5:2–4). But the Thessalonians, like all who believe in Christ, understand that they already belong to that day.

Paul plays upon the technical, **eschatological** term *day of the Lord*. The day will not surprise believers, for they are not in darkness as others are. Because they are children of the light, they are also children of the day (5:5)–not children of daytime generally, however, but children of that particular day, the day of the Lord. Needless to say, the imagery of day and night is quite appropriate to Paul's hortatory purpose. Night is the time of sleep or drunkenness (5:6 ff.). Day is the time of wakefulness and sobriety. But Paul's exhortation turns upon the point that Christians already have the day of the Lord, at least in anticipation. That is, God has destined them for **salvation**, not for wrath (5:9). Therefore, their conduct should reflect who and what they are before God. "Belonging to the day" (5:8) is more than general, metaphorical language. It has a specific reference in Paul's own thought: the day of the Lord's coming. This day is for his Christian readers an occasion for hope and therefore for encouragement. Such hope frees a person from despair, whether for himself or for his loved ones who have already died.

In 1 Thessalonians there is scarcely a suggestion of the distinctive **theological** themes and arguments found in Paul's later letters. The attitude of the Thessalonians toward Paul seems warm and receptive. He speaks of their exemplary attitude and conduct (1:4–7), not to mention their reception of him (1:9). He views them as his children in Christ (2:10–12). As yet there is no hint of the great Pauline controversy over the role of the **law**; the Thessalonian community is predominantly Gentile. Yet some typically Pauline emphases do appear. Faith, hope, and love are mentioned more than once, at the beginning as well as at the end (1:3; 5:8; cf. 1 Cor. 13:13). Paul urges converts not to repay evil for evil (5:15; cf. Rom. 12:17), reminiscent of Jesus' own teaching (cf. Luke 6:27–36). Christianity seems to be essentially belief in the true God, the shunning of immorality and impurity, the solidarity of a love that forgoes the claims of self, and vibrant hope and the expectation of Jesus' imminent return. Although in later letters, joint authorship is scarcely more than a conventional form (cf. 1 Cor. 1:1), in 1 Thessalonians 1:1 Paul may actually speak in concert with his coworkers Silvanus and Timothy, as they remind the Christians there of those essentials on which there is general agreement.

OUTLINE OF 2 THESSALONIANS

> Salutation (1:1–2)
> Thanksgiving (1:3–12)
> Eschatological Teaching (2:1–17)
> Instructions and Exhortations (3:1–16)
> Conclusion (3:17–18)

Eschatological Teaching (2 Thess. 2:1–17)

How are the Thessalonians to act in the present?

Whereas in 1 Thessalonians, Paul encourages new believers to remain steadfast and alert in their hope of Jesus' return (4:13–18; 5:1-11), in 2 Thessalonians, he faces a different problem. Now there are Christians who believe that the day of the Lord has *already* come

(2 Thess. 2:2). Paul's earlier words of encouragement may have caused some members of the Thessalonian church to think that the end or goal had already been attained and, therefore, that they might abandon all work and worldly responsibility (3:6–13). In any event, Paul must now dampen an enthusiasm that has apparently broken out in some quarters.

It is notable that Paul's earlier exhortations called not for idle waiting and watching but for responsible and upright living (1 Thess. 5:1–11). Had even these warnings been misconstrued to heighten further expectations of the end? Whatever the answer, Paul now refutes the precipitous announcement of the advent of the day of the Lord by pointing out that its necessary conditions have not been fulfilled.

Paul's portrayal of the present situation and of the anticipated events of the future is painted in conspicuously **apocalyptic** language. That the figure or forces named (the rebellion, the man of lawlessness, the son of perdition, the one who restrains him) are not further identified in terms of historical persons or entities is typical of the apocalyptic style as we know it from such books as Daniel, Revelation, and the **Qumran** *War Scroll*. Paul is capable of thinking in similar fashion and terms. Apparently the one who is restraining the son of perdition or the lawless one is a person or force already present and at work as Paul writes. Perhaps he is making a veiled reference to the Roman Empire or to the emperor, or even to the preaching of the **gospel**; it is really impossible to know. What is certain is Paul's intention to check and refute apocalyptic enthusiasm and to encourage the Thessalonians to continue to live responsibly in the present.

Although in his other letters we find nothing comparable to the mysterious apocalyptic scenario Paul suggests here, it is nevertheless clear that he expected a cataclysmic denouement of history (cf. 1 Thess. 4:13–18; 1 Cor. 15:20–28), perhaps within his own lifetime (although cf. Phil. 1:19–26). Because Paul's analysis of human experience and situations is often so acute, and occasionally paralleled in modern perceptions, we may be perplexed to find him thinking and speaking this apocalyptic language. Paul's thought, however, was deeply conditioned by scripture, ancient Jewish beliefs, and his vivid expectation of the return of Jesus; his worldview was very different from our own. That he did not refer to this sequence of apocalyptic events in 1 Thessalonians does not mean that he did not know it, or that he did not write 2 Thessalonians. There he was addressing a different problem; in 2 Thessalonians he speaks to a situation that may well have been created—quite apart from Paul's intention—by his own earlier words. "By letter, as though from us" (2:2), may allude to a misunderstanding of 1 Thessalonians.

Although Paul's attempt to straighten out misunderstanding about the coming of the day of the Lord dominates 2 Thessalonians, his attitude toward that **church** itself has not changed. His thanksgiving for them, their faith and conduct, continues to be genuine (1:3–4), as it was in 1 Thessalonians. In Galatians, there will be no such thanksgiving. If there are those who need warning that if they do not work they will not eat (3:10), most, if not all, will fall in line with Paul, who urges them not to be weary in well-doing (3:13 KJV). Even those who may continue to be recalcitrant should be treated as brothers and sisters (NRSV "believers") rather than as enemies. This is more like the Paul of the other, *genuine* letters than the Paul of the **Pastorals**.

G A L A T I A N S :   F A I T H ' S   S U F F I C I E N C Y

Background of Galatians

This letter was written to combat the influence in the Galatian churches of so-called Judaizers: believers who insisted that Christians be circumcised and keep the **law**. The exact location of these churches is in doubt. Either they were in the region of Pisidian Antioch, Lystra, and Derbe—which Paul evangelized on his first missionary journey, recounted in Acts 13–14—or they were located farther to the north in the ethnic region called Galatia, after its inhabitants (*Galatai*). The latter has seemed probable to many interpreters, but recent research has looked again at the evidence for the region around the city of Pisidian Antioch (cf. Acts 13:14–50). If the imperial cult (emperor worship) had been strong in that area, as it seems to have been, Christians as such would have felt the pressure, because they could not participate in it. On the other hand, Jews were generally exempted from the emperor cult. To "look Jewish" would have been a great advantage for believers there. Thus circumcision may have been enjoined as a strategy to avoid persecution.

The original Greek of Galatians 4:13 probably means "the first time" (NRSV "first"), implying that Paul had made not one but two previous visits to Galatia. If the North Galatia theory is accepted and two previous visits to Galatia must be posited, then the letter cannot be earlier than the third missionary journey, for the two visits would be those noted in Acts 16:6 and 18:23. This would put the writing of the letter in the period of Paul's Ephesian ministry (Acts 19), as indicated on the chronological table, probably about A.D. 54. Such a setting is supported, moreover, by the many affinities of Galatians with 1 and 2 Corinthians and Romans, which are more striking than any similarities to the early Thessalonian letters. On the other hand, if the South Galatia option is accepted—as some interpreters do—Galatians could have been written much earlier, any time after Paul's foray according to Acts. Because the Acts account is not a firm basis for chronology, certainty is impossible. Although Galatians seems to reflect issues addressed in the Corinthian correspondence and Romans, Paul's account of his missionary history (Gal. 2:1–21) strongly implies that his basic **theological** beliefs had remained unchanged from the time of his second visit to Jerusalem (2:1–10).

Galatians offers numerous points of contrast with the Thessalonian letters. Aside from the omission of the formal thanksgiving, the tenor of the letter is quite different, and that difference is immediately evident in the address. Paul no longer groups himself with other colleagues whom he names (as in 1 Thess. 1:1) but singles himself out as an **apostle** and indicates the divine origin of his apostolic calling, mentioning "all the brethren who are with me" as a kind of afterthought. After the salutation and benediction (vss. 3–5), occasioned by God's grace rather than by anything the Galatians may have done, Paul moves immediately to the business at hand without any customary thanksgiving for the Galatians—who in their conduct have given him no reason to offer thanks.

OUTLINE OF GALATIANS

Apostle by God's Revelation (Gal. 1:6–2:10)

How does Paul's own story relate to his apostolic authority?

Paul's expression of astonishment at the speed of the Galatians' defection (vs. 6) is genuine and deep. They have deserted the one true **gospel** of Jesus **Christ** in favor of another, a pseudo-gospel, apparently proclaimed by intruders in the churches Paul had founded. That those who preached this other gospel boasted an authority superior to Paul's is suggested by what he writes: first, he underscores the source of his own authority (vs. 1); second, he dismisses the possibility that anyone could possess authority sufficient to contradict or pervert his version of the message (vss. 8–9). The one who called the Galatians in the grace of Christ (vs. 6) is, of course, God, but Paul may also be alluding to the role he himself played in announcing the gospel in the first instance, particularly in view of the incursion of others who announced another gospel.

Paul's defense of his gospel as the one authentic gospel, authorized by God and agreed to by all the authorities of the church, takes the form of a narrative of his own career as an apostle (1:11–2:21). That narrative is in part a response to those who would accuse him, or who have accused him, of compromising the gospel in seeking human approval (1:10), presumably to make it more attractive and acceptable. Exactly how Paul is supposed to have done this is not said. Apparently those who preached another gospel attempted to discredit Paul by saying that he made confessing belief in Jesus easier and more palatable by not insisting on circumcision and the law. In 3:1–5:12 Paul argues against a version of the gospel in which both are necessary: he contends that such a gospel would be, in fact, no gospel at all. That is, it would reduce to insignificance what Jesus accomplished by dying upon the cross.

For the moment, however, Paul's principal concern is to establish his own authority as a preacher and, accordingly, the authority of the gospel he proclaims. He does this by narrating how he was called by God to be an apostle—one sent to preach the gospel—and by telling of his subsequent relations with other apostles in Jerusalem. The point he seeks to establish is that these negotiations in no way called into question or altered his gospel and his authority to preach it. In all essential respects the Jerusalem apostles—Peter, James the brother of Jesus, and John—approved what Paul preached as well as his authority to preach it (2:6–9).

Paul's reaction to what he has learned about events in the Galatian churches is defensive and angry. What was at stake was nothing less than Paul's life and work, which is intertwined with his faith and interpretation of the gospel. Certainly Paul's response is more than personal, but his person as well as his work were being challenged. Though Paul is on the defensive in 1:11–2:1, he is already moving to seize the initiative and go on the attack. By chapter 3, he is fully on the offensive, attacking the rival gospel that has sought to displace his own.

Fundamental to Paul's defense is the account of his conversion or call (1:13–17). In the Book of Acts *conversion* seems an appropriate enough term, although it is a visionary and auditory event that surpasses ordinary religious experience (9:1–9; 22:4–16; 26:9–18). In 1 Corinthians, Paul refers to an appearance to him of the risen Lord (15:8; cf. 9:1). In Galatians, Paul emphasizes rather the purpose and call of God: that as apostle he might preach the gospel of Jesus Christ among the **Gentiles**. Thus Paul's conversion is his commissioning as apostle to the Gentiles. Paul makes clear that he needed no Jerusalem apostles nor anyone else to interpret the meaning of the experience (vss. 16–17). He consulted with no one. As he wants his readers to understand, he heard and obeyed God without the help of human mediation.

Paul's conversion, by whatever name it be called, doubtless played a fundamental role in his understanding of the gospel. He himself had been overtaken and overcome in a manner that contradicted his expectations and reversed the course of his life. God's action toward him was perceived by Paul as something prior to, and apart from, his own will. Probably Paul's experience became paradigmatic of the way he understood God's work in Christ. God effected a fundamental change in Paul's life and perceptions, and he came to understand the gospel as God's prior action in Jesus Christ, to which a person must respond by faith or disobedience.

Although Paul strongly asserts his apostolic commission and independence of human authorization, he also believes that the gospel originated, not with him, but with God and that it is not given to him alone, but to the **church**. Thus, although he insists upon his independence of those who were apostles before him (1:17), he is eager to show that these same apostles approved his preaching of the gospel (2:7–10). In fact, he candidly says that he put his gospel before them for their approval, as if everything depended upon that (2:2).

At first glance, Paul's assertion of his independence and his concern for apostolic approval seems contradictory. Paul wants to say not that his gospel is novel or unique, but, rather, to claim God's initiative in revealing it to him and commissioning him to preach it to the uncircumcised (2:7), that is, to Gentiles (cf. 1:16). For despite the claims for his own commission and authority, which he is not in the least embarrassed to make, Paul wishes to show that his gospel is the same gospel with which the church has been entrusted. The uniqueness of his commissioning lies in the fact that God has made him apostle to the Gentiles. Paul does not even put forward his central doctrine of **justificat-**

ion by grace through faith as an original insight, but as an elementary aspect of the gospel itself, and one that anyone should have been able to make. Thus he upbraids Peter for his dissimulation (2:11 ff.) rather than his ignorance.

Paul was a charismatic figure and an original thinker; yet he wishes to set himself, not above, but only alongside those who were apostles before him. Although not dependent on them (cf. 1:17), he actively sought their approval. For Paul was a churchman, concerned for the church's unity. He enthusiastically agreed to take up a collection in his mission field for the poor in the Jerusalem church (2:10; cf. 1 Cor. 16:1–4; 2 Cor. 8, 9; Rom. 15:25–29). This act was more than charity. It was a visible, tangible expression of the oneness of the churches he had founded with the church at Jerusalem and, by implication, of the gospel's own unity.

Faith within the History of Salvation (Gal. 2:11–21)

Why is circumcision such a crucial point of controversy?

That Paul had already vigorously defended his own preaching and probably had to do so recurrently soon becomes apparent (2:11–21). Presumably the incident in Antioch had occurred some time before. There Cephas (i.e., Peter), Paul, Barnabas, and other Jewish Christians had been enjoying table fellowship among Gentile Christians until some representatives from James appeared on the scene (2:11–13). They, and perhaps James also, represented the "circumcision faction," a powerful group of Jewish Christians, probably based in Jerusalem, who regarded circumcision as a necessity for Gentile Christian males. Apparently for them, as for Paul, "circumcision" implied the obligation to keep the Jewish **law** and therefore entailed far more than the rite itself. They therefore refused table fellowship with nonobservant Gentile believers.

This same circumcision party had evidently made inroads into the Galatian church, occasioning Paul's letter. As one begins reading the letter, it is not entirely obvious that this is what has happened, although Paul immediately denounces those who preach "another gospel" (1:6–9). The nature of that other **gospel** becomes clearer, however, in chapters 3–4. Paul asks the Galatians whether the new existence to which they were introduced by his missionary preaching was based on the **works** of the law or on faith. Obviously, Paul is convinced it is based on the **Spirit** and faith, not the law (3:1–14). For Paul, the law characterizes the older order that has passed away; it was always intermediate or provisional (3:15–29). In the beginning Abraham believed God—that is, Abraham had faith—and it was reckoned to him as **righteousness** (3:6, quoting Gen. 15:6). Faith defines the proper relation to God, whether in Abraham's time or Paul's. The Galatians are being urged by some to revert to a state from which they have been rescued by **Christ** (1:4). Apparently Paul equates a return to dependence on legal observance for **salvation** by the Galatians as a return to their pre-Christian enslavement to "elemental spirits of the world" (4:3, 9), presumably pagan religion or superstition. Such a reversion is the necessary consequence of acquiescing to the demand of the intruders that the Galatians submit to circumcision (5:2; 6:12). As Paul says (5:3), the whole legal system was bound up with this rite. Circumcision had become the fitting symbol of the problem of whether Christians must be held accountable for the Jewish law.

From a modern perspective, in which Christianity and Judaism are two different religions separated for nearly two thousand years, the position of the Judaizers seems to be an aberration. Why should they be conservative, or afraid of progress? Yet the question is misplaced or anachronistic. From their perspective *Paul* was the aberration. Jesus was accepted by all believers as the **Messiah** of Israel; why should this acceptance mean abandonment of its ancestral laws and customs? Obviously, Paul had **theological** reasons for believing that it should, and he strongly argued his case in Galatians. Yet the Judaizers, or so-called circumcision party, believed they had tradition on their side and did not find Paul's arguments compelling.

The appearance of the circumcision party in Antioch (2:11) doubtless intimidated the Jewish Christians, including Peter and Barnabas, who had previously exercised their freedom in Christ by disregarding Jewish restrictions against eating with Gentiles. By doing so, the Jew inevitably exposed himself to the possibility of contamination by violating the Jewish laws concerning food and drink (cf. Lev. 11). Paul's reproach to Peter (2:14 ff.) surely shows him in a bad light, although we have only Paul's version of the story.

Paul's argument with Peter is based less on his own biases than on what he plainly believes is an understanding of the gospel that Peter also accepts. The statement that Peter and others "were not acting consistently with the truth of the gospel" (vs. 14) and the use of "we" (vss. 15–17) suggest that Paul was not trying to convince Peter of something debated but recalling him to an agreement about the gospel they had shared: the message of God's grace freely given. That this was more than merely intellectual assent is confirmed by the fact (vs. 14) that Peter himself had been living like a Gentile. Whether Peter and company later tried to force Gentiles to live like Jews or only made this a prerequisite of continued table fellowship is uncertain. Whatever the case, the net result was apparently the same. Gentiles were forced to submit to Jewish regulations to participate on an equal footing in the church's life. For Paul this development was intolerable, despite the fact that he and Peter were by birth Jews (vs. 15), not "Gentile sinners." It was unthinkable not because it was unnecessary or discourteous but, rather, because Paul and Peter knew that a person is not **justified**, judged acceptable to God, based on "works of the law" but by faith in Christ. At least Paul knew it. He thought Peter should, too.

From this point on it is clear that Paul does not entertain the possibility of two modes of salvation—one by the law, the other by faith in Christ (vss. 15–21). He is not just saying that one must choose one way or the other, although that is indeed necessary. In actuality there is only one way, because no one will be justified by works of the law. The important thing is that a new and viable access to God has been opened by his **Son** just when other avenues had shown themselves to be blind alleys. This conviction lies at the heart of Paul's gospel.

The objection that Christ was made a servant of **sin** (vs. 17) had probably been raised by the circumcision party. It would have been directed against the doctrine of justification by faith and its corollaries of freedom from the law and uninhibited free association among Jewish and uncircumcised Gentile Christians. Paul categorically rejects the view that Christ is a servant of sin. Later, in the opening chapters of Romans, Paul will argue that all people, whether they claim to keep the law or not, are really sinners apart from the grace of God in Christ. Thus, Paul concedes that people "have been found to be sinners" in seeking to be justified by Christ. Of course, it may by no means be inferred that those who seek to be justified by the law thereby escape the onus of sin. They simply do not understand their condition.

The real transgression would be to move backward, again submitting to the law and to sin after having escaped their grasp (vss. 18 ff.). Paul has died to the law and been crucified with Christ that he might live to God. Paul necessarily dies to the law that he may live to God and that Christ may live in him by faith (vs. 20). Paul ends this description of his encounter with Peter and the problem of the Galatian churches with a succinct statement of his tight theological logic. Justification does not come through the law, or else Christ died to no purpose (2:21). If one insists on observance of the law as a prerequisite to salvation, one implies that faith in Christ is not enough and that the law supplies what is lacking. For Paul, who understands the gospel to be absolutely Christocentric, that suggestion is intolerable.

If for the moment we use the somewhat anachronistic term *Christianity*, which Paul never uses, we may say that for Paul, Christianity is faith in Christ. On the other hand, faith in Christ makes possible the concept of Christianity as something new and distinct. For apart from the insistence that faith alone, not works of the law, justifies— makes one righteous before God—Christianity does not clearly distinguish itself from Judaism, as the Jewish Christians apparently neither did nor intended to do. To believe that a particular person was the Messiah was possible *within* Judaism. The Messiah, or Christ, would then be understood within the framework of Jewish messianism and **eschatology**. Paul's understanding of the essential meaning of the gospel of Jesus Christ, however, goes beyond this confession. For to say, as he does, that this faith alone is the crucial factor in determining a person's destiny breaks away from traditional messianic expectation and makes the Jewish biblical, legal requirements of no avail for salvation.

The specific question of circumcision, and Paul's rejection of it for Gentiles leads inevitably to the issue of the role and necessity of the biblical law, for scripture (the Old Testament) requires circumcision (Gen. 17:10; Lev. 12:3). Paul does not take this issue lightly. But what has heretofore been the essence and mark of Judaism is that no longer, at least not in Paul's view. The crucial event is **God's** sending of his **Son** (4:4).

Works of the Law (Gal. 3:1–29)

If faith is the only proper basis for our relation with God, then why did God give the law?

Paul presumes new circumstances in which the Galatians now live (3:1–5), namely, under the **Spirit**, as the reality governing and empowering them. This fundamental reality, characterizing their life, is not given by "**works** of the **law**" but by "the hearing of faith" (3:2, 5 RSV). What is primary is not doing but hearing. Hearing leads to believing and only then to doing. ("Believing what you heard" [NRSV] sounds too much like assenting to propositions advanced.)

As he will do again in Romans 4, Paul presents Abraham as the first and foremost person of faith, the man who "believed God and it was reckoned to him as **righteousness**" (3:6, quoting Gen. 15:6). Paul's purpose is not to extol Abraham per se but to advance the cause of faith. *Faith* for Paul means not just believing that something is true; it is entrusting one's life to that conviction. Moreover, God's promise to Abraham means the blessing of all **Gentiles** (3:8; cf. Gen 12:3; 18:18; 22:18). The fact that Genesis 18:18 and 22:18 refer to all nations except Israel (*ethnē*), or Gentiles, leads Paul to believe that not only Abraham's physical descendants, but all Gentiles, would come to God by faith (3:9).

Faith is, and really always has been, the only true access to God. And so the biblical law's necessity and role is called into question (3:10). **Christ redeems** us from the curse of the law, writes Paul (v. 13). This language must have been as repulsive to other Jews as it is strange to most people today. How or why is the law a curse for anyone? Because the **righteous** person lives not because of his obedience to the law (v. 12), but by faith (v. 11).

How does one escape the law's curse? Christ in his death on the cross ("a tree") becomes a curse for us, writes Paul (vs. 13, referring to Deut. 21:23). This is an expression of what is called vicarious atonement. Christ bears humanity's punishment or burden so that believers, including Gentiles, "might receive the promise of the Spirit through faith" (3:14).

Paul then underscores the primacy of faith by returning to Abraham and the example of a will (Greek *diathēkē*, vs. 15). What was and is true in the case of a will is true of God's **covenant** with Abraham (3:15–18). The original will, or covenant, with Abraham, made on the basis of faith, is not superseded by the giving of the law through Moses more than four centuries later. The original covenant with Abraham, based on faith in God's promise, still stands. But if so, why the law in the first place?

Beginning in 3:19, Paul tries to answer this question. The biblical law is a temporary measure (3:19, 23). In view here is no development from law to promise. To speak of a history of **salvation**, as do some interpreters, is a way of comprehending the overarching message of the Christian Bible, but it is scarcely what Paul has in view here. Righteousness does not come by way of the law's dispensation. Presumably here Paul has in mind the giving of the law to Moses on Mount Sinai (Exod. 19:16–20:20), and he is denying its ultimate significance as the means of righteousness and life. Paul calls the law "our disciplinarian" (Greek *paidagōgos*), according to the NRSV translation. The RSV instead translates "custodian"; the KJV, "schoolmaster." These different renderings reflect uncertainty of what Paul meant. The translation "confining custodian" (J. L. Martyn, *Galatians: A New Translation with Introduction and Commentary* [New York: Doubleday, 1997]) captures the term's historic meaning and Paul's estimate of the law's function in the history of salvation, so to speak—except that the law has no saving function.

That function belongs solely to the coming of Christ (3:24–29; 4:4). The Jewish, biblical law is a confining custodian. It belongs among the "guardians and trustees" (4:2) that are keeping the heirs to the promise in a state of slavery (v. 1). It is also one of the "elemental spirits of the world" that enslaves people (v. 3). All this is presumed when

Paul writes that "in Christ Jesus you are all children of God through faith" (3:26). Paul actually wrote "sons [*huioi*] of God," but he clearly means both men and women, as his subsequent statement (vs. 28) demonstrates. Paul fixes upon the cruciality of God's sending of his Son (4:4), who is the one heir (3:16) to the promise to faith that God made to Abraham.

Obviously, this is a radical affirmation of the revolutionary importance of Christ. Doubtless it is rooted in Paul's own initial apprehension of Christ, or, more accurately, *by* Christ in his conversion (see 1:11–12), which he understood as a **revelation** of the **resurrected** Jesus (1 Cor. 15:8; cf. 1 Cor. 9:1). That Paul's claim raised doubts and objections among his fellow believers who, like him, were Jews, is understandable. These disciples were Paul's antagonists, and under their questioning or criticism Paul continued to contemplate the role of the law in the economy of salvation. His further reflections are found in the letter to the Romans (Rom. 5:20–6:4; 7:1–25). Probably between his writing Galatians and Romans, Paul encountered in the Corinthian church people who believed freedom in Christ was sheer license (1 Cor. 3:16–17; 6:12–20). Still, Paul's belief in the cruciality of the coming of the **crucified Messiah**—which could not have been anticipated—remained dominant.

Christ has freed believers from **sin**, from "the elemental spirits of the world" (4:3), and from the law. All these are part of the old order. Thus Paul writes: "For freedom Christ has set us free; stand firm therefore, and do not submit again to a yoke of slavery" (5:1). As Paul lays out the practical implications of his **theological** position, he again addresses the specific and immediate problem in the churches of Galatia. Should Christians accept circumcision? In 5:2, Paul reiterates the principle enunciated in 2:21. Here circumcision stands in place of law, for to accept circumcision as the expression of membership in the Jewish community means to obligate oneself to the keeping of the whole law, thus cutting oneself off from the grace of Christ (vss. 3 ff.). Yet circumcision is not in itself bad (vs. 6; cf. 6:11–16, esp. 15). Those already circumcised have nothing to fear (cf. 1 Cor. 7:18 f.). Rather, the *desire* to have circumcision or any mark of ethnic distinction or religious accomplishment after one has already been **baptized** into Christ (3:26 ff.) is blameworthy, for it is a regression from grace back to the law, a retreat from the **Spirit** to the flesh (3:3; 5:4; 6:12). Paul regards such a retrogression as incredible and perverse: a negation of one's freedom in Christ.

This freedom is not without responsibility. But the person of faith no longer experiences responsibility as a burden and no longer lives under the law to earn salvation. The freedom for which Christ sets humanity free is not anarchy or license to do as one pleases. Paul describes this freedom as faith working through love (5:6). He states the character and purpose of freedom aptly and succinctly: "For you were called to freedom, brothers and sisters; only do not use your freedom as an opportunity for self-indulgence, but through love become slaves to one another" (5:13). Thus, despite Paul's rejection of the law as the key to salvation, his strong sense of mutual human responsibility is grounded in Israel's history and scripture—topics to which he will return in Romans.

SECOND CORINTHIANS: COURAGE AND AUTHORITY

Cosmopolitan Corinth

Corinth was the capital of the province of Achaia and a major city of Greece. In this period Corinth was larger than Athens. The Greek city had been destroyed in 146 B.C. by the Romans, who rebuilt it as a Roman colony a century later. The reconstituted city's population consisted of Roman freedmen as well as Greeks, pagans, and Jews—a cosmopolitan group. The city's religious life and traditions were diverse. Corinth was new when Paul founded the church and later wrote his letters: there were no traditions or family connections going back more than a century.

In sharp contrast to Galatians, with Paul's Corinthian letters we can be entirely confident of their destination and audience. The description of Paul's founding of the Corinthian church in Acts 18 is sketchy, but there are several points of contact with 1 Corinthians. For example, Acts 18:8 names Crispus, a ruler of the Corinthian synagogue who was converted and baptized by Paul; the same Crispus is mentioned by Paul (1 Cor. 1:14) as one of only a few persons he **baptized** in Corinth. The Sosthenes spoken of in Acts 18:17 may be the same person named with Paul in 1 Corinthians' salutation (1 Cor. 1:1). Acts 19:21 suggests the travel plans that Paul describes in 1 Corinthians 16:5–9; the latter passage indicates (16:8) that Paul is in Ephesus (Acts 19) when he writes the letter.

In this chapter, we shall examine 2 Corinthians, which affords important insights into Paul's **apostleship**, how he understood his mission and work, as well as how he was perceived by others. This letter, or most of it, was written after 1 Corinthians, which is treated in Chapter 9. There one can find more information about Corinth and Paul's correspondence with the church there.

Background of 2 Corinthians

As we shall see in 1 Corinthians (4:1–5, 14–21; 11:1), Paul occasionally defends his legitimacy as an **apostle**, as well as his conduct or lifestyle. He seems confident, however, that the Corinthians will honor him (1 Cor. 9:2). By comparison, 2 Corinthians suggests a far more serious situation for Paul. His apostleship has been attacked, and that challenge has found a reception among at least some Corinthian Christians. Although in chapter 4, Paul's meditation on his apostleship is calm and not defensive, in chapters 10–13 his attitude is markedly different. He refers explicitly to attacks upon him and counterpunches those he regards as opponents. From their general content, it is clear that 2 Corinthians followed 1 Corinthians. Moreover, in 1 Corinthians Paul anticipates another visit (16:5), while in 2 Corinthians he has apparently made that visit and anticipates a third (13:1). At least part of 2 Corinthians was written from Macedonia (cf. 1:16; 2:13; 7:5).

Second Corinthians ends on a note of urgency: Paul has dispatched Titus to Corinth (12:18) but remains apprehensive about an approaching third visit. A comparison with the first half of this letter (chaps. 1–7) reveals a notable contrast. In the first part, Paul speaks of his *past* anxiety in anticipating another visit to Corinth, presumably his third (cf. 2:1). This attitude, which he now looks back on, corresponds with what he was experiencing as he wrote chapters 10–13. Paul's brief characterization of the letter he then wrote (2:3 ff.) corresponds in part to the content of those final chapters. Moreover, Paul indicates that it was the return of Titus from Corinth that set his mind at ease and reassured him about the loyalty of the Corinthians (7:5–16; 12:18). There are, therefore, good reasons to think that chapters 1–9 were written *after* chapters 10–13 and that the letter Paul describes in 2:3–4 is now found in those latter chapters. On the other hand, the one matter that moved Paul to write the "tearful letter" (2:4)—an individual who has caused Paul or the community pain (2:5–8; 7:12)—is not mentioned at all in 2 Corinthians 10–13. Because the evidence of Paul's correspondence is fragmentary, it may not be possible to reconstruct his itinerary and changing relationships with the church at Corinth.

In addition to the tearful-letter problem, there is the question of the character and origin of chapters 8 and 9. Both chapters deal with the collection Paul was making for the Jerusalem church (cf. Gal. 2:10; Rom. 15:25–28). They do not, however, fit together very well. Paul introduces the subject in 9:1 as if he had not already been discussing it just previously. Moreover, the content of chapter 9 seems somewhat repetitive. Further, the introduction of the subject (8:1) is abrupt, although not intolerably so. Chapters 8 and 9 may be two separate letters that Paul sent to Corinth to pave the way for the consummation of the collection and its delivery to the saints (9:1) in Jerusalem. Alternatively, chapter 8 may have been a part of the letter comprising chapters 1–7 and chapter 9 a separate note. Although the unity of 2 Corinthians as a single letter is still defended, on close examination this unity tends to weaken, if not dissolve. The most significant break is between chapters 9 and 10, at 10:1. There both tone and content shift abruptly and without explanation. It is difficult to believe that chapters 10–13 did not originally constitute some part of a different letter.

If 2 Corinthians is a composite document, made up of two or more earlier letters, that raises questions about the editing of the Pauline correspondence in those later years when the **epistles** were collected. The New Testament did not appear in anything like its present form until nearly 150 years after Paul wrote, and the history of the collection and circulation of the documents during that time is largely unknown. The simplest and most likely explanation of the editing of 2 Corinthians is that the process consisted of the stitching together of two letters or parts of letters (chaps. 1–9 and 10–13) that had originally been written separately.

OUTLINE OF 2 CORINTHIANS

Introduction: Salutation (1:1–2), Blessing (1:3–11), and Assurances of Concern (1:12–2:13)
Paul's Apostolic Service (2:14–5:21)
   Courage in Ministry (4:1–15)
Personal Appeals and Assurances (6:1–7:16)
Paul's Collection for the Jerusalem Church (8:1–9:15)
Paul's Apostleship under Attack (10:1–13:10)
Conclusion (13:11–14)

At the beginning of 2 Corinthians (1:3–2:13) Paul discusses his own travel plans. Doubtless his readers would have understood, because they knew about the changes in plans to which Paul alludes. Later readers must piece things together from fragmentary information. Paul has made a painful visit and was contemplating another (2:1), both after his initial founding visit. Paul speaks of going to Macedonia (Northern Greece: e.g., Thessalonica, Philippi) in 2:13, and later of being much relieved when his colleague Titus met him there (7:5–7), because he reassured Paul about the Corinthians' loyalty to him. There had been problems in Corinth, but Paul does not describe their nature or identify a person with whom he has had difficulty (2:1–4).

Paul speaks, first, in a veiled way of his own ministry (2:14–17), then more explicitly and positively (3:1–6). God has made Paul competent to be minister of a new **covenant**. (The Greek term *kainē diathēkē* means also "New Testament"; *testamentum* is Latin for *diathēkē*.)

At this point Paul breaks off into a digression (3:7–18) about **spirit** and letter. "Letter" represents the Old Covenant or Testament (*palaia diathēkē*), the covenant represented primarily by the giving of the Mosaic **law** on tablets of stone (3:7). The proverbial contrast between spirit and letter is rooted in this passage. Paul does not reject the Old Covenant. After all, it was given by God (3:7, 13). This looks like a higher view of the law than that found in Galatians 3:19–20. Still, there is an important sense in which the law's time has come and gone. Now it cannot be rightly read until the veil that Moses put over his face (v. 13) has been removed (v. 16). This veil is the same as that over the Mosaic law (v. 14), which can be removed only when one turns to the Lord (cf. Exod. 34:34).

It is anachronistic to read "New Testament" and "Old Testament" in this passage, as if they were collections of books. Until there was a New Testament, there could be no Old Testament; it was simply the (Jewish) Bible. The New Testament did not attain anything like its present form until more than a century after Paul wrote this.

Courage in Ministry (2 Cor. 4:1–15)

How does Paul's ministry imitate that of Jesus?

Paul describes his **apostolic** ministry with moving eloquence (see 4:1–15). As a minister of **Christ** he is not relieved of the limitations and frailties of his human condition. In fact, he is plunged more deeply into them. Indeed, his work is a trial as well as a joy. Yet he is not discouraged (vs. 1). His conduct is appropriate to his ministry (vs. 2). If in some cases his preaching of the **gospel** does not meet with acceptance, the reasons lie beyond his control (vss. 3 ff.). Picking up the imagery of chapter 3, Paul says the gospel is veiled (or concealed) to those who are perishing. The significance of that veiling is then explained (vs. 4), though the explanation may provoke more questions than it resolves.

In speaking of the god of this world, Paul does not mean that there are two gods—the God of heaven, revealed in Christ, and another god of this world. When he elsewhere speaks of many so-called gods in heaven and on earth (1 Cor. 8:4–6), and of the "elemental spirits of the world" (Gal. 4:3; cf. Col. 2:8), he probably refers to supernatural beings, powers, or forces that influence human life. After all, for him Satan is personal, even as is God (2 Cor. 2:11). Paul is himself free from these powers because of Christ, whom he here calls the likeness or image (Greek, *eikōn*; cf. English icon) of God. Into the dark world controlled by the "god of this world"—who is darkness, who blinds the eyes of those who do not believe so that they must live in darkness—the light of the gospel of Christ's glory shines (vs. 4).

Not surprisingly, Paul emphasizes that, as a minister, he preaches Jesus Christ as Lord (vs. 5). This is the center and substance of the Christian message. But why does he say that he does not preach himself, stressing his servant role? Perhaps his rivals or opponents in Corinth, who are apparently trying to seize leadership of the **church** from him, extol themselves. This at least is Paul's opinion of them (see esp. chap. 11). In contrast to apostles or ministers who think they must impress the Corinthians by their letters of recommendation, mighty works, or spiritual virtuosity, Paul effaces himself to present Jesus Christ more adequately. In so doing, Paul becomes transparent to the gospel he preaches (vs. 6).

This is not merely a matter of a successful missionary technique. Paul believes his conduct and attitude are both realistic and right. The fact that Paul is an apostle makes him no less subject to human limitations (vs. 7). Paul's own afflictions demonstrate this (vs. 8). But such afflictions (vss. 8 ff.) do more than show that Paul is human; they actually recapitulate the death and **resurrection** of Jesus (vss. 10 ff.). To suffer as Paul does is to carry in the body the death of Jesus, through which the life of Jesus becomes manifest (vs. 11). By "the life of Jesus" Paul means not just his earthly life but his resurrection from the dead (cf. vs. 14). Because of Paul's dying—his giving up of himself for them—the Corinthians experience life, even as through Christ's death human beings gain life. In both cases the offering is vicarious, on behalf of others.

Paul concludes this characterization of his ministry by referring to the scriptures (4:13), calling to mind his earlier discussion of Christ's crucial role in the Bible's proper interpretation (3:16). Paul has the same spirit of faith as the psalmist who wrote, "I believed, and so I spoke" (Ps. 116:10 **LXX**). Even though Christ's coming marks the decisive turning point of history for Paul, the faith it elicits does not differ from Israel's true faith. Paul's faith, however, focuses primarily upon Jesus: here, upon his hope in Jesus. Typically, Christian hope has found its basis and warrant in the resurrection of Jesus; Paul is a pioneer in reflecting this fundamental pattern (vs. 14). This section is rounded off by the declaration, "Yes, everything is for your sake" (vs. 15). Apparently, "everything" includes God's raising of Jesus, the gospel message, and Paul's affliction in his apostolic ministry. The ultimate end of all things is the glory of God himself, as God is extolled in thanksgiving by ever increasing numbers of believers (vs. 15).

Paul's Apostleship under Attack (2 Cor. 10:1–13:10)

How does Paul's boasting of his weakness reflect his view of apostleship?

Paul's attitude and subject matter change abruptly at the start of chapter 10. At first, Paul is restrained, although his anxiety and intense concern shine through the text. He earnestly entreats the Corinthians to attend to him, while maintaining that he does not intend to frighten them by his letters (10:9 ff.). At just that point, however, Paul betrays awareness of what his Christian opponents say about him, and he cannot resist a derogatory

Shrines to Apollo were numerous (see above, p. 280; cf. pp. 36–39). While Paul never visited the one in Delphi, he doubtless saw this temple of Apollo every day that he was in Corinth.

characterization of them (10:12). Immediately he pulls back, both in tone and in his own estimate of his success (10:13–18).

Paul's feelings for the Corinthians and his unique relation to them become clear in chapter 11. He does not disavow his jealousy (11:2), which becomes almost painfully apparent (vss. 3 ff.) as he compares himself with the "super-apostles" who have bewitched the Corinthians (vss. 5 ff.). That the Corinthians have been exploited by interlopers becomes evident, not only from Paul's explicit statements (vs. 20) but also from the contrast with Paul's own practice when in Corinth (vss. 7–11). These super-apostles' conduct and boasting prompt Paul to speak unabashedly of the experiences that commend him, both as a Jew and as a servant of Christ (vss. 21–29). All the while Paul is aware of the dubious, self-contradictory nature of his own bragging. It contradicts his understanding of Christian life according to the **gospel**, conformed to the cross (vss. 21, 23). Therefore, if he boasts, Paul will boast of his weakness (vs. 30).

Before he does so, however, Paul again allows himself to speak of experiences that distinguish him from most of his colleagues and rivals (12:1–6). Presumably, Paul here describes his own experience, although he speaks in the third person. He wishes to put distance between himself and the subject of his boasting (vs. 5)—but clearly he believes he has ample reason to brag (vs. 6). What restrains his boasting is finally not his modesty. God has given him a reminder of his limitations—the "thorn in the flesh"—so that he may boast only in his weakness, that the power of **Christ** may be manifest in him (vss. 7–10). This is a recurring theme of Paul's thought, especially in 2 Corinthians: "We have this treasure in clay jars [RSV: "earthen vessels"] so that it may be made clear that this extraordinary power belongs to God and does not come from us" (4:7). Paul's self-conception is basically formed by his grasp of the gospel and his role as a servant of it, but his rivals afford a nice foil for his presentation of his own apostolic ministry. Amidst temptation to play his opponents' game, at which Paul is convinced he could excel, he is restrained—by God or Christ himself, or by his understanding of the very nature of his message.

The gospel is God's power (cf. Rom. 1:16–17) made manifest in human weakness, whether in the cross of Jesus or the life of the **apostle**. God makes himself known in this gospel, not in esoteric religious knowledge (1 Cor. 8) or in spectacular demonstrations of **Spirit**-possession (1 Cor. 14). Such **revelation** finds its natural counterpart in attitudes of humility and compassion among the faithful, for the cross of Christ is itself the ultimate expression of God's self-giving love (cf. Rom. 5:6–11). The pattern of the apostle's life expresses the character of the gospel, as it reflects the cross of Christ and affords a paradigm for every believer (1 Cor. 11:1).

Obviously, Paul's standards of what constitutes a true apostle of Jesus Christ are different from those of the super-apostles (11:5; 12:11). At the same time Paul will not for one instant concede that he is inferior to them by any standard (vs. 11). His concern for the defense of his apostleship is, however, integrally related to his commitment to the Corinthian **church** (vs. 19). As in Galatians, so here: Paul's defense of the gospel, his insistence upon his apostleship's validity, and his care for his churches' welfare are of a piece. At the conclusion of 2 Corinthians (12:14–13:14) Paul anticipates yet another visit to Corinth: a third, in which he hopes things will go well, although he is wary if not apprehensive (13:10). In Paul's view, the Corinthians' faithfulness to the gospel is inseparable from their loyalty to him, not because of any proprietary rights but because he—in contrast to the super-apostles who have intruded or sent their agents into the church—represents in his conduct as well as in his preaching the one true gospel.

Who were these super-apostles? Could they be the Jerusalem apostles—Peter and James (Jesus' brother)—who play such a large role in Galatians (cf. 1:13–2:10)? Many commentators have proposed this identification, but several factors speak against it. First, the super-apostles of 11:5 are not distinguished from the false apostles Paul describes in 11:13–14, which implies they are ministers of Satan. Paul would hardly have described Jerusalem's pillar apostles in this way. In the second place, there is no indication that these rival apostles made keeping the **law** and practicing circumcision an issue. The issues in Corinth do not appear the same as in Galatia. Moreover, in Galatians Paul emphasizes the Jerusalem apostles' approval of the terms of his mission to **Gentiles**. That these false apostles disparage Paul's rhetorical skills in comparison to their own (10:10) again suggests they were not the Jerusalem apostles, who are characterized in the Book of Acts as uneducated (4:13). In any case, these apostles were intruders in the Greek-speaking Corinthian church. That they were Jews, as Paul suggests (11:22–23), does not mean they were **Aramaic**-speaking, Palestinian Jews like Peter, James, and John. Probably they were **Hellenistic** Jews, as fluent in Greek as Paul was.

PHILIPPIANS AND PHILEMON: PERSONAL ATTITUDE AND RELATIONS

Background of Philippians

In Philippians, Paul looks back over a long and arduous ministry with at least the intuition that it is now drawing to a close. Such resentment as he harbored toward his enemies and the enemies of the **gospel** is now overshadowed by feelings of appreciation for a **church** that supported him in bad times and in good. With the end perhaps in view (cf. Phil. 1:21 ff.), Paul continues to care for those churches to which he was **Christ's apostle**. That care is expressed through gratitude, pleas for personal reconciliation, and sustained **theological** argument.

Philippians' place and date of origin may be subject to doubt, but there is no uncertainty about the Philippian destination of the letter (1:1; 4:15). According to the Acts account (16:11–40), with which Philippians 4:15 seems to agree, Philippi was Paul's first mission stop on his initial journey into Macedonia and Greece.

OUTLINE OF PHILIPPIANS

Introduction: Salutation and Thanksgiving (1:1–11)
Personal and Theological Communication (1:12–3:1)

Joy in Hardship (1:12–26)
Exhortation and Encouragement to the Philippians (1:27–2:18)
The Example of Jesus (2:1–11)
Plans to Dispatch Emissaries (2:19–3:1)

A Warning (3:2–21)

Paul's Own Life as an Example against the Evil Workers (3:2–17)
Denunciation of the Evil Workers (3:18–21)

General Exhortation and Personal Matters (4:1–20)
Conclusion (4:21–23)

Joy in Hardship (Phil. 1:12–26)

How does Paul's attitude toward his own misfortune demonstrate his understanding of the gospel?

Paul's feeling of genuine warmth for the Philippians shines even through the conventional opening thanksgiving (1:3–11). At the letter's end, he specifies the grounds of his affection for them (4:14–18). They have helped Paul generously. Now Paul is in prison (vss. 7, 13) on account of his preaching of the gospel (vs. 13; cf. Acts 21–28.) Despite his circumstances, he is not despondent. Far from having impeded his work and the gospel's advance, his opponents have done just the opposite (vs. 12)—for by his very

> ## What Are the Captivity Epistles?
>
> Ephesians, Philippians, and Colossians, as well as the brief personal letter to Philemon, claim to have been written by Paul from prison (Eph. 3:1; 4:1; Phil. 1:12–18; Col. 4:10; Philem. 1, 23). That this was the case with Philippians and Philemon is beyond reasonable doubt. Doubts about Colossians and Ephesians are related to the question of whether they were written by Paul himself or by one or more of his disciples. In the latter case, the prison setting may be a literary device.
>
> We shall treat Colossians and Ephesians together in Chapter 11. Colossians may have been penned by Paul himself or by a coworker in Paul's name. Ephesians is most likely the product of a later Paulinist. Even if Colossians was written by Paul, it is closely related to Ephesians in subject matter and style. In both there is a special emphasis upon the idea of the **church** as the body of Christ and upon Christians' being already raised with Christ. Both contain the sort of conventional ethical exhortations (Col. 3:18–4:1; Eph. 5:21–6:9) largely missing in Paul's uncontested letters, but characteristic of other early Christian writings (cf. 1 Pet. 2:18–3:7). Therefore, quite apart from questions of authorship, the letters are appropriately treated together. (Indeed, the author of Ephesians may have used Colossians as a principal source.)
>
> Philemon and Colossians are linked by personal references (e.g., the slave Onesimus in Philem. 10 and Col. 4:9; Epaphras in Philem. 23 and Col. 1:7; 4:12) and by common destination (Colossae). If Colossians was written by Paul, it and Philemon appear to have been dispatched at the same time, possibly by the same couriers (Col. 4:7–9). Philippians, on the other hand, stands somewhat apart.
>
> Although the evidence is ambiguous, tradition has it that the so-called prison epistles were written from Rome during Paul's two-year imprisonment recounted in Acts 28—that is, about A.D. 59–61. We know, however, that Paul was imprisoned at other times in other places (cf. 2 Cor. 11:23): in Caesarea (Acts 24–26), Philippi (Acts 16:19–40), and possibly Ephesus (1 Cor. 15:32; cf. Acts 19:28–41). It is, therefore, not impossible that one or more of the captivity epistles were written from different prisons. Still, there is no compelling alternative to the longstanding view that they were penned in Rome toward the end of Paul's ministry. General considerations, such as Paul's reminiscent frame of mind in Philippians, suggest a late date and point in the direction of a Roman origin. We shall proceed on the assumption that Philippians and Philemon are the last extant letters of Paul, probably written from Rome.

imprisonment Paul bears **witness** to Christ (vs. 13). Moreover, and contrary to what might have been expected, Paul's coworkers have been emboldened, not intimidated, by the treatment accorded the apostle (vs. 14).

Paul's realistic assessment of his colleagues' motivations in preaching is striking (1:15–18). We know that Paul was not welcome everywhere, even among Christians in his own churches. It comes as no surprise if his appearance among Roman Christians aroused not only love but also envy and rivalry. Paul was not modest about the importance of his own role in the apostolic preaching and suffered from no sense of personal inadequacy in comparison with his coworkers (cf. Rom. 15:17; 1 Cor. 15:10; 2 Cor. 11:5, 21 ff.). He was capable of arousing antagonisms. In all probability, therefore, he presents here a true picture.

Paul seems able to rise above petty jealousies, not because of superior personal or moral character, but on the basis of theological insight. For him, the proclamation of the gospel, not the personalities (cf. 1 Cor. 3) or even the motivations of the preachers, was primary. The gospel had validity and power independent of the one who conveys it. Thus, despite some rivals' intention to harass him, perhaps by making more converts than he could while languishing in jail, Paul can rejoice—for "whether out of false motives or true, Christ is proclaimed" (vs. 18).

Paul had confidence in the Christian community and the **Spirit**. Therefore, he had hope. The interdependence of one member of the community with another, so graphically portrayed in Paul's image of the body of Christ (1 Cor. 12; Rom. 12:3–8), finds practical expression in their prayers (vs. 19). The prayers of the church and the Spirit of Jesus work together for Paul's deliverance. Deliverance from what? It is by no means certain that Paul refers only to deliverance from a Roman executioner or from prison. The word *sōtēria,* here translated "deliverance," also means **salvation**, and Paul's use of this and related terms usually has a future, **eschatological** reference. Paul can regard death as well as life as the fulfillment of his hope for deliverance (vs. 20). He does not, however, allow himself to yearn for death. He desires only to face either life or death with courage, so that Christ will be honored in his body (vs. 20). This is a good example of Paul's distinctive use of the Greek term *sōma,* "body." Here it surely does not refer to physical shape or substance, but to Paul's individual, personal presence in the world.

Paul next explains the relative advantage of living or dying and indicates what he means by "dying is gain" (vss. 22–25). Life means labor (vs. 22), whereas death means being with Christ (vs. 23). Given the Philippians' continuing needs, Paul regards it as more urgent for now that he continue to live (vs. 24). That, apparently, is the basis of his confidence that his life will for the moment be spared, so that he may visit the Philippians again (1:25 ff.). Whether events proved him right in this expectation is debatable. If he was writing from Roman imprisonment, in all probability they did not. But the point is that Paul's eager expectation of deliverance or salvation could by no means be disappointed, whatever the outcome of his situation; he had hope because God had raised Jesus Christ from the dead. This Jesus, in his humiliation, death, and **resurrection**, was for Paul the pattern of Christian existence and the ground of hope. So at what was very likely his ministry's end, with the prospect of his own death facing him, Paul had confidence and joy (1:4, 18, 19; cf. also 1 Cor. 15:32; 2 Cor. 11:23 ff.).

The Example of Jesus (Phil. 2:1–11)

In 1:27 ff. Paul makes an easy transition from encouragement to exhortation, and in 2:1–11 (esp. vss. 5–11) he offers a **Christological** model for ethics. In doing so, he invokes the example of Jesus, though not Jesus' behavior or even his teaching. After telling the church how they should act—more important, on what basis and with what attitude (2:1–4)—Paul invokes the example or "mind" of Jesus. Then follows what is sometimes called a **Christ myth**: the story of Jesus told from a cosmic viewpoint. The subject suddenly changes, not just to Jesus, but to the heavenly Christ who descends to earth, assumes human form, and returns (2:6–11). The literary **genre** also changes. For good reason the NRSV prints vss. 6–11 in strophes, as this material is frequently referred to as a Christ-hymn.

So Paul may be drawing upon a traditional hymn. Was it sung in church worship? The prologue of the Gospel of John (1:1–18), which tells the same **cosmic** story, seems also to be based on a hymn. Perhaps it too had a liturgical origin or setting. Another Pauline passage, which like the Johannine prologue presents the role of Christ in creation, is Colossians 1:15–20. It too may be a hymn, which some English versions (like the New American Bible) present in strophic form. In each of these cases, which highlight the **preexistent** Christ's cosmic role, whether in creation or **redemption**, we seem to be dealing with a hymn, or at least with some liturgical form. It is in the church's praise of Christ in worship that his cosmic role is perceived.

Unlike the prologue of John and the Colossians hymn, the Philippians hymn dwells on Jesus' **saving** role, not his role in creation. Debate has centered on the meaning of certain expressions: the *form* (*morphē*) of God; *equality* with God; something to be *exploited* (*harpagmos*); *emptied* himself; the *form* (*morphē*) of a *slave*; *human likeness* (*homoicōma*), human form (*schēma*). These terms occur in the hymn's first part (vss. 6–7), which concerns the preexistent Christ's becoming human. The hymn's second part (vss. 8–9) refers to his death and **resurrection**, which has occurred; the last (vss. 10–11), with future worship and the confession of Jesus as Lord, which has not yet occurred but has been already anticipated in the church's worship. It is the first of these three parts (Christ Jesus' preexistence) that causes the most difficulty, for it speaks of things no one has seen or experienced. Christians have witnessed the death and resurrection of Jesus. His universal adoration has been anticipated in their worship.

Much of the theological debate abut the terms noted above has arisen because of later **theological** discussions of the nature of Jesus Christ, which came to a head only in the fourth and fifth centuries of our era. To simplify immensely these complex and theologically important debates, the question had to do with whether or how Jesus could be at once God and Man, as it has been put historically, or both divine and human. Yet "divine" and "human" are inadequate, because they are too general. God and Man is preferable. (See the comments in the Prologue: The Nature of the New Testament, p. 9.)

Does "form of God" mean that Jesus was truly God? If "equality with God" could really have been "exploited," Jesus must have been really God. (Yet "exploited" could also be translated "seized"!) The context implies Jesus was, as John 1:1, forthrightly states, God (*theos*; not just divine, *theios*). Do "form of a slave," "human likeness," and "human form" mean that Jesus was truly human? Some early Christians, later condemned as heretics, thought not. (They were called **docetists**, from the Greek verb *dokein*, to seem. For them, Jesus only *seemed* to be human.) What the Philippians hymn intends was later put more sharply and succinctly in John 1:14: "the **Word** became flesh."

Jesus' real humanity came to unmistakable expression in his death on the cross (2:8), which the docetist Christians denied. "Crucified, dead, and buried" in the **Apostles' Creed** obviously describes a historical fact but at the same time makes a theological point. The Christ-myth of Philippians 2:6–11 was widely shared by first-century Christians. It was their way of expressing the ultimate importance of Jesus Christ and his intimate relation to God. The form of this confession in Philippians is the earliest we have. This brief discussion has shown the fundamental questions and issues that it raised.

The remainder of Paul's **epistle** to the Philippians consists of encouragement, a warning against heretics (esp. in chap. 3), exhortation, personal reflections, and an expression of appreciation. This last section (4:14–20) may bespeak the occasion for the entire letter. Its tone, with the possible exception of chapter 3, is consonant with this appreciation. Indeed, Philippians evinces an ease and familiarity not often found in Paul's letters. Even chapter 3 implies no division between Paul and the church, but warns against outsiders and intruders who quite possibly had not yet appeared in Philippi. More is implied in 4:14 ff. than perfunctory thanks: there is a mutual sympathy and understanding between Paul and the first church he founded on the European continent.

Background of Philemon

By far the briefest of Paul's letters, Philemon is a personal note. Paul addresses individuals, including Philemon, who was a member of the Colossian church. Colossae is not mentioned in the letter, nor is Philemon mentioned in Colossians; but Archippus, mentioned in the greeting of Philemon, is named as a leader of the Colossian church (Col. 4:17). Many of the same people send greetings in Colossians as in Philemon (Col. 4:10–17; Philem. 23–24). Most important, Onesimus, concerning whom Paul writes to Philemon, is mentioned as having been sent to Colossae with Tychicus (Col. 4:7–8). Thus the letters to the Colossians and to Philemon are closely related.

Whereas the authenticity of Colossians is debated (see pp. 378–381), no one doubts that Paul wrote Philemon. No canonical list of Paul's letters omits this letter, and it is difficult to conceive why some other person would have written such a brief personal note in Paul's name. If Colossians is Deutero-Pauline—written by a disciple of Paul rather than Paul himself—then the author either knew Paul's letter to Philemon or was otherwise familiar with the people mentioned in it.

Traditionally, Philemon has been assigned to the period of Paul's Roman imprisonment (ca. A.D. 60), even though the people named are mostly associated with Colossae and Asian Christianity. Moreover, Paul anticipates release from prison and the possibility of visiting Philemon in the immediate future (vs. 22). For him to have anticipated release from Rome and a trip to Colossae is not unthinkable, yet another tradition attests to Paul's imprisonment in nearby Ephesus (cf. 1 Cor. 15:32; 2 Cor. 11:23), from which he could have more easily anticipated a visit to Colossae. In that case, Philemon would probably have been written in the early fifties.

Slavery and Freedom (Philem. 4–20)

Did Paul insist on Onesimus' freedom?

Philemon does not tell a story, but it implies a story about Paul's relationship to Philemon and Onesimus, Philemon's runaway slave. In the beginning Paul probably brought the good news of **salvation** to Philemon—that is, Paul converted him to the faith (vs. 16), whether at Colossae or elsewhere. (According to Colossians 2:1, Paul had not yet visited Colossae.) Subsequently, Paul was arrested and imprisoned, either in Rome or in Ephesus. Meanwhile, Onesimus, Philemon's slave, escaped or ran away (vs. 15, passim) and found his way to Paul in prison. (Again, nearby Ephesus would seem likely.) How he came upon Paul, or why he should have sought him out, we do not know. Perhaps he was apprehended and put into prison with Paul, although if he was also a prisoner one wonders how Paul could have had the authority to send him back to Philemon (vs. 12). Maybe Onesimus was not incarcerated. Whatever the case, Paul apparently befriended Onesimus while in prison and brought him to faith in Jesus Christ (vs. 10). Rather than keep Onesimus as his own servant (vs. 13; Paul here avoids "slave" terminology), which he would have had some right to do, Paul elects to send him back to Philemon (vs. 12). With Onesimus Paul sends this letter (vss. 17–19a)—actually, a letter of recommendation for Onesimus—offering to compensate Philemon for any loss or damage (vss. 17–19a) and urging him to receive his slave back without penalty or recrimination (cf. vs. 16). We may imagine that Onesimus returned to Philemon and was received according to Paul's wish (vss. 8–10). Whether he was to be regarded as a slave or a freedman is not explicitly stated, and this question has been the subject of much exegetical debate.

Paul hopes to persuade Philemon, in Colossae, to take Onesimus back as a brother (i.e., a fellow Christian), whatever his worldly status might be. Although careful to urge politely rather than command (vss. 8–10), Paul nevertheless reminds Philemon of the latter's debt to him (vs. 19b) and of Paul's own **apostolic** authority. At the end he says that he is confident of Philemon's obedience (vs. 21) and instructs him to prepare the guest room for a visit (vs. 22)! There is little doubt that Paul knows what Philemon should do, and believes he has the authority to command it, because of both his apostolic status and their earlier relationship. Yet Paul recognizes that he cannot enforce his will and must draw on his powers of persuasion, using his own authority and Philemon's debt to him adroitly and subtly, not rudely or blatantly.

Although Onesimus' status before God is that of a brother or fellow Christian, this does not necessarily mean Paul expected Philemon to manumit (free) him. Given Paul's understanding of the implications of **baptism** into Christ (cf. Gal. 3:27–28), one might think that he meant for Philemon to free Onesimus. The slavery question was, however, not as important for Paul, who expected the end of worldly conditions with the imminent return of Jesus, as it is for modern people, for whom the idea of slavery as an institution is abhorrent. Paul nowhere advocates the abolition of slavery, an enormously important institution in antiquity. Whether onc is slave or free in this world is for Paul a matter of indifference (Gal. 3:28), for "the present form of this world is passing away" (1 Cor. 7:31). In 1 Corinthians, Paul seems to recommend that Christians retain their present status (7:24), although he may quietly endorse a slave's making use of the opportunity to become free (7:21). Paul was not a submissive, quiescent person (cf. 2 Cor. 11:23–29); nor can he be said to have actively supported slavery or the other oppressive social or political conditions of this world. Nevertheless, Paul does not explicitly say that he expects Philemon to grant to Onesimus a freedman's status. Conceivably, Paul's not commanding this action has something to do with the subtlety of his rhetorical style, but it may have had more to do with his **eschatology**: God would soon end human slavery.

This brief letter reveals something about the constituency of Paul's churches, and presumably of others as well. Philemon was a householder (cf. vs. 22) and a slave owner. The two usually went together in antiquity. The householder was not just a homeowner; within his household were more than members of the nuclear family: there were also servants, slaves, more remote kin, and perhaps others. The householder was a person of acknowledged status and means. We know from Paul's letters that a fair number of householders had been converted to the new faith, for their houses served as gathering places for the Christian community. Thus Paul writes here, as he does often, of "the church in your house" (vs. 2). Not until much later did Christians have, or build, halls (i.e., "churches") in which to meet; normally they met in the homes of affluent members like Philemon (cf. Rom. 16:3–5, 23). As Paul's letter to Philemon clearly shows, slaves and poor people were gladly welcomed into the community of faith. Wealthier people were not excluded but rather played an important role in the life of the emerging church.

Philemon, like Philippians, bespeaks a warm and close relationship between Paul and the churches he founded in this case the church in Colossae (cf. vs. 2 and Col. 4:17). Probably such friendly relations were the rule, not the exception. If we think otherwise, it may be because Paul wrote when there were problems and he could not immediately visit the church affected. Thus the letters to the Galatians and the Corinthians have played such a large role—perhaps too large a role—in the interpretation of Paul's work.

C O N C L U S I O N :   W H A T   W E   K N O W   A B O U T   P A U L

We have now studied the Book of Acts and representative letters of Paul. In fact, we know more about Paul than about Jesus. Paul was converted in the early or mid-thirties. He died in the early sixties. Probably he was born about the turn of the century and was therefore about the same age as Jesus, whom he never knew personally, although he claimed to have seen the **resurrected** Lord (1 Cor. 15:8; cf. 1 Cor. 9:1; Gal. 1:12–16).

From the Book of Acts we know that his Jewish (Hebrew) name was Saul (*sha-ul*), the name of Israel's first king. His Roman cognomen was Paul (*paulos*), the name he always uses in his letters. The portrayal of Paul in Acts prepares us for what we read in his letters, although the Book of Acts does not mention his letters. Whether Luke had read any of them is a good question. Probably they had not yet been collected when Luke wrote, and it is possible that he knew none of them.

At many points Acts and Paul agree. For example, Paul was a **Pharisee** (Acts 23:6; Phil. 3:4–7), and he persecuted Christians (Acts 9:1–2; Gal. 1:13). Although Paul himself claims to have seen the risen Jesus, in Acts this is not quite so clear, although Paul hears Jesus addressing him (Acts 9:4–6) after "a light from heaven flashed around him" (Acts 9:3). In both cases, clearly it is a **revelatory** experience.

Sometimes Paul speaks of working with his own hands (1 Cor. 4:12; cf. 1 Thess. 2:9), but he never says at what—just what his work was. Acts (18:3) tell us that Paul stayed in Corinth with fellow believers Aquila and Priscilla, because they all collaborated as tentmakers.

Only from Acts do we learn that Paul was able to speak Hebrew, or perhaps **Aramaic** (Acts 22:2); that he was born in, and was a citizen of, the city of Tarsus of Cilicia, in present-day Turkey (22:3; 21:39); and that he studied in Jerusalem with Gamaliel (22:3). Moreover, we learn only from Acts that Paul was a Roman citizen, a claim he makes more than once (16:37–39; 22:25–29; cf. 25:10–12). All these data fit a picture of Paul as a person of high status and education that Luke is trying to draw. Moreover, Paul intends to be a good and faithful Jew. That all these characteristics fit what was for Luke a desirable picture of Paul does not mean, however, they have no historical basis. Nor should one draw that conclusion from the fact that Paul himself does not mention them. None is directly relevant to Paul's presentation of his understanding of the **gospel** to the **Gentile** churches of his mission field.

Paul was the first Christian **theologian**. He regarded the unfolding of his mission in light of what God had done and was doing in the sending of Jesus, his **Son** (Gal. 4:4), the **crucified messiah** of Israel. As a rule, Paul's theological thinking arose out of practical situations. Perhaps his sharpest insights come in response to severe challenge. Those who had questioned Paul's own **apostolic** credentials claimed that male converts in the Galatian churches must undergo circumcision, the mark of membership in the Jewish community. In the letter to the Galatians he rejects their claims, arguing that faith's acceptance of Jesus as God's grace is the heart and soul of the gospel. Faith is negated if one insists on circumcision, for circumcision implies acceptance of the **law** instead of grace as the way of **salvation**. Yet for Paul, the expression of faith in human relationships is love, not theological knowledge (1 Cor. 8:1–13). Love takes precedence over knowledge. Knowledge leads to the sort of confidence in one's own power that can thwart faith. Love honors the other person, whom God also loves, and is grounded upon faith. In one place Paul gives love precedence even over faith and hope (1 Cor. 13:13). By that he cannot mean that faith and hope are dispensable, but that apart from love they fail the test of genuineness.

Paul was a convert, a missionary preacher, an organizer of churches, an author and theologian, and a teacher and administrator for the churches he founded. His life was filled with hard work, travel, controversy, physical punishment and imprisonment.

Rarely, however, does any hint of what Paul endured, the fatigue he must have experienced, appear in his letters (but cf. 2 Cor. 11:23–29). Obviously, Paul's dedication was matched by a strong physical constitution. Not many people have the sheer energy to do what Paul did. When one considers that he did it in the face of such hardship and opposition, his accomplishments become even more remarkable.

SUGGESTIONS FOR FURTHER READING

The Suggestions for Further Reading at the end of Chapters 9 and 10 include works on Paul's theology.

GENERAL TREATMENTS

C. J. Roetzel, *The Letters of Paul: Conversations in Context*, 3rd ed. (Atlanta: John Knox, 1991), centers on the Apostle's correspondence. E. P. Sanders, *Paul* (Oxford: Oxford University Press, 1991), sets Paul's theology and ethics in the context of his mission. C. B. Cousar, *The Letters of Paul* (Nashville: Abingdon, 1996), considers issues and themes pervading the letters. J. A. Ziesler, *Pauline Christianity*, rev. ed. (Oxford: Oxford University Press, 1990), and M. D. Hooker, *Paul: A Short Introduction* (Oxford: Oneworld, 2003), concentrate on Pauline theology. More advanced is a fine collection of essays, J. D. G. Dunn (ed.), *The Cambridge Companion to St Paul* (Cambridge: Cambridge University Press, 2003).

Locating Paul in his Roman philosophical environment are T. Engberg–Pedersen, *Paul and the Stoics* (Edinburgh: T & T Clark, 2000), and B. W. Winter, *Philo and Paul among the Sophists: Alexandrian and Corinthian Responses to a Julio-Claudian Movement*, 2nd ed. (Grand Rapids: Eerdmans, 2002). The socio-historical constituency and organization of Paul's churches are treated in the important, comprehensive study by W. A. Meeks, *The First Urban Christians: The Social World of the Apostle Paul*, 2nd ed. (New Haven: Yale University Press, 2003). J. H. Schütz employs modern sociological theory in *Paul and the Anatomy of Apostolic Authority* (New York: Cambridge University Press, 1975). B. R. Gaventa, *From Darkness to Light: Aspects of Conversion in the New Testament* (Philadelphia: Fortress, 1986), discusses Paul's apostolic calling. G. Lüdemann, *Opposition to Paul in Jewish Christianity*, trans. M. E. Boring (Minneapolis: Fortress, 1989), considers an important, neglected topic. J. M. Bassler (ed.), *Pauline Theology*, Volume 1: *Thessalonians, Philippians, Galatians, Philemon* (Minneapolis: Fortress, 1991), is a valuable collection of essays.

1 AND 2 THESSALONIANS

E. Best, *A Commentary on the First and Second Epistles to the Thessalonians* (New York: Harper & Row, 1972), accepts 2 Thessalonians as Pauline. In contrast, E. J. Richard, *First and Second Thessalonians* (Collegeville, MN: Liturgical, 1995), and B. R. Gaventa, *First and Second Thessalonians* (Louisville: John Knox Press, 1998), do not. The collection of essays by K. P. Donfried, *Paul, Thessalonica, and Early Christianity* (Edinburgh: T & T Clark, 2002), compares Paul's thought with that of Jesus and Qumran.

GALATIANS

J. L. Martyn's *Galatians: A New Translation with Introduction and Commentary* (New York: Doubleday, 1997) is a most comprehensive and excellent technical commentary. Also notable are H. D. Betz, *Galatians: A Commentary on Paul's Letter to the Churches in Galatia* (Philadelphia: Fortress, 1979); R. B. Hays, "Galatians: Introduction, Commentary, and Reflections," *The New Interpreter's Bible*, vol. 11 (Nashville: Abingdon, 2000), 181–348, and J. D. G.

Dunn, *The Epistle to the Galatians* (Peabody, MA: Hendrickson, 1994). Galatians lies at the center of many of Martyn's essays in *Theological Issues in the Letters of Paul* (Edinburgh: T & T Clark, 1997). On the letter's theology and ethics, consult C. K. Barrett, *Freedom and Obligation: A Study of the Epistle to the Galatians* (London: SPCK, 1985), J. M. G. Barclay, *Obeying the Truth: A Study of Paul's Ethics in Galatians* (Edinburgh: T & T Clark, 1988), J. D. G. Dunn, *The Theology of Paul's Letter to the Galatians* (Cambridge: Cambridge University Press, 1993), and R. B. Hays, *The Faith of Jesus Christ: The Narrative Substructure of Galatians* 3:1–4:11 (Grand Rapids: Eerdmans, 2002). M. D. Nanos (ed.), *The Galatians Debate* (Peabody, MA: Hendrickson, 2002), takes up many of the letter's disputed issues.

2 CORINTHIANS

V. P. Furnish, *II Corinthians* (Garden City, NY: Doubleday, 1984), is now standard, though C. K. Barrett, *A Commentary on the Second Epistle to the Corinthians* (New York: Harper & Row, 1973), remains first-rate. Also see F. J. Matera, *II Corinthians* (Louisville: Westminster John Knox, 2003). In *The Opponents of Paul in Second Corinthians* (Philadelphia: Fortress, 1986), D. Georgi tries to deduce the nature of Paul's opponents from his own comments. J. Murphy-O'Connor, *The Theology of the Second Letter to the Corinthians* (Cambridge: Cambridge University Press, 1991), is a reliable survey. F. Young and D. F. Ford, *Meaning and Truth in 2 Corinthians* (London: SPCK, 1987), is perceptive and stimulating.

See also the Suggestions for Further Reading at the end of Chapter 9.

PHILIPPIANS AND PHILEMON

Increasingly commentators pair these letters: thus, C. Osiek, *Philippians, Philemon* (Nashville: Abingdon, 2000), and B. B. Thurston and J. M. Ryan, *Philippians & Philemon* (Collegeville: Liturgical, 2005). Philippians is also well served by M. Bockmuehl, *The Epistle to the Philippians* (London: A & C Black, 1997), and M. D. Hooker, "The Letter to the Philippians: Introduction, Commentary, and Reflections," NIB 11 (2000): 467–549. K. Barth's profound *The Epistle to the Philippians* (Louisville: Westminster John Knox, 2002), has been returned to print, as has R. P. Martin, *A Hymn of Christ: Philippians 2:5–11 in Recent Interpretation and in the Setting of Early Christian Worship* (Downer's Grove, IL: InterVarsity, 1999).

A Roman carving, in ivory, of the crucifixion (ca. A.D. 400), British Museum, London. This is the oldest known illustration of Christ on the cross. *(Courtesy of The Bridgeman Art Library.)*

CHAPTER 9

1 CORINTHIANS: FAITH FOR A FRACTURED CHURCH

Background of 1 Corinthians

We have already considered the setting and origin of Paul's letters to the Corinthians (see Chapter 8, pp. 292–293).

First Corinthians was at least the third letter in the correspondence between Paul and Corinth. Paul had already written the Corinthians previously (5:9), and they him (7:1). Neither of these letters survives. Much of the latter part of 1 Corinthians, from 7:1 on, is devoted to answering questions raised by the Corinthians' letter. Chapters 1–4 deal with problems in the Corinthians **church** reported by Chloe's people (1:11). Chapters 5 and 6 are concerned with moral problems Paul has learned about from some undesignated source. While some have suggested that 1 Corinthians is a composite of several letters, most scholars defend the document's original unity.

The letter was written from Ephesus in Asia (1 Cor. 16:8) in the mid-fifties of the first century, during Paul's third missionary journey (see the time-chart, p. xxv; see also p. 258). 1 Corinthians was written before 2 Corinthians. This is clear not only from their order in the New Testament but also from their content. One finds in 2 Corinthians a much-deteriorated relationship between the Corinthian church and Paul, whose once-acknowledged status as **apostle** is now being challenged. In 1 Corinthians, Paul is able to speak authoritatively; the church's acknowledgment of his apostolic authority is not yet the major question, although the problem does emerge in chapter 9. Moreover, 2 Corinthians assumes a second visit to Corinth (12:14; 13:1), which is not mentioned in 1 Corinthians. A date of **A.D.** 54 for the one and A.D. 55 for the other is likely, though it is possible that 2 Corinthians 6:14–7:1 is part of an earlier letter referred to in 1 Corinthians 5:9–11.

Corinth was a center of trade, lying on the narrow isthmus between the Gulf of Corinth and the Saronic Gulf, across which flowed traffic between the Adriatic and Aegean seas. It was also a manufacturing and banking town where social status was more likely based on economic or business achievement than on family history or connections. Perhaps too much has been made of Corinth's wide-open, immoral character. "Not for every man is the voyage to Corinth" went the ancient proverb, implying that the trip was only for the experienced or jaded. Whether cultic prostitution was actually practiced in the temple of Aphrodite on the Acrocorinth overlooking the city is a matter of dispute. (The ancient geographer Strabo's statement to that effect would have applied to the earlier Greek city, rather than to the Roman city of New Testament times.) Nevertheless, the problems and issues that Paul confronted in Corinth, as reflected in 1 Corinthians, bespeak its cosmopolitan character and tend to support the city's bawdy reputation. The ethos of the city was not Jewish, nor did it reflect the higher ideals of Greco-Roman culture.

We can deduce more about the character, as well as the problems, of the Corinthian church than about any other Pauline community. Not only do we know a great deal about the city of Corinth, but also in 1 Corinthians itself the problems of the church get a thorough airing. Moreover, we learn something from 1 Corinthians and related New Testament books about the people who made up the Corinthian church. Crispus, mentioned in 1:14, was according to Acts (18:8) prominent in the Corinthian synagogue. Gaius, whom Paul also says he **baptized**, was evidently a householder of considerable means; the church could meet in his house (Rom. 16:13). Stephanas, whom Paul mentions by way of afterthought (1:16), was also a householder. Erastus (Rom. 16:23) was a city official in Corinth and therefore a prominent citizen. Paul describes the Corinthian Christians as lowly people according to worldly standards (1:26–31). Doubtless many were. On the other hand, some were obviously more well-to-do. When Paul calls the Corinthians rich (4:8), castigates them for going to court (6:1–8), and speaks of the houses they have to eat and drink in (11:22), he further reflects this fact. The Corinthian church was a mixed group, consisting of people from varied backgrounds, and its mixed character had something to do with the difficulties that arose within it.

OUTLINE OF 1 CORINTHIANS

Introduction: Greetings and Thanksgiving (1:1–9)

Division in the Church (1:10–4:21)

The Corinthian Situation (1:10–17)
Paul's Own Practice and Example (1:18–3:4)

Paul and Apollos as Servants (3:5–4:7)
Admonition to the Corinthians (4:8–21)

Immorality in the Corinthian Church (5:1–6:20)

Flagrant Sexual Immorality (5:1–13)
Christians Suing One Another (6:1–11)

Theology of the Body (6:12-20)

Responses to the Corinthians' Letter and Other Issues (7:1–15:58)

Sexual Relations in Marriage (7:1–40)
Love and Knowledge (8:1–13)
Apostleship and Reward (9:1–27)
The Danger of Idolatry and Idol Temples
(10:1–11:1)
Conduct in Worship: Hairdress and the
Lord's Supper (11:2–34)

Spiritual Gifts (12:1–14:40)
Spirit and Body (12:1–31)
Love (12:31–13:13)
Prophecy and Speaking in Tongues (14:1–40)
The Resurrection from the Dead (15:1–58)

The Collection and Other Business (16:1–24)

INTRODUCTION: GREETINGS AND THANKSGIVING (1:1–9)

Paul begins with his usual salutation (1:1–3), followed by a typical thanksgiving (1:4–9). The salutation (1:1–3) is conventional, but not therefore meaningless. Paul first of all identifies himself as called by God to be an **apostle**. In Galatians 1:15–16 he describes that call. Sosthenes, who joins Paul in writing, may be a former synagogue official (cf. Acts 18:17), but this is uncertain. In any event, Paul himself is clearly the real author. The term **church** (Greek: *ekklēsia*; English: ecclesiastical) is based on the Greek word to call and means, literally, "called out." So Paul is called to be an apostle, and the disciples or church members are described as called (1:2). They are called to be saints and are **sanctified** in **Christ** Jesus. Here the Greek word (*hagios*; English: hagiography) could also be translated **holy** in the biblical sense of set apart. The concept of sainthood as a special holiness is as yet unknown. All are saints, who call (in prayer) on the "the name of our Lord Jesus Christ." This is the beginning of the Christian custom of praying in Jesus' name. "Grace" and "peace" are typical Christian terms, but they are meaningful. God's **saving** action is his grace, and its result is peace in and among human beings. "Peace" is a typically Jewish and Old Testament blessing; "grace" is more distinctively Christian and particularly Pauline. The thanksgiving (1:4–9) is also conventional but meaningful: Paul mentions speech and knowledge (vs. 5), as well as spiritual gifts (vs. 7), which will become major topics later on (chapters 8, 13, and 14).

DIVISION IN THE CHURCH (1:10–4:21)

The Corinthian Situation (1 Cor. 1:10–17)

If we value diversity, why are divisions in the church of Corinth bad?

In 1:10–17, Paul begins to address the problem of divisions in the **church**. Some look to Paul, others to Apollos, others to Cephas (**Aramaic** for Peter, "Rock") as their patrons. But Paul does not blame the other leaders for these divisions. Paul himself had founded the church at Corinth (3:6; cf. Acts 18:1–11). Clearly Apollos, the learned Alexandrian Jew who was converted by Priscilla and Aquila in Ephesus (Acts 18:24–28), had played an important role in the church (1 Cor. 3:4–6; 16:12). Whether Peter had is not so clear, although Paul refers to him in 3:22 and 9:5. Divisions attributable to loyalty to different leaders have led to quarrels (vs. 11). Some claim Paul, others Apollos, others Cephas (Peter), and others Christ himself. What disturbs Paul is not the other leaders themselves but the quarrels swirling around them among the Corinthians, reported to him by Chloe's people. (Chloe, a householder, was apparently a prominent woman in Corinth.)

Although most Christians were not wealthy, a few were. They were householders, with a sizable retinue of family and slaves. Paul speaks of having baptized the household of Stephanas (1:16), who were the first converts in Achaia, the province of which Corinth was the capital (16:15). While writing from Ephesus (16:8), he sends greetings from the churches there, particularly the church in the house of the married couple Aquila and Prisca, or Priscilla, as she is called in Acts (16:19; 18:1-3). Crispus and Gaius, whom also Paul **baptized** (1:14), are mentioned elsewhere: Crispus in Acts 18:8, where he is called an official of the Corinthian synagogue and Gaius in Romans (16:23), which was written from Corinth. But Paul the apostle was not sent to baptize, but to proclaim the good news (vs. 17), which he will then characterize (1:18–25).

The divisions in Corinth, which Paul does not fully or systematically describe, are troubling for more than practical reasons. The members of the community of believers are Christ's own body, as Paul will later declare (12:12–31), activated by the same **Spirit** (12:1). In Corinth, the unity of that body is threatened, as it was in the Galatian letter. There the problem was division between Jewish and **Gentile** Christians (Gal. 2:11–14; cf. 3:27–29), as the Jewish Christians separated themselves at meals. In Corinth the divisions are differently based but nevertheless serious. As this letter unfolds, one gets a clearer picture of their character and basis. But the fundamental conviction that drives Paul is the unity of the community in **Christ**, the church's one foundation (3:10–11). That unity must remain inviolate.

Paul's Own Practice and Example (1:18–3:4)

Is Paul adopting Christian humility, or is he making a theological point?

Next Paul speaks of the centrality of the message of the **crucified Christ** (1:18–25). This is the essence of what Paul has called "the **gospel** I proclaim among the **Gentiles**" (Gal. 2:2). God sent his **Son** (Gal. 4:4), the **Messiah** of Israel, as Jews expected; but Jesus was

crucified as a criminal, which no one had expected. There is a radical reversal of expectations, a transvaluation of the world's values, which Paul sums up in 1 Corinthians
1:22–25. God has intervened in human history and human affairs in a way no one, least
of all Paul before his calling, could have anticipated. For Paul, the gospel makes sense in
the aftermath of God's intervention, but it could not have been anticipated beforehand.
So then scripture (the Christian Old Testament) makes sense in light of that intervention
in a way it did not, and could not, beforehand (cf. 2 Cor. 3:12–18). (Thus, Paul quotes
Isaiah 29:14 in support of his understanding of the nature of Christian proclamation.)
One way of putting this is to say that Paul did not grasp the gospel message until he had
been grasped by the God who made known this good news. Paul's own "conversion,"
described in Acts and referred to frequently by Paul, is the basis of his **theology**. Yet Paul
himself refers to it, not as conversion, but as revelation (*apokalypsis*; Gal. 1:12). This
event shattered, and ultimately reversed and reformulated, his expectation.

Paul's own strong sense of this reversal of human expectation spills over into his
description of the Corinthians themselves (vss. 26–31). Here Paul's rhetoric can easily
lead to the conclusion that the Corinthian Christians, or early Christians generally, were
all poor or lower class people. Yet we have seen that householders, people of means, were
among Paul's converts and colleagues. The fact that households included slaves fits into
the general picture. Not all slaves were menial servants. Some were well educated and
had been prosperous. Paul does not say "none of you," but "not many of you" (vs. 26).
Probably that would have been the case, not only among the believers in Corinth, but
also among any similar Christian group. In any event, sociological conclusions should
not be too quickly deduced from Paul's theologically inspired rhetoric.

After characterizing the Corinthians, and perhaps Christians generally, Paul
reminds them of his own preaching (2:1–5). He seems to be denigrating his own skill as
an orator (vss. 3–4). In fact, some of his critics would have agreed (cf. 2 Cor. 10:10). But
just to say this is to miss Paul's point: his own weakness makes way for the power of God
(vs. 5), which is present through the Spirit (vs. 4, cf. Gal. 3:2–3). The Lord, that is, Jesus,
speaking through the **Spirit**, has told Paul, "My grace is sufficient for you, for power is
made perfect in weakness" (2 Cor. 12:9). Paul dispenses, not human wisdom, but the
wisdom of God, which is folly to those who do not know or accept the preaching of the
crucified messiah, including the "rulers of this age" (vss. 8–9) who crucified Jesus.
Whom does Paul mean? Probably the Roman and Jewish authorities in Jerusalem,
although he could allude to supernatural powers instead, or as well. The source of Paul's
apparent scripture quotation in vs. 9 cannot be identified. Perhaps he is recalling the
prophet Isaiah (cf. 64:4; 52:15). Often Paul must have cited scripture from memory. He
could scarcely have toted the scrolls of the **law** and the **prophets** around with him!

God reveals things to believers (here Paul must be referring primarily, if not solely,
to himself) through the Spirit (vs. 10). Through the Spirit, God speaks to the spirits of
human beings (vss. 11, 13, 15). Paul, as one who is inspired by the Spirit, interprets spiritual things to those who are spiritual (vs. 12–13). As the NRSV notes indicate, what Paul
actually says and means is ambiguous at this point. There are those who can understand,

and those who cannot (vs. 14). To the latter, such wisdom is foolishness. Why is there this division? To Paul it remains a mystery. He speaks of "those who are the called" (vs. 14) as if there were those who are not. And presumably there are also those to whom spiritual things are foolishness unless or until they receive the Spirit of God. In vs. 14 Paul speaks in the singular of the natural (*psychikos*) person (*anthrōpos*), who has not yet been touched by God's **revelation** and does not receive his Spirit. Paul is here speaking not of different types within the **church**, but of those within the ambit of God's revelation and those who are outside it. Will they perhaps come in? Paul does not address that question.

A strong claim (2:15) is made for those who are spiritual (NRSV; the Greek is singular, "the spiritual person"). Does Paul mean that those who claim the Spirit are beyond all human judgment? Perhaps so, insofar as their claim is valid. Yet later on Paul himself admonishes those in the Corinthian community who claim to possess God's Spirit (cf. 12:3). Paul does not, however, wish to deny the claim outright. Jesus is manifest to Paul and the churches through the Spirit, which has in some sense displaced the law as guide (cf. Gal. 3:2–5). In 2:16, Paul cites Isaiah 40:13 to support his own claim. To claim the mind of Christ (i.e., "the Lord") is to claim possession by the Spirit. Paul makes this claim for himself.

Then addressing the Corinthians directly (3:1), Paul seems to shift the ground. Apparently he is thinking back to when he first preached and founded the Corinthian church. They were not ready for solid food—but still they are not! Paul now turns from the beginning of the community to its present state (vss. 2–4). The Corinthians do not manifest true spirituality, that is, possession by the **Spirit** and mind of Christ, as their jealousy, quarrels, and divisions prove (vs. 4). Paul is joining the indicative with the imperative: "Be who you are!" The fact that the Corinthians have not attained the state to which they were called does not mean that they have not been called. Life in Christ does not mean magical formation but, rather, moral struggle. The difference from their former state is not that the battle is now won, but that it is winnable. Paul will later employ athletic imagery (9:24–26; cf. Phil. 3:12–16). The author of 2 Timothy writes in Paul's name, "I have fought the good fight, I have finished the race . . ." (4:7), words worthy of the **Apostle** and of his hope for the churches he founded.

Paul and Apollos as Servants (3:5–4:7)

How does Paul's discussion of his own role imply a criticism of the Corinthians?

Paul now returns to the rivalry between groups in the church. Interestingly, Peter (Cephas) and Christ as factional leaders now fall out of the picture. Probably Peter had not visited Corinth, or had played no major role there. Certainly Jesus Christ had not been to Corinth in any physical sense. "I belong to Christ" (vs. 12) is not a criticism of claiming Christ. All should. Paul implies that some do so, however, in a way intended to reflect credit on themselves. They rise above it all, because they feel superior to the rest: "We belong to Christ!"

In any event, the reader may infer that the Paul and Apollos parties are the ones that now must be dealt with. Paul enjoys a certain priority, because as an **apostle** he founded the Corinthian church (3:6, 10). Apollos came along later (3:6). His role, only hinted at by Paul, may be filled out from Acts 18:24–28, which briefly describes Apollos, his learning, and the role he played in Ephesus before moving to Achaia. Like Paul, Apollos' background was Jewish. He was from Alexandria, Egypt, a major center of learning with the largest library in the ancient world. Paul's treatment of his relationship to Apollos is altogether even-handed (vss. 5–9). Yet there is an implied threat of judgment against anyone who builds poorly upon the foundation that Paul has laid. "The Day" is that of Jesus' return and final judgment (cf. "the day of our Lord Jesus Christ" in 1:7–8).

The community of the church is God's temple (3:16–17): that is, the place where God dwells, as in the Jerusalem temple. (In effect, for Paul the church has replaced the temple, although the Jerusalem temple was still standing and functioning when he wrote.) The level of threat against anyone who attacks the new temple now ups the ante, so to speak. Paul will return to this warning in 6:12–20. Believers, individually and corporately, are the temple of God.

Suddenly, as if provoked by his own words, Paul's attention shifts away from himself and Apollos to the Corinthian Christians (3:18–23). The divisions in the church evidently have something to do with claims of having wisdom (vs. 18). Once more Paul invokes scripture, this time Job 5:13 and Psalm 94:11. Paul's contrasting of human wisdom with the gospel (1 Cor. 1:18–25) is now related to the problem of division in Corinth. The NRSV translation of vs. 21 ("So let no one boast about human leaders") is a loose translation, though probably correct. The RSV's "Let no one boast of men" is more literal. "Let no one boast by human standards" is also possible. "All things are yours" is rooted in the Corinthians', and all believers', existence in Christ, who is God's possession. If you already possess everything, why squabble over who is superior?

Paul pauses to reflect on his own role as apostle (4:1–7) in a passage that concludes with his making a similar point (vs. 7): "Everything comes from God as a gift." Possibly Paul's eloquent statement (4:1–5) is an anticipatory response to criticisms of him that he knows, perhaps from Chloe's people (1:11), have been lodged in Corinth. Paul is not affected by such judgments (vss. 3-4) but is content to await the judgment of the Lord, that is, Jesus Christ (vs. 5). Obviously, he still expects Jesus' return before long (cf. 1:7, 8; 16:22; 1 Thess. 4:13–5:11).

Paul then notes why he has applied all this to himself and Apollos (3:5–23). There is no conflict between Paul and Apollos, or Peter for that matter, but there are conflicts within the Corinthian church. They are "puffed up in favor of one against another" (vs. 6). "Nothing beyond what is written" is an obscure admonition, probably referring to scripture quotations Paul has earlier used in the letter (1:18, 31; 2:9, 16; 3:19, 20). What is written—scripture—forbids human boasting (cf. Rom 12:3), of which at least some in the Corinthian congregation are guilty. Boasting, for Paul, is the opposite of true Christian existence, which is based on a fundamental awareness of new life as a gift. In Galatians the problem was grace versus works of the **law** as a human accomplishment in which one might boast. Here the problem is grace versus boasting in human wisdom (vs. 7).

Admonition to the Corinthians (4:8–21)

Is Paul being sarcastic? To what end?

At this point Paul's basic contention against the Corinthians, or some in the Corinthian church, surfaces. He criticizes their lifestyle, which expresses their superior self-regard, by contrasting it with his own (vss. 8–13). The crux of the contrast is vs. 10, but Paul's description of the hardships he has endured is hardly fictitious. (In 2 Corinthians 11:22–29 he gets more specific.) Paul mentions his own self-supporting labor and his refusal to respond in kind when abused or demeaned. This reflects Paul's understanding of the meaning of the **gospel** and also his appropriation of the conduct of Jesus himself (cf. 11:1). Paul's criticism of these Corinthians goes to the very heart of the matter. He is not dealing in superficialities.

Then Paul seems to back off (vs. 14). It is perhaps a rhetorical tactic, but Paul's genuine affection for the congregation breaks through. He has begotten them in the gospel (NRSV: "became your father") and, as would any parent in antiquity, beseeches them, "Be imitators of me." To this end he has sent Timothy, his close associate, to the Corinthians. Obviously Timothy is his trusted emissary (vs. 17). From Acts (16:1) we learn that Timothy was also Jewish. His mother was Jewish, and Paul himself is said to have circumcised him (Acts 16:3). Perhaps Timothy was the bearer of this letter, although that is not explicitly said. Moreover, Paul himself plans to pay another visit to Corinth (vss. 18–21). What kind of visit will it be? Paul says, in effect, "It's up to you!" (The word translated "stick" in vs. 21 by NRSV is better left "rod," as in RSV. "Rod" still has the connotation of punishment in English: "Spare the rod and spoil the child.") Paul's contrast of talk and power is noteworthy (vss. 19–20). People in Corinth may talk, but the **kingdom of God**'s rule is power. Paul has already spoken of the imminent return of Jesus, which was associated in early Christian thought with the advent of God's powerful rule. The gospel that Paul announces is more than a subject for discussion in which people may take pride because of their wisdom. Its power already impinges upon the present.

IMMORALITY IN THE CORINTHIAN CHURCH (5:1–6:20)

Why is Paul so indignant about the Corinthians' attitude? Not only are they complacently proud; they also are engaging in conduct that Paul finds deplorable. Three instances are cited. Two (5:1–13; 6:12–20) have to do with sexual behavior that would have been intolerable under biblical **law**. They are intolerable for Paul as well, but he refrains from citing the Bible against them.

Flagrant Sexual Immorality (5:1–13)

Why was this couple's conduct tolerated by some in the church of Corinth?

"Sexual immorality" (Greek: *porneia*; English: pornography) is reported, probably again by Chloe's people. Someone is living with his father's wife. Presumably, this is not his own mother. "Someone has the woman [or wife] of his father," is what Paul literally says. Leviticus 18:8 specifically mentions such a case in distinction from incest with a parent. Paul does not cite scripture, however, but says that such immorality is not found even among pagans (or "**Gentiles**"; KJV). Even those not under the law do not do such a thing. (Indeed, Cicero expresses horror over a union between mother-in-law and son-in-law.) The flagrancy of such immorality contrasts sharply with their arrogance (vs. 2). The offender is to be excommunicated. The woman in question appears not to be a member of the **church**, since there is no further mention of her.

The protocol for excommunication is then outlined (vs. 3–5). It is to take place in Paul's physical absence, but he will be present in **spirit**. Exactly what is meant by the handing over to Satan (vs. 5), as well as what is to follow, is unclear and unknown. Yet even at this stage Paul holds out hope for the grievous offender, but only at the day of the Lord, the return of Jesus. Perhaps the destruction of the man's flesh means his physical death.

Exactly why Paul assumes that yeast symbolizes evil (vs. 6) is not obvious, though the term is similarly used in Mark 8:15. Paul calls **Christ**'s the paschal (**Passover**) lamb (vs. 7), and only unleavened bread is eaten during Passover (Exod 12:8, 15–20). Yeast or leaven does permeate the whole batch or lump of dough. The yeast analogy works well for the desired condition of the Corinthians after Christ paschal sacrifice (vs. 7). They should celebrate not with the old yeast, which has been cleaned out, but with unleavened bread. The unity, wholeness, and purity of the church are to be preserved.

Paul then anticipates an objection (vss. 9–13): How can the church maintain its purity in this evil world? He refers to an earlier letter he wrote the Corinthians, which we no longer possess (unless part of it has been incorporated into 2 Cor. 6:14–7:1). He does not intend to forbid necessary contacts with people outside the community; he writes, instead, about who should not be tolerated within the church. What Paul said in 2 Corinthians 6:14–7:1 corresponds with this, and that passage seems to interrupt the flow of 2 Corinthians at that point. In support of his contention, Paul cites Deuteronomy 17:7 (vs. 13). Remarkably, Paul continues to cite scripture as authoritative, even though he does not, as a rule, invoke scriptural law on moral issues. Distinctively Christian obedience has a different rationale: the mind of Christ (2:16).

Christians Suing One Another (6:1–11)

What does their litigation imply about the social and economic status of some Corinthian Christians?

Suddenly Paul moves to another issue: Christians are going to (secular) courts in order to sue other Christians, thus allowing pagans ("the unrighteous") to sit in judgment between them. Believers are to have a role in the coming judgment of the end times (vss. 2–3; cf. Matt. 19:28). It is inconceivable to Paul that Christian believers (church members, as we would now say) cannot settle matters among themselves (vss. 4–8). Here (vs. 6) Paul uses the term *adelphos*, brother, or brothers and sisters, as Paul clearly means. He contrasts them with unbelievers (*apistoi*). To avoid sexist language, the NRSV translates *adelphos* as "believer," the opposite of "unbelievers," but in doing so individualizes the term. Members of the community of believers are like family; they are as intimately related as siblings, brothers and sisters. As Paul reflects on the situation, he judges that it is better to be defrauded than to go to court. But the Corinthian brothers and sisters wrong and defraud each other. They disrupt family relations.

They are in danger of being wrongdoers. This leads Paul to a denunciation of wrongdoers generally. Here again the choice of the English term "wrongdoers" (NRSV) is understandable but leaves out something. The RSV uses the more literal term "unrighteous" (Greek: *adikoi*), which touches upon a major theme of Paul's **theology**, God's **righteousness** in contrast with human *unrighteousness* (cf. Rom. 1:16–18; 3:9–10). Paul now focuses upon the latter (vss. 9–11), giving a catalogue of those who will not enter the **kingdom of God**. They are wrongdoers, unrighteous persons (vs. 9). This list of wrongdoers is similar to that in 5:10–11. "Fornicators" (*pornoi*) means sexually immoral persons. The others in the list are easily identifiable, except for male prostitutes (*malakoi*) and sodomites (*arsenokoitai*). These are technical terms designating male homosexuals. (For further discussion, see Chapter 10, p. 349.) None of these, Paul reiterates, will inherit the kingdom of God. Paul's concluding statement (vs. 11) is telling. This is what at least some of the Corinthians were. But they have undergone a fundamental transformation. "You were washed" doubtless refers to the **baptism** that marked the initiates' entrance into the church as people pronounced holy and righteous. The name of the Lord Jesus Christ was pronounced over them at baptism. As Paul acknowledges this moment of transformation, however, there may remain some doubt about its actual effect on some of the new Corinthian Christians.

Theology of the Body (6:12–20)

Who in Corinth is saying that all things are lawful, and why?

The question of the present behavior or lifestyle of some Corinthian Christians now comes to the fore. Here Paul makes no specific accusation (as in 5:1–5) but warns his readers against sexual "freedom." His initial statement (vs. 12) is a kind of slogan that some in Corinth may have brandished to justify their behavior, real or contemplated. Are all things lawful? To the Galatians Paul has said, "For freedom **Christ** has set us free" (5:1). Is his emphasis on liberty now being used to justify sexual libertinism? Already in Galatians, Paul had warned against using freedom as an opportunity for the flesh (5:13; see NRSV note). Now he qualifies the slogan by saying that, although all things may be lawful, all are not beneficial, and that he (and by implication the Corinthian believers) would not be dominated by anything. The next slogan (vs. 13) concerns food, but food seems not really to be the problem. If food is for the stomach and the stomach for food, which Paul grants with qualification, is not sex for the body and the body for sex? This seems to be what Paul is getting at. The word Paul uses, *porneia*, refers not only to "fornication" (NRSV) but also connotes every kind of unlawful sexual intercourse. The translators might have done better to render Paul's statement as "the body is not for free sex but for the Lord." If some Corinthians were not already doing it, Paul suspects they were contemplating it! The term "body" (Greek: *sōma*) denotes the person's physical being, but it is more than that. The body is the whole self. Speaking of the **resurrection**, Paul will insist there is a spiritual body (15:44). When Paul says that the believers' bodies are members of Christ (6:15), he means the physical body, yet more than that. The body is one's personal identity. The sexual act involves the physical body but involves the total self (vs. 18), even as being a member of Christ's body involves the total self, physical as well as spiritual. In the course of the argument (vs. 16) Paul quotes Genesis 2:24: "The two shall be one flesh," a biblical statement also cited by Jesus (Mark 10:8 parr.), just before saying (vs. 9), "Therefore, what God has joined together, let no one separate." (The KJV version of this injunction is best known from Christian marriage services: "What therefore God hath joined together, let not man put asunder.")

For Paul there is no such thing as sex without bodily commitment, a commitment of the whole self. It is significant that Paul uses the Genesis passage about marriage and applies it to sexual relations with a prostitute. Sexual union is marriage. The terms fornication, fornicator, and prostitute in the NRSV are too narrow. Illicit sex, an immoral man, and an immoral woman are what Paul is writing about. The immoral woman Paul mentions (vs. 16) is not necessarily taking money for sexual favors. The man who joins himself with her (vs 18) is not necessarily paying for the privilege. Paul here espouses a high view of sexual relationships. Is he unrealistic? For Paul, there is no such thing as casual sex. The continuing preoccupation with sexual behavior in modern Western culture—as if sexual sins were the worst sins of all and certainly the most interesting—owes something to the Apostle Paul, and to the Bible. This modern cultural attitude is, however, obsessed with sex in a way the Bible is not.

Yet preoccupation with sex should not lead the reader to overlook Paul's principal point, which is the unity of believers in Christ as members of his body. Paul finally appropriates language about the temple, the place of God's dwelling (vs. 19): "Your body is a temple of the **Holy Spirit**." What believers are they owe to God alone, who has acted on their behalf through Jesus' death. The body is the means of giving glory to God in response to what God has done. Because of his high view of the body Paul has a high view of the importance of sex and denounces its misuse.

RESPONSES TO THE CORINTHIANS' LETTER AND OTHER ISSUES (7:1–15:58)

Suddenly the agenda shifts. Heretofore Paul, prompted by reports he received, has initiated the subjects he believed needed addressing. First, there are divisions in the Corinthian **church**: the problem is not with Paul's colleagues, but with the character of the Corinthians themselves. They suffer from spiritual pride in their own wisdom and status. Yet, in Paul's view, this pride is contradicted by the immoral behavior within the congregation.

The agora of Corinth. The agora was the forum (as in Rome) and the civic center of the city. At left center the higher edifice is the *bēma* or platform on which Paul may have been arraigned (Acts 18:12).

Beginning in chapter 7, however, Paul responds to questions raised by the Corinthians. To begin with, he writes (7:1): "Now concerning the matters about which you wrote." Then four other times (7:1; 8:1; 12:1; 16:1) Paul begins a discussion by saying, "Now concerning." In these cases, too, he is likely responding to the Corinthians' letter. In chapter 15, it becomes clear that the question of the **resurrection** has been raised by the Corinthians (15:12): ". . . how can some of you say there is no resurrection of the dead?" The question of spiritual gifts (12:1) is discussed through chapters 13 and 14 as well as chapter 12. This accounts for chapters 7–8 and 12–16. Moreover, chapter 9 clearly addresses questions raised by those who would examine Paul (vs. 3) and who have probably raised questions in the letter. Contextually, the status of chapters 10 and 11 is not as certain. There Paul returns to issues addressed in chapters 1–6, once referring to what he has heard (11:8). Was this also part of the report from Chloe's people (1:11)? In any event, most of this latter portion, which is more than two-thirds of the letter, is devoted to issues raised by the Corinthians themselves in their own letter to Paul.

Sexual Relations in Marriage (7:1–40)

Why does the question of sex within marriage come up? How can the unbelieving partner be saved?

Only here does Paul mention the Corinthians' letter to him, and we know that he had written them previously (5:9). We do not know whether Paul first addresses the topic of sexual relations because it was mentioned first by them, or because he was already addressing it (6:12–20). In 7:1–40 the issue is not sexual promiscuity, but sex within marriage or committed relationships. Again, Paul seems to cite a slogan, as the quotation marks—which are editorial additions to the translation—indicate. Paul concedes this point: celibacy is to be preferred. Nevertheless, marriage may be a necessity because of normal sexual urges (7:2). Within marriage, sex is normal and not to be avoided (vss. 2–6). Remarkably for his time, Paul treats the man and woman as mutually equal partners in sexual relations. Yet celibacy, which Paul himself practices, is preferable (vs. 7–8).

Paul's advice to the already married is an attempt to be practical and to conform to Jesus' own teaching about marriage and divorce, which Paul seems to know (vss. 10–16; cf. Mark 10:2–10 parr.). Marriage is inviolable, as Jesus taught (vss. 10–11). Marriages between believers and unbelievers should also be inviolable (vss. 12–16). The children of such mixed marriages are **holy**, not unclean, and the believing partner, whether husband or wife, may **save** the spouse. When Paul speaks of the unbelieving partner being made holy through the believing one (vs. 14), and perhaps being saved (vs. 16), modern evangelicals may assume he has conversion in mind. Perhaps he does. Yet given Paul's high view of marriage, or any sort of sexual union, could he be suggesting that this physical union might save the unbelieving partner? The unbeliever is united with the body of the believer, who is a member of the body of **Christ** (12:12–13, 27). In 6:13–20 Paul cautions the believer against uniting his (or her) body, which has become a member of (the body of) Christ, with a prostitute, or sexually immoral person. Sexual intercourse is bodily (or personal) union (6:16; cf. Gen. 2:24). Paul conveys the strictness of Jesus' own teaching in an atmosphere of reasonableness. He then uses the discussion of marriage to urge that all should remain in the state they were when called, i.e., when they became believers and members of the church (vss. 17–24). The time is short; Jesus will soon return (vss. 26-31). This state of affairs has to affect all human relationships, especially whether or not one will marry or, in the case of the death of a spouse, remarry (vs. 39). Remarriage should, however, be within the **church** ("in the Lord").

Paul's counsel is eminently sensible, given his expectation that the time remaining is very short (vss 32–35). Marriage brings with it unavoidable concerns that the single person does not have, and the latter can practice uninterrupted devotion to the Lord (vs. 35). Obviously, Paul recognizes that within the Corinthian church there are couples who are committed but not married: they have not engaged in sexual relationships (vss. 25, 36–38).

There is no indication that Paul himself had instituted or recommended such a practice. Probably it is related to the shortness of time. Like Paul, many believers expected that Jesus would return immediately (vs. 29, 31; 16:22). Under such circumstances, to marry and beget children might seem pointless. Though he recommends continuing in the celibate state as practical and preferable, Paul does not forbid marriage. Interestingly, the prospect of having children is not mentioned as a reason for marriage; Paul speaks only of the fulfillment of sexual desire. The NRSV has Paul speaking of virgins (vs. 25) and fiancées (vs. 36). In both cases the Greek word is the same, *parthenos*, usually translated "virgin." "Fiancée" was chosen because Paul seems to be speaking of committed relationships.

Paul's advice, and the Corinthian circumstances that evoked it, seem at first to find little resonance in the modern Western world of the twenty-first century. On the other hand, 9/11 and the possibility of a nuclear holocaust make the sense of a foreshortened future intelligible, and novels portraying the events leading up to the return of Jesus as happening the day after tomorrow sell by the millions in the United States of America. Apparently, millions of modern people expect to be "raptured" (1 Thess. 4:17). Yet there is not now, at least not on a mass scale, the kind of **apocalyptic** asceticism Paul faced, and which to some degree he shared, in Corinth.

The relationship between men and women is of perennial interest in most, if not all, human societies, but Paul's counsel, as well as the Corinthians' practice, has little direct applicability to modern Christians. 1 Corinthians 7 is not a model for premarital counseling. But Paul's wisdom and balanced judgment may be, given the practices and assumptions that he and the Corinthians have embraced. He is entirely evenhanded in his treatment of men and women as sexual partners (7:2-4; cf. 1 Cor. 11:8–12, where Paul clearly has Gen. 3:21–23 in view). That Paul may encounter both asceticism, a preference for celibacy, and sexual excess in the same Christian community is astonishing on its face, but on reflection perhaps not so incongruent. On the one hand, some believers may have thought that their wisdom and knowledge put them beyond ordinary standards or concerns. Others, however, pulled back from the concerns and standards of ordinary life and headed in a different direction: they abjured marriage and related responsibilities. Paul's own inclination is toward asceticism, so he naturally sides with the latter group, but without condemning those who marry (vs. 7): "Each has a particular gift from God, one having one kind and another, a different kind." Paul will extend this insight in chapter 12.

Love and Knowledge (8:1–13)

Why not eat meat offered to idols?

In Corinth, Paul faced a situation quite different from that in Galatia. The Corinthian problem was not an insistence upon the **law** but, if anything, just the opposite. As we learn from 6:12–20, freedom had become license, at least in Paul's view.

Chapter 8, dealing with the question of what to do about meat offered to idols, is even more useful than the interesting discussion of sex in revealing the fundamental character of Paul's problems at Corinth. Superficially, this may seem unlikely, inasmuch as the subject of sex is very much alive in Western culture, while the number of persons who either offer meat to idols or worry about the problem of whether to eat such meat is microscopic. (It may be an issue, however, for Christians in cultures where animal sacrifice is still practiced.) Yet a careful reading of chapter 8 reveals that far more is involved than the resolution of a practical problem faced by Christians in the ancient world. A fundamental **theological** and **ethical** question is raised. (See also Rom. 14:1–15:6.)

Christians living in a pagan world, among associates, relatives, and friends who were not Christians, were frequently placed in the position of having to eat, or refuse to eat, meat that had been offered to idols. Many poorer people could not afford meat and could eat it only on public occasions. But even if Christians avoided such feasts in the temples of pagan gods, as Paul sternly admonishes them to do (1 Cor. 10:14–22), they could not entirely escape the problem. For in the ancient world, much of the meat sold in the markets had also been offered to idols, even if in a most perfunctory way. The slaughtering of animals was frequently accompanied by a quasi-religious rite or token sacrifice. Although Paul, in instructing the Corinthians, seems to assume that some meat had not been offered to idols, it is at the same time clear that Christians could scarcely have avoided the problem of whether to eat meat that had been so offered. Sooner or later it would have been thrust upon them unless they withdrew from the world, an alternative that Paul does not recommend (1 Cor. 5:9 ff.).

Paul concedes that the consecration of meat to idols has no theological significance, because the idols themselves are nothing (vs. 4). Thus, in principle, eating meat offered to gods that are nonentities should not affect one's relation to the true God (vs. 8). However, although Paul and some Corinthian Christians know this, others do not (vs. 7). Therefore, the knowledgeable believer should refuse to eat meat offered to idols out of respect for the weaker brother (cf. 8:11), who may follow him in eating the meat and think that it really has some special potency or sanctity because it has been offered to idols. Alternatively, the weaker brother may believe that he has incurred real guilt before God for eating idol meat if he did not know that the idol has no real existence and that there is only one God, the Father, and one Lord Jesus Christ. Paul does not deny that other gods and lords exist (vs. 5); elsewhere he assumes their existence (15:24–27; Rom. 8:38 ff.). What he denies, for the Christian, is their ultimate significance: other-worldly, supernatural powers do not possess authority equal to that of the one God and Father of Jesus Christ.

Although Paul seems to countenance even eating meat in an idol's temple as a matter of indifference, except for the offense it might cause for an unknowledgeable brother (8:10), when he returns to the subject in 10:14-30, he issues a strict prohibition. There participation in any cultic act at an idol's temple is prohibited on the grounds of its conflicting with, and contradicting, the unity that believers have with Christ through participation at his table (10:16–22). Nevertheless, Paul continues to defend the believer's right to eat whatever meat is sold to him or set before him on other, non-cultic occasions (10:23–30), except that he still must have regard for the conscience of his sister or brother. Thus love takes precedence over knowledge.

Paul was aware of the potential danger of knowledge in a way that the Corinthians were not. Therefore, he makes it clear at the outset (8:1–3) that knowledge alone is a questionable gift. Some Corinthians were evidently so smitten with their newly acquired knowledge and consequent freedom that they identified knowledge and freedom *as such* with the essence of Christian existence. Paul found this intolerable.

At the beginning of this discussion, Paul puts love and knowledge in proper perspective. Paul goes so far as to agree with the Corinthians that "all of us possess knowledge" (8:1). But he immediately issues a warning: knowledge, especially knowledge that knows that it knows and takes pride in the fact, is a potential menace. The contrast between such knowledge and love is graphically put: "Knowledge puffs up, but love builds up." To be puffed up is obviously bad. (The same word, literally meaning "to be puffed up," is translated as "arrogant" in 5:2 in the NRSV—an accurate rendering that unfortunately obscures the connection with chapter 8.) To be built up, on the other hand, implies inner and outer strengthening of the church and the individual (cf. 3:10–15). The priority of love over knowledge is driven home most memorably in 1 Corinthians 13, the famous chapter on love. At the beginning of this hymn in praise of love, Paul accords it a place above prophecy, knowledge, and faith (13:2). Again in 13:8 and 9 he returns to the theme of love's superiority to knowledge. There is nothing wrong with knowledge per se, but in this world and this life it must give way to faith, hope, and love. Perfect knowledge will characterize the life to come, but in the present age the Christian must not make knowledge a primary concern (13:12 ff.). The key to 1 Corinthians 8 is not the impropriety of giving offense, but rather the supremacy of love over knowledge.

Apostleship and Reward (9:1–27)

Why doesn't Paul just accept pay and avoid criticism?

In overseeing his churches, Paul more than once dealt with the necessity of work, that is, working to support one's self (1 Thess. 4:11–2; 2 Thess. 3:7–13). Paul also prided himself that he worked rather than burden the **churches** he was founding (1 Thess. 2:9). In a case when he did not, he noted that fact with apparent regret (2 Cor. 11:8). Indeed, he took pride in not being a financial burden on his churches (1 Cor. 9:15–18).

Yet somehow Paul's practice has backfired, and he now has to defend it against those who would examine him (vs. 3). Since he is now answering questions put to him in the Corinthians' own letter (7:1), perhaps it contained reference to those who questioned Paul's credentials because he felt compelled to support himself, while other **apostles** did not (cf. vss. 4-6). This is the most likely explanation of why Paul suddenly takes on this issue. His first response is to assert quite strongly his status as an apostle (cf. Gal. 1:11–2:10). His claim to apostleship is based first of all on his having seen the risen Jesus (cf. 1 Cor. 15:8; Gal 1:15–16), but also on the success of his apostolic work (1 Cor. 9:1–2).

Paul then reveals a little about his colleagues' practice, as well as his own. They receive support and take their wives along with them as they visit churches (vs. 5). After a couple of common-sense examples of compensation for work (vs. 7), Paul cites scripture (vss. 8–10), maintaining that Moses (Deut. 25:4) is writing for Christians rather than for oxen, an interesting hermeneutical position, but one that conforms to Paul's new view of scripture. Paul draws the logical conclusion that applies to him and his colleagues (vs. 11), indeed, to them even more than to others (vs. 12a).

Nevertheless, Paul abjures his right for compensation (vs. 12b), even though **priests** in the temple are compensated and the Lord's (Jesus') command justifies it (vs. 14; cf. the word of Jesus in Luke 10:7). He will put no obstacle that impedes the success of his preaching of the **gospel** (vs. 15). Paul's rather tortuous argument (vss. 15–18) underscores this. He must preach the gospel because of divine obligation. There is no reward in that. The reward is that he has the satisfaction of offering the gospel free of charge, and in doing so is even more successful than his colleagues (vs. 19). Paul is a competitor, with other Christian apostles, but also with other philosophical teachers. He declines to accept rightful compensation, but outdoes them. He does this, however, by self-abnegation; he does not pursue his own rights (cf. 6:7–8). He does not accept the reward that is rightfully his. But there is method in his madness, for that is a key to his success. In a world of diversity, very different from our own in many ways but in that respect very much like it, Paul is engaged in a battle for hearts and minds, as are modern religious zealots, whether Jewish, Christian, or Muslim.

Is Paul, with his Christian colleagues, just one zealot among many? Yes and no. Like evangelical Christians generally, Paul is absolutely convinced that the advent of Jesus as the Christ makes all the difference in the world to humankind. The crucial question may be what is this difference. It can perhaps be articulated, but to be meaningful the difference must also be demonstrated. Paul believes it has been. He speaks elsewhere of God's proving his love for **sinners** through Christ's death (Rom. 5:8). He says that through Christ God was reconciling the world to himself (2 Cor. 5:19). Moreover, "For it is the God who said, 'Let light shine out of darkness,' who has shone in our hearts to give the light of the knowledge of the glory of God in the face of Jesus Christ" (2 Cor. 4:6). The good news of Jesus is, in Paul's view, good news, not bad news, for humanity—thus, the urgency of Paul's mission as he reflects on it in vss. 19–23. The word, good news (which is what "gospel" means), must be spread.

Paul's depiction of himself in 1 Corinthian 9:19–23 is easily subject to misinterpretation. The statement "I have become all things to all people" (vs. 23) might suggest that Paul has no real standards or goals other than success in evangelism. In King James English "all things to all men" has become a byword that signals lack of moral principle. Rather, Paul has found an alternative moral principle. But "moral principle" is not the right term. What governs Paul is his belief in a decisive event. In modern evangelical parlance "the hour of decision" emphasizes human decision. Paul lays primary stress upon God's decision and action, which governs his mission. The fundamental grounds for resisting Paul is, as Celsus the second-century critic of Christianity saw, the contention that what Paul thought had happened has not in fact happened.

Paul concludes with images drawn from ancient athletic contests. The Isthmian Games were held every two years in Corinth, and the Olympic Games in various places

Boxers from an ancient mural in Pompeii
(cf. 1 Corinthians 9:26). *(Courtesy of David Levenson.)*

in Greece every four. Was Paul a sports fan? That is doubtful, but he knew the street language of sports. His own life was like an athletic contest, and a model for other believers (9:24; cf. 11:1). Athletes receive a perishable wreath, those who are in Christ an imperishable one (vs. 25), which is the **resurrection** of the dead (chapter 15; cf. Phil. 3:11). Paul takes nothing for granted (vs. 27), and the Corinthians should not either. Victory may have been won, but life is still a struggle.

The Danger of Idolatry and Idol Temples (10:1-11:1)

Why does Paul return to the question of meat offered to idols?

The beginning of a new chapter 10 is an editorial marker that was introduced centuries after the New Testament was written. So Paul's warning to the Corinthians falls without interruption after his statement about himself (9:26–27). This can be missed, because Paul introduces the brief narrative of Israel in the wilderness (10:1–5). He assumes that the Israelites are the ancestors (Greek: "fathers") of the Christians at Corinth (and elsewhere), despite the fact that most of them are **Gentiles**. Based on his view that (Old Testament) scripture applies directly to the church (cf. 9:10), Paul summarizes the **Exodus** story (cf. Exod. 13:21–22; 14:21–29; 16:4, 35; 17:1–7; Num. 14:16, 29–30), which provides examples (*typos, typikōs*; English "type," "typologically") for the Corinthians' church (10:6, 11).

When Paul says that the rock was Christ (vs. 4), he goes far beyond anything in the Old Testament text. The rock is not an example (cf. vss. 6, 11) but a *type* of Christ. This is typological **exegesis**, where one thing is made to stand for another. Sometimes the Old Testament is treated this way in the New. Paul was doubtless aware that the original writer did not intend this meaning, but that is beside the point. Given this typology, the **baptism** is a type of the Christian baptism of the Corinthians; the eating and drinking of spiritual food and drink are types of the eating and drinking of the **Lord's Supper**. Already there is an implied warning to the Corinthians that they should not think that these two rites, baptism and the Lord's Supper, will save them despite their sinning.

Paul continues to exploit the analogy between Israel and the **church** (vss. 6–11), referring to specific scriptural episodes. The Israelites desired evil (Num. 11:4–6, 34; Ps. 106:14–15). They became idolaters (vs. 7; Exod. 32:1–6). They engaged in sexual immorality (vs. 8): Israelite men were having sex with foreign women and worshipping foreign gods (Num. 25:1–9). Though the Israelites put God to the test, the Corinthians must not put Christ to the test (vs. 9). For testing the Lord, Israelites were destroyed by serpents (Num. 21:5–6). The destruction of those who complained against God (vs. 10) may refer to the same episode (Num. 21:5) or a similar one (Num. 14:26–35). Paul does not doubt that he is referring to historical events, things that really happened (vs. 11), but their ultimate purpose was to serve as examples "to instruct us, on whom the ends of the ages have come." This is Paul's way of referring to the church. It is not conceived as a religious institution but as the community of those who believe the proclamation of the gospel, that is, the good news about what God is doing. This began with Jesus, and Paul believes he is continuing it.

Paul then exhorts the Corinthians: if you are standing, beware that you do not fall after all (vs. 12). Take nothing for granted, as Paul takes nothing for granted (cf. 9:27). Then Paul goes from warning to encouragement (vs. 13): you can do it because God will help you. The moral testing the Corinthians must go through is universal.

The emphases on idolatry, with examples drawn from the story of Israel, may seem strange, although the charge of sexual promiscuity resonates elsewhere in 1 Corinthians (5:1–5, 9; 6:9, 12–20). Now, however, Paul relates the references to idolatry to the Corinthians' situation and temptations (vs. 14–22). (Sexual promiscuity and idolatry are often linked in scripture.) Things fall rapidly into place. There is a parallel between the Israelites' apostasy in the wilderness—worshipping foreign gods—and the danger of the Corinthians' participating in worship of other gods in pagan temples more than a thousand years later.

Paul has already admonished the Corinthians not to eat food offered to idols because of the consciences of some brothers and sisters in the church. In 8:10, he seemed to countenance Christians' eating such food in pagan temples. In 10:23–24 he seemingly alludes to that earlier instruction. Whatever is sold in the meat market may be eaten without question (vs. 25), although Paul knows it may well have been offered, however perfunctorily, to idols in a pagan temple. The same goes for accepting and eating meat served by a host who is not a believer (vs. 27). One should abstain only for the sake of the conscience of another believer (vss. 28–29a). All this is in line with Paul's instructions in chapter 8. In vs. 29b, however, Paul's logic seems to break down. "Why not go ahead and eat? All right, do it!" might seem to follow. Yet Paul has already given the reason for subjecting one's freedom: respect for the conscience of another. Perhaps in vs. 30 Paul defends his conduct—eating idol meat but not in a pagan temple and not when other believers have raised questions—against other Corinthians who have objected to his practice. This exemplifies the difficulty caused by the fact that we do not know for sure the circumstances or objections to which Paul is responding.

Paul's final, general advice to the Corinthians (10:31–11:1) should be compared with the description of his own conduct and purpose (9:19–23). Their goal, like his, should be that all, or as many as possible, should be saved (10:33; cf. 9:22). Do not participate in idol worship, but beyond that simply give thanks to God for what you receive (vs. 30), for it ultimately comes from God and is good (vs. 26; cf. Ps. 24:1). The norm for the believer is Jesus Christ himself whom Paul also imitates, leading the way for others to follow (11:1).

Conduct in Worship: Hairdress and the Lord's Supper (11:2–34)

Can anything else be learned from Paul's discussion of hairstyles?

Reading 1 Corinthians, one is impressed by the distance between attitudes that are still understandable today and those that are not. The first half of this chapter represents the latter. Nevertheless, Paul has some significant things to say here, quite apart from the subject of hairdressing.

If the Corinthians are doing just as Paul wants them to (vs. 2), one wonders why Paul goes to such pains to explain to them what is proper (vss. 3–16). Probably Paul's opening statement reflects the fact that in their letter the Corinthians have given him this assurance. First, he sets out a hierarchy: God, Christ, believing man (husband), the believing woman (wife) (vs. 4). Given Paul's **theological** premises, this hierarchy is understandable, but then he begins to draw from it less than obvious conclusions about whether or not the head should be covered in worship. A man's head should not be covered, but a woman's head should be. In vs. 3 the NRSV translation alternates between man and husband in a way the original text itself does not, because in Greek, as in many languages (e.g., Hebrew, German), the same word is used for man and husband. Only context can determine meaning. It is best to stay with "man/woman" in 11:2–16, except in vs. 3, where a husband and wife seem to be in view (as the NRSV suggests).

The covering of the head with the yarmulke, now practiced by Orthodox Jewish males, dates from centuries later than Paul. Probably the Christian tradition of women who wear hats or other head coverings in church goes back to Paul and Corinth. What Paul says about men's having long hair being degrading (vs. 14) is reminiscent of an older generation's revulsion when this practice was adopted among mostly younger men in the 1960s: it violates customary expectations. Paul's reasons for women to keep their heads covered and for men to keep their hair short are several, but he invokes neither scripture nor Jesus. The most ancient portrayals of Jesus, not to mention modern paintings, show him with longer hair. Paul appeals to common sense (vs. 13), natural law (vs. 14), and his own custom as well as that of the **churches** of God (vs. 16). Paul also says that a woman should have on her head a symbol of authority, "because of the angels" (vs. 10). The mention of the angels, or why Paul would have thought of them, remains a perplexity that points to the difference between his view of the world and ours. (Angels are mentioned in 1 Cor. 4:9 and 13:1, as well as in 6:3, where it is said that Christians will judge angels, not all of whom are good.)

The most interesting, and for the reader the most significant, aspect of Paul's discussion of these matters is what he has to say about the status of women, as compared with men, before God. Typically, Paul presupposes the biblical account: here (vss. 7–12), specifically Genesis 2:18, 21–23. Woman was created from man, not the other way around (vss. 8–9). Nevertheless, the sexes are mutually interdependent "in the Lord" (vs. 11). "In the Lord" means in Jesus Christ, but in this world and age it also means "in the church." Woman came from man, man now comes through woman, "but all things come from God" (vs. 12). There is mutuality and by implication equality.

Obviously, Paul is discussing conduct in corporate worship. Prayer could be private, but not **prophecy** (cf. vss. 4–5). Paul assumes that women will pray and prophesy publicly, in services of church worship: something that is forbidden in 1 Corinthians 14:33b–36. Either Paul blatantly contradicts himself, or 14:33b–36 is a later editorial insertion to bring the real, historical Paul into line with the Paul of the Pastorals (cf. 1 Tim. 2:11–12). Probably it is the latter (see below, pp. 335–336). Paul himself believed that man and woman are equal "in the Lord" (Gal. 3:28), and this applies to worship as well as marital sex (1 Cor. 7:3–5). (On relations between husbands and wives see also Ephesians 5:21-33, where the mutuality expressed is much closer to 1 Corinthians than to the **Pastoral Epistles**.)

Of all the issues that Paul discusses in 1 Corinthians, the hair-dressing issue in 11:2–16 is probably the strangest. It is indicative of the extent to which Paul and modern readers occupy different intellectual and religious worlds. We do not share the same or even similar assumptions. Yet Paul's reasoning about the relation of the sexes is clear enough. He begins by commending the Corinthians for following his traditions (vs. 2) and ends by referring to the custom he follows along with other churches of God. Probably we are to infer that most Corinthians followed Paul, but there were some who differed. Thus the sharp edge to some of his comments.

Is the Lord's Supper a meal or a liturgical act?

There are, however, matters in which the whole Corinthian church has gone astray (11:17–34). Now Paul's objections are much clearer to the later reader. Here Paul has in view conduct at the **Lord's Supper**, observed in obedience to Jesus' command (vss.

24–25). Again Paul refers to divisions in the church (cf. 1:10–17), but now they are based not on **theology** or loyalty to different leaders. Perhaps the basis is social or economic differences (vs. 21). In any event, the occasion that should manifest the community's unity (10:16–17) results in divisions and distinction (vss. 18-19), and Paul finds this intolerable (vss. 21–22).

Here Paul speaks a language Christians of later generations would understand. Yet there is much we do not know about how Christian worship and the Lord's Supper were conducted in the first generation. The Lord's Supper, or **Eucharist**, has for most of Christian history been a part of the traditional Sunday morning service. Yet here the most natural interpretation is that it is an evening meal. (The Greek word used in vs. 20, *deipnon*, means the main or evening meal, as Jesus' last supper was; cf. Mark 14:12–25 parr.) Apparently, in Corinth it was a general, evening meal (vss. 20–22) in which some overindulged (vs. 21). Probably such a meal was commonly practiced among the earliest Christians. Paul moves in the direction of reforming the meal as practiced in Corinth. It is not, in his view, just a big dinner at which people could indulge or overindulge according to their means (cf. vss. 20–22, 34). Such behavior divides the church. Rather, the Lord's Supper expresses its unity (10:17), when rightly understood and carried out.

Paul then rehearses the beginning of the meal in Jesus' own ministry (11:23–26). This is the earliest written account of the words of institution of what, with **baptism**, has become the most commonly practiced Christian sacrament. Paul knows, and expects the reader to know, something about the events leading up to Jesus' death: this was an act Jesus performed on the night he was betrayed (vs. 23). As compared with the **Synoptic** account, particularly Mark's (Mark 14:22–25; cf. Matt. 26:26–29; Luke 22:15–20), Paul's version shows more extensive liturgical shaping. For example, after both the bread and the cup the partakers are told to do this "in remembrance of me." (One version of Luke's account has this instruction, but 1 Corinthians may have influenced it.) The last statement of Paul's version speaks of the coming of Jesus, that is, his return, and reflects Jesus' word about the coming of the **kingdom** in the synoptic accounts. These words of institution are included in most traditional Christian services down to the present, usually in the Pauline form.

Finally, Paul warns the Corinthians against unworthy participation in the supper (vss. 27–32). Down to the present day, Christians do not partake unless they have confessed or otherwise repented of their sins. It has become one of the central acts of Christian worship and discipline. (Roman Catholic political candidates who do not conform to the Church's teaching on some moral issue like abortion have sometimes been threatened with exclusion from the Eucharist, although this has been the subject of much controversy within the Church.) In Paul's view participation "without discerning the body" (vs. 29) will incur judgment, which may take quite palpable, physical form (vs. 30). Out of a general practice, we see a **sacrament** emerging, although that somewhat technical term does not yet appear in the New Testament.

Early Christian Worship

Little is known about the worship of the earliest Christians. Doubtless it was much influenced by Jewish synagogue worship, because the earliest followers of Jesus were Jews who eventually left, or were excluded from, synagogues because of their diverging beliefs and practices. 1 Corinthians 11 tells us more about early, distinctively Christian, worship than we would otherwise know. But not until a hundred years later is there a fuller description of services of **baptism**, **Eucharist**, and other church worship practices such as the reading of scripture and preaching (cf. Justin Martyr, *Apology* 1.61–67). Christians have traditionally worshipped on Sunday, but the name of the day does not occur in the New Testament. Paul, however, seems to assume that Christians gather on the first day of the week, which would be Sunday (16:2). The Seer of Revelation writes that he was in the Spirit on the Lord's Day (Rev. 1:10). According to The **Didache** or *Teaching of the Twelve Apostles*, one of the earliest Christian writings outside the New Testament, the Eucharist is to be held on the Lord's Day (14.1). Sunday as the **holy** day of Christians came to replace the Jewish Sabbath (Saturday) as Christianity separated from Judaism.

The "other things" about which Paul will give instruction (vs. 34) are not explained. Presumably they are matters about which the Corinthians have written in their letter to Paul (7:1), which Paul evidently still has in view, despite digressions.

Spiritual Gifts (12:1–14:40)

Spirit and Body (12:1–31)

Does Paul reject diversity?

With "Now concerning spiritual gifts (Greek: *pneumatika*)," Paul clearly responds to one of the questions the Corinthians put to him in their letter (7:1). At the very beginning of his own, Paul has said to the Corinthians that they "are not lacking in any spiritual gift" (1:7 NRSV), although there the Greek word is **charisma** (note the English word), gift of grace. There may be an intended difference. The Corinthians think in terms of spiritual endowment or achievement, Paul in terms of God's gracious gift.

Before their conversion the Corinthians worshipped idols (12:2), as did the Thessalonians (1 Thess. 1:9). They were pagan **Gentiles**. Their conversion to **Christ** was inspired by the **Holy Spirit** (vs. 3). Curiously, Paul first denies that anyone inspired by the Spirit might have cursed Jesus. Were some actually doing this? Probably not. Paul is giving an extreme example, to illustrate that not everything can be ascribed to the Spirit. There are limits (cf. 1 John 4:1–3). The Spirit, and Spirit–possession, is a big item with the Corinthians, but also with Paul. He asserts that not everything can be ascribed to the Spirit, while also holding that various functions necessary to the community's well-being are the work of the Spirit. One function or office should not lord itself over another.

There are varieties of services (vs. 5), but the same Lord (Jesus Christ). (Here translators seem to avoid *ministries* [for *diakonia*], perhaps because of later **ecclesiastical** usage, but it seems appropriate.) "Activities" are probably not something different, but fill out the meaning of services as ministries. All comes from God and Jesus Christ through the Spirit. Basic elements of later **Trinitarian** doctrine (Father, **Son** and **Holy Spirit**) are already found here. Paul spells out what these ministries or services and activities are (vss. 8–11). Interestingly, he ends with the gift of tongues and their interpretation, to which he will return in chapter 14. Perhaps Paul has not yet thought through carefully the gifts he names, for in most cases they concern a specific activity, but all would have the gift of faith (vs. 8; cf. vs. 3). The principle Paul invokes is stated in vs. 11: the Spirit is the source of all valid gifts.

Next Paul introduces the concept of the body of Christ. All are members of Christ's body (vs. 12); indeed, all were **baptized** into one body (vs. 13; cf. Gal. 3:27–28). The **church**, therefore, is the body of Christ. Strangely, Paul himself does not seem to make this exact equation, at least not in the letters universally acknowledged as his. (In Ephesians 1:23; 5:23, and Colossians 1:18 the church is explicitly said to be the body of Christ.) "Body" was used by human communities or societies to emphasize unity long before Paul. His readers would have readily understood his use of the term. Emphasis falls initially on unity: one Spirit, one body (12:12–13).

Having established the unity of the community as a body, the body of Christ, Paul then emphasizes that the community is made up of different and diverse members, even as the human body is (vss. 14–30). He describes various parts of the body to make the point that the members of the body are different, but complementary. The least explicit references are to be found in vss. 22–24, where Paul specifies the weaker, less honorable, less respectable, and inferior members, which are nevertheless indispensable and, therefore, treated with greater respect and honor. Which bodily members is Paul talking about? Probably the private parts. Yet their precise identification is not important. Paul obviously has in view the less prestigious members of the community. The attempt to identify them with precise body parts is unnecessary and could easily become ludicrous! Throughout 1 Corinthians, Paul has had in view the problem of those who considered themselves possessed of superior wisdom, knowledge, or even spiritual gifts, lording it over others (8:1–3). Therein lies the reason he makes for himself no claim about his preaching (cf. 2:1–5; 4:8–13). Undeniable differences are not differences of genuineness or value, but rather differences of function.

These functions are spelled out in detail (vss. 28–30) after a general, covering statement (vs. 27). Not surprisingly, these are not dissimilar to the manifestations of the Spirit for the common good, which Paul has just rehearsed in 12:8–10. The Spirit empowers the body of Christ through specific gifts. In both cases Paul ends the lists by mentioning tongues, by which he means speaking in tongues, and their interpretation (vss. 10, 30). In both cases Paul also mentions miracles or deeds of power, as well as gifts of healing (vss. 8–10, 28). In conclusion, he underscores his point about diverse gifts of the Spirit or functions of the body by asking whether all share them (vs. 29). That the answer to each query is "No" is clear enough from context in English translation; the more precise Greek makes it unmistakable that a negative answer is anticipated. Paul's title for this section (chapter 12) might well have been "Diversity within Unity."

Love (12:31–13:13)

How could anyone be against love? Are the Corinthians? What is the point?

Paul now calls on the Corinthians to pursue the greater gifts (cf. 12:4, where the same term, **charisma**, is used). But the "still more excellent way" (vs. 31b) is the way of love, something that is even more than a spiritual gift. Love validates, and lack of love invalidates, all such gifts. This great discourse on love, set between two imperatives about striving for or seeking gifts (12:31a and 14:1b), is a kind of interlude, which certainly does not make it less important. Chapter 13 is sometimes described as a hymn to love, and its frequent liturgical use, particularly in Christian weddings, supports such an appraisal. Marital love is, however, the last thing on Paul's mind. The Greek word used here for love is *agapē*, the characteristically Christian term for self-giving love. Marital love has as a major component *erōs* (English: erotic), love that desires physical fulfillment, as Paul would readily acknowledge (1 Cor. 7:2–5).

Paul's description of love (vss. 4–7) has become classic. Although love is more than a **spiritual** gift, it is ranked alongside, but above, them. It is above **prophetic** powers, knowledge, and faith so as to remove mountains (vs. 2). That qualification of faith is interesting. One thinks of Jesus' description of a faith that could cast a mountain into the sea (Mark 11:22–23 parr.). Apparently, Paul means that kind of faith, not faith as the initial reception of the **gospel**, which is a usage more typical of him (cf. 1 Cor. 12:9, where Paul mentions faith just before gifts of healing and the working of **miracles**).

After his eloquent description of love (vss. 4-7) Paul again speaks of prophecy, this time in connection with tongues, that is, speaking in tongues (cf. 14:1–25). But first of all, love never ends (vs. 8). Prophecy and tongues, along with knowledge, are necessary gifts for this age, but not for eternity (vs. 9–10). Our knowledge and speech are provisional and partial. Paul has in view the end of present conditions of life, with the return of Jesus. He reflects upon the partiality, incompleteness, and inherent inadequacy of human knowledge and speech, even prophetic speech, using the analogy of childhood as compared with adulthood (vs. 11). Then Paul changes the imagery (vs. 12). The KJV translators put it memorably: "For now we see through a glass, darkly; but then face to face. . . ." Modern translations make clear that Paul is talking about seeing indistinct images in a mirror as opposed to seeing the real thing clearly. But in the end, human understanding will be like God's understanding of us. Paul is invoking **eschatology**, the end time, when human existence will be taken up into God (cf. 15:20–28). His faith embraces the future, but unlike some **apocalyptists** ancient and modern, Paul is fully aware that he lacks knowledge of that future because he has not yet attained it. Indeed, no one has.

When Paul concludes that faith, hope, and love abide, he means that they endure until the age to come. This trinity is fundamental for Paul (cf. 1 Thess. 1:3–5; 5:8; also Gal 5:5–6). Yet love is the greatest because both faith and hope look to a future fulfillment or terminus, when God has become all in all (1 Cor. 15:28). Presumably only love would then remain. What Paul does not say is made explicit by the author of 1 John: God is love (1 John 4:8, 16).

Prophecy and Speaking in Tongues (14:1–40)

In what way does the contrast between prophecy and speaking in tongues sum up the Corinthians' problem?

Paul remains with the question of spiritual gifts, which he began to address in 12:1, presumably in response to questions raised by the Corinthians in their letter (7:1). Immediately he makes clear that two such gifts are the focus of discussion: speaking in tongues and **prophecy** (vss. 1, 2).

Christianity in its beginnings was in large part, or in many places, a charismatic movement. (Note that in 12:4, as well as 1:7, Paul uses the term **charisma**, gift of grace, which comes over into English unchanged, as a synonym with *pneumatikon* for "spiritual gifts.") Worship took place under the aegis and inspiration of the **Spirit** of God. Paul tells the Thessalonian church not to quench the Spirit, but to test everything (2 Thess. 5:19–21). Both speaking in tongues and prophecy are equally spiritual gifts. Paul can count on the Corinthians, and presumably other Christians, to acknowledge this.

Speaking in tongues has accompanied the rise of the modern charismatic movement in North America and continues to be a feature of Catholic as well as Pentecostal worship in the Third World. Prophecy is, according to Paul's own statements, speech intelligible to everyone (14:3). As such, it builds up the **church**. One could translate "edifies" (RSV), which originally meant to build up (cf. English "edifice"), but that term has come to suggest "instruct" in English. Paul is talking not so much about instructing as about building up. The Greek term (*oikodomeō*) means to build in the sense of building a house, but it also can shade over into "instruct." Paul's point throughout this section is that what goes on in church should build up the whole church and not just individuals (14:2–4). He has already spoken of building the church, which he likens to God's temple (3:10–17). The building up of the church, which is its strengthening, involves what is intelligible to the mind. Therefore, prophecy is, on the whole, more valuable than speaking in tongues (14:4–5, 18–19), although Paul himself speaks in tongues (14:18).

Several paragraphs (in the NRSV) are then devoted to explain why prophecy is superior to speaking in tongues for the building up of the church congregation (vss. 6–25). Most of this, now as then, looks like plain common sense. Why go to this much trouble? In fact, for those who deal with **glossolalia** (Greek for speaking in tongues), Paul's advice and reasoning are still quite useful. Glossolalia has the same potential for dividing congregations now as it had then.

Paul's remarks in 1 Corinthians 14 assume that what is being practiced is speech in an unfamiliar or unknown tongue, which requires translation (cf. Acts 2, which describes a miracle of audition in which persons from different countries understand one another's foreign speech). Everything makes sense except Paul's use of Isaiah

(28:11–12) in vs. 21. In fact, if vss. 21–22 are simply omitted, everything makes sense to the reader, because what Paul says in vss. 23–25 is in agreement with his whole argument. Yet it seems to be contradicted by vss. 21–22! Tongues may be a sign for unbelievers, but only in the sense that they will be put off (as in vs. 23). While prophecy may be for believers rather than unbelievers, Paul goes on to say how it may work effectively for unbelievers as well (vs. 25). Something seems to have gone wrong here, whether in Paul's mind, in his dictation to his secretary, or in its recording. In the conclusion (16:21) Paul inadvertently reveals that the letter has been dictated, as was his custom (cf. Rom. 12:22; Gal. 6:11). Were some few difficulties in interpretation actually caused by lack of careful proof-reading? How could this happen in holy scripture? Yet Paul's letters were not regarded as scripture for years to come (cf. 2 Pet 2:15–16).

Paul's next statement (vss. 26–33) continues to make perfectly good sense and also gives some further indication of the character of early Christian worship. It was sometimes, but apparently not always, centered on a meal (1 Cor. 11:12–34). Probably only later the taking of the bread and the cup were separated out and called the **Eucharist**, from the Greek word meaning "thanksgiving" (cf. *The Didache* 9:1–5, as well as 6:1–2). Here Paul speaks of a hymn (or psalm, *psalmos*; the other word for hymn is *hymnos*), a lesson (or teaching; Greek *didachē*), a revelation, a tongue, or an interpretation (presumably of the tongue). Evidently, worship was spontaneous and unscripted. That was all right with Paul, but it must be in good order (vs. 32). The fact that here Paul contrasts disorder with peace rather than order suggests that sometimes things may have gotten chaotic. Paul's final admonition ("decently and in order") has remained the same in English translations from KJV to NRSV. Paul recognizes the role of the Spirit but is confident that anyone who has the authority of the Spirit will agree with him (vs. 37). Finally, he permits speaking in tongues, but encourages prophecy (vs. 39).

In reading, one could move from 14:33a to 14:37 quite easily if vss. 33b–36 were absent. Prophets (vss. 32, 37) and spirits or spiritual powers (again in vss. 33 and 37) figure in both in such a way that the connection seems good. Moreover, the subject matter of the intervening verses changes in a way that is scarcely Pauline. Women are to be silent and subordinate in church! What is said here corresponds well with the restrictions put on women in 1 Timothy 2:8–15, but that letter was probably not written by Paul himself (see Chapter 11, pp. 388–394). As for Paul, he anticipates that women will not only pray but also prophesy publicly in church (1 Cor. 11:5, 13). Moreover, Paul knows women who are active in leadership roles in churches (16:19; Rom. 16:1, 6). While there seem to be no **manuscripts** of 1 Corinthians that lack 14:33b–36, it is nevertheless unlikely that Paul himself said this, because it does not square with his belief and practice. The fact that it agrees with the Pauline **Pastorals** actually arouses suspicion about it.

The lintel over this doorway, preserved in a museum in ancient Corinth, reads "Synagogue of the Hebrews" (cf. Acts 19:8–10). *(Courtesy of Robert Spivey.)*

We saw evidence earlier of what may go awry in the dictating of a letter (14:21–22). Now we may have evidence of what can happen in the editing of documents after they have been written. There is a problem in understanding how 2 Corinthians chapters 1–7 and 10–13 could have fit together originally. Also 2 Corinthians 6:11–7:1 seems to be out of place. It is possible they were originally parts of different letters. Nevertheless, the content of all three of those segments squares with what we otherwise know of Paul. Just at that point, however, 1 Corinthians 14:33b–36 presents problems.

We do not get Paul's letters directly from his hands. Indeed, he did not *write* them. He *spoke* them, and they were transcribed by someone else (cf. Rom. 16:22). Probably

Paul wrote only 1 Corinthians 16:21–24 with his own hand, the body of the letter having been written by the secretary. It is a reasonable assumption that Paul read what the secretary wrote before appending this conclusion; accordingly, we can be confident that, by and large, 1 Corinthians represents what Paul said as he composed the letter. It is unlikely, however, that Paul could have exercised such control over his letters' editing and publication; presumably, that happened after his ministry and death. The historical Paul was shaped into the canonical Paul, in part by the very arrangement of the letters in the New Testament. Romans—which Paul certainly wrote, though late in his career—comes first. Toward the end of the **canon** come the Pastoral letters (1 and 2 Timothy and Titus), where we see a somewhat more conservative Paul, portrayed as bringing his ministry to a close and, indeed, facing death (2 Tim. 4:6–8).

The Resurrection from the Dead (15:1–58)

What do those who say there is no resurrection believe? Is a spiritual body a contradiction in terms?

Up to this point Paul has been discussing practical, liturgical, and moral issues—often with **theological** overtones. Now he engages a theological issue, or set of issues, fundamental to distinctly Christian belief. What is at issue is the **resurrection** of the body from the dead. Some Corinthians seem to be denying or questioning this doctrine (vs. 12). But exactly what are they rejecting or disputing?

Paul does not say how he knows this. Probably he has been informed. He does not begin by saying, "Now concerning the resurrection from the dead." He introduces the subject by going back to the beginning and basis of his preaching to the Corinthians Christians (15:1–3), what he has proclaimed and they received. This is **saving** knowledge if they will hold to it (vs. 2). It concerns what Paul believes are historical facts.

Paul cites the tradition that he has delivered to them and they have received. What we now read is not a transcript of Paul's sermons, but a recital of its basic elements. Paul once sought the approval of the "pillars" of the Jerusalem Church for the gospel he proclaimed among the **Gentiles** (Gal. 2:2). Apparently this is it. These pillars, James (the brother of Jesus), Cephas (Peter), and John (presumably one of the two Sons of Zebedee) approved Paul's preaching.

The elements of this preaching can be succinctly stated (1 Cor. 15: 3–4): **Christ** died for our **sins**; he was buried; he was raised on the third day in accordance with the scriptures. Here or elsewhere, Paul never mentions the discovery of an empty tomb, recounted in all the **Gospels**. Yet the reference to the third day presumes a discrete event in which the one left in the tomb was raised. He was raised (passive voice); God raised him.

Then Paul names a series of appearances of the one who was raised, beginning with Cephas (Peter) and ending with himself, Paul (vss. 5–8). This is the oldest extant account of resurrection appearances, and it differs strikingly from the Gospel stories. Basically, it is just a list. The only item in the list that matches the Gospels' narratives is the appearance to the twelve, which corresponds generally to Matthew 28:16–20, Luke 24:33–49, or John 20:19–23, 26–29. These accounts, however, differ among themselves. A resurrection appearance to Simon (Peter) is reported secondhand in Luke 24:34, and Peter is among a group of seven who see the risen Jesus according to John 21. Of the appearances to more than five hundred, to James, to all the **apostles** (apparently more than the twelve), and finally to Paul, we learn nothing from any other New Testament source. As we have seen, Paul insists on this appearance to him as a mark of his apostleship (1 Cor. 9:1; 15:8–9; Gal 1:12).

Since the Gospel accounts differ so much among themselves, their differences from Paul should not surprise us greatly. The disciples were scattered at Jesus' death (John 16:32; cf. Mark 14:50), with no apparent expectation of seeing him again. That the appearances of Jesus to them after his death took them by surprise authenticates these experiences as real for the disciples, whatever their cause or origin.

In 15:12, Paul states what some in Corinth are saying about the resurrection of the dead: "How are some of you saying there is no resurrection of the dead?" It is possible that no one is denying the resurrection of Jesus per se, but that some do not understand this within the broader context of a Jewish and early Christian view of history and **eschatology**, in which the **righteous** dead or the dead generally will rise (Dan. 12:1–3; Isa. 26:19). Along with other early believers in Christ, Paul shared this view (1 Thess. 4:13–18; cf. John 5:28–29; 6:54). Yet the way the resurrection hope is stated varies from document to document, and even within documents, such as the Gospel of John. There is no way we can be sure what these Corinthians whom Paul opposes actually thought, but Paul viewed their position as at least contradicting faith in the resurrection of Jesus Christ. Yet for Paul the resurrection of Jesus and the resurrection of believers are bound together (vs. 13). To this extent Paul shares in **apocalyptic** thought, although he avoids the kind of speculative imagining of the future as is found, for example, in the Revelation to John.

Paul's statement in vs. 13 is revealing. As one infers from the resurrection of Christ the resurrection of the dead, or at least dead believers, so one infers from the denial of the general resurrection a denial of the resurrection of Christ. So to deny resurrection generally is to deny the resurrection of Christ (vss. 15–16), as well as the forgiveness of sins brought by his death (vs. 17).

Paul, however, affirms as a given the resurrection of Christ (vs. 20). Belief that it happened is basic to Paul's theology. On the basis of Christ's resurrection the resurrection of believers is conceivable. On the basis of the disciple's future resurrection the resurrection of Christ is intelligible. Paul insists on holding the two together. As a **Pharisee**, Paul would have already believed in the resurrection of the dead generally (cf. Phil. 3:5; cf. Acts 23:6 and 26:4–8). The particular belief in Christ's resurrection began with his own conversion experience, which he understood as a manifestation of the risen Christ. Indeed, Paul was converted by that experience into believing the truth of Jesus' followers' claims about God's raising him from the dead.

In Christ, who reversed the deadly effect of Adam's sin, the possibility of life has been restored to humankind (vss. 20–23). Then Paul sketches what follows. Following the resurrection of Christ is that of those who belong to him (vs. 23); then the rest of eschatological history, which Paul still awaits, unfolds (vss. 24–28). For Paul all parts of this eschatological drama hang together. To deny any of it is to deny it all, and specifically to deny the resurrection of Jesus Christ, on which everything hinges (vss. 29–34).

Paul then entertains a crucial question (vs. 35) and immediately seems to dismiss the questioner (vs. 36). But then he continues for about three paragraphs (in our modern NRSV) explaining how the dead are raised and what their bodies are like (vss. 35–57). Here we may find a clue to the doubts of some of the Corinthians. What they may have objected to is the claim imputed to Paul and others that flesh and blood will inherit the **kingdom of God** (vs. 50). Paul no more believes that than they do, but in rejecting such a view he has introduced the concept of a spiritual body (vs. 44). The image of the man of heaven, which God gives, is different from that of the man of dust (vs. 49). Paul concludes, characteristically, with quotations of scripture (Isa. 25:8; Hos. 13:14). Paul, of course, now knows more about the meaning of scripture than did its authors, for the meaning of scripture is seen in the light of Christ. Death is truly death because of sin, which is put into play by the **law** (vs. 56). (The interplay of the law and sin is later described by Paul in Romans 7:7–12).

In the background of Paul's argument, perhaps indeed in the foreground, is what is called federal theology. The United States government is called federal, because in it the several states are bound together. The American Civil War was a violent test of that federal union. The analogy is not exact, but the violent death of Jesus Christ was a violent test of the unity of humankind, from which, in Paul's view, we emerged united in Christ, the heavenly man, as we had been united in Adam, the man of dust. There is, in Paul's theology, no room for the individual existing in and for himself. Thus the resurrection of Christ can scarcely be believed in as something that happened to one individual human being. To make sense it must be embraced in its federal, corporate reality.

Does all that Paul says about the nature of the resurrection body—that it is a "spiritual body" rather than a "physical body"—also apply to the Risen Christ? Did Jesus die a physical body (*sōma psychikon*) to be raised a spiritual body (*sōma pneumatikon*)? Yes. Otherwise, Paul's logic breaks down. But it is a body nevertheless. No body, no individual. Thus Paul speaks of a bodily resurrection, which is different from a resurrection of the flesh or a physical resurrection. Rather than say a person has a body, Paul would prefer to say that a person *is* a body.

T H E C O L L E C T I O N A N D O T H E R B U S I N E S S
(1 6 : 1 – 2 4)

Why is the collection of special importance to Paul?

Paul has now finished dealing with issues, but not with business. The collection for the saints (16:1–4) is for the Jerusalem **church** (cf. vs. 3), which Paul had promised to carry out while visiting James (the brother of Jesus), Cephas (Peter) and John (another of Jesus' twelve **apostles**) in Jerusalem (Gal. 2:1–11). In Galatians, they are called the poor; here, the saints. Paul also mentions this collection in 2 Corinthians (8:5; 9:1), where he again speaks of the saints, meaning the Jerusalem church. All believers are saints, that is, holy to the Lord (1 Cor. 1:2), but the Jerusalem church has a certain precedence in time and space. Jerusalem is still the **holy** city of Israel. (Although Paul now reinterprets his Jewish tradition in light of God's having sent his **Messiah**, he still thinks of himself as a Jew.) The collection expresses the unity of the Gentile Christians with Israel, the root of the vine (cf. Rom 11:16). As Paul writes his letter to the Romans, he is on his way to Jerusalem to deliver this collection (Rom. 15:25–27).

Interestingly, Paul mentions the Corinthians' coming together on the first day of the week (vs. 2). This is Sunday, probably the day when the Christians met for worship, because Jesus had been raised from the dead on the first day of the week (Mark 16:2; cf. 1 Cor. 15:4). Gradually Sunday replaced the Jewish Sabbath as the Christians' holy day.

Paul next lays out his personal travel plans (vss. 5–9). He intends to visit Corinth again, but will stay a while longer in Ephesus, from which this letter was obviously written (vs. 8; cf. Acts 19:1–20:1). Paul then speaks of Timothy and Apollos, (16:10–11, 12). Both are mentioned in Acts as having been present in Ephesus (19:2 and 18:24–28). Clearly Apollos has played an important role in Corinth (1 Cor. 1:12; 3:5–6, 22; 4:56; cf. Acts 18:27–28). Paul has sent Timothy to Corinth (1 Cor. 4:17), and he now commends him.

Stephanas, mentioned earlier (1:16), is the head of a Corinthian household, whose members Paul baptized. Probably Paul baptized Stephanas first (cf. vs. 15). But now he and two others have come from Corinth to Ephesus (vs. 17), and presumably they will return to Corinth. Paul commends them warmly (vss. 16, 18).

Asia (vs. 19) is the province of which Ephesus is the capitol. Paul speaks of more than one church there, but especially the church that meets in the house of the married couple Aquila and Prisca (cf. Rom. 16:4; Acts 18:26). Churches in this earliest period met in the houses of more affluent members, because there were no church buildings as such. The holy kiss (vs. 20) is mentioned more than once in Paul's letters (Rom. 16:16; 1 Thess. 5:26), and elsewhere as well (1 Pet. 5:14).

Paul takes pen in hand (vs. 21) to write the conclusion himself (cf. Gal. 6:11). This practice authenticated the letter in question (as in 2 Thess. 3:17). Paul's concluding statements are not exactly routine, but are more or less boilerplate. He is not calling down a curse on anyone specifically (vs. 22). He and other Christians look forward to the return of Jesus (cf. 1 Thess 4:13–18; even Rom. 13:11–12). Paul's use of the **Aramaic** *Maranatha* ("Our Lord, come"), which English translations often indicate only in a note, may have been an early slogan, emanating from the original Palestinian, Aramaic-speaking church. (Similarly, Revelation 22:7, 12, 17–20 looks to the imminent return of Jesus, but does not use the Aramaic as Paul does.) A brief benediction (cf. the more familiar one in 2 Cor. 13:13) and Paul's reiteration of his love for the Corinthians end the letter (vss. 23, 24).

CONCLUSION

In 1 Corinthians, Paul addresses many matters that have arisen from the *historical situation* of the Corinthians and their **church**. Identifying those problems enable us to define that situation and to understand Paul's **epistle**. The contrast with Galatians—which seems focused on the question of circumcision and the law—is striking. From 1 Corinthians a raft of problems emerges; gradually we perceive coherence in the Corinthian situation and in Paul's basis for addressing it.

In Corinth, Paul encounters divisions among factions loyal to different leaders (1:10–17), gross immorality (5:1-2; 6:12–20), litigation among Christians (6:1–11), destructive pride in spiritual knowledge (chaps. 8. 12–14), and disorder in worship (chap. 11). All these seem to be manifestations of a more fundamental problem with a common root: a religious individualism that undermines love for one's fellow believers and confuses freedom with license.

In response, Paul unfolds a fundamental *emphasis* of his **theology**: the meaning of the cross of **Christ**, the foolishness of God that negates all human wisdom (1:18–2:6). The death of Jesus, his cross, negates all human pride, whether in knowledge or in spiritual gifts. In chapter 15, Paul takes up the complement of that conviction: Christ's **resurrection**, whose reality or significance Paul has reason to believe the Corinthians doubt. To speak of the resurrection as an emphasis is an understatement: it is a presupposition, a *sine qua non*, of Christian belief and practice. Such faith must find expression in practice. In the cross of Christ, faith and practice find their norm: God's own self-giving love (chapter 13). The believer is empowered by the **Spirit**, which binds the community together as the body of Christ (chapter 12). The Corinthians' theology leads in practice to division, while Paul's leads in practice to unity. Certainly that is Paul's point and goal.

The letter's *structure* seems to follow a recital of problems of which Paul has heard, perhaps from Chloe's people (1:11) and in a letter the Corinthians sent to him (7:1). While there is truth in this, it cannot be sheer coincidence that Paul begins with the cross of Christ and ends with Christ's resurrection. Moreover, as the letter reaches its culmination,

Paul moves from particular concerns to more general ones: the character of Christian worship and spiritual gifts (chaps. 11, 14), which brackets his depiction of the church as the body of Christ, governed by mutual love (chaps 12–13). In all cases, the stronger or more powerful in the church should have regard for the weaker and less influential, and not demean them (8:7-13; 11:20–22; 12:14–16).

Distinguishing **redaction** from *tradition* does not loom large in the interpretation of 1 Corinthians. Paul wrote the letter. Yet significant traditional elements do emerge. That Christ died for our **sins** is a given for Paul; it is received by him as tradition (15:3). The same may be said of the list of those to whom the risen Christ appeared (15:4-7), except that Paul believes the risen Christ appeared also to him. The church's unity is, or should be, grounded in liturgy and worship. The words of institution of the **Lord's Supper** (11:23–26) speak of the bread, or loaf (Greek *artos*), as Christ's body. The unity of Christ's body is manifested in the one loaf of the **Eucharist** (10:16-17).

The unity of the body of Christ, given through the Spirit, not the **law**, is the basis of conduct in the Corinthian church (6:12–20). It is this **gospel**, preached and practiced by Paul, which offers organizing coherence for the Corinthians' diversity (14:40). Faced with a wide array of practical and theological problems, Paul is forced to reason out with and for that church what life together as the body of Christ must mean. We see him thinking theologically about practical situations in 1 Corinthians as in no other letter. At the same time we catch from 1 Corinthians, more than from any letter of Paul, or of the New Testament generally, a glimpse of what life in the earliest churches must have been like.

SUGGESTIONS FOR FURTHER READING

1 CORINTHIANS

R. B. Hays, *First Corinthians* (Louisville: John Knox, 1997), is a very useful **commentary**. Another standard, somewhat more technical, treatment is G. D. Fee, *The First Epistle to the Corinthians* (Grand Rapids: Eerdmans, 1987). C. K. Barrett, *A Commentary on the First Epistle to the Corinthians* (New York: Harper & Row, 1968), still wears remarkably well. Other, more recent treatments include R. A. Horsley, *1 Corinthians* (Nashville: Abingdon, 1998), and J. P. Sampley, "The First Letter to the Corinthians: Introduction, Commentary, and Reflections," *NIB* 10 (2002): 771–1003.

J. Murphy-O'Connor, *St. Paul's Corinth: Texts and Archaeology* (Wilmington, DE: Michael Glazier, 1983), is a valuable collection and interpretation of **ancient evidence** bearing on the Corinthian correspondence. **Sociological perspectives** are employed by G. Theissen, *The Social Setting of Pauline Christianity: Essays on Corinth*, trans. J. H. Schütz (Philadelphia: Fortress, 1982). M. M. Mitchell, *Paul and the Rhetoric of Reconciliation: An Exegetical Examination of the Language and Composition of 1 Corinthians* (Louisville: Westminster John Knox, 1993), argues on **rhetorical-critical** grounds that the letter is a cohesive, deliberative argument designed to combat factionalism in the church of Corinth. By contrast, J. C. Hurd, *The Origins of I Corinthians*, 2nd ed. (Macon, GA: Mercer University Press, 1983), contends that the Corinthian controversies were largely the result of Paul's own changing position.

PAULINE THEOLOGY

C. K. Barrett, *Essays on Paul* (Philadelphia: Westminster, 1982), assembles seminal work on such topics as "Christianity at Corinth," "Cephas and Corinth," and "Things Sacrificed to Idols." More recently, there is the provocative collection edited by D. M. Hay, *Pauline Theology, Volume II: 1 & 2 Corinthians* (Minneapolis: Fortress, 1993). The central motif of Pauline theology is illumined by both C. B. Cousar, *A Theology of the Cross: The Death of Jesus in the Pauline Letters* (Minneapolis: Fortress, 1990), and A. R. Brown, *The Cross and Human Transformation: Paul's Apocalyptic World in 1 Corinthians* (Minneapolis: Fortress, 1995). G. D. Fee, *God's Empowering Presence: The Holy Spirit in the Letters of Paul* (Peabody, MA: Hendrickson, 1994), is a rich study; and V. P. Furnish, *The Theology of the First Letter to the Corinthians* (Cambridge: Cambridge University Press, 1999), an admirable summary and analysis. Furnish's *Theology and Ethics in Paul* (Nashville: Abingdon, 1968), is a classic investigation; his *The Moral Teaching of Paul: Selected Issues*, rev. ed. (Nashville: Abingdon, 1985), draws heavily from 1 Corinthians.

The Suggestions for Further Reading at the end of Chapter 10 include additional works on Paul's theology.

The Apostle Paul, by Rembrandt van Rijn ([and Workshop?] 1606–1609). *(Courtesy of © 2006 Board of Trustees, National Gallery of Art, Washington, D.C. Widener Collection, 1942.)*

ROMANS: THE RIGHTEOUSNESS OF GOD

Background of Romans

Paul's **Epistle** to the Romans was probably written during, or shortly after, his last visit to Corinth, following resolution of the problems of the Galatian and Corinthian **churches** and completion of the collection for Jerusalem (cf. Rom. 15:17–29; 2 Cor. 1:16; chapters 8 and 9; Acts 20:2 f.). Paul was heading for Jerusalem when he wrote this letter (Rom. 15:25, 28, 30 ff.). Romans was thus written in the mid- to late fifties of the first century, probably in A.D. 56. Paul regarded his work in the eastern part of the Mediterranean world as complete and was looking forward to a subsequent journey to Spain, but his plans would be foreclosed by his arrest and imprisonment (cf. Rom. 15:23–29 and Acts 20:25, 38). Romans is addressed, not to a church lying within what had theretofore been Paul's missionary orbit, but rather to an already established church that Paul expected to visit. Paul wished to present himself and his **gospel** to Christians at Rome. He also hoped to use Rome as a center for his future missionary endeavors in Europe. Thus he sought the approval of the Roman church (15:24). Romans is the fullest presentation of Paul's **theological** views that we possess.

Galatians, especially its account of Paul's earlier dispute with Peter (Gal. 2:11–21), indicates that the seeds of Romans had already been planted in Paul's thought long before. Yet Paul was likely driven by experiences with his churches in Galatia and Corinth to formulate more carefully his understanding of the gospel. The basic theological themes set forth in Galatians receive more extensive and considered treatment in Romans, whereas some of the themes as well as the practical counsel of the Corinthian correspondence also appear here (e.g., the body of **Christ** in Rom. 12:3–8; love in 12:9 ff., 13:8 ff.; conscience and the weaker brother in chap. 14). Romans conveys Paul's relatively later and more considered reflection, written at a time when the fires of controversy had been dampened.

345

OUTLINE OF ROMANS

INTRODUCTION:
RIGHTEOUSNESS BY FAITH (1:1–17)

How does Paul use the introduction of Romans to introduce his message?

Romans opens with a long, formal salutation (1:1–7), containing a confessional statement (vss. 2–4) as well as Paul's description of his **apostolic** office. Non-Pauline elements such as reference to Jesus' Davidic sonship and the term "**Spirit** of **holiness**" suggest that this confessional statement may represent an earlier tradition. On the other hand, the equally rare phrase "obedience of faith" (vs. 5) sets out an important emphasis of Romans. By that phrase, Paul means the obedience to, or acknowledgment of, God accomplished through faith.

The customary thanksgiving (vss. 8–15) builds toward the statement of the letter's primary theme (vss. 16–17). Paul praises the Romans' faith and offers elaborate assurances of his own prayers for them. Although such expressions were conventional in **Hellenistic** correspondence of the time, Paul is not engaging in mere pleasantries, as shown by the specific content of his prayers (vs. 10) and by the appropriateness of his praise for the Roman Christians.

The full meaning and import of the thematic statement (vss. 16 ff.) can be seen only in the light of the entire letter. Yet several points stand out. Paul's interpretation of the Christian **gospel** is here sumarized in a kind of **theological** shorthand: "the power of God for **salvation**" (vs. 16). The gospel is God's grace, something freely given rather than earned. The pairing of Jew and Greek is a further extension of the same line of thought. God grants salvation impartially, without regard for merit or ethnic origin, without regard even for special religious distinction. It is bestowed universally. Although *Jew* means for Paul "an Israelite according to the flesh," *Greek* is virtually a synonym for **Gentile**. The substance of Paul's gospel is then spelled out more fully (vs. 17). It is the revelation of God's **righteousness** (Greek: *dikaiosynē*). By this Paul could mean a doctrine about God, that he is righteous rather than unrighteous, which Paul would have by no means denied. But for Paul the term *righteousness of God* has a specific, dynamic meaning (cf. Rom. 3:26). It primarily refers to how God acts in human history.

The gospel displays and interprets God's righteousness, and it is this theme that Paul develops in Romans. God's righteousness is made known to, and appropriated by, faith. Faith has now become a universal possibility. As we have already seen in Galatians, emphasis on the importance and indispensability of faith is characteristic of Paul. Romans will further develop and refine the theme of the righteousness of faith.

GOD'S WRATH: THE PROBLEM OF SIN (1:18–3:20)

How does homosexuality, in Paul's view, typify the sinful human condition?

Paul speaks of the **revelation** of God's **righteousness** in 1:17; in 1:18 he turns to the revelation of God's wrath. Both terms, *righteousness* and *wrath*, are **eschatological**. That is, they refer to **apocalyptic** manifestations expected in the last days of this world as signs that God is bringing human history to a climactic, perhaps catastrophic conclusion. Paul places God's righteousness and his wrath over against each another as if he believed that their presence already marked the final turning point of world history. Indeed, Paul can refer to Christians as those upon whom the end of the ages has come (1 Cor. 10:11) and can advise against marriage or other too close attachments to this world on the grounds that it is passing away (1 Cor. 7:31).

Although the primary tension in 1:17 ff. is between God's righteousness and his wrath, Paul introduces a secondary tension between God's righteousness and the wickedness of humanity. Paul plays upon the *dikaiosynē* ("righteousness") of God and the *adikia* ("wickedness") of humanity. With the setting up of these tensions or polarities, the problem of Romans is posed, and the fundamental **theological** questions are raised. What is the relation between God's wrath and his righteousness? Moreover, how is it possible for humanity, characterized by *adikia*—lack of righteousnes—to stand before a **holy** God, whose very essence is righteousness?

Paul does not yet deal fully with these questions. He first characterizes humankind as the object and occasion of God's wrath (Rom. 1:18–3:20). At the outset (vs. 18) he makes clear that the characterization will not be favorable, even though he does not yet indicate the extent of wickedness. Paul speaks of a present outpouring of God's wrath, parallel with the revelation of his righteousness just mentioned. Actually, he describes the condition of humankind from the standpoint of the revelation of God's righteousness and wrath in and through the gospel. He does not present the human condition from the perspective of the neutral and strictly objective onlooker. Thus Paul could scarcely have expected everyone to subscribe to his description. The wrath of God against human wickedness accompanies the revelation of his righteousness, and only against the background of this norm—the righteousness of God as revealed in Jesus Christ—does human wickedness stand out in bold relief.

This wickedness is first said to be suppression of the truth (vs. 18): failure to acknowledge the Creator implicit in the creation (vss. 19–20). It is not as if the world had no access to knowledge of God. Precisely the opposite is the case. Thus Paul can say, "They are without excuse" (vs. 20). Not only do people generally have the possibility of knowing God but fail to exercise it; Paul goes so far as to attribute to them an actual knowledge of God (vs. 21). What they lack, however, is proper *acknowledgment:* "They did not honor him as God or give thanks to him." Instead they became senseless and practiced disobedience—namely, idolatry (vss. 22 ff.)—with the resulting defilement or dishonoring of their bodies (vs. 24). The grounds for this existing state of affairs lie in the fact that human values and loyalties have become perverted, even inverted, since they "exchanged the truth about God for a lie and worshiped and served the creature rather than the Creator" (vs. 25). This inversion of the "natural order"—worship of the Creator—concludes the first stage in Paul's analysis of the human situation.

Dionysius, the Greek god of wine. Paul condemns the worship of such pagan gods in Romans 1:18–25. *(Courtesy of the British Museum.)*

Three important points now emerge. First, Paul speaks of wickedness, or unrighteousness, without yet saying it is universal. Paul leaves open the option of extending the condemnation of human wickedness to include all people but does not yet explicitly do so. Second, although Paul speaks initially of the present revelation of God's wrath (vs. 18), he switches to the past tense in describing the course of **sin** in the human race. He thereby indicates that the present situation, against which God's wrath is directed, did not come about in a day but has a long and significant past. Third, Paul asserts that God gives people up to their lusts, an idea that occurs first in verse 24 and recurs in verses 26 and 28. He does not mean that God is the cause of sin. Rather, God allows people to fall prey to the overt sinning already implicit in their misdirected loyalty and worship.

Paul and Homosexuality

Paul's singling out of homosexuality as typical of the inversion of the natural order is not accidental. The Bible condemns homosexuality in the strictest terms (cf. Lev. 18:22; 20:13), which in itself indicates it was not unheard of in Old Testament times (Gen. 19:4–8; Judg. 19:22–26). Apparently, this practice was fairly prevalent in the Greco-Roman world, as, for example, Plato's *Symposium* implies. Paul does not speak simply as a pious Jew, enraged at what he regards as a most heinous violation of law and nature. Paul has already argued that people's lack of **righteousness** results from their lack of a proper acknowledgement of God—a failing that bears its expected fruit in idolatry. For him idolatry, a worshiping and serving of the creature rather than the Creator (vs. 25), is literally a perversion or, as we have suggested, a glaring manifestation of the inversion of the order of things that God created. The result of this reversal of the created order is the disordering and confusion of human life in general. Homosexual practices also appear to reverse the order in which sexual relations were intended. Thus in antiquity, as today, "unnaturalness" is the basis for the popular condemnation of homosexuality. So not just a puritanical disposition but Paul's understanding of wickedness and idolatry as inversion of a God-given order suggests to him homosexuality as the most characteristic manifestation of human sinfulness. **Sin** is not merely the breaking of commandments or laws, although it certainly involves that. Rather, sin is a complete disorientation of life such that human existence and behavior become altogether divorced and estranged from the ground of their being, the God who creates and orders all things. Yet it cannot be emphasized too strongly that Paul does *not* cite homosexuality specifically because it is the worst of sins, but because in his view it best exemplifies the nature of sin.

Such disorientation does not stop with sexual aberrations but extends to all life. "Things that should not be done" (vs. 28) translates a Stoic expression (*ta mē kathēkonta*) meaning things out of accord with humanity's proper nature. Human perversity in refusing to acknowledge God is thus manifest in homosexuality and no less strikingly in the general disordering of life: most especially of human relationships, the subject of the catalog of vices (vss. 29–31). Paul describes people turned toward one another in animosity and suspicion rather than love. This unnatural way of relating to others violates the intended order of creation.

Paul has not yet expressly extended his condemnations to include all of humanity. From the prominence given to homosexuality and the subsequent catalog of vices, the Jewish reader would be justified in suspecting that Paul has in mind the **Gentile** and is making an exception of the Jew. After all, Paul was not above referring disparagingly to "Gentile sinners" (Gal. 2:15), as if those terms were practically synonymous. Probably Paul does have in mind here the sinful conduct of the Gentile. For the Jewish or Jewish-Christian reader, what he says might seem quite convincing. In fact, in the **apocryphal** book the Wisdom of Solomon, one can find ideas akin to those that Paul sets forth here. Its author, in agreement with Paul, seems to assume that knowledge of God should be attainable from creation, although people by and large do not attain it (Wisdom 13:6–9). He renders a similar assessment of the relation between idolatry and immorality (Wisdom 14:12) and presents a catalog of specific sins (Wisdom 14:22 ff.) not unlike that of Romans 1:29 ff. (cf. also 13:13; 1 Cor. 5:10 ff.; 6:9 ff.; 2 Cor. 12:20 ff.; Gal. 5:19 ff.). So far in Romans there is little to make the Jewish reader uneasy, for Paul has written an eloquent condemnation of Gentile sin.

That Paul intends something more, however, is already clear from the first few verses of chapter 2 (vss. 1–4). As Paul has the Gentile in the back of his mind in 1:18–32, so he seems here to be thinking of the Jew. That Paul would apply his harsh words to any presumptuous and self-righteous human being need scarcely be said—but that he specifically intends them for the Jew as well as the Greek soon becomes apparent (2:6 ff.). The idea that God shows no partiality (2:11) means that the Jew is brought

A mural on the wall of an ancient Pompeiian house, located near Rome. Alongside it are much less modest portrayals of sexual indulgence. Such art represents a climate against which Paul vigorously inveighed (cf. Romans 1:26–27; 1 Corinthians 6:9–10, 12–20).

under judgment on the same basis as the Greek (i.e., Gentile), as Paul in fact makes quite explicit (vss. 9–10). This naming of the Jew alongside the Gentile probably indicates that the Jew has been in mind from the beginning of chapter 2 in Romans.

What Paul has already stated (vss. 9–11) he now develops by setting forth the basis for God's impartial judgment of Jew and Gentile (vss. 12–16). Interestingly, the **law**— and Paul means here scriptural, Jewish law—is accepted as the definitive expression of God's will, according to which he will judge all people on the last day (but cf. vs. 16). Mere possession of the law has, however, no particular value. Therefore, if any Gentile fulfills the law's requirements, even without knowing its concrete form (vss. 14–15), that obedience is perfectly acceptable. The idea that God's election of Israel constitutes a special privilege and advantage even if Jews do not respond appropriately is already rejected (vss. 12 ff.). In the two closing paragraphs (vss. 17–24 and 25–29) this point is driven home with the clear implication (esp. in vss. 17–24) that the Jews also stand condemned. Despite their advantage as the recipients and bearers of God's law, they do not in fact do what the law commands. Thus their desire to instruct or reprove others is sheer presumption. Really to be a Jew is to obey God. Such obedience is not a matter of outward show, but "a matter of the heart . . . spiritual and not literal" (vs. 29). This statement does not mean that obedience has no visible form or tangible expression. The true Judaism of which Paul speaks can be nothing less than obedience to God in the real world, not a specious and amorphous spirituality without concrete manifestations. Clearly, however, being a real Jew cannot be identified with belonging to an institution or nation, or with fleshly marks, such as circumcision. Significantly, however, "Jew" is still a positive term in Paul's vocabulary.

Paul's questions (3:1) are now well motivated. From what has so far been said, we might expect negative replies: the Jew has no advantage. In a sense such an assertion would be fitting, because the Jew has no advantage just because he is a Jew, and circumcision, the distinguishing mark of every Jewish male, has no merit in and of itself. Yet the Jewish possession of the scriptures (the "oracles of God," vs. 2) is in and of itself a considerable advantage. Paul mentions this benefit as the first of what was apparently intended to be a series of items. But he immediately becomes sidetracked and does not mention the remaining advantages in this context (graphic proof of the more or less occasional character of even Romans). For the moment (vss. 3–8) Paul is obviously concerned with matters about which he has probably been challenged or attacked. Thus we encounter a series of embarrassing questions (vss. 3, 5, 7) that Paul was neither the first nor the last to ponder. The unfaithfulness of the Jews constitutes a problem, because they do not now receive the promises vouchsafed to them (vs. 3): "Will their faithlessness nullify the faithfulness of God?" To resolve this problem by blaming Israel rather than God, so that God's righteousness is not impugned but rather established (vs. 4), raises the further problem of how God can justly condemn the transgressor when the wickedness really serves to vindicate God's righteousness (vs. 5). In other words, "if through my falsehood God's truthfulness abounds to his glory, why am I still being condemned as a sinner?" (vs. 7). Paul hardly answers these questions at this point. Indeed, he dismisses the questioner rather rudely (vs. 8). Yet, as we shall see, these questions are pivotal points in Paul's argument in Romans, and at length he returns to them in chapters 9–11.

The argument concerning the universality of sin, which Paul has been developing since the introductory part of the letter, is now concluded (3:9–20). Uncertainty about the meaning of the particular form of a Greek verb makes it unclear whether, in verse 9, Paul is asking whether the Jews are better or worse off than others. Whatever the question, however, Paul's basic contention is unaltered, as his positive statement shows (vs. 9): the Jews are actually no better off. To clinch his demonstration, Paul characteristically calls upon the scriptures (vss. 10–18). If there has been any doubt about what Paul is trying to prove, these verses dispel it. Scriptural quotations from many different sources have been skillfully woven together to describe the general state of humanity (vss. 10–12) and to specify the details of that condition (vss. 13–18). Next comes an interpretative clarification (vs. 19) that removes any uncertainty as to their applicability, for they apply not only to Gentiles but particularly to those under the law—that is, to Jews. Finally, Paul makes his own **theological** statement about what the law can and cannot do (vs. 20; see also 4:15; 5:20; 7:8, 10 ff.). Clearly this long section, extending from 1:18 to 3:20, is intended to demonstrate humanity's universal sinfulness as the backdrop for the proclamation of the **gospel** (cf. 3:23), which reveals God's **righteousness** and also his wrath (1:17–18).

At first glance it may appear that this lengthy prolegomenon is only a frightening diagnosis intended to induce the patient to accept the radical new cure. Yet Paul has already referred to the present, rather than the past, revelation of the wrath of God (1:18) precisely as proof that the revelation of God's righteousness is also taking place. For Paul, human sinfulness becomes fully apparent only now with the revelation of God's righteousness in Christ (see 3:26). Paul did not understand his own pre-Christian life as a period of disappointment over sinful humanity and disillusionment with his own sin (cf. Gal. 1:14 and Phil. 3:4–6). His darker view of the human predicament and his own past situation apparently arose only after his conversion. Thus Paul does not think the hearer of the Christian preaching could be convinced of the seriousness of his plight apart from the message that the **crucified** one was the **Christ**. By not recognizing in Jesus the **Messiah**, **God's Son**, but by crucifying him, the depth of the world's wickedness is revealed.

On the other hand, not everything in this section (Rom. 1:18–3:20) is the result of Paul's *ex post facto* thinking, in the light of God's **revelation** and on the basis of Christian faith. Paul's condemnation of Gentile sinfulness and his admission of the theoretical possibility of Gentile righteousness apart from the law are not unique to Paul, the **apostle** of Christ. Probably he could have said as much before his conversion. Jewish condemnation of Gentile sin was not uncommon in New Testament times; it appears in the New Testament itself (cf. Matt. 5:47; 6:7; Gal. 2:15). More unusual are Paul's inclusion of the Gentile *and the Jew* under the same standard of judgment, and his view that, when the Jew and Gentile are judged on the same basis before God, the Jew will have no particular advantage. Even that assertion might not have seemed so offensive to his religious kins-men had Paul not gone on to say that the Jew actually falls short of fulfillment of God's will and consequently stands condemned with the Gentile. In the light of the revelation of God's righteousness in the gospel of his Son, all are sinners. Paul's affirmative answer to the question about the advantage of the Jew (3:1) scarcely seems convincing in the light of his wholesale condemnation of Jew and Gentile.

Even if we grant that Paul's condemnation—as he understands it, God's condemnation—of human sinfulness is just, given his unique perspective, the origin of sin remains a mystery. Paul could have maintained that human nature in itself is evil. If so, what Paul calls wickedness, unrighteousness, or sin would be not a human possibility but a necessity. There would then be no such thing as meaningful human responsibility. Such a position with respect to some portion of humanity may have been possible for some of Paul's contemporaries, but this sort of determinism does not account for Paul's thought. On the one hand, the corruption of which he speaks extends to all humanity, not just a portion. On the other, Paul goes to great pains to maintain that humanity's plight is the result not of a corrupt nature but of concrete sinning. Thus the point of verse 1:19 is, as we have seen, the establishment of humankind's responsibility for the human condition. God's giving people over to certain forms of wickedness (1:24, 26, 28) does not mean that God causes them to be evil, but that he permits them to be. Therefore, Paul proclaims that humanity stands in a state of universal sinfulness because of actual sinning. That specific acts of sinning carried with them ominous consequences for future generations is implied by verses 1:24, 26, 28, where Paul doubtless has more than one generation in view. Is sin then some disease that has infected the human race at the outset, transmitted from one gen-eration to the next? If so, then every person would be born with an inclination toward sin. Perhaps Paul would have agreed that this is the case. But he does not set out that venerable conception of original sin, according to which a sinful nature is inherited by each generation from its predecessor. That is a later development in the history of Christian doctrine.

Still, Paul does not regard sin simply as personal wickedness or transgression resulting from the ill will of individuals. Although he indicates that individuals are responsible for their sin and do not sin inevitably or by nature, Paul is well aware of the suprapersonal character of evil among the human race. Specifically, he traces the origin of this evil or sin to Adam (Rom. 5:12–21; cf. 1 Cor. 15:45 ff.). Elsewhere, without ever mentioning Adam, he refers to creation's bondage to decay (8:21) or to the present evil age (Gal. 1:4). Also apart from Adam, Paul speaks of sin as an external power that enslaves humanity (chap. 6) and describes how it insidiously attacks through the **law** (chap. 7). Nevertheless, in view of his specific references to Adam, it is probable that Paul's understanding of sin's corporate character owes much to the strand of Jewish thought that laid responsibility for humanity's corruption at Adam's doorstep (esp. *4 Ezra* 3:20–21; 7:116–126; cf. Baruch 54:15–19).

Accordingly, Paul's conception of sin has two foci, which remain in paradoxical and unresolved tension with one another: people sin willingly, but inevitably. Paul never speaks of sin so as to relieve all of humanity, or the individual sinner, of responsibility for it. Yet he would by no means subscribe to a purely personal or individualist concept of sin. Like his predecessors among Israel's prophets, Paul was fully aware of both its individual and corporate dimensions.

Paul's conceptual categories may seem foreign to us. We like to "explain" human evil in terms of historical cause and effect and environmental influence. Generally, we do not describe our own situation, no matter how evil or dangerous, in terms of oppression by **mythological** demonic powers (Rom. 8:38). Yet awareness of the awful depth and mystery of human evil, illumined but by no means exhausted by historical and sociological explanation, comes to expression in works of art, literature, and the theater. Rational efforts, significant as they may be, do not suffice to exorcise or even to comprehend the demonic dimensions of our society and our world. Far from being utterly strange, Paul's awareness of being beset by mysterious forces outside human control corresponds to the experience of our contemporary existence. Moreover, his refusal to release humanity from responsibility for sin, paradoxical as it may appear, also characterizes our apprehension of life. We know that injustice, racism, sexism, and violence are our heritage, but also our responsibility.

GOD'S RIGHTEOUSNESS AND THE RESPONSE OF FAITH (3:21–4:25)

For Paul, God's wrath is not the last word. Although God has every reason to display righteous wrath against human rebelliousness and perversity, he does not leave the human race to its deserved condemnation. Instead, God turns in mercy and compassion. According to Paul, the evidence of this grace is Jesus Christ. The historic and public **crucifixion** of the expected Jewish **Messiah** reveals God's **righteousness** and his power for **salvation** (1:16). At a pivotal point of Romans, Paul announces this manifestation of God's righteousness in terms drawn largely from the Jewish sacrificial system (3:21–31). In a world gone profoundly wrong, God sets things right.

Justification by Faith (3:21–31)

Why is Jesus Christ offered as a sacrifice to God for human sin?

Paul now spells out his concept of God's righteousness and how it is effected through Jesus Christ. The bleak picture of humankind held captive under the power of **sin**, set forth in preceding chapters, is presupposed. Although knowledge of God is given to everyone in creation (1:19 ff.), and despite the fact that knowledge of God's will is accessible to Jew and **Gentile** (2:12 ff., 17 ff.), the plight of both is a dire one (3:19 ff.). Paul challenges fundamentally those who consider themselves righteous by virtue of their own accomplishments. That righteousness is shown to be unrighteousness. For "now apart from the law the righteousness of God has been disclosed, and is attested by the law and the prophets" (Rom. 3:21).

Paul is intrigued by paradox. The **revelation** of God's righteousness is attested in advance by the **law** and the **prophets** (the Old Testament), although that revelation does not come *through* the law. Neither is this righteousness gained through works of the law. Rather, it is accessible only through faith in Christ (vs. 22). Human wisdom, power, and righteousness all stand in opposition to the cross of Christ, because they represent humanity's attempt to establish life as secure apart from God (cf. 1:25). Faith is the means by which one may receive God's righteousness. That this is the only possibility of righteousness and life is spelled out by Paul (3:22b–23) in a summation of his argument of the preceding section (1:18–3:20). In verse 24, Paul then specifies how God makes his righteousness accessible as a gift, that is, "by his grace." Only now does Paul refer to the historic event of the cross of Christ, in which, according to his **gospel**, this grace is bestowed.

The concise series of assertions in vss. 24–26 is as difficult as it is important, for here (and especially in verse 25) Paul introduces unfamiliar terminology taken largely from Jewish **sacrificial** practice. The word **redemption** (vs. 24) literally means a buying back from slavery, although its specific meaning in this context is not certain. Redemption may simply have the general meaning of deliverance, for in the next verse Paul quickly drops this marketplace term and switches back to a sacrificial vocabulary. Thus (vs. 25) he says that God put Christ forth as a sacrifice of atonement by his blood (vs. 25). The conviction that sin must be dealt with concretely is deeply embedded in biblical religion and doubtless in the consciousness of Paul and the earliest Christian community. Paul's reference to blood makes clear that the sacrifice of the altar is in view. This model for conceiving the significance of Christ's death is the sacrifice of the animal on the altar and the sprinkling of his blood. Paul, however, qualifies this idea of ritual sacrifice with the phrase "effective through faith," showing that for Paul the effect of the sacrifice is dependent on the manner of its reception. Christ is an **expiation**—but for faith alone.

Yet the power of the sacrifice itself is not thereby dissipated. The event of Christ's death, understood as a sacrifice, shows God's righteousness (vs. 25). This righteousness needed to be demonstrated or vindicated, because God had not dealt with sin in the past (vs. 25b). This is apparently what was meant by God's divine forbearance in passing over former sins. God exercises patience with sin, but not tolerance. In the face of human sin and evil, which has been allowed to go unchecked and unpunished, God must act to demonstrate his righteousness (vs. 26). This could only have been done by an event within human history. It is effected in the cross of Christ, which God set forth as an expiation—literally, a means of dealing with sin.

Not only the word translated "sacrifice of atonement" (Greek: *hilastērion*) but a number of other words and expressions found in verse 24 are rare in Paul. For example, even the term redemption is not common in his letters. Moreover, Paul does not typically speak of the blood of Christ, but of Christ's cross, death, or body. Paul has probably drawn upon traditional terms and concepts in this definitive statement of the nature and effect of Christ's work. The source of his language may be the words of institution of the **Lord's Supper** (1 Cor. 11:23–26; Matt. 26:26–28; Mark 14:22–24; Luke 22:17–19), where Jesus interpreted his own coming death as a sacrifice. Jewish sacrificial language was used early on to interpret Christ's death. Indeed, the belief that Christ's death was a sacrifice for sin is common in the New Testament (cf. 1 Cor. 15:3; John 1:29; 1 Pet. 2:24; 1 John 2:2; and the theme of the entire Epistle to the Hebrews). Paul identifies his own view of the work of Christ with commonly accepted ideas (cf. also 2 Cor. 5:21; Gal. 3:13), if he is not drawing directly upon earlier creedal or liturgical formulations. Elsewhere he develops other interpretations of the significance of Christ's death independent of cultic imagery (cf. 1 Cor. 1:18–25; 2 Cor. 5:16 ff.). Already in this passage he places emphasis on faith (vs. 25). Although the first clause of verse 26 only reiterates what has been said in the previous verse, the second and concluding clause takes the thought further and in a decidedly Pauline direction. God shows himself to be righteous in justifying the person of faith.

The Greek verb translated "justify" (*dikaioun*) has exactly the same stem as the Greek noun translated "righteousness" (*dikaiosynē*). Therefore, according to the literal sense of the Greek word, to justify means "to make righteous." In Paul's thought, however, **justification** is not simply an infusing or a miraculous re-creation or transformation. It is in the first instance a reckoning. As one can see (chap. 4), God reckons faith as righteousness and thus puts the believer in the right before him.

Here the model Paul has in mind is the law court, with God as the righteous judge. Thus it is a *forensic* righteousness, the verdict of righteousness pronounced over a person on trial. Quite clearly, therefore, this righteousness is less an ethical quality than a relationship. A person who is righteous in this sense is one who is vindicated in the court of law, or acquitted. That person is declared righteous. He is put in the right before God.

That righteousness has this forensic meaning in Paul is plain in such passages as Romans 3:4, where Paul quotes Psalm 51:4 (here we find the verbal form translated "justified"), and 8:34, where the act of justifying is set against that of condemning in the context of a court scene when the judge pronounces a verdict. (Cf. Gal. 3:11 and Rom. 3:20, where the forensic meaning is also clear, and 1 Cor. 4:4, where the verb *dikaioun* is best translated "acquitted," as in NRSV.) The scriptural precedent for this understanding of righteousness in the sense "to pronounce righteous" can be seen in Isaiah 43:9 (cf. also Isa. 50:8 ff.; 58:2):

> Let all the nations gather together, and let the peoples assemble
> Let them bring their witnesses to *justify them* [i.e., pronounce them righteous], and let them hear and say, "It is true."

Although this quotation shows an affinity of the Pauline and an older biblical understanding of righteousness, there is also an important difference with respect to God's righteousness. For the Old Testament and Judaism generally, it is self-evident that the *sinner* is not to be acquitted ("justified") but rather the *righteous person* (Exod. 23:7; Prov.

10:27 ff.; Ps. 1). By contrast, Paul maintains that God pronounces precisely the *ungodly* as righteous (Rom. 4:5; 5:7 ff.). This is the marvel of the gospel.

Paul does not, however, envision God merely as a judge who sits somewhere in heaven, aloof from human affairs, holding court and pronouncing verdicts. The righteous God is a saving God, and his righteousness and **salvation** are closely related. The scriptural background of this relationship can be seen in the Hebrew literary construction known as synonymous parallelism, in which the second line of a couplet is synonymous with the first:

> The Lord has made known his victory, he has revealed his vindication
> [**Septuagint** *dikaiosynē*= righteousness] in the sight of the nations (Ps. 98:2).
> I bring near my deliverance [righteousness], it is not far off, and my salvation will not tarry (Isa. 46:13).
> I will bring near my deliverance [righteousness] swiftly, my salvation has gone out . . . (Isa. 51:5).

In such passages God's righteousness is understood as a saving act or event. Similarly, God **reveals** his righteousness in the gospel (Rom. 1:17) while at the same time manifesting his wrath against sin (1:18). Thus, for Paul, God's righteousness is not primarily an abstract quality. Although a judgment, it is not a disinterested judicial pronouncement. It is an event in which God goes forth to judge and save—indeed, the climactic deed of salvation in the history of God's dealing with humanity.

That verdict of righteousness which was expected or hoped for in the final judgment (cf. Rom. 2:12) has already been spoken in favor of humankind through Jesus Christ. Although Paul believes that salvation is only consummated at the day on which the Lord returns in judgment (Rom. 13:11; cf. 2 Cor. 5:10), he nevertheless maintains that those who trust in what God has already done find themselves in a decisively new situation. Thus they live in a creative tension characterized by past assurances and hope for the future.

Since Paul is dealing with such basic biblical motifs as God's righteousness and human sin, it may seem surprising that he has so little to say about repentance and even forgiveness. The absence of these themes is not coincidental. They are important, not only in the Old Testament and Judaism, but for much of early Christianity. In Luke 24:47, for example, the Christian message is understood to be the proclamation of repentance and forgiveness in Jesus' name. For Paul, however, human sin requires a more radical change than repentance can bring about. Indeed, the human situation is so dire that a true repentance is virtually impossible. Therefore, God's forgiveness comes not in response to such repentance but only as a sheer act of grace. Only God can rectify the fallen state of the human race. Thus God takes the initiative where human initiative is no longer possible, creating a radically new situation and relationship.

The Colosseum in Rome was inaugurated by the Emperor Titus in A. D. 80. *(Courtesy of David Levenson.)*

Abraham and the Promise to Faith (4:1–25)

Why does Paul use Abraham rather than Jesus as the example of faith?

God's saving act in Jesus Christ is appropriated by faith rather than by **works** of the **law** (3:27 ff. and chap. 4). That this is no novel idea is shown by the example of Abraham, the father of Israel (chap. 4; cf. Gal. 3). Long before the law was given or even the requirement of circumcision established, "Abraham believed God and it was reckoned to him as righteousness" (4:3; cf. Gen. 15:6). As Paul has already argued in his letter to the Galatians (see Chapter 8, pp. 287–291), a person is accounted **righteous** before God by faith, not works. One is pronounced righteous before God not on the basis of the character or quantity of one's deeds—much less the accident of birth—but on the basis of that fundamental conviction or allegiance that determines life.

Faith and Believing in Romans

Much of what was said of faith (Greek *pistis*) as *trust*, with respect to Mark's presentation of Jesus' gospel, applies also to Paul's view of trust. See Chapter 2, "Faith and Believing in Mark," p. 64.

In view of Christ's **crucifixion** and **resurrection** this allegiance must focus upon a specific historical person and event. Paul sees Abraham's faith as a general prototype of specifically Christian faith and the **righteousness** reckoned to him as a model of what the Christian receives by faith—that is, apart from works. Abraham, Israel's father, shows that faith in God's promise has from the beginning of the story of **salvation** been one of proper attitude before God.

GOD'S GRACE AND HUMAN FREEDOM (5:1–8:39)

For Paul, faith is not just believing a set of facts, much less adhering to a theory. Faith is trust in God's faithfulness, living confidently in the new situation that God has created. After having shown the appropriateness and indispensability of faith by his argument based upon Abraham (chap. 4), Paul underscores the reality of this new situation (chap. 5). In fact, chapters 5–8 can profitably be viewed as Paul's effort to show that such a new situation actually exists, despite indications to the contrary.

The New Situation (5:1–21)

How has life been changed by the coming of Christ?

As he speaks of this new reality (5:1–5), Paul's style changes. To this point he has set forth the **revelation** of God's wrath and righteousness, arguing that the latter can be apprehended only in faith. Now Paul speaks from the standpoint of the community of faith and in the first person plural. What he has previously sought to establish now becomes his working assumption: "Therefore, since we are justified by faith." On the basis of the new reality, Paul refers to "this grace in which we stand." Having been put in the right through God's act in **Christ**, the person of faith has peace with God and enjoys his grace. For Paul "grace" encompasses the entire Christ–event and its effects. Grace is the mode of God's working and the resulting state in which believing humanity is placed. Grace is God's benevolent disposition and action on humanity's behalf, prior to and apart from any human effort and accomplishment—the framework, so to speak, for the response of faith.

The nature of grace is then spelled out (vss. 6–11). Not merely an abstraction, grace has to do with a real and specific event in human history, and recent history at that. Moreover, this event, the death of Christ, took place for the sake of sinful people (vss. 6–8). The pathos of this death is deeply felt by Paul himself (vs. 7). Significantly, Paul does not reckon Christ's death as showing his own love for us, but rather God's (vs. 8). Paul thus emphasizes not the personal motivation of the man Jesus as he went to the cross but the underlying purpose and disposition of God. For God, even the cross is not wanton and meaningless violence. It is, instead, the means by which judgment and **salvation** are made known to and for sinners.

The distinction between salvation as future fulfillment and **justification** as present assurance of this future reality now comes to light (vs. 9). "Blood" refers to Christ's death, again alluding to the **sacrificial** system. Between verses 9 and 10, however, a shift of terminology occurs. Paul first speaks of being justified (vs. 9), the term used in the key statement of 3:21–23 and in his discussion of Abraham in chapter 4. Now, however, the key words for the same state of affairs become "reconciled" and "reconciliation" (vss. 10 ff.). The work of Christ is no longer described in terms of the sacrificial cultus, but of the reorientation of the person. The one who was at odds with God is put in the right ("justified"), thereby at peace with God (5:1) and no longer under the dire threat of his wrath (1:18; 5:9). Paul thus maintains that the death of Christ directly affects the individual, who is transformed from a state of hostility to one of reconciliation and peace. Because the future is no longer in jeopardy but secure by virtue of Christ's accomplished act, the believer already has grounds for rejoicing in God through the Lord Jesus Christ (vs. 11). Yet Paul carefully avoids saying that salvation is already present (cf. Rom. 13:11).

In Romans 5:12–21 Paul completes the transition from discussing the righteousness of faith (3:21–4:25) to describing the new life that results from God's power and grace. The sentence structure and train of thought break off abruptly at the end of verse 12, but the basic idea is picked up again in verses 15–18. The digression of verses 13 ff. is puzzling, because Paul's relatively simple, earlier statements about Christ and Adam (1 Cor. 15:21 ff. and 45 ff.) seem needlessly complicated introducing the ideas of **sin** and the **law**. Paul, however, introduces the complication because he does not see the human problem as one of mortality and its solution as **resurrection** or assurance of eternal life. The intrusion of sin and the law, which are integrally related to death (cf. 1 Cor. 15:56), render the human problem more complex, and more deadly.

Death is not simply the termination of vital bodily functions. Rather, death follows from sinfulness and ultimately negates and condemns human life. In turn, sin is accentuated rather than removed by the law (vs. 13; cf. Rom. 3:20). Over against this hopeless oppression and bondage, Paul places the assurance of God's all-sufficient grace in Jesus Christ. This power (cf. 1:16), effective for humanity in Jesus' righteous obedience, frees people from the oppressive and enslaving bondage of sin, death, and law. Against this triumvirate are arrayed righteousness, life, and grace. As through one man, Adam, humanity was enslaved, so in one man, Jesus, humanity is set free. If condemnation and death could follow from one man's disobedience, then freedom and life can follow from one man's obedience.

Paul sees death as the ultimate threat to human life and sin as the ultimate problem; he knows that the two are interrelated. The human predicament is not just death, for death occurs in a state of rebellion against the Creator and in alienation from one's fellow human beings. This plight is not helped, but worsened, by the law, which says what to do but cannot give the power to do it. Thus, not only death but sin and dying in sin become the human fate, without God's ceasing to hold people responsible for their waywardness. One is at the same time responsible for sin and fated to die in it.

Paul has first testified that those who are accounted righteous by faith can live in grace with confidence about their ultimate destiny (5:1–11). Now he has declared that those powers that oppressed humanity are overcome (5:12–21). Thus the rejoicing and reigning of the justified (see 5:2, 3, 11, 17) are not flights of fancy but a genuine, palpable reality. Whether this assertion can be maintained in the face of life's hard facts and whether conditions have actually changed so that the power of sin, law, and death are overcome are the fundamental questions to which Paul next addresses himself (chaps. 6, 7, and 8).

This entire section (chaps. 5–8) is the center and the heart of Romans. Here Paul sets forth and describes "this grace in which we stand" (5:2). Chapter 5 dealt with this new state in a general way. Chapters 6–8 take up specific problems and objections, phrased by Paul in the form of a battery of questions that punctuate these chapters: "Should we continue in sin in order that grace may abound?" (6:1); "Should we sin because we are not under the law but under grace?" (6:15); "Do you not know . . . that the law is binding on a person only during that person's lifetime?" (7:1); "What then shall we say? That the law is sin?" (7:7); "Did what is good, then, bring death to me?" (7:13); "Wretched man that I am, who will rescue me from this body of death?" (7:24); "What then are we to say about these things? If God is for us, who is against us?" (8:31); "Who will separate us from the love of Christ?" (8:35). From these questions the reader may correctly infer that chapter 6 deals with the new life under grace and the problem of sin, chapter 7 with the newly found freedom from the oppression of the law, and chapter 8 with the role of the **Spirit** and the ground of the believer's hope.

Freedom from Sin (6:1–23)

Why not sin to increase God's outpouring of grace?

Paul now poses a problem that probably had been raised already by others: if the believer receives grace in proportion to the **sin** that must be overcome (5:20 ff.), why not continue sinning to increase the supply of grace (6:1)? Paul understands the question, but not the motivation of the questioner (6:2 ff.). The grace of God in Jesus Christ is indeed freedom (6:15 ff.; cf Gal. 4–5) but freedom *from* sin, not freedom *for* sin. Paul understands sin as an oppressive, finally fatal enemy of humankind, a bondage and a burden. Therefore, he declares that **baptism**, understood as dying and rising with Christ, is a dying to sin and a rising to "newness of life." Paul assumes that all believers have been baptized and share his understanding that baptism is the event through which the new believer is united with Christ, particularly with his death and **resurrection** (vss. 3, 6). From this idea Paul draws his own ethical conclusion. For him it is most important that baptism be not an end, but a beginning. Anyone who in baptism has died to sin is henceforth freed from it. Life is no longer lived under sin's dominion. Sin, to be sure, continues to exist as a power and a reality. But to revert to sin after having been freed from it in Christian baptism would be a contradiction of the new basis of one's existence. Such a reversal is for Paul unthinkable (vs. 2).

Even though newness of life is already a reality, it calls forth a personal human response. Paul does not believe that this response is automatic; an automatic response would nullify human freedom and genuine responsibility. He therefore exhorts his readers not to let sin reign over them (vs. 12), not to yield themselves to sin (vs. 13). Instead they should yield themselves to God as instruments of **righteousness** and not allow sin to exercise dominion over them (vs. 14). For Paul there is no question of obtaining newness of life through right behavior, as a reward. What God gives in Christ, he gives freely. Further, the acceptance of that free gift takes the form of yielding one's own life to the power and reality to which one has been joined in baptism—that is, to God's **redemptive** act in Jesus Christ.

Although Paul speaks of believers' having died with Christ and having risen to "newness of life," he does not say they have already risen with Christ, that is, experienced his resurrection (cf. also Phil. 3:10–11). In Colossians (2:12) and Ephesians (2:4–6), however, believers are said to have already risen with Christ. Admittedly, the difference is not absolute, for in Colossians and Ephesians, **ethical** implications are drawn from Christians' new, risen status, while clearly in Romans, Paul believes that believers are now empowered in ways they had not been previously.

Freedom from the Law (7:1–25)

If the law is from God, why does it not save?

A question repeatedly implied, if not explicitly stated (cf. 3:31), in Paul's discussion so far concerns the place of the **law**. Paul's statements about the law seem to contradict one another. On the one hand, he obviously takes the law—the law as contained in the Hebrew scriptures—to be the definitive expression of God's will for the ordering of human life (Rom. 2; 3:31). On the other, he maintains that the law does not enable one to escape the sinful and death-oriented existence that is now the human lot (cf. 3:20; 4:15; 5:13, 20). Moreover, as we shall see, the law itself becomes an oppressive factor in humankind's plight.

Paul begins his extended discussion of the law by describing how death sets aside a former legal obligation (7:1–6). The marriage analogy that Paul introduces in verses 1–3 is not completely apt for the point he wants to make and, therefore, must not be pressed. What Paul says here makes sense when we see that his point is simply that a legal obligation is set aside by means of a death. Therefore, as the law binding a woman to a man is set aside by his death, so the law to which allegiance was once owed is set aside through dying with Christ (7:4).

The subsequent discussion of the law (vss. 7–25) ought to be understood in the light of the basic contention that death sets aside the law. Why should this fact be so important to Paul? This long excursus, answering the question of whether the law is **sin**, implies the prior question of why one must die to the law, or, conversely, why one may not be saved by it. Why does not life, in the fullest sense of the word, result from keeping the law? The Jew believed that it did, and as a Jew, Paul had once believed this, too. Because his own view of the law's effect had been so radically reversed, however, he has a great deal at stake in showing that death cancels law. After having shown this annulment (vss. 1–6), he proceeds to explain why the law cannot bring about the life it intends (7–25). Paul's question (7:7) introduces this explanation. Is the law sin? To maintain his position and avoid the charge of **antinomianism**, he must answer in such a way as to maintain the law's integrity (3:31) but at the same time refuse to concede that the law in the present situation can rescue humankind from its predicament.

Paul's position is that the law is good, but sin undermines it. This subversion of the law takes place because people are under the power of sin that works in their flesh (7:14). This flesh is not simply to be equated with the physical side of being human any more than is the body of death from which one yearns to be free (7:24). Sin has laid claim upon life's intangible as well as tangible aspects. When Paul says that "nothing good dwells within me, that is, in my flesh" (vs. 18), the "me" he speaks of is the fleshly person in Adam, as contrasted to the person in Christ. This individual knows that the law is good, but cannot keep it. Life is a conflict between what is intended and what is actually accomplished (7:13 ff., 21 ff.). Entrapped under sin and flesh, the law only adds to the predicament, for in the very hearing of the law one disobeys and is led further into sin. So, although the law continues to be **holy**, just, and good (7:12), for the person "under the law" in the specifically Pauline sense it is nevertheless fatal (vss. 11, 13).

Significantly, Paul also relegates religious acts and attitudes to the realm of the flesh; thus, in Philippians 3:4–6 he refers to his own Jewish background as "reason for confidence in the flesh." Moreover, the Judaizers' demand that Galatian Christians accept circumcision is due to their desire to make a show in the flesh (6:12 ff.). Here the twofold connotation of flesh is apparent: on the one hand, the body's physical substance (2 Cor. 12:7), on the other, a way of life (Gal. 3:3). "Flesh" can also be a way of referring to humanity, in the style of the Hebrew scriptures (cf. Rom. 3:20, where NRSV's "no human being" aptly translates what is literally "no flesh").

The Wretched "I" in Romans 7:7-25

A central problem of this portion of Romans is that Paul everywhere speaks in the first person singular, even in the present tense. Is he, as at first we might think, recounting his own present experience, or does 7:9 indicate that he is speaking of his earlier life as a Jew under the **law**? Or is it possible that by "I" Paul does not really refer to himself at all? In Paul's speech "I" may not mean the speaker or writer personally but could mean people generally ("one," the German *Man*; or the French *on*). Paul uses the first-person pronoun in a similar sense in 1 Corinthians 13, where the "I" includes himself but is not limited to him personally. Notwithstanding a long history of interpretation that sees Paul as grappling with his own inadequacy and sin in 7:7–25, nothing else in the context or in Paul's writings generally indicates that he held such a pessimistic view of his own possibilities *in* **Christ**. Quite the contrary! Moreover, it is unlikely that this description is a passing moment or phase of his consciousness. The passage hardly refers to his previous experience as a Jew, for in Philippians 3:4 ff. and Galatians 1:14 Paul talks about his earlier life and does not indicate that he was anxious or depressed.

Probably the correct explanation of this difficult passage is that Paul writes of his own, or any person's, experience under the law, *now regarded retrospectively from a new, Christian perspective*. Thus, Paul speaks of this experience as he could not have before his conversion. Paul the believer writes about his earlier, preconversion experience as he now sees it, not as he understood it at the time. While the passage cannot apply to Paul's current, Christian awareness, many people have found their own experience echoed in it. This viewpoint is not surprising, for to retreat into a life under law, rather than under grace, remains a possibility for the believer.

Life in the Spirit (8:1–39)

How does the Spirit affect the believer?

If we take Romans 7:7–25 as a description of the way in which **sin** works through the **law**, rather than as an autobiographical confession or reminiscence, the problem of how to fit it (esp. 7:14) into Paul's personal experience disappears. This reflection is not about something he has felt; Paul is analyzing law, sin, and existence under their dominion rather than portraying his own state of mind. The opening of chapter 8 bears out this interpretation, for here the reverse of the situation described in chapter 7 is presented as typical of Paul and others in **Christ**. For them a great revolution has occurred (vss. 1–4). Life is no longer dominated and defined by flesh, sin, law, and death—that is, by the old Adam—but instead by **Spirit**, **righteousness**, grace, and life—that is, by new life in Christ. God himself has brought about this revolution in the human estate, for the Spirit is God's Spirit. (Paul also speaks of the Spirit of Christ and does not distinguish between them; see vs. 9.)

The conviction that God has acted decisively on humankind's behalf in the historical appearance of Jesus as the Christ leads Paul to encourage his fellow Christians. He speaks of the Spirit and its assuring role (vss. 16, 23, 26 ff.), of the hope that lies ahead (vss. 18–25), and of God's invincible plan and purpose (vss. 28–30), grounded in God's love (vss. 28, 35, 37, 39). With the magnificent peroration of verses 35–39, Paul ends this central section of his letter, having maintained that the **revelation** of God's grace as righteousness in Christ has brought about a truly new situation in which the bondage of the old age has been broken and the promise of a new age is finding fulfillment. For Paul, the knowledge of this new reality is given in and by the Spirit. The term *spirit* translates the Greek *pneuma*, which, like the Hebrew *ruach*, can also mean "wind" or "breath." Accordingly, in the Old Testament and earliest Christianity the appearance of the Spirit implied the advent of extraordinary divine power (cf. Acts 2 and its discussion on pp. 247–251; also 1 Cor. 14 and its consideration on pp. 334–335). Usually Paul means by *spirit* the Spirit of God or Christ. Because he also uses the word in the more general sense of a human faculty (body, soul, and spirit), it is sometimes difficult to know whether one should speak of spirit with a small or capital letter. For Paul, the Lord is the Spirit (2 Cor. 3:17); that is, Paul does not differentiate precisely between the risen Lord Jesus Christ and his Spirit. The Spirit is Christ's and God's active and supporting presence in the individual believer and the whole community. As such, the Spirit is also the first fruits (Rom. 8:23) and guarantee (2 Cor. 1:22; 5:5) of the **salvation** that lies just ahead. In the interim between the earthly appearance of Jesus the **Messiah** and his coming in glory, the Spirit is given.

In Paul's view the Spirit is both the life-giving power and the ethical guide for the believer's life (Gal. 5:25). Elsewhere Paul contrasts Spirit and letter as if the Spirit had taken over the role of the law (2 Cor. 3:7 ff.). Those who live in or by the Spirit live out of God's resources rather than their own and are able to break free from the power of the flesh—that is, the fate of human existence estranged from God ("the law of sin and death" of Rom. 8:2)—and to attain life (8:9–11). Paul's comprehensive view of the Spirit's function allows him to interpret the believer's whole life in terms of the Spirit (Rom. 8:3–8) and its gifts (1 Cor. 12–14, esp. 12:4–11; cf. Gal. 5:22 f.). Thus, he can also think of human spirits as attuned to God's Spirit (Rom. 8:16) and of Christians as "spiritual" in this specific sense (Gal. 6:1). Nevertheless, Paul does not portray life in the Spirit as invulnerable to sin. One's willing and doing must be in accord with the Spirit in its particular character as the Spirit of God and Christ. Spirit is not merely God's power in the **eschatological** age. The Spirit's presence is marked by such qualities as love, joy, peace, and patience (Gal. 5:22) in human relationships. The opposite qualities in human relationships are a sign of dominance of the flesh (Gal. 5:19 ff.). Paul exhorts his readers to live not, according to the flesh (Rom. 8:12 ff.), but in the Spirit given in the new age for a new obedience (see 12:1 ff.).

GOD'S FAITHFULNESS (9:1–11:36)

Why does Paul not concede that God has abandoned the Jewish people?

With the coming of the new age in **Christ** and the consequent fulfillment of God's promises in the new Christian community, a serious question is raised about the promises of God to the old community, Israel (see 3:1 ff.). Paul sees the event of Christ's coming within the framework of a larger history of interaction between God and humanity that centers in Israel and is recorded in the Hebrew scriptures. For him the question now revolves around that history and those promises. Were they meaningless? Are they now null and void?

Before Paul seriously tackles this question, he makes clear by way of introduction (9:1–5) his abiding kinship with Israel, the Jewish people. He assumes, however, that

This wall is part of the original wall of Herod that enclosed the temple area. Known as the Wailing Wall, it has become sacred to adherents of Judaism.

most Jews have not accepted Jesus as the **Messiah**; thus, they remain outside the circle of the new community (vss. 1–3). This situation is the crux of the problem with which Paul wrestles in Romans 9–11. He will not write off his kinsfolk, nor will he concede that God has written them off. While Paul discounts his own Jewish religious pedigree and accomplishments because of Christ (Phil. 3:7), he refuses to discount the distinctive position of Israel as a people before God (9:4 ff.; cf. 3:1 ff.).

Yet Paul's fundamental reason for regarding the given situation as a problem has more to do with God than with Israel. For if the word of God has in fact failed—if God has simply canceled his promises—then everything Paul has said to this point is called into question, because God's **righteousness** is then jeopardized by his infidelity (9:6). Paul will not countenance such blasphemy (cf. 3:3 ff.). If *God* were unjust (9:14), the note of supreme confidence struck in chapter 8 would be undermined. To put it bluntly: if God had reneged on promises made to Israel, how could the Christian be certain that God would not change his mind again? At stake is nothing less than the validity of God's promises and, by implication, God's trustworthy character as righteous deliverer. For if the promises of God are revocable, then how can one have faith in his righteous judgment on humanity's behalf in Jesus Christ? Paul now turns to the questions of the faithfulness and righteousness of God in history (cf. Rom. 3:1–8). Romans 9–11 is by no means an appendix dealing with a question that has become peripheral. Rather, for the **gospel** to make sense, Paul must show that God's faithfulness vindicates itself in history.

In four different ways Paul meets the implied charge that the **word** of God has failed. In the first place, he argues that God's promise was always based on the principle of election or choice (9:5–26). Moreover, this promise is not automatically passed down from one generation to the next; it is a dynamic process in history by which God continues to call and to choose (9:6b–13). It might appear that Paul thought God somewhat capricious in this respect (vs. 5:18). Indeed, he seems to defend that capriciousness (vss. 19 ff.). Yet here Paul grounds election in a prior faith in God as Creator and Lord of creation (vss. 20 ff.), for what Paul ultimately has in view is not God's arbitrary rigor but his mercy (vss. 22 ff.). Moreover, the rejection of large numbers of Israel's children is predicted by the **prophets** Hosea and Isaiah (vss. 25–29). Thus God himself has declared that it must occur.

In the second place, sufficient grounds for Israel's rejection can be found in her own misguided effort to please God. In 9:30–10:4 Paul clarifies the concept of God's righteousness. Because Israel has not understood that God's righteousness is to be received by faith (9:30 ff.), she has sought to establish her own by **works** (10:3). But Paul insists that God's righteousness cannot be earned. God pronounces people righteous and thus brings them into the right before himself through the cross of Jesus. Christ becomes "for us . . . righteousness" (1 Cor. 1:30), and in the **apostles'** preaching the cross of Jesus is said to be the **revelation** of God's righteousness (1:16 ff.; cf. 1 Cor. 1:18 ff.). If there is any effort to establish one's own righteousness, then the gift of God is refused. Israel thus brings reprobation upon herself (9:30–10:4; cf. 3:3 f.). To make clear that the responsibility rests fully upon Israel, not God, Paul contends that Israel has in fact heard the preaching of the gospel and rejected it (10:5–21, esp. 14–21). He drives home this point not by making specific reference to the preaching of good news to the Jews, as he certainly could have, but by once again referring to scripture (10:18–20).

So far Paul has assumed Israel's unbelief as a condition calling for explanation. Beginning with chapter 11, however, Paul's argument takes a new tack as he makes his third point. To the question of whether God has rejected his people, Paul now says no. He himself is an Israelite (11:1). The example of Elijah (vss. 2–4) shows that Paul is not alone: "So too at the present time there is a remnant, chosen by grace" (vs. 5). Paul combines Isaiah's concept of the remnant with the idea of election, already set forth in chapter 9, and his own understanding of the gospel as God's grace. Indeed, what Paul says here fits well with the election doctrine of chapter 9. God's grace in Jesus Christ is the point at which the process of election in history takes another step forward, while the remnant from Israel provides continuity with the Old Testament people of God. Paul's exposition of the way in which God works in history does not differ in principle from the Hebrew scriptures' understanding, or at least his interpretation of them. God elects according to his own free choice rather than according to national, ethnic, or familial principles. The only unhappy aspect of this doctrine is that God's election seems to work through a process of elimination, whereby the number of the elect becomes progressively fewer—hardly a happy outcome, except that presumably God could have elected to save no one at all.

The discussion then takes a decisive, even surprising turn as Paul makes his fourth point (11:11). The prospect is not pessimistic, as we might have expected. Paul expounds his expectation of God's continuing work in history for the **salvation** of Jew as well as Greek (vss. 11–32). The salvation of the **Gentiles** will make the Jews jealous and thus bring them back into the fold. Paul looks forward to the salvation of all Israel (11:26), quoting the prophecy of Isaiah (59:20-21; cf. 27:9).

How seriously one can take this view of history is a legitimate question. For one thing, Paul did not anticipate an indefinite continuation of world history (see Rom. 13:11 ff.). He thought history was coming rapidly to a close and that Christ would soon return. Of course, the sequence of **eschatological** events that Paul anticipated has not occurred. The conversion of the Gentiles does not seem to be complete, although "the full number of the Gentiles" (vs. 25) may not mean every Gentile. Moreover, there is not yet any indication of the conversion of Israel. Paul's image of the olive tree (vss. 17–24; cf. Jer. 11:16) nevertheless provides a graphic picture of his understanding of Gentile Christianity's relationship to contemporary Judaism and to the true Israel of God represented by the root of the tree. Gentile Christians are branches grafted in only because some original branches were broken off. The olive tree itself is the new universal people of God, intended to comprise both Jew and Greek. The imagery ought not to be taken as Paul's attempt to predict the future. Instead we have here an affirmation of faith in the ultimate fulfillment of God's purposes.

In concluding his argument, Paul neatly summarizes an important paradox of Christian faith: "For God has imprisoned all in disobedience, so that he may be merciful to all" (11:32). This astounding statement is neither a passing thought nor a means of easing a rough patch into which Paul's argument has led him. (The same basic idea occurs elsewhere, notably in 5:18–20 and Gal. 3:22). Even at its most extreme severity, God's purpose, the end and goal of his activity, is mercy. In the history of peoples, as of individuals, God's saving activity is grace: surpassing and contradicting human expectation and hopes, appearing where least expected and on behalf of the ungodly (4:5). For Paul, the ungodly are in the end all people: ". . . so that he may be merciful to all" (vs. 32).

The final paragraph of this chapter and of this section of Romans is a confession in almost hymnic form (vss. 33–36). Paul wishes to emphasize the continuing mystery, over which his exposition has only skimmed. The seeming triumph of iniquity in the human race is deceptive. The complete revelation, which is God's alone to give, is not yet fully disclosed. God continues to work in history to the end that he may have mercy upon all. Yet Paul's faith is not in his own **theology** of history, but in the God who makes his mercy known in Christ: "For from him and through him and to him are all things. To him be the glory forever. Amen" (11:36).

THE OBEDIENCE OF FAITH (12:1–15:13)

Why not just accept God's grace and be done with moral striving?

A major division in the structure of Romans occurs after the hymn of praise that concludes Paul's discussion of Israel's destiny (11:33–36). With a general exhortation (12:1–2) Paul introduces a series of instructions that concludes at 15:13. The character of this long section and its relation to what precedes can best be grasped by examining the introductory exhortation.

Paul bases his appeal (vs. 1) on the "mercies of God." The most likely clue to the meaning of this term is to be found in the word "therefore," which suggests that Paul grounds what he now proposes to say in what has gone before. Chapters 1–11 might then be understood as an exposition of God's mercies, in the sense of God's merciful activity on behalf of sinful and wayward humanity. Paul bases his ethical appeals on the prior claim that God has on believers by virtue of the grace shown them in Jesus Christ. The indicative ("what God has done for you") becomes the ground for the imperative ("what you must do for your fellow human being"). This is altogether characteristic of Paul's thought. Such an interpretation of the mercies of God also suggests that Paul picks up in 12:1 the theme of mercy from 11:32: "For God has imprisoned all in disobedience so that he may be merciful to all."

"To present your bodies as a living sacrifice" and "spiritual worship" (vs. 1) are perplexing phrases. Here, as previously (cf. 3:21 ff.), Paul appropriates the language of the **sacrificial** cult at a crucial point of his treatment. Obviously, such language cannot be taken literally, for it is quite clear that Paul is not talking about a material sacrifice when he speaks of "spiritual worship." Paul means a personal commitment or offering to God in response to his mercy in Jesus Christ. By the sacrifice of the body Paul means the surrender of the self, which has heretofore been subjected to **sin**, flesh, and death (cf. 8:9–11; 7:21–25). Thus the sacrificial language is quite appropriate when understood in terms of "spiritual worship."

Paul next introduces the tension between present and future that is characteristic of early Christian **eschatology** (vs. 2). The NRSV's alternative translation, "Do not be conformed to this *age*," is almost surely more accurate than "this *world*." As we have seen, the coming of Christ has inaugurated a new age, even though the old age continues. Believers must conform no longer to the old age as their regulative principle of life, but to the new, which they have entered. They should be transformed by the *renewal* of the mind.

The mind here evidently means both the knowing and willing faculties, but the importance of the mind as the seat of intelligence and common sense should not be understated. Paul does not believe that anyone can come to God through rational means alone. Nevertheless, he deems it possible and necessary for the one who has come to God in faith to exercise his mind in God's service, to discern God's will. "What is the will of God . . . good and acceptable and perfect" is to be discerned and then proved (cf. RSV) in the doing of the deed as well as in contemplating it.

This appeal (12:1–2) forms the connecting link between Paul's long **theological** discourse in chapters 1–11 and the **ethical** exhortations of chapters 12–15. These dicta are of a general, more or less stereotyped nature. Whether they reflect Paul's own firsthand knowledge of the situation among the Christians in Rome is a good question. Doubtless they indicate the state of Paul's own thinking and perhaps to a considerable degree the problems that he encountered in other churches. Probably they also contain certain pre-Pauline, traditional materials.

Paul's use of the image of the body to illumine the relation of Christians to one another and to Christ (12:3–8) recalls its earlier and more extensive elaboration in 1 Corinthians 12 and forms the basis for further exhortations (vss. 9–13). The general ethical injunctions of 12:14–21 recall the Old Testament and (vs. 20) the words of Jesus (Matt. 5:44; Luke 6:27). Yet Paul may be quoting directly from Proverbs 25:21 ff. rather than giving Jesus' own words. This would account for the inclusion of the "burning coals" clause, which is not found in Jesus' sayings.

The discussion of the governing authorities (13:1–7) is strikingly similar to that in 1 Peter (2:13–17). If 1 Peter is not dependent upon Romans, it probably indicates the existence of a common viewpoint and tradition regarding the church's relation to worldly authority (cf. 1 Tim. 2:1–2; Tit. 3:1). Romans 13:7 may be a dim reflection of Jesus' teaching in Mark 12:13–17. Similarly, 13:8–10 evokes Mark 10:19, as well as 12:31, but without conforming closely enough to suggest any direct dependence. The eschatology of 13:11 ff. is quite Pauline (cf. 1 Cor. 7:31; 1 Thess. 4:13–18), as is the manner in which eschatology and ethics are combined (cf. 12:2).

Chapter 14 continues the ethical reflections about the Christian's responsibility to his brother or sister that we already have witnessed in 1 Corinthians (esp. chaps. 8 and 10). Paul regards the theological position of the strong (15:1) as correct, as he does in 1 Corinthians, but admonishes others who consider themselves strong on their responsibilities to the weak, who have dietary or similar scruples. In 15:1–3, as he brings his exhortations to a close, Paul introduces the example of Christ himself (Phil. 2:5–11; cf. 1 Pet. 2:21; Mark 8:34, 10:38 ff.). The principle of scriptural interpretation enunciated here (vs. 4) is stated more extensively in 1 Corinthians 9:8–10; 10:6, 11; and 2 Corinthians 3. Paul then introduces the subject of the **Gentile** mission by means of further scriptural quotations

(15:7–13), preparing the way for his reflections upon his own missionary accomplishments and plan (15:14–33).

These hortatory chapters of Romans are not merely perfunctory admonitions. Faith for Paul is no abandonment of moral responsibility, but the way to come to obedience to God (Rom. 1:5; 15:18). As he stresses repeatedly, faith in Christ does not overthrow the **law** but upholds it. Paul has absolutely no tolerance for a Christianity that is morally lax or indifferent. That would be as much "another gospel" or "no gospel" as the legalism of the Judaizers in Galatia. Thus the concrete ethical exhortations and advice in Romans 12:1–15:13 are entirely in accord with—in fact, the outgrowth of—Paul's fundamental theological stance. The **gospel** must elicit a faithful response that is obedient to God, and this obedience of faith must have specific relevance for the actual situations of life.

CLOSING (15:14–16:27)

How does the closing relate to the rest of Romans?

Paul's discussion of his accomplishments and plans for the immediate future is important for setting Romans in its *historical context* (see "Background of Romans"). Paul obviously regards his work as entering a new phase, to be marked by a visit to Jerusalem (vs. 25), his long-awaited journey to Rome (vss. 28–29), and further missionary endeavors in

The statue of St. Paul Outside the Walls in Rome commemorates the burial place of the apostle. The church building itself was constructed in the early nineteenth century to replace the Constantinian church (fourth century) that burned. A serious effort was made to replicate the older structure.

Spain (vs. 28). The concluding chapter of Romans (16) is a series of personal greetings and commendations to and from Christians either in Rome or with Paul. In this letter Paul introduces the Romans to his **theology**, his understanding of the **gospel**, while at the same time correcting misinterpretations by his opponents within the **church**. He clearly intends to gain Roman Christians' approval and moral support—perhaps also their financial or logistical support—for his mission to Spain. Thus Romans apparently was written after the Corinthian crisis was resolved, probably while Paul was still in Corinth (cf. 16:23) but anticipating his delivery of the collection to the poor among the saints in Jerusalem (Rom. 15:25–26; cf. Acts 20:2–6; 21:4, 11–19; 24:17).

CONCLUSION

We have just considered Romans' *historical context*, which is closely related to its character and purpose. In Romans more than in any other letter, Paul is in conversation and debate with his Jewish heritage and theological background. Not surprisingly, he makes a concerted effort to do justice to his traditional roots, both Jewish and Jewish Christian. Thus Romans contains a considerable amount of traditional material of which 1:2–4 and 3:24–26, as well as much of the hortatory material of chapters 13–15, afford good examples. Yet one cannot make much headway in distinguishing *tradition* from *redaction* in Romans, for Paul is more likely to pick up traditional language and concepts than to use extended sources. Moreover, such traditional materials or concepts as he adopts have been well assimilated to his thought. It is more profitable to ask what Paul has stated and what he intended. Although there are real difficulties of interpretation, the broad outline of his thought are clearly discernible from the Romans' structure and emphases.

The *structure* of Romans is actually a kind of theological argument, and in that respect unlike most of the books in the New Testament. Romans has to be studied in its entirety to be understood, and such a study is outlined in this chapter. After a long introduction, in which the letter's themes, especially the **righteousness** of God, are set forth, Paul gives an extensive account of the human condition, in which he concludes that **sin** has pervaded the entire human race, leaving all Jews as well as **Gentiles** in need of **redemption** (1:18–3:20). Paul then turns to the **sacrificial** and saving death of Jesus (3:21–26) and to the necessity of faith as the only way the benefits of that death can be appropriated. Abraham is summoned as the key witness and confirmation of the faith's saving efficacy: "Abraham believed God, and it was reckoned to him as righteousness" (Rom. 4:3; cf. Gen. 15:6).

The beginning of chapter 5 marks a turning point in the letter. Paul shifts from an argumentative to a confessional style, and from the second and third persons to the first. Chapters 5 through 8 are concerned with whether and how the conditions of human existence have been changed by **Christ**'s coming. According to Paul, because of God's love and deed in Christ (chap. 5), believers live a new life in this world even before **salvation** has fully arrived and while the world continues to decay. They are able to overcome sin (chap. 6); they are no longer under a **law** they cannot fulfill (chap. 7); they are full of the **Spirit** of life and free from death (chap. 8). Thus in chapters 5 through 8, Paul spells out the nature and effects of "this grace in which we stand" (5:2).

Chapters 9 through 11 deal with the question of God's faithfulness to his promises to Israel, a question lurking in the background since 3:3 ff. This is an urgent matter, because on Paul's own terms Israel does not seem to be inheriting the promise. If God has been faithless with Israel, can he be counted on to be faithful to the Christian **church**? Yet it is not God but Israel who has defaulted on the terms of the promise. Moreover, Paul maintains that at length even a wayward Israel, whose seeming apostasy will lead to the salvation of the Gentiles, will return to God's favor and be saved.

The letter's final major section spells out the meaning of Christian faith for life's various circumstances (12:1–15:13). Paul scarcely strives for comprehensiveness; rather, he lays down guidelines and directions, often relying on earlier and traditional formulations to specify what the obedience of faith (1:5) demands in concrete situations. Here as elsewhere the imperative, what the person in Christ is to do, flows from the indicative, what God in Christ has done. Thereafter, Paul gives an insight into his view of his own groundbreaking **apostolic** work, sketches out his plans to visit Rome and eventually to go to Spain (15:14–33), and ends with sundry words of personal greeting and a final general exhortation (chap. 16).

The principal *emphases* of Romans should be readily apparent from our study of the text and its structure, but can now be stated more succinctly. Romans concerns the meaning of the event of the **Messiah's** coming, particularly the fact of his death and the faith that he is risen. This event throws light backward, to illumine the enormity of human sin, and forward, to display the richness of human freedom and life under grace. Paul elaborates his discussion against the background of problems and assumptions arising out of his Jewish heritage. Thus the meaning of Jesus' coming as the **Christ** is discussed not in abstraction, nor simply over against the problems of human existence in general, but primarily with the history of Israel and her understanding of God and humanity in view. The principal question arising from that heritage, in the light of the **revelation** of God's righteousness and wrath in Christ, is how sinners can be accounted righteous before God. For Paul, God's righteousness is revealed in Jesus Christ; it is an action and pronouncement of God, freely bestowed. Thus he shows himself to be a righteous and gracious God. Faith is the proper response to God's graciousness. This means, first of all, that one must trust in what God has done in Jesus Christ. But this trust is not intellectual assent in the abstract. It finds expression in a new life. The possibility and power of the new life are already given. Still, life must actually be lived out in the community of faith and love. Thus Paul speaks not only to his hearers in the indicative mood, to tell them what God has done; he also appeals to them in the imperative, to draw their lives into conformity with this new reality. Meanwhile, God continues to work, sometimes in mysterious ways, for the salvation of both Jew and Greek.

SUGGESTIONS FOR FURTHER READING

ROMANS

Much of the letter's path-breaking study has taken the form of **commentaries**. E. Käsemann, *Commentary on Romans*, trans. G. W. Bromiley (Grand Rapids: Eerdmans, 1980), is a major work, but of limited usefulness for the student without Greek. The same is true of C. E. B.

Cranfield's *A Critical and Exegetical Commentary on the Epistle to the Romans*, 2 vols. (Edinburgh: T & T Clark, 1975–1979), and J. D. G. Dunn's *Romans 1–8* and *Romans 9–16* (Dallas: Word, 1988). Cranfield has compressed his longer work into *Romans: A Shorter Commentary* (Edinburgh: T. & T. Clark, 1991). Also more accessible are P. J. Achtemeier, *Romans* (Atlanta: John Knox, 1985), J. A. Fitzmyer, *Romans* (Garden City, NY: Doubleday, 1993), B. Byrne, *Romans* (Collegeville, MN: Liturgical, 1996), N. T. Wright, "The Letter to the Romans: Introduction, Commentary, and Reflections," *NIB* 10 (2002): 393–770, and L. E. Keck, *Romans* (Nashville: Abingdon, 2006). Brief but penetrating is the commentary in P. W. Meyer, *The Word in This World: Essays in New Testament Exegesis and Theology*, ed. J. T. Carroll (Louisville: Westminster John Knox, 2004), which also includes many of Meyer's important contributions to Pauline interpretation.

Other studies flesh out the background of Romans. K. P. Donfried (ed.), *The Romans Debate*, rev. ed. (Peabody, MA: Hendrickson, 1991), is a stimulating collection of essays on Paul's purposes in writing to Rome. A. J. M. Wedderburn probes the same question in *The Reasons for Romans* (Edinburgh: T & T Clark, 1988). On the Roman church to which Paul wrote, consult P. Lampe, *From Paul to Valentinus: Christians at Rome in the First Two Centuries*, trans. M. Steinhauser (Minneapolis: Fortress, 2003); on the broader political context, see R. A. Horsley (ed.), *Paul and Empire: Religion and Power in Roman Imperial Society* (Harrisburg, PA: Trinity Press International, 1997).

PAULINE THEOLOGY

Major works that view Pauline thought against his **Jewish background** are A. Schweitzer, *The Mysticism of Paul the Apostle*, trans. W. Montgomery (New York: Holt, 1931), K. Stendahl, *Paul Among Jews and Gentiles and Other Essays* (Philadelphia: Fortress, 1976), E. P. Sanders, *Paul and Palestinian Judaism* (Philadelphia: Fortress, 1977) and the same author's *Paul, the Law, and the Jewish People* (Philadelphia: Fortress, 1983), and W. D. Davies, *Paul and Rabbinic Judaism*, 4th rev. ed. (Philadelphia: Fortress, 1980). On Paul's use of scripture (i.e., the Christian Old Testament), see especially R. B. Hays, *Echoes of Scripture in the Letters of Paul* (New Haven: Yale University Press, 1989); on his understanding of Israel's law, a good orientation is V. Koperski, *What Are They Saying About Paul and the Law?* (New York: Paulist, 2001).

Among **synthetic studies**, R. Bultmann, *Theology of the New Testament*, vol. 1, trans. K. Grobel (New York: Scribner's 1951) is still important. J. C. Beker, *Paul the Apostle: The Triumph of God in Life and Thought* (Philadelphia: Fortress, 1980), deals with Paul's theology in its Jewish apocalyptic framework and addresses the problem of drawing out the coherence of thought from letters addressed to specific occasions and problems. J. D. G. Dunn, *The Theology of Paul the Apostle* (Grand Rapids: Eerdmans, 1998), is heavily structured on Romans. E. Käsemann's *Perspectives on Paul*, trans. M. Kohl (London: SCM, 1971), contains classic essays, most in interaction with Romans. D. M. Hay and E. E. Johnson (eds.), *Pauline Theology*, Volume 3: *Romans* (Minneapolis: Fortress, 1991), harvests some of the best recent scholarship. A good summary is K. Haacker, *The Theology of Paul's Letter to the Romans* (Cambridge: Cambridge University Press, 2003).

The Suggestions for Further Reading at the end of Chapter 9 include additional works on Paul's theology.

The center panel of the "Isenheim Altarpiece" (1510–1515), by Matthias Grünewald, now housed in the Musée d'Unterlinder, Colmar, France. Represented are Mary the mother of Jesus, embraced by the disciple John; Mary Magdalene, kneeling; the crucified Jesus; and John the Baptist, who repeats John 3:30. The letters INRI above the cross are the initial Latin letters of the inscription, "Jesus of Nazareth, King of the Jews." *(Courtesy of The Art Resource, New York.)*

CHAPTER 11

DEUTERO-PAULINE LETTERS: THE EMERGING CHURCH

Comments on Pseudonymous Writings

Even the most casual reader of the New Testament is impressed by how much of it is related to the **Apostle** Paul. Thirteen letters are ascribed to him. Another, Hebrews, came into the **canon** under his banner, while more than half the Book of Acts is devoted to his missionary labors. Paul is the apostle to the **Gentiles**, not only by his own claim but also by virtue of the place he holds in the New Testament. The reader who goes straight through the New Testament first encounters Paul in Acts, and then after Romans, reads the numerous letters addressed to special situations and crises of Paul's **churches**, and finally in the **Pastorals** meets the ministerial Paul, concerned with church office and administration. Hebrews, which deals extensively with the **sacrificial** work of Jesus—also a theme of Paul's **theology**—and exhorts believers to continued faithfulness, stands at the boundary of the Pauline corpus. It is not, however, attributed to Paul.

To this point we have considered the letters that Paul himself wrote. (Of these, only 2 Thessalonians is at all questionable.) In this chapter, we treat letters whose authorship is more dubious (Colossians and Ephesians) and those that he almost certainly did not pen (the three Pastoral letters). For several reasons, however, these letters can be considered "Pauline," even if not from Paul's own hand. They claim Pauline authorship. They have been so ascribed to him by tradition. Important themes of Pauline theology are developed or adjusted in them; matters that might have concerned Paul had he lived into the subsequent generation are addressed. These later, Deutero–Pauline letters, as well as the Book of Acts, attest the existence of a Pauline tradition or school that flourished after the Apostle had passed from the scene.

Paul had Christian opponents during his lifetime, and his legacy was not at first universally accepted. In the Epistle of James (2:8–26), perhaps even in parts of the Sermon on the Mount (Matt. 5:18–19; 7:13–23), we possibly find polemic against, or correction of, a Pauline point of view. Ebionite (derived from the Hebrew word for "poor"; cf. Gal. 2:10) Christians, who survived into the second century and later, apparently represented a Jewish version of Christianity that was unfriendly to Paul. Manifestly anti-Pauline sentiments are found in the so-called Clementine Christian literature of the second and third centuries.

Against such a background, consisting of pro-Pauline and anti-Pauline forces, we should read these later letters ascribed to him. In this chapter, they are treated in roughly their chronological sequence, which is also their descending order of proximity to Paul. That is, the order runs from Colossians, which is closest chronologically and substantially—and still regarded by many as **authentically** Pauline—to the Pastorals, concerned with accountable structures within the emerging church and regarded as authentic by a small minority of scholars.

What's in a Name?

A pseudonymous writing is one written under the name of someone other than the actual author. All the Pauline letters treated in this chapter are probably pseudonymous. This state of affairs differs from that in Gospels and Acts, which are instead anonymous. That is, within the documents themselves no one is actually named as author. This is true even of the Gospel of John, where the anonymous Beloved Disciple is never identified with John (21:24), and of Luke–Acts, whose author is never named but who refers to his own literary endeavors in those books' prologues (Luke 1:1–4; Acts 1:1–5). The Gospels' traditional titles appear to have been added only as those books were incorporated into the New Testament.

In the next two chapters, we shall consider other writings whose authorship is uncertain, though only a couple may be clearly pseudonymous. Both 1 and 2 Peter contain explicit references or allusions to the **Apostle** Peter as their author (e.g., 1 Pet. 1:1; 5:1; 2 Pet. 1:1; 1:17 ff.). The letters of James and Jude seem to represent themselves as works of Jesus' brothers, but this is only possible, not certain, since the names are common and no fraternal connection with Jesus is claimed (although in Jude 1 the author identifies himself as a servant of Jesus **Christ** and brother of James). Hebrews is properly considered anonymous: it makes no express authorial claim. The Revelation to John explicitly names a John as author (1:1) but does not identify him as the disciple of Jesus or as an apostle. The Johannine letters, unlike the Pauline, do not name an author, although in 2 and 3 John the author is identified simply as "the elder," as if he were well known to his readers.

The most acute problems are found in the Pauline and Petrine letters. Of these as many as eight may be pseudonymous (2 Thessalonians, Colossians, Ephesians, the three **Pastorals**, and both 1 and 2 Peter). According to the current consensus of biblical scholarship, at least five are pseudonymous (Ephesians, the Pastorals, 2 Peter). These not only name Paul or Peter as author but also contain several self-references or allusions that seem intended to underscore their authorship. Not surprisingly, some suggest that, if they are **pseudepigrapha** (written under an assumed name), they are forgeries, with all that implies. Most scholars, however, are reluctant to go that far, although it is the case that literate people in antiquity were aware of forgeries. In fact, some later Christian books, written under the names of apostles but known to have been written by others, were eventually rejected by the church as **apocryphal**.

New Testament pseudepigrapha should be viewed in light of Old Testament and ancient Jewish practice and tradition. All **law** was ascribed to Moses, although he did not write the Pentateuch in its present form. Similarly, wisdom books were ascribed to Solomon and Psalms to David. Prophetic books like Isaiah contain material originating with that eighth-century B.C. prophet but also literary layers from later centuries as well. Jewish **apocalyptic** books were characteristically written under the names of ancient worthies, such as Daniel and Enoch, rather than their actual authors.

Obviously, these Jewish scriptures establish a precedent, not of forgery, but for the ascription of sacred writings to ancient figures whom tradition holds to be their source. For example, there can be no doubt that Paul is the source of Ephesians, for apart from Paul that letter would be inconceivable. The same may be said of the Pastorals, although their differences from the writings of Paul himself are more pronounced. Yet the Pastorals clearly intend to apply the Pauline message and tradition to a later generation, when matters of **church** organization and ministerial office have become increasingly crucial. Many personal details of the Pastorals, such as the relationship of Paul to his subordinates Timothy and Titus, establish them as Pauline in tenor if not authorship. The Apostle is not only a source of tradition; in the Pastorals he becomes a part of the tradition itself. For early Christians, like their Jewish forebears, literary origin was less important than continuity of tradition. In other words, Paul and Peter continue to speak to new situations in the life of the church through letters ascribed to them, much as Moses or Isaiah continued to speak to Israel.

Although questions of literary property were regarded as of secondary importance, they did not disappear from Christian consciousness. Thus, in the second and third centuries false claims of apostolic authorship were recognized, and writings such as the *Gospel of Peter* and *3 Corinthians* (in the New Testament **Apocrypha**) were discredited on the grounds of their inconsistency with normative Petrine and Pauline traditions.

COLOSSIANS: STEADFASTNESS AGAINST HERESY

Background of Colossians

Several arguments have been lodged against the **authenticity** of Colossians: (1) stylistic differences from the undoubtedly Pauline letters, (2) differences in its development of theological thought, (3) the complex character of the erroneous teaching that the **Apostle** combats (could it have developed in Paul's lifetime?), and (4) the close relation both in style and thought to Ephesians, which is probably the work of a later Paulinist rather than of Paul himself.

Taken singly, none of these arguments is decisive. Taken together, they constitute strong reasons for doubting that Paul himself wrote Colossians. That Paul had never visited Colossae (2:1–5) does not speak decisively on either side, for neither had he visited Rome. In recent scholarship, however, Pauline authorship of Colossians has been increasingly rejected, without its necessarily being dated much later than Paul. One of the problems in denying Pauline authorship is to identify a plausible alternative setting a generation or so later. The question arises whether Colossians was actually composed in his name by one of Paul's fellow workers. (Timothy joins him in the salutation, but that is commonplace; cf. Phil. 1:1). For conveninece, we shall continue to refer to the author as Paul, despite the valid reasons for doubting that traditional claim.

Stylistic considerations raise doubts about Pauline authorship that even a reading of the English text will sustain. Colossians contains a number of long, well-rounded Greek periods, or sentences, unlike the rough-hewn eloquence of the unquestioned letters. Such differences, scarcely attributable to secretarial styles, are impressive, especially because they are shared to a striking degree by Ephesians. There is another simple but telling bit of evidence: in neither Colossians nor Ephesians does the author address his readers as *brethren* (NRSV: "brothers and sisters"; Greek: vocative plural, *adelphoi*)—a form of address found in all the genuine letters.

If Colossians was written by Paul himself, or by an associate in his name, it was apparently occasioned by the return of Epaphras from Colossae, bearing news to an imprisoned Paul of the circumstances in that church (1:7; 4:10, 12 ff.). Mention of Archippus (4:17) suggests a relationship to the letter of Philemon, where a person of the same name is addressed in its salutation (vs. 2). In fact, a number of the same persons are mentioned in Philemon (vss. 23–24) and Colossians (4:10–17). If Colossians is a later pseudonymous letter, it is difficult to conceive of its setting except in very general terms.

OUTLINE OF COLOSSIANS

Introduction: Salutation and Extended Thanksgiving (1:1–14)
Doctrine of Christ (1:15–2:7)

Christ's Status (1:15–20)
Christ's Saving Work (1:21–23)
Christ's Ministry—Paul's Service (1:24–2:7)

Warning against Erroneous Teaching (2:8–23; esp. 2:8–15)
Exhortation to Good Conduct (3:1–4:6)

Death and Resurrection the Basis for Christian Conduct (3:1–11)
General Advice (3:12–17)
Advice to Families (3:18–4:1)
Further General Admonitions (4:2–6)

Conclusion: Instructions and Personal Matters (4:7–18)

Warning against Erroneous Teaching (Col. 2:8–15)

What is harmful in the heresy Paul attacks?

Colossians appears to have been written in part to warn the church of Colossae against the dangers inherent in an aberrant form of Christianity, which, for want of a better term, we shall call the Colossian heresy. (*Heresy* and *heretic* are somewhat anachronistic terms, as they presuppose a creedal orthodoxy that did not exist at the beginning of the development of Christian thought. They are nevertheless useful in describing Paul's Colossian opponents, who seek to put obstacles in the way of true faith.) As our knowledge of this heresy must be gleaned from the letter's own statements, the task of understanding it and of fully understanding Colossians is difficult. Still, in 2:8–23, especially 2:8–15, Paul gives some hints about its nature. He characterizes it as "philosophy and empty deceit," having to do with "human tradition" and the "elemental spirits of the universe" and not with Christ (vs. 8.). There is a fundamental opposition between this teaching and the Christian **gospel** as Paul understands it.

The key phrase (in vss. 8, 20) seems to be "elemental spirits of the universe" (Greek, *stoicheia tou kosmou*). Paul uses the term elsewhere only in Galatians 4:3, 9, where he apparently regards the observance of Jewish ceremonial **law** as submission to such spirits. This may also be the case in Colossians (2:20 ff.), though here such observance also expresses a philosophy or worldview in which Christ occupies a subordinate place. The elemental spirits of the universe may have been natural phenomena that were thought to sustain or determine life and, therefore, were endowed with a semireligious aura—for example, the heavenly bodies, which, like the sun, sustain life, or, like the stars, determine it. Within these natural phenomena, divine influences that work upon humanity were deemed to be active and accessible. Ritual demands, taboos, and calendar observances accompanied this "philosophy" (2:16 ff., 20 ff.). As the universe was filled with such numinous powers, it behooved people to **propitiate** them through the appropriate ritual. Paul seems to be dealing with what we consider a super-charged astrology.

Most disturbing was not ritual observance as such, although Paul would have rejected any insistence upon that, but the heretics' apparent willingness to subsume Christ under a system of elemental spirits. Ancient religious syncretism habitually absorbed strange deities, and **Christ** was subject to such confiscation. Paul seems to counter the Colossian heretics' claim that the deity dwelt or subsisted in the elemental spirits of the universe when he asserts that the whole fullness of deity dwells in Jesus Christ (vs. 9). The term *bodily* probably does not refer to the earthly body of Jesus Christ but to the dwelling of the deity in Christ, understood as the body of the church or universe. In Colossians both **church** (1:18) and the universe (1:15–17; 2:10) are described as the body of Christ, or the body of which Christ is the head.

The heretics may have propounded "fullness" (vs. 10) through subservience to the elemental spirits of the universe. Against this contention Paul argues that such "fullness" comes only from Jesus Christ. Far from being subordinate to these elemental spirits, he is the head of every ruler and authority. Paul does not directly deny the existence of such forces, but insists that they have been subordinated to Christ. There is no reason, therefore, for the Christian to have any regard for them. In a different context Paul has already stated the same basic idea (see 1 Cor. 8:5 ff.).

Colossians reminds the readers, perhaps on the verge of succumbing to this misleading teaching, of the real ground of their hope and confidence (vss. 11 ff.). The reference to "circumcision made without hands" (vs. 11; NRSV: "spiritual circumcision") may imply that the Colossian heretics, like the so-called Judaizers of Galatia, demanded that Christians submit to circumcision in the flesh. Christian circumcision, replies Paul, is not "in the flesh" but has the effect of "putting off the body of flesh" (vs. 11). This does not mean leaving this mortal life but, rather, putting off the life that is determined by the flesh. (See the discussion of flesh and spirit in Chapter 10, pp. 364–365. and the reference to "a human way of thinking," literally "mind of the flesh," in 2:18.) The death of the body (and mind) of the flesh occurs in **baptism**, where the new believer is buried and raised with Christ in a recapitulation of Christ's death and **resurrection** (vs. 12; cf. Rom. 6). Typically, Paul does not claim that this dying and rising is an automatic or magical occurrence. It takes place through faith. Notice the close relation between **sin** and death, forgiveness and life (vs. 13), a pattern typical of Paul, who nevertheless usually speaks of **righteousness** or **justification** rather than forgiveness.

Christ as God's saving act is a familiar idea to Paul's readers. In verse 15, we are given another interpretation of Christ's work, one better suited to the Colossian situation. Christ has decisively triumphed over the "rulers and authorities." These are doubtless included among the elemental spirits of the universe, if not identical with them. Christ's **redemptive** work means not only freedom from flesh, sin, death (vs. 13), and the law (vs. 14), but also freedom from the oppressive powers of the universe that have held humanity under their dominion (cf. also Gal. 4:1 ff.). For the baptized believer, subjection to such worldly spirits, powers, or authorities is a thing of the past; they had been conquered and rendered harmless, or "disarmed." Christ is the universal or *cosmic* redeemer.

The remainder of the **epistle** (2:16–4:6) is largely concerned with the **ethical** implications of Paul's **theological** argument. In 2:16–23 he rejects the spurious asceticism of the Colossian heretics, which takes no account of Christ's lordship over the world but is simply subservient to the things that Christ has already overcome (2:20). Such religiosity, ascetic though it may be, does not finally escape the lordship of the flesh (2:23; note the NRSV's alternative reading: "of no value, serving only to indulge the flesh"). The believer is not, however, subject to the elemental spirits of the universe. Instead he lives in the realm of the resurrected Christ (3:1 ff.). With Christ and the believer now portrayed as sitting at the right hand of God, Paul seems to flirt with speculative fancy. But such resurrection life is interpreted as this-worldly existence, free from the power of sin, death, and "things that are on earth" (vs. 2; Paul probably has in mind those elemental spirits of which he has already spoken). To all these the believer has died. Life is now secure with God (vs. 3), and the believer hopes to share in the **eschatological** glory of Christ (vs. 4).

Emphasis on the present reality of resurrection life is nevertheless somewhat strange in Paul, who elsewhere hesitates to speak of believers as if they had already attained resurrection glory (cf. the future tense applied to resurrection in Rom. 6:5; also 1 Cor. 4:8). On the other hand, this idea is common in Ephesians (2:4–9), where believers are also said to *have been* saved (2:8). In the undisputed letters of Paul, **salvation** is reserved for the eschatological future (Rom. 13:11). Believers are in this age justified and reconciled to God so that their future salvation is assured.

Like Ephesians, Colossians makes much of the church as the body of Christ (Col. 1:18, 24; 3:15), an idea that is surely rooted in Pauline thought (1 Cor. 12; Rom. 12:4–8). Yet it is an interesting and perhaps significant fact that the earlier Paul says, "You are the body of Christ" (1 Cor. 12:27) or "We are one body in Christ" (Rom. 12:5) but never makes the more abstract claim that the church is the body of Christ, although the latter is the apparent meaning of his conception. It is as if Colossians and Ephesians were developing a doctrine of the church as the body of Christ from a Pauline metaphor. In Colossians (3:18) and Ephesians (5:23) that metaphor is extended, as Christ becomes the *head* of the church, which is his body.

EPHESIANS: LOOKING TO THE FOUNDATION
Background of Ephesians

Although Colossians does not clearly imply a time and church situation subsequent to Paul's ministry, unless the erroneous teaching is regarded as post-Pauline **Gnosticism**, Ephesians does seem to presuppose a different and later setting. It also manifests other points of divergence from Paul. The indications of this changed situation are subtle but nonetheless real.

The style of the author's Greek, which is clearly reflected in a good English translation (especially the RSV), is elaborate to the point of ostentation (cf. esp. 1:15–23, which the RSV preserves in one sentence, as it is in Greek, while the NRSV breaks the passage down into several English sentences). The sentences also lack the pungency, abruptness, and punch of Paul's rough but eloquent style. In this respect Ephesians is farther removed from Paul than Colossians, while at the same time bearing such a close resemblance to it at several points that the possibility of literary dependence on Colossians cannot be dismissed (cf. Col. 1:21–22 and Eph. 2:11; Col. 1:25–27 and Eph. 3:4–7; Col. 2:19 and Eph. 4:15–16). Paul sometimes has difficulty ending a sentence (cf. Gal. 2:6–10) because so many thoughts and considerations pile into his mind. In Ephesians, however, the long sentence seems to be a deliberate and eloquent development based on the study of Paul.

There are other differences, which betray a somewhat different theological perspective. For example, the "mystery" spoken of in Ephesians (3:3) is the incorporation of Gentiles, along with Jews, into the body of Christ (3:6), whereas the "mystery" of which Paul speaks in 1 Corinthians (15:51) is **apocalyptic**; it concerns the transformation of the **resurrection**. When Paul uses the term in 1 Corinthians 4:1, its meaning is scarcely the same as in Ephesians. This apparent shift in terminology typifies the ecclesial focus of Ephesians; that is, emphasis shifts toward the **church** as the center of **theological** interest. This shift is clearly evident in the text that we treat below (2:11–22). There the church is said to be founded upon the **apostles** and **prophets**, as if these were ancient worthies rather than contemporaries (cf. 1 Cor. 12:28–29).

A final characteristic of Ephesians sets it apart from the other Pauline letters: it is a general **epistle**, not a letter written to a specific church. The oldest manuscripts do not contain "Ephesus" in the salutation, and this omission corresponds with the lack of specific reference to persons and places at the end of the letter. (The RSV's omission of "in Ephesus" better represents the textual tradition than the NRSV's inclusion of it.) Aside from Tychicus (6:21) the conclusion contains no references to persons or events (cf. Col. 4:7–8). When "Ephesus" falls out of the salutation, Ephesians becomes a letter addressed by Paul to all Christians. Its general, even universal, salutation then corresponds to its content. It is a compendium of Pauline ideas and theology, having close parallels not only with Colossians but also with the other, genuine Pauline letters (cf. Eph. 1:3 and 2 Cor. 1:3; Eph. 4:4, 11 and 1 Cor. 12 or Rom. 12:5; Eph. 6:13–17 and 1 Thess. 5:8).

We can no longer say for what specific purpose Ephesians was written. E. J. Goodspeed's suggestion that it was devised as a covering letter for the first, or an early, collection of Paul's letters is plausible but cannot be proven (*The Meaning of Ephesians* [Chicago: University of Chicago Press, 1933]). The earliest known collection of Paul's letters, that of Marcion (ca. A.D. 140), whose views came to be regarded as heretical, contained Ephesians (although not Hebrews or the Pastorals). Thus we can be certain that its reputation and authority had been established less than a century after its composition.

OUTLINE OF EPHESIANS

Address (1:1–2)
Thanksgiving and Praise of God and Christ (1:3–23)
Christ's Work and Its Results (2:1–3:21)

Christ's Saving Work (2:1–10)
The Unity of the Church (2:11–22)
Paul's Ministry (3:1–13)
Prayer for the Church (3:14–21)

Ethical Instructions and Exhortations (4:1–6:20)

Basis for Ethics in Christ and the Church (4:1–16)
General Instructions for Christians (4:17–5:20)
Instructions for Families (5:21–6:9)
Final Summary Exhortations (6:10–20)

Conclusion and Benediction (6:21–24)

The Unity of the Church (Eph. 2:11–22)

How does Ephesians interrelate the topics of Jew, Gentile, and church?

The introductory hymn of praise (1:3–23) elaborates the characteristic Pauline thanksgiving. Whereas the typical thanksgiving makes contact with the concrete situation of the church Paul is addressing, the Ephesian thanksgiving does not. It is long, solemn, and liturgical. The thanksgiving ends with chapter 1, and the second major phase of the letter begins. It is a kind of declaration or address to the readers. The author starts in the second person, "you," but more than once slips over into the confessional first person plural, "we" or "us" (cf. 2:3–7, 10).

The next section (2:1–10) relates God's **saving** act in Jesus Christ, already set forth in Old Testament imagery (1:15–23; cf. Ps. 110), to believers. The Pauline language and conceptuality are clearly visible. No single passage from Paul's **epistles** is the source or model of this passage, but many familiar Pauline themes appear. For obvious reasons, 2:8 ff. is often quoted as a succinct statement of Pauline theology. It is, even though it was probably not written by Paul. This whole section is to be placed alongside others in the genuine letters (Rom. 3:21–31; 5:1–11; 1 Cor. 1:18–25; 2 Cor. 5:16–21; and Gal. 2:14–21) as a classic summation of Pauline theology.

The same solemn tone that has so far dominated the letter continues, but in 2:11–22 a subtle shift of emphasis occurs. Whereas 2:1–10 deals with the work of Christ on behalf of individuals, in 2:11–22 attention shifts to the church. Of course, the church was already in view (cf. 1:22 ff.), and the individual is not now lost from sight. Nevertheless, the passage in question (2:11–22) focuses upon the church. Even though the word *church* does not appear, emphasis falls upon the idea of community and the creation of this community through the death of Jesus.

The marble street in Ephesus originally ran down to the sea, which has receded several miles since Paul's day. Because Paul had a significant ministry in Ephesus (Acts 18:18–19:41), later Pauline letters were thought to have been sent there (cf. Ephesians 1:1) or refer to others (Timothy) being sent there (1 Timothy 5:13).

The author envisions the church as composed primarily of **Gentiles** rather than Jews (2:11, see also 3:1; cf. 4:17). Inasmuch as he speaks for Paul, he naturally takes the position of the Jew. Already in this verse we read of the existence of two groups, distinguished by their circumcision or lack of circumcision in the flesh. They are both communities in and of the flesh: that is, ethnic communities. As far as the author is concerned, the circumcision made in the flesh by hands does not give those circumcised any particular advantage. Yet this does not mean that Israel as God's people has no theological significance. Here the author remains quite close to Paul's own thought. Israel as an ethnic group, as the circumcision, has no particular advantage, but the same may not be said of Israel as the inheritor of God's promises. The advantage of the Jew or of Israel in the latter sense (cf. Rom. 3:1, 9, and 9:1 ff.) is apparent in the statement that follows immediately (vs. 12). Even the phrase "without Christ" implies the advantage of the Jew over the Gentile, because the **Messiah** is promised to Israel. To be "aliens from the commonwealth of Israel" is also to be separated from the messianic hope, as is indicated by the phrase "strangers to the covenants of promise." Obviously what is meant are the covenant promises to Israel. Significantly, Gentiles are characterized as "aliens" and "strangers." Their situation is one of being alone, cut off, lost in the most profound and far-reaching sense of the word. Moreover, they are hopeless and godless. Although the author does not grant any particular advantage or significance to fleshly circumcision per se, he ascribes the greatest significance to Israel as the object of God's redemption and the community of God's people. To be alienated from Israel is to be without hope and without God in the world.

The work of Christ is interpreted as the recovery of the estranged (vs. 13). "By the blood of Christ" refers to Christ's death understood as a **sacrifice** on behalf of humanity. The concept of being "far off" can be understood in the light of what immediately precedes (vss. 11–12). But what is meant by "have been brought near"? Naturally, one would suspect that, since the estrangement was defined in terms of separation from Israel, reconciliation and **salvation** would be described as union or reunion with Israel. Thus, "being brought near" would mean the Gentiles' association, or incorporation, with the covenant people. This is partly what is meant; however, Christ is peace for both Jew and Gentile (vs. 14). He effects reconciliation (vs. 16) between them, making them one (vs. 14) by breaking down the "dividing wall, that is, the hostility between us." Moreover, he sets aside the Jewish **law**, the commandments and ordinances (2:15). Jesus' abolishing them in his flesh doubtless refers to his death. The author has in mind other, similar Pauline statements (cf. Gal. 3:13; Rom. 7:4 and 8:3).

The Temple: Transforming a Religious Catastrophe into a Theological Confession

Ephesians 2:14 refers to a breakdown of the dividing wall of hostility. This is often taken to be an allusion to the destruction of the wall of the Jerusalem temple that separated the court of the **Gentiles** from the inner court open only to Jews (Josephus, *Jewish War* V. 190–200). The removal of that wall would allow those who were far off—the Gentiles—to be brought near (2:13). Rome's destruction of Jerusalem in A.D. 70 and the ensuing demolition of the temple walls may have suggested this way of describing Christ's work. The intent of such an allusion is suggested by the extensive use of temple imagery in verses 20–22. It also comports with our suggestion that Ephesians is pseudonymous, not the work of Paul, and was written after the temple's destruction.

Jesus' death marks the end of the period in which the law holds sway. Christ is the end of the **law** (Rom. 10:4). By bringing the law to naught, Christ does away with the hostility that separates Jew from Gentile, and thus becomes their peace. It is not simply a matter of Gentiles becoming Jews, for the fundamental status of the believing Jew is also changed. The author's careful qualification of the law as the "law with its commandments and ordinances" implies that Christ sets aside the particular, Jewish formulation of the law of God, but without introducing an era of lawlessness. The result of abolition of any distinction between Jew and Gentile is the creation of "one new humanity" in Christ (vs. 15). The creation of the "new humanity" is the prerequisite for peace among all peoples (vs. 15), as well as with God (vs. 16). This new human being (4:24; NRSV: "the new self") can obey God. (The same Greek word, *anthrōpos*, whence the English *anthropology*, is used in 2:15 and 4:24.) The *creation* (vs. 15) of the "new" man in place of the "old" man probably intends to recall 2 Corinthians 5:17: "So if anyone is in Christ, there is a new creation; everything old has passed away; see, everything has become new!"

The idea that reconciliation comes through the cross of Christ is what we might have expected from a Paulinist (vs. 16), and the term *body* (Greek, *sōma*) is thoroughly Pauline. In fact, Ephesians here combines different Pauline uses. The primary reference, obviously, is to the **crucified** body of Jesus, who becomes a curse for us (Gal. 3:13)— who becomes **sin**, or a sin–offering, for our sake (2 Cor. 5:21). Christ died for our sins (1 Cor. 15:3), whose death is our reconciliation: "while we were enemies, we were reconciled to God through the death of his Son" (Rom. 5:10). In addition, the peculiar wording of Ephesians 2:16, "in one body," implies an identification of those being reconciled with the reconciler. Again the union of the believer with the crucified is a typical Pauline motif: "I have been crucified with Christ" (Gal. 2:19); "you have died to the law through the body of Christ" (Rom. 7:4). Moreover, the body is an important Pauline image, signifying the unity of Christians in Christ—that is, the **church** (Eph. 1:22; 1 Cor. 12; Rom. 12:3–8; see Chapter 10, pp. 368–370). The initial theme of this passage was community, and the recitation of Christ's work has focused upon its effect in reconstituting unity or community between God and humanity and, especially, among different peoples.

This emphasis on restored community is reiterated (vss. 17 ff.). Those who are far off are doubtless Gentiles, and those who are near, Jews (vs. 17). The present unified status before God of both Jew and Gentile is described as "access in one spirit" (vs. 18). Once again, the thought is a legitimate echo of Pauline theology. The idea of a new access to God through Jesus has appeared already (Rom. 5:2). That the mode of this access to God is the **Spirit** is a thought that pervades Paul's writings (e.g., Rom. 8; 1 Cor. 12). The Spirit assures the reality of the new condition enjoyed by the believer. The Spirit and Christ are not to be identified, but the Spirit is the means or mode of Christ's presence, and therefore of access to God.

Mention of the one Spirit leads to the theme of the unity of the new community (vss. 20–22) constituted by the new humanity. Again we have a Pauline web of ideas. For the new community is characterized by the possession of the Spirit, and the Spirit-possessed community is the body of Christ (cf. vs. 16 and 1 Cor. 12:12 ff.). The idea of

Spirit and body is not, however, developed immediately. Instead, another typical Pauline image, that of the house or temple, is invoked, though as we shall see with some uncharacteristic variations.

The author solemnly declares (vs. 19) that the situation of separation (vss. 11 ff.) is no more. The Gentiles have been incorporated into the reconstituted humanity that is the church. They are now "citizens with the saints"—that is, Israel. Yet "Israel" herself has been thoroughly redefined through Christ, who puts an end to the law and by implication to the "circumcision made in the flesh by human hands" (2:11). "Saints" (vs. 19) now simply means "those consecrated to God," a biblical idea and Paul's common designation of Christians (1 Cor. 1:2).

"Household of God" (vs. 19; literally "householders of God") evokes the temple imagery, developed in verses 20–22. The foundation of the building that is to be the temple is first described (vs. 20). The description given here may be contrasted to 1 Corinthians 3:11, where Paul emphatically maintains that Jesus Christ alone is the foundation of the building that is the church. Although the sharpness of the disagreement is softened by the designation of Christ as the chief cornerstone (probably the keystone that holds the entire structure together, as in an arch; cf. vs. 21), there is still an important difference. That difference is heightened when the **prophets** and **apostles** are called "**holy**" (3:5). In contrast to Paul, for whom every true member of the church is holy or a saint (the two words are the same in Greek), the word is here used to set apart the apostles and prophets as a special and superior group within the church—much in the manner in which the words are used in medieval and modern ecclesiastical parlance. The prophets and apostles appear to be elevated as a special group (vs. 20). Even though in Paul's own thought the apostle plays a key role and the prophet is second only to him (1 Cor. 12:28), Paul goes out of his way to maintain that there are no fundamental distinctions among members of Christ's body (1 Cor. 12, esp. 12:13). Probably the author of Ephesians would not have denied this. Yet the idea of a special status of the apostolate slips into his understanding of the church's structure.

Ephesians does not, however, consciously downgrade the role of Jesus Christ in favor of the apostles (cf. vs. 21). The church is held together in Christ and grows in him. Although being in Christ is a Pauline concept, the new twist in Ephesians is that the church grows in Christ (vs. 21; cf. 4:13, 15). Again, Pauline imagery is developed further in Ephesians: in this passage, by a combining of motifs. The temple, not the body, is the explicit subject. Yet the concept of growth obviously relates to the body, as is made plain at other points in this letter (cf. 4:12, 16, where the building imagery also appears). Apparently, the image of the body lies in the background (cf. 1:22 ff.; 2:16) and enriches the temple image.

The Gentiles, who once were aliens but later were brought near and made fellow citizens, are now built into a new building or structure, which is to be a dwelling place for God (vs. 22). The notion that God or his glory dwells in his temple stems from the Old Testament and was applied to the Jerusalem temple until its destruction. Although that temple had probably been destroyed by the time Ephesians was written, Paul had previously anticipated the designation of Christ's church as the new temple by his use of such imagery in relation to the new community and its members (1 Cor. 3:16 ff.; 6:19 ff.; 2 Cor. 6:16). The older view of God's dwelling in his temple envisioned his abiding in a building; in this new conception the "building" is the community of persons, the church. In 1 Peter 2:4 ff., the figure of the building or temple is taken yet a step farther: individual Christians, like Christ, are described as "living stones."

The passage we have considered marks the culmination of theological themes that Ephesians has developed. Formally, the theological section of the **epistle** continues to the benediction at the end of chapter 3. But that chapter is basically a recapitulation of what has gone before, with special reference to Paul's ministry.

Significantly, the drama of salvation just narrated is now described as Paul's insight into the mystery of Christ (3:6): "that is, the Gentiles have become fellow heirs, members of the same body, and sharers in the promise in Christ Jesus through the gospel." Clearly the author regards this as the peculiarly Pauline understanding of the **gospel**. It is true that for Paul the gospel implies the church, and the church abolishes the distinctions of an age already passing away. Moreover, the scriptural prophecies are directed to persons of faith, not to Israel according to the flesh. Paul, however, does not regard the incorporation of the Gentiles into the body of Christ as his *central* insight into the mystery of the gospel. The elements of thought are Pauline, but the focus has shifted. There has been a subtle change in the center of interest and emphasis in Ephesians from Christ to the church. This does not mean that Christ's importance is lessened, or that the church was unimportant to Paul, but that the church as the outcome of Christ's work and Christ's historical embodiment increasingly becomes the main subject of the author's theological concern. Hence he takes Paul's central insight to be **ecclesiological**. He returns to the theme of the church again and again (1:22 ff.; 2:11–22; 3:6, 10; 4:1–16; 5:21–33; 6:10–20). After chapter 2, the church may not be so explicitly discussed, though it is exhorted. And this exhortation seems directed not to individual problems or specific situations, but to the church in general. Even practical instructions regarding the relationship of husband and wife are seen as expressing the exemplary relation of Christ and the church—"the two shall become one flesh" (5:31 ff.).

Ephesians develops Paul's thought in the light of a new situation. Its concentration of interest upon the church is not un-Pauline so much as it is a development on the basis of Paul. It is, moreover, a development in the light of a peculiar state of affairs that Paul did not anticipate. That, in a real sense, makes us and the author of Ephesians closer to each other than to Paul. The Apostle anticipated Christ's imminent return and the end of the age. Ephesians reflects no such urgent anticipation. The church will have to exist as an institution in this world for quite a while. The solemn injunction to put on the whole armor of God indicates that the author expects a long fight. (Similar imagery appears in 1 Thess. 5:8, but in an **eschatological** context missing in Ephesians.) Yet Ephesians manifests no weakening of conviction or attenuation of the faith.

THE PASTORALS: THE COMMUNITY AS INSTITUTION
Background of the Pastoral Epistles

Whereas Ephesians was originally addressed to Christians generally, the **Pastorals** are cast in the form of letters to Timothy and Titus, Paul's fellow workers, who are mentioned frequently in the other Pauline letters. According to Acts, Paul found Timothy in Lystra, Asia Minor (16:1, cf. 2 Tim. 3:11). Because his mother was a Jewish believer, and thus Timothy was considered Jewish, Paul circumcised him (16:3). According to Paul, Titus, a **Gentile**, was not required to be circumcised (Gal. 2:3). He is not mentioned in Acts.

Unlike the letters previously considered, the Pastorals do not quite fit any situation described in the Book of Acts. According to 1 Timothy, Timothy is in Ephesus, where he has been urged to remain (1:3). Paul himself seems to write from Macedonia (1:3). Perhaps the situation envisioned corresponds to 1 Corinthians 16, where Paul plans to travel to Macedonia (vs. 5) and anticipates Timothy's return to Ephesus (vs. 11)—although this is entirely hypothetical.

In 2 Timothy, Paul is imprisoned in Rome (1:17), where he has survived one trial (4:16–18) but apparently awaits further proceedings and his own death (4:6–8). Various coworkers of Paul are located, but we are not told Timothy's whereabouts. Possibly he is still in Ephesus (1:15, 18). In any event, Paul urges him to join him (4:9).

Titus is in Crete when Paul writes him (1:5) from Nicopolis (3:12), on the Adriatic shore of Greece, a city mentioned in neither Acts nor the other Pauline letters. According to Acts, Paul did not visit Crete until his final journey to Rome (27:7); there is no mention of Titus' accompanying him on that journey. The Epistle to Titus might have been composed during a period of Paul's ministry not recorded in Acts, perhaps after his "first defense" (2 Tim. 4:16), assuming he then gained his freedom temporarily. Such reconstructions are highly speculative, however, and are probably unnecessary, for there are significant grounds for doubting that the Pastorals were composed during Paul's lifetime.

Marcion did not include the Pastorals in the first known collection of Paul's letters (ca. 140), and one of the earliest papyrus manuscripts of the Greek New Testament (P^{46}, dating from the end of the second century) does not have and perhaps never contained them. Of course, Marcion was condemned as a heretic because he believed that the God of the Old Testament was not the Father of Jesus Christ, and denied the goodness of creation. Had he known them, Marcion might have rejected the Pastorals as inauthentic for **theological** reasons (cf. 1 Tim. 4:1–5). We cannot be certain he knew them, but even if he was acquainted with them, evidently he believed he could reject them without sacrificing his own credibility.

The Greek style and especially the language of the Pastorals are markedly different from the other Pauline letters, including Colossians and Ephesians. The Pastorals have a vocabulary of just over 900 words (848, exclusive of proper names). Of these, 306 are not found elsewhere in the Pauline letters (as compared with 177 words not found elsewhere in the **authentic** 2 Corinthians, which is a much longer). About 175 words are not found elsewhere in the New Testament; 211 are common to second-century Christianity; only about 50 are distinctly Pauline. There are no dialogues with an imaginary opponent. The syntax does not reflect Paul's emotional involvement. Occasionally there is an obviously poor imitation of Paul (1 Tim. 2:7, where Paul's claim that he is not lying seems pointless; cf. Gal. 1:20). Style, as well as vocabulary, are somewhat different from the other Pauline letters.

Moreover, the theology of the Pastorals differs from that of the other letters even, perhaps especially, where the same words are used. For example, in Paul *faith* (Greek, *pistis*) means the acceptance of God's grace, trusting what God has done in Jesus (see also Chapter 8, pp. 287–289). It refers primarily to a believing, faithful relationship. In the Pastorals, however, *faith* means primarily the content or object of belief. Thus the author speaks of "the faith" (1 Tim. 3:9; 4:1; 2 Tim. 4:7), meaning a body of doctrine. This change signals a significant theological difference, suggesting a later time in which the defense of correct belief had become a primary concern. Indeed, the danger of heresy has become acute (1 Tim. 6:20–21). Moreover, **righteousness** has become a virtue (1 Tim. 6:11) along with godliness, faith, love, steadfastness, and gentleness (cf. 2 Tim. 3:16: "training in righteousness"). It is no longer tied to an action or **revelation** of God. The statement about the **law** in 1 Timothy 1:7–11 may sound Pauline but on closer examination is unlike what Paul says elsewhere. The **Spirit** is spoken of rarely (cf. 2 Tim. 1:14); the body (or body of Christ), not at all. Religion or godliness (*eusebeia*) plays an important role; by contrast, the term does not figure in Paul's other letters.

OUTLINE OF 1 TIMOTHY

Address (1:1–2)
Warning against Heresy and Heretics (1:3–20)
Manual of Church Order (2:1–3:16)

Worship (2:1–15)
Qualifications and Duties of the Clergy (3:1–16)

Manual for Ministers (4:1–6:19)

Heresy and Right Teaching in the Church (4:1–16)
Dealing with Elders and Widows (5:1–22)
Personal Advice (5:23–24)
Advice to Slaves (6:1–2)
Dangers of False Teachers and Teachings (6:3–10)
Exhortation to Ministers (6:11–19)

Conclusion (6:20–21)

Heresy and Right Teaching in the Church (1 Tim. 4:1–16)

Why was an ordained ministry necessary and important?

In the **Pastorals,** the development of **church** organization runs parallel to the development of doctrine. In the other Pauline letters there are various functions and offices in the church, all of which are equally gifts of the Spirit (1 Cor. 12). Although Paul singles out **apostles**, along with **prophets** and teachers, as having priority (12:28), he does not distinguish clergy from laity. Apparently, he does not know an ordained Christian clergy; even where he mentions deacons and bishops (Phil. 1:1) it is not clear he regards them as a distinct group. In the Pastorals, on the other hand, specific qualifications for bishops and deacons are set forth (1 Tim. 3:1–13). Timothy himself is called a servant of Jesus Christ (1 Tim. 4:6; *diakonos* or deacon), and his ordination by elders is mentioned (1 Tim. 4:14). Directions concerning "elders who rule" are given to him, and he is in charge of their ordination (5:17–22). Timothy is obviously a church officer of the highest rank who presides over bishops and elders (cf. Titus 1:5). As such, he is the guardian of the church's faith and doctrine (1 Tim. 6:20–21; 2 Tim. 1:13–14).

That the faith has attained creedal formulation is evident from several statements in the Pastorals (e.g., 1 Tim. 2:4–6; 2 Tim. 2:11–13). Distinctively Christian writings may be used and extolled in the churches of the Pastorals (2 Tim. 3:15), and all scripture, including the Old Testament, is commended (2 Tim. 3:16). Timothy's faith began with his grandmother Lois and apparently came down to him through her and his mother Eunice (2 Tim. 1:5). This does not necessarily mean that Timothy was a third-generation Christian, but when we first meet him in Acts (16:1–3) he is already a believer, as was his mother. In Acts, there is no mention of his grandmother, but the picture of Timothy as the descendant of a Christian family of long standing fits what the Pastorals otherwise convey: the church is well established and has been for some time. It is girding itself to live in the world for a period of indefinite duration. This attitude contrasts sharply with that of Paul himself, who thought the **parousia** was at hand (Rom. 13:12) and prayed for Jesus' return (1 Cor. 16:22).

The exterior of the Theater at Ephesus (for its interior, see p. 265) conveys a sense of its immense size. It could seat 25,000 or more spectators.

The concern to establish church order and church office, thus ensuring the continuity and stability of church doctrine against aberration or heresy, reflects the recognition of the changed conditions under which the church was living. 1 Timothy 4 is a good cross-section of the letter, as it reveals most of the Pastorals' distinguishing features. The first five verses deal with heresy—false teaching—that has arisen within the Christian community. The remainder of the chapter is the opening of a section designated in the outline as a manual for ministers.

When the author says that the heretics against whom he struggles were to be anticipated (4:1), the edge is taken off the hard and discouraging fact that even within the community of faith error persists. This unhappy circumstance occurs with God's foreknowledge; the Spirit predicts it. The same motif appears elsewhere in the New Testament (Mark 13:5 ff.; Acts 20:28–30; 2 Pet. 3:3; 1 John 2:18; Jude 18). The common element in these texts is the fact that the church has been duly warned of the appearance of evil persons within its midst. In an earlier period Paul recognized the existence and danger of such persons (Phil. 3:1 ff.) but said nothing about their having been predicted.

The attitude of our author is intolerant, because the heretics have "renounced the faith" by attending to "deceitful spirits" and "teachings of demons" (vss. 1–2). The luxury of allowing each his or her own view in religious matters is impossible for the Pastor. He is a churchman concerned about the truth of the Christian message, the church's proper preservation of it, and the obedient ordering of church life in the **gospel**'s light. The false doctrine he denounces and deplores has immediate practical ramifications, for heretical beliefs lead inevitably to the wrong ordering of life (vss. 3–5).

The ascetic, world-denying character of this heresy is apparent (vs. 3). The heretics' asceticism—avoidance of sex and certain food—suggests that they are closely related to, if not identical with, the **Gnostics** denounced by the Christian Fathers in the second century. The earlier description of false teachers (1:3–7) corresponds rather well with this aberrant form of Christianity. Confirmation is also found at the end, where Timothy is advised to "avoid the profane chatter and contradictions of what is falsely called knowledge" (6:20). The Greek word translated *knowledge* is *gnōsis*, whence the name of this heresy—Gnosticism. The widespread appearance of this heretical version of the Christian gospel, which defined the Christian message as a program of escape from this evil world to a good one above, was one of the most important developments in the history of second-century Christianity. First Timothy probably represents an early stage in the emergence, identification, and rejection of the Gnostic viewpoint. We cannot assume, however, that Gnosticism is the only heresy attacked in the Pastoral letters.

In opposition to this specious and harmful asceticism, the author lays out his own position (vss. 4 ff.). His view had been adumbrated in verse 3 ("received with thanksgiving"; cf. the same phrase in vs. 4), where the phrase "by those who believe and *know the truth*" may be consciously formulated in opposition to the claims of the Gnostics. First Timothy (4:4 ff.) vigorously reasserts the claim of the Old Testament (Genesis 1:29), Judaism, and Jesus himself that God's creation is fundamentally good. Though not denied by the earliest generation of Christians, this belief was relegated to the periphery because of their eager expectation of further revelations from the Lord and a correspondingly low estimate of this world. What has become the classical Christian position is clearly formulated in 1 Timothy: "Everything created by God is good, and nothing is to be rejected, provided it is received with thanksgiving." "Thanksgiving" involves consecration by God's **word** and by prayer (vss. 4 ff.). What "God's word" means in this context is not obvious; possibly it signifies scripture. Although the New Testament had not yet been formed, the Old was the Bible of the Christian community.

The next two paragraphs (vss. 6–10 and 11–16) instruct Timothy, and therefore the clergy, about the church's ministry and administration. The following section (5:1–6:2) contains specific guidance for dealing with various groups in the church, especially widows, who were considered the responsibility of the community. Thus we have a kind of manual for the minister.

"These instructions" (4:6) may refer to all that has preceded in the letter or to what follows. Either makes good sense. The term *servant* or *minister* apparently designates an office or class of offices in the church. In chapter 3 the qualifications for ministry, the offices of bishop and deacon, have been outlined. "Timothy" is himself such a "minister" in the official clerical sense. He has been ordained to this ministry through the laying on of hands (vs. 14). The investiture of the historical Timothy by a board of elders seems unlikely and does not agree with the account of Paul's enlistment of Timothy in Acts 16:1–3. This section of the letter is more intelligible on the assumption that it was written for the benefit of the church's nascent official ministry, a generation or two after Paul.

The emphasis on right doctrine (vs. 6b) supports this view. "The words of the faith," an un-Pauline expression, refers to the right formulation of the confession of faith, as the immediately following mention of sound teaching (or doctrine) shows. For Paul, faith implies belief, trust, obedience, an orientation of life, and a relationship. Of course, faith for Paul has an object toward which it is directed and about which intelligible things can be said. Yet Paul does not emphasize the correct doctrinal formulation in the manner in which the Pastorals do. Even less does he understand faith in the sense of "*the faith*"—the correct doctrinal formula.

A major reason for this difference between Paul and the Pastorals appears in the reference to profane myths and old wives' tales (vs. 7). Doubtless the rise of strange teachings leads to the emphasis upon right doctrine that we find in the Pastorals. The appearance of contradictory beliefs necessitates the definition of the true teaching. Now we may use the term *heresy* in its proper sense: a contradiction of, or departure from, established doctrine (cf. pp. 395 ff.). The false teachers are considered beyond the pale (cf. 4:1–5; 6:3 ff.); indeed, there is no question of discussion with them, much less of winning them back. They must be prevented from contaminating the church and pulling others down with them. It is a good question whether the difference between the Pastorals and their opponents and Paul and his foes is more than one of degree. In any event the gulf separating them is deeper, the lines of separation more sharply drawn.

Attention next focuses upon the relative merits of physical training and training in godliness (vss. 7b–10). The Pastorals regularly underscore an important saying with some such assertion as "the saying is sure" (vs. 9; cf. 1:15; 3:1; 2 Tim. 2:11; Titus 3:8). Probably this formula indicates a traditional saying. The KJV's "bodily exercise profiteth little" is closer to the Greek original than is the NRSV (vs. 8); 1 Timothy wishes to contrast the little profit of bodily training with the great values of training in godliness. "Godliness" (*eusebeia*) is a word found not at all in Paul, and quite rarely in the New Testament outside the Pastorals and 2 Peter . It is, in fact, a term more at home in ancient **Hellenistic** piety than in specifically biblical or Christian faith. "Piety" might be an equally good translation of the Greek word in question. The high value that the Pastorals ascribe to this quality is significant, underscoring how their thought differs from Paul's own outlook. For him, the mode of Christian existence is faith, life in Christ or in the **Spirit**; the term for godliness or piety does not occur. In the Pastorals the mode of Christian existence is godliness and piety; faith is the body of right doctrine. The concepts "in Christ" and "in the Spirit" play little or no role in the Pastorals. It is typical of them that the promise for the present life and the life to come is directly related, not to Christ and the Spirit, but instead to godliness (vs. 8b).

The toiling and striving of those whose exercise is godliness have as their goal the believers' hope in the living God and Savior (vs. 10). The anti-Gnostic character of the Pastorals' polemic may appear again in this affirmation of God as the Savior of all. Commonly in Gnosticism, only an elect group with a disposition for and capability of possessing knowledge could attain **salvation**. Here God is the Savior of all, not a special class. That God actually saves only those who believe is the probable meaning of the last clause (cf. 2:1–6). But 1 Timothy declares quite clearly that no one stands presumptively outside the potential realm of God's **redemption**.

The specific referent of "these things" in the following exhortation is unclear (vs. 11; cf. vs. 6). Does it refer to what precedes or what follows, or is it a general exhortation without any specific point of reference? The latter is more likely. At any rate, what immediately follows (vss. 12–16) is not material that Timothy would command and teach but rather advice to him personally. The injunction to Timothy to let no one despise his youth (vs. 12) and the indication that Paul plans a visit (vs. 13) lend a note of verisimilitude to the correspondence, but they are probably part of the cloak of pseudonymity in which the letter is clad. The rest is general instruction to the pastor, like much of the Pastorals. We have already noted that verse 14 presupposes the existence of an ordained ministry.

The word here translated *gift* is the Greek **charisma**, which implies a special spiritual endowment. Paul held that the *charismata*, "spiritual gifts," were distributed among all the members of the community, so that, although there are varieties of gifts and services, all Christians are, so to speak, gifted (1 Cor. 12). Here, however, the charismatic gift is limited, whether consciously or not, to the particular power and authority of an all-male ministerial office (cf. 1 Tim. 2:11–12; again, contrast Paul: Rom. 16:1; 1 Cor. 11:5). The gift is granted by the laying on of hands as well as by **prophecy**. "Prophecy" is probably an allusion to the Spirit-inspired designation of people for certain tasks, characteristic of earliest Christianity (Acts 13:12; 1 Cor. 12:28; 14:1). But in spite of the continuation of prophetic utterance, the Spirit's dispensation appears tied to institutional office and ordination. What, then, of the Spirit's free movement and authority in the community? Is spontaneity being sacrificed to the church's need for unity and order? If so, is this necessary? Is the price too great to pay? The Pastorals do not represent the only period in the church's history that has entertained such questions as these.

The other injunctions (vss. 12 ff. and 15 ff.) mirror the continuing life of the community, now a religious institution. Official leaders are to set the example in faith, conduct, and related matters (vs. 12), seeing after their duties of conducting public worship (vs. 13) and supervising the education of the people in sound doctrine (vss. 13–16) to the end that both minister and people will be saved (vs. 16). The model of the church as a continuing community composed of leaders and followers, clergy and laity, making its way through the world toward greater things that God has in store, is the legitimate legacy of the Pastoral Epistles.

Finally, the reader is left with the impression of Paul as pastor. This Paul cares for and provides for the indefinite continuation and survival of the church. He instructs Timothy, his coworker, to establish the clergy, to guard true doctrine, to resist error, and to preserve discipline and order among the faithful. This Paul is not without strong positive ties to the historical Paul of the **authentic** letters. Nevertheless, expectations had changed as conditions had changed. It was tacitly acknowledged that, although Jesus would return (1 Tim. 6:14; 2 Tim. 4:1), in the meantime generations might come and go, as perhaps they already had (2 Tim. 1:5). In 1 Timothy 4, we find an excellent sample of the concern for the church's continuing life and teaching that characterizes these letters. The Paul of the Pastorals extends his authority and ministry to the ongoing church.

CONCLUSION: SOLIDIFYING CHRISTIANITY'S IDENTITY

The formation of Christian identity and the problem of its maintenance are themes shot through all of the New Testament documents. They are manifest in writings like 1 Corinthians, as Paul struggles to clarify Christian responsibilities within a pagan world, and in Matthew, which serves as a kind of manual of discipline for that evangelist's church. In the Deutero-Pauline **epistles**, however, these issues and the manner of dealing with them become more explicit. By the second or third Christian generation—the era roughly spanning the Deutero-Pauline letters and the **Catholic Epistles**, to be taken up in the next chapter—various strategies had come to be adopted for defining and maintaining Christian identity.

The Distinction of Orthodoxy and Heresy

Although anachronistic at its earliest stage, "heresy" (understood as fallacious opinion) and "orthodoxy" (straight thinking), their definitions and boundaries, become increasingly important within churches of the late first and early second centuries. As we have seen, it appears to have been a primary occasion for the writing of Colossians. Though difficult to identify with precision, the opponents defied in that letter appear to advocate a "philosophy" that subordinates Christ to "the elemental spirits of the universe" (Col. 2:8). Endeavoring to follow in Paul's footsteps, the author of the **Pastoral Epistles** repeatedly repudiates "godless and silly myths" (1 Tim. 4:7; also 1:4; 2 Tim. 4:4; Tit. 1:14). Indeed, he appears certain enough of his own orthodoxy that he can denounce those whom he regards as corrupters of the faith, placing upon them a ban of excommunication (Titus 3:10 ff.). The challenge of aberrant teaching will reappear in 1 John (2:18–19), Jude (vv. 5–16), and Revelation (1:1–3:21). Jude writes forcefully "to contend for the faith which was once for all delivered to the saints" (v. 3): an indication, not only of the ever-pressing task of attempting to say what Christianity is and what it is not, but also of a tendency, under occasional pressures, to harden that important distinction.

Organs of Authority

Early Christians did not all say and believe the same things. In the face of different understandings, there was a growing pressure to regulate the new religion and its bounds of acceptable belief. The situation may have been analogous to twenty-first century North America, where groups of widely divergent, even opposing, views style themselves "Christian" without an overall authority to adjudicate differences. Primitive Christianity dealt with this problem through three organs of authority: clergy, creeds, and scripture.

Clergy

The movement begun by Jesus had always had leaders: Jesus himself; the twelve whom he formed to propagate his ministry (Mark 3:13 ff. and parr.); James, Paul, and other **apostles** (1 Cor. 15:5–9). First Corinthians (12:28) and Ephesians (2:20) highlight apostles and **prophets**, among other congregational leaders. In the second century and thereafter, organizational structures emerged with clearly appointed leaders, ordained and set aside for special tasks, who were differentiated from the rest of their congregations.

As we have seen, the **Pastoral Epistles** already evince awareness of a distinction between ordained clergy and laity; moreover, those letters imply that Paul's apostolic authority is exercised through Timothy and Titus, who in turn delegate it to ordained bishops and elders (1 Tim. 3:1–13; 4:11–5:22; 2 Tim. 1:6; Tit. 1:5–9). Even today the language of the Pastorals appears in the liturgies and certificates of ordination of some Christian denominations. Following a path opened in 1 Timothy (3:1–7) and Titus (1:7–9), the bishop, the church's leader in a given city or region, gained recognition as the guardian of tradition and the custodian of the true faith. This organizational development was quickly solidified in the corpus known as the **Apostolic Fathers**. For Ignatius of Antioch, an early second-century bishop, the essence of the church resides, so to speak, in the person of the bishop (*To the Ephesians* 3–6). In *1 Clement*, written by a bishop of Rome near the end of the first century, the concept of apostolic succession acquires initial clarity: apostles appoint bishops to succeed them and, in effect, to continue and extend their authority in the church across space and time.

Creeds

Concise New Testament confessions planted the seeds for creedal formulations of basic beliefs through which the church sought to unify itself. Summaries of early Christian preaching appear in Acts (2:22–36), 1 Corinthians (15:3–5), and 1 Timothy (3:16). Early liturgies of the **Lord's Supper**, encapsulating basic Christian beliefs about Jesus' death, may be preserved in 1 Corinthians (11:23–26) and in the **Synoptics** (Mark 14:22–24 and parr.). The proto-**Trinitarian** wording of Matthew 28:19 may express an early **baptismal** or creedal formulation. The Pastoral and Johannine Epistles place heavy emphasis on true and trustworthy confession (1 Tim. 1:15; 4:9; 1 John 2:21–23; 4:1–3, 15). In 1 Timothy "the words of the faith and good doctrine" have themselves become a source of nourishment (4:6), clear evidence that authentic Christianity may be equated with something like creedal orthodoxy. That tendency thrives in the second-century writings of Justin Martyr and Irenaeus of Lyon; the well-known **Apostles' Creed** has its roots in this era, even though its present form is not traceable until centuries later. The original function of creeds was both to exclude the erroneous and to articulate the valid—an important instrument in the church's struggle to define orthodoxy and rule out heresy.

Scripture

In speaking of "scripture," most of the New Testament authors referred to the Bible of the synagogue, what would later be called the Old Testament (see 1 Cor. 15:3). Only in the latest New Testament document, 2 Peter (ca. A.D. 130), does a collection of Paul's letters seem to be, not only in circulation, but regarded among "the other scriptures"

(3:15–16). We have seen that, while Christian preaching about Jesus referred to Jewish scripture for its intelligibility, Christian preachers subordinated interpretation of those scriptures to their prior convictions about what God was doing in Jesus. In that sense, early creedal formulations of a rule of faith and life guided Christians' appropriation of the Jewish Bible, their writing of many New Testament books, and the process by which some of those books were eventually collected into a **canon** (Greek, *kanōn*, meaning "rule") of distinctively Christian scriptures as a New Testament counterpart for the Old.

The compilation of the New Testament canon was fitful, progressing more speedily in some regions with some books and more slowly elsewhere with others. Much of the process remains shrouded in obscurity. We know that, soon after the end of the first century, most of the books now in the New Testament had been written. About a century later, the four Gospels, Acts, and thirteen letters of Paul were widely recognized as authoritative; other books were also used, some of which were eventually canonized, others not.

There were four primary criteria that most Christians in most places effectively, if not always self-consciously, applied in canonizing certain literature. *Inspiration* was one such criterion. As early as 2 Timothy 3:16–17, scripture inspired by God was recognized for its usefulness in equipping the **church** to live in a manner pleasing to God. Inspiration, however, was never the sole criterion: many books thought by some to be inspired were not finally canonized. Moreover, inspiration was believed to lie not merely in the creation of documents but also in their correct interpretation. Thus, another important criterion for canonization was *apostolicity*: not merely a book's association with a recognized apostle, but its contents' coherence with a normative Christian witness, expressed in its liturgy and creeds, extending from the earliest testimonies through each successive Christian generation. In essence, the concern for a book's apostolicity expressed the church's hope for its own integrity across time.

A third criterion lent canonical authority to a book: its wide currency and acceptance in churches throughout the Christian world. This is what was originally meant by *catholicity*: a general, if not universal, consensus on the book's expression of authentic Christian belief and practice. Finally, a *rule of faith*—expressed in its creeds, by its clergy, among believers at worship—guided the church's decisions about canonization. Under competing pressures exerted by **Gnostics** like Marcion and ecstatic movements like the **Montanists**, the emerging Great Church of the second and third centuries was forced to decide which writings were orthodox, creating a canon that, while including the Jewish Bible, encompassed a spectrum of Christian beliefs (four Gospels, not one; divergent voices including Paul and James) within acceptable limits. Christian scripture—authorized by inspiration, apostolicity, and catholicity—emerged from dynamic encounters of creedal orthodoxy with aberrant heresies, overseen by clergy dedicated to "the sound words of our Lord Jesus Christ and the teaching that accords with godliness" (1 Tim. 6:3).

SUGGESTIONS FOR FURTHER READING

GENERAL RESOURCES

Using the insights of Peter Berger and Thomas Luckmann, (*The Social Construction of Reality* [Garden City, New York: Anchor Books, 1966]), M. Y. MacDonald, *The Pauline Churches: A Socio-Historical Study of Institutionalization in the Pauline and Deutero-Pauline Writings* (Cambridge: Cambridge University Press, 1989), is a valuable introduction to letters and communities in the Pauline tradition. A.-J. Levine and M. Blickenstaff have edited *A Feminist Companion to the Deutero-Pauline Epistles* (Sheffield: Sheffield Academic Press, 2003). General theological assessments of this literature are G. A. Krodel (ed.), *The Deutero-Pauline Letters: Ephesians, Colossians, 2 Thessalonians, 1–2 Timothy, Titus* (Minneapolis: Fortress, 1993), and A. T. Lincoln and A. J. M. Wedderburn, *The Theology of the Later Pauline Letters* (Cambridge: Cambridge University Press, 1993). D. G. Meade, *Pseudonymity and Canon: An Investigation into the Relationship of Authorship and Authority in Jewish and Earliest Christian Tradition* (Grand Rapids, MI: Eerdmans, 1987), offers a superb analysis of that topic.

COLOSSIANS

The standard **commentary** remains E. Lohse, *Colossians and Philemon* (Philadelphia: Fortress, 1971), though now see also J. D. G. Dunn, *The Epistles to the Colossians and to Philemon: A Commentary on the Greek Text* (Grand Rapids: Eerdmans, 1996). Perceptive theological commentaries include E. Schweizer, *The Letter to the Colossians: A Commentary*, trans. A. Chester (Minneapolis: Augsburg, 1982), P. Pokorný, *Colossians: A Commentary*, trans S. S. Schatzmann (Peabody, MA: Hendrickson, 1991), and D. M. Hay, *Colossians* (Nashville: Abingdon, 2000). On the so-called **Colossian heresy**, see C. E. Arnold, *The Colossian Syncretism: The Interface between Christianity and Folk Belief at Colossae* (Tübingen: Mohr-Siebeck, 1995).

EPHESIANS

Superb **commentaries** on Ephesians have lately been published. The standard technical treatment is now E. Best, *Ephesians: A Critical and Exegetical Commentary* (Edinburgh: T & T Clark, 1998), whose essence Best has distilled as *Ephesians: A Shorter Commentary* (London: T & T Clark, 2003). See also P. Perkins, *Ephesians* (Nashville: Abingdon, 1997), P. T. O'Brien, *The Letter to the Ephesians* (Grand Rapids: Eerdmans, 1999), M. Y. MacDonald, *Colossians and Ephesians* (Collegeville, MN: Liturgical, 2000), and J. Muddiman, *Ephesians* (New York: Continuum, 2001).

THE PASTORAL EPISTLES

The classic **commentary** by M. Dibelius, *The Pastoral Epistles*, rev. H. Conzelmann and trans. P. Buttolph and A. Yarbro (Philadelphia: Fortress, 1972), is now updated by I. H. Marshall and P. H. Towner, *A Critical and Exegetical Commentary on the Pastoral Epistles* (Edinburgh: T & T Clark, 1999). Equally technical are J. D. Quinn, *The Letter to Titus: A New Translation with Notes and Commentary* (New York: Doubleday, 1990), and L. T. Johnson, *The First and Second Letters to Timothy: A New Translation with Introduction and Commentary* (New York: Doubleday, 2001). By upholding Pauline authorship of the Pastorals, Johnson challenges the critical consensus. J. M. Bassler, *1 Timothy, 2 Timothy, Titus* (Nashville: Abingdon, 1996), and R. F. Collins, *1 and II Timothy and Titus: A Commentary* (Louisville: Westminster John Knox, 2002), are especially sensitive to the Pastorals' **theology**, as is F. M. Young, *The Theology of the Pastoral Letters* (Cambridge: Cambridge University Press, 1994). A good **overview** is M. Harding, *What Are They Saying about the Pastoral Epistles?* (Mahwah, NJ: Paulist, 2001).

SOLIDIFYING CHRISTIAN IDENTITY

W. Bauer, *Orthodoxy and Heresy in Earliest Christianity*, trans. and ed. R. A. Kraft and G. Krodel, 2nd ed. (Philadelphia: Fortress, 1971), is a classic attempt to reconstruct the diversity of **early Christian beliefs**; its hypotheses and results are challenged by J. D. G. Dunn, *Unity and Diversity in the New Testament: An Inquiry into the Character of Earliest Christianity*, 2nd ed. (Harrisburg, PA: Trinity Press International, 1990). H. von Campenhausen, *Ecclesiastical Authority and Spiritual Power in the Church of the First Three Centuries*, trans. J. A. Baker (London: A. & C. Black, 1969) is another standard study. The development of **the Christian canon of scripture** is comprehensively treated by H. von Campenhausen, *The Formation of the Christian Bible*, trans. J. A. Baker (London: A/ & C. Black, 1972), and B. M. Metzger, *The Canon of the New Testament: Its Origin, Development, and Significance* (New York: Oxford University Press, 1987). Various dimensions of **the early church at worship** are explored by L. W. Hurtado, *At the Origins of Christian Worship: The Context and Character of Early Christian Devotion* (Grand Rapids: Eerdmans, 1999), R. N. Longenecker (ed.), *Community Formation in the Early Church and in the Church Today* (Peabody, MA: Hendrickson, 2002), P. A. Harland, *Associations, Synagogues and Congregations: Claiming a Place in Ancient Mediterranean Society* (Minneapolis: Fortress, 2003), and R. W. Gehring, *House Church and Mission: The Importance of Household Structures in Early Christianity* (Peabody, MA: Hendrickson, 2004).

A mosaic of the head of St. Peter, Byzantine (1210), housed in Museo Regionale, Messina. *(Courtesy of The Bridgeman Art Library.)*

CHAPTER 12

THE CATHOLIC EPISTLES: FAITH AND ORDER

What's Catholic About the Catholic Epistles?

James, 1 Peter, and the Epistles of John are all in different ways concerned with the life, doctrine, and discipline of the early Christian communities. Because they are not addressed to individual Christian **churches**, they, along with 2 Peter and Jude, are traditionally called the **Catholic** (general) **Epistles**. James insists that faith should be accompanied by good **works**, and lays heavy emphasis on the **ethical** demands under which Christians should live. Like the writer of the **Pastoral** letters, the author tends to construe faith as believing in certain doctrines.

1 Peter addresses itself to similar moral concerns, but is much more directly **Christological**—that is, a doctrine of Christ is fundamental. The author shows a distinct consciousness of the unfriendly environment in which believers must live. Christians are to give no cause for offense, and at the same time they are to live courageously in the face of external hostility.

In different ways both 1 Peter and James deal with the threat posed by false doctrine and false teachers within the church. Such interests have already been encountered

401

in the Pastorals and Colossians, and recur also in the Johannine letters. Possibly forms of the ancient **Gnostic** heresy constitute the opposition against which most of these letters warn. The Johannine letters are, however, principally concerned with the quality of the community's inner life—whether it is characterized by love. In this respect, as in others, they stand very close to the Gospel of John, where there is also a striking emphasis on the unity of the community that finds expression in mutual love among the members.

JAMES: INNER DISCIPLINE

Background of the Letter of James

The very first verse of the letter of James presents problems. Who is James? There are several possibilities: the brother of Jesus himself, one of the two disciples of Jesus bearing that name, or someone else. Who or what are the twelve tribes in the **Dispersion** (1:1)? The reference is obviously to the twelve tribes of Israel dispersed around the Greco-Roman world, but James is not a letter to Jews (cf. 1:1; 2:1; 2:14–26). Apparently Christians could also be referred to as the "Dispersion" (1 Pet. 1:1). The letter is addressed to Christians but to no single Christian congregation. The conditions existing in a single **church** or in specific congregations are no more reflected in the letter as a whole than in the salutation. The conclusion tells us nothing; the "letter" stops quite abruptly.

Although tradition has ascribed the book to James the brother of the Lord, it does not seem to have been known and quoted by other Christian writers until the early third century. The fourth-century church historian Eusebius of Caesarea indicates that some Christians of his day doubted that it belonged in the New Testament at all. The Protestant reformer Martin Luther criticized the letter because of its emphasis on good **works** at the expense of faith and apparently did not regard it as the work of Jesus' brother. In fact, the letter itself nowhere explicitly claims to be the work of this particular James. Nor is the ascription to Jesus' brother supported by considerations of language and style. The style and quality of the Greek are reasonably good, probably better than what an **Aramaic**-speaking Galilean would produce. The content is nevertheless Jewish. The **law** and moral rectitude are extolled. Furthermore, the address to "the twelve tribes in the Dispersion" implies a **Hellenistic** Jewish readership. The ascription of the letter to James is intelligible, even if it should turn out to be incorrect.

Probably James represents a form of Jewish Christianity at the end of the first century or the beginning of the second. Its **ethical** exhortations reflect a knowledge and use of what had by then become an extensive ethical tradition. The best-known section (2:14–26) betrays a knowledge of Pauline **theology**, perhaps of Galatians and Romans. If so, then the author very likely knew the collected Pauline corpus, which would date his writing toward the end of the first century at the earliest. On the other hand, Paul or the views of Paulinists are not above criticism (contrast 2 Pet. 3:15–17), making a much later date seem unlikely. Because the kind of Judaism that formed the background of James existed in many parts of the Hellenistic world, it is futile to try to locate the book's place of origin.

Despite the Jewish cast of James, references and quotations from the Old Testament are not frequent. There are, however, a number of possible references or allusions to Jesus' sayings and teachings, particularly the Matthean version (e.g., 5:12; cf. Matt.

5:34–37). Whether these indicate a knowledge of any of our **Gospels**, or only of an independent tradition, is uncertain.

OUTLINE OF JAMES

Address (1:1)
Exhortation to Christian Practice (1:2–27)
Faith and Ethics (2:1–26)

Faith and the Poor (2:1–7)
The Importance of the Law (2:8–13)
Faith and Action (2:14–26)

Teaching and Wisdom (3:1–18)
Condemnation of Pride and Passion (4:1–12)
Concluding Exhortation (4:13–5:20)

Warning against Boasting and Riches (4:13–5:6)
Exhortation to Practice, Prayer, and the Restoration of the Sinner (5:7–20)

Faith and Action (James 2:14–26)

Does James oppose or complement Paul in emphasizing works?

The letter of James seems to have been written to meet the actual needs of the expanding and consolidating Christian church, even though it is addressed to no specific congregation. Members of newly formed churches needed concrete guidance about what to do in actual life situations that required ethical decisions. For the Christian converted from Judaism, the problem was less acute, because such a person possessed the powerful and comprehensive tradition of the biblical and Jewish law. In addition, in wide circles of the early Christian church, the teachings of Jesus were circulated for their moral and spiritual guidance. The existence of a substantial tradition of Jesus' teaching in the **Gospels**, especially Matthew and Luke, is ample testimony to this fact. The appropriation of the Jesus tradition in the Gospels and the incorporation of all four Gospels into the church's **canon** naturally resulted in the increasing availability and use of the tradition of Jesus' ethical teaching as a norm and guide for Christian life. Already in James we may see this development in those passages that are similar to sayings of Jesus known from the **Synoptic** Gospels, although James may have known earlier **oral tradition** rather than the Gospels.

From Paul's letters we can already see that there were various ideas about what it meant to be Christian. The character of Christian life had to be defined, and for the individual this definition by and large took place after, not before, the experience of conversion. James helps to define Christian life by concrete advice and admonition. The ethical exhortations of James have much in common with those of other Christian documents, such as the Pauline **epistles** (cf. 1 Thess. 4:1–12), Ephesians (4:25–6:20), and Hebrews (13:1–8), as well as the *Letter of Barnabas* and the ***Didache*** of the so-called **Apostolic Fathers**.

Perhaps the ethical interest and character of James are portrayed most graphically at that point where the author combats what he considers to be a dangerous form of

Christianity, which holds that a person is **justified** before God by faith alone rather than by conduct as well (2:14–26). The initial hypothetical situation (described in vss. 14–17) and the moral lesson drawn from it have a timeless appeal to pious, practical Christian people. On the other hand, a quite narrow understanding of faith is presupposed; for James, faith equals belief (vs. 19). This view of faith, similar to that of the **Pastorals** (1 Tim. 4:6; Tit. 1:13; 2:1), takes faith to be primarily assent to certain propositions. This understanding is different from that of Paul, for whom faith is the *act of believing* and the *relationship* between the believer and the one believed (Rom. 3:21-26).

The contrast between faith and works reminds the reader of Paul's intense **theological** discussion of this subject. Perhaps James's arguments are directed against the position of Paul, who would have surely agreed with the intention of James (cf. vss. 18 and 20). Yet the use of the example of Abraham (vss. 21 ff.) as well as the citation of the same Old Testament passage (Gen. 15:6) that Paul used to prove a quite different point (Rom. 4 and Gal. 3) suggests some sort of contact and disagreement with Paul or some interpretation of him. The disagreement, of course, concerns the relationship of faith and **works** and the place of works in the economy of **salvation** (vss. 21–24).

We have already noted the discrepancy between James's and Paul's views of faith. We must now ask how James understands works and in what sense they are considered necessary for salvation. Paul, of course, espouses **justification** by faith alone and

The south wall of the Jerusalem temple. Excavations have exposed the enormous stones of the Herodian reconstruction at its base. According to early Christian tradition, James the brother of Jesus was killed by being thrown down from the pinnacle of the temple, just to the right of this picture.

excludes "**works** of the **law**" as a means of justification before God (Gal. 2:15–16). James, on the other hand, does not oppose justification by works to justification by faith. He does not accept Paul's posing of the alternatives. Rather, he regards the performance of works of the law, along with faith, as indispensable for justification (2:24; cf. 2:10). Interestingly, James (2:8) brings forth the same scripture passage (Lev. 19:18) with which both Jesus (Matt. 22:34–40; Mark 12:28–31; Luke 10:25–28) and Paul (Rom. 13:8–10; Gal. 5:14) sum up the law and, like Paul, he does not attribute it to Jesus.

Paul's actual controversies over "works of the law" had to do with the specifics of food laws and circumcision, which apparently no longer concern James, who is interested in the necessity of good conduct as well as belief. Still, Paul and James really differ on the question of justification. Whether James would have expressed himself in this fashion, had he understood Paul's view of faith or faced Paul's situation in the controversy with Jewish Christians, is a moot question. There is, however, a kind of practical agreement between them. James says (vs. 24) that belief alone is not enough; pure religion, as he styles it (1:27), involves faith and ethics. Paul would have certainly agreed: "For in **Christ** Jesus neither circumcision nor uncircumcision counts for anything; the only thing that counts is faith working through love" (Gal. 5:6). James insists on works as the proof of faith (vs. 18): faith without works is dead. Paul would prefer to say that faith without obedience is not genuine faith.

James seems to be fighting a misunderstood Paulinism—whether his own or someone else's—that divorces faith from life. Such a misunderstanding of Paul's thought may have been prevalent in the church of his day (cf. 2 Pet. 3:15–17). Among his own converts in Corinth, Paul encountered those who thought that their knowledge or possession of the **Spirit** put them beyond paltry considerations of right and wrong, **sin** and **righteousness**. They separated faith or piety from this-worldly ethical questions. Thus Paul had to exhort the Corinthian Christians to abstain from, or give up, immoral practices. It would not be at all surprising if the subtleties of Paul's theological and ethical reflection were lost on a later generation of Christians.

Whether the simple correspondence of faith and works in James is satisfying depends on how one understands the human situation and what one takes to be the essential problem in human life. If one is free to do and to believe according to one's own choice, without any predisposition to good or evil, then James certainly makes more sense than Paul. On the other hand, if present existence in the world is to be understood in terms of oppressive bondage to sin, as alienation and rebellion, then the simple view of James does not suffice, at least not as a **theological** analysis of humanity's state in the world and the manner of redemption. In the final analysis, however, James is a manual for Christian conduct, not a fundamental theological treatise.

FIRST PETER: CONTINUING STRUGGLE FOR THE FAITH
Background of 1 Peter

First Peter presents itself as the work of the great disciple and **apostle**, and no grounds for doubting this claim were advanced until modern times. Yet there are at least three reasons for questioning this tradition:

1. The Greek of 1 Peter is very good. Could a Galilean fisherman have written it? **Aramaic**, Peter's native tongue, differs at least as much from Greek as Greek differs from English.

2. First Peter contains many Pauline motifs and ideas, especially the concept of Jesus' death atoning for **sin** and effecting **righteousness** (1:18 ff.; 2:24). The Pauline expression "in **Christ**" also occurs in 1 Peter (3:16; 5:10, 14), and there is a striking similarity between the view expressed in 2:14 ff. and the attitude toward the state commended by Paul in Romans 13:1–7. If the author knew the collected Pauline letters, such knowledge would imply that 1 Peter was written perhaps a generation later and could not be the work of Peter, who is reported to have died in the sixties in Rome (cf. *1 Clem.* 5.1; Ignatius, *Rom.* 4.3). Nevertheless, the possibility that Peter, in Rome (5:13), might have known only Paul's letter to the Romans cannot be excluded.

3. First Peter contains no indication of acquaintanceship with the historical Jesus of the sort we would expect from the disciple who in many ways was closest to him. The claim to be a witness of the suffering Christ (5:1) does not necessarily mean an eyewitness. According to the **Gospels**, Peter fled Jesus on the night he was betrayed and presumably did not see the **crucifixion**. Moreover, the passage that deals with Christ's suffering and death (2:22 ff.) is apparently based on the suffering-servant passages of Isaiah rather than on historical observation. Although this observation does not disprove Peter's authorship, for he was not present at the crucifixion, the text can scarcely be taken as evidence for it.

Modern defenders of Petrine authorship acknowledge the weight of at least the first and second arguments and suggest that these factors are due to the role played by Silvanus (5:12), a coworker of Paul (1 and 2 Thess. 1:1), who as secretary actually composed the letter in its present form. But if Silvanus is the same figure as the Silas of Acts, as is usually supposed, then he too was originally an Aramaic-speaking Palestinian (Acts 15:22, 27, 40), and the first difficulty would not be entirely removed.

If the letter is by Peter, it must date from about A.D. 60, or a few years later. The suffering of Christians to which the letter refers would be the persecution of the Emperor Nero. In that case the warnings and admonitions would seem misdirected, for Nero's persecution took place in Rome—the probable place of origin ("Babylon," 5:13; cf. Rev. 18)—not in Asia Minor, to which the letter is addressed. If the letter is not Petrine, the period of the Emperor Domitian's persecution would be the probable time of composition. This situation would date 1 Peter in the last decade of the first century and also make knowledge of the Pauline letters a possibility. Whatever the conclusion concerning 1 Peter's origin, the author's purpose was to encourage early Christians in their faith.

Structurally, 1 Peter presents some peculiarities. The salutation (1:1–2) and **epistolary** conclusion (5:12–14) easily fall away. At 4:11 there is a conclusion of sorts, and 4:12 makes a new beginning. The fact that in 4:12 ff. persecution seems an imminent possibility, whereas in the preceding part of the letter it is more remote, has prompted the suggestion that the different parts were written at different times. The hortatory, even homiletical, character of much of the letter suggests that it may have originated in a **baptismal** sermon, with the epistolary form a later editorial addition. The explicit reference to the hearers' or readers' baptism (3:21) is accompanied by several other baptismal allusions (1:3, 8–9, 22–23), and the entire piece makes sense as an address to newly baptized converts. Although plausible, the hypothesis falls short of proof, however, and the book is known only in epistolary form.

OUTLINE OF 1 PETER

> Address (1:1–2)
> The Hope of Salvation (1:3–12)
> The Holiness of Christians (1:13–2:10)
> Instructions and Appeal for Good Conduct (2:11–4:11)
>> *Proper Social Relationships (2:11–3:7)*
>> *Servants and the Suffering Servant (2:11–25)*
>> *Wives and Husbands (3:1–7)*
>> *Christian Conduct before the World (3:8–4:6)*
>>> In the Face of Hostility (3:8–22)
>>> In the Face of Immorality (4:1–6)
>> *Concluding Exhortation (4:7–11)*
> Conduct in the Face of Persecution (4:12–5:11)
> Conclusion (5:12–14)

Servants and the Suffering Servant (1 Pet. 2:11–25)

Why should Christians accept persecution?

Whether or not one reckons it to be the work of the **Apostle** Peter, 1 Peter is one of the choice writings of the early Christian period and of the New Testament. The document is written with good taste and restraint, and bespeaks a realistic, if critical, understanding of the world. The author calls Christians to obedient work and witness in the world without surrendering to its standards and demands.

The main body of 1 Peter falls into four sections, the last three having to do with conduct. Of these, the first (1:13–2:10) is more explicitly **theological**, dealing with the basis of the **ethical** demand of the **gospel**, and culminating in the hortatory use of the image of a building or temple (2:4–10), an image already noted in Ephesians and 1 Corinthians. The second (2:11–4:11) is specific and practical, without losing contact with its theological roots or becoming banal or trivial. Throughout this section the theme of submissiveness recurs (2:13, 18; 3:1). This submission is no cowardly groveling before worldly power, but rather an acceptance of divinely ordained structures of order and authority in the world. Christians submit without capitulating and without surrendering their conscience. That they may have to suffer is a real possibility, reflected throughout the letter. The final section (4:12–5:11) deals specifically with conduct in the face of persecution. The central point is that Christians should be obedient to God, conducting themselves in a manner beyond reproach and enduring with patience and courage the evil that unrighteous people may inflict.

In our passage (2:11–25), the author writes clearly and impressively. There is first a general introductory exhortation (vss. 11–12). "Aliens and exiles" possibly alludes to Genesis 23:4 (**LXX**), where Abraham calls himself an alien and exile (cf. also Heb. 11:13 and Ps. 39:12). The Christian **church** is a pilgrim people, as was the people of Israel. The language and conceptuality applied to Israel in scripture are adopted for the Christian community, which regards itself as heir to those ancient promises of God. The author's main interest (vs. 12), however, is that Christians' behavior before the world should be above reproach. It is anticipated that Christians will be denounced by the **Gentiles**. "Gentiles" here seems to mean non-Christian rather than non-Jew, an indication that the church regards itself either as a "third race," distinguishable from both Jew and Gentile, or as the true Israel. In any case, the church sees itself against the background of a largely Gentile culture, and the problem of Jew and Gentile within the church seems to have been left behind. This viewpoint bespeaks a second rather than first-generation origin for 1 Peter. "When he comes to judge" refers to the last judgment, an event still anticipated in the near future (4:7). It is implied that there may be some hope for those Gentiles who have previously maligned Christians if in the end they are led by their good **works** to an acknowledgment of God (which seems to be the meaning of "glorify"). Such a humane and hopeful view would accord with 1 Peter's doctrine of Christ's preaching to the dead (i.e., "the spirits in prison"; cf. 3:19; 4:6).

In line with the kind of conduct expected of Christians in this world, the author urges subjection to and support of civil authority (2:13–17). This passage finds a close parallel in Romans (13:1–7). If the author of 1 Peter did not know Romans, the similarity may rest on a common tradition concerning church and state reflected also in 1 Timothy (2:1 ff.), perhaps going back to Jesus himself (Mark 12:17). In any event, 1 Peter makes clear that Christianity is not a politically revolutionary movement. The government is ordained by God for the enforcement of order and justice (2:14; cf. Rom. 13:1–5). Whereas Paul assumed that the civil authority would carry out this function, such an assumption is not quite so clear in 1 Peter. Nevertheless, fundamental confidence in the emperor is affirmed (vss. 13, 17).

Obedience is not urged for the sake of sheer conformity, however, and is therefore not fundamentally self-serving. It is intended to silence the calumnies against the church and to contribute to its inner stability and unity. Moreover, its ultimate end is not that Christians should be docile and enslaved to whatever worldly order exists at any given time or place. The twofold injunction, "As servants of God, live as free people, yet do not use your freedom as a pretext for evil" (vs. 16), exhorts Christians to blameless behavior in the world so that charges brought against them from any quarter may be shown to be palpably false. The author does not blandly assume that all will be well in this world for Christians whose conduct is unexceptionable. The prospect of unmerited punishment and suffering is already a real one (1:6; 4:12 ff.; 5:9 ff.). The Christian is to *respect* the secular ruler, along with all people, but to *fear* only God and to *love* fellow Christians in the church (2:17).

The following paragraph (vss. 18–25) is directed to servants, likely slaves, but has implications for other Christians that extend beyond the institution of slavery. Within the established order, Christians conform to the legitimate demands that are placed upon them. Yet even in the face of illegitimate demands and punishment they accept their lot without rebelling. The person who has done wrong and suffers has nothing of which to boast, but the **righteous** one who suffers unjustly has God's approval (vss. 19, 20). The warrant for such an assertion is the example of Jesus Christ. Because Christ has suffered for them, believers follow in his steps (vs. 21) by suffering willingly also.

Mention of Christ's suffering leads into a series of descriptive and theological statements about the suffering of Jesus (vss. 21–24). These claims are largely constructed out of the **Septuagint** version of the servant songs of Isaiah. If they seem appropriate when applied to the suffering and death of Jesus, it is partly because from 1 Peter on— and perhaps earlier—these Isaiah passages have been used in describing and interpreting Jesus' death. We have in 1 Peter the *locus classicus* for the interpretation of the death of Jesus in terms of suffering, and with reference to Isaiah's suffering servant. Indeed, in relating Christ and Christians, this passage marks an important point in the development of **Christological** thought and its ethical implications—the recognition that Jesus' death is the norm and model for Christian conduct.

The author's immediate purpose, to speak a **redeeming** and comforting word, a word of encouragement, is accomplished by pointing to the real and meaningful relation between the slave who is unjustly beaten and Christ, who was also unjustly punished, but by whose wounds the same servants or slaves are healed. As they are united with him in suffering, so they will be united in his glory (1:3–9; 5:10). The relevance of Christ's suffering is not, however, limited to slaves who are being unjustly punished. Any person of faith who unjustly suffers evil for righteousness' sake will be blessed (3:14), for it is better to suffer for doing good than for doing evil (3:17). Such a one, who suffers according to God's will, is comparable to Christ himself (3:18). Indeed, that person may be said to share in the sufferings of Christ (4:13).

We have already considered the question of what historical circumstance evoked this emphasis on suffering (cf. 1:6). It is sometimes suggested that 1 Peter reflects a situation similar to that described in correspondence between the Roman governor Pliny and the Roman emperor Trajan (ca. **A.D.** 112), in which Pliny asks Trajan for instructions on handling the problem presented by Christians: although both display an admirable desire to act fairly, they concur on executing Christians who refuse to recant (Pliny, *Letters* X.96–97). Such harassment of its readers *as Christians* is anticipated in 1 Peter, although it is uncertain whether the author expects a general state-sponsored persecution of Christians. The references to suffering as a Christian (4:14, 16) and the coming "fiery ordeal" (4:12) suggest as much. On the other hand, the letter's positive attitude to Roman authority, expressed in 2:13–17, implies that the authority of the state is not behind the persecution of Christians, or at least the state is not recognized as hostile. In any case, 1 Peter intends to encourage Christians and to promote their sense of inner strength and cohesiveness in the midst of an unfriendly environment.

To this end, much of the letter concerns the normal, day-to-day business and behavior of individual Christians and congregations. Thus we find in 1 Peter something

St. Peter's Basilica in Rome. This huge edifice was built in the sixteenth century to replace an older fourth-century structure. It stands over the traditional tomb of Peter, which actually contains the bones of a large elderly man who lived and died about two thousand years ago. *(Courtesy of Robert Spivey.)*

already seen in Colossians, Ephesians, and James: the more or less stereotyped, probably traditional ethical exhortation directed to various persons or groups. In fact, despite its originality in appealing to the suffering of Christ, this passage (2:18–25) is just such an **paraenesis**, addressed specifically to slaves. Similar exhortations to wives (3:1–6), husbands (3:7), and the whole congregation (3:8–12) follow. Possibly also the exhortations to patience, courage, and steadfastness in the face of suffering are of a traditional character.

THE LETTERS OF JOHN:
LOVE, DOCTRINE, AND CHURCH POLITICS
Background of the Johannine Letters

Although 2 and 3 John seem to be genuine letters, it is not clear that 1 John was originally conceived as a letter. It lacks the customary **epistolary** introduction as well as a conclusion. In fact, 1 John seems to end in midair with no conclusion at all. Nevertheless, the text more than once indicates that the author is writing to someone (2:12 ff., 26; 5:13). At least in that respect, the document has the appearance of a letter.

Significant similarities of 1 John to the Gospel of John are pointed out in the discussion of the text. These resemblances are both formal and substantial, stylistic and **theological**. While there are also some differences in their perspectives and interests, the close relation of the **Gospel** and letters cannot be denied. In all probability the letters were written after the Gospel; 1 John in particular seems to presuppose the teaching of the Gospel. Its prologue is immediately intelligible in light of John 1:1–18, especially verse 14. The play on old and new commandments (2:7–8) seems to presuppose John 13:34. The problem posed by heterodox teachers or prophets claiming to speak through the **Spirit** may result from the promise of the Spirit (or **Paraclete**) as given by Jesus in the Fourth Gospel (cf. 14:15–17, 26; 16:12–15). The writer of 1 John has learned that the claim to be spiritually inspired does not guarantee orthodox teaching. In all likelihood 1 John was written to clarify the message of the Gospel of John and to make sure that it was not misinterpreted by those whom the writer considered false **prophets**.

The place and date of origin of the Johannine letters are uncertain. According to ancient church tradition, both the Gospel and the letters were written in Ephesus by the **Apostle** John. But most of the same reservations cited in connection with the tradition of the Gospel's origin and authorship apply also to the letters. There was a noted Asian churchman called the Elder John, who flourished at the end of the first or the beginning of the second century; he may have been confused with the Apostle John in ancient times (Eusebius, *EH* III.39). It is tempting to suggest that he is the "John" who wrote the Gospel and letters, as the author of the brief second and third letters identifies himself as "the Elder." At best the evidence for identifying the author of 2 and 3 John with this ancient, largely unknown figure is inconclusive. *Elder* was a common ecclesiastical title and *John* a common name. (The Greek noun *presbyteros*, elder, yields the term *presbyterian* to designate churches governed by elders.)

The very brief second and third letters yield little data about their origin. Their obvious theological and stylistic similarities to 1 John strongly suggest that they were written by the same author. Although 2 John seems to presuppose and resist the same heretical views opposed by 1 John, this problem is not discussed in 3 John. In the latter, some question of ecclesiastical politics seems to be the center of attention. Diotrephes (3 John 9) is resisting the Elder's spiritual authority. Unlike the Gospel and Revelation, 1 John has little distinct structure or pattern. Nevertheless, the identification of the following major thematic units may assist the reader in understanding the book.

OUTLINE OF 1 JOHN

Prologue: Christian Fellowship (1:1–4)
The Nature and Essence of Christianity (1:5–2:29)
The Marks of True Life in the Community (3:1–24)
Criteria for Certainty and Assurance Among the Faithful (4:1–5:12)

The Spirit of Jesus as Love (4:1–21)
Obeying the Commandments (5:1–5)
The Three Witnesses (5:6–12)

Postscript: Sin and Forgiveness (5:13–21)

The Spirit of Jesus as Love (1 John 4:1–21)

How does one distinguish the bad spirit from the good?

After the introductory prologue, which is strikingly reminiscent of that of the Fourth Gospel, the author treats two basic themes, Christian life and Christian faith. He defines Christian faith so as to exclude certain erroneous views, including the notion that it is possible to have faith without its taking concrete form in a distinct manner of life.

Chapter 4 is typical in that it treats these major themes. First, there is a warning to test the spirits (vss. 1–6). The spirits are ultimately only two, the spirit of truth and the spirit of error (vs. 6). The spirit of error manifests itself in false **prophets** (vs. 1). This is the spirit of the **antichrist**, whose coming was predicted (vs. 3; cf. 1 Tim. 4:1; also pp. 389–394). It is now in the world, and those who obey it are of the world (vss. 4 ff.), whereas the intended readers are of God (vs. 6). The opposition of world and God in 1 John is irreconcilable (cf. 2:15–17).

A fuller understanding of this passage necessitates some acquaintance with the phenomenon of prophecy in the early church. The role of the Christian prophet has probably been underestimated, because none of the New Testament books except Revelation seems to have been written by a person who was primarily a prophet. Yet Paul ranks prophets immediately after **apostles** in importance (1 Cor. 12:28). When the author of Ephesians speaks of the **church**'s being built upon the foundation of the prophets and the apostles (2:20), he may mean not Old Testament but Christian prophets. Although prophets were doubtless important figures (cf. Acts 11:27 ff.; 21:10 ff.), they constituted a potential problem. Their claim to speak inspired words of **Christ** or the **Spirit** (cf. Rev. 1:1–3; 22:18 ff.) might result in confusion, especially if divinely inspired prophets disagreed. Thus, the early Christians saw the necessity of distinguishing them—"test[ing] the spirits" (4:1). The idea of discerning among the spirits, or among prophets claiming to speak in the Spirit, is already present in Paul (1 Thess. 5:19–22), who laid down some fundamental rules for distinguishing the inspiration of the Holy Spirit in 1 Corinthians 12:3 and went on to outline procedures for regulating Spirit-inspired prophecy (1 Cor. 14). A half-century or so later, the author of the ***Didache*** suggests that prophets who stayed in one place for longer than a brief period, sponging off the community, were very likely false prophets—not to mention those who, while purporting to speak in prophetic ecstasy, ordered a meal or demanded money (cf. *Didache* xi, 7–12; xii–xiii).

John's criterion for distinguishing the Spirit of God from that of the antichrist (4:2 ff.) reveals a great deal about the understanding of Christianity he opposed. His own positive affirmation or confession is apparent (vs. 2): the person inspired by the Spirit of God confesses that Jesus Christ has come in the flesh. The contrary confession would thus deny that Jesus had come in the flesh, presumably in favor of the view that he was actually a spirit or matterless manifestation that had only appeared to take on an actual human body. In the **apocryphal** New Testament literature of the second century one may clearly see the burgeoning of this **docetic** view (*docetic* from the Greek verb *dokein*, meaning "to seem or appear"; that is, Christ only seemed to be human). It was characteristic of **Gnostic** Christianity and went hand in hand with an abhorrence of this world and all things material (cf. 1 Tim. 4:3–5; p. 391). John rejects such **Christology** as the work of the antichrist. Not confessing Jesus means to deny the genuinely human dimension of the Christ event. An important textual variant (vs. 3) reads "dissolves Jesus" instead of "does not confess Jesus"; it was understood by interpreters of the ancient church to refer to a gnosticizing division between the human Jesus and the divine Christ. Although this reading is probably not original, it would be an accurate commentary on our text, if the heretics denied that God had actually revealed himself in Jesus—that the **Word** had become flesh (John 1:14).

The antichrist (vs. 3), whose spirit speaks through the false prophets, is the antithesis of God's revelation in Jesus. Therefore, the typically Johannine dualism or polarity of God and the world can be used in describing the antichrist and his adherents (vss. 4 ff.). The world in this sense is not the good creation of God but the bad creation of human beings. The world so regarded represents human society organized and operating without reference to, or concern for, the existence and will of God. World and Christ, world and church, are pitted sharply against one another. In the Fourth Gospel, we have observed that this world is nevertheless described as the object of God's love (3:16 ff.). 1 John is not so explicit, yet even here Jesus is called "the Savior of the world" (4:14).

The antichrist is an **apocalyptic** figure, whose traces appear elsewhere in the New Testament. Although the actual term *antichrist* is found only in the Johannine letters, the idea of an individual or collective opponent of God's purposes, especially of his **Messiah**, appearing as a prelude to the winding-up of world history, is not uncommon in Jewish and early Christian apocalyptic literature (cf. Mark 13:5 ff.; 2 Thess. 2:1–12; and Rev. 20:7–10). Both 1 John (2:18–25) and 2 John (7) presuppose a tradition concerning the appearance of antichrist at the last hour. But rather than regarding this figure as a purely supernatural, apocalyptic being, the author now equates it with the emergence of false teachers (2:18) or false teaching—that is, with historical events or personages. Teaching that denies the humanity of the **Son of God**, and in effect denies Jesus, is the spirit of the antichrist.

In the face of this powerful movement, represented by the antichrist, which is "of the world" (vs. 5 RSV), the believer can be of good courage. The true believer has overcome the spirits (vs. 4), for as the author elsewhere says, "the darkness is passing away, and the true light is already shining" (2:8). The effective power of the new life that God gives through Christ is already present and available. With Christ, the believer has already overcome the power of the world (cf. John 16:33). The concept of the world evolves (vss. 3ff.) from a simple statement that the antichrist is in the world, and a neutral concept of world, to an idea of the indwelling of the antichrist (or perhaps Satan) in the world, analogous to God's dwelling in the believer (vs. 4). Now the world becomes a hostile power. Thus it can be said that those heretics who have the spirit of the antichrist are "of the world" in the negative sense so characteristic of John's understanding of the term. As they are of the world, so the Christian is of God (vs. 6). Those who do not "listen to us," but instead presumably listen to the heretics (namely, those who do not accept the orthodox teaching about Christ), thereby show themselves to be, not of God, but of the world.

A second major motif is now introduced (4:7–12). Being born of God is joined to the exhortation to love. The act of love determines one's relationship to God. Who is born of God and knows God? The person who loves. The possibility of knowing God in lovelessness is absolutely excluded (vs. 8): "God is love." The very character of love is to be understood with reference to the way in which God has shown love by sending his Son as the **expiation** for **sin** (vs. 9; cf. John 3:16 ff. and Rom. 3:25). Love is not a quality by which God is to be defined. Rather, in the sending of the Son, God is the active subject by whom love is to be defined. Therefore, the question of human love toward God is secondary (vs. 10). Yet human love is by no means a matter of indifference. Because God loves, Christians ought to love one another (vs. 11). The primary responses to God's love are faith in Jesus, as God's **revelation** in the flesh, and love for the other person. The real Christian, as distinguished from the pretender, is the one who believes in Jesus and practices love. Through such human love, God and his love become real and accessible, despite the fact that no one sees God (vs. 12; cf. John 1:18). The characteristically Christian belief that human love is grounded in the love of God finds no clearer expression than in 1 John.

The assurance that God abides in the believer and the believer in God is the possession of the Spirit (vs. 13). Obviously, one cannot possess the Spirit without love. What is more, neither love nor Spirit is an abstract quality. Both are based upon a particular confession of Jesus. The confession of Jesus, or of God's action toward the world in Jesus (vss. 15 and 14, respectively), is the basis for true understanding of both love and the Spirit. Of course, no one can truly claim the Spirit who does not believe in Jesus and live in love. The Spirit gives the believer assurance (vs. 13), but not in abstraction from faith and love (vs. 16). Those who lack faith and love can only be possessed of the spirit of the antichrist (4:1, 3; cf. 2:18–19).

First John refers again (4:17) to the ground of the Christian's confidence, which is ultimately confidence before God in the day of judgment. Presumably, the perfecting of love is based upon a relation to Jesus: as Jesus is in this world, so is the Christian. One's pattern of life is modeled after Christ's (cf. John 13:12–17). The thought of confidence is carried a step forward by the introduction of a new idea, the incompatibility of love and fear (vs. 18). The perfecting of love means confidence in the day of judgment, because love excludes fear. Of course, one could think that perfect love casts out fear because it does away with the danger of judgment. Yet the author's initial statement, "There is no fear in love," indicates an intrinsic incompatibility between fear and love. "Perfect love casts out fear," because the one who loves is born of God and knows God (vs. 7), and because love eliminates the concern for self that breeds anxiety. Therefore, the presence of fear means that one is not perfected in love. Here the terms "perfected" (vs. 17) and "reached perfection" (vs. 18) are based on a Greek stem meaning "complete," in the sense of finished. In the person who is perfected, love has reached its desired fulfillment: it determines life.

The author returns to the theme of God's prior love and the way in which it motivates people to love (vs. 19). The chapter ends with a succinct but pointed statement on the relationship of love of God and love of other people (vss. 20 ff.). The commandment (vs. 21) is presumably Jesus' "new commandment" of John 13:34, which the author sometimes calls the old commandment (e.g., 2:7). The commandment is old from the author's perspective because it goes back to the beginning, i.e., to Jesus. Either way, the commandment concisely conveys the burden of Jesus' teaching. At the same time it effectively reiterates a central conviction of our author: faith and obedience, religion and **ethics**, must not be separated from one another but always belong together.

Comparing First John with the Fourth Gospel

The similarities of 1 John 4 to the Fourth **Gospel** are numerous. Some have been noted; in conclusion, we should call attention to the most important. The concept of the **Spirit** (1 John 4:1 ff.) plays a prominent role in the Gospel. "Spirit of truth" (1 John 4:6) occurs several times in the farewell discourses (John 14–16), although it is not set over against the spirit of error or the **antichrist**, as in 1 John. The idea of Jesus' coming in the flesh (1 John 4:2) is reminiscent of John 1:14. The negative valuation of the world (1 John 4:5) is typical of the Fourth Gospel (John 4:6; cf. esp. John 17). The idea of birth (1 John 4:7) as spiritual regeneration also appears in John (esp. chap. 3). We have witnessed the importance of the theme of love (1 John 4:7 ff.) in the Fourth Gospel. Most remarkably, 1 John 4:9 reflects the basic motifs and even the language of John 3:16. That no one has ever seen God (1 John 4:12) is also affirmed in the Gospel's prologue (1:18). The concept of abiding in Christ (1 John 4:13, 15 ff.) and the themes of seeing and testifying, or **witnessing** (4:14), are commonplace in John. We have noted the connection of "this commandment" (1 John 4:21) and the "new commandment" of the Fourth Gospel. Moreover, the Greek text reveals many common stylistic traits that cannot be easily reproduced in English.

Church Doctrine and Politics (2 and 3 John)

Why is hospitality to be tied to right doctrine?

These briefest letters of the New Testament deal with different problems. One (2 John) is **theological** and **ethical**; the other (3 John), more practical or political. Although they are similar in style and vocabulary to 1 John, because of their brevity one cannot be absolutely certain that they were written by the same author. In both letters, the author identifies himself as the Elder, although in 1 John there is no salutation and therefore no self-identification.

The "elect lady and her children" addressed in the salutation of 2 John are often taken to be a **church**. (The Greek word *kyria* is the feminine form of *kyrios*, the title applied to Jesus and usually translated "Lord.") This reference seems confirmed by the terminology "the children of your elect sister" in the conclusion (vs. 13)—that is, the church from which the Elder writes.

2 John

The very brief 2 John takes up the two principal concerns of 1 John: love within the community (vss. 5–6) and the threat of false teaching (vss. 7–11). Once again the readers are reminded of the commandment they have had "from the beginning" to love another (cf. 1 John 2:7–11; 3:11). Clearly this is understood as the fundamental teaching of Jesus himself (vs. 6; cf. John 13:34), the commandment that defines the community in its conduct over against the world. The true community is, however, also defined by its correct doctrine, which begins with the affirmation of "the flesh," the real humanity of Jesus (vs. 7; cf. 1 John 1:1–3; 4:2–3; John 1:14). From this doctrine "the deceivers" have departed (cf. 1 John 4:1, 3), and such persons are to be shunned personally as well as theologically. They are not to be received or given hospitality (vs. 10). Whether or not 2 John was actually written by the author of the First Epistle, it seems to have been written subsequently to reinforce its teaching. Even as 1 John seems to presuppose, or to be based upon, the Fourth Gospel, so 2 John seems to presuppose 1 John.

3 John

The equally brief note known to us as 3 John is rather different, in that it does not address theological or ethical matters. It begins with a relatively lengthy, and genuinely personal, salutation addressed to Gaius, a church leader loyal to and dependent upon (vs. 4) the Elder. The Elder has just received a reassuring report about Gaius from traveling Christians (vs. 3).

The burden of 3 John has to do with such travelers and the obligation of offering hospitality to them (vss. 5–8). After reading Acts and Paul's letters, it comes as no surprise to learn that Christians, particularly some church leaders, frequently traveled from church to church or from city to city, exercising **apostolic** or pastoral oversight and preaching the gospel. Hospitality to such travelers ("strangers," vs. 5), frequently along dangerous routes, was therefore more than a matter of courtesy, although it was that as well.

The background of 3 John seems to have involved the refusal of one local church leader, Diotrephes, to receive the Elder's emissaries (vss. 9–11). No love is lost between the Elder and Diotrephes. Whether their conflict was based on theological or ethical matters, on questions of church polity or leadership, or merely on personal distaste, we are not told. Presumably the dispute had nothing to do with the substance of the **gospel**, otherwise the Elder would surely have denounced Diotrephes on such grounds. Nor does the Elder defend himself against charges made by Diotrephes. 3 John may attest to a struggle over jurisdiction and authority between church leaders. Interpreters have devoted considerable energy and imagination to reconstructing the circumstances or causes of this dispute. Unfortunately, those reasons remain hidden.

One clear purpose of 3 John is to commend Demetrius (vs. 12), who seems to be the bearer of the letter. Apparently the Elder anticipated that, while his emissary would not find the welcome mat out at Diotrephes' doorstep, Gaius would take him in. Again 3 John shows the social importance of the house-church and householder, which we have already encountered in Paul's letters. The relatively well-off Christian who possessed a house was an important figure, who could not only host a church meeting but who could also provide hospitality for traveling missionaries and others. This letter also raises the question of itinerant versus local leaders in the early church. Obviously, Paul as an apostle was an itinerant leader, traveling from city to city and church to church, but he and the churches he founded had to rely on local, indigenous leadership as well (cf. Phil. 1:1). In 3 John we may well see evidence of conflict between a traveling leader, the Elder (and his emissaries), and a local church authority, Diotrephes. Such tensions would have developed as the church organized itself to live and work in the world.

CONCLUSION: CHRISTIANITY'S SUCCESS AS A RELIGIOUS MOVEMENT

From the start, Christianity was an outward-oriented or missionary movement. That fact merits critical reflection. Any understanding of Christianity as merely an **ethical** system or way of life based on Jesus' teaching misses the point, as important as that teaching may have been. The Christian movement was motivated by a **gospel**—a message of good news to be promulgated—with many of the connotations that the word still evokes. Had it not been, many of the New Testament books would have been vastly different or would not have existed at all.

The writings treated in this chapter presuppose the good news that was the basis and impetus of the Christian missionary movement. That impetus is more directly reflected in the writings of the first century, particularly Paul's **epistles**, than in those considered here and in the preceding chapter. In the second and third generations there was a growing emphasis on consolidation, looking both within and without. First Peter especially was concerned with how the Christian community presented itself to outsiders. All the others, as well as the Deutero-Pauline letters (see Chapter 11), deal mainly with the church's inner life: its organization, doctrine, and discipline.

James draws upon existing ethical traditions, stemming at least in part from Jesus, to instruct believers in how they should behave. Practice is, if anything, more important than belief. The Johannine letters have similar interests, except that they—especially 1 John—insist upon the maintenance of a true confession of faith. Jesus Christ *did* come in the flesh. No claim to spirit inspiration can ignore or contradict that fact. Like Judaism, Christianity was an exclusive faith. Its adherents could worship no other gods nor participate in the cults of such gods. The author of 1 John writes: "Little children, keep yourselves from idols" (5:21), his concluding line. Interpreters have long puzzled over this unexpected conclusion, but it reflects a basic premise of New Testament Christianity, as well as Judaism. Indeed, the premise of all New Testament writings is the exclusivity of Christianity. The new faith was inclusive, in that it welcomed all, both Jew and Greek (Gentile)—as Paul said (Rom 1:16)—but demanded that adherents give up other gods and forms of worship. This austerity may account for much of the polemic against heresy. It was perceived as compromising with the world's, or other religions', expectations or standards by importing them into Christian belief or observance.

In spite of such rigorousness, however, the influence of common worldly practices crept in. The Paul of 1 Timothy, not the historical Paul, denies women the right to speak and, therefore, to exercise leadership roles, in **church**; rather, they are to be kept barefoot and pregnant (2:9-15). By the same token, 1 Peter, although seemingly less harsh, requires women to be submissive to their husbands and modest (3:1-7). By contrast, as we have seen, women played a prominent role in the ministry of Jesus and the churches of Paul. Doubtless such restrictions reflected the growing churches' practice.

Nevertheless, the Christianity of the end of the first century could scarcely have made a stronger effort to maintain its identity through continuity with the past.

SUGGESTIONS FOR FURTHER READING

JAMES

L. T. Johnson contributes two superb **commentaries**: one, in *The New Interpreter's Bible*, volume 12 (Nashville: Abingdon, 1998), pp. 175–225; the other, more technical *The Letter of James: A New Translation with Introduction and Commentary* (New York: Doubleday, 1995). The same author's *Brother of Jesus, Friend of God: Studies in the Letter of James* (Grand Rapids: Eerdmans, 2004) assembles his perceptive essays on different dimensions of the letter. Another fine commentary is by P. J. Hartin, *James* (Collegeville: Liturgical, 2003), who also offers an astute **theological assessment** of James in *A Spirituality of Perfection: Faith in Action in the Letter of James* (Collegeville: Liturgical, 1999). J. Painter's *Just James: The*

Brother of Jesus in History and Tradition, 2nd ed. (Columbia, S.C.: University of South Carolina Press, 2004), locates that important figure in the history and literature of the first three Christian centuries.

1 PETER

Originally completed over twenty-five years ago, L. Goppelt, *A Commentary on 1 Peter*, trans. J. E. Alsup (Grand Rapids: Eerdmans, 1993), is still an important work. The standard technical **commentaries** in English are now P. J. Achtemeier, *1 Peter: A Commentary on the First Epistle of Peter* (Minneapolis: Fortress, 1996), and J. H. Elliott, *1 Peter: A New Translation with Introduction and Commentary* (New York: Doubleday, 2000). M. E. Boring, *1 Peter* (Nashville: Abingdon, 1999), is also well worth consulting, as is A. Chester and R. P. Martin, *The Theology of James, Peter, and Jude* (Cambridge: Cambridge University Press, 1994).

THE JOHANNINE LETTERS

The standard **commentaries** have been R. E. Brown, *The Epistles of John* (Garden City: Doubleday, 1982), and R. Schnackenburg, *The Johannine Epistles: Introduction and Commentary*, trans. R. and I. Fuller (New York: Crossroad, 1992). One must now also consult the excellent commentary of J. Painter, *1, 2 and 3 John* (Collegeville: Liturgical, 2003). Briefer in scope and more theologically focused are D. M. Smith, *First, Second, and Third John* (Louisville: John Knox, 1991), and C. C. Black in *The New Interpreter's Bible*, volume 12 (Nashville: Abingdon, 1998), pp. 363–469. See also J. M. Lieu, *The Theology of the Johannine Epistles* (Cambridge: Cambridge University Press, 1991), as well as the bibliography at the end of Chapter 5.

St. John the Evangelist on the Island of Patmos (c.1618; oil on canvas), by Diego Rodriguez de Silva y Velásquez, (1599–1660). National Gallery, London. *(Courtesy of The Bridgeman Art Library.)*

CHAPTER 13

OTHER APOSTOLIC WRITINGS: VISION AND DISCIPLINE

Back to the Future: Comments on Christian Eschatology

Fittingly, the New Testament ends with The Revelation to John: the longest, most sustained, and most overtly **apocalyptic** writing in the New Testament. Yet the difference of Revelation from the rest of the New Testament is more of degree than of kind. As we have witnessed throughout our study, **eschatology**—discourse about the last things or the end of the age—is a distinguishing and pervasive characteristic of primitive Christianity and the **Hellenistic** Judaism from which it grew.

As we saw in Chapter 1, an abiding hope sustained many Jews during the New Testament period. Those expectations took different forms, from **Qumran**'s fervent hope for God's imminent, cataclysmic intervention in history to many **Pharisees**' less heated though no less devout expectations of a **messianic** age to come. The earliest Christians inherited such views, not only from their general environment and such figures as John the Baptist (Luke 3 3:7–9), but also and quite specifically from Jesus, whose own ministry and teaching were saturated in eschatological expectation, at times apocalyptically couched (Luke 11:2, 20; Mark 13 parr.). The **kingdom of God**—its revelation and activation by Jesus, its privileges and tribulations for his disciples—is a dominant theme in the **Q** tradition (e.g., Luke 6:20–49; 7:18–35; 10:24; 11:14–22, 26–27). Luke regards **Pentecost** (Acts 2:1–42) as only the first in a series of dramatic, saving events among the **church** and in the world "in the last days" (vs. 17). Paul's counsel to his churches (e.g., 1 Cor. 7) presupposes their living at the age's end, initiated by God's **resurrection** of Jesus as "the first fruits of those who have fallen asleep" (15:20). "For salvation is nearer to us now than when we first believed; the night is far spent, the day is at hand" (Rom. 13:11–12).

As years, then decades, melted away, Christian eschatology persisted even if its intense tone of imminence faded. In different ways, Matthew (24:36–51; 25:1–13), Paul (1 Thess. 4:13–5:11, and Paul's successors (2 Thess. 2:1–12, if not written by Paul) came to terms with the delay of the **parousia** (Christ's glorious second coming). While retaining apocalyptic elements more familiar to us from the **Synoptics** (5:27–29; 6:54; 12:48), John's **Gospel** may be the New Testament's most consistent specimen of realized eschatology: belief in the fulfillment, in this present age, of God's promises through the first advent of Jesus Christ (1:14; 5:24; 14:15–17, 25–27). Ephesians extols the mystery of God's will now disclosed to Christians who, in Christ Jesus, have already been "raised up with him and made to sit with him in the heavenly places" (Eph. 1:3–10; 2:6; cf. Col. 1:26–27; 3:1). From its earliest book (1 Thessalonians) to its latest (2 Peter), the New Testament is remarkable for the durability and vagaries of eschatological thought.

The four documents considered in this chapter display the pervasiveness of early Christianity's eschatology, the variety of its expression, the problems it raised, and its practical implications for the church's life in the world. That, too, is a constant in the books that were ultimately **canonized**: instead of relaxing or dissipating their strength, Christian hope in the New Testament consistently drives its adherents to love and a high level of moral conduct, in grateful response to God's gracious disposition and in anticipation of a judgment yet to come (Matt. 25:14–46; John 15:12–17; Acts 20:17–35; Rom 12:9–13:14; Eph. 5:1–20; Jas. 1:17–18; 3:13–18; 1 Pet. 4:7–19; 1 John 3:11–24).

HEBREWS: THE MINISTRY OF THE TRUE HIGH PRIEST
Background of the Letter to the Hebrews

Traditionally Hebrews has been ascribed to the **Apostle** Paul, but Origen, the great theological scholar of the third-century church, knew that it was not his work. Indeed, Origen stated that only God knew the identity of the author of Hebrews. The letter itself does not claim Pauline authorship. Even less than the **Pastorals**, and far less than Ephesians, does it express typically Pauline ideas and interests. For example, in the Pastorals, faith has become belief in doctrine about Jesus instead of a relationship to **Christ**; in Hebrews, faith is simply steadfastness. Neither expresses Paul's view of faith as the acceptance of God's grace in Christ. The identity of the author remains unknown. Apollos of Alexandria, Paul's coworker (Acts

18:24; 1 Cor 1:12; 3:4 ff.), has been suggested by some, including Martin Luther in the sixteenth century. The suggestion is reasonable though unprovable.

The readers suggested by the title would be Jewish Christians, not Jews. The title is a later addition, however, and the author's argument does not necessarily demand a Jewish background for his readers, only a Christian one. The reference to those from Italy sending greetings (13:24) suggests that Rome may have been the destination of Hebrews, as does its use in the late first-century letter of Clement of Rome. Because of the similarities in biblical exegesis and thought patterns between Hebrews and Philo of Alexandria, it is often conjectured that the document was composed in or near Alexandria in Egypt. References to persecution (10:32–34; 12:4) do not help very much in placing or dating the letter.

The situation and mood of the intended readers and the kind of **ethical** exhortations suggest second-generation Christianity, perhaps about A.D. 80–90. Yet Hebrews does not mention the destruction of the Jerusalem temple (A.D. 70) in the course of the argument concerning the new **priesthood** in Jesus Christ, and an earlier date is therefore sometimes proposed. Its concern with the Old Testament tabernacle, and not with the contemporary temple, may explain this silence.

Despite the lack of an **epistolary** salutation, Hebrews concludes as if it were a letter (cf. 13:22–25). Yet without chapter 13 Hebrews would probably be taken for a tract or perhaps a sermon. Extensive exhortations are scattered throughout the book. Hebrews differs from many other New Testament writings, however, in that such passages are integrally related to the author's **theological** thought. They do not appear to be merely traditional admonition or conventional bits of ethical wisdom.

The thought of Hebrews is complex, subtle, and sophisticated. The author was skilled in the use of the Greek language and the then-current methods of biblical interpretation. We should not expect to grasp the full range and complexity of Hebrews on first reading. Despite its obvious qualities, Hebrews was not everywhere accepted as Pauline or authoritative in the early **church**. Particularly in Western Christendom, it was slow in gaining recognition as **canonical**.

OUTLINE OF HEBREWS

Prologue: God's Final Word (1:1–2)

Argument: Jesus as Son and High Priest (1:3–10:18)

The Person of the Son (1:3–4:13)
His Superiority to Angels (1:3–2:18)
His Superiority to Moses (3:1–6)
Warning and Admonition (3:7–4:13)
The Son as High Priest (4:14–10:18)
Jesus' Qualifications as High Priest (4:14–5:10)
Exhortation to Maturity (5:11–6:20)
The Superiority of Christ's Priesthood (7:1–28)
The High Priestly Work of Jesus (8:1–10:18)

Application: The Necessity of Faithfulness (10:19–12:29)

> *The Response of Faith (10:19–39)*
> *Forerunners in Faithfulness (11:1–12:11)*
> > *Examples from Israel (11:1–40)*
> > *The Example of Jesus (12:1–11)*
> *Exhortation and Warning (12:12–29)*

Conclusion: Final Exhortation, Personal Matters, and Benediction (13:1–25)

Jesus' Qualifications as High Priest (Heb. 4:14–5:10)

Why is the humanity of Jesus indispensable to his high-priestly work?

Because Hebrews deals extensively with the saving significance of Jesus' **sacrifice**, his **crucifixion**, this book shares common ground with Paul, for whom Christ's death on the cross is of central importance. Hebrews' elevated view of Jesus—its **Christology**—also bears some resemblance to that of John's Gospel: both books begin with exalted claims for **Christ** as the reflection of God's glory and as instrumental in the world's creation, claims with parallels made for the figure of eternal Wisdom in **Hellenistic** Judaism (Wis. 7:26; cf. John 1:1–14; 1 Cor. 1:24; 8:6; Col. 1:15–20). Like Paul and John, Hebrews also places Jesus' death as a **redemptive** sacrifice at its **theological** center. Yet the differences between Hebrews and these other writings are considerable. Neither Paul nor John relates Jesus to the old **covenant** in the same way as does Hebrews. John comes closer by portraying Jesus as the substantial fulfillment of Judaism's foreshadowing institutions (cf. John 7:1–8:59). Hebrews seems to draw a hard line against the possibility of forgiveness for believers who **sin** (6:1–8; 10:26–27), a rigorist stance absent from Paul and John. The greatest difference that Hebrews presents, however, lies in its distinctive presentation of Jesus Christ as, simultaneously, high **priest** and sacrifice. Of all the books in the New Testament, that idea and its development are unique to Hebrews.

The book's first three chapters announce a basic theme to which the author will repeatedly return: the superiority of Jesus as God's eternal **Son** over other Old Testament figures. The author's mode of argument involves a series of tightly interwoven scriptural verses, which may have come to the author already linked (Pss. 2:7; 104:4; 45:6–7; 102:25–27; 110;1; 8:4–6; 22:22; Isa. 8:17–18; Ps. 95:7–11). Similar scriptural daisy chains have been discovered in biblical interpretation among the **Dead Sea Scrolls** (4Q *Florilegium*). The author of Hebrews uses these verses, however, to make a fundamental point: the Son of God's superiority over the angels (1:4–7, 13; 2:5, 7, 9, 16). So insistent is the author in this matter that Hebrews seems almost to be correcting its readers of a misapprehension that Jesus was subordinate to the angels (cf. Col. 2:18). Once that possibility is laid to rest, however, the author never again returns to it. For only a little while was Jesus made lower than the angels, when he suffered and tasted death for all, after which God crowned him with glory and honor (Heb. 1:9).

In chapter 3, Jesus' superiority over Moses is asserted: while Moses was a faithful servant in God's house, Jesus was faithful over that house as a Son (3:1–6). Mention of Moses and of Jesus' surpassing faithfulness lead the author to issue his readers an extended warning, anticipated in 2:1–4, on the dire consequences of their own infidelity (3:7–4:13). A careful argument is unfolded, in which the church's situation is compared with that of Israel in its forty years of wandering in the wilderness. Although based on an interpretation of the Old Testament, this conception is also related to the actual situation of the **church** to which the author wrote. That church needs challenging and is in peril of losing faith and never reaching the promised rest (2:3; 4:1–11; see also 5:11–6:12; 10:19–12:29). It faced the potential of sluggishness after the enthusiasm and hope of the earliest days had faded—perhaps when the first **apostles** died. The road ahead was long, and many were tempted to abandon the journey. There was a danger that they would retreat into Judaism or perhaps merely into conventional, lifeless piety.

Here and elsewhere, the author's method of paralleling the Christian church with characters or episodes drawn from the Old Testament is typological: that is, an Old Testament figure or institution is understood as the type or prototype of some aspect of Christian revelation. Still, the driving force of the appeal is not adherence to the Old Testament, but to Jesus, "the apostle and high priest of our confession" (3:1). Only here in the New Testament is Jesus identified as an "apostle," though the idea bears affinity with the Fourth Gospel's presentation of Jesus as the Son sent (Greek, *apostellō*, "send") by the Father (John 4:34; 5:24, 30, 37; 6:38, 44; and elsewhere). Yet, in contrast with John, the **Synoptics**, Acts, Paul, and even James, faith is not directly related to Jesus in the manner we would expect. For Hebrews, faith means steadfastness or persistence in hope, with the end in view. This becomes especially clear in chapter 11, where faith is considered at length quite apart from Jesus or faith specifically in him. Indeed, Jesus himself is the prime example of faith, "its pioneer and perfecter" (12:2), through his endurance of suffering and the shame of the cross.

Ultimately, however, Jesus Christ remains the ground of faith. Apart from him, the confession to which the church must "hold fast" (4:14 ff.) would be without meaning or point. Central to the author's presentation of Jesus is the image of the "great high priest who has passed through the heavens" (4:14), introduced in Hebrews at 2:17. As high priest, Jesus is the guarantor of God's promised **salvation**. The description of Jesus' heavenly enthronement as Son (chaps. 1–2) precedes an extended discussion of the heavenly Christ's high-priestly activity. Hebrews seeks to show in detail how Jesus' heavenly high priesthood directly affects the church and the Christian. Jesus' ministry as high priest is the surety supporting Christians' life in the world and sustaining their hope for the future. With such encouragement they can hold fast to their confession, which is the church's expression of faith in God and hope through Jesus Christ.

The Christology of Hebrews is well-summarized in 4:14–16, especially in the two very different assertions about Jesus in verses 14 and 15. On the one hand, he is the great heavenly high priest (vs. 14), whose stature derives from his bearing "the exact imprint of

God's very being" (1:3 NRSV). On the other, Jesus is the "one who in every respect has been tested as we are, yet without sin" (4:15). It is necessary that Jesus exercise heavenly ministry on humanity's behalf, for only such ministry is efficacious in dealing with the human condition. Alone, however, confidence in Jesus' heavenly ministry could have no effect, no relevance for people on earth. Already the author's logic impresses itself upon the reader: Christ could not act for others unless he sympathized with them—and he could not sympathize with them unless he had actually shared human nature and experience (thus, 2:14). The heavenly high priesthood of Jesus affects humankind because it is the supernal high priesthood of a real human being. Hebrews contains perhaps the earliest, clear, straightforward New Testament statement of what later came to be called the **Incarnation**: God's human presence in Jesus of Nazareth. God is present in his earthly and in his heavenly ministry, but not in such a way that Jesus ceases to be a man and becomes by this fact a heavenly supernatural being, removed from the human condition, unbelievable or irrelevant to ordinary mortals. Yet in spite of Jesus' complete participation in human life, he is not overcome by its temptation; he does not sin (cf. 2 Cor. 5:21). "Without sin" means that Jesus did not succumb to the fundamental temptation to abandon God in faithlessness; to the contrary, he is the very model of faithfulness (Heb 12:2). Both Christological claims in 4:14–15 are necessary and inseparable: Because Jesus fully partakes of divinity, he is able to redeem humankind. Because he fully partakes of humanity, in every respect except sin, Jesus is willing and disposed to do so.

The twofold assertion that Christ has passed through the heavens and yet is like other human beings (4:14–15) lays the basis for subsequent exhortation and invitation (vs. 16). The expression *throne of grace* implies the presence of Christ the high priest at God's right hand (1:3). Understanding the **gospel** as God's grace is, of course, thoroughly and typically Pauline. That the concept of grace was from the first recognized as Pauline is shown by its presence not only in the genuine Pauline letters but also in Ephesians, the Pastorals, and Acts (chaps. 13–20, which deal with Paul). The use of grace (Greek: *charis*) in 1 Peter and Hebrews may indicate that these documents, though not authored by Paul, belong within the sphere of Pauline influence, for elsewhere in the New Testament the term is surprisingly infrequent. (By contrast, the term occurs not at all in Matthew and Mark, and only a few times in Luke and John.) Even though grace is not the object of theological discussion in Hebrews, it seems to have Pauline roots. Grace is God's graciousness, his love freely given. As in the case of faith, however, in Hebrews grace does not appear to be tied explicitly to the event of Christ's coming. Instead, it signifies the continuing availability of God's strength, which makes possible faith, understood as faithfulness.

The heart of Hebrews and its climactic theological moments have to do with the book's presentation of Jesus, the Son of God, as the heavenly high priest. The argument proceeds in this fashion: Jesus' qualifications for the high priesthood, introduced in 4:14–16, are elaborated in 5:1–10. This section falls into two distinct parts: first, a general statement of the qualifications for high priesthood (vss. 1–4); second, a declaration of the way in which Jesus satisfies these qualifications (vss. 5–10). Following an extended, well-integrated exhortation to Christian maturity (5:11–6:20), in 7:1–28, the author picks up a thread left dangling in 5:10 and develops a case for the superiority of Christ's high priesthood. Then, in 8:1–10:18, the nature of Christ's priestly ministry is articulated.

The Function of a Priest

The prototype of the high-priestly ministry (Heb. 5:1–4) is the biblical priesthood. In this tradition Jewish **priests** administered the temple cult in Jerusalem according to the Old Testament's mandates until the siege and eventual destruction of the city and its temple during the Roman war (**A.D.** 66–73). Hebrews can assume its readers' familiarity with the idea of a priest as mediator between God and humanity, especially in matters of **sin** and purification, if only from the Old Testament. Moreover, the office of priest and its justification as one who performs ritual **sacrifice** for the community are widespread in the history of religions. The function of a priest, whether ancient or modern, is to maintain an open channel of communication with the divine and, by offering sacrifice for sin and abolishing impurity, to ensure divine favor.

The succinct definition of the high priest's function (Heb. 5:1) equally applies to the entire priesthood. Although the high priest held a special office, embedded in the Levitical lineage, he could effectively exercise this office only because of his common lot with the people as a whole (vs. 2). This was the high priest's first qualification. Because what he shared with the people led him, too, to sin, he had to offer sacrifice on his own behalf (vs. 3). By contrast, Christ was without sin, although subject to human temptations (4:15). The high priest's second qualification was the divine calling (5:4).

To demonstrate that Christ fulfills both qualifications for the high priesthood (vss. 5–10), the author begins with the second. With the New Testament generally, Hebrews affirms that Christ's honor and glory are not things he claimed for himself. Quite the contrary: Jesus' own life was one of self-giving service, not arrogance. His peculiar dignity has no human basis but stems from God's call and appointment. For proof, the author returns to the Old Testament, which he regards as the definitive expression of God's will and intent—when rightly understood and interpreted (3:7; 9:8; 10:15). Quoted in both 1:5 and 5:5, Psalm 2:7 appears to have been a key Christian proof text (see also Acts 13:33). Even more critical for the author's argument is the quotation from Psalm 110:4 (Heb. 5:6, 10), which lays the foundation for the presentation (in chap. 7) of Jesus' high priesthood after the order of Melchizedek. As for Christ's fulfillment of the high priest's first qualification, the author describes Jesus' human nature (vss. 7–9), developing ideas previously introduced (2:9, 11, 14, 17 ff.). Though its details may not correspond exactly to the Synoptics (cf. John 12:27), undoubtedly Hebrews 5:7–8 refers to Jesus' agony in Gethsemane (Mark 14:32–42 parr.). The emphasis is on what Jesus holds in common with humanity—his anguish and suffering—not what distinguishes him from others. Like 1 John (4:2), Hebrews stresses Jesus' full solidarity with the human experience. He was really human, terrified by a real death.

Why does the author assert (5:10) and then explain (6:19–7:28) Jesus' service at God's right hand as a high priest after the order of Melchizedek? The key is concealed in the quotation of Psalm 110:4 in Hebrews 5:6. This Psalm is addressed to King David, the Lord's anointed (that is, the **Messiah**); David is called a priest forever according to the order of Melchizedek (110:4). Since Jesus was believed to be the Davidic Messiah, the Christ, what is said of the Messiah in Psalm 110 is said of him. Thus, the title of Melchizedek is taken as a messianic designation of Jesus. But why refer to Melchizedek at all? The answer lies in Hebrews' reference (7:1–10) to Genesis 14:17–20, a brief story about Abraham's gift of a tithe (a tenth) to Melchizedek, a non-Levitical priest "having neither beginning of days nor end of life": "a priest forever," just like Jesus, the Son of God (vss. 3–6). Because "the inferior [Abraham] is blessed by the superior [Melchizedek]" (vs. 7), scripture shows that Jesus' Melchizedekian (i.e., messianic and eternal) high priesthood is superior to its earthly and transitory, Levitical counterpart. Some first-century Jewish texts, including the Dead Sea Scrolls (11Q *Melchizedek*), suggested Melchizedek's eternality, based on scripture's silence about his birth and death.

Thus the stage is set for Hebrews' portrayal of Christ's high priestly ministry (8:1–10:18). Necessary for understanding this climactic section of Hebrews is the complex character of its author's **eschatology**. On the one hand, he assumes a horizontal, Jewish concept of "two ages," consisting of promises of good things and their ultimate realization in the messianic age to come. Thus, the author speaks of "these last days" (1:2), in which the promised "Sabbath rest for the people of God" (4:9) will be realized for those who maintain their confidence in God to the end (3:14; 4:1, 6, 11; 6:11–12; 7:28; 11:1–12:2). On the other hand, Hebrews also presupposes a vertical, Platonic schema of "two worlds": the earthly theater of everyday appearances, which is but a shadowy copy of an unseen, heavenly realm that is more real and substantial than the visible world. In a sense, Hebrews' famous definition of faith (11:1) correlates both of these eschatological dimensions: "the assurance of things hoped for" (the temporal mode of two ages), "the conviction of things not seen" (the eternal mode of two realms).

The more typically Jewish aspect of Hebrews' eschatology permeates the book. Jesus is called the pioneer of salvation (2:10; also 12:2), leading the readers into a promised glory. Though the Israelites departed from Egypt, because of their unbelief they did not enter God's Sabbath rest (3:16–19). (For the author, as for later rabbinic tradition, the "Sabbath" is a metaphor for the eschatological rest into which God's faithful will enter.) In Hebrews, the promise of entering that rest remains unfulfilled (4:1), "apart from us" (11:40). Those who have believed—the book's readers—will enter that rest and, in some sense, have already begun to do so (4:1–10; 12:25–29). As it was with Abraham (6:13–20), indeed with all the worthies in Israel's history (11:4 ff.), entering that rest depends on patient endurance, with eyes set upon Jesus, "a forerunner on our behalf" (6:20), and with confident assurance that God, the one "who has promised, is

The Roman siege ramp can be seen leading up to the top of Masada, where the last Jewish resistance to the Roman assault ended in A.D. 74. The defeat of the Jews and their conquest by Roman power occurred without the longed-for divine intervention, a fact that must have given pause to early Christians as well as ancient Jews. *(Courtesy of David Levenson.)*

faithful" (10:23). This is the motivation for patient endurance, to which Hebrews repeatedly returns: "so that you may do the will of God and receive what was promised" (10:36). In a manner similar to what is encountered in Revelation (3:10; 14:1; 21:1 ff.), that rest is also described as approaching Mount Zion, "the city of the living God, the heavenly Jerusalem" (Heb 12:22).

Accordingly, with the rest of the New Testament, Hebrews exhorts its readers to love and good conduct, in preparation for a day on which Christ will return in judgment (6:9–12; 9:27–18; 10:23–25; 13:1–17). Yet it is a Platonic coloring, the "vertical" dimension of the book's eschatology, which suffuses Hebrews' description of Christ's high-priestly ministry in chapters 8–10: "we have such a high priest, one who is seated at the right hand of the throne of the Majesty in the heavens, a minister in the sanctuary and the true tent that the Lord, and not any mortal, has set up" (8:1–2; cf. 4:14). Repeatedly, the earthly tent, the central place of Israel's worship (Exod. 26), pales in comparison with the heavenly sanctuary in which Jesus now presides (8:5–6; 9:1–14; 10:1). "For Christ has entered, not a sanctuary made with hands, a copy of the true one, but into heaven itself, now to appear in the presence of God on our behalf" (9:24).

The Day of Atonement

Far from leaving the argument at the level of an assumption that what is unseen and heavenly is superior to matters on the visible earth, Hebrews engages, in a manner unique within the New Testament, the rites prescribed for the Day of Atonement in Leviticus 16 (cf. Heb 9:1–10). The purpose of the Day of Atonement (Hebrew: *yom kippur*) was to cover, ritually, all sins committed by Jews throughout the preceding year for which individual restitution had not been made. Protocols for its observance in the third-century **Mishnaic** tractate *Yoma* indicate that, even after the temple's destruction in A.D. 70—and perhaps before, throughout **Diaspora** Judaism—the Day of Atonement was celebrated annually by Jews for the restoration of their fellowship with God and with one another. It remains an important annual ritual in contemporary Judaism.

Hebrews offers many reasons for the superiority of Christ's atoning sacrifice over those of all other high priests. First, his offering was made by entering into "the greater and more perfect tent" (9:11), "not into a sanctuary made with hands, a copy of the true one, but into heaven itself, now to appear in the presence of God on our behalf" (9:24; also 8:3–5). Second, Christ himself is "holy, blameless, unstained, separated from sinners, exalted above the heavens" (7:26). Other priests are many, mortal, and replaceable; Christ alone holds his priesthood permanently (7:23–24). Third, his sacrifice was once for all, without need of either daily offerings or annual repetition (7:27; 10:1–3, 11–14); "he has appeared once for all at the end of the age to put away sin by the sacrifice of himself" (9:26). Fourth, Jesus is not only the untainted priest but is also the perfect sacrifice itself: "he offered up himself" (7:27), "securing an eternal **redemption**" that surpasses any and all sacrifice of the blood of bulls and goats (9:12–14; 10:4). Fifth, the life that Jesus voluntarily offered to God conveys **holiness**: it sets Christians apart and draws them into the sphere of God's holy domain (7:25; 10:10; 11:14). "For by a single offering [Christ] has perfected for all time those who are **sanctified**" (10:14). Finally, Jesus' self-sacrifice inaugurates a new and enduring **covenant** between God and humanity: a covenant foreshadowed in Exodus 24:3–8 and promised by the prophet Jeremiah (31:31–34; cf. Heb. 8:8–13; 9:15–21; 10:15–17). To a degree greater than other New Testament writings, Hebrews explicitly correlates God's old covenant with Israel with his new covenant with the church through Jesus Christ. The previous covenant was neither fraudulent nor without purpose; through the hindsight of Christian faith, however, it was a frail copy, an imperfect shadow, of a better hope and a better covenant, enacted on better promises (7:18–22; 8:6; 10:1–10).

The assertion of the incomparable sufficiency of Christ's ministry, in contrast with the work of other priests, once again prompts serious exhortation to those who have benefited from his priestly offering (10:19–31), followed by recollection of the readers' earlier courage and confidence (vss. 32–39). This challenge to keep the faith leads into a catalogue of numerous examples of faith, brought forward from the Old Testament (chap. 11), culminating in Jesus' own example (12:2–3) and yet another encouragement for holiness and the strengthening of a droopy faith (12:4 ff.). With its long hortatory section (13:1–19), consisting of disconnected instructions, concluding with a benediction (vss. 20 ff.) and an **epistolary** farewell (vss. 22–25), Hebrews' final chapter sounds more like Paul than the rest of the document. That, plus the reference to "our brother Timothy" (vs. 23), may have prompted the traditional view that Hebrews was Paul's own work.

In a way that is unique and theologically profound, the Epistle to the Hebrews expresses many of the New Testament's central beliefs about Christ's significance and the character of Christian hope. Its Christological reading of scripture, drawing upon techniques used by Philo of Alexandria and the sectarians at **Qumran**, set the terms of much biblical interpretation in the church's patristic and middle ages. Its understanding of perfection as dynamic maturity by which the believer grows into the life of Christ would be taken up and developed especially in the theology of the Eastern Orthodox Church. Its emphasis on Christ as both subject and object of perfect sacrifice to God is particularly resonant with Roman Catholics and all religious traditions that take seriously human consciousness of sin and the consequent need for the restoration of broken fellowship with God. According to the **gospel**, Jesus offers to God his life for the life of all others. Historically, that claim has made sense to Christians. Few documents have probed its implications more intensely, or with greater theological acuity, than Hebrews.

2 PETER AND JUDE:
DEALING WITH THE LORD'S DELAY
Background of 2 Peter and Jude

The second letter attributed to Peter, which follows 1 Peter in the New Testament, is now almost universally regarded as pseudonymous. 2 Peter contains material remarkably similar to the Epistle of Jude and is probably an elaboration of the content of that brief letter. Moreover, the author struggles against skepticism about the return of Jesus in the light of its delay (3:3–10). He also knows a collection of the **Apostle** Paul's letters, which he apparently regards as scripture (3:15–16), and may know one or more of the **Synoptic Gospels** (cf. 1:17–18), as well as John (1:14; cf. John 21:18). All these facts point in the direction of composition in the first half of the second century rather than during the Apostle Peter's lifetime.

The Epistle of Jude, probably earlier than 2 Peter, is a writing of the late first century at the earliest. The "false teachers" (2 Pet. 2:1) who bring in heresies are likely the same as Jude's ungodly people "who pervert the grace of our God into licentiousness and deny our only Master and Lord, Jesus Christ" (Jude 4). Jude's denunciation accurately, if generally, describes what certain early **Gnostic** groups would have been perceived as doing, thereby attesting to their probable existence (cf. 1 Tim. 6:20–21), although that term is not used. The invective of 2 Peter is directed at similar opponents. Such Gnosticism became an important force in the second century, although it had roots in the first. By its explicit linkage with James (Jude 1), Jude is tied to the Letter of James as well. Probably the reader is to understand it as emanating from the brother of James of Jerusalem, and thus, by extension, from a brother of Jesus. This implied identification is difficult to confirm, however, given the character of the letter, especially its opposition to Gnosticism. There is no way of knowing where Jude and 2 Peter were written. Although the two letters are related, they are separated in the New Testament by the Johannine **epistles**.

Historically, neither Jude nor 2 Peter has played an important role in later interpretation of the New Testament. Indeed, there were doubts about the **authenticity** and authority of both in antiquity—of 2 Peter even more than of Jude. Possibly their eventual acceptance as authoritative and **canonical** had something to do with their vigorous, and useful, denunciation of Gnostic or other aberrations from the faith. Such denunciation, which shades into a vilification of opponents unexampled elsewhere in the New Testament, could easily be applied by later interpreters to other opponents. In the history of polemics, therefore, 2 Peter and Jude have, unfortunately, provided controversialists with a rich source of fierce invective.

OUTLINE OF 2 PETER

> Address (1:1–2)
> Exhortation and Reminder (1:3–21)
> Warning and Condemnation of False Teachers (2:1–22)
> The Coming of the Day of the Lord (3:1–13)
> Concluding Exhortation (3:14–18)

The Coming of the Day of the Lord (2 Pet. 3:1–10; Jude 3)

What is the relation between the delay of Jesus' return and the importance of true doctrine?

The third chapter of 2 Peter reveals a great deal about the letter's situation and purpose. At the outset the author speaks of a previous letter, presumably 1 Peter, which he may have known as an authoritative book. Toward the end his reference to Paul clearly indicates that he knows a collection of the Apostle's letters that now have the status of holy scripture (3:16).

Already we have noticed some indications that 2 Peter presupposes knowledge of the **Synoptic Gospels** and even the Gospel of John. The reference to Jesus' having spoken of Peter's death (1:14) seems to reflect knowledge of John 21:18 or of a related tradition in which Jesus gives Peter to understand that he will die a martyr's death. Immediately thereafter, the Johannine narrative deals with the question of the Beloved Disciple's fate (21:20–23). The reader discovers that some Christians believed that he would not die but would live to see Jesus' return in glory (vs. 23). John, however, goes out of his way to make clear that Jesus did not actually say that. Apparently, the Gospel writer here deals with a real or potential disappointment at the failure of Jesus' **parousia**.

A similar concern is met in 2 Peter 3:3–10, where the "scoffers" who raise questions about Jesus's return are probably disillusioned Christians (vss. 3–4). Perhaps some were beginning to think that the promise of Jesus' return had somehow already been fulfilled. Second Thessalonians 2:1–2 and 2 Timothy 2:17–18 give evidence of such belief, as do some of the words of Jesus in the farewell discourses of the Gospel of John (chaps. 14–17). We are confronting an understandable problem among Christians living a generation or more after Jesus' death. Clearly, many of the first Christians believed that Jesus would return before they, or at least their generation, had died out (cf. Mark 9:1; 1 Cor. 11:30; 1 Thess. 4:15). When he did not, troubling doubts arose.

The author of 2 Peter answers the questions raised by the so-called scoffers on the basis of scripture or scriptural **exegesis**. First, he maintains that all things have not continued "as they were from the beginning of creation" (3:4) and points to the destruction of the world by flood (in the time of Noah: Gen. 7:11–21). Then he reiterates that a fiery judgment is still to come (vs. 7). Its seeming delay has resulted from a failure to reckon according to God's time (vs. 8). The basis for this reckoning is Psalm 90:4, although it is not explicitly cited, where one day is equated with a thousand years. The author thus shows that the scoffers do not know or understand scripture. Moreover, if the Lord seems slow—actually he is not—it is just another manifestation of his patience (vs. 9). In the meantime, let the scoffers and all others take warning! The comparison of the Lord's coming to a thief (vs. 10) presupposes the motif of "a thief in the night," found in earlier New Testament traditions (Matt. 24:43–44; 1 Thess. 5:2, 4; Rev. 3:3; 16:15).

In 2 Peter, the typical concern of early Christians for pure doctrine, which we have already observed in the **Pastorals**, comes to expression quite openly. This letter reflects a situation in which the church had begun to think in terms of a long, indeterminate future. For such a future the church needed to ready itself by emphasizing inner discipline, correct doctrine, and the rejection of heresy. Both 2 Peter and Jude share these emphases. The latter two become particularly clear in Jude, where the author appeals to his readers or hearers to defend "the faith that was once for all entrusted to the saints" (Jude 3). Such defense is necessary in the face of what both authors would consider the rankest heresy.

Jude, like 2 Peter, is convinced that the **church**, or Christians, must dig in for a long siege. The concept of faith as "the faith" (i.e., doctrine), already found in the Pauline Pastorals, here comes to completion: "faith" is understood as a deposit of doctrine given to the church ("the saints") at the beginning of the Christian era. The word *orthodoxy* is not used, but the author is plainly thinking in terms of the opposition of orthodoxy and heresy that has characterized the development of Christian doctrine throughout much of its history. Interestingly, whereas the concept of faith foreshadows later developments, the designation of the church as "the saints" reflects a very primitive manner of thinking and speaking (cf. Rom. 1:7). Saints are not yet a special or elite group within the church. All true believers are saints: that is, they are set apart as holy and dedicated to the Lord (cf. Heb. 6:10; 13:24).

THE REVELATION TO JOHN:
FAITH'S VISION OF A NEW ORDER

Background of Revelation

The last book of the Christian Bible, the Revelation to John, belongs to the genre and thought-world of apocalypticism, to which it has given its name. The term *apocalypticism* comes from the Greek word *apokalypsis*, which is the Greek title of the book and means "revelation." Thus Revelation (note the singular) is rightly said to be an **apocalypse**, and its thought is apocalyptic.

The literary **genre** of apocalypse is marked by four features: (1) the **revelation** itself, which is given by God; (2) a mediator between God and the world (in Revelation either Jesus Christ or an angel); (3) a prophet or seer who receives the revelation (in Revelation, John of Patmos); (4) disclosure of future events. This definition is actually based on Revelation, but it fits a number of documents, Jewish and Christian, written before and since. In the Hebrew Bible one thinks particularly of Daniel 7–12 and of Isaiah 24–27; in the **Pseudepigrapha**, parts of *1 Enoch* (chaps. 14–15), *4 Ezra*, and *2 Baruch*. In early second-century Christianity, the *Shepherd of Hermas* followed Revelation, as did the *Apocalypse of Peter*.

Apocalyptic **eschatology** was much more widespread in antiquity than the apocalypse as a literary genre. As noted above, the entire New Testament, or most of it, is either written from the standpoint of apocalyptic eschatology or takes a position with respect to it. But within the New Testament only Revelation is an apocalypse, belonging to that literary genre. Because biblical apocalyptic presupposes the Old Testament, especially the **prophets**, it is fitting that Revelation is shot through with Old Testament language, though without explicit quotations.

The origins of the apocalyptic view of the world and history have been much debated, with several possibilities proposed: Persian (Iranian) dualistic influence on late biblical thought; the disappointment of this-worldly hopes for a free Jewish state; the impetus of ancient Hebrew prophecy. Without doubt apocalyptic ideas appear in Judaism as a consequence of the **Exile**, and under foreign influence and the pressure of the disappointment of worldly, historical hopes. Daniel, for example—at least the Daniel apocalypse—was written under the influence of the Seleucid repression of Jewish religion in the early second century B.C. The **Qumran** community felt oppressed by the **Hasmonean** dynasty, which it considered illegitimate, and produced its own, sharply dualistic, apocalyptic writings, perhaps under Persian, Zoroastrian influence.

To what extent the entire Christian movement is a response to a sense of oppression and alienation—first, as experienced by and within Judaism; second, as experienced in the wider Roman world—is an important historical and theological question. The Gospel of John, which reflects a profound alienation of Jesus' followers from Judaism, does not promote an apocalyptic eschatological point of view. Instead, John reinterprets apocalyptic eschatology. Jesus' own proclamation of the coming of God's **kingdom**, as it is presented in the **Gospels**, can be understood as an expression of apocalyptic thought. Yet Jesus' kingdom proclamation does not share the dismal alienation from this world fostered by apocalyptic assumptions. Nor does the Jesus of the New Testament develop the detailed symbolism of apocalyptic imagery. Still, Jesus' own kinship to the apocalyptic perspective is apparent, as can be seen from his words about the kingdom and judgment (see pp. 202–210). Paul also expects God to intervene decisively within history in a very short space of time. Yet Paul, like Jesus, for the most part avoids detailed apocalyptic symbolism.

To understand and appreciate Revelation, we need to read it within the context of biblical and early Christian thought. Revelation echoes the language of scripture, especially the prophetic books of the Old Testament. Although its world may seem strange, it was not foreign to early Christian readers. It stand much closer to the world and thought of first-century Christians, and to Jesus, Paul, and even the Fourth Gospel, than modern Christians are likely to suppose.

Revelation's concentration upon the eschatological future and its use of vivid apocalyptic language stand in contrast to the Gospel of John, in which eschatological fulfillment is emphasized and apocalyptic imagery is avoided. As we have seen, the language and theology of the Johannine letters are closely related to the Gospel. Although the Revelation to John, traditionally ascribed to the same author, seems remote from the other Johannine writings, some important points of similarity or lines of connection exist. In 1 John there is still an expectation of Jesus' return (2:8, 18, 28), and the circle of disciples that preserved and published the Gospel of John evidently had at one time cherished the hope that he would return before the death of the Beloved Disciple (21:23). Moreover, in Revelation, as in the Fourth Gospel and 1 John, Jesus is called the **Word**, *logos* (Rev. 19:13). **Witness** (or testimony) and *witnessing* are also important concepts in all these writings. In the Gospel, Jesus promises the **Spirit** to his disciples (e.g., in 14:15–17). In 1 John, the claim of spiritual inspiration by those who espouse erroneous doctrine is challenged (4:1–3), whereas the Revelation to John claims to be a Spirit-inspired book in its entirety (1:10). One could go on, but these instances are enough to indicate that the Johannine writings—Gospel, letters, and apocalypse—are related by content and perspective as well as by tradition.

Although some scholars have expressed doubt, the Book of Revelation was probably written during a period of crisis in the **church**, occasioned by the Roman government's active opposition. Tradition ascribes its message of resistance and hope in times of hardship and persecution to the reign of the Emperor Domitian, near the close of the first century (Eusebius, *EH*, III, 18, 3, citing Ignatius). As to the place and conditions of writing and the identification of those addressed, there is no reason to doubt its own statements (1:9). Nor is there any reason to doubt what the author says about himself in the same chapter. Clearly he is an important church figure of Asia, a prophet, whose name is John. The traditional identification with John the son of Zebedee is not impossible, but nothing in the book itself either indicates or demands this. This John does not call himself an **apostle**; instead, he seems to refer to the apostles as revered figures of the past (18:20; 21:14). Moreover, he gives no indication of having accompanied Jesus or having known those who did. Nevertheless, the later identification of this John with the apostle and author of the Gospel paved the way for Revelation's acceptance into the **canon** of the New Testament.

The structure of Revelation is complex, and there is some reason to suspect that the original order has at points been disrupted or augmented. The following outline is developed in terms of a simple time–scheme.

OUTLINE OF REVELATION

Introduction: The Vision of the Prophet on Patmos (1:1–20)

The Present Time of the Church's Struggle: The Letters to the Seven Churches (2:1–3:22)

The Time between the Present and the End (4:1–18:24)

> *The Vision of Heaven (4:1–5:14)*
> *The Opening of the Seven Seals (6:1–8:1)*
> *The Blowing of the Seven Trumpets (8:2–11:19)*
> *Apocalyptic Vision of Happenings on Earth (12:1–13:18)*
> *Preparatory Vision of the End (14:1–20)*
> *The Pouring Out of the Seven Bowls of Wrath (15:1–18:24)*

The End: Future Victory (19:1–22:5)

> *The Judgment and Christ's Return (19:1–20:15)*
> *The New World (21:1–22:5)*

Conclusion: Present Time and the Prophet on Patmos (22:6–21)

The Vision of the Prophet on Patmos (Rev. 1:1–20)

What is the relationship of the present to the future?

From stem to stern this is an **apocalyptic** work, a **revelation**. Thus John declares that his book will show the servants of God what must soon take place (vs. 1). The true author of the revelation is not John, but rather God, who delivers it to Jesus **Christ**, who gives it to his angel, who in turn relays it to John (cf. 22:6, 8, 16). John has borne witness or testified (1:2), a reference to the writing of this book; the object of this witness is the **word** of God and the testimony of Jesus Christ—that is, the revelation (cf. vs. 1), as is clear from the explanatory phrase "even to all that he saw." The same Greek word, or stem (*martyr-*), may be translated by the English words "**witness**" or "testimony." A blessing is pronounced on anyone who reads aloud, hears, and keeps (obeys) this **prophecy** about the future (vs. 3), and the imminence of what is to be narrated is again emphasized. Similar blessings, with attendant warnings, conclude the book (22:7, 14, 18–19, 21).

Several important characteristics of Revelation may be observed in its opening paragraph. The author's own title, "the revelation of Jesus Christ," expresses the book's apocalyptic

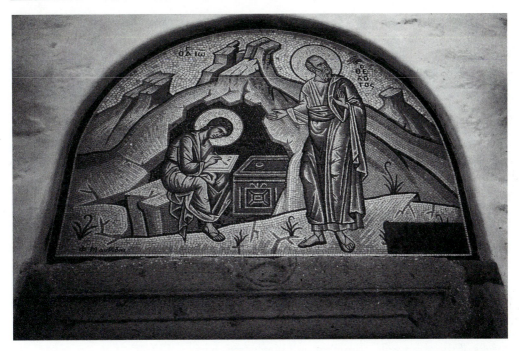

The entrance to the Tomb of St. John on the Greek Island of Patmos, just off the coast of present-day Turkey. According to local tradition, in this cave John had the visions that led to the writing of the Book of Revelation.

character. This emphasis is indicated in several other ways. The content is to be revealed only to the faithful ("his servants"). It has to do with things that are soon to take place. The mediator between the divine realm (represented by God and Christ) and the human (represented by John and other servants of God) is an angel. What the angel communicates, John somehow sees, presumably as a vision. All these traits are typical of the Jewish–Christian apocalyptic tradition. Furthermore, in the apocalyptic understanding of history, events unfold according to the plan and purpose of God ("what *must* soon take place"). John sees a preenactment of the unfolding culmination of world history. In keeping with the book's apocalyptic character, Jesus Christ (vs. 1) is primarily the heavenly Christ, who later appears in great splendor (1:12 ff.) and will return from heaven at the end of the age (22:20).

Using an epistolary salutation John then addresses himself to the seven churches of Asia (vss. 4 ff.; cf. 1:11 cf. end map). This mixing of apocalyptic and **epistolary** forms is not unprecedented. (The **pseudepigraphical** *2 Baruch*'s chapters 76–87, while apocalyptic, are cast in the form of a letter.) It is very unusual, however, that John writes in his own name: most authors of apocalypses adopted names of famous persons out of the past (e.g., Daniel, Enoch, Ezra, Baruch, or Peter). By assuming the stance of an earlier figure, the writer thus could "predict" the intervening events—which had actually already occurred—thus lending credence to his descriptions of the actual future. John, by contrast, writes confidently under his own name and from the standpoint of his own time to the churches of Asia. Although he is an authoritative figure, his confidence lies not in himself but, rather, in his conviction that prophetic inspiration has been reborn in the **church**. He seems to have been a Christian prophet in the tradition of those mentioned in the letters of Paul, Ephesians, 1 John, and the ***Didache***. As the Lord of Israel spoke through prophets in ancient times, so now the Lord Jesus Christ speaks through prophets to the church and to the world. Although the prophet is addressed through angels, this mediation does not dilute his own experience and awareness of the Lord's powerful presence.

The greeting "Grace to you and peace" (vs. 4) is typical of the New Testament, especially of Paul. "Who is and who was and who is to come" is God. Judaism and the pagan world, as well as Christianity, afford examples of such speaking of God in the past, present, and future tenses. As for the seven spirits, they are probably the author's unique way of referring to the **Holy Spirit**. The number seven may be suggested by the seven churches to which John addresses the letters (chapters 2–3), though elsewhere (4:5; 5:6) he speaks of seven spirits where the context excludes any reference or allusion to the churches. Perhaps the seven spirits can be explained on the basis of John's fondness for the number seven, a symbol of completeness in antiquity. In later chapters Revelation speaks of the seven seals, trumpets, and bowls (see chart, p. 442).

The description of Jesus as a faithful witness (vs. 5) recalls the "testimony" or "witness" of Jesus (1:2; Greek, *martyria*). **Witness** is the term used of a person who testifiies in the sense either of observing an event or of bearing witness on someone's behalf. In early Christian usage, however, it soon took on a specific connotation. For example, in Revelation (see 2:13, 11:3–7, and 17:6), the witness has often died as a result of witnessing. The extent to which the idea of dying became integral to the term itself, because of the early Christian experience of persecution, is indicated by the meaning of the word *martyr* in English. Jesus Christ is the archetypal witness and martyr, the one who gives his life as his testimony, and others follow in his footsteps. Thus the historical death of Jesus is crucial for John.

Jesus' martyrdom is not, of course, just the end of a great and good person. As the first-born from the dead (cf. Col. 1:18) he is the exalted **Messiah**, the ruler of earthly kings. Moreover, his **resurrection** is related to the resurrection of the believer (cf. 1 Cor. 15). The believer, especially the person whose faith and testimony have led to death, is to share Christ's glory. In Revelation this triumph is often referred to as conquering (cf. 2:26 and *passim*). This is not, however, an immortality easily gained. The resurrection life is attained through conquest of this world's power, especially through martyrdom by this world's hands (cf. John 16:33 and 1 John 5:4). It is, therefore, a hidden conquest, at least to the eyes of the world. Significantly, John's vision of Christ as the victorious Lamb does not cancel out the Lamb's having been slain (5:6–14).

Christ's present rule over earthly kings (vs. 5) is as hidden as the martyr's conquest. Yet it is nonetheless real. And in the one case as in the other, what is already real in God's eyes will be made manifest before the eyes of humankind. In words made famous by Handel's *Messiah* (1741), "the Lord God omnipotent reigneth" (19:6 KJV). God's reign is exercised through Christ, who, though crucified, dead, and buried, nevertheless now lives and rules. That God through Christ actually does reign, and that this reign will be made manifest to bring all peoples into subjection, whether for their weal or woe, is Revelation's basic theme. Of course, this message is either the hope or the assumption of almost every book in the New Testament. The uniqueness of Revelation, however, is that in one way or another this theme is constantly in the foreground and is always dressed in apocalyptic imagery.

The remainder of the **Christological** confession (1:5b–7) appears to be traditional (cf. vs. 5b with Rom. 3:23 ff.; 8:35 ff.; Gal. 2:20; vs. 6 with 1 Pet. 2:9). That Christians in some sense already possess the good things promised is typical of the New Testament's realized or partially realized **eschatology**, which we have already observed in Hebrews (4:1–10; 12:25–29). Yet the future-oriented apocalyptic point of view, more characteristic of this author, appears again in verse 7. Jesus' return to earth as a conqueror "coming with the clouds" is not a new idea (cf. Daniel 7:13; Mark 13:26; 14:62; Matt. 24:30; 25:31). That every eye shall see him forecasts the future universal recognition of the lordship of Christ (cf. 1 Cor. 15:25 ff. and Phil. 2:10 ff.). The references to piercing and wailing allude to the **crucifixion** (cf. Zech. 12:10 and John 19:37) and the implied future judgment of the nations.

The end of the epistolary salutation is indicated by the "So it is to be. **Amen**," a liturgical formula. The prophetic word (vs. 8) has no obvious connection with what precedes or follows. In a sense the verse is related to the prediction of Jesus' **parousia** (vs. 7), because it affirms that God is the sure ground of this hope. The first and last parts of the statement, the word of the Lord God ("I am the Alpha and the Omega") and the description of him in terms of past, present, and future, are more closely related than may initially appear. Alpha and omega are the first and last letters of the Greek alphabet, the equivalent of the English expression "from A to Z." God is the first and last (cf. 22:13, where this explanation is given), the one who was and is and is to come. Thus God is the Lord of history at the beginning, at its end, and during the interim.

The abuse of Revelation by ancients and moderns obsessed with predicting the future has obscured the indispensable link with the *past* and the significance of the *present* as real and important aspects of the author's thought. We have already observed the importance of the past (vss. 4–7): church tradition, the historical Jesus, and scripture. As for the present, the author's message for the contemporary churches of Asia unfolds in the next chapters (2–3). Although chapters 19–22 plainly have to do with the future return of Christ and the end of the world history, the long central section (chaps. 4–18) does not deal solely with the end time. Although the end is constantly in view, the author is equally concerned with his own period. For example, John's apocalyptic interpretation of past and present historical events can be seen in the portrayal of Jerusalem's destruction (chap. 11), the destiny of the Messiah and the church in the world (chap. 12), and the depredations of the Roman Empire (chaps. 13, 17, and 18). All history—past, present, and future—is under the sign of the Alpha and the Omega, the lordship of the God who was and is and is to come. Nothing falls outside the scope of God's revelation to John.

The author's own involvement in that history becomes clearer in 1:9–11, where the reader learns that it includes participation in the world's events as well as in the church's life. This section marks the beginning of the revelatory book proper, for it serves to introduce the visions, which comprise chapters 2 and 3 as well as the rest of his work. The so-called letters to the seven churches are no less visions (1:11–20) than the sighting of New Jerusalem (chap. 21). Yet the naming of the locations of the churches (vs. 11) makes graphic and concrete the this-worldly dimension of Revelation.

Crucial for grasping John's situation as he writes, and therefore for understanding this book, is the statement that he was on Patmos "because of the word of God and the testimony of Jesus" (vs. 9). Probably he means that he was exiled to Patmos as punishment for preaching the word of God and testifying to Jesus; this is especially likely in view of the fact that such preaching and testifying had led to martyrdom (cf. 6:9 and 20:4). John speaks of sharing not only the **kingdom** but also the persecution and the patient endurance.

The persecutions perpetrated against God's people call for steadfast endurance. Hebrews also mentioned the need for endurance with the possibility of persecution already in view (10:34 ff.; 12:4). In Revelation persecution seems to have become the predominant reality. Moreover, we know from the Roman historian Tacitus (*Annals* III.68; IV.30; XV.71) that Patmos was used as a penal colony, a place of banishment, by the Romans. Ancient church tradition also understood John to have been incarcerated for his Christian preaching. We are justified in accepting this tradition as an accurate interpretation of Revelation 1:9.

John receives his revelation "in the Spirit" (vs. 10); the association of the **Spirit** with visions and ecstatic utterances is common to primitive Christianity (Acts 2:1 ff.; 1 Cor. 14). By "the Lord's day" John evidently means Sunday. If so, this is one of the earliest references to Sunday as the distinctly Christian holy day (cf. Acts 20:7; 1 Cor. 16:2). In the New Testament as in the Old, "the sabbath" always means the Jewish Sabbath, Saturday. Sunday has appropriately replaced Saturday as the Christian Sabbath, for according to tradition it was on Sunday—the third day after, and including, Friday— that Jesus rose from the dead. The voice like a trumpet that John hears is that of the Son of Man (vs. 13), the heavenly Christ.

John writes by divine command (vs. 11) and by mandate sends what he writes to the seven churches of Asia. The command is to "write in a book what you see," rather than what you hear. The mode of the communication of revelation is not verbal, as is usual in the earlier Old Testament prophets, but visual, as in the tradition of Ezekiel, the later, postexilic prophets, and, above all, the Jewish apocalyptic writers.

The visionary scenes now begin (vs. 12), and we encounter for the first time the problem of how to understand them. On the one hand, the narrations of the visions seem to be carefully constructed literary works, replete with scriptural allusions and language (again, see chart, p. 442). On the other hand, the possibility that ecstatic or visionary experiences were the basis for what the author has written cannot be excluded. Unlike other apocalyptic writers, John does not find it necessary to accredit his message by concealing himself; nor does he attempt to gain credence for his prophecy of things to come by dressing out as predictions the recitation of generally known historical facts.

The seven golden lampstands (vs. 12) recall the seven-branched lampstand (Hebrew, *menorah*) that was said to stand outside the second veil of the Israelite tabernacle (Exod. 25:31–40; cf. Zech. 4, a passage dealing with the messianic hope). In all likelihood the allusion is intentional despite the fact that here we seem to be dealing with seven separate stands, not one. The presence of the lampstands indicates an approach to the holy place (see chap. 4). But John's explicit interpretation is that the seven lampstands represent the seven churches soon to be addressed (chaps. 2 and 3).

The appearance of the Christ (vs. 13) evokes Daniel 7:13, "one like the son of man." We are not told that this figure is the Christ, and John does not favor "**Son of Man**" as a messianic title (but cf. 14:14); yet 1:17 ff. makes this identification with Christ certain. The clothing of this still-mysterious figure (vs. 13) may have been suggested by Ezekiel 9:2 and 11 and Daniel 10:5. The remainder of the description (vss. 14–15) is for the most part derived from the appearance of the one who was the Ancient of Days or an Ancient One (Dan. 7:9, NRSV), although the comparison of his voice to the sound of many waters probably comes from Ezekiel 1:24 and 43:2. Obviously John's mind was steeped in the language and imagery of the Old Testament, even though, remarkably, nowhere in this book does he cite scripture explicitly.

The seven stars (vs. 16) are interpreted in verse 20. The sharp two-edged sword recalls Genesis 3:24 (cf. Ezek. 21:9–10) and especially Hebrews 4:12. In the latter passage, as apparently here, the sword symbolizes the word of God. Christ's shining face indicates nearness to, if not possession of, the glory of God himself (cf. Matt. 13:43; 2 Cor. 3:7–18; 4:6). With this verse the description of the vision of the Son of Man is complete. John's reaction and Christ's response in identifying himself and explaining the vision to John follow (vss. 17–20).

John's prostration at his vision of the heavenly Christ (vs. 17) is not only understandable but also liturgically appropriate. Daniel 10:7–10 is the immediate background if not the direct inspiration of this verse. Christ reaches out, restores John (vs. 17), and identifies himself to him (vss. 17b–18). That Christ is the first and the last implies that like God, and with him, he exercises lordship over history from beginning to end. "Living one" and "alive forever and ever" in conjunction with the statement "I was dead" refer unmistakably to the crucifixion and resurrection. The power of the keys (in Matt. 16:19, given to Peter) is here reserved

The Seven-Fold Pattern of Visions in Revelation

	Chapters 6-11			Chapters 16-18
	7 SEALS	7 TRUMPETS		7 BOWLS
The Initial Unit of Four Catastrophes	6:1–2: First Seal Opened white horse, bow, crown: to conquer	8:7: First Trumpet Blown hail, fire, blood 1/3 earth burned up	Chapters 12-15: Visions, Reassurance, Preparation for final series	16:2: First Bowl Poured sores on the unfaithful
	6:3–4: Second Seal Opened red horse, sword to take peace from earth	8:8–9: Second Trumpet Blown fiery mountain in sea, 1/3 sea became blood		16:3: Second Bowl Poured sea turns to blood
	6:5–6: Third Seal Opened black horse, pair of scales	8:10–11: Third Trumpet Blown star falls on 1/3 of rivers 1/3 rivers became wormwood		16:4-7: Third Bowl Poured rivers become blood
	6:7–8: Fourth Seal Opened pale horse, sword, famine, pestilence, wild animals	8:12: Fourth Trumpet Blown 1/3 sun, 1/3 moon, 1/3 stars struck into darkness		16:8-9: Fourth Bowl Poured sun scorches people
The Woes Intensify as the End Approaches	6:9–11: Fifth Seal Opened martyrs under altar "how long?" "a little longer"	8:13: Fifth Trumpet Blown Eagle, "woe, woe, woe," demon locusts from the bottomless pit		16:10: Fifth Bowl Poured darkness upon the beast's kingdom
	6:12–17: Sixth Seal Opened great earthquake, sun and moon, stars fall, all fear	9:13–21: Sixth Trumpet Blown Voice: "Release four angels" 200,000,000 demonic cavalry from Euphrates		16:12-16: Sixth Bowl Poured kings of east cross Euphrates to prepare at Armageddon
INTERLUDE	7:1–17 sealing of the 144,000 a great multitude's acclamation	eating scroll (10:1-11) 2 witnesses (11:1-3)		(pattern broken)
The End	8:1: Seventh Seal Opened silence	11:15: Seventh Trumpet Blown end announced and celebrated		16:17-21: Seventh Bowl Poured lightning, earthquake, "God remembered great Babylon"
				17–18 Elaboration: The Fall of Babylon

The Seven-Fold Pattern of Visions in Revelation. *(Adapted from M. Eugene Boring,* Revelation *[Louisville: John Knox Press, 1989], pp.120–121. Reproduced by permission.)*

for Christ. As a result of his own death and resurrection, Christ assumes power over death and Hades (cf. Rom. 6:9 ff.) His resurrection is no mere resuscitation, but an exaltation to supreme power and authority. The divine ascriptions and prerogatives applied to Christ imply that humanity's ultimate destiny depends upon and is assured by him. The claim to possess the keys of death and Hades (vs. 18) may also be related to the primitive Christian concept of Christ's descent into hell and his freeing of the captives there (1 Pet. 3:18–22; 4:6; cf. Eph. 4:8–10).

Attention returns to the prophet's task as Christ commands him to write (vs. 19). Once again the Book of Revelation concerns not only the unfolding of the future but also the interpretation of present events: "what is" as well as "what is to take place after this." Christ interprets the seven stars and seven lampstands to John (vs. 20). The notion that nations, communities, or even individuals had guardian angels was not uncommon in the ancient world (cf. Acts 12:15; Tob. 5:21); so each **church** has its angel, who serves it as a medium of **revelation** or communication with God. The letters to the seven churches (chaps. 2 and 3) are then directed to them through these guardian angels.

The seven letters are no ordinary letters but are as much supernatural in their source and delivery as the rest of the book. Nevertheless, they again show the author's concern, not only with heavenly things and things to come, but with the this-worldly life and problems of the churches. This concern is directed both toward the inner life of the church and toward its witness to a hostile world. Naturally, the two are related, for no church with chinks in its moral armor would be strong enough to stand before such a world and resist the demand to worship its gods.

The remainder of Revelation presents a jarring juxtaposition of the heavenly and the earthly, the historical or worldly and the eschatological. Chapters 4 and 5 picture the heavenly court. The seer describes the throne of God himself and the momentous events taking place there, particularly the designation of the Lamb (Christ) who had been slain as worthy to open the scroll. The opening of six of these seals is described in chapter 6. Heavenly events and realities have their earthly counterparts and consequences. With the opening of the seals catastrophes break out across the earth. Then there follows an interlude (chap. 7). The first part (7:1–8) shows the gathering of the elect from the four corners of the earth; the latter (vss. 9–17), their appearance in heaven. At the beginning of chapter 8, we have the opening of the seventh seal—and silence. After about half an hour of silence, the sounding of the seven trumpets begins (chaps. 8 and 9; 11:15–19) with disasters erupting upon the earth.

Chapters 10–13 deal with contemporary events or those of the recent past. The prophet's own experience (chap. 10) is like that of the prophet Ezekiel (Ezek. 2:8–3:3). Since Ezekiel's word of the Lord had to do with lamentations and woes, especially against Jerusalem (cf., e.g., Ezek. 4:1 ff.), it is no surprise that Revelation 11 reflects that city's devastation. The birth and persecution of the Messiah and of his church are envisioned in chapters 12 and 13. In chapter 12, the heavenly dimension of the conflict is paramount, whereas in chapter 13, attention focuses on Rome, described under the apocalyptic symbol of the beast. The sounding of the seventh trumpet is delayed by intervening scenes, just as the opening of the seventh seal was delayed. The seventh and final stage of each sequence has a peculiar significance, for apparently it stands symbolically at the borderline between the apocalyptic, catastrophic dissolution of this world and the coming of God's kingdom. The events that follow the sounding of the trumpets recapitulate those that follow the opening of the seven seals. Yet there may also be a progression. After the seventh seal there is only silence; after the seventh trumpet, however, we get a preview of the glory that is to come (11:15–19).

From chapter 14 on, the apocalyptic interpretations are no longer of the immediate past or present, but of the future. Again the seer has a vision of heaven (14:1–5), this time followed by a series of warnings from angels flying in heaven and the command that the heavenly Christ reap the harvest of the earth (14:14–20). Chapters 15 through 18 describe in appropriately symbolic terms the final upheavals to be wrought on earth by the outpouring of the bowls of divine wrath.

The seer's prophecy about the remainder of world history is completed with the outpouring of the seventh bowl of wrath and the destruction of Babylon, which is presumably Rome (chaps. 17 and 18; cf. 1 Pet. 5:13). Yet we can discern no clear distinction between world history as we understand it and the last days. John understands *his own time* to be the last days. He does not conceive the present as a period of secular history where everything is governed by natural, social, or psychological laws of cause and effect. For him there is no secular history, for all time is ultimately under the lordship of God. Nevertheless, the immense powers of evil, with otherworldly origins and dimensions (e.g., the beast, the dragon or serpent, who is called the Devil and Satan, 12:9), presently hold sway in the world. Their sovereignty is, however, ephemeral. God's wrath is directed against them, and they are overthrown. What happens in heaven anticipates God's ultimate triumph on earth.

Victory does not occur easily or without vast repercussions. Chaos and disaster break out upon the earth as the power of God overwhelms the forces of evil (cf. 2 Thess. 2:1–12). Even the advent of Christ, traditionally called the second coming, does not put an end to the struggle once and for all (chap. 19). After Christ's thousand-year reign, the millennium (after the Latin word for "thousand"), there is yet another outbreak of evil, led by Satan himself (chap. 20) before God finally brings everything into subjection, renewing both heaven and earth (21:1–22:5; cf. 1 Cor. 15:20–28). Nevertheless, the substance of the seer's message is not that the end is a long way off, but that the night is already far spent, the day is at hand (cf. Rom. 13:12). The apocalyptic drama is underway and moves inexorably toward its conclusion. "Surely I am coming soon. **Amen.** Come, Lord Jesus!" (22:20).

Christians of John's day were willing, at the risk of their lives, to resist the demand that they worship the Roman emperor (13:1–15; cf. 18:24): the incarnation of worldly order and power, the epitome of human self-deification. Why did they dare to do so? Such worship seems little more than a perfunctory gesture, although it was a significant token of subjection to the power and authority of this world. These

Rome from the Capitoline Hill. The Romans conquered Jewish resistance in Palestine, and their conquest is memorialized by the Arch of Titus (Chapter 1, p. 10). Yet the once omnipotent Roman empire lives on only in classical law and literature and in grand ruins, like the Colosseum on the horizon above (see also Chapter 10, p. 358).

Christians resisted because they believed in an authority that transcends this world, an authority revealed in the death of Jesus upon the cross and in his exaltation from the dead to God's own right hand. The Book of Revelation shows that for many, if not most, of them this conviction and the refusal to fall down and worship the beast were set in the context of a lively future hope, not primarily for their own personal survival of physical death, but for the manifestation of God's authority and rule before all humanity. God's Christ and his saints were to be vindicated before the eyes of a skeptical and evil world.

Far from offering a fantastical timetable, as some persist in reading it—in spite of Mark 13:32–33—Revelation gives testimony to faith in God's lordship over history. The author is convinced that the apparent confusion of events does in fact lead somewhere; history is not meaningless. Yet such meaning is not apparent in individual events, for it can only be grasped when history is viewed in its entirety—that is, from the standpoint of its expected end. Christ is the light by which all history is illuminated for John. The Old Testament provides the imagery by means of which he portrays the end. For John of Patmos, as for other writers of the New Testament, faith meant not only looking upward to God and Christ, and backward to the manifestations of God's reality and fidelity in the past, but forward in expectation to his further and final revelation in the future.

SUGGESTIONS FOR FURTHER READING

ESCHATOLOGY AND APOCALYPTICISM

Three **standard treatments** are P. D. Hanson, *The Dawn of Apocalyptic: The Historical and Sociological Roots of Jewish Apocalypticism*, rev. ed. (Philadelphia: Fortress, 1979), C. Rowland, *The Open Heaven: A Study of Apocalyptic in Judaism and Early Christianity* (New York: Crossroad, 1982), and J. J. Collins, *The Apocalyptic Imagination: An Introduction to Jewish Apocalyptic Literature*, 2nd ed. (Grand Rapids: Eerdmans, 1998). Of these, Rowland stands out by emphasizing the revelation of heavenly secrets, not predictions of the future, as the essence of apocalyptic thought. Helpful overviews of the subject are S. L. Cook, *The Apocalyptic Literature* (Nashville: Abingdon, 2003), and S. M. Lewis, *What Are They Saying about New Testament Apocalyptic?* (Mahwah, NJ: Paulist, 2004).

HEBREWS

H. W. Attridge, *The Epistle to the Hebrews: A Commentary on the Epistle to the Hebrews* (Minneapolis: Fortress, 1989), and C. R. Koester, *Hebrews: A New Translation with Introduction and Commentary* (New York: Doubleday, 2001), are now the standard **commentaries**. For concentration on Hebrews' **theology**, consult L. T. Johnson, *Hebrews: A Commentary* (Louisville: Westminster John Knox, 2006). G. Hughes, *Hebrews and Hermeneutics* (Cambridge: Cambridge University Press, 1979), locates Hebrews amid significant theological issues; B. Lindars, *The Theology of the Letter to the Hebrews* (Cambridge: Cambridge University Press, 1991), offers a succinct treatment of the subject in its literary and historical contexts. A classic work is E. Käsemann, *The Wandering People of God: An Interpretation of the Letter to the Hebrews*, trans. R. A. Harrisville and I. L. Sundberg (Minneapolis: Augsburg, 1984). An important **social–scientific approach** is D. A. deSilva, *Despising Shame: Honor Discourse and Community Maintenance in the Epistle to the Hebrews* (Atlanta: Scholars, 1995). D. J. Harrington, *What Are They Saying about the Letter to the Hebrews?* (Mahwah, NJ: Paulist, 2005) offers an orientation to a range of interpretive questions.

JUDE AND 2 PETER

These letters are usually treated together, as in R. J. Bauckham, *Jude, 2 Peter* (Waco, TX: Word Books, 1983), J. H. Neyrey, *2 Peter, Jude: A New Translation with Introduction and Commentary* (New York: Doubleday, 1993), S. J. Kraftchick, *Jude, 2 Peter* (Nashville: Abingdon, 2002), and D. Senior, *1 Peter, Jude, 2 Peter* (Collegeville: MN: Liturgical, 2003). D. F. Watson, *Invention, Arrangement, and Style: Rhetorical Criticism of Jude and 2 Peter* (Atlanta: Scholars Press, 1988), is an important **literary study**.

THE REVELATION TO JOHN

Note the **commentaries** by M. E. Boring, *Revelation* (Louisville: John Knox, 1989), J. Roloff, *Revelation: A Continental Commentary*, trans. J. Alsup (Minneapolis: Fortress, 1993), L. L. Thompson, *Revelation* (Nashville: Abingdon, 1998), and the compendious contribution of D. E. Aune, *Revelation*, 3 vols. (Dallas: Word Books, 1997–1998). A. Y. Collins, *Crisis and Catharsis: The Power of the Apocalypse* (Philadelphia: Westminster, 1984), E. F. Schüssler Fiorenza, *The Book of Revelation: Justice and Judgment* (Philadelphia: Fortress, 1985), S. J. Friesen, *Imperial Cults and the Apocalypse of John: Revelation in the Ruins* (Oxford: Oxford University Press, 2001), and C. J. Hemer, *The Letters to the Seven Churches of Asia in Their Local Setting* (Grand Rapids, MI: Eerdmans, 2001) all explore important **social dimensions** of the Johannine Apocalypse. On its **theology**, consult R. J. Bauckham, *The Theology of the Book of Revelation* (Cambridge: Cambridge University Press, 1993), and C. R. Koester, *Revelation and the End of All Things* (Grand Rapids: Eerdmans, 2001). For the book's **history of interpretation**, consult A. W. Wainwright, *Mysterious Apocalypse: Interpreting the Book of Revelation* (Nashville: Abingdon, 1993).

An early third-century fresco depicting the Eucharistic banquet in the Catacombs of Priscilla, Rome. *(Courtesy of the Bridgeman Art Library.)*

THE ANATOMY OF THE NEW TESTAMENT— MEANING, STRUCTURE, AND IDENTITY

MEANING

The meaning of the New Testament as a whole is more than that of each of its parts, but different levels of meaning within the New Testament are not unrelated. The New Testament as a collection of authoritative books, a **canon** of holy scripture, was born out of **theological** interests and practical needs of the **church** in the second and third centuries. But these interests and needs were not simply imposed from without upon the New Testament books. Doubtless the **Apostle** Paul, for example, did not think that he was composing holy scripture when he wrote to the Corinthians or to the Romans. Yet he was quite consciously asserting his apostolic authority to say what distinctively Christian faith was and what it implied for the life of believers under specific circumstances. Similarly, those who preserved the sayings of Jesus may not have thought of themselves as setting

449

up a rival to the books of Moses. Nevertheless, they regarded Jesus' sayings as faithful guides to the will of God and applied them like holy scripture to the situations that arose in the church's life. The impulses to establish a canon, and thus to provide resources for the church's guidance and enrichment, did not begin long after the writing of the last New Testament book, but in some form actually preceded and motivated the writing of many of those books. In the long run, the purposes of a Matthew or a Paul found fulfillment when their books were incorporated into a larger whole.

Of course, the various New Testament writings do not all say the same thing. In fact, there are real differences and even disagreements among them. For the most part, however, the New Testament books show an interest in what is apostolic, authoritative, and original. They attach importance to the earthly life and ministry of Jesus, even if, as in the case of Paul, that interest concentrates mainly upon his death. They regard Jesus' death and **resurrection** as the central **saving** event. They look upon Christ and the church as the fulfillment of Old Testament **prophecy**, and they look forward to the final **revelation** of God's power and glory. Moreover, they agree in attaching fundamental importance to the moral life. It is by no means a safe assumption, however, that all early Christians or their literature agreed on these points. Increasing evidence that they did not continually comes to the fore. We have discovered that Paul encountered Christians who thought the **gospel** presumed acceptance of the traditions and scriptures of Israel as binding law, and others who found in it a license to do as they pleased. The **Pastoral Epistles**, 2 Peter, and Revelation all lash out at wrongheaded and dangerous ideas held by fellow Christians. The Christian **Gnostic** texts recently discovered in Egypt reveal a divergent form of Christianity with ancient roots. Significantly, some words of Jesus in the **Synoptic Gospels**, especially Matthew, are applied against misguided Christians.

The New Testament itself is a result of the effort of the early Christian church to define its faith and draw out its consequences for life. Intended to lay down certain directions and set boundaries, it is neither a random nor even a representative specimen of opinion. The New Testament goes beyond the purposes of its individual constituents, thereby embodying and affirming them. When we think of the New Testament's meaning, therefore, we concern ourselves not simply with what the authors intended but with the canon as a whole.

STRUCTURE

The structure of the New Testament is simple. Its twenty-seven books are divided into four Gospels, the Book of Acts, twenty-one Epistles, and the Revelation to John. Ancient canonical lists give different orders within the **Gospels** and **Epistles**, but the integrity of the groupings is always observed. As we have noticed already, the **canonical** order makes a certain sense and is therefore helpful to the reader. Although the genuine Pauline letters were written first, the Gospels stand at the head of the canon. From a historical perspective on the beginnings of Christianity this may be misleading, but for the Christian **church-es** that over a period of many years brought the New Testament to its present shape this order makes sense. Jesus is primary, **theologically** as well as chronologically, for Christian faith. The New Testament is centered upon Jesus.

Within the fourfold Gospel canon, Matthew stands first. Despite traditional and occasional scholarly theories supporting Matthew's chronological priority, Mark was likely the first Gospel written. Yet Matthew's primacy in the Gospel canon and in the New Testament is understandable, and, from the standpoint of the church that formulated the canon, quite proper. Matthew presents Jesus as the fulfillment of the Hebrew scriptures and the founder and teacher of the church. By its opening genealogy, Matthew suggests both continuity with the Old Testament and the assumption of scriptural authority. (Genealogy is itself a biblical **genre**.) The final Gospel, John, may well be the last of the four to have been written; its character as a theological reflection in narrative form suits it admirably for the final position in the Gospel canon. For most of the church's history John has provided the theological and **Christological** perspective and terminology for understanding Jesus. It is the key to the other Gospels, as the Protestant reformer John Calvin put it in the preface of his commentary. Moreover, John's prologue is a recapitulation of Genesis 1, in which God's speaking is transformed into the presence of the **Word** with God as the agent of creation (John 1:1–5). Subsequently, John's text appears to serve as scripture for the presentation of Jesus in 1 John.

Although Acts was written after at least two of the Gospels (Mark and Luke), and at least a generation after the genuine Pauline letters, it appropriately bridges the gap between Gospels and Epistles. Although the Pauline letters are to be preferred to Acts as historical sources, those letters provide only fragments of each congregation's history. The Book of Acts is the first attempt to write a continuous account of the earliest church, and for at least two centuries there was no successor. As such, Acts provides a rudimentary framework and background for reading and understanding the Epistles. Its emphasis upon the missionary work of Paul, to whom fourteen of the New Testament Epistles have traditionally been ascribed, is quite appropriate.

Among the Epistles, Romans stands first in the order that has become standard among Christian churches. Again, it was not written first, but it has valid claim to that position as the most thorough exposition of Paul's theology. After Romans the Pauline letters tend to group themselves in descending order of length or importance. Not coincidentally the **Pastorals**, written a generation or so after Paul, come near the end, and Hebrews, whose ascription to Paul was seriously doubted in antiquity, is last of all. Moreover, Hebrews points into the future (4:1–11) to a sabbath rest for the people of God. The Pauline corpus is then followed by the **Catholic Epistles**, all of which are in fact later than Paul and represent the interests of emerging, institutional Christianity.

As though the claims and interests of that institution should not have the last word, the New Testament concludes with Revelation. In all probability its position in the canon is related to the fact that in antiquity serious doubts were raised about its **apostolicity** and therefore its right to be included. Apart from such considerations, however, its position at the end is quite appropriate. Revelation, drawing upon heavenly visions, points toward the future, toward the end or goal of history, and expresses in **apocalyptic** imagery the fundamental early Christian conviction that God rules, appearances to the contrary notwithstanding.

The *meaning* of the New Testament is, therefore, more than its *structure*, but its meaning cannot be separated from the structure, which expresses the shape of Christian **revelation** and belief. Christianity began, not with Jesus' ministry to Israel, but with his death and the reports of **resurrection** appearances, faith quickly spread beyond the ethnic, geographical, and religious bounds of Judaism. Thus the new religion eventually established itself as a distinct confession, with adherents drawing on ancient, traditional roots and hopes represented by its holy scripture, in Testaments both Old and New. Yet the new faith looked finally not to the past for its vindication but to the future advent of God's **salvation**. The New Testament ends fittingly with an apocalypse, the Revelation to John. The fulfillment of hope that Revelation portrays in such graphic imagery does not, of course, misrepresent the Gospels and Epistles, for an evangelist (Mark 13 and parr.) or an apostle (1 Cor. 15) could speak with equal assurance of the coming of God's deliverance.

It is quite apparent that the New Testament as a whole embodies certain emphases that to a considerable extent determine its meaning. Some things were underscored, whereas others were omitted. That we have in the New Testament no letters from Paul's converts in Corinth (1 Cor. 7:1), much less his opponents, is not coincidental. Certain viewpoints were ruled out in the course of the doctrinal development that produced the New Testament canon, the ancient creeds of the church, and its carefully articulated **sacramental** and clerical organization. Nevertheless, theological viewpoints that at one time seemed at odds with one another gained representation within the canon. Thus the Epistle of James, which in fact and perhaps by intention differs from Paul, stands in the same New Testament with Romans and Galatians. If the opponents of Paul in 2 Corinthians were **miracle**-working **charismatics**, their opposition to him did not prevent a similar point of view from finding expression in the miracle traditions of Mark and John, though even there the tradition is modified and redirected. The New Testament represents no strict doctrinal unity. Yet there is nevertheless a remarkable continuity of perspective and emphasis in most of the canonical writings.

IDENTITY

Of all the Mediterranean religions of that period, only Judaism and Christianity survive today. In view of the Roman persecution that the church faced until the fourth century, and what Judaism has endured before and since, it is remarkable that either has survived from antiquity. In an age when people easily combined religious allegiances and when religions themselves were syncretistic (i.e., inclined to borrow from one another), Judaism and Christianity stood out in their insistence on complete and undivided devotion from their followers. To many observers, both ancient and modern, such an attitude seemed unnecessarily intolerant. There were, of course, defections from both, but neither religion harbored fundamental doubts about its identity and distinctiveness. As we have seen, however, one question of identity was debated during the first century and later, at least among Christians, and possibly also among Jews (although adequate evidence on the Jewish side is lacking): Were Christianity and Judaism mutually incompatible? What we might call the principle of *exclusivity* did not, however, lead to the demise of these religions, but was rather an important factor in their survival.

Along with this sense of identity in Judaism and Christianity there went a *communal consciousness*. Israel or Judaism has been from the beginning a people, and a people with a common history, particularly in their dealing with God. The same was immediately true of early Christianity, which appropriated that common heritage. Moreover, Paul describes the Christian community as a body, and organic unity (1 Cor. 12; Rom. 12:3ff.), using a figure of speech well known in antiquity. All the members are interrelated. This corporate concept was an extremely important aspect of early Christianity's strength, as it had been of Judaism. The unity was always subject to dissension if not division, but at the same time was regarded as essential.

In both cases the unity was buttressed by *common worship*, whether in synagogue or **church**. Of course, a crucial point in Christianity's separation from Judaism was the role played by Jesus in such worship. For the early Christians, Jesus the **Christ** was not merely a figure of the past, but a living presence at the community's heart, particularly in its worship (cf. 1 Cor. 1:2). In effect, they worshiped him, not to the exclusion of the God of Israel, but alongside him as God **incarnate**. The seeds of an irrevocable split with the parent religion were thus planted, as in a **Gentile** environment Christianity became liturgically, as well as **theologically**, increasingly Christ-centered. **Baptism** was required of Jew as well as Gentile. The **Lord's Supper** was a peculiar liturgical means of partaking of "the body and blood of our Lord Jesus Christ," an idea that would have been more tolerable to many former pagans than to Jews. Nevertheless, early Christian worship was modeled on synagogue worship. Apart from the **sacraments**, as they came to be called, services centered upon the reading of scripture, preaching, and congregational prayer.

Early churches also shared with the synagogue concern for *the moral life*. For both this concern was central and constitutive, although for both it was based on God's initiative and grace, whether through Moses and the **Exodus** from Egypt or through the career and death of Jesus, also a Jew. For both the **law** of God was a pivotal issue, if understood in different ways. Paul could call Christ the end of the law (Rom. 10:4), although by this he meant its fulfillment rather than its termination. The intrinsically moral character of early Christianity manifests itself in various ways in the New Testament. Notably, in the Gospel of Matthew, but to some extent in all the Gospels, the teaching of Jesus, understood as the expression of God's will, is remembered and repeated, and his life becomes a template for Christian morals, if not law.

The idea that a person survives death in some manner was widely held by people in antiquity, pagan as well as Jewish. Paul, with other **Pharisees**, believed in the **resurrection** of the dead (Acts 23:6). Yet Paul and other Christians were distinguishable by their belief that Jesus had already conquered death, as witnesses to his resurrection could testify, and that through faith in him and in unity with him they too could overcome its power (1 Cor. 15; John 11:25–36). The resurrection of Jesus meant for his disciples that they too had conquered death, though it meant much more. It was not only individualistic in its implications. It established the reality of the *hope* that Jesus would return and that God's **kingdom** would be established for the **redemption** of this world and its history.

Before the end of the first century, Christianity had become a distinct religion with its own identity, although rooted in Judaism and its scripture. It took various forms as it spread across the Mediterranean world, as it does today, appealing to large numbers of people in different walks of life. Of course, the New Testament did not produce Christianity; rather, Christianity produced the New Testament. Yet the New Testament and the churches that style themselves Christian have an obvious common ground, which is a fundamental sense of the importance of identity and purpose. The New Testament in its parts and as a whole represents an effort to address the question of the identity and character of the new faith, and that question is a fundamental component of the consciousness of Christian churches, whether ancient or modern. In the midst of some diversity, in antiquity and ever since, the New Testament bespeaks a sense of a purposeful unity and commonality that churches share.

The anatomy of the New Testament reflects this sense, as well as the origin and growth of Christianity. First there are the **Gospels**, the churches' testimony to the founder and foundation, Jesus. Then comes the Book of Acts, a narrative of the church's beginnings and faith in its universality. Emphasizing an exclusiveness of faith that nevertheless projects itself as universal and inclusive, **epistles** attest that faith's vitality as well as the problems encountered within Christian communities in attempting to realize their goal of universality. Finally, the New Testament ends with the Book of Revelation, which looks at once to heaven and to the future to reveal the hope for the coming of a new and universal community, the New Jerusalem, the City of God.

Abba: the intimate, familiar Aramaic word for father. In the normal piety of first-century Judaism, this form of address was too intimate to be used of God. But Jesus (see Mark 14:36) and the early Christians (see Rom. 8:15; Gal. 4:6) used it in this way.

A.D.: abbreviation of the Latin *Anno Domini*, which means "in the year of our Lord." In the Western world, the birth of Christ is the point of reference for dating events. Events occurring before the birth of Jesus are indicated by the abbreviation B.C., "before Christ." Alternatively, one may speak of C.E. (Common Era) or B.C.E. (Before the Common Era).

Agrapha: literally, unwritten words or sayings. The term refers to words and sayings of Jesus not contained in the canonical Gospels.

Allegory: a story whose details or actions illustrate or tell about something quite different. Each element of an allegory possesses its own distinct meaning, which is determined by something outside the story: for example, the Christian faith in the case of Bunyan's *Pilgrim's Progress* (1678).

Amen: the transliteration of a Greek word that in turn transliterates a Hebrew word. In common usage *amen* is either a solemn confirmation of what has been said or a response of assent to words of another.

Antichrist: an apocalyptic figure, the archenemy of Christ, who will appear shortly before the parousia to wage war against the friends of Christ. (1 John 2:22; 4:4; *see* Parousia.)

Antinomianism: the belief that the Christian who has been freed by Christ has no ethical or moral obligations at all.

Antitheses: the six contrasts with ancient teaching that Jesus proclaims in the Sermon on the Mount (see Matt. 5:21–48) in the antithetical form, "You have heard. . . . But I say to you. . . ."

Apocalypse: an uncovering or a revelation (e.g., the Apocalypse or Revelation to John). The term "apocalyptic" is applied to a type of literature that is pessimistic about humanity's possibilities and hence discloses God's plan for the last days. Although related to prophecy and eschatology, apocalyptic thought stresses more precisely and forcefully the future intervention of God in the end time. (*See* Eschatology; Revelation.)

Apocrypha: the fourteen books of the Septuagint Bible not found in the Hebrew Bible; usually it is a part of the Catholic Bible but not the Protestant Bible. More generally, the adjectival form *apocryphal* means "hidden or spurious." (1 John 2:22; 4:4; *see* Pseudepigrapha.)

Apocryphal New Testament: noncanonical books such as the *Gospel of Peter* that claim apostolic authorship, but were known in antiquity to be inauthentic.

Apostle: a term meaning "one who is sent," specifically applied to the twelve disciples who were close to Jesus (see Mark 3:14 ff.). Paul also appropriates this designation for himself because of the risen Christ's appearance to him (see 1 Cor. 15:1 ff.).

Apostles' Creed: an ancient Christian creed expressing belief in God the Father, Son, and Spirit, the church, and the resurrection of the dead. Although the name implies that it was composed by the apostles, it does not appear in its present form until centuries later. Nevertheless, its roots go back to an ancient Roman baptismal creed that was already taking shape in the second century. The creed emphasizes the death and resurrection of Jesus, as did much early Christian preaching (see 1 Cor. 15:3–5).

Apostolic Fathers: a collection of second-century noncanonical writings, such as the Letters of Ignatius, that do not claim apostolic authorship. They are apostolic in the sense that they were generally accepted as representing the apostolic faith.

Aramaic: the language of Palestine during the time of Jesus and the early church. A Semitic tongue, it is closely related to Hebrew.

Archaeology: the scientific study of ancient cultures on the basis of their material **remains, such** as fossil relics, artifacts, monuments, pottery, and buildings.

Ascension: traditionally, the visible departure of Jesus into heaven forty days after his resurrection (see Acts 1:9).

Authentic: in biblical criticism the term is applied to writings that are believed to have been written by the person to whom they are traditionally attributed. For example, Romans is without doubt an *authentic* letter of Paul.

Baptism: the act or sacrament of immersion into water by which a person was received into the early Christian church. The Greek term *baptizō* means "dip" or "immerse."

B.C.: the abbreviation of "before Christ." (*See* A.D.)

Beatitudes: the nine blessings that stand at the beginning of Jesus' Sermon on the Mount (see Matt. 5:3–12).

Canon: a term originally applied to a reed used for measuring. It was later used of those books or writings that became standard or authoritative for the early Christians. By the close of the fourth century the Christian canon was largely fixed. (*See* Apocrypha; Pseudepigrapha.)

Catholic: universal, affecting humankind as a whole; an adjective used by the early church to refer to whatever was universally shared among the various churches.

Catholic Epistles: James; 1 and 2 Peter; 1, 2, and 3 John; and Jude. These seven letters are supposedly "general" in destination and in character and hence Catholic.

Charisma: "gift of grace." The term came to be used in the early church for the various gifts of the Spirit, such as wisdom, knowledge, faith, healing, and speaking in tongues (see 1 Cor. 12).

Christ: See Messiah.

Christology: that aspect of Christian thought concerned specifically with the revelation of God in Jesus the Christ.

Church: the community of believers in Jesus Christ. The term is used of individual congregations and of the entire fellowship of Christians.

Cosmos: the world or universe; a Greek term frequently used in ancient philosophical discussion. In the New Testament, it often takes on a negative sense as the world standing in opposition to God (see John 1:10; 1 John 2:15–17).

Council of Jamnia: the group of rabbinical scholars who settled in the coastal town of Jamnia shortly after the fall of Jerusalem in A.D. 70 and helped to standardize the Jewish religion. They are usually credited with having fixed the Hebrew canon of the Old Testament, now followed by Protestants as well as Jews.

Covenant: a solemn agreement that binds two parties together. The Old Testament (Covenant) depicts the agreement by which God and the people of Israel were bound together, and the New Testament (Covenant) tells the story of the new agreement effected by God with the new Israel through Jesus the Christ. Ordinarily in biblical usage a covenant is sealed in blood.

Crucifixion: a Roman form of execution in which the victim was nailed or bound to a wooden cross and left to die.

Dead Sea Scrolls: ancient Jewish documents from the period of Christian origins, discovered near the Dead Sea since 1947. (*See* Essenes; Qumran.)

Decalogue or Ten Commandments: the name given to the ten words Moses received, according to tradition, from God on Mt. Sinai (see Exod. 20:1–17 and Deut. 5:6–21).

Diaspora or dispersion: the Jewish community scattered (dispersed) outside the holy land of Palestine. This dispersion originated in the Babylonian exile of 587 B.C.

***Didache* or *Teaching of the Twelve Apostles*:** an anonymous, early second-century Christian manual for church life.

Docetism: derived from the Greek word *dokein* meaning "to seem," an early Christian heresy according to which Jesus Christ only seemed to suffer and die. A divine being, it was thought, could not suffer.

Ecclesiology: the aspect of Christian theology concerned specifically with the formation and character of the church (Greek, *ekklēsia*), the community of believers.

Epistle: a letter of a formal or didactic nature; the term is traditionally applied to the New Testament letters.

Eschatology: discourse about the last things or the end of the age (Greek, *eschatos*, meaning "last"). Traditionally, the term is used of Christian thought concerning all the events and actions associated with both the end of history and the end of human life. (*See* Apocalypse; Parousia.)

Essenes: an ascetic, Jewish religious group existing at the time of the New Testament. They stressed radical obedience to the Jewish law. (*See* Qumran.)

Ethics: a broad term applied to such related matters as moral codes and practices, theories of value, and the imperatives of Christian faith as they pertain to relations of one person to another.

Eucharist: derived from the Greek word meaning "thankfulness" and, beginning in the second century, used of the sacrament of the Lord's Supper, in which bread and wine are consecrated and distributed to the faithful Christians. (*See* Lord's Supper; Sacrament.)

Exegesis: the critical interpretation of a text. Literally the term means "to lead out" the meaning from the text.

Exile: specifically the removal of defeated Israelites by the Babylonians in 587 B.C.

Exodus: a going out; used specifically of Israel's departure from Egypt under the leadership of Moses about the thirteenth century B.C.

Expiation: "covering," or "making right," by means of some act or rite, the offense done by one party to another, especially expiation for sin before God. (*See* Propitiation; Sacrifice.)

Form Criticism: the classification of the "forms" in which the tradition, especially the Gospel tradition, circulated before being written down and the attempt to determine the "setting in life" of the church that they reflect. (*See* Pericope; Redaction Criticism.)

Genre: the literary type or form of a document. For example, in modern critical discussion the question of whether the Gospels fit the genre of ancient biography or constitute a distinct and different genre has been widely debated.

Gentile: a non-Jew. The original Greek term tranlated "Gentiles" means "nations."

Glossolalia: literally, speaking in tongues, regarded by Luke (Acts 2) and Paul (1 Corinthians 14) as a gift of the Holy Spirit.

Gnosticism: a religious movement or attitude widespread about the time of the emergence of the Christian faith. Believers possessed a secret knowledge *(gnōsis)* and sought to escape the ephemeral earthly world for the eternal heavenly world.

God-Fearers: A term (Greek *sebomenoi*) used by ancient Jews with reference to Gentiles who were attracted to synagogues and their worship of one God, yet who did not submit to the whole **law** or, in the case of males, circumcision.

Gospel: originally the message of good news that God has revealed himself as gracious in the event of Jesus Christ. (The NRSV translators have generally used "good news" to translate the Greek *euangelion*, formerly translated "gospel.") The term later came to designate also the literary form in which the good news of Jesus' life, death, and resurrection is narrated; for example, the Gospel According to Matthew.

Haggadah: a Hebrew term designating rabbinic traditions, usually in narrative form (stories or legends) that illustrate the moral teaching of the Torah. (*See* Midrash.)

Halakah: a Hebrew term (from the verb meaning "to walk") designating rabbinic tradition regulating conduct. (*See* Midrash; Mishnah.)

Hasmonean: the actual family name for the Maccabees, leaders of the Jewish revolt against the Seleucid heirs of Alexander the Great in the second century B.C.. (*See* Maccabees.)

Hellenization: the process or result of the spread of Greek language and culture in the Mediterranean world during and after Alexander the Great (died 323 B.C.).

Historical Criticism: the science, perspective, or method that approaches the Bible with historical questions. Typically, its goal is to understand the historical setting of the writings in the history of Israel or the early church. (*See* Exegesis; Literary Criticism.)

Holy: that which has to do with, or is set apart for, God or the divine power and majesty.

Immanence: the nearness or involvement of God in the world. (*See* Transcendence.)

Incarnation: literally "becoming flesh"; the embodiment of God in Jesus of Nazareth.

Justification: the act or process by which God brings people into proper or right relationship with himself. In Paul's letters, the justification or righteousness of God is to be received by faith, not works. (*See* Righteousness.)

Kērygma (literally "proclamation"): the early Christian preaching about Jesus as the Christ, intended to elicit the decision of faith.

Kingdom of God or "Rule of God": God's lordship over humankind and the world. The kingdom is the central theme of Jesus' message in the Synoptic Gospels.

Koinē ("common" in Greek): the everyday Greek speech used throughout the Hellenistic world during the period of early Christianity. The New Testament books are written in *koinē* Greek.

Law: in the New Testament generally the revelation of God through Moses to the people of Israel embodied in the cultic, ritual, and moral commandments of the Old Testament. (*See* Gospel; Torah.)

Literary Criticism: the science, perspective, or method that seeks to determine the literary character or development of the books of the Bible. It has traditionally been practiced in conjunction with historical criticism, although recently it has become more independent as modes of literary criticism and theory developed outside biblical scholarship have been applied to the Bible. (*See* Exegesis; Historical Criticism.)

Lord's Supper: the church's continuing reenactment of the last supper of Jesus with his disciples. (*See* Eucharist.)

LXX: *See* Septuagint.

Maccabees: the name given the priestly family who successfully led a revolt against Hellenistic rule beginning in 167 B.C. It is derived from Judas Maccabeus, the Hasmonean brother who first led the revolt. They ruled over Palestine from 142 B.C. to 63 B.C. (*See* Hasmonean.)

Manuscripts: handwritten documents, especially the ancient New Testament documents from which our present text is determined. The earliest complete New Testament manuscripts come from the fourth century, although there are sizable fragments of earlier date.

Messiah: from the Hebrew term meaning "anointed one." It was used of the Davidic king, whose restoration was expected in Jesus' day. Its Greek equivalent is *Christos* (Christ), the basic designation of Jesus in the New Testament. He was believed to be the expected Messiah of Israel.

Midrash: the form, activity, or product of biblical interpretation, particularly as carried out in rabbinic Judaism. *Midrashim* (pl.) may be legal (*halakic*) or illustrative and even narrative (*haggadic*) in character.

Miracle: an extraordinary event, contrary to normal expectations; a manifestation of the activity of God.

Mishnah: the authoritative Jewish legal, or halakic traditions, ascribed ultimately to Moses, that developed in rabbinic and Pharisaic Judaism (cf. Mark 10:5–13) and were codified in the early third century. The term is usually applied to the written form. The Mishnah and the learned commentary upon it *(Gemara)* constitute the Talmud. (*See* Talmud.)

Montanism: an ascetic, apocalyptic movement in the second half of the second century A.D., whose adherents, following Montanus of Phrygia, believed themselves the prophets of a fresh outpouring of the Holy Spirit, or Paraclete, upon the church.

Myth: the result of efforts to communicate faith in transcendent reality by means of story and symbol. This technical use of the term should be distinguished from the popular meaning of a fantastic or untrue story.

Natural Theology: Discourse about God which assumes that human reason, unaided by revelation, is adequate to discern certain religious truths.

Oral Tradition: any teaching or similar material transmitted from person to person or generation to generation by word of mouth rather than by use of writing; also the process of such transmission.

Parable: a brief story that makes its point by the unusual development or imagery of the narrative. The various details do not function as allegory but are significant for the story itself. Although the parable was already known to the Jewish religious tradition, Jesus made extensive use of it. (*See* Allegory.)

Paraclete: helper, comforter, or mediator. The term is used in the Fourth Gospel of the Holy Spirit as the Christian community's helper after the death of Jesus (see John 14:16; 15:26; 16:7).

Paraenesis: a Greek term meaning moral exhortation. It is frequently applied to those parts of New Testament letters devoted to moral instruction.

Parousia (literally "presence" or "coming"): the early Christian belief in the appearance or second coming of Christ, a glorious advent in power and judgment at the end of the age. (*See* Eschatology; Son of Man.)

Passion: suffering, particularly the suffering of Jesus during the last week of his life in Jerusalem and especially the suffering leading to his death.

Passover: the annual Jewish celebration of the deliverance from slavery in Egypt under the leadership of Moses. Jesus was crucified at the time of the Passover. (*See* Exodus.)

Pastoral Epistles: 1 and 2 Timothy and Titus. These letters give advice to the church leader or pastor concerning matters of church government and discipline.

Patriarch: the father of a people, especially the three great ancestors of the people of Israel (Abraham, Isaac, and Jacob). The period of Israel's history before the Exodus from Egypt is frequently called the patriarchal period.

Pentecost: the Jewish Feast of Weeks, beginning on the fiftieth day after Passover. According to the Book of Acts it was the occasion of the descent of the Holy Spirit upon the disciples of Jesus, and thus it is looked upon as the beginning of the church.

Pericope (p. **pericopae**): a "cutting around" or section. The term is used of the individual, complete units of tradition about Jesus that circulated separately in the early church and that were ultimately joined together to form the Gospels. (*See* Form Criticism; Redaction Criticism.)

Pharisees: a prominent Jewish religious group at the time of Jesus, who practiced strict observance of both the written and oral law of Judaism. The name probably comes from a Semitic term meaning "separated." (*See* Sadducees.)

Preexistence: the term used to designate the New Testament belief that Jesus of Nazareth in some way existed with God before his earthly advent (see John 1:1–3; 17:24).

Priest: a holy person authorized to perform ritual and cultic acts whereby human beings and God are enabled to commune with another. (*See* Holy; Sacrifice.)

Procurator: an official of the Roman Empire, responsible to the emperor, exercising administrative authority over a province or district.

Prophet: someone who speaks or acts for God. In general, the prophet not only predicted God's action but also pleaded with the people to respond to God's will. Prophets existed in the early church as well as in ancient Israel.

Propitiation: a placating or pacifying of the deity; a sacrifice that induces God to be favorable or beneficent to the sacrificer. (*See* Expiation.)

Pseudepigrapha: literally "false writings," particularly a group of late Jewish writings claiming Old Testament figures as their authors. They reflect Jewish religious thought in the intertestamental period. (*See* Apocrypha.)

Q Source: the hypothetical source, consisting primarily of sayings of Jesus, used by both Matthew and Luke in the writing of their respective Gospels.

Qumran: the site on the northwest shore of the Dead Sea where a Jewish sect, the Essenes, lived in strict obedience to the law of its covenant community until approximately A.D. 70. The Dead Sea Scrolls (part of the library of the community) were discovered near this site. (*See* Essenes.)

Rabbi: "master," a Jewish religious leader or teacher (cf. John 1:38) especially trained and qualified to expound and apply the law of Moses.

Redaction Criticism: the separating of tradition from redaction (editorial work) especially in the Gospels. One who edits, revises, or shapes the literary or oral sources at hand is called a redactor. (*See* Form Criticism; Pericope.)

Redemption: literally "to buy" or "take back," particularly the act or process of God's taking back sinful or rebellious humanity by means of the event of Jesus Christ.

Resurrection: a rising from the dead: a central hope in the New Testament based upon the early Christians' belief that Jesus was raised from the dead by God. In general the New Testament view of resurrection of the body or person should be distinguished from the widely held notion of the immortality of the soul.

Revelation (translated from the Greek word *apokalypsis*): an uncovering, revealing, or laying bare. It refers to the uncovering of the transcendent God in human events, particularly the event of Christ in the Christian tradition. (*See* Apocalypse.)

Righteousness: primarily the quality and action of God; hence human righteousness proceeds from God's initiative in Christ and is based upon a relation with God as revealed in Christ. Righteousness and justification translate the same Greek noun *dikaiosynē* in the New Testament. (*See* Justification.)

Sacrament: a sacred rite, "an outward and visible sign of an inward and spiritual grace," namely, the presence of the transcendent God. The term *sacrament* does not occur in the New Testament, but it is commonly used to refer to the acts of baptism and the Lord's Supper, which are reported there. (*See* Baptism; Eucharist.)

Sacrifice: the act of offering something valuable to the deity. By the act of sacrifice, communion with the divine is initiated, reestablished, or continued. (*See* Priest.)

Sadducees: a religious group of the intertestamental period who represented the priestly aristocracy of Jewish life. In distinction from the Pharisees, they held only to the written Mosaic law and did not believe in resurrection.

Salvation: the state of complete liberation from sin, brokenness, and estrangement between humanity and God. In general, the New Testament locates salvation in the future, although its inauguration is already effected in Christ.

Sanctification: the process of being made holy. The term refers to the life of the Christian under the guidance of the Holy Spirit as the effects of Christ's work, especially the love of God and of others, become more and more manifest.

Scribes: a title applied to learned men in postexilic Judaism who studied and copied the law and exercised judgment in matters pertaining to the law (see Ezra 7:6). (*See* Pharisees.)

Second Coming: See Parousia.

Semitism: in the New Testament, a stylistic or linguistic feature characteristic of Hebrew or Aramaic, possibly indicating that the writer was influenced by one of these Semitic languages or used a source that was written in one of them.

Septuagint (usually designated LXX, "seventy"): the Greek translation of the Hebrew Old Testament for Diaspora Jews. According to the legend of the *Epistle of Aristeas*, the translation was accomplished by seventy-two Jewish scholars who worked for seventy-two days; hence the title. The translation originated in the third century before the rise of Christianity.

Sin: generally any act that violates the law or will of God. In the New Testament, however, it denotes particularly the broken or estranged relation between the human race and God. (*See* Righteousness.)

Sitz im Leben ("setting in life"): the term is employed widely by form critics to refer to the community setting and, implicitly, the function of traditions. (*See* Form Criticism.)

Son of God: in Hebraic thought, someone especially selected or anointed by God for a task, such as the king of Israel, a prophet, or the people of Israel. In Hellenistic religious thought, the term refers frequently to a male offspring of the gods. In the New Testament, Jesus functions as the Son of God primarily in the Hebraic sense.

Son of Man: the title by which Jesus refers to himself in the Gospel narratives. Possibly in Jewish thought the term referred to an apocalyptic figure who was to come at the end of the ages to serve as judge between the righteous and the wicked (cf. Daniel 7:13 RSV; Mark 8:38; John 5:27), although its meaning may be more enigmatic. In the Gospels the use of the title Son of Man is confined almost entirely to Jesus. (*See* Apocalypse; Parousia.)

Soteriology: discourse about salvation (Greek, *sōtēria*). Soteriology refers to the New Testament understanding of the righteousness of God, sin, the work of Christ, the response of faith, and the work of the Spirit in sanctification.

Soul: a spiritual entity, distinct from the body, within each person. This concept of the soul, even the notion of the soul's immortality, plays little role in Hebraic or New Testament thought. Its prominence in Christian thought derives from later Greek influence.

Source Criticism: the work of identifying the written sources that were used in the composition of any given document, such as one of the Gospels.

Spirit: the dynamic power and activity of God directed toward the world, especially active in the history of Israel, the life of Jesus, and the early church; in the Christian tradition usually referred to as the Holy Spirit.

Synoptic Gospels: Matthew, Mark, and Luke: those Gospels that see Jesus' ministry together.

Synoptic Problem: the problem of understanding the relationship among the Synoptic Gospels, taking account of their great similarities as well as their distinct differences. The generally accepted solution is that both Matthew and Luke used Mark, the Q source consisting largely of Jesus' sayings, and distinct material to which each had access separately.

Talmud (meaning instruction or study): the authoritative body of Jewish tradition consisting of Mishnah and *Gemara* (commentary upon it) that developed in the several centuries immediately preceding and following the beginning of the Christian era. It exists in Palestinian (early fifth century) and Babylonian (late fifth century) forms. (*See* Mishnah.)

Targum: an ancient translation of the Hebrew scriptures (Old Testament) into the related Aramaic language that was generally spoken in first-century Palestine.

Theology: discourse on God; the study of or reflection upon the nature of God and the nature of God's relationship to humanity.

Torah: the Hebrew term meaning law or teaching, especially law as divine revelation. (*See* Law.)

Transcendence: in theology, God's distance from the world; alternatively, God's holiness or "otherness" as distinct from the secular or profane. (*See* Immanence.)

Trinity: the Christian doctrine that God exists in three persons: the Father, Jesus Christ as the Son, and the Holy Spirit. The developed doctrine is not found in the New Testament, although Father, Son, and Spirit are spoken of frequently.

Virgin Birth: the miraculous birth of Jesus to Mary, his mother, without the participation of a human father in the conception.

Witness: in the New Testament includes both observation and testimony, especially to the life, death, and resurrection of Jesus. In one sense, martyrdom is an especially appropriate witness to Jesus. The English term *martyr* is based on the Greek word for "a witness."

Word: a technical, literary designation of a complete saying, especially a saying of Jesus. In the Johannine literature Jesus himself is called the Word (John 1:1–18).

Word of God: frequently a designation for the Bible. In the New Testament, however, it is used in close connection with the event of Jesus Christ, especially the preaching about that event. (*See* Kerygma.)

Works, or "works of the law": in Pauline theology, the means of earning righteousness before God instead of acknowledging sin and relying on his grace. (*See* Justification.)

Zealots: a term applied to Jewish revolutionaries who sought to overthrow Roman rule of Palestine by means of violent resistance. Although the term may have come into use only during the Roman War (A.D. 66–70), it is often applied to earlier revolutionary figures.

I. TOOLS FOR NEW TESTAMENT STUDY

Concordances, which cite the occurrences of every significant word in the Bible, are indispensable when one wishes to determine what a particular word means in the New Testament or one of its constituent books. Two particularly valuable concordances that indicate the original Greek word on which two standard English versions are based are C. Morrison, *An Analytical Concordance to the Revised Standard Version of the New Testament* (Philadelphia: Westminster, 1979), and R. E. Whitaker and J. R. Kohlenberger III, *The Analytical Concordance to the New Revised Standard Version of the Bible* (Grand Rapids and Cambridge: Eerdmans, 2000).

Among high-quality one-volume Bible **dictionaries**, P .J. Achtemeier (ed.), *The HarperCollins Bible Dictionary* (San Francisco: HarperSanFrancisco, 1996), and W. R. F. Browning (ed.), *Oxford Dictionary of the Bible*, 2nd ed. (Oxford: Oxford University Press, 2004) are recommended. D. N. Freedman (ed.), *The Anchor Bible Dictionary*, 6 vols. (New York: Doubleday, 1992), is the largest general dictionary. For the meaning of theological terms, see X. Leon-Dufour (ed.), *Dictionary of Biblical Theology*, trans. J. P. Cahill (New York: Desclee, 1967). Even those without Hebrew and Greek can profit from G. Kittel et al. (eds.), *Theological Dictionary of the New Testament*, trans. G. W. Bromiley (Grand Rapids, MI: Eerdmans, 10 vols., 1964–76). This work's one-volume abridgment, G. M. Bromiley, *Theological Dictionary of the New Testament: Abridged in One Volume* (Grand Rapids, MI: Eerdmans, 1985), translates all Greek and Hebrew words and provides a comprehensive English index so that the reader who knows no Greek can find any entry. H. Balz and G. Schneider (eds.), *Exegetical Dictionary of the New Testament*, 3 vols. (Grand Rapids, MI: Eerdmans, 1990–93), also provides English transliterations of the Greek, as well as an English index.

Most reliable among **atlases** are H. G. May (ed.), *The Oxford Bible Atlas*, 3rd ed., rev. J. Day (New York: Oxford University Press, 1984), J. B. Pritchard, *The Harper Concise Atlas of the Bible* (New York: HarperCollins, 1991), and Y. Aharoni and M. Avi-Yonah, *The Macmillan Bible Atlas*, rev. ed. (New York: Macmillan, 1977). Perhaps the best general guide is J. Murphy-O'Connor, *The Holy Land: An Archaelogical Guide from Earliest Times to 1700*, rev. ed. (New York: Oxford University Press, 1992).

General treatments of **archaeological matters** include G. E. Wright, *Biblical Archeology*, rev. ed. (Philadelphia: Westminster, 1962), and J. Finegan, *The Archaeology of the New*

Testament: The Life of Jesus and the Beginning of the Early Church, rev. ed. (Princeton, NJ: Princeton University Press, 1992). G. F. Snyder, *Ante Pacem: Archaeological Evidence of Church Life Before Constantine* (Macon, GA: Mercer University Press, 1985), is a reliable guide to what can be known with some certainty.

II. COMMENTARIES

Among the tools for New Testament study, none is more important than a reliable commentary on the primary text. Serious but nontechnical series include *Black's New Testament Commentaries* (Peabody, MA: Hendrickson), *Sacra Pagina* (Minneapolis: Liturgical Press), *Abingdon New Testament Commentaries* (Nashville: Abingdon), and *The New Testament Library* (Louisville: Westminster John Knox). *Interpretation: A Bible Commentary for Teaching and Preaching* (Atlanta: John Knox) and L. E. Keck (ed.), *The New Interpreter's Bible: A Commentary in Twelve Volumes* (Nashville: Abingdon), will interest many readers who value the Bible as scripture yet wish to understand it critically. A technical series based on the Greek text, *Hermeneia—A Critical and Historical Commentary on the Bible* (Minneapolis: Fortress), is generally excellent; because all Greek and other foreign language citations are translated, it can be used by the student who lacks specialized languages. Uncompromisingly based on the Greek New Testament is the venerable *International Critical Commentary* (Edinburgh: T & T Clark). *The Anchor Bible* (Garden City, NY: Doubleday) is an ambitious and now much improved series. Among one-volume Bible commentaries, consult R. E. Brown, J. A. Fitzmyer, and R. E. Murphy (eds.), *The New Jerome Biblical Commentary* (Englewood Cliffs, NJ: Prentice Hall, 1990), J. L. Mays (ed.), *The HarperCollins Bible Commentary*, rev. ed. (San Francisco: HarperSanFrancisco, 2000), and J. D. G. Dunn and J. W. Rogerson (eds.), *Eerdmans Commentary on the Bible* (Grand Rapids and Cambridge: Eerdmans, 2003). W. A. Meeks (ed.), *The HarperCollins Study Bible: New Revised Standard Version* (New York: HarperCollins, 1993), offers concise but reliable introductory articles and annotations.

III. TEXT AND CANON

Textual history and criticism are thoroughly treated by B. M. Metzger and B. D. Ehrman, *The Text of the New Testament: Its Transmission, Corruption, and Restoration*, 4th ed. (New York: Oxford University Press, 2005). A standard, text-critical handbook is K. and B. Aland, *The Text of the New Testament*, trans. E. F. Rhodes, rev. ed. (Grand Rapids, MI: Eerdmans, 1989). L. M. MacDonald and J. A. Sanders, *The Canon Debate: On the Origins and Formation of the Bible* (Peabody, MA: Hendrickson, 2002) is a useful collection of studies.

IV. CHRISTIANITY AS A RELIGIOUS MOVEMENT

Recent and reliable treatments of early Christian history include W. H. C. Frend, *The Rise of Christianity* (Philadelphia: Fortress, 1984), J. Becker (ed.), *Christian Beginnings: Word and Community from Jesus to Post-Apostolic Times*, trans. A. S. Kidder and R. Krauss (Louisville: Westminster/John Knox, 1993), and H. Chadwick, *The Church in Ancient Society: From Galilee to Gregory the Great* (Oxford: Oxford University Press, 2001). D. Senior and C. Stuhlmueller helpfully concentrate on *The Biblical Foundations for Mission* (Maryknoll, NY: Orbis, 1983). As its subtitle suggests, E. W. Stegemann and W. Stegemann, *The Jesus Movement: A Social History of Its First Century*, trans. O. C. Dean, Jr. (Minneapolis: Fortress, 1999), is a comprehensive treatment of social aspects of earliest Christianity; R. Stark, *The Rise of Christianity: How the Obscure, Marginal Jesus Movement Became the Dominant Religious Force* (San Francisco: Harper San Francisco, 1997), another social-scientific study, tends to confirm Acts' picture of the burgeoning of early Christianity. Recurring features of that context are considered in the important handbook edited by F. Young, L. Ayres, and A. Louth, *The Cambridge History of Early Christian Literature* (Cambridge: Cambridge University Press, 2004). W. A. Meeks, *In Search of the Early Christians* (ed. A. R. Hilton and H. G. Snyder; New Haven and London: Yale University Press, 2002), assembles that scholar's seminal essays; J. Pelikan, *Christianity and Classical Culture: The Metamorphosis of Natural Theology in the Christian Encounter with Hellenism* (New Haven and London: Yale University Press, 1993), is a learned, lucid investigation of a complex subject. In general, E. Ferguson, M. McHugh, and F. W. Norris (eds.), *Encyclopedia of Early Christianity*, 2nd ed. (London: Taylor & Francis, 1998), is an exceptionally useful reference work.

V. NEW TESTAMENT THEOLOGY AND ETHICS

R. Morgan, *The Nature of New Testament Theology* (London: SCM, 1973), contains translations of the seminal but critically divergent essays of W. Wrede and A. Schlatter. H. Räisänen, *Beyond New Testament Theology: A Story and a Programme* (Philadelphia: Trinity Press International, 1990), advocates a return to Wrede's history-of-religions perspective and goals. Schlatter's more confessional approach is evidenced in N. T. Wright's series *Christian Origins and the Question of God*, which includes *The New Testament and the People of God* (Minneapolis: Fortress, 1992), *Jesus and the Victory of God* (Minneapolis: Fortress, 1996), and *The Resurrection of the Son of God* (Minneapolis: Fortress, 2003). D. O. Via, *What Is New Testament Theology?* (Minneapolis: Fortress, 2002), is a concise statement of the methdological issues involved.

R. Bultmann, *Theology of the New Testament*, trans. K. Grobel, 2 vols. (New York: Scribners, 1951, 1955), has not been superceded as the single most important work, although it virtually ignores the Synoptics and concentrates on Paul and John. Important recent treatments include J. D. G. Dunn, *Unity and Diversity in the New Testament: An Inquiry into the Character of Earliest Christianity*, 2nd ed. (Harrisburg, PA; Trinity Press International, 1990), G. B. Caird, *New Testament Theology*, completed and edited by L. D. Hurst (Oxford: Oxford University Press, 1994), and G. Strecker, *Theology of the New Testament*, trans. M. E. Boring (New York and Louisville: Walter de Gruyter/Westminster John Knox, 2000). Lately reissued is the classic work by Paul S. Minear, *The Kingdom and the Power: An Exposition of the New Testament Gospel* (Louisville: Westminster John Knox, 2004). On Christology, see M. de Jonge, *Christology in Context: The Earliest Christian Response to Jesus* (Philadelphia: Westminster, 1988), J. D. G. Dunn, *Christology in the Making: A New Testament Inquiry into the Origins of the Doctrine of the Incarnation*, rev. ed. (London: SCM, 1989), R. Bauckham, *God Crucified: Monotheism and Christology in the New Testament* (Grand Rapids: Eerdmans, 1999), and L. W. Hurtado, *Lord Jesus Christ: Devotion to Jesus in Earliest Christianity* (Grand Rapids: Eerdmans, 2003).

Major studies on New Testament ethics include V. P. Furnish, *The Love Commandment in the New Testament* (Nashville: Abingdon, 1972), W. Schrage, *The Ethics of the New Testament*, trans. D. E. Green (Philadelphia: Fortress, 1988), and R. B. Hays, *The Moral Vision of the New Testament: A Contempoirary Introduction to New Testament Ethics* (New York: HarperCollins, 1996).

VI. HISTORY OF CRITICISM AND INTERPRETATION

W. G. Kümmel, *The New Testament: The History of the Investigation of Its Problems*, trans. S. M. Gilmour and H. C. Kee (Nashville: Abingdon, 1972), is a classic survey concentrating on German scholarship. Better balanced is William Baird's three-volume *History of New Testament Research*, which to date includes *From Deism to Tübingen* (Minneapolis: Fortress, 1992) and *From Jonathan Edwards to Rudolf Bultmann* (2002). *The Cambridge History of the Bible*, 3 vols. (New York: Cambridge University Press, 1963–70), traces the story back to its biblical beginnings, with essays by appropriate specialists. Reliable but more cursory is R. M. Grant with D. Tracy, *A Short History of the Interpretation of the Bible*, rev. ed. (Philadelphia: Fortress, 1984). J.H.Hayes (ed.), *Dictionary of Biblical Interpretation*, 2 vols. (Nashville: Abingdon, 1999) is a useful reference work. The modern history of the hermeneutical issues involved in biblical interpretation is subjected to intensive scrutiny by A. C. Thiselton, *The Two Horizons:*

New Testament Hermeneutics and Philosophical Description with Special Reference to Heidegger, Bultmann, Gadamer, and Wittgenstein (Grand Rapids, MI: Eerdmans, 1980). In *Is There a Meaning in This Text? The Bible, the Reader, and the Morality of Literary Knowledge* (Grand Rapids: Zondervan, 1998), Kevin J. Vanhoozer takes into account even more recent philosphical developments.

VII. OTHER RESOURCES

D. M. Scholer, *A Basic Bibliographic Guide for New Testament Exegesis*, 3rd ed. (Grand Rapids, MI: Eerdmans, 1995), J. A. Fitzmyer, *An Introductory Bibliography for the Study of Scripture*, rev. ed. (Rome: Biblical Institute Press, 1981), and F. W. Danker, *Multipurpose Tools for Bible Study*, rev. ed. (Minneapolis: Fortress, 1993) are basic bibliographical handbooks. The invaluable ATLA Religion Database is now available on CD-ROM. The journal *New Testament Abstracts*, published at Weston College, Weston, Massachusetts, catalogs and summarizes articles and important books on the New Testament as they appear.

The standard scholarly journals in North America are *Journal of Biblical Literature*, the official journal of the Society of Biblical Literature, and *Catholic Biblical Quarterly* of the Catholic Biblical Association (which includes non-Catholic scholars among its membership). Both journals publish critical reviews of books as well as articles. *Interpretation: A Journal of Bible and Theology* also publishes articles and reviews of general interest. *Biblical Archaeologist*, which contains articles by scholars aimed at the general reader, is published by the American Schools of Oriental Research. The standard European journals are *New Testament Studies*, published by the international *Studiorum Novi Testamenti Societas* (Society for New Testament Studies), and *Zeitschrift für die Neutestamentliche Wissenschaft*, which often publishes articles in English. These journals are available in college, university, and theological seminary libraries, as well as in large public libraries.

The most reliable and comprehensive Web-based resource is *New Testament Gateway* (www.ntgateway.com), edited by Mark Goodacre. As its name implies, this electronic directory provides links to online texts and translations, journals, scholars and societies, bibliographies and e-lists, as well as resources devoted to specific New Testament books and authors. For other ancient texts and classical resources, *The Perseus Digital Library* (www.perseus.tufts.edu), edited by Gregory Crane, is highly recommended.

Sabbath question, 70–71, 166
sinfulness, 22, 350–54
with sinners, 26, 69–70, 134,
138
suffering, 68, 73–83, 104, 107,
144–45, 220–36
teaching, 27, 100, 101, 103, 152,
201–20
temptation (*See* Temptation of
Jesus)
tradition about, 68, 76–77, 128,
188–93
transfiguration, 74, 77, 83, 99
trial, 141, 176–78, 228
Jewish Christians, 252, 257, 276,
287–88, 312, 408, 423
Jews. *See also* Israel, Judaism
advantages of, 284, 385
in John, 153, 163–65, 177–78,
182
in Matthew, 111
in Paul, 331, 350–52, 365–66
reconciliation in Ephesians,
385–87
role in Jesus' crucifixion, 222,
228–29
Johannine letters, 411–18. *See also*
John, The First Letter of
historical circumstances, 411,
416–17
hospitality, 416–17
relation to John, 153, 411,
414–16
Johannine literature, 151–84, 402,
411–18. *See also* John, The
First Letter of, John, The
Gospel According to,
authorship, 151–52, 181, 411
John, son of Zebedee, 151, 172,
181, 435
John, The First Letter of, 411–16
antichrist, 412–14
Christology, 413
dualism, 413
heresy combatted, 412
literary character, 411
outline, 412
purpose, 411
relation to Gospel, 411–16
Spirit and spirits, 411, 412–15
John, The Gospel According to,
151–84. *See also* Johannine
literature
acceptance as scripture, 151–52
authorship, 151–52, 181

background, 151, 153–54
Christology, 152, 158, 167, 189
community, 162, 169–80
composition and order, 154–55,
158
dialogue and discourse, 164, 167,
169
dualism, 157
emphases, 182
eschatology, 163, 181
eternal life, 175
farewell discourses, 170, 174–76
Galilee and Judea, 170
and Genesis, 156–57
glory, 161, 172, 176
grace, 158
historical setting, 153–54, 182,
183–84
historicity, 153–54, 178, 181
"I am" sayings, 165
Jesus' prayer for church, 175–76
Judaism, 153, 157
Last Supper, 171–73
love, 172–73, 181
man born blind, 164–69
miracles, 164–69, 183
misunderstanding as writing
technique, 162
motif of Jesus' origin, 167
outline, 154
place of composition, 158
prologue, 155–59
Qumran, 153, 157
resurrection, 162, 180
soteriology, 162
Spirit, 244
structure, 155, 182
and Synoptics, 152, 158,
165–69, 171, 183–84
theological development of
miracles, 165, 168
tradition and redaction, 158,
165, 183–84
truth, 176
unity of church, 176
world, 176
John, The Second Letter of, 411,
416
John, The Third Letter of, 411, 416
John Mark, 60
John of Patmos, 209
John the Baptist, 25, 249
baptism of Jesus, 62–63, 96–99,
132
birth, 126

and Christian baptism, 249
and early Christianity, 424–25,
430
eschatology, 205
identified with Law and
prophets, 100
and Jesus, 96–99, 100, 152, 158,
196, 214
in John, 152, 157, 159–60
in Luke, 96, 126
in Matthew, 96
mentioned by Jesus, 202
preaching, 96–99, 132–33
prophetic character, 62–63
John the Elder. *See* Elder John
Joseph, recognized as Jesus' father,
93–94, 127
Joseph of Arimathea, 83, 180, 230
Josephus, Flavius, 18, 25, 188
Against Apion, 124
Jewish Antiquities, 14, 18, 21, 45,
188
Jewish War, The, 19, 23, 26
Judaism, 11–28, 91, 156, 157. *See
also* Essenes, Israel, Jews,
Pharisees, Qumran
community, Sadducees,
Temple
covenant, 28
diaspora, 13, 14, 44–46, 430
eschatology, 25, 205, 434
and Hellenism, 15, 17, 19, 31
history, 11–12, 14–25
land, 14, 18–19
law, 12–13, 17, 19, 21–22, 24, 44
worship, 12–13, 19, 21–22
Judaizing Christians, 284, 288–89.
See also Jewish Christians
in Galatia, 284, 288–89
Judas, Gospel of, 80
Judas Iscariot, 171, 172, 227, 245,
269
betrayal of Jesus, 80
Judas Maccabeus, 16
Judas the Galilean, 16
Jude, The Letter of, 431–33
authorship, 377, 431
date, 431
faith, 433
Gnosticism, 431
relation to James and James of
Jerusalem, 431–32
relation to 2 Peter, 431
Judea, 17, 33, 63, 78
in John, 170

ADRIATIC SEA

DALMATIA

ILLYRICUM

DACIA

MOESIA

MACEDONIA

Rome
Three Taverns
Appii Forum
Puteoli *Naples*

ITALY

Dyrrhachium

Brindisi

Philippi
Amphiopolis
Thessalonica
Nea

Beroea

Apollonia

AEGEAN SEA

ACHAIA

Nicopolis

SICILY

Rhegium

Corinth
Cenchreae

Athens

Syracuse

CRETE

Phoenix
Fair Ha

MEDI

THE MEDITERRANEAN WORLD AT THE TIME OF THE NEW TESTAMENT

NAMES OF ROMAN PROVINCES THUS: LYCIA

| 0 | 100 | 200 | 300 |

SCALE OF MILES

Modern place names are shown in italics, thus: *Cairo*

Cyrene

LYBIA

BLACK SEA

CIA

Istanbul

BITHYNIA

et PONTUS

GALATIA

REGNUM
POLEMONIS

Ankara

ASIA

Adramyttium

Pergamun

Thyatira

Philadelphia

Sardis

Hierapolis

Colossae

Laodicea

iletus

LYCIA

PAMPHILIA

Attalia

dus

IODES

Patara

Myra

Perga

Antioch

Iconium

Lystra

Derbe

REGNUM

CAPPADOCIA

ANTIOCHI

Tarsus

CILICIA

Seleucia

Aleppo

Antioch

SYRIA

CYPRUS

Salamis

Paphos

Beirut

PHOENICIA

Damascus

Sidon

Tyre

Ptolemais

R A N E A N   S E A

PALESTINE

Joppa

Jerusalem

Gaza

Alexandria

one

EGYPT

ARABIA

Cairo